JOHN WILLIS

THEATRE WORLD

1980–1981 SEASON

VOLUME 37

CROWN PUBLISHERS, INC.
ONE PARK AVENUE
NEW YORK, N.Y. 10016

Maureen Stapleton in "Antony and Cleopatra" (1948); with Melvyn Douglas in "The Bird Cage" (1950); with Eli Wallach in "The Rose Tattoo" (1951); with Brandon DeWilde in "The Emperor's Clothes" (1953); with Arthur Kennedy in "The Crucible" (1953)

in "Richard III" (1953); in "The Seagull" (1954); with Myron McCormick in "27 Wagons Full of Cotton" (1955); with Cliff Robertson in "Orpheus Descending" (1957)

with Tim Everett in "The Cold Wind and the Warm" (1958); with Jason Robards in "Toys in the Attic" (1960); "The Glass Menagerie" (1965); with Harry Guardino in "The Rose Tattoo" (1966 City Center)

with George C. Scott in "Plaza Suite" (1968); with Lou Jacobi in "Norman, Is That You?" (1970); with Michael Lombard in "The Gingerbread Lady" (1970); with George Grizzard in "The Country Girl" (1972)

2

with Florence Stanley and Neil Flanagan in "The Secret Affairs of Mildred Wild" (1972); with Pamela Payton-Wright in "The Glass Menagerie" (1975); with E. G. Marshall in "The Gin Game" (1978); with Elizabeth Taylor in "The Little Foxes" (1981)

T O
MAUREEN STAPLETON

whose humor, generosity, and friendship are as deeply appreciated and treasured as are her critically acclaimed performances

Photos by Fletcher Drake, Fred Fehl, Friedman-Abeles, Alix Jeffry, George Karger, Inge Morath, Ottomar, Martha Swope, Talbot, Zodiac

1953   1960   1970   1975   1981

LIZBETH MACKAY, MARY BETH HURT, MIA DILLON
in "Crimes of the Heart"
1981 winner of Pulitzer Prize and New York Drama Critics Circle Award

CONTENTS

EDITOR: JOHN WILLIS

Assistant Editor: Stanley Reeves

Staff Photographers: Joseph Abeles, Bert Andrews, J. M. Viade, Van Williams

THE SEASON IN REVIEW
June 1, 1980–May 31, 1981

For the fifth consecutive year, both theatre boxoffice and attendance, on Broadway and on tour, produced record-breaking statistics. There was a nationwide renewal of interest in live theatre, in spite of the inflationary effect of rising costs in all contributing factors of the productions. Ticket prices rose again ($50 top) to meet labor agreements and cost-of-living stipulations. Nevertheless, tickets became more easily accessible through computerization, and television advertising made seeing the productions more attractive and desirable. Satiated with inept, boring television programming, viewers were more eager for a night out with live entertainment.

Artistically and intellectually the season was less successful. Seldom had there been a year with so many long-running hits. This created a theatre shortage, especially for large musicals, and limited the number of openings for new comedies and serious plays, very few of which achieved hit status. Of the more than sixty new productions, there was a paucity of American playwrights. Films and television have been luring the prospective new writing talent to the Elysian fields of enormous salaries. Beth Henley's "Crimes of the Heart," presented Off Broadway by the Manhattan Theatre Club, received the Pulitzer Prize, as well as the New York Drama Critics Circle citation for best American play. The latter group voted "A Lesson from Aloes" by South Africa's Athol Fugard as best play, and gave special citations to "Lena Horne: The Lady and Her Music," and the revival of "Pirates of Penzance."

Coveted "Tonys" went to the English import "Amadeus" and to its star Ian McKellen (Outstanding Actor), to the musical "42nd Street," the revival of "Pirates of Penzance," and its star Kevin Kline (Outstanding Actor in a Musical). Lauren Bacall and Marilyn Cooper, both in "Woman of the Year," received Tonys for outstanding actress and featured actress in a musical, respectively. Outstanding featured actor in a musical was Hinton Battle of "Sophisticated Ladies." Other Tonys for performances in plays went to Jane Lapotaire (Outstanding Actress) in the British importation "Piaf," Swoosie Kurtz (Outstanding Featured Actress) in "5th of July," and Brian Backer (Outstanding Featured Actor) in "The Floating Light Bulb." Special Tonys were awarded Lena Horne for her one-woman show, and the Trinity Square Repertory Company of Providence, RI. The Drama Desk also chose "Amadeus" as best play and "Pirates of Penzance" as best musical. Outstanding performers who were honored were Joan Copeland ("The American Clock"), Ian McKellen, Brian Backer, Swoosie Kurtz, Kevin Kline, Lena Horne, and Marilyn Cooper, and Tony Azito of "Pirates of Penzance."

In addition to the above-mentioned imports, there were notable appearances by Derek Jacobi in "The Suicide," Roy Dotrice in "A Life," David Bowie in "The Elephant Man," Tim Curry and Jane Seymour in "Amadeus," Glenda Jackson in "Rose," and brilliant solo performances by Emlyn Williams as Charles Dickens, Frank Barrie as Macready, Alec McCowen reading St. Mark's Gospel, and Ian McKellen in "Acting Shakespeare," a benefit to help rebuild Shakespeare's Globe Theatre in London. Other outstanding Broadway performers were Maureen Anderman, Beatrice Arthur, William Atherton, Roderick Cook, Keene Curtis, Michael Allen Davis, Blythe Danner, Leslie Denniston, Tammy Grimes, Julie Harris, Gregory Hines, Phyllis Hyman, James Earl Jones, Eva LeGallienne, Cynthia Nixon, Carrie Nye, Tony Orlando, Geraldine Page, Lee Roy Reams, Adam Redfield, Wanda Richert, John Rubinstein, Rex Smith, Maureen Stapleton, Helen Stenborg, Jessica Tandy, and Elizabeth Taylor in her Broadway debut.

Broadway also experienced a record-breaking season of costly failures, the most notable being "Frankenstein" with a loss of over two million dollars. Other productions failing to please critics and public were "Broadway Follies," "Charley and Algernon," "Onward Victoria," "Bring Back Birdie," "Can-Can," "Moony Shapiro Songbook," and "Copperfield," all musicals. Among the plays were George C. Scott in "Tricks of the Trade," Neil Simon's "Fools," Donald Sutherland and Ian Richardson in Edward Albee's "Lolita." Praiseworthy musicals included "Tintypes" transplanted from Off Broadway, "Sophisticated Ladies," Richard Burton's return in "Camelot," and a beautiful revival of "Brigadoon" with Meg Bussert and Martin Vidnovic.

Although it was good to have Lincoln Center's Vivian Beaumont Theater re-activated, the productions by its new theatre company were less than enthusiastically received. The Brooklyn Academy of Music's repertory company productions were equally unsuccessful, and at the termination of its season the company was disbanded. Because of financial difficulties, the Chelsea Theater Center was forced unfortunately to discontinue its activities after sixteen years of valuable work for the theatrical community.

Off Broadway and Off Off Broadway, where productions are generally less commercial and more artistic, continued to be a potpourri of new and established talent in all facets of theatre, and presented numerous worthy productions and performances. Among the stars appearing Off Broadway were Malcolm McDowell in "Look Back in Anger," Julie Haydon in "The Glass Menagerie," Rosemary Harris and Christopher Walken in "The Seagull," Arlene Francis in "Don Juan in Hell," Meryl Streep in "Alice in Concert," Nicol Williamson in his original role in "Inadmissible Evidence," and Susannah York in "Hedda Gabler," which closed an outstanding season at the Roundabout Theatre. Other Off-Broadway performers who deserve mention are: Lisa Banes, Barbara Bryne, Maxwell Caulfield, Stephen Collins, Lindsay Crouse, Mia Dillon, Giancarlo Esposito, Gloria Foster, Peter Francis-James, Valerie French, Beulah Garrick, Daniel Gerroll, Keith Gordon, Bob Gunton, John Heard, Barnard Hughes, Mary Beth Hurt, William Hurt, Earle Hyman, Tommy Lee Jones, John Lone, Carl Lumbly, Lizabeth Mackay, Joseph Maher, Joe Morton, Amanda Plummer, Remak Ramsay, Michele Shay, John Shea and Sigourney Weaver.

Off-Broadway productions of varying quality, in addition to others previously mentioned, include: "Album," "American Days," "Between Daylight and Boonville," "Beyond Therapy," "Billy Bishop," "Chekhov Sketchbook," "Childe Byron," "Close of Play," "Cloud 9," "Knuckle," "Long Day's Journey into Night," "Meetings," "Slab Boys," "Summer," "A Taste of Honey," "Waiting for the Parade," "The Winslow Boy," "Zooman and the Sign," and the musicals "Haggadah," "Hijinks," "I Can't Keep Running in Place," "March of the Falsettos," "Randy Newman's Maybe I'm Wrong," "Real Life Funnies," "Really Rosie," and "Trixie True."

Notations during the season: Actors Equity and the League of New York Theatres and Producers reached a three-year agreement on salary increases. In addition, AEA settled with the Off-Broadway League on salary increases. It also raised its annual membership dues. . . . Frank Rich became theatre critic for *The New York Times* with Walter Kerr appearing only in the Sunday editions. . . . Demolition of the Helen Hayes, Morosco, and Bijou theatres appears imminent with final arrangements being made for construction of the Portman Hotel—a sad loss to the theatre district! . . . The 35th Tony Awards were presented on Sunday, June 7, 1981 at the Mark Hellinger Theatre with the accustomed exemplary telecast.

Ian McKellen in "Amadeus"

Kevin Kline in "The Pirates of Penzance"

BROADWAY CALENDAR
June 1, 1980 through May 31, 1981

Lee Roy Reams, Wanda Richert in "42nd Street"

Lauren Bacall in "Woman of the Year"

Harris Yulin, James Earl Jones
in "A Lesson from Aloes"

Christopher Reeve, Swoosie Kurtz,
Amy Wright in "5th of July"

AMBASSADOR THEATRE

Opened Monday, June 2, 1980.*

Tom Mallow in association with James Janek presents:

YOUR ARMS TOO SHORT TO BOX WITH GOD

Conceived from the book of St. Matthew by Vinnette Carroll; Music and Lyrics, Alex Bradford; Additional Music and Lyrics, Micki Grant; Director, Vinnette Carroll; Choreography, Talley Beatty; Sets and Costumes, William Schroder; Lighting, Richard Winkler; Sound, Abe Jacob; Musical Direction, Michael Powell; Orchestrations and Dance Music, H. B. Barnum; Producing Director, Anita MacShane; Production Supervisors, Jerry R. Moore, Richard Martini; Artistic Production Coordinator, Ralph Farrington; Originally produced by Urban Arts Theatre; Wardrobe, Altamiro Costa; Sound, Bruce Greenhut; Production Assistant, Arthur Katz; Props, Joe Cannon; Assistant to Ms. Carroll, Linda Vanterpool

CAST

Adrian Bailey, Julius Richard Brown, Cleavant Derricks, Sheila Ellis, Ralph Farrington, Jamil K. Garland, Elijah Gill, William-Keebler Hardy, Jr., Jennifer-Yvette Holliday, Linda James, Garry Q. Lewis, Linda Morton, Jai Oscar St. John. Kiki Shepard, Leslie Hardesty Sisson, Ray Stephens, Quincella Swyningan, Faruma S. Williams, Marilynn Winbush, Linda Young, Swing Dancers: Adrian Bailey, Linda James

MUSICAL NUMBERS: Beatitudes, We're Gonna Have a Good Time, There's a Stranger in Town, Do You Know Jesus?, He's a Wonder, Just a Little Bit of Jesus Goes a Long Way, We Are the Priests and Elders, Something Is Wrong in Jerusalem, It Was Alone, I Know I Have to Leave Here, Be Careful Whom You Kiss, Trial, It's Too Late, Judas' Dance, Your Arms Too Short to Box with God, Give Us Barabbas, See How They Done My Lord, Come on Down, Can't No Grave Hold My Body Down, Beatitudes, Didn't I Tell You, When the Power Comes, Everybody Has His Own Way, Down by the Riverside, I Love You So Much Jesus, The Band

A musical in two acts.

General Manager: James Janek
Company Manager: Sheila R. Phillips
Press: Max Eisen, Barbara Glenn
Stage Managers: Robert Borod, Robert Charles, Ralph Farrington

* Closed Oct. 12, 1980 after 149 performances and 4 previews. For original production see THEATRE WORLD Vol. 33.

Martha Swope, Jay Thompson Photos

Left: Gwendolyn Nelson Fleming, Quincella Swyningan, Elijah Gill Top: Jennifer-Yvette Holliday

William-Keebler Hardy, Jr.

MARTIN BECK THEATRE
Opened Tuesday, June 3, 1980.*
Jay Julien, Arnon Milchan, Larry Kalish present:

IT'S SO NICE TO BE CIVILIZED

By Micki Grant; Director, Frank Corsaro; Choreography, Mabel Robinson; Associate Producer, Danny Holgate; Musical Director, Coleridge-Taylor Perkinson; Scenery and Visuals, Charles E. Hoefler; Lighting, Charles E. Hoefler; Ralph Madero; Costumes, Ruth Morley; Orchestrations, Danny Holgate, Neal Tate; Choral Arrangements, Tasha Thomas; Dance Arrangements, Carl Maultsby; Sound, Palmer Shannon; Assistant Conductor, William Gregg Hunter; Hairstylist, Phyllis Della; Wardrobe, Toni Baer;

CAST

Sharky	Obba Babatunde
Mollie	Vivian Reed
Larry	Larry Stewart
Sissy	Vickie D. Chappell
LuAnne	Carol Lynn Maillard
Grandma	Mabel King
Mr. Anderson	Stephen Pender
Blade	Dan Strayhorn
Rev. Williams	Eugene Edwards
Mother	Deborah Burrell
Dancing Bag Lady	Juanita Grace Tyler

ENSEMBLE: Daria Atanian, Paul Binotto, Sharon K. Brooks, P. L. Brown, Jean Cheek, Vondie Curtis-Hall, Paul Harman, Esther Marrow, Wellington Perkins, Dwayne Phelps, Juanita Grace Tyler
UNDERSTUDIES: Jean Cheek (Grandma), Esther Marrow (Mollie), Vondie Curits-Hall (Sharky/Larry/Blade), Deborah Burrell (LuAnne), P. L. Brown (Rev. Williams), Paul Harman (Joe/Anderson), Allison Renee Manson (Bag Lady), Sharon K. Brooks (Mother/Sissy), Dance Alternates: Allison Renee Manson, Steiv Semien
MUSICAL NUMBERS: Step into My World, Keep Your Eye on the Red, Wake-Up Sun, Subway Rider, God Help Us, Who's Going to Teach the Children?, Out on the Street, Welcome Mr. Anderson, Why Can't Me and You?, When I Rise, World Keeps Going Round, Antiquity, I've Still Got My Bite, Look at Us, The American Dream, Bright Lights, It's So Nice to Be Civilized, Like a Lady, Pass a Little Love Around

A Musical in two acts. The action takes place on Sweetbitter Street over a weekend in late summer.

General Manager: John Larson
Press: Merlin Group, Cheryl Sue Dolby, Sandra Manley, Marguerite Wolfe, Eileen McMahon, Glen Gary
Stage Managers: Jack Gianino, Carolyn Greer, Paul Harman

* Closed June 8, 1980 after 8 performances and 23 previews.

Tom Keller Photos

Paul Binotto, Wellington Perkins, Obba Babatunde, Dan Strayhorn, Dwayne Phelps
Top: Mabel King (C), Obba Babatunde, Vivian Reed Below: Obba Babatunde, Vivian Reed

Dick Van Dyke
(also above)

CITY CENTER
Opened Thursday, June 5, 1980.*
James M. Nederlander, Raymond Lussa, Fred Walker present:

THE MUSIC MAN

By Meredith Willson; Book in collaboration with Franklin Lacey; Direction and Choreography, Michael Kidd; Music and Vocal Direction, Milton Rosenstock; Sets, Peter Wolf; Costumes, Stanley Simmons, Lighting, Marcia Madeira; Sound, Barry Rimler; Orchestrations, Don Walker; Assistant to Mr. Kidd, Bonnie Evans; Wardrobe, Warren Morrill, Dean Jackson; Hairstylists, Dale Brownell, Frank A. Melon, Naomi Slavin; Associate Conductor, Alyce Billington; Production Assistant, Jay Binder; Assistant to Mr. Kidd, Randy Doney; Projections, Marcia Madeira

CAST

Traveling Salesman/Constable Locke	Dennis Holland
Traveling Salesman/Jacey Squires	Lee Winston
Traveling Salesman/Oliver Hix	Randy Morgan
Traveling Salesman/Olin Britt	Ralph Braun
Traveling Salesman/Ewart Dunlop	Larry Cahn
Traveling Salesmen	Michael J. Rockne, Tom Garrett, Andy Hostettler
Charlie Cowell	Jay Stuart
Conductor	Peter Wandel
Harold Hill	Dick Van Dyke
Mayor Shinn	Iggie Wolfington
Marcellus Washburn	Richard Warren Pugh
Tommy Djilas	Calvin McRae
Marian Paroo	Meg Bussert
Mrs. Paroo	Carol Arthur
Amaryllis	Lara Jill Miller
Winthrop Paroo	Christian Slater
Eulalie MacKecknie Shinn	Jen Jones
Zeneeta Shinn	Christina Saffran
Alma Hix	Marcia Brushingham
Maude Dunlop	Mary Gaebler
Ethel Toffelmier	P. J. Nelson
Mrs. Squires	Mary Roche

RIVER CITY TOWNSPEOPLE: Victoria Ally, Carol Ann Basch, Dennis Batutis, David Beckett, Mark A. Esposito, Tom Garrett, Liza Gennaro, Dennis Holland, Andy Hostettler, Tony Jaeger, Wendy Kimball, Ara Marx, Darleigh Miller, Gail Pennington, Rosemary Rado, Michael J. Rockne, Coley Sohn, Peter Wandel
UNDERSTUDIES & STANDBYS: Jay Stuart (Harold Hill), Dennis Holland (Charlie/Ewart), J. J. Jepson (Conductor/Marcellus/-Constable), Larry Cahn (Salesmen), Ralph Braun (Mayor), Michael Rockne (Olin), Randy Morgan (Jacey), Tom Garrett (Oliver), Tony Jaeger (Tommy), Mary Gaebler (Mrs. Paroo/Eulalie), Darleigh Miller (Marian), Ara Marx (Zaneeta), Coley Sohn (Amaryllis/Winthrop), Mary Roche (Alma), Wendy Kimball (Maude/Ethel/Mrs. Squires), Swing Dancers: Alis Elaine Anderson, J. J. Jepson
MUSICAL NUMBERS: Rock Island, Iowa Stubborn, Trouble, Piano Lesson, Goodnight My Someone, Seventy-Six Trombones, Sincere, The Sadder-but-Wiser Girl, Pickalittle, Goodnight Ladies, Marian the Librarian, My White Knight, Wells Fargo Wagon, It's You, Shipoopl, Lida Rose, Will I Ever Tell You, Gary Indiana, Till There Was You, Finale.

A musical in 2 acts and 17 scenes. The action takes place during 1912 on a railway coach and in River City, Iowa.

General Managers: Jack Schlissel, James Walsh
Company Manager: David Hedges
Press: Solters/Roskin/Friedman, Milly Schoenbaum, Anne Obert Weinberg, Kevin Patterson
Stage Managers: Conwell S. Worthington II, John M. Galo, Charles Reif

* Closed June 22, 1980 after 21 performances and 8 previews. For original Broadway production, see THEATRE WORLD Vol. 14.

Jay Thompson Photos

Top Left: Dick Van Dyke, Meg Bussert

PRINCESS THEATRE
Opened Sunday, June 15, 1980.*
David Black and Robert Fabian in association with Oscar Lewenstein and Theodore P. Donahue, Jr. present:

FEARLESS FRANK

Book and Lyrics, Andrew Davies; Music, Dave Brown; Director, Robert Gillespie; Musical Staging, Michael Vernon; Scenery, Martin Tilley; Costumes, Carrie F. Robbins; Lighting, Ruth Roberts; Orchestrations, Michael Reed; Musical Direction and Additional Arrangements, Michael Rose; Associate Producers, Norma Adler, Michael A. Riddell; Wardrobe, Mark Immens; Assistant to Producers, Liz Nickson

CAST

Frank Harris . . . . Niall Toibin
French Waiter/Headmaster/Kendrick/Lord
  Folkestone/Whistler . . . . Alex Wipf
Secretary/School Girl/Jessie/Lilly . . . . Valerie Mahaffey
Nellie/Kate/Laura . . . . Kristen Meadows
Tobin/Whitehouse/Smith/Chapman/Oscar Wilde . Steve Burney
Nursemaid/Actress/Bootblack/Topsy/Newsboy/
  Enid . . . . Ann Hodapp
Cowboy/Carlyle/Clapton/deMaupassant/Dowson . Olivier Pierre
Mrs. Mayhew/Mrs. Clapton/Mrs. Clayton . . . . Evalyn Baron

UNDERSTUDIES: Ralph Bruneau (Wipf/Burney), Valerie Beaman (Mahaffey/Hodapp), Susan Elizabeth Scott (Meadows/Baron)
MUSICAL NUMBERS: The Man Who Made His Life into a Work of Art, Nora the Nursemaid's Door, The Examination Song or Get Me on That Boat, Halted at the Very Gates of Paradise, Dandy Night Clerk or How to Get on in the Hotel Trade, Riding the Range, Oh Catch Me Mr. Harris, The Greatest Man of All, My Poor Wee Lassie, My Own or True Love at Last, Evening News, Le Maitre de la Conte or Maupassant Tells All, Oh Mr. Harris You're a Naughty Man!, Great Men Great Days or The King of the Cafe Royal, Free Speech Free Thought Free Love, Mr. Harris It's All Over Now!, Fearless Frank

A musical in two acts. The action takes place in 1921 in Nice and in the memory of Frank Harris.

General Management: Theatre Now, Inc.
Press: Hunt/Pucci Associates, James Sapp
Stage Managers: Larry Forde, Steven Beckler, Ralph Bruneau

* Closed June 25, 1980 after 12 performances and 13 previews.

Roger Greenawalt Photos

**Left: Ann Hodapp, Alex Wipf, Olivier Pierre,
Top: Niall Toibin with (clockwise from
lower left) Kristen Meadows, Valerie
Mahaffey, Ann Hodapp, Evalyn Baron**

**Kristen Meadows, Niall Toibin,
Evalyn Baron**

**Kristen Meadows, Steve Burney,
Alex Wipf**

11

CIRCLE IN THE SQUARE
Opened Thursday, June 26, 1980.*
Circle in the Square (Theodore Mann, Artistic Director; Paul Libin, Managing Director) presents:

THE MAN WHO CAME TO DINNER

By Moss Hart and George S. Kaufman; Director, Stephen Porter; Scenery and Costumes, Zack Brown; Lighting, Jeff Davis; Wigs and Hairstyles, Paul Huntley; Wardrobe, Millicent Hacker

CAST

Mrs. Ernest W. Stanley	Patricia O'Connell
Miss Preen	Anita Dangler
Richard Stanley	Josh Clark
June Stanley	Amanda Carlin
John	Bill McCutcheon
Sarah	Yolanda Childress
Mrs. McCutcheon	Dorothy Stinnette
Mr. Stanley	Richard Woods
Maggie Cutler	Maureen Anderman
Dr. Bradley	Robert Nichols
Sheridan Whiteside	Ellis Rabb
Harriet Stanley	Kate Wilkinson
Bert Jefferson	Peter Coffield
Professor Metz/Westcott	Nicholas Martin
Luncheon Guests	Jason Jerrold, Jeffrey Rodman
Mr. Baker	Robert O'Rourke
Expressmen	John Hallow, Jeffrey Rodman
Lorraine Sheldon	Carrie Nye
Sandy	Jamey Sheridan
Beverly Carlton	Roderick Cook
Banjo	Leonard Frey
Radio Technician	Jeffrey Rodman
Plainclothesman	Charles Hardin
Choir	Dorothy Stinnette, Lilli Syng, Kate Wilkinson
Deputies	Robert O'Rourke, George Spelvin

STANDBYS & UNDERSTUDIES: James Cahill (Whiteside), Amanda Carlin (Maggie), Gwyn Gilliss (Lorraine), Bill McCutcheon (Beverly), John Hallow (Bradley/Stanley), Yolanda Childress (Preen), Jeffrey Rodman (Banjo/Sandy/Richard/Metz/Westcott), Robert O'Rourke (Technician/Expressman/Deputy), Jamey Sheridan (Jefferson)

A comedy in three acts and four scenes. The action takes place in the home of Mr. & Mrs. Stanley in a small town in Ohio during December of 1938.

Company Manager: William Conn
Press: Merle Debuskey, David Roggensack
Stage Managers: Randall Brooks, Nicholas Russiyan, Robert O'Rourke

* Closed Sept. 7, 1980 after 85 performances and 19 previews. Original production opened Oct. 16, 1939 at the Music Box and played 739 performances. The cast included Monty Woolley, Edith Atwater, Carol Goodner and John Hoysradt.

Martha Swope Photos

**Top Right: Carrie Nye, Ellis Rabb,
Peter Coffield, Maureen Anderman
Below: Carrie Nye Right: Rabb,
Patricia O'Connell, Richard Woods**

**Ellis Rabb, Anita Dangler,
Leonard Frey**

**Maureen Anderman, Ellis Rabb,
Roderick Cook**

RADIO CITY MUSIC HALL
Opened Monday, June 30, 1980.*
Radio City Music Hall Productions (Robert F. Jani, President-/Executive Producer) presents:

MANHATTAN SHOWBOAT

Conceived and Produced by Robert F. Jani; Executive Musical Director, Donald Pippin; Production Executive, John J. Moore; Choreography, Linda Lemac, Howard Parker, Debra Pigliavento, Frank Wagner; Rockettes Choreography, Violet Holmes; Principals Staged by Frank Wagner; Dialogue, Stan Hart; Special Material, Nan Mason; Musical Routining, Stan Lebowsky; Scenery, Robert Guerra; Costumes, Frank Spencer, Michael Casey; Lighting, David F. Segal; Orchestrations, Elman Anderson, Michael Gibson, Arthur Harris, Philip J. Lang; Conductor, Elman Anderson; Original Music and Lyrics, Donald Pippin, Sammy Cahn, Nan Mason

CAST

Belle	Karen Anders
Edgar	Louis Carry
Hiram Boggs	Thomas Ruisinger
Tree	Steven Williford
Daisy	Herself
P. T. Barnum	Tony Moore
Buffalo Bill	Buddy Crutchfield
Annie Oakley	Lou Ann Csaszar
Annie	Laurie Stephenson
Organists	Timothy Stella, David Messineo

ROCKETTES: Pauline Achillas, Carol Beatty, Catherine Beatty, Dottie Belle, Karen Berman, Susan Boron, Deniene Bruck, Barbara Ann Cittadino, Eileen Collins, Brie Daniels, Susan DiGilio, Susanne Doris, Jacqueline Fancy, Alexis Ficks, Mary Ann Fiordalisi, Prudence Gray, Carol Harbich, Ginny Hounsell, Cynthia Hughes, Pam Kelleher, Dee Dee Knapp, Judy Little, Leslie Gryszko McCarthy, Barbara Moore, Ann Murphy, Lynn Newton, Pam Stacey Pasqualino, Joan Peer, Cindy Peiffer, Geraldine Presky, Sheila Rodriguez, Maryellen Scilla, Terry Spano, Lynn Sullivan, Sunny Summers, Susan Theobald, Carol Toman, Darlene Wendy, Rose Anne Wolsey, Phyllis Wujko

THE NEW YORKERS: Pam Cecil, Joanna Coggins, Lou Ann Csaszar, Buddy Crutchfield, Alvin Davis, Rick Emery, Dale Furry, Bobby Grayson, Phil Hall, Nina Hennessey, Stephen Hope, Deirdre Kane, Dale Kristien, Andrea Lyman, James Mahady, Tony Moore, Sylvia Nolan, Denise O'Neill, Susan Powers, Cleo Price, Jeffory Robinson, Laurie Stephenson, Bob Teterick, Kay Walbye, Scott Whiteleather, Bob Wrenn

DANCERS: Dennis Angulo, Phillip Bond, Ron Chisholm, Angie Daye, Danute Debney, John Michael Doyle, Glenn Ferrugiari, Doug Fogel, Neisha Folkes, Linda Kay Hamil, Kristie Hannum, Edward Henkel, Olgalyn Jolly, Elisa Lenhart, Kim Leslie, Gail Lohla, Cary Lowenstein, Margaret McGee, Terry McLemore, Ron Meier, Lorena Palacios, James Parker, Debra Pigliavento, Michele Pigliavento, Sam Singhaus, Cassie Stein, Alan Stuart, Karen Toto, Barry Weiss

PROGRAM

Opening, The Circus, Nightclubs and Floorshows, Vaudeville, Sing-a-long, Musical Theatre, Great Reviews, Rockettes, Belle's Turn, Finale

General Managers: Robert A. Buckley, Jeff Hamlin, Patricia Morinelli
Press: Gifford/Wallace, Keith Sherman
Stage Managers: Neil Miller, Peter Rosenberg, Ray Chandler, Peter Aaronson

* Closed Oct. 15, 1980 after 191 performances.

Martha Swope Photos

Paxton Whitehead

NEW YORK STATE THEATER
Opened Tuesday, July 8, 1980.*
Mike Merrick and Don Gregory by arrangement with James M. Nederlander present:

CAMELOT

Book and Lyrics, Alan Jay Lerner; Based on "The Once and Future King" by T. H. White; Music, Frederick Loewe; Director, Frank Dunlop; Choreography, Buddy Schwab; Sets and Costumes, Desmond Heeley; Lighting, Thomas Skelton; Musical Director, Franz Allers; Conductor, James Martin; Sound, John McClure; Orchestrations, Robert Russell Bennett and Phil Lang; Musical Coordinator, Robert Kreis; Production Supervisor, Jerry Adler; Artistic Consultant, Stone Widney; A Dome/Cutler-Herman Production; Assistant to Producers, Ruthann M. Barshop; Technical Supervisor, Arthur Siccardi; Special Effects, Robert Joyce; Wardrobe, Josephine Zampedri, Robert Mooney; Hair Designs, Vincenzo Prestia; Incidental Music, Robert Kreis; Assistant Choreographer, Dee Erickson

CAST

Arthur	Richard Burton
Sir Sagramore	Andy McAvin
Merlyn	James Valentine
Guenevere	Christine Ebersole
Sir Dinidan	William Parry
Nimue	Jeanne Caryl
Lancelot Du Lac	Richard Muenz
Mordred	Robert Fox
Dap	Robert Molnar
Friar	James Valentine
Lady Anne	Nora Brennan
Lady Sybil	Deborah Magid
Sir Lionel	William James
King Pellinore	Paxton Whitehead
Horrid	Bob
Sir Lionel's Squire	Davis Gaines
Sir Sagramore's Squire	Steve Soborn
Sir Dinidan's Squire	Herndon Lackey
Tom	Thor Fields
Knights of the Investiture	Ken Henley,

Gary Jaketic, Jack Starkey, Ronald Bennett Stratton

KNIGHTS, LORDS & LADIES: Nora Brennan, Jeanne Caryl, Melanie Clements, Stephanie Conlow, Van Craig, John Deyle, Debra Dickinson, Richard Dodd, Cecil Fulfer, Davis Gaines, Lisa Ann Grant, Ken Henley, John Herrera, Gary Jaketic, William James, Kelby Kirk, Herndon Lackey, Deborah Magid, Andy McAvin, Laura McCarthy, Robert Molnar, Steve Osborn, Patrice Pickering, Janelle Price, Nancy Rieth, Patrick Rogers, Deborah Roshe, D. Paul Shannon, Jack Starkey, Ronald Bennett Stratton, Sally Ann Swarm, Sally Williams, Alternates: Lynn Keeton, Richard Maxon
UNDERSTUDIES: William Parry (Arthur), Janelle Price (Guenevere), Gary Jaketic (Lancelot), James Valentine (Pellinore), Andy McAvin (Mordred), Robert Molnar (Merlyn), Deborah Magid (Nimue), D. Paul Shannon/Herndon Lackey (Dinidan), John Deyle (Lionel), Herndon Lackey (Sagramore), John Herrera (Dap)
MUSICAL NUMBERS: Guenevere, I Wonder What the King Is Doing Tonight, The Simple Joys of Maidenhood, Camelot, Follow Me, C'Est Moi, The Lusty Month of May, How to Handle a Woman, The Jousts, Before I Gaze at You Again, If Ever I Would Leave You, The Seven Deadly Virtues, What Do the Simple Folk Do, Fie on Goodness, I Loved You Once in Silence, Finale

A musical in 2 acts and 14 scenes. The action takes place in and near Camelot, a long time ago.

Company Manager: James Awe
Press: Seymour Krawitz, Patricia McLean Krawitz, Joel W. Dein
Stage Managers: Jonathan Weiss, Cathy Rice

* Closed Aug. 23, 1980 after a limited engagement of 56 performances and 6 previews to tour. Original production opened at the Majestic Theatre Dec. 3, 1960 with Julie Andrews, Richard Burton, Robert Goulet, and played 873 performances. See THEATRE WORLD Vol. 17.

Martha Swope Photos

**Top Left: Christine Ebersole, Richard Burton,
and below with Richard Muenz
Left Center: Richard Muenz, Christine Ebersole**

WINTER GARDEN THEATRE
Opened Monday, August 25, 1980.*
(moved March 30, 1981 to Majestic Theatre)
David Merrick presents:

FORTY-SECOND STREET

Songs, Harry Warren, Al Dubin; Lead Ins and Crossovers, Michael Stewart, Mark Bramble; Based on novel by Bradford Ropes; Direction and Choreography, Gower Champion; Scenery, Robin Wagner; Costumes, Theoni V. Aldredge; Lighting, Tharon Musser; Musical Direction and Vocal Arrangements, John Lesko; Orchestrations, Philip J. Lang; Dance Arrangements, Donald Johnston; Sound, Richard Fitzgerald; Dance Assistants, Karin Baker, Randy Skinner; Assistant to Producer, Jon Maas; Wardrobe, Gene Wilson, Kathleen Foster; Assistant to Mr. Champion, Larry Carpenter; Assistant Conductor, Donald Johnston; Hairstylists, Ted Azar, Robert DiNiro, Dale Brownell, Anne Sampogna; Original Cast Album by RCA Records.

CAST

Andy Lee	Danny Carroll
Oscar	Robert Colston
Mac	Stan Page
Annie	Karen Prunczik
Maggie Jones	Carole Cook
Bert Barry	Joseph Bova
Billy Lawlor	Lee Roy Reams
Peggy Sawyer	Wanda Richert
Lorraine	Ginny King
Phyllis	Jeri Kansas
Julian Marsh	Jerry Orbach
Dorothy Brock	Tammy Grimes
Abner Dillon	Don Crabtree
Pat Denning	James Congdon
Thugs	Stan Page, Ron Schwinn
Doctor	Stan Page

ENSEMBLE: Carole Banninger, Steve Belin, Robin Black, Joel Blum, Mary Cadorette, Ronny DeVito, Denise DiRenzo, Mark Dovey, Rob Draper, Brandt Edwards, Jon Engstrom, Sharon Ferrol, Cathy Greco, Dawn Herbert, Christine Jacobsen, Jeri Kansas, Ginny King, Terri Ann Kundrat, Shan Martin, Beth McVey, Maureen Mellon, Sandra Menhart, Bill Nabel, Tony Parise, Don Percassi, Jean Preece, Vicki Regan, Lars Rosager, Linda Sabatelli, Nikki Sahagen, Ron Schwinn, Yveline Semeria, Alison Sherve, Robin Stephens, David Storey, Karen Tamburrelli
UNDERSTUDIES: Leila Martin (Dorothy/Maggie), James Congdon (Julian), Mary Cadorette/Nancy Sinclair (Peggy), Joel Blum (Billy), Bill Nabel (Bert/Mac), Don Percassi (Andy), Stan Page (Abner/Pat), Karen Tamburrelli (Annie), Donald Johnston (Oscar), Ensemble: Lorraine Person, Rick Pessagno
MUSICAL NUMBERS: Audition, Young and Healthy, Shadow Waltz, Go into Your Dance, You're Getting to Be a Habit with Me, Getting Out of Town, Dames, I Know Now, We're in the Money, Sunny Side to Every Situation, Lullaby of Broadway, About a Quarter to Nine, Pretty Lady Overture, Shuffle Off to Buffalo, 42nd Street

A musical in 2 acts and 16 scenes. The action takes place during 1933 in New York City and Philadelphia.

General Manager: Helen L. Nickerson
Company Managers: Louise M. Bayer, Leo K. Cohen
Press: Fred Nathan, Louise Weiner Ment, Solters/Roskin/Friedman, Joshua Ellis, Milly Schoenbaum, Bud Westman, Kevin Patterson
Stage Managers: Steve Zweigbaum, Arturo E. Porazzi, Jane E. Neufeld, Barry Kearsley, Debra Pigliavento

* Still playing May 31, 1981. Recipient of 1981 "Tonys" for Best Musical, and for Outstanding Choreography.

Martha Swope Photos

Top Right: Jerry Orbach (L), Wanda Richert (C), Lee Roy Reams, Danny Carroll (R) Below: Don Crabtree, Jerry Orbach, Tammy Grimes Right Center: Lee Roy Reams (C) and dancers

Carole Cook and chorus

HELEN HAYES THEATRE

Opened Sunday, September 14, 1980.*
The Kennedy Center, Isobel Robins Konecky, Fisher Theatre Foundation and the Folger Theatre Group present:

CHARLIE AND ALGERNON

Book and Lyrics, David Rogers; Music, Charles Strouse; Based on novel "Flowers for Algernon" by Daniel Keyes; Director, Louis W. Scheeder; Musical Director-Conductor, Liza Redfield; Choreography, Virginia Freeman; Orchestrations, Philip J. Lang; Scenery, Kate Edmunds; Costumes, Jess Goldstein; Lighting, Hugh Lester; Sound, William H. Clements; Assistant Conductor, Tom Fay; Wardrobe, Linda Lee; Projections, Jim Hobbs

CAST

Charlie	P. J. Benjamin
Alice Kinnian	Sandy Faison
Dr. Strauss	Edward Earle
Dr. Nemur	Robert Sevra
Mrs. Donner	Nancy Franklin
Lita	Loida Santos
Frank	Patrick Jude
Charlie's Mother	Julienne Marie
Little Charlie	Matthew Duda
Charlie's Father	Michael Vita

STANDBYS: Phillip Alan Witt (Charlie/Nemur/Father), Michael Vita (Strauss/Frank), Sydney Anderson (Mrs. Donner/Lita/-Mother), R. D. Robb (Little Charlie), Dance Captain, Sydney Anderson

MUSICAL NUMBERS: Have I the Right, I Got a Friend, Some Bright Morning, Jelly Donuts and Chocolate Cake, Hey Look at Me, Reading, No Surprises, Midnight Riding, Dream Safe with Me, Not Another Day Like This, Somebody New, I Can't Tell You, Now, Charlie and Algernon, The Maze, Whatever Time There Is, Everything Was Perfect, Charlie, I Really Loved You

A musical performed without intermission.

General Management: Theatre Now, Inc.
Company Manager: Michael Lonergan
Press: Michael Alpert, Marilynn LeVine, Mark Goldstaub, Alan Hale

* Closed Sept. 28, 1980 after 17 performances and 12 previews.

Right: Julienne Marie, Matthew Duda, Michael Vita Top: Nancy Franklin, Loida Santos, Patrick Jude, P. J. Benjamin

P. J. Benjamin

P. J. Benjamin

MOROSCO THEATRE
Opened Tuesday, September 23, 1980.*
John Wulp, Roger Berlind, Richard Horner, Hinks Shimberg present:

PASSIONE

By Albert Innaurato; Director, Frank Langella; Scenery, David Gropman; Costumes, William Ivey Long; Lighting, Paul Gallo; Sound, Alex McIntyre; Special Effects, Scott Glenn; Assistant to Director, Gail Obenreder; Hairstylist, James Nelson; Production Assistant, Rickie Grosberg; Wardrobe, Rosemary Canarelli

CAST

Little Tom	Richard Zavaglia
Oreste	Daniel Keyes
Berto	Jerry Stiller
Sarah	Sloane Shelton
Aggy	Angela Paton
Renzo	Dick Latessa
Francine	Laurel Cronin

STANDBYS & UNDERSTUDIES: Ed Kovens (Berto/Renzo), Vera Lockwood (Aggy/Sarah), William Daprato (Oreste), Karen Shallo (Francine), Robert Iammarino, Louise Lipman, Rose Roffman

A comedy in two acts. The action takes place at the present time in South Philadelphia.

General Manager: Malcolm Allen
Company Manager: Stanley D. Silver
Press: Bob Ullman, Daisy Bacall
Stage Managers: Jay Adler, Charles Kindl

* Closed Oct. 5, 1980 after 15 performances and 11 previews.

Susan Cook Photos

Right: Angela Paton, Jerry Stiller
Top: Angela Paton, Dick Latessa, Jerry
Stiller, Sloane Shelton

Sloane Shelton, Dick Latessa

Jerry Stiller, Laurel Cronin

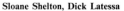

BIJOU THEATRE
Opened Monday, September 29, 1980.*
Arthur Shafman International Ltd. presents:

INSIDEOUTSIDEANDALLAROUND
with
SHELLEY BERMAN

Production Supervisor, Kitzi Becker; Production Adviser, Richard G. Miller; Production Associates, Evelyn Gross, Eileen Jaffe, Susan Balsam

A one-man show presented in two acts.

General Manager: Christopher Dunlop
Company Manager: John Larson
Press: Jeffrey Richards, Robert Ganshaw, C. George Willard, Ben Morse, Ted Killmer, Helen Stern

* Closed Oct. 25, 1980 after limited engagement of 24 performances and 4 previews.

Shelley Berman

CIRCLE IN THE SQUARE
Opened Thursday, October 2, 1980.*
Circle in the Square (Theodore Mann, Artistic Director; Paul Libin, Managing Director) presents:

THE BACCHAE

By Euripides; Translated and Directed by Michael Cacoyannis; Set and Costumes, John Conklin; Lighting, Pat Collins; Music, Theodore Antoniou; Wardrobe, Millicent Hacker

CAST

Dionysus (also referred to as Bacchus and
    Bromius) . . . . Christopher Rich
Tiresias . . . . Tom Klunis
Cadmus . . . . Philip Bosco
Pentheus . . . . John Noah Hertzler
Guards . . . . Peter Efthymiou, Alfred Karl, Gary Tacon
Herdsman . . . . Richard Kuss
Messenger . . . . Paul Perri
Agave . . . . Irene Papas

CHORUS OF BACCHAE: Sheila Dabney, Elain Graham, Ernestine Jackson, Jodi Long, Karen Ludwig, Valois Mickens, Socorro Santiago, Catherine Lee Smith, Michele-Denise Woods
UNDERSTUDIES: Gary Tacon (Dionysus/Messenger/Guard), Alfred Karl (Cadmus/Tiresias/Herdsman), Peter Efthymiou (Pentheus)

Performed without intermission.

Company Manager: William Conn
Press: Merle Debuskey, David Roggensack
Stage Managers: Randall Brooks, Rick Ralston

* Closed Nov. 23, 1980 after 61 performances and 20 previews.

Martha Swope Photos

Above: Irene Papas, Philip Bosco
Left: Christopher Rich, John Noah Hertzler

Philip Bosco, Irene Papas

AMBASSADOR THEATRE

Opened Wednesday, October 8, 1980.*
Emanuel Azenberg, The Shubert Organization, The Mark Taper Forum, Gordon Davidson present:

DIVISION STREET

By Steve Tesich; Director, Tom Moore; Set, Ralph Funicello; Costumes, Robert Blackman; Lighting, Martin Aronstein; Associate Producers, William P. Wingate, Kenneth Brecher; Assistant to Director, Nancy Robbins; Wardrobe, Karen Lloyd; Hairstylist, John Quaglia; Production Assistant, Cecile Cook

CAST

Chris	John Lithgow
Mrs. Bruchinski	Theresa Merritt
Yovan	Keene Curtis
Betty	Justin Lord
Nadja	Murphy Cross
Roger	Joe Regalbuto
Dianah	Christine Lahti
Sal	Anthony Holland

UNDERSTUDIES: Raymond Baker (Chris), Barbara Meek (Bruchinski), Stephen Burks (Betty), George Touliatos (Yovan), Stephen Van Benschoten (Roger/Sal), Joy Rinaldi (Dianah/Nadja)

A comedy in two acts. The action takes place at the present time in Chicago.

General Managers: Jose Vega, Linda Cohen
Press: Bill Evans/Howard Atlee, Leslie Anderson-Lynch, Jim Baldassare, Bruce Cohen
Stage Managers: Franklin Keysar, Mary Michele Miner

* Closed Oct. 25, 1980 after 21 performances and 19 previews.

Martha Swope Photos

Right: Keene Curtis, Christine Lahti, Joe Regalbuto, John Lithgow, Anthony Holland, Theresa Merritt, Justin Lord, Murphy Cross
Top: John Lithgow, Keene Curtis

Justin Lord, Murphy Cross

John Lithgow, Theresa Merritt

ANTA THEATRE
Opened Thursday, October 9, 1980.*
The Aurora Stage Wing Inc. presents:

THE SUICIDE

By Nikolai Erdman; Translated by George Genereux, Jr. and Jacob Volkov; Adapted by Trinity Square Repertory Co. (Adrian Hall, Director) and Jonas Jurasas; Director, Jonas Jurasas; Producers, Bill Dyer, Dick De Benedictis; Setting and Costumes, Santo Loquasto; Lighting, F. Mitchell Dana; Sound, Jack Shearing; Music, Richard Weinstock; Movement, Ara Fitzgerald; Executive Producers, James L. Stewart, Rich Irvine; Associate Producers, R. Tyler Gatchell, Jr., Peter Neufeld; Lyrics, Bill Dyer; Assistant to Director, Johno Bard Manulis; Assistant to Producers, Ronald Taylor; Technical Coordinator, Arthur Siccardi; Wardrobe, Henry Arango; Hairstylist, J. Roy Helland; Off-stage Musicians, Bill Moersch, Andy Seligson

CAST

Semyon Semyonovich Podsekalnikov (Senya) ...... Derek Jacobi
Maria Lukyanovna Podsekalnikova (Masha).. Angela Pietropinto
Serafima Ilyinishna, his mother-in-law .... Grayson Hall
Alexander Petrovich Kalabushkin............ Clarence Felder
Margarita Ivanovna, his dear friend .... Carol Mayo Jenkins
Aristarkh Dominikovich Grand-Skubik........ John Heffernan
Yegor Timofeevich, a Marxist......... John Christopher Jones
Waldemar Arsenyevich Pugachov, butcher .... David Sabin
Victor Victorovich, a writer..................... Chip Zien
Father Yelpidy, a priest..................... William Myers
Cleopatra Maximovna, a fading beauty .... Laura Esterman
Raisa Filippovna, her rival............ Mary Lou Rosato
Pervaya, gypsy with balalaika .... Leda Siskind
Vtoraya, gypsy with violin................... Susan Edwards
Tretya, gypsy with tambourine .... Cheryl Giannini
Pervy, gypsy with mandolin............ David Patrick Kelly
Vtoroy, gypsy with violin.................... Derek Meader
Woman with young boy..................... Leda Siskind
Trety, gypsy with guitar........................ Jeff Zinn
Young Boy......................... David Patrick Kelly

UNDERSTUDIES: Russell Horton (Senya), Cheryl Giannini (Serafima/Cleopatra), Leda Siskind (Maria), Christopher Loomis (Alexander/Pugachov/Yelpidy), Susan Edwards (Raisa), Derek Meader (Victor), Polly Pen (Pervaya, Vtoraya, Tretya), John Seeman (Yegor/Pervy/Trety/Vtoroy/Young Boy)

A comedy in two acts. The action takes place during the 1920's in a Moscow tenement.

General Management: Gatchell & Neufeld
Associate: Douglas C. Baker
Company Manager: Mark Andrews
Press: Jeffrey Richards, C. George Willard, Robert Ganshaw, Ben Morse, Helen Stern, Ted Killmer
Stage Managers: Peter Lawrence, Jim Woolley, Sarah Whitham
* Closed Nov. 29, 1980 after 60 performances and 20 previews.

Peter Cunningham Photos

Left: Clarence Felder, Carol Mayo Jenkins
Above: Chip Zien, David Sabin, Clarence Felder,
Derek Jacobi, John Heffernan, William Myers,
Mary Lou Rosato Top: Angela Pietropinto, Jacobi

Derek Jacobi

John Heffernan, Derek Jacobi

MAJESTIC THEATRE
Opened Thursday, October 16, 1980.*
Zev Bufman and The Shubert Organization present the Wolf
Trap production of:

BRIGADOON

Book and Lyrics, Alan Jay Lerner; Music, Frederick Loewe; Director, Vivian Matalon; Choreography and Musical Staging, Agnes deMille; Choreography re-created by James Jamieson; Scenery, Michael J. Hotopp, Paul dePass; Costumes, Stanley Simmons; Lighting, Thomas Skelton; Musical Direction-Vocal Arrangements, Wally Harper; Assistant to Miss deMille, David Evans; Orchestrations, Mack Schlefer, Bill Brohn; Sound, T. Richard Fitzgerald; Hairstylist, Paul Huntley; Executive Producer for Wolf Trap, Craig Hankenson; Wardrobe, Randy Beth; Assistant Conductor, Thomas Helm; Assistant to Director, Victoria Bussert

CAST

Tommy Albright	Martin Vidnovic
Jeff Douglas	Mark Zimmerman
Angus McGuffie	Kenneth Kantor
Archie Beaton	Casper Roos
Sandy Dean	Michael Cone
Maggie Anderson	Marina Eglevsky
Harry Beaton	John Curry
Meg Brockie	Elaine Jausman
Andrew MacLaren	Jack Dabdoub
Fiona MacLaren	Meg Bussert
Jean MacLaren	Mollie Smith
Charlie Dalrymple	Stephen Lehew
Mr. Lundie	Frank Hamilton
Frank	Mark Herrier
Jane Ashton	Betsy Craig
Bagpiper	Larry Cole

SINGERS: Michael Cone, Betsy Craig, Larry French, Linda Hohenfeld, Michael Hayward-Jones, Joseph Kolinski, Diane Pennington, Cheryl Russell, Linda Wonneberger
DANCERS: Bill Badolato, Cherie Bower, Amy Danis, Tom Fowler, John Giffin, Mickey Gunnersen, Jennifer Henson, David Hughes, Phil LaDuca, Elena Malfitano, Susi McCarter, Jerry Mitchell, Eric Nesbitt, Holly Reeve, Dale Robbins, Harry Williams, Swing Dancers/Singers: Randal Harris, Suzi Winson
STANDBYS & UNDERSTUDIES: Linda Wonneberger (Fiona), Jack Dabdoub (Lundie), Eric Nesbitt (Harry), Mark Zimmerman (Tommy), Mark Herrier (Jeff), Diane Pennington (Meg), Casper Roos (MacLaren/Lundie), Linda Hohenfeld (Fiona/Jane), Joseph Kolinski (Charlie), Hayward-Jones (Angus/Sandy), Kenneth Kantor (Archie), Larry French (Frank), Holly Reeve (Jean), Tom Fowler (Harry), Amy Danis (Maggie)
MUSICAL NUMBERS: Once in the Highlands, Brigadoon, Down on MacConnachy Square, Waitin' for My Dearie, I'll Go Home with Bonnie Jean, Bonnie Jean, Heather on the Hill, Rain Exorcism, The Love of My Life, Jeannie's Packing Up, Come to Me Bend to Me, Almost Like Being in Love, Wedding Dance, Sword Dance, The Chase, There But for You Go I, Steps Stately, Drunken Reel, Funeral Dance, From This Day On

A musical in 2 acts and 12 scenes. The action takes place in Scotland and New York City.

General Manager: Theatre Now, Inc.
Company Manager: Hans Hortig
Press: Fred Nathan, Louise Weiner Ment
Stage Managers: Joe Lorden, Jack Gianino, David Rosenberg
*Closed Feb. 8, 1981 after 133 performances and 8 previews. Original production opened at the Ziegfeld Theatre March 13, 1947 with David Brooks, George Keane, Priscilla Gillette and James Mitchell, and played 581 performances. See THEATRE WORLD Vol. 4.

Martha Swope Photos

**Right Center: Mollie Smith, John Curry, Meg Bussert,
Casper Roos Above: Elaine Hausman, Mark Zimmerman
Top: Martin Vidnovic, Meg Bussert**

Stephen Lehew and company

TOWN HALL
Opened Sunday, October 19, 1980.*
Shalom Yiddish Musical Comedy Theatre, Raymond Ariel,
David Carey, Theo Roller present:

WISH ME MAZEL-TOV

Book by Moshe Tamir; Music, D. Blitenthal, A. Lustig; Lyrics, Y.
Alperin; Musical Arrangements, Horia Alexander, A. Lustig; Direc-
tor, Michal Greenstein; Musical Direction, Renee Solomon; Sets and
Costumes, Adina Reich; Choreography, Yankele Kaluski

CAST

Daliah	Mary Soreanu
Rivkah	Reizl Bozyk
Yankl	Karol Latowicz
Pinye	Solo-Moise Aron
Estee	Eleanor Reissa
Tzvikah	Sandy Levitt
Jeanette	Raquel Yossifon
Ryah	Ruth T. Kaminska
Emanuel Kaufman	David Ellin
Captain Shimon Kaufman	David Carey
Boys and Girls	Shelly Pappas, Luis Manuel,
	Kari Petersen, Mark Rubin

MUSICAL NUMBERS: Yafo Ballet, Honesty's the Hard Way,
Daliah, A Yiddish Yingele, Ver S'iz Avek, Soldier's Dance, What-
ever You Want, We Went Forth, My Dearest, God Will Provide,
Peace, I Need a Husband, Wish Me Mazel-Tov

A musical in two acts.

Press: David Lipsky
Stage Manager: Dan Shemer

* Closed Jan. 11, 1981 after 84 performances.

Jerry Goodstein Photos

**Right: Karol Latowicz, Reizl Bozyk,
Solo-Moise Aron Top: David
Carey, Mary Soreanu**

Stephen Wade

CENTURY THEATRE
Opened Tuesday, October 21, 1980.*
Stuart Oken, Jason Brett & The Klezmer Corporation present:

BANJO DANCING

or the 48th Annual Squitters Mountain Song Dance Folklore Con-
vention and Banjo Contest . . . and how I lost; Devised by Stephen
Wade with Milton Kramer; Director, Milton Kramer; Settings, David Emmons; Lighting, Dennis Parichy; An Apollo Group Production in association with Jeffrey Wachtel

CAST

Stephen Wade

A one-man show presented in two acts.

General Management: Frank Scardino
Press: Jeffrey Richards, Robert Ganshaw, Ben Morse, Helen
Stern, C. George Willard, Ted Killmer
Stage Manager: Annette Jops

* Closed Nov. 30, 1980 after 37 performances and 10 previews.

Jennifer Girard Photo

JOHN GOLDEN THEATRE
Opened Thursday, October 23, 1980.*
Richmond Crinkley and Royal Pardon Productions, Ivan Bloch, Larry J. Silva, Eve Skina in association with Joan F. Tobin present the American National Theatre and Academy production of:

TINTYPES

Conceived by Mary Kyte, Mel Marvin, Gary Pearle; Director, Gary Pearle; Musical Staging, Mary Kyte; Settings, Tom Lynch; Costumes, Jess Goldstein; Lighting, Paul Gallo; Sound, Jack Mann; Musical and Vocal Arrangements, Mel Marvin; Orchestrations and Vocal Arrangements, John McKinney; Production Coordinator, Brent Peek; Wardrobe, Cindy Steffens; Hairstylist, Peg Schierholz, Susan Kellett; Assistant Conductor, Clay Fullum

CAST

Carolyn Mignini
Lynne Thigpen
Trey Wilson
Mary Catherine Wright
Jerry Zaks
Mel Marvin at the piano

MUSICAL NUMBERS

ACT I: Ragtime Nightingale, The Yankee Doodle Boy, Ta-Ra-Ra Boom-Dee-Ay!, I Don't Care, Come Take a Trip in My Airship, Kentucky Babe, A Hot Time in the Old Town Tonight, Stars and Stripes Forever, Electricity, El Capitan, Pastime Rag, Meet Me in St. Louis, Solace, Waltz Me Around Again Willie, Wabash Cannonball, In My Merry Oldsmobile, Wayfaring Stranger, Sometimes I Feel Like a Motherless Child, Aye Lye Lyu Lye, I'll Take You Home Again Kathleen, America the Beautiful, Wait for the Wagon, What It Takes to Make Me Love You—You've Got It, The Maiden with the Dreamy Eyes, If I Were on the Stage (Kiss Me Again), Shortnin' Bread, Nobody, Elite Syncopations, I'm Goin' to Live Anyhow 'Til I Die

Act II: The Ragtime Dance, I Want What I Want When I Want It, It's Delightful to Be Married, Fifty-Fifty, American Beauty, Then I'd Be Satisfied with Life, Narcissus, Jonah Man, When It's All Goin' Out and Nothin' Comin' In, We Shall Not Be Moved, Hello Ma Baby, Teddy Da Roose, A Bird in a Gilded Cage, Bill Bailey Won't You Please Come Home, She's Gettin' More Like the White Folks Every Day, You're a Grand Old Flag, The Yankee Doodle Boy, Toyland, Smiles

UNDERSTUDIES: Marie King (Mignini/Wright), Wayne Bryan (Wilson/Zaks), S. Epatha Merkerson (Thigpen)

General Management: Elizabeth I. McCann, Nelle Nugent
Company Manager: James A. Gerald
Press: Betty Lee Hunt, Maria Cristina Pucci, James Sapp
Stage Managers: Steve Beckler, Bonnie Panson, Marie King

* Closed Jan. 11, 1981 after 93 performances and 11 previews. For original Off-Broadway production, see THEATRE WORLD Vol. 36.

Susan Cook, Roger Greenawalt Photos

**Trey Wilson, Carolyn Mignini, Jerry Zacks,
Mary Catherine Wright, Lynne Thigpen**
(also at top)

BIJOU THEATRE
Opened Thursday, October 30, 1980.*
Arthur Shafman International Ltd. presents:

QUICK CHANGE

Written by Bruce Belland, Roy M. Rogosin, Michael McGiveney; Director, Roy M. Rogosin; Music, Roy M. Rogosin; Lyrics, Bruce Belland; Costumes, Mary Wills; Set, John Shipley, Chris Flower; Sound, Alan Chapman, Eric Neufeld; Production Adviser, Richard G. Miller; Production Associates, Evelyn Gross, Eileen Jaffe, Susan Balsam

CAST

Michael McGiveney
assisted by Judith Hudson, Mark Bodine, Chris Flower

ACT I: Carnival, The Triumph of Arthur, The Lady Recites, Bill Sikes from "Oliver Twist"

ACT II: Pitchman and the Cop, Quicker Than the Eye, A Misunderstood Minority, Shoot-Out at Belle's Saloon

Company Manager: John Larson
Press: Jeffrey Richards, Robert Ganshaw, C. George Willard, Ben Morse, Ted Killmer, Helen Stern
Stage Manager: Ernie Guderjahn

* Closed Nov. 1, 1980 after 4 performances and 3 previews.

Jay Thompson, Toni Wade Photos

Michael McGiveney

MOROSCO THEATRE
Opened Sunday, November 2, 1980.*
Lester Osterman, Richard Horner, Hinks Shimberg and Freydberg-Cutler-Diamond Productions present:

A LIFE

By Hugh Leonard; Director, Peter Coe; Scenery and Costumes, Robert Fletcher; Lighting, Marc B. Weiss; Associate Producer, Spencer Berlin; Associate Producer and Casting, Lynne Stuart; Wardrobe, Josephine Dolan; Hairstylist, James Nelson

CAST

Drumm	Roy Dotrice
Dolly	Helen Stenborg
Mary	Aideen O'Kelly
Mibs (Young Mary)	Lauren Thompson
Desmond (Young Drumm)	Adam Redfield
Lar (Young Kearns)	David Ferry
Kearns	Pat Hingle
Dorothy (Young Dolly)	Dana Delany

A drama in two acts. The action takes place at the present time in a small town just south of Dublin, Ireland.

General Manager: Malcolm Allen
Company Manager: Stanley D. Silver
Press: Seymour Krawitz, Patricia McLean Krawitz, Martin Shwartz, Joel W. Dein
Stage Managers: Elliott Woodruff, Eileen Haring

* Closed Jan. 3, 1981 after 64 performances and 8 previews.

Top: Helen Stenborg, Roy Dotrice, Dana Delany,
Right: Pat Hingle, Aideen O'Kelly,
Stenborg, Roy Dotrice Below: David Ferry, Lauren
Thompson, Delany, Adam Redfield

Pat Hingle, Roy Dotrice

NEW APOLLO THEATRE

Opened Wednesday, November 5, 1980.*

Jerry Arrow, Robert Lussier, Warner Theatre Productions present the Circle Repertory Theatre production of:

FIFTH OF JULY

By Lanford Wilson; Director, Marshall W. Mason; Setting, John Lee Beatty; Costumes, Laura Crow; Lighting, Dennis Parichy; Sound, Chuck London; Song by Jonathan Hogan; Assistant to Director, Bruce McCarty; Production Assistant, Liz Rothberg; Wardrobe, Warren Morrill; Hairstylist, Jan Shoebridge; Technical Consultant, Michael Sulsona

CAST

Kenneth Talley, Jr.	Christopher Reeve[1]
Jed Jenkins	Jeff Daniels
John Landis	Jonathan Hogan
Gwen Landis	Swoosie Kurtz
June Talley	Joyce Reehling
Shirley Talley	Amy Wright
Sally Friedman	Mary Carver
Weston Hurley	Danton Stone[2]

UNDERSTUDIES: Tanya Berezin (Gwen/June), Phillip Clark (Kenneth/Jed/John), Jane Fleiss (Shirley), Edith Larkin (Sally), Lindsey Ginter (Weston/John)

A comedy in two acts. The action takes place at the Talley Place, a farm near Lebanon, Missouri, early evening of July 4, 1977 and the following morning

General Management: Belbrook Management
Company Manager: Thomas Shovestull
Press: Max Eisen, Barbara Glenn, Francine Trevens, Maria Somma
Stage Managers: Fred Reinglas, Jody Boese

* Still playing May 31, 1981. Miss Kurtz received a 1981 Tony for her performance as an Outstanding Featured Actress.
†Succeeded by: 1. Phillip Clark, Richard Thomas, 2. Ben Siegler

Martha Swope/Albert Bray Photos

Right: Amy Wright, Joyce Reehling, Mary Carver, Richard Thomas Top: Jeff Daniels, Christopher Reeve, Swoosie Kurtz, Jonathan Hogan, Amy Wright

Christopher Reeve, Swoosie Kurtz, Amy Wright

Richard Thomas, Swoosie Kurtz

BROOKS ATKINSON THEATRE
Opened Thursday, November 6, 1980.*
Gilbert Cates in association with Matthew Alexander presents:

TRICKS OF THE TRADE

By Sidney Michaels; Director, Gilbert Cates; Sets and Lighting, Peter Dohanos; Costumes, Albert Wolsky; Incidental Music, Charles Fox; Sound, Peter Berger; Production Associate, Tom Folino; Associate to Producer, Nancy B. Dodds; Wardrobe, Sally D. Smith; Assistant to Producer, Peggy Griffin

CAST

Dr. August Browning . . . . George C. Scott
Diana Woods . . . . Trish Van Devere
Howard . . . . Lee Richardson
Paul . . . . Geoffrey Pierson

Standbys: Lloyd Battista, Breon Gorman

A "romantic mystery" in two acts and ten scenes. The action takes place at the present time in the office of Dr. Browning in New York City.

General Manager: Paul Libin
Company Manager: Sally Campbell
Press: Merle Debuskey, Leo Stern
Stage Managers: Martin Gold, Carlos Gorbea

*Closed Nov. 6, 1980 after one performance and 9 previews.

Jay Thompson Photos

Left: Trish Van Devere, George C. Scott

Lee Richardson, Geoffrey Pierson, Trish Van Devere, George C. Scott

ETHEL BARRYMORE THEATRE
Opened Wednesday, November 12, 1980.*
Robert Whitehead and Roger L. Stevens present:

LUNCH HOUR

By Jean Kerr; Director, Mike Nichols; Scenic Design, Oliver Smith; Costumes, Ann Roth; Lighting, Jennifer Tipton; Assistants to Producers, Doris Blum, Jean Bankier; Assistant to Director, Charles Suisman; Wardrobe, Penny Davis; Hairstylist, Lyn Quiyou; Production Assistant, Bill Becker

CAST

Oliver	....	Sam Waterston
Nora	....	Susan Kellermann
Carrie	....	Gilda Radner
Leo	....	Max Wright
Peter	....	David Rasche

Standby: Jack Gilpin

A comedy in two acts. The action takes place at the present time in Oliver's house in the Hamptons.

General Manager: Oscar E. Olesen
Press: Seymour Krawitz, Patricia Krawitz, Joel W. Dein
Stage Managers: Nina Seely, Wayne Carson

* Closed June 28, 1981 after 263 performances and 8 previews.

Martha Swope Photos

Top: Susan Kellermann, Sam Waterston, Gilda
Radner, David Rasche, Max Wright

Gilda Radner, Sam Waterston

VIVIAN BEAUMONT THEATER
Opened Friday, November 14, 1980.*
The Lincoln Center Theater Company (Richmond Crinkley,
Producer) presents:

THE PHILADELPHIA STORY

By Philip Barry; Director, Ellis Rabb; Setting, John Conklin; Costumes, Nancy Potts; Lighting, John Gleason; Sound, Richard Fitzgerald; Incidental Music, Claibe Richardson; Played by The Roslyn Artists String Quartet; Production Supervisor, Helaine Head; Production Coordinator, Linda Strohmier; Assistant to Director, Edward Fabry; Executive Producers, McCann & Nugent

CAST

Edward	Edward Fabry
Elsie	Anne Sargent
May	Kim Beaty
Thomas	Robert Burr
Dinah Lord	Cynthia Nixon
Tracy Samantha Lord	Blythe Danner
Margaret Lord	Meg Mundy
Alexander (Sandy) Lord	Michael Gross
William (Uncle Willie) Tracy	George Ede
Macaulay (Mike) Connor	Edward Herrmann
Elizabeth (Liz) Imbrie	Mary Louise Wilson
George Kittredge	Richard Council
C. K. Dexter Haven	Frank Converse
Seth Lord	Douglass Watson
Mac	Count Stovall

STANDBYS & UNDERSTUDIES: Kim Beaty (Tracy), J. Kenneth Campbell (Dexter/Mike/George), Robert Burr (Seth/Uncle Willie), Anne Sargent (Margaret), Edward Fabry (Sandy/Thomas), Tiffany Bogart (Dinah/Elsie/May), Count Stovall (Edward/Thomas)

A comedy in two acts and four scenes. The action takes place in the summer room and garden of the Lord's home in the country outside Philadelphia during a period of 24 hours in the late 1930's.

Company Managers: Mario De Maria, Joey Parnes
Press: Betty Lee Hunt, Maria Cristina Pucci, James Sapp
Stage Managers: Peter Glazer, Count Stovall

* Closed Jan. 4, 1981 after limited engagement of 60 performances and 4 previews. Original production opened at the Shubert Theatre, March 28, 1939 and played 417 performances. In the cast were Katharine Hepburn, Shirley Booth, Van Heflin and Joseph Cotten.

Roger Greenawalt Photos

Top: Edward Herrmann, Michael Gross, Blythe Danner, **Below:** Douglass Watson, Meg Mundy, Cynthia Nixon

Frank Converse, Blythe Danner

Edward Herrmann, Blythe Danner

PLAYHOUSE THEATRE
Opened Tuesday, November 18, 1980.*
Jay J. Cohen, Richard Press, Louis Busch Hager Associates in
association with Yale Repertory Theatre (Lloyd Richards, Artistic Director) present:

A LESSON FROM ALOES

Written and Directed by Athol Fugard; Set, Michael H. Yeargan;
Costumes, Susan Hilferty; Lighting, William Armstrong; Executive
Producer, Ashton Springer; Wardrobe, Delores Gamba; Production
Supervisor, Ray Cook; Production Assistants, Larry Walden, Alan
R. Markinson

CAST

Piet Bezuidenhout . . . . Harris Yulin
Gladys Bezuidenhout . . . . Maria Tucci
Steve Daniels . . . . James Earl Jones†

UNDERSTUDIES: Linda McGuire (Gladys), Baxter Harris (Piet),
Zekes Mokae (Steve)

A drama in two acts. The action moves between the backyard and
the bedroom of a small house in Algoa Park, Port Elizabeth, South
Africa in 1963.

Company Manager: Stephanie S. Hughley
Press: Max Eisen, Irene Gandy, Francine L. Trevens
Stage Manager: Neal Ann Stephens

* Closed Feb. 8, 1981 after 96 performances and 14 previews. Cited
by the New York Drama Critics Circle as Best Play of the season.
†Succeeded by Zekes Mokae

Gerry Goodstein Photos

**Right: James Earl Jones, Maria
Tucci, Harris Yulin**

James Earl Jones, Marie Tucci, Harris Yulin

BILTMORE THEATRE

Opened Thursday, November 20, 1980.*

Jack Garfein, Warner Theatre Productions, Herbert Wasserman present the Harold Clurman Theatre production of:

THE AMERICAN CLOCK

By Arthur Miller; Inspired by Studs Terkel's "Hard Times"; Director, Vivian Matalon; Scenery, Karl Eigsti; Costumes, Robert Wojewodski; Lighting, Neil Peter Jampolis; Hairstylist, Charles LoPresto, Robert Cybula; Incidental Music, Robert Dennis; Executive Assistant to Producer, Cheryl Faraone; Assistant to Director, Sally Burnett; Wardrobe, Clarence Sims

CAST

Lee Baum	William Atherton
Moe Baum	John Randolph
Clarence/Waiter/Isaac/Jerome/Piano Mover	Donny Burks
Rose Baum	Joan Copeland
Frank/Livermore/Man in Welfare Office/ Stanislaus	Ralph Drischell
Grandpa/Kapush	Salem Ludwig
Fanny Margolies/Myrna	Francine Beers
Clayton/Sidney Margolies/Ralph	Robert Harper
Durant/Sheriff/Piano Mover/Toland	Alan North
Tony/Taylor/Dugan	Edward Seamon
Waiter/Bicycle Thief/Rudy/Piano Mover/Ryan	Bill Smitrovich
Joe/Bush	David Chandler
Irene	Rosanna Carter
Jeanette Ramsey/Edie/Lucille/Attendant	Susan Sharkey

STANDBYS & UNDERSTUDIES: Tresa Hughes (Rose), Suzanne Reichard (Doris/Jeanette), Lil Henderson (Irene/Myrna), Peter Francis-James (Clarence/Piano Mover/Ryan/Frank)

A "mural for theatre" in two acts.

General Management: Jack Schlissel/Jay Kingwill
Company Manager: Al Isaac
Press: Joe Wolhandler, Steven Wolhandler, Kathryn Kempf
Stage Managers: Robert LoBianco, Jane Neufeld

* Closed Nov. 30, 1980 after 12 performances and 11 previews.

Inge Morath Photos

**Top Right: William Atherton, Joan Copeland
Below: John Randolph, Joan Copeland**

"The Living Nativity"

RADIO CITY MUSIC HALL

Opened Sunday, November 23, 1980.*

Radio City Music Hall Productions presents:

THE MAGNIFICENT CHRISTMAS SPECTACULAR

Conceived and Produced by Robert F. Jani; Executive Musical Director, Donald Pippin; Staging and Choreography, Violet Holmes, Linda Lemac, Frank Wagner; Scenery, Charles Lisanby; Costumes, Frank Spencer; Lighting, Ken Billington; Narration Material, James Engelhardt; Production Coordinator, Linda Lemac; Wardrobe, Barbara Van Zandt, Donna Peterson; Conductor, Elman Anderson

PROGRAM

Christmas Caroling, Organists Robert MacDonald and David Messineo, Overture, The Christmas Tree, The Nutcracker, A Christmas Carol, Traditions of Santa Claus, The Night Before Christmas, International Holiday Traditions, Hanukkah, Twelve Days of Christmas, The New Yorkers Sing a Little Song, The Rockettes in the Parade of the Wooden Soldiers, The Living Nativity

Presented without intermission.

Stage Managers: Neil Miller, Peter Rosenberg, Ray Chandler, Peter Aaronson
Press: Gifford/Wallace, Keith Sherman

*Closed Jan. 4, 1981 after 97 performances.

Rivka Photos

HELEN HAYES THEATRE
Opened Sunday, November 30, 1980.*
Gladys Rackmil and Fred Levinson in association with Emhan Inc. present:

PERFECTLY FRANK

Conceived and Written by Kenny Solms; Music and Lyrics, Frank Loesser; Scenery and Costumes, John Falabella; Lighting, Ken Billington; Musical Director, Yolanda Segovia; Director, Fritz Holt; Choreography, Tony Stevens; Music Consultant, Larry Grossman; Orchestrations, Bill Byers; Dance Arrangements, Ronald Melrose; Sound, Larry Spurgeon; Hairstylist, Ted Azar; Associate Producer, Vivian Serota; Wardrobe, Joseph Busheme; Assistant to Producers, Dan Mizell; Production Assistant, Susan Lehner; Assistant Conductor, Marvin Laird

CAST

Andra Akers	David Ruprecht
Wayne Cilento	Virginia Sandifur
Jill Cook	Debbie Shapiro
Don Correia	Jo Sullivan
David Holliday	Jim Walton

UNDERSTUDIES: Robert Brubach (Cilento/Correia), Michael Byers (Holliday/Ruprecht/Walton), Emily Grinspan (Akers/-Shapiro/Sandifur/Sullivan), Barbara Hanks (Cook/Sandifur)

ACT I: Prologue, Screen Test, USO Show, Dressing Room, Understudy Rehearsal, Manhattan
ACT II: Entr'Acte, Rumble Rumble, Marriage, Rosabella, Dressing Room, Blues, Finale

General Management: Leonard Soloway/Allan Francis
Company Manager: Michael O'Rand
Press: Shirley Herz, Jan Greenberg, Sam Rudy
Stage Managers: A. Robert Altshuler, T. L. Boston, Michael Byers

* Closed Dec. 13, 1980 after 16 performances and 24 previews.

Martha Swope/Jay Thompson Photos

**Top Right: Don Correia, Jill Cook,
Wayne Cilento**

Jill Eikenberry, Martha Jean Sterner
Above: Edmond Genest, Jill Eikenberry

MARTIN BECK THEATRE
Opened Sunday, December 14, 1980.*
John N. Hart, Jr. in association with Hugh J. Hubbard and Robert M. Browne presents:

ONWARD VICTORIA

Book and Lyrics, Charlotte Anker, Irene Rosenberg; Music, Keith Herrmann; Director, Julianne Boyd; Musical Staging, Michael Shawn; Scenery, William Ritman; Costumes, Theoni V. Aldredge; Lighting, Richard Nelson; Music Direction, Larry Blank; Orchestrations, Michael Gibson; Dance Arrangements, Donald Johnston; Vocal Arrangements, Keith Herrmann, Larry Blank; Hairstylist, Robert DiNiro; Sound, Lewis Mead; Technical Supervisor, Jeremiah J. Harris; Wardrobe, William Campbell; Assistant Conductor, Donald Rebic; Production Assistant, Howard P. Lev

CAST

Little Girl/Mrs. Randolph	Lora Jeanne Martens
Victoria Woodhull	Jill Eikenberry
Tennie Claflin	Beth Austin
Telegraph Boy/Randolph	Marty McDonough
Jim	Dan Cronin
Cornelius Vanderbilt	Ted Thurston
Mrs. Fleming	Carrie Wilder
Mrs. Baxter	Karen Gibson
Fleming	Gordon Stanley
Baxter	John Kildahl
Woman Investor #1	Carol Lurie
Johnson	Scott Fless
Perkins	Ian Michael Towers
William Evarts	Rex Hays
Woman Investor #2	Dru Alexandrine
Beth Tilton	Martha Jean Sterner
Theodore Tilton	Edmond Genest
Elizabeth Cady Stanton	Laura Waterbury
Jim's Girlfriend	Lauren Goler
Congressman Butler/Grant Speaker/Maginnes/ Judge	Kenneth H. Waller
Henry Ward Beecher	Michael Zaslow
Susan B. Anthony	Dorothy Holland
Eunice Beecher	Linda Poser
Charlie Delmonico/Fullerton	Lenny Wolpe
Anthony Comstock	Jim Jansen

UNDERSTUDIES: Dorothy Holland (Victoria), Lora Jeanne Martens (Tennie), Rex Hays (Beecher/Tilton), Kenneth H. Waller (Delmonico)
MUSICAL NUMBERS: The Age of Brass, Magnetic Healing, Curiosity, Beecher's Processional, I Depend on You, Victoria's Banner, Changes, A Taste of Forever, Unescorted Women, Love and Joy, Everyday I Do a Little Something for the Lord, It's Easy for Her, You Cannot Drown the Dreamer, Respectable, Another Life, Read It in the Weekly, A Valentine for Beecher, Beecher's Defense

A musical in 2 acts and 17 scenes. The action takes place in New York City and Washington, D.C., during 1871.

General Management: Joseph Harris/Ira Bernstein
Press: Shirley Herz, Jan Greenberg, Sam Rudy
Stage Managers: Ed Aldridge, Joseph Corby, Renee F. Lutz

* Closed Dec. 14, 1980 after 1 performance and 23 previews.

Martha Swope Photos

31

BROADHURST THEATRE

Opened Wednesday, December 17, 1980.*
The Shubert Organization (Gerald Schoenfeld, Chairman; Bernard B. Jacobs, President), Elizabeth I. McCann, Nelle Nugent, Roger S. Berlind present:

AMADEUS

By Peter Shaffer; Director, Peter Hall; Production Design, John Bury; Associate Scenic Designer, Ursula Belden; Associate Costume Designer, John David Ridge; Associate Lighting Designer, Beverly Emmons; Music Directed and Arranged by Harrison Birtwistle; Production Coordinator, Brent Peek; Assistant Director, Giles Block; Wardrobe, Rosalie Lahm; Special Effects, Chic Silber; Production Assistant, Virlana Tkacz; Sound, Jack Mann; Wigs and Hairstylist, Paul Huntley

CAST

Antonio Salieri	Ian McKellen
The Venticelli	Gordon Gould, Edward Zang
Salieri's valet	Victor Griffin
Salieri's cook	Haskell Gordon
Joseph II, Emperor of Austria	Nicholas Kepros
Johann Kilian von Strack	Paul Harding†1
Count Orsini-Rosenberg	Patrick Hines
Baron van Swieten	Louis Turenne
Priest	Michael McCarty†2
Giuseppe Bonno	Philip Pleasants†3
Teresa Salieri, wife of Salieri	Linda Robbins
Katherina Cavalieri, Salieri's pupil	Caris Corfman†4
Constanze Weber, wife of Mozart	Jane Seymour†5
Wolfgang Amadeus Mozart	Tim Curry†6
Major Domo	Martin LaPlatney†7
Valets	Ronald Bagden, Rick Hamilton, Richard Jay-Alexander, Peter Kingsley, Mark Nelson,†8 Mark Torres
Citizens of Vienna	Caris Corfman, Michele Farr†9, Russell Gold, Haskell Gordon, Victor Griffin, Martin LaPlatney, Warren Manzi†10, Michael McCarty, Philip Pleasants, Linda Robbins

STANDBYS & UNDERSTUDIES: Jeremiah Sullivan/Daniel Davis (Salieri), Warren Manzi/John Pankow (Mozart/Venticello), Caris Corfman (Constanze), Philip Pleasants (Joseph II/Venticello), Russell Gold (von Strack/van Swieten/Salieri's valet), Michael McCarty (Count/Cook), Michele Farr (Teresa/Katherina), Martin LaPlatney (Major Domo/Valets), Mark Nelson (Mozart)

A drama in two acts. The action takes place in Vienna in November 1823, and in recall, the decade 1781–1791.

General Management: McCann & Nugent
Company Manager: Susan Gustafson
Press: Merle Debuskey, William Schelble
Stage Managers: Robert L. Borod, Robert Charles, Richard Jay-Alexander

* Still playing May 31, 1981. Recipient of 1981 Tonys for Best Play, Outstanding Actor in a Play (Ian McKellen), Outstanding Scenic Design, and Outstanding Lighting Design (John Bury).
† Succeeded by: 1. Jonathan Moore, 2. Donald C. Moore, 3. Russell Gold, 4. Michele Farr, 5. Caris Corfman, Amy Irving, 6. Peter Firth, 7. Brad O'Hare, 8. David Bryant, 9. Kristin Rudrud, 10. John Pankow

Zoe Dominic Photos

Left Center: Michael McCarty, Tim Curry, Caris Corfman, Ian McKellen, Russell Gold Below: Louis Turenne, Paul Harding, Tim Curry, Nicholas Kepros, Ian McKellen, Patrick Hines Top: Jane Seymour, Ian McKellen Below: Ian McKellen, Tim Curry

Nicholas Kepros, Jane Seymour

CIRCLE IN THE SQUARE THEATRE
Opened Thursday, December 18, 1980.*
Circle in the Square (Theodore Mann, Artistic Director; Paul Libin, Managing Director) presents:

JOHN GABRIEL BORKMAN

By Henrik Ibsen; Translated by Rolf Fjelde; Director, Austin Pendleton; Set, Andrew Jackness; Costumes, Jennifer Von Mayrhauser; Lighting, Paul Gallo; Production Assistant, Phil Seward; Wardrobe, Millicent Hacker; Wigs, Paul Huntley, Charles LoPresto, Michael Wasula

CAST

Mrs. Gunhild Borkman	Rosemary Murphy
Malene, Mrs. Borkman's maid	Brittain McGowin
Miss Ella Rentheim	Irene Worth
Mrs. Fanny Wilton	Patricia Cray Lloyd
Erhart Borkman	Freddie Lehne
John Gabriel Borkman	E. G. Marshall
Frida Foldal	Viveca Parker
Vilhelm Foldal	Richard Kuss

STANDBYS & UNDERSTUDIES: George Morfogen (Borkman), Elizabeth Hubbard (Gunhild/Ella), Brittain McGowin (Frida), Joseph Adams (Erhart)

A drama in three acts and four scenes. The action takes place during a late 1890's winter evening in the Rentheim family mansion outside the Norwegian capital

Company Manager: William Conn
Press: Merle Debuskey, David Roggensack
Stage Managers: Randall Brooks, Rick Ralston

* Closed Feb. 8, 1981 after 61 performances and 16 previews.

Brownie Harris Photos

Top: E. G. Marshall, Freddie Lehne, Rosemary Murphy Right: Marshall, Richard Kuss Below: Patricia Cray Lloyd, Lehne Left: Irene Worth, Marshall, Rosemary Murphy

Irene Worth, E. G. Marshall

BROOKS ATKINSON THEATRE
Opened Sunday, December 28, 1980.*
Frederick Brisson in association with the John F. Kennedy Center for the Performing Arts presents:

MIXED COUPLES

By James Prideaux; Director, George Schaefer; Set, Oliver Smith; Costumes, Noel Taylor; Lighting, Martin Aronstein; Assistant to Producer, Dwight Frye; Dance Consultant, Judith Haskell; Assistant to Director, Donald Smith; Production Assistant, Alexandra Isles; Wardrobe, Linda Lee; Hairstylist, Ray Iagnocco

CAST

Pilot	John Stewart
Alden	Michael Higgins
Elberta	Geraldine Page
Don	Rip Torn
Clarice	Julie Harris

STANDBYS: M'el Dowd, Peter McRobbie

A comedy in two acts. The action takes place in a workshop hangar at an airfield in New Jersey during September of 1927.

General Manager: Victor Samrock
Press: Jeffrey Richards, C. George Willard, Robert Ganshaw, Ben Morse, Helen Stern, Ted Killmer
Stage Managers: Robert Townsend, Charles Kindl

* Closed Jan. 3, 1981 after 9 performances and 7 previews.

Right: Geraldine Page, Julie Harris

Geraldine Page, Julie Harris

Julie Harris, Rip Torn
Above: Geraldine Page, Michael Higgins

34

PALACE THEATRE
Opened Sunday, January 4, 1981.*
Terry Allen Kramer, Joseph Kipness, James M. Nederlander, Stewart F. Lane in association with Twentieth Century-Fox Productions present:

FRANKENSTEIN

By Victor Gialanella; Director, Tom Moore; Scenery, Douglas W. Schmidt; Costumes and Puppets, Carrie F. Robbins; Lighting, Jules Fisher; Special Effects and Sound, Bran Ferren; Music, Richard Peaslee; Fight Coordination, B. H. Barry; Associate Producer, Marvin A. Krauss; Assistant to Director, Nancy Robbins; Production Assistant, Kathleen C. Shannon; Production Associate, Charlotte Dicker; Wardrobe, Peter J. FitzGerald; Hairstylist, John Quaglia; Special Effects Director, William McDonough; Puppet Master, Peter Baird

CAST

Hans Metz, a villager .... John Seitz
Peter Schmidt, a villager .... Dennis Bacigalupi
Henry Clerval, friend of Victor .... John Glover
Elizabeth Lavenza, Victor's adopted cousin ...... Dianne Wiest
William Frankenstein, Victor's younger brother .. Scott Schwartz
Justine Moritz, a maidservant .... Jill P. Rose
Victor Frankenstein, a scientist ...... William Converse-Roberts
Lionel Mueller, magistrate .... Richard Kneeland
Frau Mueller, his wife .... Kate Wilkinson
Alphonse Frankenstein, Victor's father .... Douglas Seale
The Creature .... Keith Jochim
DeLacey, a blind hermit .... John Carradine

UNDERSTUDIES: Leslie Barrett (Alphonse/Mueller/DeLacey), Michael Davidson (William), Anne Kerry (Elizabeth/Justine), Barbara Lester (Frau Mueller), Eric Uhler (Metz/Schmidt), Stephen Van Benschoten (Creature), Mark Winkworth (Victor/Henry)

A drama in 2 acts and 10 scenes. The action takes place in and around the Frankenstein estate, Geneva, Switzerland, in the mid-1800's.

General Management: Marvin A. Krauss, Eric Angelson, Gary Gunas, Steven C. Callahan
Press: Merle Debuskey, Leo Stern
Stage Managers: Michael Martorella, John Fennessy, Stephen Van Benschoten

* Closed Jan. 4, 1981 after 1 performance and 29 previews.

Martha Swope Photos

Right: Keith Jochim, Dianne Wiest
Above: Dennis Bacigalupi, John Seitz,
John Carradine Top: John Glover, David Dukes

CENTURY THEATRE
Opened Wednesday, January 14, 1981.*
Arthur Cantor presents:

EMLYN WILLIAMS
as
CHARLES DICKENS

A solo performance of scenes from the novels and stories of Charles Dickens; Production Supervisor, Robert Crawley; Assistant to Producer, Peninah Serrill; Production Assistants, Marilyn Rosenberg, Ken Bryant; The desk used is an exact copy of the one used by Dickens.

PART I: Scenes from "Our Mutual Friend," " The Black Veil," "Martin Chuzzlewit," "Dombey and Son"

PART II: Scenes from "The Tale of a Little Person," "The Battle of Life," 'Little Dorrit," "A Tale of Two Cities," "The Uncommercial Traveller"

General Manager: Harvey Elliott
Company Manager: Arthur Cantor
Press: Arthur Solomon, Marguerite Wolfe
Stage Manager: Robert Crawley

* Closed Feb. 1, 1981 after limited engagement of 23 performances.
Bryan Heseltine Photo

**Emlyn Williams
as Charles Dickens**

35

Estelle Parsons

URIS THEATRE

Opened Thursday, January 8, 1981.*
Joseph Papp presents the New York Shakespeare Festival production of:

THE PIRATES OF PENZANCE

Lyrics, W. S. Gilbert; Music, Arthur S. Sullivan; Director, Wilford Leach; Music Adapted and Conducted by William Elliott; Choreography, Graciela Daniele; Scenery, Bob Shaw, Wilford Leach; Supervised by Paul Eads; Costumes, Patricia McGourty; Hair and Makeup, J. Roy Helland; Lighting, Jennifer Tipton; Sound, Don Ketteler; Production Supervisor, Jason Steven Cohen; Wardrobe, Barrett Hong; Assistant to Director, John Albano; Production Assistant, Chris Sinclair; Original Cast Album by Elektra/Asylum Records

CAST

The Pirate King	Kevin Kline
Samuel, his lieutenant	Stephen Hanan
Frederic	Rex Smith
Ruth, a pirate maid	Estelle Parsons

Major-General Stanley's Daughters:

Edith	Alexandra Korey
Kate	Marcie Shaw
Isabel	Wendy Wolfe
Mabel	Linda Ronstadt†

Robin Boudreau, Maria Guida, Nancy Heikin, Bonnie Simmons

Major-General Stanley	George Rose
The Sergeant	Tony Azito

PIRATES & POLICE: Dean Badolato, Mark Beudert, Brian Bullard, Scott Burkholder, Walter Caldwell, Tim Flavin, Ray Gill, George Kmeck, Daniel Marcus, G. Eugene Moose, Joseph Neal, Walter Niehenke, Joe Pichette, Ellis Skeeter Williams, Michael Edwin Willson

UNDERSTUDIES: Ray Gill (Pirate King), G. Eugene Moose (Samuel), Wendy Wolfe (Ruth), Scott Burkholder (Frederic), Nancy Heikin (Edith), Joe Pichette (Stanley), Daniel Marcus (Sergeant), Karla DeVito (Mabel), Bonnie Simmons (Kate), Maria Guida (Isabel), Swings: Laurie Beechman, Roy Alan

MUSICAL NUMBERS: Our the Pirate Sherry, When Frederic Was a Little Lad, Oh Better Far to Live and Die, O False One You Have Deceived Me, Climbing over Rocky Mountain, Stop Ladies, Oh Is There Not One Maiden Breast, Poor Wandering One, Ought We to Do, How Beautifully Blue the Sky, We Must Not Lose Our Senses, Hold Monsters!, I Am the Very Model of a Modern Major-General, Men of Dark and Dismal Fate, Dry the Glistening Tear, Then Frederic, When the Foreman Bares His Steel, Now for the Pirates Lair, When You Had Left Our Pirate Fold, My Eyes Are Fully Open, Away! My Heart's on Fire, All Is Prepared, Stay Frederic!, Sorry Her Lot, No I Am Brave, When a Felon's Not Engaged in His Employment, A Rollicking Band of Pirates We, With Cat-Like Tread, Not a Word!, Sighing Softly to the River, Finale

An operetta in two acts.

General Manager: Robert Kamlot
Company Manager: Charles Willard
Press: Merle Debuskey, Richard Kornberg, John Howlett, Ed Bullins
Stage Managers: Zane Weiner, Frank DiFilia, Roy Alan

* Still playing May 31, 1981. Recipient of 1981 Tony for Outstanding Reproduction of a Play or Musical, Outstanding Actor in a Musical (Kevin Kline), Outstanding Direction of a Musical, and a Special Citation from the New York Drama Critics Circle.
†Succeeded by Karla DeVito

Martha Swope Photos

Left Center: Rex Smith, Linda Ronstadt, George Rose Above: Tony Azito, Linda Ronstadt Top: Linda Ronstadt, George Rose, (back) Kevin Kline, Rex Smith

BILTMORE THEATRE
Opened Wednesday, January 14, 1981.*
Doris Cole Abrahams and Burry Fredrik in association with
Leon Becker present:

TO GRANDMOTHER'S HOUSE
WE GO

By Joanna M. Glass; Director, Clifford Williams; Setting, Ben Edwards; Costumes, Jane Greenwood; Lighting, Marc B. Weiss; Technical Supervisor, Jeremiah Harris; Wardrobe, Bill Campbell; Set Decorations, Michael Sharp

CAST

Grandie	Eva LeGallienne
Harriet	Kim Hunter
Muffy	Pamela Brook
Clementine	Ruth Nelson
Jared	Shepperd Strudwick
Beatrice	Anne Twomey
Paul	David Snell
Twyla	Leslie Denniston

UNDERSTUDIES: Ruth Nelson (Grandie), Betty Low (Clementine/Harriet/Grandie), Edward Earle (Jared), Alex Wipf (Paul), Lise Hilboldt (Muffy/Beatrice/Twyla)

A drama in two acts and four scenes. The action takes place at the present time in Grandie's home in a small town outside of Hartford, Connecticut.

General Management: Frank Scardino, Phil Leach, Corinne Edgerly
Press: Shirley Herz, Jan Greenberg, Sam Rudy, Peter Cromarty
Stage Managers: Robert Corpora, Audrey Koran, Edward Earle

* Closed March 8, 1981 after 61 performances and 19 previews.
† Succeeded by Lise Hilboldt

Meryl Joseph Photos

Left: Kim Hunter, Eva LeGallienne
Above: Anne Twomey, Kim Hunter, David
Snell, Pamela Brook Top: Shepperd
Strudwick, Eva LaGallienne, Kim Hunter,
David Snell

Shepperd Strudwick, David Snell, Pamela Brook, Leslie Denniston, Ruth Nelson,
Anne Twomey, Kim Hunter, Eva LeGallienne

BIJOU THEATRE

Opened Wednesday, January 21, 1981.*
Arthur Shafman presents:

SHAKESPEARE'S CABARET

Concept and Music by Lance Mulcahy; Director, John Driver; Choreography, Lynne Taylor-Corbett; Scenery and Costumes, Frank J. Boros; Lighting, Marc B. Weiss; Orchestrations, Vocal Arrangements, and Musical Direction, Don Jones; Wardrobe, Debbie Fisher; Production Assistants, Jacqueline Biberman, Nina R. Lederman; Production Adviser, Richard G. Miller; Production Associates, Evelyn Gross, Susan Balsam; Originally produced at Colonnades Theatre Lab

CAST

Alan Brasington
Catherine Cox
Pauletta Pearson
Patti Perkins
Larry Riley
Michael Rupert
Weyman Thompson (Understudy)

MUSICAL NUMBERS: If Music and Sweet Poetry Agree, What Thou Seest When Thou Dost Awake, All That Glisters, Why Should This a Desert Be?, Crabbed Age and Youth, Orpheus and His Lute, Music with Her Silver Sound, Come Live with Me and Be My Love, Have More Than Thou Showest, Venus and Adonis Suite, Tell Me Where Is Fancy Bred?, If Music Be the Food of Love, Epitaph for Marina, the Phoenix and the Turtle, Now, The Willow Song, Immortal Gods, Tomorrow Is St. Valentine's Day, Fathers That Wear Rags, The Grave Digger's Song, Come Unto These Yellow Sands, Shall I Compare Thee to a Summer's Day?, Lawn as White as Driven Snow, Rosalynde, Let Me the Canakin Clink, Shakespeare's Epitaph, Fear No More the Heat of the Sun

A musical cabaret performed without intermission.

General Manager: Sherman Gross
Press: Jeffrey Richards, Robert Ganshaw, C. George Willard, Ben Morse, Ted Killmer, Helen Stern
Stage Managers: Kitzi Becker, John Handy

* Closed March 8, 1981 after 54 performances and 12 previews.

Stephanie Saia Photos

**Top Right: Patti Perkins, Michael Rupert
Below: Pauletta Pearson, Catherine Cox,
Patti Perkins**

VIVIAN BEAUMONT THEATER

Opened Thursday, January 22, 1981.*
The Lincoln Center Theater Company (Richmond Crinkley, Producer) presents:

MACBETH

By William Shakespeare; Director, Sarah Caldwell; Settings, Herbert Senn, Helen Pond; Costumes and Apparitions, Carrie Robbins; Lighting, John Gleason; Sound, Richard Fitzgerald; Fight Director, B. H. Barry; Music, Edward Barnes; Technical Coordinator, Jack Lines; Wardrobe, Joseph Busheme; Hairstylist, Frank Melon; Special Effects, Chic Silber; Production Coordinator, Brent Peek

CAST

Lady Macbeth	Maureen Anderman
Macbeth, a Scottish army general	Philip Anglim†1
Caithness/Nobleman/Murderer	Ivar Brogger
Young Siward/Rosse Aide	Robert Burns
Macduff, nobleman of Scotland	J. Kenneth Campbell
Seyton, officer attending Macbeth	Jarlath Conroy
Witch	Michael Dash
Lennox, a nobleman	Kelsey Grammer
Witch	Ellen Gould
Witch/Lady	Cordis Heard
Rosse, a nobleman	James Hurdle
Gentlewoman/Witch/Lady	Dana Ivey
Sewer/English Soldier	Esquire Jauchem
English Soldier/Duncan Attendant	Randy Kovitz
Lady Macduff	Kaiulani Lee
Angus, a nobleman	Kevin McClarnon
Fleance/Son of Macduff	William Morrison
Duncan Attendant/Shield Bearer	Conal O'Brien
Donalbain/Monteith	Eugene Pressman
Witch/Lady	Judith Roberts
Banquo, a Scottish army general	Norman Snow†2
A Porter	Roy K. Stevens
Bishop/Old Siward	Sam Stoneburner
Scottish Doctor/Old Man/Murderer	Peter Van Norden
Malcom, son of Duncan	John Vickery
Duncan, King of Scotland	Neil Vipond
Acolyte/Macduff child	Jonathan Ward

A tragedy performed in two acts. The action takes place in Scotland and in England.

Company Managers: Mario DeMaria, Joey Parnes, Jean Passanante
Press: Betty Lee Hunt, Maria Cristina Pucci, James Sapp
Stage Managers: Robert Bennett, Nancy Finn, Esquire Jauchem

* Closed March 8, 1981 after 61 performances and 9 previews.
† Succeeded by: 1. Kelsey Grammer during illness, 2. Fritz Sperberg

Roger Greenawalt Photos

Maureen Anderman, Philip Anglim

HELEN HAYES THEATRE
    Opened Wednesday, January 28, 1981.*
    Rodger H. Hess presents:

THE FIVE O'CLOCK GIRL

Book, Guy Bolton, Fred Thompson; Music and Lyrics, Bert Kalmar, Harry Ruby; Director, Sue Lawless; Musical Staging and Choreography, Dan Siretta; Scenery, John Lee Beatty; Costumes, Nanzi Adzima; Lighting, Craig Miller; Sound, Richard Fitzgerald; Assistant Producer, Jamey Cohan; Music Research, Alfred Simon; Production Associate, Sheila Tronn Cooper; Orchestrations and Dance Arrangements, Russell Warner; Assistant Choreographer, Larry McMillian; Musical Direction, Lynn Crigler; Production Consultant, Warren Pincus; Originally produced by the Goodspeed Opera House; Wardrobe, John Riccucci; Assistant to Director, France Burke; Production Assistant, Allen Haines

CAST

Madame Irene	Sheila Smith
Hudgins (Mr. Brooks' valet)	Ted Pugh
Susan Snow	Pat Stanley
Patricia Brown	Lisby Larson
Gerald Brooks	Roger Rathburn
Ronnie Webb	Barry Preston
Cora Wainwright	Dee Hoty
Jasper Cobb	Timothy Wallace
Jeanie	Teri Corcoran
Pete, the waiter	James Homan
Rodney, Madame Irene's escort	Richard Ruth
Sam	Rodney Pridgen
Ethel/Molly/Maid	Annette Michelle
Elsie	Lora Jeanne Martens
Bunnie	Jean McLaughlin
Polly	Debra Grimm
Maisie	Carla Farnsworth-Webb
Jules, Maitre d'	Jonathan Aronson
Detective	G. Brandon Allen
Bobby/Policeman	Gary Kirsch

UNDERSTUDIES: Jean McLaughlin (Sue), Lora Jeanne Martens (Pat), Carla Farnsworth-Webb (Cora), Richard Ruth (Gerry), Jonathan Aronson (Ronnie), Teri Corcoran (Mme. Irene), Timothy Wallace (Hudgins), G. Brandon Allen (Jasper), Swings: Danute Debney, Robert Rabin
MUSICAL NUMBERS: Overture, In the Old Neighborhood, Keep Romance Alive, Thinking of You, Up in the Clouds, I'm One Little Party, My Sunny Tennessee, Any Little Thing, Manhattan Walk, Long Island Low Down, Who Did? You Did!, Nevertheless, All Alone Monday, Dancing the Devil Away, Finale

A musical in 2 acts and 10 scenes. The action takes place in New York City in the 1920's.

General Management: Theatre Now, Inc.
Press: Shirley Herz, Jan Greenberg, Sam Rudy, Peter Cromarty
Stage Managers: John J. Bonanni, Peter Weicker, Danute Debney

* Closed Feb. 8, 1981 after 12 performances and 7 previews.

Peter Cunningham Photos

Barry Preston (3rd from left), Sheila Smith, Ted Pugh, Pat Stanley, Lisby Larson, Roger Rathburn, Dee Hoty, Timothy Wallace Top: Ensemble

TOWN HALL
    Opened Thursday, February 19, 1981.*
    Lily Turner Attractions presents:

JACQUES BREL IS ALIVE AND WELL AND LIVING IN PARIS

Music, Jacques Brel; Conception, English Lyrics, Additional Material, Eric Blau, Mort Shuman; Based on Brel's lyrics and commentary; Original Direction, Moni Yakim; Production Supervisor, Eric Blau

CAST

Joe Masiell	Betty Rhodes
Sally Cooke	Shawn Elliott

MUSICAL NUMBERS: Marathon, Alone, Madeleine, I Love, Mathilde, Bachelor's Dance, Timid Frieda, My Death, Girls and Dog, Jackie, The Statue, Desperate Ones, Sons of, Amsterdam, The Buffs, Old Folks, Marieke, Brussels, Fannette, Funeral Tango, Middle Class, You're Not Alone, Next, Carousel, If We Only Have Love

A musical in two acts.

General Management: Lily Turner
Press: M.J. Boyer, Rosemary Carey
Stage Managers: Steve Helliker, Greg Villone

* Closed March 8, 1981 after 24 performances.

Elizabeth Marshall Photos

Sally Cooke, Shawn Elliott, Betty Rhodes, Joe Masiell

39

PLYMOUTH THEATRE

Opened Thursday, February 5, 1981.*
Elizabeth I. McCann, Nelle Nugent, The Shubert Organization, Ray Larsen in association with Warner Theatre Productions present:

PIAF

By Pam Gems; Director, Howard Davies; Assistant Director, Helaine Head; Musical Direction and Arrangements, Michael Dansicker; Setting, David Jenkins; Costumes, Julie Weiss; Lighting, Beverly Emmons; Produced originally by the Royal Shakespeare Co.; Production Coordinator, Brent Peek; Wardrobe, Margot Moore; Hairstylist, Stephen Camanella; Special Effects, Chic Silber; Sound, Jack Mann; Wigs, Paul Huntley

CAST

M.C./Manager	David Leary
Piaf	Jane Lapotaire
"Papa" Leplee, owner of Cluny Club	Peter Friedman
Toine	Zoe Wanamaker
Emil, maitre d' of Cluny Club	Nicholas Woodeson
Legionnaire/Pierre/Agent	Stephen Davies
Jacques/German Soldier/Angelo	Lewis Arlt
Eddie/Butcher/Marcel/Barman	Robert Christian
Little Louis/German Soldier/Lucien/Dope Pusher	Michael Ayr
Police Inspector/Georges/Physiotherapist	Kenneth Welsh
Paul/American Soldier/Theo	David Purdham
Marlene	Jean Smart
American Soldier	Peter Friedman
Madeleine	Judith Ivey
Jacko	Nicholas Woodeson
Nurse	Sherry Steiner

STANDBYS & UNDERSTUDIES: Judith Ivey (Piaf), Lewis Arlt (Man at rehearsal), Cynthia Carle (Marlene/Nurse/Madeleine), Robert Christian (Physiotherapist/Paul), Stephen Davies (Eddie), Peter Friedman (Dope Pusher/German Soldier), Michael Hammond (Manager/Inspector/Georges), Christopher McHale (Marcel/Jacques/Theo), David Purdham (Leplee), Sherry Steiner (Toine/Madeleine/Piaf), Robert Thaler (Pierre/Jacko/Emil/Lucien), Kenneth Welsh (Angelo), Nicholas Woodeson (Barman/Butcher)

A drama in two acts. A celebration of the life of Edith Piaf from the late 1920's through 1963.

General Management: McCann & Nugent
Company Manager: James A. Gerald
Press: Solters/Roskin/Friedman, Joshua Ellis, David LeShay
Stage Managers: Helaine Head, William Gammon, Christopher McHale

* Closed June 28, 1981 after 165 performances and 9 previews. Jane Lapotaire received a 1981 "Tony" Award as Outstanding Actress in a Play.

Martha Swope Photos

Left: David Purdham, Jane Lapotaire,
Peter Friedman Top: Jane Lapotaire,
Zoe Wanamaker

Jane Lapotaire, Nicholas Woodeson

Jane Lapotaire

J. C. Quinn, Sean Penn, Larry Nicks

CENTURY THEATRE
Opened Monday, February 23, 1981.*
Gretl Productions Inc. and Ned Davis in association with Ken Cotthoff and Boyd Ralph present:

HEARTLAND

By Kevin Heelan; Director, Art Wolff; Scenery and Lighting, Bill Ballou; Special Visual and Audio Effects, Tom Brumberger; Costumes, Kiki Smith; Wardrobe, Lucille Gabriel

CAST

Earl .... Larry Nicks
Skeet .... J. C. Quinn
James .... Sean Penn
Cotton .... Keith Jochim
Pauline .... Martyn St. David

A drama in two acts. The action takes place at the present time during late spring in a small town in the Midwest.

General Management: Jeff Evans
Company Manager: Delman Hendricks
Press: Glenna Freedman, Judy Jacksina, Angela Wilson, Dolph Browning
Stage Managers: Christine Devereux, David Higlen

* Closed March 15, 1981 after 24 performances and 5 previews.

Martha Swope Photos

MOROSCO THEATRE
Opened Tuesday, March 3, 1981.*
Craig Anderson and Stafford Productions present:

THE SURVIVOR

By Susan Nanus; Based on book by Jack Eisner; Music, Gary William Friedman; Director, Craig Anderson; Scenery, Steven Rubin; Costumes, Bill Walker; Lighting, John Gleason; Sound, Jan Nebozenko; Associate Producer, Buddy Bloom; Assistant Director, Robert Caprio; Production Associate, David Thalenberg; Wardrobe, Karen Lloyd; Hairstylist, John Herrmann; Production Assistants, Ava Hordyk, Charles Johnson

CAST

Jacek .... David Marshall Grant
Zlatke .... Joanna Merlin
Rudy's Mother .... Ruth S. Klinger
Lutek's Mother .... Rochelle Parker
Sevek's Mother .... Nada Rowand
Hela .... Loren Brown
Rudy .... Lonny Price
Lutek .... Joseph Adams
Sevek .... Mark Bendo
Yankele .... Zeljko Ivanek
Halina .... Ann Lange
Grandma Masha .... Lilia Skala
Polish Blackmailer/Rudy's Father/Jewish
  Collaborator .... Ralph Drischell
Lutek's Father/Markowsky/Escapee ..... Richard M. Davidson
Markowsky .... Richard Greene

UNDERSTUDIES: Joseph Adams (Jacek), Richard M. Davidson (Aron), Joan de Marrais (Rudy's mother/Sevek's mother/Lutek's mother), Ralph Drischell (Markowsky), Richard Greene (Escapee), Zeljko Ivanek (Rudy), Ruth S. Klinger (Grandma), Wendy Rosenberg (Hela/Halina), Nada Rowand (Zlatke), Jeff Marcus (Lutek/Sevek/Yankele), Hal Sherman (Lutek's Father/Blackmailer/Collaborator/Stash)

A drama in two acts. The action takes place in and around the Warsaw Ghetto from November 1940 to April 1943.

General Manager: Harris Goldman
Company Manager: Harold Sogard
Press: Howard Atlee/Bill Evans, Jim Baldassare, Leslie Anderson
Stage Managers: Louis D. Pietig, Shari Genser

* Closed March 8, 1981 after 8 performances and 16 previews.

Martha Swope/Ken Howard Photos

Top Right: Lonny Price, Joseph Adams, Ann Lange, Zeljko Ivanek, David Marshall Grant (front) Below: Lilia Skala, Grant

Ann Lange, David Marshall Grant

41

LUNT-FONTANNE THEATRE
Opened Sunday, March 1, 1981.*
Robert S. Berlind, Manheim Fox, Sondra Gilman, Burton L. Litwin and Louise Westergaard in association with Belwin Mills Publishing Corp. and Norzar Productions present:

SOPHISTICATED LADIES

Concept by Donald McKayle; Based on music of Duke Ellington; Director, Michael Smuin; Musical Staging and Choreography, Donald McKayle, Michael Smuin; Co-Choreography and Tap Choreography, Henry LeTang; Musical Director, Mercer Ellington; Settings, Tony Walton; Costumes, Willa Kim; Lighting, Jennifer Tipton; Sound, Otts Munderloh; Hairstylist, Howard Leonard, Danny Wintrobe; Orchestrations, Al Cohn; Musical and Dance Arrangements, Lloyd Mayers; Vocal Arrangements, Malcolm Dodds, Lloyd Mayers; Associate Choreographer, Bruce Heath; Assistant Choreographer, Mercedes Ellington; Musical Consultant and Additional Arrangements, Paul Chihara; Wardrobe, Jennifer Bryan; Production Assistants, Michael Harrod, Mark Saraceni

CAST

Hinton Battle	Terri Klausner
Gregg Burge	P. J. Benjamin
Gregory Hines	Phyllis Hyman
Judith Jamison	Priscilla Baskerville
Mercedes Ellington	

SOPHISTICATED LADIES & GENTLEMEN: Claudia Asbury, Mercedes Ellington, Paula Lynn, Wynonna Smith, Adrian Bailey, Michael Lichtefeld, Michael Scott Gregory, T. A. Stephens
UNDERSTUDIES: Hinton Battle/Gregg Burge (Gregory Hines), Wynonna Smith/Valerie Pettiford (Judith Jamison), Michael Scott Gregory, Faruma S. Williams (Gregg Burge), Paula Lynn (Terri Klausner), Michael Lichtefeld (P. J. Benjamin), T. A. Stephens/Faruma S. Williams (Hinton Battle)
MUSICAL NUMBERS: Overture, I've Got to Be a Rug Cutter, Music Is a Woman, The Mooche, Hit Me with a Hot Note, Love You Madly, Perdido, Faty and Forty, It Don't Mean a Thing, Bli-Blip, Cotton Tail, Take the "A" Train, Solitude, Don't Get Around Much Anymore, I Let a Song Go Out of My Heart, Caravan, Something to Live For, Old Man Blues, Drop Me Off in Harlem, Rockin' in Rhythm, Duke's Place, Diminuendo in Blue, In a Sentimental Mood, I'm Beginning to See the Light, Satin Doll, Just Squeeze Me, Dancers in Love, Echoes of Harlem, I'm Just a Lucky So-and-So, Hey Baby, Imagine My Frustration, Kinda Dukish, Koko, I'm Checking Out Goombye, Do Nothing 'Til You Hear from Me, I Got It Bad and That Ain't Good, Mood Indigo, Sophisticated Lady, Finale

A musical in two acts.

General Managers: Joseph Harris, Ira Bernstein, Steven E. Goldstein
Press: Fred Nathan, Eileen McMahon, Sam Ross, Karen Johnson
Stage Managers: Martin Gold, Carlos Gorbea, Kenneth Hanson

* Still playing May 31, 1981. Recipient of 1981 Tonys for Outstanding Featured Actor in a Musical (Hinton Battle) and Outstanding Costume Design.

Martha Swope Photos

**Top Right: Gregory Hines, Judith Jamison
Below: Adrian Bailey, Michael Lichtefeld,
T. A. Stephens, Michael Scott Gregory,
Phyllis Hyman**

Terri Klausner, Gregg Burge

Paula Lynn, P. J. Benjamin, Claudia Asbury, Wynonna Smith, Mercedes Ellington

MARTIN BECK THEATRE
Opened Thursday, March 5, 1981.*
Lee Guber, Shelly Gross, Slade Brown and Jim Milford present:

BRING BACK BIRDIE

Book, Michael Stewart; Music, Charles Strouse; Lyrics, Lee Adams; Conceived and Directed by Joe Layton; Scenery, David Mitchell; Costumes, Fred Voelpel; Lighting, David Hays; Sound, Otts Munderloh; Video Sequences, Wakefield Poole, Frank O'Dowd; Musical Direction-Vocal Arrangements, Mark Hummel; Dance Music Arrangements, Daniel Troob; Hairstylist, Werner Sherer, Stephen Bishop; Associate to Director, Wakefield Poole; Video Consultant, Lee M. Erdman; Film Coordinator, Zev Guber; Wardrobe, Patricia Britton; Assistant Conductor, Linda Twine; Production Associate, Helen Meier; Dance Assistant, Michon Peacock; Assistants to Producers, Laurie Kaufman, Michele Jacobson; Production Assistants, Victor Lukas, Peter Loewy

CAST

Storyteller/Reporter	Donna Monroe
Albert	Donald O'Connor
Rose	Chita Rivera
Mtobe	Maurice Hines
Hogan/Guard/Marshall	Howard Parker
Albert, Jr.	Evan Seplow
Jenny	Robin Morse
Gary	Jeb Brown
Girl Friends	Barbara Dare Thomas, Vanessa Bell, Julie Cohen, Christine Langner
Porter/Rev. Sun/Reporter	Frank DeSal
Sunnie/Chorus Girl/Birdette	Betsy Friday
Tourist/Reporter	Bill Bateman
His Wife/Effie	Zoya Leporska
Shopping Bag Lady/Birdette	Rebecca Renfroe
Indian Squaw	Janet Wong
Indian Brave/Reporter	Larry Hyman
Mae Peterson	Maria Karnilova
Mayor C. B. Townsend	Marcel Forestieri
"Filth" Group	Evan Seplow, Jeb Brown, Cleve Asbury, Leon Evans, Mark Frawley
House Manager	Peter Oliver Norman
Rose II	Lynnda Ferguson
Cameraman	Michael Blevins
Walter	Kevin Petitt

STANDBYS & UNDERSTUDIES: Howard Parker (Albert), Michon Peacock (Rose), Zoya Leporska (Mae), Peter Oliver Norman (Mtobe), Bill Bateman (Conrad), Michael Blevins (Albert, Jr.), Cleve Asbury (Gary), Betsy Friday (Rose II), Swings: Donna Ritchie, Porter Hudson

MUSICAL NUMBERS: Twenty Happy Years, Movin' Out, Half of a Couple, I Like What I Do, Bring Back Birdie, Baby You Can Count on Me, A Man Worth Fightin' For, You Can Never Go Back, Filth, Back in Show Biz Again, Middle Age Blues, Inner Peace, There's a Brand New Beat in Heaven, Well I'm Not!, When Will Grown-Ups Grow Up?, Young, I Love 'Em All

A musical in 2 acts and 15 scenes.

General Managers: Theatre Now, Inc.
Company Manager: Stephen Arnold
Press: Solters/Roskin/Friedman, Milly Schoenbaum, Joshua Ellis, Kevin Patterson

* Closed March 7, 1981 after 4 performances and 31 previews.

Martha Swope Photos

**Top: Chita Rivera, Donald O'Connor
Below: Chita Rivera**

Donald O'Connor, Robin Morse

MITZI E. NEWHOUSE THEATER
Opened Thursday, March 5, 1981.*
The Lincoln Center Theater Company (Richmond Crinkley, Producer; Edward Albee, Artistic Director) presents:

THE ONE ACT PLAY FESTIVAL

Settings, John Wright Stevens; Costumes, David Murin; Lighting, Marc B. Weiss; Sound, Richard Fitzgerald; Production Coordinator, Brent Peek

CAST

"Stops Along the Way" by Jeffrey Sweet
Director, Kevin Conway
Donna .... Kathleen Widdoes
Larry .... Graham Beckel
Ray...................................... William Newman
Waiter .... Michael Egan
Gas Station Attendant .... Marilyn Rockafellow
Clerk..................................... Michael Egan
Bartender.............................. Marilyn Rockafellow
Intermission
"In Fireworks Lie Secret Codes"
Written and Directed by John Guare
#1 .... William Newman
#2 .... Kathleen Widdoes
#3 .... James Woods
#4 .... Barbara Andres
#5 .... Graham Beckel
Pause
"Vivien" by Percy Granger
Directed by Kevin Conway
Vivien.................................... Michael Egan
Paul .... James woods
Mrs. Tendesco........................... Barbara Andres
Company Manager: Mario DeMaria
Press: Betty Lee Hunt, Maria Cristina Pucci, James Sapp
Stage Managers: Rita Calabro, Robin Miller, Joey Parnes, Jean Passanante

* Closed April 5, 1981 after 37 performances and 8 previews.

Roger Greenawalt Photos

James Woods, Michael Egan in "Vivien"
Top: William Newman, Marilyn Rockafellow,
Kathleen Widdoes, Graham Beckel in
"Stops Along the Way"

Jeff Johnson, Iris Revson, Mark Morales,
Reed Jones, Wendy Edmead Above: Rockettes

RADIO CITY MUSIC HALL
Opened Friday, March 6, 1981.*
Radio City Music Hall Productions presents:

AMERICA

Conceived and Produced by Robert F. Jani; Musical Direction and Routines, Tom Bahler; Choreography, Violet Holmes, Linda Lemac, Frank Wagner; Principals Staged by Frank Wagner; Scenery, Robert Guerra; Costumes, Michael Casey; Lighting, Ken Billington; Special Material and Dialogue, Harvey Jacobs; Original Music and Lyrics, Tom Bahler, Mark Vieha; Wardrobe, Barbara Van Zandt, Donna Peterson; Organists, Robert Maidhof, George Wesner; Director of Rockettes, Violet Holmes

PROGRAM

The Opening, The Story of America, Fifty Great Places All in One Place, The Spirit of America, A Tour de Force of America, Hawaii Is the 50th Star, The Electro-Live-Synthomagnetic Radio City Music Hall Orchestra, Freedom, A New American Spirit Is Alive, On Parade, America the Beautiful

Press: Gifford/Wallace, Keith Sherman
Stage Managers: Donald Christy, Ray Chandler, Peter Aaronson, Jack Horner

* Closed Sept. 7, 1981 after 284 performances and 11 previews.

Martha Swope Photos

44

NEDERLANDER THEATRE
Opened Sunday, March 15, 1981.*
Edgar Lansbury, Joseph Beruh, James Nederlander present:

BROADWAY FOLLIES

Music and Lyrics, Walter Marks; Concept and Direction, Donald Driver; Choreography, Arthur Faria; Scenery, Peter Larkin; Costumes, Alvin Colt; Lighting, Roger Morgan; Sound, Abe Jacob; Musical Direction-Vocal and Dance Arrangements, Marvin Laird; Orchestrations, Bill Byers; Talent Coordinator, Gilbert Miller; Production Supervisor, Robert Straus; Hairstylist, Joe Tubens, Calvin Trahan; Assistant to Director, Nina Faso; Assistant to Producers, Darrell Jonas; Production Assistants, Kim Larimore, John Nassivera; Wardrobe, Peter J. FitzGerald

CAST

Robert Shields	Lorene Yarnell
Tessie O'Shea	Michael Allen Davis
Milo & Roger	Scott's Royal Boxers
Los Malambos	Gaylord Maynard & Chief Bearpaw

ACT I: Broadway Follies, Vaudeville, Wonderful U, Picadilly, The Oasis, The Pampas, The Toyshop, The Paper Bag Rag

ACT II: At Home with the Clinkers, The Barnyard, Specialty, The Saloon, Tap My Way to the Stars, The Rest of Michael Davis, Grand Parade

General Manager: Marvin A. Krauss, Gary Gunas, Eric Angelson, Steve Callahan
Company Manager: Sally Campbell
Press: Gifford/Wallace, Keith Sherman, Valerie Warner
Stage Managers: Robert V. Straus, John Actman, Joel Tropper

* Closed March 15, 1981 after one performance and 14 previews.

Topix Photos

Robert Shields, Lorene Yarnell

Donald Sutherland, Blanche Baker

BROOKS ATKINSON THEATRE
Opened Thursday, March 19, 1981.*
Jerry Sherlock presents:

LOLITA

By Edward Albee; Adapted from the novel by Vladimir Nabokov; Director, Frank Dunlop; Scenery, William Ritman; Costumes, Nancy Potts; Lighting, David F. Segal; Executive Producer, Robert Hartman; Associate Producer, Kee Young; Wardrobe, Joe Busheme; Assistant to Producer, Jean Norihiko Sherlock; Assistant to Director/Casting, Jay Binder; Hairstylist, Gerry Leddy

CAST

A Certain Gentleman	Ian Richardson
Humbert Humbert	Donald Sutherland
Lolita	Blanche Baker
Charlotte	Shirley Stoler
Annabel	Alaina Wojek
Louise	Marcella Lowery
Clare Quilty	Clive Revill
Constance	Bella Jarrett
Head Nurse	Yvette Hawkins
Nurse #1	Colette Alexander
Nurse #2	Barbara Ware
Dick	Kevin Conroy
Bill	Joe Pagano
Doctor	Norman Abrams

STANDBYS & UNDERSTUDIES: Tresa Hughes (Charlotte), William Mooney (Humbert/Certain Gentleman/Quilty), Barbara Ware (Lolita/Annabel), Yvette Hawkins (Louise), Joe Pagano (Dick), Norman Abrams (Bill)

A play in two acts.

General Management: Leonard Soloway/Al Francis
Press: Henry Luhrman, Bill Miller, Terry M. Lilly, Kevin P. McAnarney
Stage Managers: Jon R. Hand, Sally Hassenfelt, Norman Abrams

* Closed March 28, 1981 after 12 performances and 31 previews.

CORT THEATRE
Opened Thursday, March 26, 1981.*
Elizabeth I. McCann, Nelle Nugent, The Shubert Organization in association with Colin Brough for the Lupton Theatre Company, Ltd. and Warner Theatre Productions Inc. present:

ROSE

By Andrew Davies; Director, Alan Dossor; Setting, John Gunter; Costumes, Linda Fisher; Lighting, Andy Phillips; Set Supervision, Tom Lynch; Production Coordinator, Brent Peek; Management Associates, Claire Calkins, Ann Dorszynski, David Domedion, Elizabeth Hermann, Sondra Katz; Wardrobe, Cindy Steffens; Hairstylist, Joseph Dal Corso; Special Effects, Chic Silber; Sound, Jack Mann; Production Assistant, Robert E. Goldberg.

CAST

Rose	Glenda Jackson
Mother	Jessica Tandy
Smale	Beverly May
Malpass	Margaret Hilton
Jim Beam	J. T. Walsh
Sally	Jo Henderson
Jake	Guy Boyd
Geoffrey	John Cunningham
School Caretaker	Don McAllen Leslie
Teachers	Cynthia Crumlish, Lori Cardille

STANDBYS: Myanwy Jenn (Smale/Mother), Jo Henderson (Rose), Don McAllen Leslie (Jake)

A play in two acts. The action takes place in and around a Midlands town at the present time.

General Management: McCann & Nugent
Company Manager: Veronica Claypool
Press: Solters/Roskin/Friedman, Joshua Ellis, Becky Flora, Cindy Valk
Stage Managers: Steven Beckler, Arlene Grayson

* Closed May 23, 1981 after 68 performances and 12 previews.

Martha Swope Photos

Top: Jessica Tandy, Glenda Jackson
Right: Beverly May, Glenda Jackson

Glenda Jackson, Jessica Tandy
Above: John Cunningham, Jackson

PALACE THEATRE
Opened Sunday, March 29, 1981.*
Lawrence Kasha, David S. Landay, James M. Nederlander,
Warner Theatre Productions/Claire Nichtern, Carole J. Sho-
renstein, Stewart F. Lane present:

WOMAN OF THE YEAR

Book, Peter Stone; Music, John Kander; Lyrics, Fred Ebb; Based on
MGM film by Ring Lardner, Jr., Michael Kanin; Director, Robert
Moore; Musical Staging, Tony Charmoli; Settings, Tony Walton;
Costumes, Theoni V. Aldredge; Lighting, Marilyn Rennagel; Sound,
Abe Jacob; Musical Direction and Vocal Arrangements, Donald
Pippin; Orchestrations, Michael Gibson; Dance Arrangements,
Ronald Melrose; Animations, Michael Sporn; Assistant to Mr.
Charmoli, Ed Nolfi; Hairstylists, Masarone, Paul Warden; Assistant
to Producers, Donald Martocchio; Production Assistant, Michael
Gavenchak; Wardrobe, Stephanie Edwards; Assistant to Director,
George Rondo; Production Associate, Melinda Sherwood; Original
Cast Album on Arista records and tapes

CAST

Chairperson	Helon Blount
Tess Harding	Lauren Bacall
Floor Manager	Michael O'Gorman
Chip Salisbury	Daren Kelly
Gerald	Roderick Cook
Pinky Peters	Gerry Vichi
Phil Witaker	Tom Avera
Sam Craig	Harry Guardino
Ellis McMaster	Rex Hays
Abbott Canfield	Lawrence Raiken
Maury	Rex Everhart
Helga	Grace Keagy
Alexi Petrikov	Eivind Harum
Cleaning Women	Helon Blount, Marian Haraldson
Jan Donovan	Marilyn Cooper
Larry Donovan	Jamie Ross

CHORUS: DeWright Baxter, Joan Bell, Helon Blount, Sergio Cal,
Donna Drake, Richard Glendon-Larson, Marian Haraldson, Mi-
chael Kubala, Paige Massman, Gene Montoya, Michael O'Gorman,
Susan Powers, Daniel Quinn, Robert Warners, Swings: Ed Nolfi,
Karen Giombetti
STANDBYS & UNDERSTUDIES: Jamie Ross (Sam), Marian Ha-
raldson (Helga), Robert Warners (Alexi), Richard Glendon-Larson
(Chip), Ralston Hill (Phil/Ellis/Larry), Michael Davis (Abbott-
/Pinky/Maury), Paige Massman (Jan)
MUSICAL NUMBERS: Woman of the Year, The Poker Game, See
You in the Funny Papers, You're Right You're Right, Shut Up
Gerald, So What Else Is New?, One of the Boys, Table Talk, The
Two of Us, It Isn't Working, I Told You So, I Wrote the Book,
Happy in the Morning, Sometimes a Day Goes By, The Grass Is
Always Greener, We're Gonna Work It Out

A musical in 2 acts and 15 scenes. The action takes place at the
present time.

General Management: Marvin A. Krauss Associates
Company Manager: G. Warren McClane
Press: Merle Debuskey, Leo Stern, Diane Judge
Stage Managers: David Taylor, Robert LoBianco, T. L. Boston

* Still playing May 31, 1981. Recipient of 1981 Tonys for Best
Musical Book, Best Musical Score, Outstanding Actress in a Musical
(Lauren Bacall), Outstanding Featured Actress in a Musical (Mari-
lyn Cooper)

Martha Swope Photos

**Right Center: Marilyn Cooper, Jamie Ross,
Lauren Bacall Above: Eivind Harum, Lauren
Bacall, Roderick Cook Top: Cook, Bacall,
Daren Kelly**

Harry Guardino, Lauren Bacall

CIRCLE IN THE SQUARE THEATRE
Opened Thursday, April 2, 1981.*
Circle in the Square (Theodore Mann, Artistic Director; Paul Libin, Managing Director) in its thirtieth season presents:

THE FATHER

By August Strindberg; Translated by Harry G. Carlson; Director, Goran Graffman; Scenery, Marjorie Kellogg; Costumes, Jennifer von Mayrhauser; Lighting, Arden Fingerhut; Music, Kirk Nurock; Wig and Hairstylists, Paul Huntley, Michael Wasula; Wardrobe, Millicent Hacker

CAST

Captain	Ralph Waite
Laura, his wife	Frances Sternhagen
Bertha, his daughter	Kate Purwin
Margret, his old nurse	Pauline Flanagan
Dr. Ostermark	W. B. Brydon
Pastor	Richard Woods
Noyd	Peter Crombie
Emma	Jessica Allen
Svaird	David Faulkner
Laura's Mother	Molly Adams

A drama in two acts and three scenes. The action takes place during late December in the 1880's in a small town in Sweden.

Company Manager: William Conn
Press: Merle Debuskey, David Roggensack
Stage Managers: Randall Brooks, Rick Ralston

* Closed Apr. 26, 1981 after 29 performances.

Brownie Harris Photos

**Left: Pauline Flanagan, Ralph Waite,
Frances Sternhagen**

Richard Woods, Frances Sternhagen

EUGENE O'NEILL THEATRE
Opened Monday, April 6, 1981.*
Emanuel Azenberg presents:

FOOLS

By Neil Simon; Director, Mike Nichols; Scenery, John Lee Beatty;
Costumes, Patricia Zipprodt; Lighting, Tharon Musser; Music, John
Rubinstein; Technical Supervisor, Arthur Siccardi; Wardrobe, Max
Hager; Production Assistant, Jim Hogarty; Assistant to Producer,
Leslie Butler; Hairstylist, John D. Quaglia

CAST

Leon Tolchinsky	John Rubinstein
Snetsky	Gerald Hiken
Magistrate	Fred Stuthman
Slovitch	David Lipman
Yenchna	Florence Stanley
Dr. Zubritsky	Harold Gould
Lenya Zubritsky	Mary Louise Wilson
Sophia Zubritsky	Pamela Reed
Gregor Yousekevitch	Richard B. Shull

STANDBYS: Jeff Abbott (Leon/Snetsky), Diaan Ainslee (Lenya-
/Yenchna), Deborah Allison (Sophia)

A comedy in two acts. The action takes place long ago in the
village of Kulyenchikov.

Managers; Jose Vega, Bruce Birkenhead, Jane Robison
Press: Bill Evans, Howard Atlee, Sandra Manley, Leslie
Anderson, Jim Baldassare
Stage Managers: Martin Herzer, Cathy B. Blaser, Jeff Abbott

* Closed May 9, 1981 after 40 performances and 14 previews.

Martha Swope Photos

**Top: John Rubinstein, Pamela Reed, Harold
Gould, Mary Louise Wilson Below: David Lipman,
Gerald Hiken, Richard B. Shull, Rubinstein, Fred
Stuthman, Reed, Gould, Wilson, Joseph Leon,
Florence Stanley**

**John Rubinstein, Pamela Reed
Top: Rubinstein, Gerald Hiken**

ANTA THEATRE
Opened Thursday, April 16, 1981.*
Don Gregory and Mike Merrick present:

COPPERFIELD

Book, Music and Lyrics, Al Kasha, Joel Hirschhorn; Based on novel "David Copperfield" by Charles Dickens; Direction and Choreography, Rob Iscove; Scenery, Tony Straiges; Costumes, John David Ridge; Lighting, Ken Billington; Musical Direction-Vocal Arrangements, Larry Blank; Orchestrations, Irwin Kostal; Dance Arrangements-Incidental Music, Donald Johnston; Sound, John McClure; A Dome Production; Production Coordinator, Arthur Anagnostou; Assistant Director, Harold deFelice; Assistant Choreographer, Vera Mazzeo; Technical Director, Arthur Siccardi; Wardrobe, Penny Davis, Linda Lee; Associate Conductor, Donald Johnston; Hairstylists, Ray Iagnocco, Michael Heller; Assistants to the Producers, Ruthann M. Barshop, Yolande Zenon, Elaine Garvey

CAST

Dr. Chilip/Baker	Richard Warren Pugh
Peggotty	Mary Stout
Nurse/Julia Mills	Katharine Buffaloe
Aunt Betsey Trotwood	Carmen Mathews
Young David	Evan Richards
Clara Copperfield	Pamela McLernon
Mr. Murdstone	Michael Connolly
Jane Murdstone	Maris Clement
Mr. Micawber	George S. Irving
Victoria	Spence Ford
Bootmaker	David Horwitz
Butcher	Bruce Sherman
Mrs. Micawber	Linda Poser
Vanessa	Dana Moore
Constable	Michael Danek
Mick Walker	Gary Munch
Mealy Potatoes	Brian Quinn
Billy Mowcher	Christian Slater
Mr. Quinion	Ralph Braun
Mr. Dick	Lenny Wolpe
Janet	Darleigh Miller
Adult David	Brian Matthews
Mrs. Heep	Beulah Garrick
Uriah Heep	Barrie Ingham
Mr. Wickfield	Keith Perry
Agnes Wickfield	Leslie Denniston
Dora Spenlow	Mary Mastrantonio
Ticket Taker	Michael Gorman

ENSEMBLE: David Ray Bartee, Ralph Braun, Katharine Buffaloe, Maris Clement, Michael Danek, Spence Ford, Michael Gorman, David Horwitz, Pamela McLernon, Darleigh Miller, Dana Moore, Gary Munch, Keith Perry, Linda Poser, Richard Warren Pugh, Brian Quinn, Lynne Savage, Bruce Sherman, Claude Tessier, Missy Whitchurch
UNDERSTUDIES: Christian Slater (Young David), Linda Poser (Aunt Betsey), Ralph Braun (Murdstone), Missy Whitchurch (Peggotty), Keith Perry (Uriah), Lenny Wolpe (Micawber), Richard Warren Pugh (Mr. Dick), Katharine Buffaloe (Mrs. Heep), Pamela McLernon (Dora), David Horwitz (Adult David), Darleigh Miller (Agnes), Swing Dancers: Heather Lee Gerdes, Daniel Dee
MUSICAL NUMBERS: I Don't Want a Boy, Mama Don't Get Married, Copperfield, Bottle Song, Something Will Turn Up, Anyone, Here's a Book, Umble, The Circle Waltz, Up the Ladder, I Wish He Knew, The Lights of London, Villainy Is the Matter, With the One I Love

A musical in 2 acts and 19 scenes. The action takes place in 1812 and 1822 in England.

Company Managers: Martin Cohen, Jill Cohen
Press: Seymour Krawitz, Patricia Krawitz, Warren Knowlton
Stage Managers: Peter Lawrence, Jim Woolley, Edward Isser, Sarah Witham

* Closed April 26, 1981 after 13 performances and 26 previews.

Martha Swope Photos

Right Center: Leslie Denniston, Lenny Wolpe, Barry Ingham, George S. Irving, Brian Matthews, Linda Poser, Carmen Mathews **Above:** Ingham, Irving **Top:** Pamela McLernon, Evan Richards

Carmen Mathews, Leslie Denniston, Mary Mastrantonio, Brian Matthews

BIJOU THEATRE
Opened Thursday, April 9, 1981.*
Arthur Shafman presents:

AAAH OUI GENTY!

Production Supervisor, Christopher Dunlop; Administrator, Musty Hafner; Production Adviser, Richard G. Miller; Production Associates, Evelyn Gross, Craig Harvey, Susan Balsam

CAST

Philippe Genty
Mary Genty
Michel Guillaume
Jean-Louis Heckel

A program of puppet theatre presented in two acts.

General Manager: Sherman Gross
Company Manager: Jim Awe
Press: Jeffrey Richards, Robert Ganshaw, Ben Morse, Helen Stern, C. George Willard, Ted Killmer, Richard Humleker, Stanley Evans
Stage Manager: Remi Jullien

* Closed May 3, 1981 after 29 performances and 3 previews.

Top Right: Genty puppets

PRINCESS THEATRE
Opened Wednesday, April 22, 1981.*
Steve Salvatore and Michael Jordan in association with Joel B. Leff present:

ANIMALS

Written and Directed by Eddie Lawrence; Scenery, John Wright Stevens; Costumes, Marilyn Bligh-White; Lighting, Marc B. Weiss; Associate Producers, Jeffrey Madrick, Steven Kent Goldberg, Anthony Mazzarella; Elephant Head, Jane Stein; Duck Bill, Rodney Gordon; Sound, Christopher J. Chambers; Assistant to Mr. Lawrence, Glenn Taranto; Wardrobe, Toni Baer; Hairstylist, Armand Bouton

CAST

"The Beautiful Mariposa"
Maria Rios . . . . Cecilia Flores
Juan Ribera . . . . Lazaro Perez
Maid . . . . Cara Duff-MacCormick
Manuelo Ribera . . . . Demo DiMartile
First State Trooper . . . . Ben Kapen
Second State Trooper . . . . Victor Argo
 The action takes place at the present time in a motel room in Kansas.

"Louie and the Elephant"
Louie Bengal . . . . Dan Frazer
Thaddeus . . . . Victor Argo
Elephant . . . . Joel Kramer
Lulu Hopper . . . . Barbara Erwin
 The action takes place in The Tusk, a San Francisco nightclub.

"Sort of an Adventure"
Harriet Greshaw . . . . Jeanne Wechsler
Hester Cable . . . . Barbara Erwin
Eddie Greshaw . . . . Ben Kapen
Hedda Webb-Winters . . . . Cara Duff-MacCormick

 The action takes place in the dining-living room of an apartment in West Greenwich Village, NYC.

Company Manager: Barbara Carrellas
Press: Solters/Roskin/Friedman, Milly Schoenbaum, Kevin Patterson, Maurice Turet
Stage Managers: Jack Timmers, Margaret Peckham

* Closed Apr. 22, 1981 after one performance and 9 previews.

Ken Howard Photos

Right Center: Ben Kapen, Cara Duff-MacCormick

Dino Laudicina, Joel Kramer,
Barbara Erwin, Dan Frazer

VIVIAN BEAUMONT THEATER
Opened Monday, April 27, 1981.*
The Lincoln Center Theater Company (Richmond Crinkley, Producer) presents:

THE FLOATING LIGHT BULB

By Woody Allen; Director, Ulu Grosbard; Setting and Costumes, Santo Loquasto; Lighting, Pat Collins; Sound, Richard Fitzgerald; Production Coordinator, Brent Peek; Technical Coordinator, Jack Lines; Wardrobe, Midge Marmo; Hairstylist, Werner Sherer; Assistant to Director, Jenny-Anne Martz; Magic Design, Robert Aberdeen

CAST

Paul Pollack	Brian Backer
Steve Pollack	Eric Gurry
Enid Pollack	Beatrice Arthur
Max Pollack	Danny Aiello
Betty	Ellen March
Jerry Wexler	Jack Weston

Understudy: Tresa Hughes (Enid)

A drama in two acts. The action takes place in the Canarsie section of Brooklyn during 1945.

Company Managers; Mario De Maria, Joey Parnes, Jean Passanante
Press: Betty Lee Hunt, Maria Cristina Pucci, James Sapp
Stage Managers: Franklin Keysar, Wendy Chapin

* Closed June 21, 1981 after 65 performances and 16 previews. Mr. Backer received a 1981 Tony for Outstanding Featured Actor in a Play.

Roger Greenawalt Photos

Danny Aiello, Ellen March Top: Eric Gurry, Beatrice Arthur, Jack Weston, Brian Backer

MINSKOFF THEATRE
Opened Thursday, April 30, 1981.*
James M. Nederlander, Arthur Rubin, Jerome Minskoff, Stewart F. Lane, Carole J. Shorenstein, Charles D. Kelman present:

CAN-CAN

Music and Lyrics, Cole Porter; Book, Abe Burrows, Entire Production Staged and Choreographed by Roland Petit; Director, Abe Burrows; Scenery, David Mitchell; Costumes, Franca Squarciapino; Lighting, Thomas Skelton; Music Direction-Vocal Arrangements, Stanley Lebowsky; Orchestrations, Philip J. Lang; Dance Arrangements-New Dance Music, Donald York; Sound, Larry Spurgeon; Hairstylist, Ronald DeMann, Lorraine Oleinyk; Costume Supervisor, Patricia Adshead; Wardrobe, Joseph Busheme; Production Assistants, Julia B. Flamm, Andy Feigen, James Dawson; Associate Conductor, Nick Archer; Assistant to Director, Melinda Sherwood

CAST

Bailiff/Waiter/Chief Justice	Joseph Cusanelli
Judge Paul Barriere	David Brooks
Court President/Monarchist	Tom Batten
Judge Aristide Forestier	Ron Husmann
Claudine/Eve	Pamela Sousa
Hilaire Jussac	Swen Swenson
Boris Adzinidzinadze	Avery Schreiber
Waiter/Policeman/Guard	John Remme
La Mome Pistache	Zizi Jeanmaire
Hercule	Michael Dantuono
Theophile	Mitchell Greenberg
Etienne/Policeman	Tommy Breslin
Photographer	James Dunne
Model	Deborah Carlson
Adam	Darrell Barnett
Mimi	Donna King
Apache Leader	Luigi Bonino
Patrons	Nealey Gilbert, Dennis Batutis

ENSEMBLE: Deborah Carlson, Pam Cecil, Edyie Fleming, Nealey Gilbert, Linda Haberman, Nancy Hess, Brenda Holmes, Donna King, Manette LaChance, Meredith McIver, Gail Pennington, Rosemary Rado, Daryl Richardson, Linda Von Germer, Darrell Barnett, Dennis Batutis, John Dolf, James Dunne, James Horvath, Steven LaChance, Kevin McCready, Gregory Schanuel, Swings: Kim Noor, Bob Renny
UNDERSTUDIES: Michael Dantuono (Aristide), Mitchell Greenberg (Boris), Donna King (Claudine), Tom Batten (Barriere), Joseph Cusanelli (Hercule), John Remme (Theophile)
MUSICAL NUMBERS: Maidens Typical of France, Never Give Anything Away, C'Est Magnifique, Quadrille Dance, Come Along with Me, Live and Let Live, I Am in Love, Montmartre, Garden of Eden Ballet, Allez-vous En, Never Be an Artist, It's All Right with Me, Apache Dance, I Love Paris, Can-Can, Finale

A musical in 2 acts and 17 scenes. The action takes place in Paris in 1893.

General Managers: Marvin A. Krauss, Gary Gunas, Eric Angelson, Steven C. Callahan
Company Manager: Duke Kant
Press: Merlin Group, Cheryl Sue Dolby, Merle Frimark
Stage Managers: Mortimer Halpern, Nate Barnett, Sherry Lambert

* Closed May 3, 1981 after 5 performances and 16 previews. Original production opened May 7, 1953 at the Shubert Theatre and played 892 performances. In the cast were Lilo, Peter Cookson, Gwen Verdon and Hans Conreid. See THEATRE WORLD Vol. 9.

Martha Swope Photos

Right Center: Zizi Jeanmaire (C) Above: Pamela Sousa and dancers Top: Zizi Jeanmaire, Ron Husmann

Avery Schreiber, Pamela Sousa

MOROSCO THEATRE
Opened Sunday, May 3, 1981.*
Stuart Ostrow in association with T.A.T. Communications
Company presents:

THE MOONY SHAPIRO SONGBOOK

Book, Monty Norman, Julian More; Music, Monty Norman; Lyrics, Julian More; Setting, Saul Radomsky; Costumes, Franne Lee; Director, Jonathan Lynn: Musical Numbers Staged by George Faison: Lighting, Tharon Musser; Musical Direction, Elman Anderson; Technical Supervisor, Jeremiah Harris;Wardrobe, Bill Campbell; Dance Arrangements, Timothy Graphenreid; Vocal Arrangements, Ray Cook; Associate Conductor, Irving Joseph; Production Assistant, Howard P. Lev; Musical Supervisor, Stanley Lebowsky; Sound, Otts Munderloh; Projections, Wendall K. Harrington; Hairstylist, Lyn Quiyou; Assistant to Director, Nina Lightstone

CAST

Jeff Goldblum
Judy Kaye
Timothy Jerome
Annie McGreevey
Gary Beach

STANDBYS & UNDERSTUDIES: Christopher Chadman (Goldblum), Maureen Moore (Kaye/McGreevey), Philip Hoffman (Jerome/Beach), Audrey Lavine (Kaye), Brenda Pressley (McGreevey)
MUSICAL NUMBERS: Songbook, East River Rhapsody, Talking Picture Show, Meg, Mister Destiny, Your Time Is Different to Mine, Pretty Face, JeVous Aime, Les Halles, Olympics '36, Nazi Party Pooper, I'm Gonna Take Her Home to Momma, Bumpity-Bump, The Girl in the Window, Victory, April in Wisconsin, It's Only a Show, Bring Back Tomorrow, Happy Hickory, When a Brother Is a Mother to His Sister, Climbin', Don't Play That Lovesong Anymore, Lovely Sunday Mornin', Rusty's Dream Ballet, A Storm in My Heart, The Pokenhatchit Public Protest Committee, I Accuse, Messages, I Found Love, Golden Oldie, Nostalgia, Finale

A musical in two acts.
General Managers: Joseph Harris, Ira Bernstein, Peter T. Kulok, Nancy Simmons
Press: John Springer, Meg Gordean, Suzanne Salter, Jeffrey Wise
Stage Managers: Phil Friedman, Perry Cline, Philip Hoffman

* Closed May 3, 1981 after one performance and 15 previews.

Martha Swope Photos

Gary Beach, Judy Kaye, Jeff Goldblum, Annie McGreevey Also Top with Timothy Jerome

Barbara Perry

BIJOU THEATRE
Opened Tuesday, May 5, 1981.*
Arthur Shafman and Shelly Maibaum present:

PASSIONATE LADIES

Written and performed by Barbara Perry; Director, Edmund Balin; Introductions, Regis Cordie; Incidental Music and Recording Consultant, Leonora Shildkraut; Associate Producer, Andrea Shapiro; Production Adviser, Richard G. Miller; Wardrobe, Debbie Fisher; Production Associates, Evelyn Gross, Craig Harvey, Susan Balsam

CAST

Barbara Perry

ACTI: The Stripper, My Friend Shakespeare

ACT II: Modern Acting, Con Amore, Betty Bruce Is Dead

General Manager: Sherman Gross
Press: Jeffrey Richards, Robert Ganshaw, Ben Morse, Helen Stern, C. George Willard, Ted Killmer, Richard Humleker, Stanley Evans

* Closed May 10, 1981 after 8 performances.

BILTMORE THEATRE
Opened Wednesday, May 6, 1981.*
Gloria Hope Sher, Marjorie Moon and Jay J. Cohen in association with Zaida Coles Edley and Spirit Will Productions present:

INACENT BLACK

By A. Marcus Hemphill; Original Music and Lyrics, McFadden & Whitehead & Moore; Director, Mikell Pinkney; Set, Felix E. Cochren; Costumes, Marty Pakledinaz; Lighting, Tim Phillips; Sound, Joseph Donohue; Hairstylist, Gene Sheppard; Musical Conductor, Barry Eastmond; Originally produced by the Billie Holiday Theatre; Executive Producer, Ashton Springer; Production Assistant, James Carter

CAST

Helwin Rydell	Gregory Miller
Mama Essie Rydell	Barbara Montgomery
Mary Rydell	Reginald Vel Johnson
Charles Rydell	Count Stovall
Percy Rydell	Bruce Strickland
Waitress	Rosanna Carter
Inacent Black	Melba Moore
Pretty Pete	Ronald "Smokey" Stevens
Carmen Casteel	Joyce Sylvester
Sally-Baby Washington	Lorey Hayes
Voice of Hamilton Rydell	Ed Cambridge

UNDERSTUDIES: Skip Waters (Charles/Helwin/Percy), Elaine Graham (Inacent), Nora Cole (Carmen/Sally-Baby)

A comedy in 2 acts and 9 scenes. The action takes place at the present time in the Rydell Estate Mansion in Old Westbury, Long Island, and in New York City.

General Manager: Theatre Management Associates
Company Managers: Mary Card, Young T. Hughley, Jr.
Press: Judy Jacksina, Glenna Freedman, Dolph Browning, Angela Wilson
Stage Managers: Ed Cambridge, David Blackwell

* Closed May 17, 1981 after 15 performances and 14 previews.

Marcus DeVoe Photos

Melba Moore, Reginald Vel Johnson
Top Right: Melba Moore

Ronald Stevens, Joyce Sylvester

MARTIN BECK THEATRE
Opened Thursday, May 7, 1981.*
Zev Bufman with Donald C. Carter and Jon Cutler presents:

THE LITTLE FOXES

By Lillian Hellman; Director, Austin Pendleton; Setting, Andrew Jackness; Costumes, Florence Klotz; Lighting, Paul Gallo; Hairstylist, Patrik D. Moreton, Michael Kriston; Music Adapted by Stanley Silverman; Sound, Jack Mann; Assistant Director, Kimothy Cruse; Technical Supervisor, Jeremiah J. Harris; Wardrobe, Agnes Farrell; Production Assistant, Teresa Conway

CAST

Addie	Novella Nelson
Cal	Joe Seneca
Birdie Hubbard	Maureen Stapleton
Oscar Hubbard	Joe Ponazecki
Leo Hubbard	Dennis Christopher
Regina Giddens	Elizabeth Taylor
William Marshall	Humbert Allen Astredo
Benjamin Hubbard	Anthony Zerbe
Alexandra Giddens	Ann Talman
Horace Giddens	Tom Aldredge

UNDERSTUDIES: Carol Teitel (Regina/Birdie), Conrad L. Osborne (Horace/Oscar/William), William Youmans (Leo), Louise Stubbs (Addie), Hugh L. Hurd (Cal)

A drama in three acts. The action takes place in the living room of the Giddens house in a small town in the South in the spring of 1900.

General Management: Theatre Now Inc.
Company Manager: Michael Lonergan
Press: Fred Nathan, Patt Dale, Eileen McMahon, Charles Cinnamon, Nora Peck, Chen Sam
Stage Managers: Patrick Horrigan, Brian Meister

* Closed Sept. 6, 1981 after 123 performances and 8 previews.

Left: Humbert Allen Astredo, Elizabeth Taylor, Maureen Stapleton, Ann Talman, Joe Seneca, Novella Nelson, Dennis Christopher, Anthony Zerbe, Joe Ponazecki Top: Maureen Stapleton, Elizabeth Taylor

Joe Ponazecki, Maureen Stapleton,
Tom Aldredge

Elizabeth Taylor, Novella Nelson,
Ann Talman

HELEN HAYES THEATRE
Opened Sunday, May 10, 1981.*
David Merrick presents:

I WON'T DANCE

By Oliver Hailey; Direction and Incidental Music, Tom O'Horgan; Stage Movement, Wesley Fata; Scenery, Bill Stabile; Costumes, Marty Pakledinaz; Lighting, Craig Miller; Associate Producer, Neal DuBrock; Wardrobe, Clarence Sims; Assistant to Director, Nan Penman; Production Assistant, Larry Fulton

CAST

Dom .... David Selby
Lil .... Gail Strickland
Kay .... Arlene Golonka

A comedy in two acts. The action takes place at the present time in Los Angeles, California.

Press: Solters/Roskin/Friedman, Joshua Ellis, Louise Ment
Stage Managers: Alan Hall, Ruth E. Rinklin

* Closed May 10, 1981 after one performance and 7 previews.

Martha Swope Photos

**Left: Arlene Golonka, Gail Strickland
Top: David Selby, Arlene Golonka**

JOHN GOLDEN THEATRE
Opened Sunday, May 10, 1981.*
Allen Klein and Julian Schlossberg with Isobel Robins present:

IT HAD TO BE YOU

By Renee Taylor, Joseph Bologna; Director, Robert Drivas; Scenery, Lawrence King, Michael Yeargan; Costumes, Carrie F. Robbins; Lighting, Roger Morgan; Sound, Richard Fitzgerald; Associate Producer, Iris W. Keitel; An ABKCO Theatre Production; Production Supervisor, Jeremiah J. Harris; Wardrobe, Peter FitzGerald; Production Assistants, Linda Belickis, Karen Jezewski, Jody H. Klein; Assistants to Director, Emily Baratta, Martin Jackman

CAST

Theda Blau .... Renee Taylor
Vito Pignoli .... Joseph Bologna

A comedy in two acts. The action takes place at the present time in New York City on Christmas Eve.

General Management: Theatre Now Inc.
Company Manager: Robb Lady
Press: Solters/Roskin/Friedman, Milly Schoenbaum, Kevin Patterson

* Closed June 21, 1981 after 48 performances and 15 previews.

Martha Swope Photos

Joseph Bologna, Renee Taylor

Lena Horne (also top)

NEDERLANDER THEATRE
Opened Tuesday, May 12, 1981.*
James M. Nederlander, Michael Frazier, Fred Walker in association with Sherman Sneed and Jack Lawrence present:

LENA HORNE:
THE LADY AND HER MUSIC

Musical Direction, Harold Wheeler; Scenery, David Gropman; Costumes, Stanley Simmons; Lighting, Thomas Skelton; Musical Conductor, Coleridge T. Perkinson; Musical Consultant, Luther Henderson; Hairstylist, Phyllis Della; Miss Horne's Wardrobe, Giorgio Sant'Angelo; Production Staged by Arthur Faria; Production Assistant, Brenda Braxton; Assistant Conductor, Linda Twine; Recorded by Qwest Records

COMPANY

LENA'S TRIO: Grady Tate (Drums), Steve Bargonetti (Guitar), Bob Cranshaw (Bass)
THE COMPANY: Clare Bathe, Tyra Ferrell, Vondie Curtis-Hall, Deborah Lynn Bridges (Alternate), Peter Oliver-Norman (Alternate)

MUSICAL NUMBERS

Life Goes On, I'm Going to Sit Right Down and Write Myself a Letter, Stormy Weather, As Long as I Live, Push de Button, Fly, I'm Glad There Is You, That's What Miracles are All About, From This Moment On, Just One of Those Things, Love, A Lady Must Live, Where or When, The Surry with the Fringe on Top, Can't Help Loving Dat Man of Mine, Copper Colored Gal of Mine, Deed I Do, I Got a Name, If You Believe, Lady with a Fan, Raisin' the Rent, Watch What Happens, I Want to Be Happy, Better Than Anything

Presented with one intermission.

General Management: James Walsh
Company Manager: Sheila R. Phillips
Press: Solters/Roskin/Friedman, Joshua Ellis, Louise Ment, Cindy Valk
Stage Managers: Joe Lorden, Jack Gianino

* Still playing May 31, 1981. Miss Horn received a 1981 Special Tony Award and a special Citation from the New York Drama Critics Circle for her performance.

Martha Swope Photos

LONGACRE THEATRE
Opened Tuesday, May 8, 1978*
(Moved January 29, 1979 to Plymouth Theatre)
Emanuel Azenberg, Dasha Epstein, The Shubert Organization, Jane Gaynor and Ron Dante present:

AIN'T MISBEHAVIN'

Conceived and Directed by Richard Maltby, Jr.; Based on an idea by Murray Horwitz and Richard Maltby, Jr.; Musical Numbers Staged by Arthur Faria; Associate Director, Murray Horwitz; Music Supervision, Orchestrations, Arrangements, Luther Henderson; Vocal Arrangements, William Elliott, Jeffrey Gutcheon; Sets, John Lee Beatty; Costumes, Randy Barcelo; Lighting, Pat Collins; Sound, Otts Munderloh; Hairstylists, Michael Weeks, Paul Lopez; Wardrobe, Max Hager, Warren S. Morrill; Technical Coordinator, Arthur Siccardi; Assistant to Producers, Leslie Butler; Production Assistant, Jane Robison; Production Supervisor, Clint Spencer; Original Cast Album on RCA Records.

CAST

Nell Carter†1	Ken Page†4
Andre De Shields†2	Charlaine Woodard†5
Armelia McQueen†3	Luther Henderson (Pianist)†6

STANDBYS: Ellia English, Annie Joe Edwards, Ms. Heaven, George Merritt, Eric Riley
MUSICAL NUMBERS: Ain't Misbehavin', Lookin' Good but Feelin' Bad, "Tain't Nobody's Bizness If I Do, Honeysuckle Rose, Squeeze Me, Handful of Keys, I've Got a Feelin' I'm Fallin', How Ya Baby, Jitterbug Waltz, The Ladies Who Sing with the Band, Yacht Club Swing, When the Nylons Bloom Again, Cash for Your Trash, Off-Time, The Joint Is Jumpin', Spreadin' Rhythm Around, Lounging at the Waldorf, Viper's Drag, Mean to Me, Your Feet's Too Big, That Ain't Right, Keepin' Out of Mischief, Find Out What they Like, Fat and Greazy, Black and Blue, Finale

A musical entertainment based on the music of Thomas "Fats" Waller, presented in two parts.

Managers: Jose Vega, Bruce Birkenhead
Press: Bill Evans, Howard Atlee, Leslie Anderson, Jim Baldassare
Stage Manager: D. W. Koehler

*Still playing May 31, 1981. For original production see THEATRE WORLD, Vol. 34. Recipient of 1978 Tonys for Best Musical, Featured Actress (Nell Carter), Director, and voted Best Musical by NY Drama Critics, Drama Desk, and Outer Critics Circle.
†Succeeded by: 1. Avery Sommers, Zoe Walker, Yvette Freeman, Roz Ryan, 2. Alan Weeks, 3. Yvette Freeman, Teresa Bowers, Loretta Bowers, 4. Ken Prymus, Jason Booker, 5. Debbie Allen, Adriane Lenox, 6. Frank Owens, Hank Jones

Martha Swope Photos

Right Center: Lonnie McNeil Above: Teresa Bowers, Ken Prymus Top: Roz Ryan, Ken Prymus

Teresa Bowers, Roz Ryan, Adriane Lenox

ALVIN THEATRE
Opened Thursday, April 21, 1977.*
Mike Nichols presents:

ANNIE

Book, Thomas Meehan; Based on "Little Orphan Annie" comic strip; Music, Charles Strouse; Lyrics, Martin Charnin; Director, Mr. Charnin; Musical Numbers-Choreography, Peter Gennaro; Producers, Irwin Meyer, Stephen R. Friedman, Lewis Allen, Alvin Nederlander Associates, JFK Center for the Performing Arts, Icarus Productions, Peter Crane; Sets, David Mitchell; Costumes, Theoni V. Aldredge; Lighting, Judy Rasmuson; Musical Direction, Arnold Gross; Dance Music Arrangements, Peter Howard; Orchestrations, Philip J. Lang; Assistant Conductor, Arthur Wagner; Assistant to Choreographer, Don Bonnell; Technical Coordinator, Arthur Siccardi; Wardrobe, Adelaide Laurino, Jeane Frisbie; Hairstylists, Ted Azar, Sonia Rivera, Hector Garcia; Assistant to Director, Janice Steele; Props, Abe Einhorn; Production Assistants, Sylvia Pancotti, Stephen Graham; Sandy owned and trained by William Berloni; Original Cast Album by Columbia Records.

CAST

Molly	Jennine Babo†1
Pepper	Caroline Daly
Duffy	Stacey Lynn Brass†2
July	Martha Byrne
Tessie	Tiffany Blake†3
Kate	Tara Kennedy
Annie	Allison Smith
Miss Hannigan	Alice Ghostley†4
Bundles McCloskey/Ickes/Sound Effects	R. Martin Klein
Apple Seller/Jimmy Johnson/Howe	David Brummel†5
Dog Catcher/Fred McCracken/Honor Guard	Larry Ross
Dog Catcher/Hull	Richard Walker
Sandy	Himself
Lt. Ward/Bert Healy/Morgantheau/Brandeis	Richard Ensslen
Sophie/Annette/Ronnie Boylan	Shelly Burch
Grace Farrell	Mary Bracken Phillips†6
Drake	Edwin Bordo
Mrs.Pugh/NBC Page/Perkins	Henrietta Valor
Miss Greer/Bonnie Boylan	Donna Thomason
Cecille/Connie Boylan	Marianne Sanazaro
Oliver Warbucks	John Schuck†7
Rooster Hannigan	Gary Beach†8
Lily	Rita Rudner†9
FDR	Raymond Thorne

UNDERSTUDIES: Raymond Thorne (Warbucks), Roy Meachum (FDR/Alternate), Henrietta Valor (Miss Hannigan), Donna Thomason (Grace), Sonia Bailey (Orphans), Sherry Dundish (Molly), Larry Ross (Rooster), Jane Robertson (Lily), Drake (Timothy Jecko), Richard Walker (Healy), O'Malley (Sandy), Ensemble: Don Bonnell, Jane Robertson

MUSICAL NUMBERS: Maybe, It's the Hard-knock Life, Tomorrow, We'd Like to Thank You, Little Girls, I Think I'm Gonna Like It Here, N.Y.C., Easy Street, You Won't Be an Orphan for Long, You're Never Fully Dressed Without a Smile, Something Was Missing, I Don't Need Anything But You, Annie, A New Deal for Christmas

A musical in 2 acts and 13 scenes. The action takes place December 11–25, 1933 in New York City.

General Management: Gatchell & Neufeld, Douglas C. Baker
Company Managers: Douglas C. Baker, Steven H. David
Press: David Powers, Barbara Carroll
Stage Managers: Brooks Fountain, Barrie Moss, Roy Meachum, Larry Mengden

* Still playing May 31, 1981. For original production see THEATRE WORLD, Vol. 33. Recipient of 1977 NY Drama Critics Circle, and "Tony" Awards for Best Musical.
† Succeeded by: 1. Roxanne Dundish, 2. Sherry Dundish, 3. Jennine Babo, 4. Betty Hutton, Marcia Lewis, 5. Timothy Jecko, 6. Anne Kerry, 7. Harve Presnell, Rhodes Reason, 8. Richard Sabellico, 9. Dorothy Stanley

Martha Swope Photos

**Top Right: John Schuck, Allison Smith,
Sandy Below: Marcia Lewis**

Betty Hutton, Sandy

60

Opened Wednesday, April 30, 1980.*
Judy Gordon, Cy Coleman, Maurice Rosenfield, Lois F. Rosenfield, in association with Irvin Feld and Kenneth Feld present:

BARNUM

Music, Cy Coleman; Lyrics, Michael Stewart; Book, Mark Bramble; Directed and Staged by Joe Layton; Scenery, David Mitchell; Costumes, Theoni V. Aldredge; Lighting, Craig Miller; Sound, Otts Munderloh; Orchestrations, Hershy Kay; Vocal Arrangements, Cy Coleman, Jeremy Stone; Music Director, Peter Howard; Production Supervisor, Mary Porter Hall; Hairstylists, Ted Azar, Alan Schubert, Vincent Esoldi, Chris Calabrese; Technical Supervisor, Peter Feller; Assistant to Producers, Erik P. Sletteland; Wardrobe, Mary P. Eno; Production Assistants, Michael Gill, Marsha Best; Assistant Conductor, Peter Phillips; Assistant to Director, John Mineo; Original Cast Album by CBS Masterworks Records.

CAST

Phineas Taylor Barnum	Jim Dale†1
Chairy Barnum	Glenn Close†2
Ringmaster/Julius Goldschmidt/	
James A. Bailey	William C. Witter†3
Chester Lyman/Humbert Morrissey	Terrence V. Mann†4
Joice Heth	Terri White†5
Amos Scudder/Edgar Templeton	Kelly Walters
Lady Plate Balancer	Catherine Carr
Lady Juggler	Barbara Nadel†6
Chief Bricklayer	Edward T. Jacobs†7
White-faced Clown	Andy Teirstein
Sherwood Stratton	Dirk Lumbard
Mrs. Sherwood Stratton	Sophie Schwab
Tom Thumb	Leonard John Crofoot
Susan B. Anthony	Karen Trott
Jenny Lind	Marianne Tatum†8
One-Man Band	Steven Michael Harris
Wilton	Bruce Robertson
Lady Aerialist	Robbi Morgan
Pianists	Karen Gustafson, Peter Phillips, Ted Kociolek
Pre-curtain Entertainers	R. J. Lewis, Catherine Carr, Andy Teirstein, Barbara Nadel, Bruce Robertson, Fred Garbo Garver, Mary Testa, Dirk Lumbard

STANDBYS AND UNDERSTUDIES: Harvey Evans, Jess Richards (Barnum), Suellen Estey (Chairy/Jenny), Bruce Robertson (Lyman), Dirk Lumbard (Bailey/Goldschmidt/Templeton/Morrissey), Mary Testa (Joice), Sophie Schwab (Chairy/Jenny), Fred Garbo Garver (Tom), Barbara Nadel (Mrs. Stratton/Susan B. Anthony), Steven Michael Harris (Scudder), Kelly Walters (Wilton), R. J. Lewis (Stratton), Ensemble: Mary Testa, Navarre Matlovsky, Fred Feldt, Colleen Flynn

MUSICAL NUMBERS: There's a Sucker Born Every Minute, Thank God I'm Old, The Colors of My Life, One Brick at a Time, Museum Song, I Like Your Style, Bigger Isn't Better, Love Makes Such Fools of Us All, Out There, Come Follow the Band, Black and White, The Prince of Humbug, Join the Circus

A musical in two acts. The action takes place all over America and the major capitals of the world from 1835 through 1880.

General Management: James Walsh
Company Manager: Susan Bell
Press: David Powers, Barbara Carroll
Stage Managers: Marc Schlackman, Bethe Ward, Michael Mann

* Still playing May 31, 1981. Recipient of 1980 "Tonys" for Best Actor in a Musical (Jim Dale), Best Scenic Design, and Best Costumes.
† Succeeded by: 1. Tony Orlando during vacation, 2. Catherine Cox, 3. Terrence V. Mann, 4. R. J. Lewis, 5. Lillias White, 6. Mary Testa, 7. Fred Garbo Garver, 8. Suellen Estey during vacation

Martha Swope Photos

Top Right: Jim Dale, Marianne Tatum
Below: Catherine Cox, Jim Dale

Tony Orlando

FORTY-SIXTH STREET THEATRE
Opened Monday, June 19, 1978.*
Universal Pictures presents:

THE BEST LITTLE WHOREHOUSE IN TEXAS

Book, Larry L. King, Peter Masterson; Music and Lyrics, Carol Hall; Direction, Peter Masterson, Tommy Tune; Musical Staging, Tommy Tune; Set, Marjorie Kellogg; Costumes, Ann Roth; Lighting, Dennis Parichy; Musical Supervision-Direction-Vocal Arrangements, Robert Billig; Hairstylists, Michael Gottfried, John Barker, Ralph Stanzione; Associate Choreographer, Thommie Walsh; Wardrobe, Beverly Meyer; Associate Producers, Bonnie Champion, Danny Kreitzberg; Conductor, Pete Blue; Props, Michael Durnin; Assistant to Director, Janie Rosenthal; Production Assistant, Allan Williams; Original Cast Album by MCA Records.

CAST

Rio Grande Band . . . . Craig Chambers, Racine Romaguera, Harvey Shapiro, Pete Blue, Chuck Zeuren, Marty Laster
Girls . . . . Monica Tiller, Karen Sutherland, Valerie Leigh Bixler, Nancy Lynch, Rebecca Seay
Cowboys . . . . Peter Heuchling, Stephen Bray, Beau Gravitte
Farmer/Melvin P. Thorpe . . . . Clinton Allmon
Shy Kid . . . . Gerry Burkhardt
Miss Wulla Jean . . . . Debra Zalkind
Traveling Salesman/C. J. Scruggs/
Chip Brewster/Governor . . . . Patrick Hamilton
Slick Dude/Soundman . . . . Gene O'Neill†1
Choir . . . . Jay Bursky, Diana Broderick, Candace Tovar, Edwina Lewis, Jan Merchant, Peter Heuchling
Angel . . . . Tina Johnson
Shy . . . . Cheryl Ebarb
Jewel . . . . Delores Hall
Mona Stangley . . . . Fannie Flagg†2
Her Girls:
Linda Lou . . . . Donna King†3
Dawn . . . . Monica Tiller
Ginger . . . . Becky Gelke†4
Beatrice . . . . Jan Merchant†5
Taddy Jo . . . . Karen Sutherland
Ruby Rae . . . . Candace Tovar†6
Eloise . . . . Diana Broderick
Durla . . . . Debra Zalkind
Leroy Sliney . . . . Stephen Bray
Dogettes . . . . Gerry Burkhardt, Jay Bursky, Peter Heuchling, Andy Parker
Stage Manager/Cameraman/Specialty Dancer . . . Tom Cashin†7
Mayor Poindexter/Senator Wingwoah . . . . J. Frank Lucas
Melvin Thorpe Singers . . . . Susann Fletcher, Beau Allen, Karen Sutherland, Stephen Bray, Diana Broderick, Clare Fields
Sheriff Ed Earl Dodd . . . . Gil Rogers
Edsel Mackey . . . . John Newton
Doatsey May . . . . Bobbi Jo Lathan†8
TV Announcer . . . . Larry L. King
Angelette Imogene Charlene . . . . Monica Tiller
Governor's Aide . . . . Jay Bursky
Reporters . . . . Peter Heuchling, Becky Gelke, Beau Allen

AGGIES: Peter Heuchling, Beau Allen, Jay Bursky, Roger Berdahl, Stephen Bray, Gerry Burkhardt, Thomas Griffith, Andy Parker
ANGELETTES: Susann Fletcher, Diana Broderick, Debra Zalkind, Karen Sutherland, Valerie Leigh Bixler
UNDERSTUDIES: Becky Gelke (Mona), John Newton (Sheriff/-Scruggs/Mayor/Senator), Diana Broderick (Ginger), Rebecca Seay (Shy/Doatsey), Gerry Burkhardt (Governor/Thorpe), Monica Tiller (Angel), Edwina Lewis (Jewel), Roger Berdahl (Mackey/Narrator), Karen Sutherland (Dawn), Alternates: Steve McNaughton, Patti D'Beck
MUSICAL NUMBERS: Prologue, 20 Fans, A Lil Ole Bitty Pissant Country Place, Girl You're a Woman, Watch Dog Theme, Texas Has a Whorehouse in It, 24 Hours of Lovin', Doatsey Mae, Angelette March, Aggie Song, Bus from Amarillo, Sidestep, No Lies, Good Old Girl, Hard Candy Christmas, Finale

A musical in two acts. The action takes place in the State of Texas.

General Management: Schlissel & Kingwill
Company Manager: Leonard A. Mulhern
Press: Jeffrey Richards, C. George Willard, Ben Morse, Robert Ganshaw, Helen Stern, Ted Killmer, Richard Humleker, Stanley Evans
Stage Managers: Paul J. Phillips, Jay Schlossberg-Cohen, Nancy Lynch

* Still playing May 31, 1981. For original production, see THEATRE WORLD, Vol. 34.
† Succeeded by: 1. Paul Ukena, Jr., Roger Berdahl, 2. Candace Tovar, 3. Valerie Leigh Bixler, 4. Rebecca Seay, 5. Clare Fields, 6. Susann Fletcher, 7. Thomas Griffith, 8. Becky Gelke

Delores Hall Top: Candace Tovar, Gil Rogers

LONGACRE THEATRE
Opened Sunday, March 30, 1980.*
Emanuel Azenberg, The Shubert Organization, Dasha Epstein,
Ron Dante present the Center Theatre Group/Mark Taper
Forum production of:

CHILDREN OF A LESSER GOD

By Mark Medoff; Director, Gordon Davidson; Set, Thomas A.
Walsh; Costumes, Nancy Potts; Lighting, Tharon Musser; Associate
Producers, William P. Wingate, Kenneth Brecher; Wardrobe, Jim
Hodson; Technical Supervisor, Arthur Siccardi; Assistant to Pro-
ducers, Leslie Butler; Assistant to Director, April Webster; Produc-
tion Assistant, Neila Ruben; Management Assistant, Jane E.
Cooper; Sign Language Consultant, Lou Fant; Interpreters, Jean
Worth, Susan Freundlich.

CAST

Sarah Norman	Phyllis Frelich
James Leeds	John Rubinstein[1]
Orin Dennis	Lewis Merkin
Mr. Franklin	William Frankfather[2]
Mrs. Norman	Scotty Bloch[3]
Lydia	Julianne Gold
Edna Klein	Lucy Martin

STANDBYS: Elizabeth Quinn (Sarah), Robert Steinberg (James),
Janice I. Cole (Lydia), Ron Trumble, Jr., Patrick D'Avanzo (Orin),
Jill Andre (Edna/Mrs. Norman)

A drama in two acts. The action takes place at the present time.

General Manager: Jose Vega
Company Manager: Lilli Afan
Press: Bill Evans, Sandra Manley, Howard Atlee, Leslie
Anderson, Jim Baldassare
Stage Managers: Frank Marino, Judith Binus, Janice I. Cole

* Still playing May 31, 1981. Recipient of 1980 "Tonys" for Best
Play, Best Actress (Phyllis Frelich), Best Actor (John Rubinstein)
† Succeeded by: 1. Robert Steinberg, David Ackroyd, John Rubin-
stein, 2. Howard Brunner, 3. Augusta Dabney

Martha Swope Photos

David Ackroyd, Phyllis Frelich, Howard Brunner
Top: Phyllis Frelich John Rubinstein

SHUBERT THEATRE
Opened Sunday, October 19, 1975.*
Joseph Papp in association with Plum Productions presents the
New York Shakespeare Festival production of:

A CHORUS LINE

Conceived, Choreographed and Directed by Michael Bennett; Book, James Kirkwood, Nicholas Dante; Music, Marvin Hamlisch; Lyrics, Edward Kleban; Co-Choreographer, Bob Avian; Musical Direction-Vocal Arrangements, Don Pippin; Associate Producer, Bernard Gersten; Setting, Robin Wagner; Costumes, Theoni V. Aldredge; Lighting, Tharon Musser; Sound, Abe Jacob; Music Coordinator, Robert Thomas; Orchestrations, Bill Byers, Hershy Kay, Jonathan Tunick; Assistant to Choreographers, Baayork Lee; Musical Direction, Robert Rogers; Wardrobe, Alyce Gilbert; Production Supervisor, Jason Steven Cohen; Original Cast Album by Columbia Records

CAST

Roy	Dennis Daniels†1
Kristine	Christine Barker†2
Sheila	Bebe Neuwirth†3
Val	Deborah Henry†4
Mike	Buddy Balou'
Butch	Kevin Chinn†5
Larry	T. Michael Reed†6
Maggie	Marcia Lynn Watkins
Richie	Ralph Glenmore†7
Tricia	Diane Frantantoni
Tom	Tim Millett†8

Zach	Scott Pearson†9
Mark	Timothy Wahrer†10
Cassie	Cheryl Clark†11
Judy	Angelique Ilo†12
Lois	Tracy Shayne†13
Don	Dennis Edenfield
Bebe	Karen Meister†14
Connie	Janet Wong†15
Diana	Chris Bocchino
Al	James Warren†16
Frank	Troy Garza†17
Greg	Danny Weathers
Bobby	Ronald Stafford†18
Paul	Rene Clemente
Vicki	Joanna Zercher
Ed	Jon Michael Richardson
Jarad	T. Michael Reed†19
Linda	Diane Duncan†20
Sam	James Beaumont†21
Jenny	Jannet Horsley†22
Ralph	Dennis Parlato†23

UNDERSTUDIES: Buddy Balou (Al), Rene Ceballos (Cassie), Jerry Colker (Mike), Catherine Cooper (Cassie/Sheila/Val), Dennis Edenfield (Mike), Diane Fratantoni (Diana/Val/Connie/Bebe/-Maggie), Morris Freed (Mark), Troy Garza (Mark/Paul/Larry-/Al), Roscoe Gilliam (Richie), J. Richard Hart (Mike/Al), Danny Herman (Mike), Don Mirault (Don/Zach/Al), Jannet Moranz (Sheila), Philip C. Perry (Mark/Don/Al), Jon Michael Richardson (Bobby/Greg), Ann Louise Schault (Cassie/Judy/Kristine), Tracy Shayne (Bebe/Diana/Maggie), Zoanna Zercher (Judy/Kristine/-Sheila/Val)

MUSICAL NUMBERS: I Hope I Get It, I Can Do That, and. . . ., At the Ballet, Sing!, Hello 12 Hello 13 Hello Love, Nothing, Dance 10 Looks 3, Music and the Mirror, One Tap Combination, What I Did for Love, Finale

A musical performed without intermission. The action takes place at the present time during an audition in the theatre.

General Manager: Robert Kamlot
Company Manager: Bob MacDonald
Press: Merle Debuskey, William Schelble, Richard Kornberg
Stage Managers: Tom Porter, Wendy Mansfield, Jon Michael
Richardson, Morris Freed

* Still playing May 31, 1981. Cited as Best Musical by NY Drama Critics Circle, Winner of Pulitzer Prize, 1976 "Tonys" for Best Musical, Best Book, Best Score, Best Director, Best Lighting, Best Choreography. A Special Theatre World Award presented to each member of the creative staff and original cast. See THEATRE WORLD Vol. 31 for original production.
† Succeeded by: 1. Philip C. Perry, Don Miralt, 2. Kerry Casserly, 3. Susan Danielle, 4. Mitzi Hamilton, 5. Roscoe Gilliam, 6. Michael-Day Pitts, Don Simione, J. Richard Hart, 7. Kevin Chinn, 8. Stephen Crenshaw, James Young, 9. Tim Millett, 10. Gregory Brock, Danny Herman, 11. Deborah Henry, 12. Jannet Horsley, Jannet Moranz, 13. Ann Louise Schaut, 14. Rene Ceballos, 15. Lauren Tom, 16. James Young, 17. Philip C. Perry, 18. Matt West, 19. Morris Freed, 20. Tracy Shayne, 21. Troy Garza, 22. Catherine Cooper, 23. T. Michael Reed.

Martha Swope Photos

**Chris Bocchino, Deborah Henry, Rene Clemente,
Tim Millett, Susan Danielle, Mitzi Hamilton**

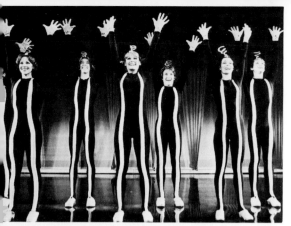

BROADHURST THEATRE
Opened Monday, March 27, 1978*
(Moved Dec. 4, 1980 to the Ambassador Theatre)
Jules Fisher, The Shubert Organization, and Columbia Pictures present:

DANCIN'

Conceived, Directed and Choreographed by Bob Fosse; Scenery, Peter Larkin; Costumes, Willa Kim; Lighting, Jules Fisher; Associate Producer, Patty Grubman; Music Conducted and Arranged by Gordon Lowry Harrell; Orchestrations, Ralph Burns; Sound, Abe Jacob; Hairstylist, Romaine Greene; Wardrobe, Joseph Busheme; Production Assistant, Vicki Stein; Assistants to Mr. Fosse, Kathryn Doby, Christopher Chadman, Gwen Verdon; Associate Conductor, Michael Camilo

CAST

Janet Eilbert†	Christine Colby
P. J. Mann	Terri Treas
Wendy Edmead	Bruce Anthony Davis
Barbara Yeager	Richard Korthaze
Michael Kubala	Michael Ricardo
Chet Walker	Gail Mae Ferguson
Eileen Casey	Robert Warners
Clif de Raita	Hinton Battle

MUSICAL NUMBERS: Prologue (Hot August Night), Crunchy Granola Suite, Mr. Bojangles, Chaconne, Percussion, Ionisation, I Wanna Be a Dancin' Man, Big Noise from Winnetka, If It Feels Good Let It Ride, Easy, I've Got Them Feelin' Too Good Today Blues, Was Dog a Doughnut, Sing Sing Sing, Here You Come Again, Yankee Doodle Dandy, Gary Owen, Stouthearted Men, Under the Double Eagle, Dixie, When Johnny Comes Marching Home, Rally Round the Flag, Pack Up Your Troubles, Stars and Stripes Forever, Yankee Doodle Disco, Dancin'

A"musical entertainment" in 3 acts and 13 scenes.

General Managers: Marvin A. Kraus, Gary Gunas, Eric Angelson
Company Manager: G. Warren McClane
Press: Merle Debuskey, William Schelble, Leo Stern, Diane Judge
Stage Managers: Peter B. Mumford, Richard Korthaze, Karen DeFrancis

* Still playing May 31, 1981. Recipient of 1980 "Tonys" for Best Choreography, Best Lighting. For original production, see THEATRE WORLD, Vol. 34.
† During the season members of the cast were succeeded by: Eileen Casey, Bruce Anthony Davis, John De Luca, Lisa Embs, Bill Hastings, Richard Korthaze, Edmund LaFosse, Dana Moore, Stephen Moore, Maryann Neu, Cynthia Onrubia, Michael Ricardo, Adrian Rosario, Beth Shorter, Laurie Dawn Skinner, Barbara Yeager, Alternates: Penny Fekany, Laurent Giroux, Jodi Moccia, Keith Keen, Gale Samuels, Chet Walker

Martha Swope Photos

Top Left: Clif de Raita, Gail Benedict, Michael Kubala, Deborah Phalen, Chet Walker, Gail Mae Ferguson, Robert Warners Below: Bruce Anthony Davis Bottom: Katherine Meloche, Clif de Raita, Gail Benedict, Shanna Reed, P. J. Mann, Eileen Casey, Robert Warners, Michael Kubala

JOHN GOLDEN THEATRE
Opened Thursday, May 1, 1980.*
(Moved to Royale Theatre Thursday, June 17, 1980.)
Alexander H. Cohen and Hildy Parks present:

A DAY IN HOLLYWOOD/
A NIGHT IN THE UKRAINE

Book and Lyrics, Dick Vosburgh; Music, Frank Lazarus; Scenery, Tony Walton; Lighting, Beverly Emmons; Costumes, Michel Stuart; Sound, Otts Munderloh; Musical Direction-Vocal and Dance Arrangements, Wally Harper; Hairstylists, Joseph Dal Corso, Eileen Tersago; Production Associate, Seymour Herscher; Direction and Choreography, Tommy Tune; Co-Choreographer, Thommie Walsh; Co-Producer, Roy A. Somlyo; Associate Producer, Philip M. Getter; Assistants to Producers, Margaret Barrett, Annette Burgess, Victoria Street; Production Assistant, Linda Dannenberg; Technical Coordinator, Arthur Siccardi; Technical Supervisor, Joseph Monaco; Wardrobe, Elonzo Dann; Music Conducted by Rod Derefinko; Original Cast Album by DRG Records

CAST

"A Day in Hollywood"

Priscilla Lopez	John Sloman
Frank Lazarus	Celia Tackaberry
Brad Moranz	Kate Draper
Niki Harris	Albert Stephenson

MUSICAL NUMBERS: Just Go to the Movies, Famous Feet, I Love a Film Cliche, Nelson, The Best in the World, It All Comes Out of the Piano, Richard Whiting Medley, Thanks for the Memory, Another Memory, Doin' the Production Code, A Night in the Ukraine

"A Night in the Ukraine"- loosely based on Chekhov's "The Bear"
Mrs. Pavlenko, a rich widow . . . . Celia Tackaberry
Carlo, her Italian footman . . . . Frank Lazarus
Gino, her gardener . . . . Priscilla Lopez
Serge B. Samovar, a Moscow lawyer . . . . Brad Moranz
Anina, Mrs. Pavlenko's daughter . . . . Kate Draper
Constantine, a coachman . . . . John Sloman
Masha, the maid . . . . Niki Harris
Sascha, a manservant . . . . Albert Stephenson

UNDERSTUDIES AND STANDBYS: Mark Fotopoulos (Mr. Moranz), Brooks Baldwin (Mr. Moranz), Tudi Roach (Lopez/-Draper), Karen Harvey (Ms. Harris), Jack Magradey (Sloman/Stephenson), Elizabeth Hansen (Tackaberry) The action takes place in the morning room of the Pavlenko residence in the Ukraine before the revolution.

General Manager: Roy A. Somlyo
Company Manager: Joel Wyman
Press: Alpert/ LeVine, Mark Goldstaub
Stage Managers: Thomas Kelly, Christopher A. Cohen, Jack Magradey

* Closed Sept. 27, 1981 after 588 performances and 9 previews. Recipient of 1980 "Tonys" for Best Featured Actress in a Musical (Priscilla Lopez), and Best Choreography.

Martha Swope Photos

Top Right: Priscilla Lopez, David Garrison, Frank Lazarus Below: Stephen James, Priscilla Lopez, David Garrison Bottom: Albert Stephenson, Frank Lazarus, Niki Harris

THE MUSIC BOX

Opened Sunday, February 26, 1978.*
Alfred de Liagre, Jr. and Roger L. Stevens present:

DEATHTRAP

By Ira Levin; Director, Robert Moore; Set, William Ritman; Costumes, Ruth Morley; Lighting, Marc B. Weiss; Wardrobe, Mariana Torres; Assistant to Director, George Rondo; Assistants to Producers, Dorothy Spellman, Jean Bankier; Props, Bruce Becker, Eoin Sprott

CAST

Sidney Bruhl .... John Wood†1
Myra Bruhl .... Marian Seldes
Clifford Anderson .... Victor Garber †2
Helga ten Dorp......................... Marian Winters†3
Porter Milgrim .... Richard Woods†4

STANDBYS: Donald Barton (Sidney), Patricia Guinan (Myra/-Helga), Ernest Townsend (Clifford)

A "comedy thriller" in 2 acts and 6 scenes. The action takes place at the present time in Sidney Bruhl's study in the Bruhl home in Westport, CT.

General Manager: C. Edwin Knill
Company Manager: Constance Coble
Press: Jeffrey Richards, Robert Ganshaw, Ben Morse, Helen Stern, C. George Willard, Ted Killmer, Richard Humleker, Stanley Evans, Robert Ganshaw
Stage Managers: Robert St. Clair, Steven Shaw

* Still playing May 31, 1981. For original production see THEATRE WORLD Vol. 34
† Succeeded by: 1. Patrick Horgan, Stacy Keach, John Cullum, Robert Reed, Farley Granger, 2. Daren Kelly, Steve Bassett, 3. Elizabeth Parrish, 4. William LeMassena

Ken Howard Photos

Marian Seldes, Elizabeth Parrish, Farley Granger Above: Robert Reed, Marian Seldes, Steve Bassett

Steve Bassett, Farley Granger Top: Robert Reed, William LeMassena

BOOTH THEATRE

Opened Thursday, April 19, 1979.*
Richmond Crinkley, Elizabeth I. McCann, Nelle Nugent present the American National Theatre Academy production of:

THE ELEPHANT MAN

By Bernard Pomerance; Director, Jack Hofsiss; Setting, David Jenkins; Costumes, Julie Weiss; Lighting, Beverly Emmons; Associate Producers, Ray Larsen, Ted Snowdon; Production Supervisor, Brent Peek; Wardrobe, Lillias Norel; Hairstylists, Frank A. Melon, Patrick D. Moreton, Hiram Ortiz; Wigs, Paul Huntley; Production Coordinator, Scott Steele; Assistant to Director, Eugene Draper; Projections, Wendall Harrington; Music, Bach, Sammartini, Saint-Saens, Faure, Elgsr, Heiss; Musical Arrangements, David Heiss; Props, Timothy Abel; Dialect Consultant, Elizabeth Smith

CAST

Belgian Policeman/Dr. Frederick Treves . . . . . . Kevin Conway†1
Carr Gomm/Conductor . . . . Richard Clarke
Ross/Bishop/Snork . . . . I. M. Hobson†2
John Merrick . . . . Philip Anglim†3
Pinhead Manager/Policeman/Will/
 Earl/Lord John . . . . John Neville-Andrews†4
Pinhead/Miss Sandwich/Countess/
 Princess Alexandra . . . . Cordis Heard†5
Pinhead/Mrs. Kendal . . . . Carole Shelley†6
Orderly . . . . Dennis Creaghan†7
Cellist . . . . David Heiss†8

STANDBYS & UNDERSTUDIES: Mitchell Litrofsky (Merrick), Jeffrey Jones (Traves/Policeman), Dennis Creaghan (Pinhead Manager/Will/Lord John), Etain O'Malley (Mrs. Kendal), JoAnne Belanger (Pinhead/Sandwich/Princess Alexandra), Peter Vogt (Gomm/Ross/Snork), Michael Goldschlager (Cellist)

A drama in 2 acts and 21 scenes. John Merrick was a real person who spent the years 1886 to his death in 1890 in the London Hospital, Whitechapel.

Company Manager: Sam Pagliaro
Press: Solters/Roskin/Friedman, Joshua Ellis, David LeShay, Becky Flora, Cindy Valk
Stage Managers: William Dodds, William Chance

* Closed June 28, 1981 after 916 performances and 8 previews. Recipient of NY Drama Critics Circle Award, 1979 "Tonys" for Best Play, Best Direction, Best Actress (Carole Shelley). For original production see THEATRE WORLD Vol. 35.
† Succeeded by: 1. Donal Donnelly, 2. Danny Sewell, 3. Jack Wetherall, Bruce Davison, Jeff Hayenga, David Bowie, Benjamin Hendrickson, Mark Hamill, 4. John C. Vennema, Jeffrey Jones, 5. Concetta Tomei, Judith Barcroft, 6. Patricia Elliott, Carole Shelley, 7. Munson Hicks, Dennis Creaghan, 8. Michael Goldschlager, David Heiss

Susan Cook Photos

Carole Shelley, Mark Hamill, Donal Donnelly Above: Hamill, Shelley

Top: Benjamin Hendrickson Left: David Bowie

BROADWAY THEATRE
Opened Tuesday, September 25, 1979.*
Robert Stigwood in association with David Land presents:

EVITA

Lyrics, Tim Rice; Music, Andrew Lloyd Webber; Director, Harold Prince; Choreography, Larry Fuller; Set, Costumes and Projections, Timothy O'Brien, Tazeena Firth; Executive Producers, R. Tyler Gatchell, Jr., Peter Neufeld; Orchestrations, Hershy Kay, Andrew Lloyd Webber; Musical Director, Paul Gemignani; Lighting, David Hersey; Sound, Abe Jacob; Production Associates, Tim Rice, Andrew Lloyd Webber; Assistant Musical Director, Edward Strauss; Projects Coordinator, Arlene Caruso; Wardrobe, Adelaide Laurino; Hairstylist, Richard Allen; Production Assistant, Wiley Hausam; Original Cast Album by MCA Records

CAST

Eva	Patti LuPone†1, Terri Klausner†2
Che	Mandy Patinkin†3
Peron	Bob Gunton†4
Peron's Mistress	Jan Ohringer†5
Magaldi	Mark Syers†6
Children	Megan Forste, Lilo Grunwald, Michael Pastryk, Colette Sena Heyman, Christopher Wooten

PEOPLE OF ARGENTINA: Seda Azarian, Dennis Birchall, Tom Carder, Susan Cella, Frank Cruz, Kim Darwin, Anny DeGange, Mark East, Scott Fless, Robert Frisch, Carole Garcia, Teri Gill, Michael Hayward-Jones, Robert Hendersen, Ken Hilliard, Morgan MacKay, Jack Neubeck, Amy Niles, Marcia O'Brien, Nancy Opel, Dawn Perry, Martie Ramm, Morgan Richardson, Davia Sacks, James Sbano, David Staller, Michelle Stubbs, Wilfredo Suarez, Susan Terry, Ian Michael Towers, Philip Tracy, Kenneth W. Urmston, Mark Waldrop, Sandra Wheeler, Brad Witsger, John Yost

UNDERSTUDIES: Susan Cella (Eva), Tom Carder, James Sbano (Che), Robert Frisch (Peron), Jack Neubeck (Magaldi), Amy Niles (Peron's Mistress)

MUSICAL NUMBERS: A Cinema in Buenos Aires, Requiem for Evita, Oh What a Circus, On This Night of a Thousand Stars, Eva Beware of the City, Buenos Aires, Goodnight and Thank You, Art of the Possible, Charity Concert, I'd Be Surprisingly Good for You, Another Suitcase in Another Hall, Peron's Latest Flame, A New Argentina, On the Balcony of the Casa Rosada, Don't Cry for Me Argentina, High Flying Adored, Rainbow High, Rainbow Tour, The Actress Hasn't Learned, And the Monkey Kept Rolling In, Santa Evita, Waltz for Eva and Che, She Is a Diamond, Dice Are Rolling, Eva's Final Broadcast, Montage, Lament

A musical in two acts. Based on the life of Eva Peron, the second wife of Argentine dictator Juan Peron.

General Manager: Howard Haines
Company Manager: John Caruso
Press: Mary Bryant, Philip Rinaldi
Stage Managers: George Martin, John Grigas, John-David Wilder, Kenneth W. Urmston

*Still playing May 31, 1981. Winner of 1980 NY Drama Critics Circle Award for Best Musical, and 7 "Tonys" for Best Musical, Best Actress (Patti LuPone), Director, Score, Book, Featured Actor in a Musical (Mandy Patinkin), and Lighting.
† Succeeded by: 1. Derin Altay, 2. Nancy Opel (matinees), 3. James Stein, 4. David Cryer, 5. Cynthia Hunt, 6. James Whitson

Martha Swope Photos

Right Center: Derin Altay, David Cryer, James Stein Above: David Cryer, James Stein Top: Derin Altay

David Cryer, Derin Altay

THE LITTLE THEATRE
Opened Saturday, May 21, 1977*
Jerry Arrow by arrangement with Circle Repertory Company
and PAF Playhouse presents:

GEMINI

By Albert Innaurato; Director, Peter March Shifter; Supervised by
Marshall W. Mason; Setting, Christopher Nowak; Costumes, Ernest
Allen Smith; Lighting, Larry Crimmins; Sound, Leslie A. De-
Weerdt, Jr.; Production Assistants, Richard Groff, Thomas Bain;
Wardrobe, Phoebe Hunter; Hairstylist, Peter Brett

CAST

Francis Geminiani	Philip Cates†
Bunny Weinberger	Jessica James
Randy Hastings	Bill Randolph†2
Judith Hastings	Marilyn McIntyre†3
Herschel Weinberger	Wayne Knight
Fran Geminiani	Frank Biancamano
Lucille Pompi	Barbara Coggin†4

UNDERSTUDIES: Maralyn Dossey (Bunny/Lucille), Larry Singer
(Francis/Herschel/Randy), Anne Newhall (Judith), John LaGioia
(Fran)

A comedy in 2 acts and 4 scenes. The action takes place June 1
& 2, 1973 in the Geminiani-Weinberger backyard in South Philadelphia, Pa.

General Manager: R. Robert Lussier
Press: Max Eisen, Francine L. Trevens, Maria Somma
Stage Managers: John F. Weeks, Larry Singer, Anne Newhall

* Closed Sept. 5, 1981 after 1819 performances. For original production, see THEATRE WORLD, Vol. 33.
†Succeeded by: 1. Steve Singer, 2. John Geter, 3. Lucinda Jenney,
4. Kaye Kingston

Martha Swope Photos

**Right: John Geter, Frank Biancamano, Jessica James,
Steve Singer, Kaye Kingston, Lucinda Jenney
Also at Top with Jessica James, Wayne Knight**

Frank Biancamano, Jessica James

Jessica James, John Geter,
Wayne Knight

David Rounds

LYCEUM THEATRE
Opened Thursday, April 10, 1980.*
Elizabeth I. McCann, Nelle Nugent, Ray Larsen present:

MORNING'S AT SEVEN

By Paul Osborn; Director, Vivian Matalon; Set, William Ritman;
Costumes, Linda Fisher; Lighting, Richard Nelson; Wardrobe, Rosalie Lahm; Hairstylists, Karol Coeyman, Paul Huntley

CAST

Theodore Swanson	Maurice Copeland
Cora Swanson	Teresa Wright†1
Aaronetta Gibbs	Elizabeth Wilson†2
Ida Bolton	Nancy Marchand†3
Carl Bolton	Richard Hamilton†4
Homer Bolton	David Rounds†5
Myrtle Brown	Lois de Banzie†6
Esther Crampton	Maureen O'Sullivan
David Crampton	Gary Merrill†7

STANDBYS & UNDERSTUDIES: Frances Helm (Esther), Harriet Rogers (Ida/Cora), Martha Miller (Aaronetta/Myrtle), Jonathan Farwell (Theodore/Carl), Robert Moberly (Homer)

A play in three acts. The action takes place in two adjacent backyards in a small midwestern town during 1922.

Company Manager: Robert Wallner
Press: Solters/Roskin/Friedman, Joshua Ellis, Becky Flora,
David LeShay, Cindy Valk
Stage Managers: Marnel Sumner, Ellen Raphael

* Closed Aug. 16, 1981 after 564 performances and 16 previews.
Recipient of 1980 "Tonys" for Best Revival, Best Direction, Best
Featured Actor (David Rounds). Original production opened at
Longacre Theatre Nov. 30, 1939 with Dorothy Gish, Jean Adair,
Kate McComb, Enid Markey and Effie Shannon and ran for 44
performances.
† Succeeded by: 1. Carmen Mathews, 2. Nancy Kulp, 3. Harriet
Rogers, Kate Reid, 4. King Donovan, 5. Robert Moberly, 6. Charlotte Moore, 7. Shepperd Strudwick

Martha Swope Photos

**Top: (standing) Kate Reid, Richard Hamilton, Lois
de Banzie, Elizabeth Wilson, Shepperd Strudwick,
(seated) David Rounds, Teresa Wright, Maurice
Copeland, Maureen O'Sullivan**

EDISON THEATRE
Opened Friday, September 24, 1976.*
Hillard Elkins, Norman Kean, Robert S. Fishko present:

OH! CALCUTTA!

Devised by Kenneth Tynan; Conceived and Directed by Jacques Levy; Contributors, Robert Benton, David Newman, Jules Feiffer, Dan Greenburg, Lenore Kandel, John Lennon, Jacques Levy, Leonard Melfi, Sam Shepard, Clovis Trouille, Kenneth Tynan, Sherman Yellen; Music and Lyrics, Robert Dennis, Peter Schickele, Stanley Walden, Jacques Levy; Choreography, Margo Sappington; Musical Director, Stanley Walden; Scenery and Lighting, Harry Silverglat Darrow; Costumes, Kenneth M. Yount; Supervised by James Tilton; Musical Conductor, Norman Bergen; Sound, Sander Hacker; Assistant to Director, Nancy Tribush; Projected Media Design, Gardner Compton; Live Action Film, Ron Merk; Production Assistants, Marcia Edelstein, Andrea Ladik; Assistant Musical Conductor, Dan Carter; Technical Directors, Thomas Healy, Charles Moran; Wardrobe, Susan J. Wright

CAST

Jacqueline Carol, Richert Easley, Cheryl Hartley, David Heisey, Tom Lantzy, Gary Meitrott, Ann Neville, Lee Ramey, Julie Ridge, Dara Norman

ACT I: Taking Off the Robe, Will Answer All Sincere Replies, Playin', Jack and Jill, Paintings of Clovis Trouille, Delicious Indignities, Was It Good For You Too?

ACT II: Suite for Five Letters, One on One, Spread Your Love Around, Four in Hand, Coming Together Going Together

An "erotic musical" in two acts.

Company Manager: Doris J. Buberl
Press Les Schecter, Barbara Schwei
Stage Managers: Ron Nash, Maria DiDia

* Still playing May 31, 1981. For original production, see THEATRE WORLD Vol. 33.

Martha Swope, Kenn Duncan Photos

Gary Meitrott, Ann Neville

MARK HELLINGER THEATRE

Opened Monday, October 8, 1979.*
Terry Allen Kramer and Harry Rigby in association with Columbia Pictures present:

SUGAR BABIES

Conceived by Ralph G. Allen, Harry Rigby; Book, Ralph G. Allen; Based on traditional material; Music, Jimmy McHugh; Lyrics, Dorothy Fields, Al Dubin; Additional Music and Lyrics, Arthur Malvin; "Sugar Baby Bounce" by Jay Livingston and Ray Evans; Staged and Choreographed by Ernest Flatt; Sketches Directed by Rudy Tronto; Production Supervisor, Ernest Flatt; Associate Producer, Jack Schlissel; Scenery and Costumes, Raoul Pene du Bois; Lighting, Gilbert V. Hemsley, Jr.; Vocal Arrangements, Arthur Malvin, Hugh Martin, Ralph Blane; Musical Director, Glen Roven; Orchestrations, Dick Hyman; Dance Music Arranged by Arnold Gross; Associate Producers, Frank Montalvo, Thomas Walton Associates; Assistant Choreographer, Toni Kay; Associate Conductor, Bill Grossman; Wardrobe, Florence Aubert, Irene Ferrari; Hairstylists, Stephen LoVullo, Vincent Tucker

CAST

Mickey Rooney†1		Ann Miller†3
Scot Stewart		Jimmy Mathews
Anita Morris†2		Sid Stone
Tom Boyd		The Agostinos
Peter Leeds		Elizabeth Hermines
Maxie Furman	Chaz Chase	Michael Allen Davis

GAIETY QUARTET: Hank Brunjes, Bob Heath, Eddie Pruett, Michael Radigan, Alternate: Edward Pfeiffer
SUGAR BABIES: Carol Ann Basch, Christine Busini, Kaylyn Dillehay, Chris Elia, Lesley Kingsley, Clare Leach, Barbara Mandra, Robin Manus, Faye Fujisaki Mar, Melanie Montana, Regina Newsome, Linda Ravinsky, Michele Rogers, Rose Scudder, Alternates: Laurie Sloan, Carole Cotter
UNDERSTUDIES: Rose Scudder (Ann Miller), Michele Rogers (Jane Summerhays), Maxie Furman (Sid Stone/Jimmy Mathews), Tom Boyd (Sid Stone/Peter Leeds/Jimmy Mathews), Michael Radigan (Scot Stewart), Hank Brunjes (Tom Boyd)
SONGS AND SKETCHES: A Memory of Burlesque, A Good Old Burlesque Show, Welcome to the Gaity, Let Me Be Your Sugar Baby, Meet Me 'Round the Corner, I Want a Girl, Travelin', In Louisiana, I Feel a Song Comin' On, Goin' Back to New Orleans, Home Sweet Home, Feathered Fantasy, Sally, Scenes from Domestic Life, A Very Moving Love Story, Don't Blame Me, Orientale, Little Red Schoolhouse, Springboard Sisters, Sugar Baby Bounce, Madame Rentz and Her All Female Minstrels, Mr. Banjo Man, Candy Butcher, Girls and Garters, Exactly Like You, Court of Last Resort, In a Greek Garden, Warm and Willing, Presenting Madame Alla Gazaza, Tropical Madness, Cuban Love Song, Cautionary Tales, Bon Appetit, Old Glory, You Can't Blame Your Uncle Sammy

A "burlesque musical" in two acts.

General Management: Jack Schlissell, Jay Kingwill
Company Manager: Alan Wasser
Press: Henry Luhrman, Terry M. Lilly, Kevin McAnarney
Stage Managers: Kay Vance, Bob Burland, David Campbell

* Still playing May 31, 1981.
† Succeeded by: 1. Joey Bishop and Rip Taylor during vacation, 2. Jane Summerhays, 3. Jane Summerhays for Miss Miller's illness

Martha Swope Photos

**Top Right: Ann Miller, Mickey Rooney
Center: Michael A. Davis, Chaz Chase**

Ann Miller, Joey Biship

IMPERIAL THEATRE
Opened Sunday, February 11, 1979.*
Emanuel Azenberg presents:

THEY'RE PLAYING OUR SONG

Book, Neil Simon; Music, Marvin Hamlisch; Lyrics, Carole Bayer Sager; Director, Robert Moore; Musical Numbers Staged by Patricia Birch; Scenery and Projections, Douglas W. Schmidt; Costumes, Ann Roth; Lighting, Tharon Musser; Music Director, Steven Margoshes; Music Supervisor, Fran Liebergall; Orchestrations, Ralph Burns, Richard Hazard, Gene Page; Production Supervisor, Philip Cusack; Assistant to Director, George Rondo; Sound, Tom Morse; Music Coordinator, Earl Shendell; Wardrobe, Chip Mulberger; Hairstylists, John Quaglia, David Brown; Assistant to Producer, Leslie Butler; Original Cast Album by Casablanca Records; "I Still Believe in Love" sung by Johnny Mathis

CAST

Vernon Gersch	Robert Klein†1
Sonia Walsk	Lucie Arnaz†2
Voices of Vernon Gersch	D. Michael Heath, John Hillner, Wayne Mattson
Voices of Sonia Walsk	Helen Castillo, Dorothy Kiara, Celia Celnik Matthau
Voice of Phil the Engineer	Hal Shane

STANDBYS & UNDERSTUDIES: John Hammil (Vernon), Pat Gorman (Sonia), Wayne Mattson (Engineer), John Hillner (Vernon), Swing Singers/Dancers: Pat Gorman, Connie Gould, Max Stone, Hal Shane
MUSICAL NUMBERS: Fallin', Workin' It Out, If He Really Knew Me, They're Playing Our Song, Right, Just for Tonight, When You're in My Arms, I Still Believe in Love, Fill in the Words

A comedy in 2 acts and 13 scenes. The action takes place at the present time in Vernon's New York City apartment, in Le Club, Sonia's apartment, on the street, the road, in a beach house in Quogue, Long Island, in a recording studio, in a Los Angeles hospital.

General Manager: Jose Vega
Company Managers Maurice Schaded, Louise Bendall
Press: Bill Evans, Howard Atlee, Sandra Manley, Leslie Anderson, Jim Baldassare
Stage Managers: Craig Jacobs, Bernard Pollock, Pat Trott

* Closed Sept. 6, 1981 after 1082 performances and 11 previews. For original production, see THEATRE WORLD Vol. 35.
† Succeeded by: 1. John Hammil, Tony Roberts, Ted Wass, Victor Garber, 2. Stockard Channing, Rhonda Farer, Diana Canova, Marsha Skaggs

Martha Swope Photos

Left: John Hillner, Wayne Mattson, D. Michael Heath, Ted Wass (C), Helen Castillo, Dorothy Kiara, Celia Celnik Matthau, Diana Canova (seated)
Top Left: Ted Wass, Diana Canova

PRODUCTIONS FROM PAST SEASONS THAT CLOSED THIS SEASON

Title	Opened	Closed	Performances
I'm Getting My Act Together	6/14/78	3/15/81	1165
Peter Pan	9/6/79	1/4/81	578
I Ought to Be in Pictures	4/3/80	1/11/81	341
West Side Story	2/14/80	11/30/80	341
Home	5/7/80	1/4/81	288
Talley's Folly	2/20/80	10/19/80	286
Fourtune	4/27/80	11/23/80	242

PLAYHOUSE 46
Wednesday, June 4,-29, 1980. (28 performances)
Howard J. Burnett by arrangement with The Philadelphia Company presents:

CASSATT

By Dorothy Louise; Director, Robert Hedley; Scenery, John Jensen; Costumes, Gerry Leahy; Lighting, Ronald Wallace; Assistant Producer, Maggi Burnett; General Manager, Paul B. Berkowsky; Associate, Sheala N. Berkowsky; Technical Director, James A. Burnett; Company Manager, Paul P. Matwiow; Stage Managers, Kender Jones, G. Leslie Muchmore; Press, Susan L. Schulman, Kate MacIntyre

CAST

Tony Musante (Edgar Degas), Esther Benson (Zoe), Carlin Glynn (Mary Cassatt), Barbara A. Spiegel (Taudy), Jeanne Ruskin (Lydia), Marcia Mahon (Katherine), Elek Hartman (Robert), Understudies: Francine Farrell, G. Leslie Muchmore

A play in two acts. The action takes place in Paris from 1877 to 1918.

Susan Cook Photo

Tony Musante, Carlin Glynn

Fredricka Weber

WONDERHORSE THEATRE
Wednesday, June 4 - 14, 1980 (10 performances)
Fredricka Weber and Jenny Deyo present:

SIX WOMEN ON A STAGE

By Fredricka Weber; Director, Hiram Taylor; Production Design, Donald Montgomery; Costumes, Carol Wenz; Composer, Victoria de Lissovoy; Associate Producer, Audre Johnston; Stage Manager, Scott A. Wiscamb; Production Assistants, Alice Rafner, Linda Madama; Harpist, Boris Goldman

CAST

Maggie Askew (Jamie), Marie Cheatham (Audrey), Joy Bond (Carole), Sally Schermerhorn (Sally), Jill Larson (Barbara), Judy Guyll (Amy), Fayn Le Veille (Mother), Larry Conroy (Dad)

A portrait of six women: who they think they are, who they're afraid they are, and who they really are.

THEATRE DE LYS
Wednesday, June 4,-8, 1980.(6 performances and 7 previews)
New World Theatre presents:

KNITTERS IN THE SUN

By George Bemberg; Director, Jane Stanton; Scenery, Bob Phillips; Lighting, Mal Sturchio; Costumes, Kim Walker; General Management, Dorothy Olim Associates; Press, Max Eisen, Francine L. Trevens; Manager Associate, Thelma Cooper; Production Assistant, Mary O'Leary; Technical Director, William Pastor; Sound, Richard Loyd; Stage Managers, Mark Keller, Andrew Krawetz; Company Manager, Gail Bell; Management Assistant, Robert Grant

CAST

Alexandra O'Karma (Marriet Carsters), Joan Shepard (Mrs. Riley), Evan Thompson (Bayard Carsters), Kelly Fitzpatrick (Andrew Carsters), Will Jeffries (Eric North)

A drama in 2 acts and 4 scenes. The action takes place in the Carsters' ancestral home in Wilmot, a small university town in rural New England at the present time.

Martha Swope Photo

Kelly Fitzpatrick, Alexandra O'Karma,
Joan Shepard, Evan Thompson

"Practice"

PERRY STREET THEATRE
Thursday, June 5,-29, 1980 (26 performances)
Nicola-Maria Barthen, Karen E. Etcoff present the New Playwrights' Theatre Production of:

PRACTICE

By Jack O'Donnell; Director, John Noah Nertzler; Set, Russell Metheny; Costumes, Peter J. Zakutansky; Lighting, John R. Enea; Associate Producer, Richard Norton; Production Consultants, Steven Block, Douglas A. Lobel; Technical Director, Neil Mazzella; Stage Managers, Ronnie Yeskel, Ada H. Citron; Press, Becky Flora

CAST

William Badgett (Preacher), Donald F. Campbell (Smith), Ron Canada (Doctor), Kevin Fisher (McNeary), Alexandra Gersten (Maureen), Andre Deon Jones (Dahveed), Doug McCoy (Terranzano), Ernie Meier (Durant), Owen Parmele (Sheridan), Daetano Provenzano (Hefferly), Stoney Richards (Gillen), Michael Sharkey (Doyle), Gary Alan Shelton (Hayes), William Steel (Rappaport), Gary Telles (McGrath), Ted Widlanski (Barnes), Eric Zengota (Geiger)

A play in two acts. The action takes place in a public playground in Jackson Heights, New York during the Fall of 1950.

George Lange/Murfitt Photos

ORPHEUM THEATRE
Tuesday, June 10 - 15, 1980. (8 performances and 5 previews)
The Guardian Company presents:

THE COCKTAIL PARTY

By T. S. Eliot; Director, Christopher Cade; Set, Evelyn Sakash; Costumes, Carol Oditz; Lighting, Tony Quintavalla; Music, George David Weiss; Arrangements, Robert Stecko; Speech Consultant, Binnie Ravitch; General Management, Marilyn S. Miller, Berenice Weiler; Manager, Barbara Carrellas; Wardrobe, Judy Brusseau; Production Supervisor, Paul H. Everett; Stage Managers, Mark Lucas, Richard Lockwood; Press, Shirley Herz, Jan Greenberg, Sam Rudy

CAST

Alexander Scourby (Sir Henry Harcourt-Reilly), Jay Bond (Alexander), Elizabeth Brigulio (Miss Barraway), Kathryn Callaghan (Lavinia Chamberlayne), Richard Lockwood (Caterer), Joan Matthiessen (Celia Coplestone), Edward Morehouse (Edward Chamberlayne), Naomi Riordan (Julia Shuttlethwaite), James Umphlett (Peter Quilpe)

A play in 3 acts and 5 scenes. The action takes place at the present time in Chamberlayne's London flat and in Sir Henry Harcourt-Reilley's consulting room.

Right: Edward Morehouse, Kathryn Callaghan

THEATRE FOUR
Thursday, June 12,-15, 1980. (6 performances and 8 previews)
Joan Dunham and Segue Productions present:

CHASE A RAINBOW

Book, Music and Lyrics, Harry Stone; Director, Sue Lawless; Choreography, Bick Goss; Settings, Michael Rizzo; Musical Director, John Franceschina; Costumes, Rita Watson; Lighting, Jeff Davis; Sound, Martin Feldman; Assistant Musical Director, Jeremy Harris; Production Assistants, Heidi Dunham, Ron Ray; General Management, Sylrich Management; Stage Managers, Marcia McIntosh, Bill McComb; Press, Seymour Krawitz, Patricia McLean Krawitz

CAST

Ted Pugh	Virginia Sandifur
Suzanne Dawson	Stephen McNaughton
Chuck Karel	Jan Neuberger

MUSICAL NUMBERS: Let's Hear It for Me, The People You Know, You've Gotta Have a Passion, We're #1, Masquerade, Segue, Everything Happens for the Best, Out of Love, Whenever You Want Me, The Big City, The Happiest People, Have a Good Day, Listen Little Boy, I'm in Showbiz, I Just Want to Know That You're All Right, Life on the Rocks, To Be or Not to Be, I've Been Around the Horn, My Meadow, Mack Sennett Where Are You, All the Years, Listen World

A musical in two acts.

Martha Swope Photo

Virginia Sandifur, Suzanne Dawson, Stephen McNaughton, Ted Pugh, Jan Neuberger, Chuck Karel

THEATRE DE LYS
Tuesday, June 17, - August 24, 1980. (78 performances)
Mike Nichols and Lewis Allen present:

BILLY BISHOP GOES TO WAR

Written, Composed and Directed by John Gray in collaboration with Eric Peterson; Co-produced by Vancouver East Cultural Centre; Scenery, David Gropman; Lighting, Jennifer Tipton; Sound, Robert Kerzman; Associate Producers, Stephen Graham, Ventures West Capital, Inc.; General Management, Robert S. Fishko; Wardrobe, Dolores Gamba; Company Manager, Harris Goldman; Press, David Powers, Barbara Carroll

CAST

Eric Peterson†1
John Gray†2

A play in two acts. All characters and incidents are based on actual facts.

† Succeeded by: 1. Cedric Smith, 2. Ross Douglas

Left: Cedric Smith, Ross Douglas

CITY LIGHTS THEATRE
Tuesday, June 24, - August 24, 1980. (44 performances)
Barbara Gittler in Association with Morris Jaffe presents:

JAZZBO BROWN

Book, Music and Lyrics by Stephen H. Lemberg; Directed and Choreographed by Louis Johnson; Scenery, Harry Lines; Lighting, Bill Mintzer; Costumes, Karen Roston, Vel Riberto; Assistant Choreographer, Mercedes Ellington; Additional Musical Arrangements, Zulema Cusseaux; Musical Conductor, Tod Cooper; Musical Supervision, Orchestrations, Arrangements, Luther Henderson; General Management, Theatre Now, Inc; Art Director, Mark Balet; Wardrobe, Gail Palmiere; Company Manager, Corwith Hammill; Stage Managers, Corwith Hamill, Adrian Turner; Technical Consultant, Dan Ketting; Press, Shirley Herz, Jan Greenberg, Sam Rudy

CAST

Andre DeShields (Billy "Jazzbo" Brown), Chris Galloway (Maxine McCall), Jerry Jarrett (D. D. Daniels), Zulema (Rachael Brown), Ned Wright (Rev. Raymond W. Brown), and Charles Bernard, Deborah Lynn Bridges, Rodney Green, Janice Nicki Harrison, Dennis A. Morgan, Gayle Samuels, Wynonna Smith, Allysia C. Sneed
MUSICAL NUMBERS: Jazzbo Brown, Broadway, I'm Bettin' on You, Million Songs, Born to Sing, He Had the Callin', Bump Bump Bump, The Same Old Tune, When You've Loved Your Man, The Best Man, Give Me More, When I Die, Dancin' Shoes, Precious Patterns, Funky Bessie, Harlem Follies, First Time I Saw You, Pride and Freedom, Take a Bow

A musical in two acts. The action takes place during a 48 hour period and moves back and forth between a Broadway theatre and a prosperous church in Harlem in 1924.

Brownie Harris/Bill Coupon Photos

Andre DeShields

CHERRY LANE THEATRE
Wednesday, June 25, - September 14, 1980. (95 performances and 7 previews)
Sally Beychok and Tom Nolan present:

TO BURY A COUSIN

By Gus Weill; Director, Philip Oesterman; Scenery, Douglas W. Schmidt; Lighting, David F. Segal; Costumes, Robert Wojewodski; Incidental Music, Hayden Wayne; General Manager, Albert Poland; Company Manager, Pamela Hare; Stage Managers, Tom Capps, Lauren Craig; Press, Solters/Roskin/Friedman, Milly Schoenbaum, Kevin Patterson, Anne Obert Weinberg

CAST

Harry Goz (Bert), Annie Deutsch Abbott (Sister), Robert Bloodworth (Ben), Lauren Craig (Lita), Virginia Daly (Mama), Harvey Pierce (Papa), Reuben Schafer (Rabbi), Diane Tarleton (Hilda), Walter Williamson (W. A. Simpson)

A drama in two acts. The action takes place in the mind of a man in a deserted train station in the South in 1954.

Martha Swope Photos

Harry Goz, Diane Tarleton

MITZI E. NEWHOUSE THEATER
Tuesday, June 24,-29, 1980. (7 performances)
The Byrd Hoffman Foundation presents:

DIALOG/CURIOUS GEORGE

Text, Christopher Knowles; Directors, Robert Wilson, Christopher Knowles; Sound, Dale Ward; Choreography and Decor from original drawings by Christopher Knowles; Realized by Robert Wilson; Lighting, Beverly Emmons; Production Manager, Robert Lo Bianco; Costumes, Fred Bosschaart; Projections designed by Robert Wilson; Realized by Jacob Burkhardt; General Management, McCann & Nugent; Company Manager, James Gerald; Stage Managers, Philippe Chemin, Joanne McEntire; Press, Bob Ullman, Craig Macdonald

CAST

Christopher Knowles	Robert Wilson
Robert Barnet Anderson	Michael J. Nesline
Joanne McEntire	Bradley Wester

A play in 4 sections and 14 parts. The characters were inspired by a collection of books for children by Margret and H. A. Rey.

Robert Wilson, Christopher Knowles

Constance Towers

JONES BEACH THEATRE
Thursday, June 26, - August 31, 1980.
Richard Horner in association with Long Island State Park and Recreation Commission presents:

THE SOUND OF MUSIC

Music, Richard Rodgers; Lyrics, Oscar Hammerstein 2nd; Book, Howard Lindsay, Russel Crouse; Suggested by "The Trapp Family Singers" by Maria August Trapp; Director, John Fearnley; Musical Staging, Frank Wagner; Scenery and Costumes, Robert Fletcher; Lighting, Marc Weiss; Associate Producer, Lynne Stuart; Musical Director, Jack Gaughan; Managing Director, Alvin Dorfmann; General Manager, Malcolm Allen; Assistant Staging, Marsha Wagner; Production Coordinator, Jack Kauflin; Wardrobe, Catherine Maher, Joseph Tripolino; Hairstylist, James Nelson; Associate Conductor, Douglas Finney; Stage Managers, Mary Koenig, Elliott Woodruff, Garon Douglass; Press, Henry Luhrman, Terry M. Lilly, Kevin P. McAnarney, Craig Macdonald, John Rogers

CAST

Constance Towers (Maria), Irma Rogers (Sister Berthe), Joanne Highley (Sister Margaretta), Mary Leigh Stahl (Mother Abbess), Dixie Stewart (Sister Sophia), Earl Wrightson (Capt. Georg von Trapp), William Ryall (Franz), Toni Darnay (Frau Schmidt), Mary Lou Belli (Liesl), Scott Perrin (Friedrich), Laura Condon (Louisa), Krista Haun (Brigitta), Evan Seplo (Kurt), Susan Keenan (Marta), Amy Dolan (Gretl), Michael C. Booker (Rolf Gruber), Lois Hunt (Elsa Schraeder), Christina Britton (Ursula), George Maguire (Max Detweiler), Bill Galarno (Zeller), Kim Fairchild (Frau Zeller), William Bush (Baron Elberfeld), Christina Britton (Baroness Elberfeld), Byron Grant (Admiral von Schreiber)
VILLAGERS & GUESTS, ETC.: Ellyn Arons, Christina Britton, Amy Danielle, Kim Fairchild, Catherine Gaines, Linda Griffin, Joanne Highley, Sheila Loggie, Patricia Ludd, Judith Malafronte, Marsha Miller, Meredith Rawlins, Irma Rogers, Dixie Stewart, Maggie Stewart, Mary Stout, Paul Ward, Peter Allemano, Marc Bowen, Peter Clark, Paul Flores, William Kirk, Douglas O'Grady, Edward Prostak, Gary Ridley, David Wahl, Garon Douglass
MUSICAL NUMBERS: Praeludium, The Sound of Music, Maria, My Favorite Things, I Have Confidence, Do Re Mi, You Are Sixteen, Lonely Goatherd, How Can Love Survive?, Laendler Waltz, So Long Farewell, Climb Every Mountain, No Way to Stop It, Something Good, Processional, Edelweiss

A musical in two acts. The action takes place in Austria early in 1938, in and near Nonnberg Abbey and the von Trapp Villa.

Left Center: Lois Hunt, Earl Wrightson

QUAIGH THEATRE
Wednesday, July 9,-16, 1980. (14 performances)
The Barwyck Company presents:

MISS STANWYCK IS
STILL IN HIDING

By Larry Puchall, Reigh Hagen; Set and Lighting, Jay Klein; Sound, George Jacobs; Director, William E. Hunt; Stage Manager, Jacqueline van den Bovenkamp; Press, Max Eisen, Francine L. Trevens

CAST

David Craig (Everett), William Glenn (Tony), Joan Golomb (Doris), Bill Henry (Henry), Randy Holden (Donald), Mackenzie Lee (Brian), Margery Meyer (Eleanor), Len Stanger (Barney)

A comedy in 2 acts and 6 scenes. The action takes place at the present time in Brian and Donald's apartment in Manhattan.

Ken Howard Photo

Margery Meyer, Len Stanger,
Randy Holden

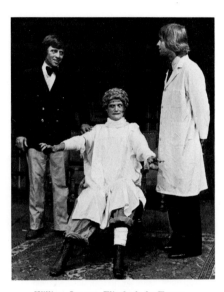

William Joerres, Elizabeth de Charay,
Jim Quinn

STAGE 15
Thursday, July 10,-27, 1980. (12 performances and 4 previews)
Stage 15 in association with Jean Claude LeBlanc presents:

THE PASSION OF FRANKENSTEIN

By Robert Kornfield; Director, Alan A. Gabor; Set, Joseph Ingellis; Costumes, A. Gabor; Lighting, Paul Merwin; Art Work, Joseph Turoczy; Stage Managers, Jean Hammer, Peter Mortlock; Press, Jeffrey Richards, C. George Willard, Robert Ganshaw

CAST

Elizabeth DeCharay (Victoria), Jim Quinn (Victor Frankenstein), Gloria Dearburne (Claire), William Joerres (Harold), George Dunlap (Igor), Katya Colman (Mrs. Telcher), Abby Aldridge (Nurse), John Edwards (Officer Krale)

A melodrama in 2 acts and 6 scenes. The action takes place at the present time in the living room of Victor Frankenstein's mansion in Stony Harbor, Long Island, New York.

PLAYHOUSE 46
Tuesday, July 15,-27, 1980. (12 performances)

TIME AND THE CONWAYS

By J. B. Priestley; Director, Warren Monteiro; Assistant Director, William Hopkins; Costume Coordinators, Marilyn Hemenway, Karen Gastiaburo; Lighting and Sound, Warren Monteiro, William Driscoll; Stage Manager, Eileen Reader

CAST

Carol Poppenger (Mrs. Conway), Jim Fitzpatrick (Alan), Marilyn Hemenway Downs (Madge), Kenneth Marks (Robin), Mary Portser (Hazel), Valerie Piacenti (Kay), Lisa Driscoll (Carol), Andrea Browne (Joan), John C. Introcaso (Ernest), Douglas R. Nielsen (Gerald)

A play in three acts. The action takes place in the sitting room of Mrs. Conway's house in 1919 and in 1938.

John C. Introcaso, Mary Portser

Patricia Routledge

DELACORTE THEATER

Tuesday, July 15, - August 31, 1980. (35 performances and 10 previews)
The New York Shakespeare Festival (Joseph Papp, Producer) presents:

THE PIRATES OF PENZANCE

Book, W. S. Gilbert; Music, Arthur Sullivan; Director, Wilford Leach; Orchestrations and Musical Direction, William Elliott; Choreography, Graciela Daniele; Sound, Don Ketteler; Lighting, Jennifer Tipton; Costumes, Patricia McGourty; Scenery, Bob Shaw, Jack Chandler, Wilford Leach; Make-up and Hairstylist, J. Roy Hellend; Assistant Choreographer, Adam Grammis; Wardrobe, Barrett Hong; Technical Director, David Lawson; Production Assistants, Lindy Rollo, Christine Sinclair; Assistant Director, Jack Chandler; Assistant Musical Director, Dan Berlinghoff; Stage Managers, Zane Weiner, Frank Difilia; General Manager, Robert Kamlot; Company Managers, Roger Gindi, Rheba Flegelman; Production Supervisor, Jason Steven Cohen; Press, Merle Debuskey, Bob Ullman, Richard Kornberg, Ed Bullins

CAST

Kevin Kline (Pirate King), Stephen Hanan (Samuel), Rex Smith (Frederic), Patricia Routledge (Ruth, a pirate maid), Major-General Stanley's Daughters: Robin Boudreau, Maria Guida, Nancy Heikin, Audrey Lavine, Bonnie Simmons, Alice Playten (Edith), Marcie Shaw (Kate), Wendy Wolfe (Isabel), Linda Ronstadt (Mabel), George Rose (Major-General Stanley), Tony Azito (Sergeant), Pirates and Police: Dean Badolato, Mark Beudert, Brian Bullard, Walter Caldwell, Keith David, Tim Flavin, G. Eugene Moose, Joseph Neal, Walter Niehenke, Joe Pichette, Barry Tarallo, Michael Edwin Wilson
UNDERSTUDIES: Keith David (King), G. Eugene Moose (Samuel), Barry Tarallo (Frederic), Tim Flavin (Sergeant), Walter Niehenke (Stanley), Wendy Wolfe (Ruth), Nancy Heikin (Mabel), Maria Guida (Edith/Kate/Isabel), Swing: Audrey Lavine

Martha Swope Photos

LION THEATRE

Monday, July 28, - August 16, 1980. (16 performances)
Nexus Theatre Associates, Ltd. presents:

OPTION

By Joyce A. Whitcomb; Director, James Bohr; Set, James Finguerra; Lighting, Salvatore A. Lupo; Costumes, James D. Collum; Associate Producer, Gail Bell; General Management, Clyde Kuemmerle; Technical Director, Michael Nesline; Props, Ron Davis; Wardrobe, Mary Leyendecker; Stage Manager, Tri Garraty; Press, Marguerite Wolfe

CAST

Eileen Albert (Gerda), Carlissa Hayden (Lydia), Walker Hicklin (Sandy), Hilary J. James (Harriet), Mel Jurdem (Lester), Eugene Kallman (Franz), James Lawrence Kelly (Steve), Dean Kyburz (Roger), Laura MacDermott (Lotta), Christy Newland (Melanie)

A drama in two acts. The action takes place during a winter and spring in the early 1960's.

Rifka Shiffman Photo

Eugene Kallman, Carlissa Hayden

"Three Forked Road"

METROPOLITAN OPERA HOUSE

Tuesday, August 12,-24, 1980. (14 performances)
The Metropolitan Opera and ICM Artists present:

THE PEKING OPERA THEATRE

Director, Zhao Yianzia; Leader of Group, Zhang Menggeng; Mangers, Hou Dian, Meng Guanghui; Stage Managers, Jiang Yuanrong, Li Shaolou; Costumes, Sun Haisong, Guo Qishan; Lighting, Wang Shifang, Rong Yongchun; Settings, Wang Zhijiang; General Managers, Theatre Now; Associate General Manager, Charlotte W. Wilcox; Company Manager, Peter Inkey; Production Stage Manager, Leonard Stein; Management Associate, Sam Ross; Press, Marilynn LeVine, Michael Alpert, Mark Goldstaub, Alan Hale

REPERTOIRE

The Monkey King Fights the Eighteen Lo Hans (Demons), The Jade Bracelet, Yen Tang Mountain, The White Snake, The Three-Forded Crossroad, The Goddess of the Green Ripples

Joanne Jacobson, David Bostick

WONDERHORSE THEATRE
Tuesday, August 12,-16, 1980. (6 performances and 21 previews)
Cynthia and Clay Smith present:

NAOMI COURT

By Michael Sawyer; Director, Ted Weiant; Set, Bob Phillips; Lighting, Ned Hallick; Costumes, George Potts; Original Score, David McHugh; Assistant to Director, Jerry Campbell; Technical Director, Derald G. Plumer; Stage Managers, Marcy Stoeven, Mike Boak; Press, Judy Jacksina, Glenna Freedman, Angela Wilson, Dolph Browning

CAST

Katharine Balfour succeeded by Rica Martens (Sally), Charles Douglass succeeded by Bruno Ragnacci (Lenny), Joanne Jacobson (Florence), Ron Johnston (Bunny), David Bostick (Harper)

A "thriller" in two acts. The action takes place in Naomi Court, a tenement in the Yorkville section of New York during the last days of August in apartments 2C and 5C.

Lee Snider Photo

ORPHEUM THEATRE
Thursday, August 14,-17, 1980. (6 performances and 10 previews)
Scott Goldstein, Lee Schneider and Property Productions present:

A SLEEPLESS NIGHT WITH AN HONEST MAN

By Lee Schneider; Director, Scott Goldstein; Set, Charles Powell; Costumes, Johnetta Lever; Lighting, D. Schweppe; Art Direction, Ditto; Hairstylist, Hiram Ortiz; Dialogue Direction, Van Hinman; Make-up, Bill O'Shea; Wardrobe, Alicia Richardson; General Manager, David Smith Mayhew; Stage Managers, William Ickes, Arely Martinez; Press, Max Eisen, Francine L. Trevens

CAST

Edmond Collins (Benedict Arnold/George Washington/John Andre), Robin Harvey (Peggy Arnold), Gisele Richardson (Anna Hawks)

A play in two acts. The action takes place in Benedict Arnold's home in London on October 2, 1784.

Ken Howard Photo

Robin Harvey, Edmond Collins

Lorna Johnson, Kevin McClarnon,
Georgia Southcotte, Rebecca Guy

WONDERHORSE THEATRE
Thursday, September 11,-28, 1980. (16 performances)
Cherubs Guild Corporation (Carol Avila, Robert Avila, Lesley Starbuck, Hillary Wyler) presents:

BETWEEN DAYLIGHT AND BOONVILLE

By Matt Williams; Director, John David Lutz; Set and Costumes, James Stewart; Lighting, Jo Mayer; Sound, Michael Jay; Producers, Carol Avila, Lesley Starbuck, Hillary Wyler; Technical Director, Joe Riemer; Stage Manager, Toni Press; Press, Susan Bloch, Adrian Bryan-Brown, Walter Vatter

CAST

Wendy Ann Finnegan (Stacy), Rebecca Guy (Carla), Lorna Johnson (Marlene), Kevin McClarnon (Cyril), Sean Mullane (Bobby), Laurie Ross (Wanda), Christian Slater (Jimmy), Georgia Southcotte (Lorette)

A drama in two acts. The action takes place at the present time in a trailer court in the strip-mining country of Southen Indiana.

Peter Krupenye Photo

HAROLD CLURMAN THEATRE

Thursday, September 11, - October 12, 1980. (38 performances)
Charlotte Bunin and Marvin Gutin present:

AN ACT OF KINDNESS

By Joseph Julian; Director, Mark Gordon; Associate Producer, Joyce Beauvais; Scenery, Gregory William Bolton; Lighting, Carol B. Sealy; General Management, Dollars and Sense Productions; Company Manager, Joe Restuccia; Sound, David Bunin; Production Assistant, Ricky Cody; Costumes, Steven Birnbaum; Stage Manager, Priscilla Guastavino; Press, David Lipsky, Victoria R. Sanders, Steven Bruce

CAST

Scotty Bloch
Eddie Jones

A drama in two acts. The action takes place at the present time on a cold winter night in a furnished room of what was once a fashionable apartment house on lower Fifth Avenue in New York City.

Stephanie Saia Photo

Scotty Bloch, Eddie Jones

Ruby Wax, Beverly Penberthy,
Brenda Currin

COLONNADES THEATRE

Wednesday, September 17, - October 12, 1980. (28 performances)
Seven Oaks Productions presents:

DESPERATELY YOURS,

By Ruby Wax; Director, Alan Rickman; Costumes, Robert Anton; Lighting, Randy Becker; General Management, Marilyn S. Miller, Berenice Weiler; Manager, Barbara Carrellas; Technical Director, Randy Becker; Original Music and Sound Design, Noble Shropshire; Stage Managers, Meryl Schaffer, Lucille Rivin; Press, Judy Jacksina, Glenna Freedman, Angela Wilson, Dolph Browning

CAST

Beverly Penberthy (The Lady in Purple), Brenda Currin (The Lady in Green), Ruby Wax (The Lady in Pink)

A play performed without intermission.

Bert Andrews Photo

PLAYHOUSE 46

Wednesday, September 24, - November 2, 1980. (42 performances)
The Production Company (Norman Rene, Artistic Director; Caren Harder, Managing Director) and Force Ten Productions present:

CASUALTIES

By Karolyn Nelke; Director, Norman Rene; Set, Roger Mooney; Costumes, John Carver Sullivan; Lighting, Debra J. Kletter; Music Composed by Jared Bernstein; Technical Director, Tim Odell; Production Manager, David L. Nathans; Stage Managers, David L. Nathans, Gus Kaikkonen; Press, Clarence Allsopp

CAST

Randy Danson (Claire), Monique Fowler (Lynnie), George Hall (Robert Crawford), Georgine Hall (Jenny Crawford), Stephen McHattie (Mark Crawford), Brad O'Hare (Owen Wilson), Lillie Robertson (Jessie Wilson)

A play in two acts. The action takes place in Garrison, a small town on the Hudson upstate in New York from July to December of 1919 with a flashback to the winter of 1918.

Chip Goebert Photo

Lillie Robertson, Stephen McHattie

PROVINCETOWN PLAYHOUSE
Thursday, September 25, - October 5, 1980. (14 performances and 4 previews)

Frank Gero and Mark Gero in association with the Provincetown Playhouse present The Asolo State Theater production of:

TRANSCENDENTAL LOVE

By Daryl Boylan; Director, Robert Strane; Set, Bennet Averyt; Costumes, Catherine King; Lighting, Martin Petlock; Original Music, John Franceschina; Technical Director, Victor Meyrich; Assistant to Director, Maggi Guran; Company Manager, Wofi Gero; Stage Manager, Stephanie Moss; Press, Shirley Herz, Jan Greenberg, Sam Rudy

CAST

Robert Murch (Ralph Waldo Emerson), Deborah Fezelle (Lydia Emerson), Monique Morgan (Margaret Fuller), Tom Brennan (Horace Greeley)

A comedy in two acts and five scenes. The action takes place in Ralph Waldo Emerson's study in Cambridge, Massachusetts, in 1840-1841.

Monique Morgan, Robert Murch

PLAYERS THEATRE
Tuesday, September 30, - October 5, 1980. (12 performances and 2 previews)

Miracle Expressions, Inc. presents:

A MATTER OF OPINION

Book and Lyrics, Mary Elizabeth Hauer; Musical Supervisor and Composer, Harold Danko; Musical Director and Composer, John Jacobson; Direction and Choreography, Shari Upbin; Production Supervisor, David S. Rosenak; Set and Costumes, John Arnone; Lighting, Joanna Schielke; General Manager, Albert Poland; Production Assistant, Pippin Parker; Wardrobe, Mary Anne Travaglione; Assistant Choreographer, Alan Miller; Musical Arranger, Dan Palkowsky; Company Manager, Erik Murkoff; Stage Managers, Michael Spellman, Charles Randolph Wright; Press, Solters/Roskin/Friedman, Milly Schoenbaum, Kevin Patterson

CAST

David Anchel (Hobo), Andy Bey (Prophet), Janet Bliss (Mrs. Gentle/Bag Lady), Ralph Braun (Mr. Fate), Vickie D. Chappell (Fantasy Child), Leigh Finner (Mrs. Finished), Kate Klugman (Fact Child), Seymour Penzner (Judge), Suzanne Smartt (Ms. Easily), Charles Randolph Wright (Mr. Merrily)

MUSICAL NUMBERS: Opening, Not Every Day Can Be a Day of Shine, Almost Working, No Thank You from a Mocking Sun, If the Sun Didn't Shine Each Day, The Average Man, Free Time, Mrs. Finished Lament, Determination, Hobo's Song, Shopping Bag Lady, Gotta Pretend, ABC to XYZ, The Wanderer, The Sandman, Just the Facts, I Am Here, Humanity, Matter of Opinion, Hooray for the Judge

A musical in two acts. The action takes place in the townsquare.

Martha Swope Photo

HAROLD CLURMAN THEATRE
Saturday, September 27, - October 19, 1980. (14 performances and 3 previews)

The Harold Clurman Theatre (Jack Garfein, Artistic Director) presents:

THE TWO-CHARACTER PLAY

By Tennessee Williams; a re-write of his play "Outcry"; Director, Alfred Ryder; Set, Tom Schwinn; Costumes, Beba Shamash; Lighting, Adam Gross; Sound, Sam Agar; Production Coordinator, Lisa Sanders; Assistant to Director, Paul Lussier; Stage Managers, Nancy Finn, Nicholas Eastman; Company Manager, Pamela C. Billig; Press, Joe Wolhandler, Steven Wolhandler, Douglas Urbanski

CAST

Clare . . . . Olive Deering
Felice . . . . Alfred Ryder

A play in two acts. The action takes place before and after the performance on an evening in an unspecified locality; during the performance: a nice afternoon in a deep Southern town called New Bethesda.

Chip Goebert Photo

Left: Alfred Ryder, Olive Deering

Janet Bliss, Andy Bey, Suzanne Smartt

CHELSEA THEATER CENTER/UPSTAIRS

Tuesday, September 30, 1980 - June 13, 1981. (274 performances and 15 previews)
(Moved Tuesday, November 25, 1980 to American Place Theatre)
John H. P. Davis and Sheldon Riss in association with Alexander S. Bowers and the Chelsea Theater Center present:

REALLY ROSIE

Book and Lyrics, Maurice Sendak; Music, Carole King; Direction and Choreography, Patricia Birch; Entire Production Designed by Maurice Sendak; Scenery supervised by Douglas W. Schmidt; Lighting, John Gleason; Costumes supervised by Carrie Robbins; Musical Arrangements and Direction, Joel Silberman; General Management, Howard Haines; Production Supervisor, Peggy Peterson; Assistant to General Manager, David Musselman; Production Assistants, Stephen John Boyle, Henry Sutro; Wardrobe, Gayle Palmieri; Stage Managers, Janet Friedman, Alison Price, Bibi Humes; Press, Shirley Herz, Jan Greenberg, Sam Rudy

CAST

Tisha Campbell (Rosie), B. J. Barie (Pierre), Lara Berk (Neighborhood Kid), Jermaine Campbell (Chicken Soup), Ruben Cuevas (Neighborhood Kid), Bibi Humes (Mother), Matthew Kolmes (Lion/Neighborhood Kid), Joe LaBenz IV (Alligator), April Lerman (Kathy), Alison Price (Mother), Wade Raley (Johnny) Understudies: April Lerman (Rosie), Ruben Cuevas (Chicken Soup), Lara Berk, Matthew Kolmes
MUSICAL NUMBERS: Really Rosie, Simple Humble Neighborhood, Alligators All Around, One Was Johnny, Pierre, Screaming and Yelling, The Awful Truth, Very Far Away, Avenue P, Chicken Soup with Rice

A musical performed without intermission.

Left: April Lerman, Joe LaBenz IV, B. J. Barie, Tisha Campbell, Wade Raley Top: Tisha Campbell, B. J. Barie

CHERRY LANE THEATRE

Opened Wednesday, October 1, 1980.*
Gene Persson, Richard S. Bright, John Loesser in association with Twentieth Century-Fox Productions and by special arrangement with the WPA Theatre present:

ALBUM

By David Rimmer; Director, Joan Micklin Silver; Sets, David Potts; Costumes, Susan Denison; Lighting, Jeff Davis; Sound, Alex McIntyre; Props/Production Assistant, John Masterson; Assistant to Producers, Peggy Murphy; General Manager, Gene Persson; Company Manager, Jolly Nelson; Stage Managers, Bethe Ward, Bruce MacVittie; Press, Jeffrey Richards, Ben Morse, C. George Willard, Robert Ganshaw, Helen Stern, Ted Killmer

CAST

Peggy	Tracy Pollan†1
Trish	Jan Leslie Harding
Billy	Kevin Bacon†2
Boo	Keith Gordon†3

Understudies: Jennifer Grey, Bruce MacVittie

A comedy in 2 acts and 8 scenes. The action takes place in the girls' bedrooms and the boys dormitories from October 1963 to graduation day, June 1967.

* Closed May 10, 1981 after 254 performances and 5 previews.
† Succeeded by: 1. Jenny Wright, 2. Ralph Davies, 3. Sam Robards

Chip Goebert Photos

Keith Gordon, Jan Leslie Harding, Jenny Wright, Kevin Bacon

NORMAN THOMAS THEATRE

Sunday, October 12, - December 28, 1980. (33 performances)
Ben Bonus presents:

ONE OF A KIND

By Al Springer; Director, Leo Fuchs; Scenery, Jerry Rothman; Production Manager, Michael Lamonaco; Based on play by Louis Freiman; Music and Lyrics, Leo Fuchs; Lighting, Andrea Randall; Musical Director, William Gunther; Stage Manager, Rebecca Springer; Press, Max Eisen, Irene Gandy

CAST

Leo Fuchs (David), Mina Bern (Tsipe), Sylvia Feder (Miriam), Israel Welichansky (Rabbi), Evelyn Kingsley (Nadia), Baruch Blum (Mendel), Gerri-Ann Frank (Rebecca)

A traditional Yiddish musical comedy in two acts. The action takes place in the Rabbi's house, Israel, and a Greenwich Village studio.

Top Right: Mina Bern, Leo Fuchs

ORPHEUM THEATRE

Monday, October 13,-19, 1980. (8 performances and 10 previews)
Lorin E. Price in association with Roberta Weissman presents:

RICHIE

By Robert Somerfeld; Director, Sherwood Arthur; Scenery, Rene D'Auriac; Lighting, Eric Gertner; Costumes, Margo LaZaro; General Manager, Paul B. Berkowsky; Company Manager, Paul P. Matwiow; Stage Managers, Bill McComb, Ira Lewis; Press, Merlin Group, Cheryl Sue Dolby, Eileen McMahon, Glen Gary

CAST

Eric Brown (Richie), Stephen Pearlman (Ike), Delphi Harrington (Debra), George Bamford (Matt), Lisa Michaelis (Corry), Bea Tendler (Pam)

A comedy/drama in 3 acts and 13 scenes. The action takes place at the present time from mid-June to mid-September.

Roger Greenawalt Photo

Right: Lisa Michaelis, Eric Brown

HAROLD CLURMAN THEATRE

Wednesday, October 22, 1980 - January 25, 1981 (94 performances and 6 previews)
Jack Garfein (Artistic Director) presents:

THE CHEKHOV SKETCHBOOK

Translated and Adapted by Luba Kadison and Joseph Buloff; Director, Tony Giordano; Settings, Hugh Landwehr; Costumes, David Murin; Lighting, Frances Aronson; Sound, George Hansen; Wardrobe, Lisa Ledwich; Administrative Assistant, Laura Livingston; General Manager, Heather Ganzer; Technical Director, Stephen P. Edelstein; Stage Managers, Johnna Murray, Sheila Gowan; Press, Joe Wolhandler, Steven Wolhandler, Douglas Urbanski

CAST

"The Vagabond" with John Heard (The Vagabond) succeeded by Jeffrey DeMunn, Frank Bara (Ptakh), Jack O'Connell (Nik), "The Witch" with Penelope Allen (Raisa) succeeded by Julie Garfield, John Heard (Savely) succeeded by Jeffrey DeMunn, Stephen D. Newman (Postman), "In a Music Shop" with Frank Bara (Shopkeeper), Joseph Buloff (Ivan)

Chip Goebert Photos

Frank Bara, Joseph Buloff
Above: Frank Bara, John Heard

TROUPE THEATRE

Sunday, October 26, - November 18, 1980. (12 performances)
The Actors Workshop of the New York Chapter of the National Academy of Television Arts and Sciences presents:

A PRAYER FOR MY DAUGHTER

By Thomas Babe; Director, Richard Edelman; Producer, George A. Heinemann; Set and Lighting, Tim Galvin; Costumes, Margarita Delgado; Production Coordinator, Jeremiah Newton; Stage Managers, Betsy English, Susie Zeigler

CAST

Toby Tompkins (Kelly), Ron Comenzo (Jack), Paul Greco (Jimmy, a.k.a. James Rosario, Jimmy Rosehips), James Selby (Sean, a.k.a. Simon Cohn, Sean de Kahn)

A drama in two acts. The action takes place at the present time in the squad room of a downtown precinct.

(No photos available)

LION THEATRE

Tuesday, November 4, - December 18, 1980. (46 performances and 3 previews)
Twin Oak Productions Ltd. presents:

THE GLASS MENAGERIE

By Tennessee Williams; Director, Tom Kamm; Scenic and Costume Design, Nancy Thun; Composer, Bruce Coughlin; Lighting, Todd Elmer; Technical Director, Anthony Diemont; Stage Manager, Christopher Barns; Press, Howard Atlee, Tom Trenkle, James Baldassare

CAST:

Julie Haydon (Amanda Wingfield), Anthony Heald (Tom), Patricia Angelin (Laura), William Anton (Gentleman Caller), Understudy: Susannah Halston

A drama in two acts. The action takes place in the Wingfield apartment on an alley in St. Louis, Missouri.

Martha Swope Photo

Top: Anthony Heald
Left: Julie Haydon

WONDERHORSE THEATRE

Friday, November 7, - 23, 1980. (16 performances)
New World Theatre (Producer/Artistic Director, Jane Stanton) presents:

THE BEETHOVEN

By Y York; Director, Richard Harden; Set, Bob Phillips; Lighting, Jeffrey McRoberts; Costumes, Amanda J. Klein; Technical Director, Stephen Caldwell; Stage Managers, Karen E. Nothmann, Gail Arthur; Press, Max Eisen, Francine L. Trevens

CAST

Steven Ryan (Harold), Dan Ahearn (Jeremy), Alexandra O'Karma (Sara), Susanne Peters (Annie), John Madden Towey (Marvin), Trinity Thompson (Roberta), Peter J. Saputo (Leo)

A drama in two acts. The action takes place in New York City at the present time in Harold's apartment and in a Broadway theatre.

Esther Bubley Photo

John Madden Towey, Alexandra O'Karma

GRAND CENTRAL TERMINAL TRACKS 39–42
Sunday, November 9, 1980. (1 performance and 23 previews)
Dodger Productions, John L. Haber, Louis Busch Hager present:

FRIMBO

Conceived, Adapted and Directed by John L. Haber; Based on book "All Aboard with E. M. Frimbo" by Rogers E. M. Whitaker and Anthony Hiss; Music, Howard Harris; Lyrics, Jim Wann; Scenery, Karl Eigsti, Fred Buchholz; Costumes, Patricia McGourty; Lighting, Fred Buchholz; Musical Arrangement and Direction, Howard Harris; Associate Musical Director, Bill Komaiko; Sound, Roscoe Harring; Technical Director, Roger Bardwell; Stage Managers, Herb Vogler, Nancy Harrington, Melissa Davis; Production Assistants, Peggy Jacobsen, Norman Frisch; Press, Jeffrey Richards, Robert Ganshaw, Ben Morse, Helen Stern, C. George Willard, Ted Killmer

CAST

Richard B. Shull (E. M. Frimbo), Larry Riley (Conductor), Deborah May (Contessa), Trio: Pattie D'Arcy, Pauletta Pearson, Cass Morgan

MUSICAL NUMBERS: Frimbo Special, Ballad of Frimbo, The Train, Train Walking, Trains or Me, Going Home, Lady by Choice, On a Train at Night, I Hate Trains, Mama Frimbo, The Mileage Millionaire, Gone Everywhere But Home, Siberia, Ode to Steam, That's the Way to Make It Move, Names of the Trains

A musical performed without intermission.

Richard B. Shull, Pauletta Pearson, Pattie D'Arcy, Cass Morgan in "Frimbo"

THEATER AT ST. PETER'S CHURCH
Wednesday, November 19,-23, 1980. (6 performances; returned for 6 additional performances Tuesday, December 9,-14, 1980) ANTA presents:

JUDGEMENT

By Barry Collins; Director, Ellen Burstyn; Setting, Raymond C. Recht; Costumes, Jane Greenwood; Lighting, Jeff Davis; Producer, Richmond Crinkley; General Manager, Scott Steele; Company Manager, John Parsons; Production Assistant, Diane Asadorian; Stage Manager, Doug Gray; Press, Betty Lee Hunt, Maria Cristina Pucci, James Sapp

CAST

Captain Andrei Vukhov . . . . Philip Anglim

Performed without intermission.

Roger Greenawalt Photo

CARTER THEATER
Thursday, November 20, 1980 - January 18, 1981. (70 performances and 16 previews)
Jim Payne in association with Sherie Seff and Bruce Kluger presents:

KA-BOOM!

Book and Lyrics, Bruce Kluger; Music, Joe Ercole; Director, John-Michael Tebelak; Choreography, Lynne Gannaway; Sets, Ken Holamon; Costumes, Erica Hollmann; Lights, Kirk Bookman; Associate Director, Nina Faso; Musical Director and Vocal Arrangements, John Lehman; Musical Arrangements, Joe Ercole; General Manager, Jim Payne; Business Manager, Maureen McDonald; Assistant Musical Director, Curtis McKonly; Technical Supervisor, Duke Durfee; Stage Managers, Matthew Causey; Press, Herb Striesfield

CAST

Ken Ward (Matt), Fannie Whitehead (Hattie), John Hall (Tony), Andrea Wright (June), Judith Bro (Jasmine), Terry Barnes (Avery)

MUSICAL NUMBERS: Now We Pray, Oh Lord, A Little Bit O' Glitter, Maybe for Instance, With a World to Conquer, Smile, Let Me Believe in Me, Believe Us Receive Us, A Few Get Through, Ballad of Adam and Eve, Gimme a "G", The Soft Spot, You Are You, The Light Around the Corner, Those ABC's, Judgement Day, Bump and Grind for God, Let the Show Go On!

A musical in two acts.

Ken Howard Photo

Philip Anglim in "Judgement"

Andrea Wright, Judith Bro, John Hall,
Ken Ward, Fannie Whitehead

Peter Burnell, Shelley Wyant

PROVINCETOWN PLAYHOUSE
Monday, November 24,-26, 1980. (3 performances and 21 previews)
Bob Lampel in association with the Provincetown Playhouse presents:

BOHEMIAN HEAVEN

By Jan Novak; Director, Gerald Mast; Set, Bob Phillips; Costumes, Sydney Brooks; Lighting, Gerard C. Klug; Sound, Christopher Andersen; General Manager, Bob Lampel; Company Manager, Robert Breslo; Technical Director, Bill Paster; Stage Managers, N. Michael Swafford, Peter Noel-Duhamel; Press, Valerie Warner

CAST

Douglas Parvin (Jarousek), Peter Burnell (Franta), Shelley Wyant (Vlasta), Peter Noel-Duhamel (Peter and Almost Everyone Else), Dave Florek (Jerry Adamec), John Watson (Jarousek alternate),

A comedy in two acts. The action takes place yesterday afternoon and that evening in Cicero, Illinois, a suburb on the west side of Chicago.

Jack Mitchell Photo

PLAYERS THEATRE
Tuesday, November 25, - December 7, 1980. (16 performances and 6 previews)
David Matthew presents:

NAOMI COURT

By Michael Sawyer; Director, Ted Weiant; Set, Bob Phillips; Lighting, Ned Hallick; Costumes, George Potts; Original Score, David McHugh; Production Assistants, Richard Kane, Debra Bucher; Fight Coach, Michael Katz; Stage Managers, Michael Spellman, Joanne Jacobson; Press, Fred Nathan, Louise Ment

CAST

B. Constance Barry (Sally Dugan), Bruno Ragnacci (Lenny Santini), Joanne Jacobson (Florence), John A. Coe (Bunny Berry), David Bostick (Harper)

A drama in two acts. The action takes place in Naomi Court, a tenement house in the Yorkville section of New York City, in Apartment 2B and Apartment 5C during the last Wednesday and Thursday of August.

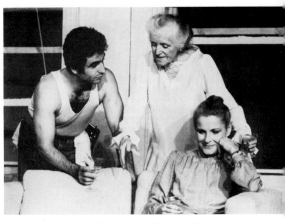

Bruno Ragnacci, B. Constance Barry,
Joanne Jacobson

Lorraine Spritzer (seated), Mary Anisi,
Pat Legere

THREE MUSES THEATRE
Tuesday, November 25, 1980 - November 30, 1980. (16 performances)
M. W. A. J. presents:

MOMA

By Tom Coble; Director, Joe Nikola; Set and Lighting, Steve M. Curt; Costumes, Joan Harris; Stage Manager, Don Buschmann; Press, Max Eisen, Maria Somma

CAST

Lorraine Spritzer (Mrs. Lucille Gamble/Moma), Pat Legere (Her Son), Mary Anisi (Her Daughter)

A drama in 2 acts and 5 scenes with a prelude. The action takes place at the present time in Pacific Grove, California, and New York City, except for a flashback to the day President Carter granted amnesty to the war resisters.

Dortha Duckworth, Ralph Farnworth

WEST SIDE MAIN STAGE
Friday, November 28, - December 4, 1980. (15 performances)
Susan L. Elrod and Robert E. Ankrom present:

BLUE HEAVEN

By Stephanie Glass Solomon; Director, Thom Mitchell; Costumes, Leslie Day; Set, Jim Schmidt; Lighting, Ronald M. Katz; Sound, Harvey S. Wilson; Production Manager, Susan Mowrer; Stage Managers, Karin D. Levitt, Susan M. Helsell; Press, Sara R. Morgan, Jeff Tarran

CAST

Dortha Duckworth (Betty), Virginia Robinson (Zola), Joan Kendall (Shirley), Betty Pelzer (Marge), Ralph Farnworth (Perry), David Ellis (Maurice), Tish Lee (Hattie), Avery Wood (Reverend), Hugh Karraker (Michaels)

A play in 2 acts and 8 scenes. The action takes place at the present time in a large city.

Lewellyn Harrison Photo

CHELSEA THEATER CENTER
Wednesday, December 2, 1980 - March 29, 1981 (103 performances)
Leavin/Davis Productions in association with Chris Silva and Chelsea Theater Center present:

WE WON'T PAY! WE WON'T PAY!

By Dario Fo; Translated and Directed by R. G. Davis; Production Design, Wolfgang Roth; Costumes, Denise Romano; Light and Sound, Terry Alan Smith; General Manager, Paul Eric Leavin; Company Manager, Chris Silva; Production Assistants, Alan Dourmashkin, Betty Diamond, Carol Selkowitz; Stage Manager, William Hare; Press, Edward T. Callaghan, Jacqueline Burnham

CAST

Bonnie Braelow (Margherita), Robert DeFrank (Luigi), Harris Laskawy (Giovanni), W. T. Martin (Sergeant/Caribineri/Undertaker-/Old Man), Karen Shallo (Antonia)

A comedy in two acts. The action takes place in a working class apartment in Milan, Italy, during 1974.

Carol Rosegg Photo

Karen Shallo, Harris Laskawy

Jean Smart

ACTORS PLAYHOUSE
Wednesday, December 2, 1980 - March 1, 1981. (80 performances)
John Glines and Lawrence Lane present The Glines production of:

LAST SUMMER AT BLUEFISH COVE

By Jane Chambers; Director, Nyla Lyon; Set, Reagan Cook; Costumes, Giva R. Taylor; Lighting, Jeffrey Schissler; Sculpture, Dorothy Abbott; Associate Producers, Bill Blackwell, Peter Pope; Company Manager, Lawrence Lane; Assistant to Producers, Jacqueline Cooper; Hairstylist, George Kryoneris; Stage Managers, Paula Ellen Cohen, Laura Burroughs; Press, Max Eisen, Francine L. Trevens

CAST

Jean Smart (Lil) succeeded by Holly Baron, Susan Slavin (Eva), Janet Sarno (Kitty) succeeded by Jane Chambers, Holly Baron (Annie) succeeded by Susan Blommaert, Lauren Craig (Rae), Dulcie Arnold (Rita), Celia Howard (Sue), Robin Mary Paris (Donna)

A drama in two acts. The action takes place at the present time on Bluefish Cove from early summer through late fall.

Ken Howard Photo

WONDERHORSE THEATRE

Thursday, December 4,-22, 1980. (15 performances and 3 previews)
Cherubs Guild Corporation presents:

VERA, WITH KATE

By Toni Press; Director, Matt Williams; Set, Loy Arcenas; Lighting, Jo Mayer; Costumes, Cheryl Henderson; Original Music, Mudra Lipari; Producers, Carol Avila, Lesley Starbuck, Hillary Wyler; Technical Director, Edmond Ramage; Stage Manager, Phil Funkenbusch; Press, Susan Bloch, Adrian Bryan-Brown, Ellen Zeisler

CAST

Helen-Jean Arthur (Vera), Tanny McDonald (Kate), John Wesley Shipp (Greg), Maeve McGuire (Maggie)

A drama in two acts. The action takes place at the present time in a church and adjacent graveyard in Southern Missouri.

Peter Krupenye Photo

**Helen-Jean Arthur, Tanny McDonald,
John Wesley Shipp, Maeve McGuire**

David Silber, Elizabeth DeBruler

THEATRE DE LYS

Sunday, December 7, 1980 - February 15, 1981. (94 performances)
Doug Cole, Joe Novak, Spencer Tandy, Joseph Butt present:

TRIXIE TRUE TEEN DETECTIVE

Book, Music and Lyrics, Kelly Hamilton; Director, Gill Gile; Musical Staging, Arthur Faria; Scenery, Michael J. Hotopp, Paul DePass; Costumes, David Toser; Lighting, Craig Miller; Orchestrations, Eddie Sauter; Music Direction and Vocal Arrangements, Robert Fisher; Associate Producer, Peter Alsop; Dance Arrangements, Jimmy Roberts; Technical Consultant, Dale E. Ward; General Management, Dorothy Olim Associates; Hairstylist, Karol Coeyman; Stage Managers, John Brigleb, Tim Cassidy; Press, Jeffrey Richards, Ben Morse, C. George Willard, Robert Ganshaw, Helen Stern, Ted Killmer

CAST

Marilyn Sokol (Miss Snood/Olga), Gene Lindsey (Joe), Kathy Andrini (Trixie), Keith Rice (Dick), Jay Lowman (Al/Wilhelm), Alison Bevan (LaVerne), Keith Caldwell (Bobby), Marianna Allen (Maxine)

MUSICAL NUMBERS: Trixie's On the Case!, This Is Indeed My Lucky Day, Most Popular and Most Likely to Succeed, Mr. and Mrs. Dick Dickerson, Juvenile Fiction, A Katzenjammer Kinda Song, You Haven't Got Time for Love, In Cahoots, The Mystery of the Moon, The Secret of the Tapping Shoes, Rita from Argentina, Trixie True Teen Detective!

A musical comedy in two acts. The action takes place during the mid-1940's in the New York offices of Snood Publishing, and in the mythical town of Cherry Hill, New Jersey.

Stephanie Saia Photo

AMDA STUDIO ONE

Friday, December 5,-22, 1980. (19 performances and 1 preview)
Gryphon Theatricals Inc. (Maryellen Flynn, Producing Director: William J. Lentsch, Artistic Director) presents:

THE STORY OF THE GADSBYS

By Rudyard Kipling; Adapted and Directed by William J. Lentsch; Scenery, Wendy Walker; Costumes, Sandy Handloser; Lighting, Rick Gray; Technical Director, John Reed; Production Staff, Cindy Tennenbaum, Kathy Ryan, Amy Whitman, John Beaupre; Stage Managers, Linda Becket, Randy Etheredge, Sarah Goodyear; Press, Judy Jacksina, Glenna Freedman, Angela Wilson, Dolph Browning

CAST

Nari Avari (Bearer/Khitmatgars), Peter Basch, Jr. (Junior Chaplain), Stephen C. Bradbury (Capt. Jack Mafflin), Mark Brandon (Dr. J. Allen Anthony), Marian Clarke (Mrs. Harriet Herriott), Elizabeth DeBruler (Minnie Threegan), Stephen Gabis (Capt. William Blayne), Russell Hill (Commissioner Doone), George Holmes (Edward MacKesy), Patricia Hunter (Poor Dear Mama), Maggie Jakobson (Emma Deercourt), Parvin Khokhar (Ayah), Aaron Lustig (Capt. Peter Curtiss), David Silber (Capt. Theo Philip Gadsby)

A drama in 2 acts and 9 scenes with an epilogue. The action takes place in British India from 1888 to 1890.

F. Laun Maurer Photo

**Marianna Allen, Keith Caldwell,
Keith Rice, Alison Bevan**

90

CHERYL CRAWFORD THEATRE

Thursday, December 18, 1980 - January 18, 1981. (37 performances and 7 previews)
Chelsea Theater Center (Robert Kalfin, Producing Director; A. Harrison Cromer, Managing Director), The Fisher Theatre Foundation and Roger L. Stevens present:

HIJINKS!

By Robert Kalfin, Steve Brown, John McKinney; Adapted from Clyde Fitch's play "Captain Jinks of the Horse Marines"; Director, Robert Kalfin; Dances and Musical Staging, Larry Hayden; Set, Sandro LaFerla; Costumes, Elizabeth P. Palmer; Lighting, Paul Everett; Musical Arrangements, John McKinney; Musical Director, Michael O'Flaherty; Stage Managers, Tony Melchior, Allison Sommers, Bruce Conner; Assistant to Director, Jane Hadley; Production Supervisor, Robert W. Baldwin; Press, Edward T. Callaghan, Michael Albano, Jeffrey Dershowitz, Erica Simpson

CAST

Evelyn Baron (Frau Hochspits/Sailor), Sal Basile (Policeman/Sun Reporter), Bruce Conner (Sailor), Michael Connolly (Fitch/Times Reporter/Papa Belliarti), Elizabeth Devine (Mrs. Maggitt/Sailor), Randall Easterbrook (Charlie/Herald Reporter), Scott Ellis (Gussie/Tribune Reporter), Christopher Farr (Peter), Joseph Kolinski (Capt. Jinks), Sarah Lowman (Jenny), Michael O'Flaherty (Musical Director/Pianist/Detective), Elaine Petricoff (Miss Pettitoes/Sailor), Marian Primont (Mrs. Greenborough/Mrs. Jinks), Jeannine Taylor (Aurelia Johnson/Madame Trentoni)

MUSICAL NUMBERS: Love's Old Sweet Song, Take Them Away They'll Drive Me Crazy, If You've Only Got a Moustache, Dad's a Millionaire, Walking Down Broadway, Star Spangled Banner, Home Sweet Home, A Mother's Smile, The Hour for Thee and Me, Capt. Jinks of the Horse Marines, Will You Love Me in December as You Do in May?, Champagne Charlie, Shew Fly! Don't Bother Me, Last Rose of Summer, Those Tassels on Her Boots, Beautiful Dreamer, Wilt Thou Be Gone Love?, A Boy's Best Friend Is His Mother, Then You'll Remember Me, La Traviata Waltzes, Silver Threads Among the Gold, That Gal Is a High Born Lady, Whispering Hope, Poor Kitty Popcorn, Mermaid's Evening Song, Auld Lang Syne, Goodbye My Lady Love, Wait Till the Sun Shines Nellie

A musical in three acts. The action takes place during 1872 at the landing dock of the Cunard Steamship Co. in New York, and at Madame Trentoni's in the Brevoort House.

Carol Rosegg Photo

Right: Robert Silver, Andrea Abbott, James Rebhorn in "Period of Adjustment" Above: Jeannine Taylor, Joe Kolinski in "Hijinks!"

WONDERHORSE THEATRE

Wednesday, January 14,-31, 1981. (20 performances)
New World Theatre presents:

OH ME, OH MY, OH YOUMANS

Conceived by Darwin Knight and Tom Taylor; Staged by Darwin Knight; Musical Direction and Arrangements, Sand Lawn; Set, Bob Phillips; Lighting, Eric Cornwell; Costumes, Andrew Marlay; Producer, Jane Stanton; Technical Director, Darald Plummer; Stage Manager, Mark Keller; Press, James R. Smith; Company Manager, Andrew Krawetz

CAST

Jo Ann Cunningham   Sally Woodson
Todd Taylor   Ronald Young

MUSICAL NUMBERS: Two Little Girls in Blue, Wildflower, Mary Jane McKane, Lollipop, A Night Out, No No Nanette, Oh Please, Hit the Deck, Rainbow, Great Day, Smiles, Through the Years, Take a Chance, Flying Down to Rio

Performed with one intermission.

Esther Bubley Photo

PERRY STREET THEATRE

Monday, December 21, 1980 - January 4, 1981. (17 performances)
High Point Productions presents:

PERIOD OF ADJUSTMENT

By Tennessee Williams; Director, Priscilla Gustavino; Settings, Michael C. Smith; Lighting, Carol Sealey; Assistant to Director, Richard Cody; Stage Manager, Dan Kirsch; Press, Joe Wolhandler Associates, Kathryn Kempf, Douglas Urbanski

CAST

Andrea Abbott (Isabel), Khandi Alexander (Susie), Virginia Mary Angelovich (Dorothea), Betsy Bell (Mrs. McGillicuddy), John Cooper (Policeman), James Rebhorn (George), Dylan Ross (Mr. McGillicuddy), Robert Silver (Ralph), Singhi (Bessie)

A drama in three acts. The action takes place in Ralph Bates' home in a suburb of a mid-southern city on Christmas Eve of 1959.

H. R. Santacoloma Photo

Todd Taylor, Sally Woodson,
Jo Ann Cunningham, Ronald Young

ORPHEUM THEATRE

Tuesday, January 20, - February 8, 1981. (15 performances)
Joe Bianco in association with Monroe Arnold presents:

AN EVENING WITH JOAN CRAWFORD

Conceived and Directed by Julian Neil; Music, Joseph Church, Nick Branch; Set, J. Patrick Mann; Lighting, Paul Everett; Costumes, Barbara Gerard; Choreography and Musical Staging, Sydney Smith; Musical Direction, Joseph Church; Associate Producer, Philip S. Kaufman; General Management, Dorothy Olim Associates; Company Manager, Doug Ellis; Management Associate, Thelma Cooper; Production Associate, Judi Arnold; Assistant Conductor, Jonathan Helfand; Assistant Choreographer, Gary Cowan; Hairstylist, John Sahag; Make-up, Tom Brumberger; Stage Managers, Richard Schiff, Ana Marie Bailey; Press, Susan L. Schulman, Glenna Freedman, Sandi Kimmel, Jeffrey Richards Associates, Ted Killmer

CAST

Lee Speaks (Joan Crawford), Joyce Fullerton (Christina), Michael J. Hume (Christopher), Fracaswell Hyman (Jacques), Michael Kemmerling (Jules Beemis/Alfred Steele), Frances Robertson (God), Kristine Zbornik (Lucifer)

MUSICAL NUMBERS: Blame It All on Me, Hollywood Lullaby, Give 'Em Hell, Too Much Money Blues, Except of Course Men, You're One of a Kind, Ain't No Place Like Home, Take a Vacation, What's It to Be a Legend

A musical in 2 acts and 19 scenes.

Martha Swope Photo

Lee Sparks, Fracaswell Hyman, Michael Kemmerling, Michael J. Hume, Frances Robertson, Kristine Zbornik, Joyce Fullerton

AMDA STUDIO I

Friday, February 20, - March 15, 1981. (20 performances)
Bandwagon presents:

FLORODORA

Music, Leslie Stuart; Lyrics, Paul Rubens, Ernest Boyd-Jones; Book, Owen Hall; Director, Lester Malizia; Scenery, Patrick Dearborn; Costumes, Jeanette Oleksa; Lighting, Larry Johnson; Vocal and Dance Arrangements, Bruce Kirle; Orchestrations, Paul Jensen; Book Adapted by Lester Malizia; Producer, Jerry Bell; Stage Managers, Arlene C. Ritz, Dan Zittel; General Manager, Jon Hutcheson; Choreography, Denny Shearer; Technical Director, Jiri Shubert; Assistant to Director, Leslie Blake; Assistant Musical Director, Katherine Morrison; Production Coordinator, Sandra Starr

CAST

J. Michael Blakely (Capt. Donegal), Judith Brow (Lotta), Byron Conner (Syms), Mary D'Arcy (Angela), Marilyn Hemenway Downs (Claire), Douglas Fisher (Cyrus), Cathryn Ann Fleuchaus (Lady Holyrood), Sally Funk (Mamie), David Gebel (Langdale), Deborah Gerard (Daisy), Peter Jack (Prof. Tweedlepunch), Steven Jacob (Pym), Patricia Landi-Iacobazzo (Valleda), Tom McKinney (Frank), Mark Monroe (Crogan), Theresa Rakov (Dolores), Aetna Thompson-Collins (Lucy), Ian Michael Towers (Leandro), Robert Urbanowicz (Herr Apfelbaum)

MUSICAL NUMBERS: Opening Chorus, The Credit's Due to Me, Silver Star of Love, Somebody, Chorus of Welcome, When I Leave Town, Galloping, I Want to Marry a Man I Do, Prenology, The Shade o the Palm, Tact, When You're a Millionaire, Tell Me Pretty Maiden, The Fellow Who Might, We Get Up at 8 A. M., When We're on the Stage, Queen of the Philippine Islands, I Want to Be a Military Man, Finale

A musical in two acts. The action takes place during the early spring of 1899 on Florodora, a mythical island in the Philippines, and in the garden of Abercoed Castle in Wales.

Jerry Bell Photo

"Florodora"

LION THEATRE

Wednesday, February 25, - March 22, 1981. (24 performances)
Lion Theatre Company (Gene Nye, Artistic Director; Eleanor Meglio, Producing Director) presents:

DECLASSEE

By Zoe Atkins; Director, Gene Nye; Settings, Linda Skipper; Costumes, Molly Maginnis; Lighting, Frances Aronson; Stage Managers, Mark Schorr, Dede Miller; Assistant to Director, David Skovron; Press, Jeffrey Richards, C. George Willard

CAST

Andrew Arnault (Jean/Servant), Helen-Jean Arthur (Charlotte), Bill Buell (Harry), Eileen Burns (Lady Wildering), Maria Cellario (Zellito), Ken Costigan (Sir Bruce/Misha), Francine Farrell (Miss Timmins), Michael Fischetti (Rudolph), Colin Leslie Fox (Sir Emmet), Sharon Laughlin (Lady Helen Haden), Julia MacKenzie (Rena/Woman), Allan Manning (Brandon/Man), Paul Murray (Count Paolo/Man/Waiter), Kevin O'Rourke (Edward), Lorraine Totaro (Alice)

A drama in three acts. The action takes place in the Haden's drawing-room in London during the spring of 1919; in the lounge of NYC's Ritz Hotel in 1922; in the reception room of Rudolph Solomon's Fifth Avenue house in NYC.

Roderick Robinson Photo

Michael Fischetti, Sharon Laughlin

ST. MALACHY'S THEATRESPACE
Thursday, February 26, - March 14, 1981. (15 performances)

MURDER IN THE CATHEDRAL

By T. S. Eliot; Director, Gregory Abels; Producer, Kristin Murphy; Scenery and Costumes, Loy Arcenas; Lighting, Kathleen Giebler; Stage Manager, Kayla Evans; Sound, Robert Casey; Production Assistants, C. C. D'Arcy, Patricia Belfanti, David Courier; Press, Warren Knowlton

CAST

Catherine Byers (4th Tempter), David Courier (Attendant), Bairbre Dowling (Chorus), Igors Gavon (3rd Tempter/William de Traci), John Genke (2nd Tempter/Hugh de Morville), William Hanauer (Messenger/Richard Brito), Peter Harrer (3rd Priest), Cynthia Hopkins (Chorus), Jane Ives (Chorus), Arnold Johnston (2nd Priest), Erika Petersen (Chorus), Lee Richardson (Becket), Bill Roberts (1st Priest), Daniel Tamm (1st Tempter/Reginald Fitz Urse)

A drama in two parts performed without intermission. The action takes place in the Archbishop's Hall, and in Canterbury Cathedral on December 29, 1170.

Gregory Abels Photo

Igors Gavon, Daniel Tamm, Lee Richardson (front), John Genke, William Hanauer

Peter Francis-James, Gloria Foster, Earle Hyman, Samantha McKoy, Al Freeman, Jr.

THEATER AT ST. PETER'S CHURCH
Tuesday, March 3,-8, 1981. (9 performances and 7 previews) (Re-opened at the Public/Anspacher Theater, Wednesday, March 18, and closed May 31, 1981 after 86 performances) The Richard Allen Center for Culture and Art presents:

LONG DAY'S JOURNEY INTO NIGHT

By Eugene O'Neill; Director, Geraldine Fitzgerald; Set, John Scheffler; Lighting, Paul Mathiesen; Costume Coordinator, Myrna Colley-Lee; Producer, Hazel J. Bryant; Managing Director, Shirley J. Radcliffe; Artistic Director, Mical Whitaker; Assistant to Producer/Casting, Glenn Johnson; Production Assistants, Count Stovall, Timothy Strong, Al Sturgess; Wardrobe, Jane Scott; Wigs, Jessica Fassman; Technical Coordinator, Thommie Blackwell; Technical Director, Dickson Lane; Company Manager, Ty Collins; Stage Managers, Harrison Avery, Dwight R. B. Cook; Press, Glenn Johnson, Merle Debuskey, Richard Kornberg, John Howlett, Ed Bullins

CAST

Earle Hyman (James Tyrone), Gloria Foster (Mary Tyrone), Al Freeman, Jr. (Jamie Tyrone), Peter Francis-James (Edmund Tyrone), Samantha McKoy (Cathleen)

A drama in four acts performed with one intermission. The action takes place in the living room of the Tyrones' summer home during August of 1912.

Bert Andrews Photo

WESTBETH THEATRE CENTER
Thursday, March 5,-29, 1981. (14 performances) Westbeth Theatre Center (Arnold Engelman, Executive Director; William Hoffman, Ian McColl, Artistic Directors) presents;

CURTAINS!

By David Meranze, Marc Alan Zagoren; Director, Michael Hoover; Scenery, Cecelia Gilchriest; Costumes, Julia Tribe; Lighting, Tim Alger; Sound, David Payne; Dance Coordinator, Celeste Miller; Staff Coordinator, Gilbert Stafford; Stage Managers, Charles Paul Gollnick, Amy Whitman; Press, The Arts Market, Beatrice DaSilva, Donald A. Harris.

CAST

Wesley Addy (Forbes Marston), Jean Buchalter (Thea Hjortz), Winnip Cook (Allison Gordon), Joy Franz (Daphne Ferguson), Howard Hagan (Samuel Faffner), Estelle Harris (Shirley Faffner), Chuck Kelsley (Edgar Wald), Peter Hooten (Chester Tomkins), John Michel (Parker King), Lynn Oliver (Victoria Del Popolo), Gilbert Stafford (Leon Hunter), Edith Wolfe (Lily Sullivan).

A mystery-comedy in 2 acts and 9 scenes. The action takes place during the late 1960's in the Drama School of Mayhew University.

Carol Rosegg Photo

Wesley Addy, Lynn Oliver

Janice Fuller, Jack Davidson,
Lois Diane Hicks, John Corey

PROVINCETOWN PLAYHOUSE

Sunday, March 8, - May 17, 1981. (81 performances and 9 previews)
Veronica Productions Company in association with the Provincetown Playhouse presents:

VERONICA'S ROOM

By Ira Levin; Director, Arthur Savage; Set, M. Cabot McMullen; Lighting, Fred Jason Hancock; Costumes, Timothy Dunleavy; Technical Director, Sam Buccio; Executive Producer, Barbara Savage; Associate Producers, Wendy Borow, Kenneth Borow; General Management, Weiler/Miller, Barbara Carrellas; Company Manager, Marshall B. Purdy; Production Supervisor, Meryl Schaffer; Production Assistant, John Lebeaux; Stage Manager, Judeth Erwin; Press, Shirley Herz/Jan Greenberg, Sam Rudy

CAST

Georgine Hall (The Woman), John Milligan (The Man), Innes-Fergus McDade (The Girl), Claude-Albert Saucier (The Young Man)

A mystery in two acts. The action takes place during the spring in a room in a house about a half hour's drive from Boston, Massachusetts.

Meryl Joseph Photo

Right: John Milligan, Innes-Fergus McDade, Claude-Albert Saucier

Liz Callaway, Michael Corbett

PLAYERS THEATRE

Sunday, March 8,-13, 1981. (5 performances and 22 previews)
International Media Studies Foundation (William B. O'Boyle, Executive Producer) presents:

MARCHING TO GEORGIA

By Barbara Daniel; Director, Milton Moss; Assistant Producer, Dennis Luzak; Set, Kenneth E. Lewis; Lighting, Robby Monk; Costumes, Gail Cooper-Hecht; General Manager, Robert S. Fishko; Company Manager, Michael O'Rand; Management Assistant, Susan M. Dorsey; Wardrobe, Kim Kaldenberg; Hairstylist, Patrik D. Moreton; Stage Manager, Richard W. Van Wyk; Press, Howard Atlee/Bill Evans, Patt Dale, Jim Baldassare

CAST

Janice Fuller (Georgia), Kristin Griffith (Jackie), Moultrie Patten (Daddy Pulliam), Jack Davidson (Curtis Pulliam), Joseph Daly (Floyd), Lois Diane Hicks (Betty), John Corey (Dodd Collier), Understudies: Judith Drake (Georgia), John Corey (Daddy/Floyd), Jeff Reade, Sherry Skinner

A comedy in 2 acts and 6 scenes. The action takes place at the present time in a small house on a side street in a small town in Virginia.

Martha Swope Photo

BTA THEATRE

Tuesday, March 10,-20, 1981. (15 performances and 9 previews)
Fisher Theatre Foundation presents;

THE MATINEE KIDS

Book and Lyrics, Garry Bormet, Gary Gardner; Music and Lyrics, Brian Lasser; Conceived and Staged by Garry Bormet, Brian Lasser; Musical Staging, Carol Marik; Scenery, Nancy Winters; Lighting, Peter Anderson; Costumes, Bruce H. Brumage; Keyboard Arrangements, Don Jones; Musical Direction, Laurence J. Esposito; Lighting, Ronald M. Bundt; General Management, Dorothy Olim, Gar Bell; Company Manager, Doug Ellis; Management Associate, Thelma Cooper; Technical Director, Carrington Bibuld; Stage Managers, Tom W. Picard, Judy Rice; Press, Jeffrey Richards, Robert Ganshaw, Ben Morse, Helen Stern, C. George Willard, Ted Killmer

CAST

Karen Mason (Chris), Liz Callaway (Chrissy), Colleen Dodson (Movie Woman), Scott Baker (Movie Man), Will Jeffries (Tom), Michael Corbett (Tom as a boy), Standby: Judy Rice

MUSICAL NUMBERS: Lucky Love, The Date, Just to Look at Him, A Couple of Years from Now, Favorite Son, Hello Tom, Footprints, Hi!, Alborada, Lucky Baby, Hold Me, First to Walk Away, Matinee

A musical in two acts.

Stephanie Saia Photo

Joan MacIntosh

ENTERMEDIA THEATRE
Thursday, March 12,-15, 1981. (6 performances)
Victor Lurie and Alex Van Lerberg present:

BLACK ELK LIVES

By Christopher A. Sergel; Based on "Black Elk Speaks" by John G. Neihardt; Director, Tom Brennan; Designed by Julie Taymor; Costumes, David Murin; Lighting, William Armstrong; Additional Staging, Jane Lind; General Manager, Robert S. Fishko; Wardrobe, Dolores Gamba; Stage Technician/Drummer, Michael Trammel; Props, Warren Jorgensen; Production Assistant, Maryellen Lurie; Stage Managers, Ed Preston, Teresa Moring; Manager, Marty Salzberg; Press, Merlin Group, Cheryl Sue Dolby, Emily Hacker

CAST

Manu Tupou (Black Elk), Sal Anthony (Wominapa/Custer/Brave), Carl Battaglia (Cramer/Crazy Horse), Clayton Corbin (Tecumseh/Little Crow/Red Cloud/Sheridan), Carlo Grasso (Manuelito/Black Kettle/Galbraith/Wovaka), Tino Juarez (Carrington/Young Navajo/Tosawi/Brave), Michael Lamont (Bent/Taylor/Musician), Jane Lind (Navajo/Yellow Woman/Girl), W. T. Martin (Jackson/Carlton/Sibley/Wynkoop), Christina Moncarz (Magpie/Pte/Girl), Edward O'Ross (Columbus/Shakopee/Sherman/Chivington/Finerty), Lee Maurice Rozie (Soldier/Indian/Musician)

Ken Howard Photo

Craig Lucas, Suzanne Henry

INTERART THEATRE
Wednesday, March 11, - July 12, 1981 (123 performances)
Interart Theatre (Margot Lewitin, Artistic Director; Abigail Franklin, Managing Director) presents:

REQUEST CONCERT

By Franz Xaver Kroetz; Translated by Peter Sander; Director, Joanne Akalaitis; Designed by Manuel Lutgenhorst, Douglas E. Ball; Dramaturg, Colette Brooks; Sound, L. B. Dallas; Technical Director, Judith Snyder; Production Manager, B. Yeager Blackwell; Stage Manager, M. C. Miller; Press, Susan Bloch, Adrian Bryan-Brown; Production Assistant, Mary Demas

CAST

Joan MacIntosh

A solo performance without intermission. The action takes place at the present time in a studio apartment.

Peter Krupenye Photo

Manu Tupou (seated left)

ACTORS PLAYHOUSE
Thursday, March 12, - May 31, 1981. (96 performances and 6 previews)
Diane de Mailly in association with William B. Young presents:

MARRY ME A LITTLE

Songs by Stephen Sondheim; Conceived and Developed by Craig Lucas, Norman Rene; Director, Norman Rene; Musical Direction, E. Martin Perry; Choreography, Don Johanson; Setting, Jane Thurn; Lighting, Debra J. Kletter; Costumes, Oleksa; General Manager, Albert Poland; Company Manager, Erik Murkoff; Assistant to Producers, Douglas Aibel; Stage Managers, David L. Nathans, Carole Doscher; Press, Solters/Roskin/Friedman, Milly Schoenbaum, Kevin Patterson

CAST

Suzanne Henry
Craig Lucas
Standbys: Carole Doscher, Michael Pace

MUSICAL NUMBERS: Two Fairy Tales, Saturday Night, Can That Boy Foxtrot!, All Things Bright and Beautiful, Bang!, The Girls of Summer, Uptown Downtown, So Many People, Your Eyes Are Blue, A Moment with You, Marry Me a Little, Happily Ever After, Pour Le Sport, Silly People, There Won't Be Trumpets, It Wasn't Meant to Happen

Performed without an intermission. The action takes place at the present time in a New York City apartment house.

Kenn Duncan Photo

THE CUBICULO
Friday, March 14, - April 2, 1981. (12 performances)
The Chelden Theater Group presents;

A FORCE OF NATURE

By Paul Lambert; Director, Ben Kapen; No other credits submitted.

CAST

James Rosin
Jon White

James Rosin

David Knapp, Kelly Wood,
Richard Lupino

THE HAROLD CLURMAN THEATRE
Tuesday, March 17, - April 12, 1981. (28 performances and 5 previews)
Choctow Productions presents:

THE TANTALUS

By Ian Cullen and Catherine Arley; Director, Stephen Joyce; Set, David Loveless; Costumes, Robert Anton; Lighting, John Hickey; Technical Director, Steven Edelstein; General Manager, David Lawlor; Producer, Billie Joyce; Stage Managers, Mary G. Koenig, Jodee Steffensen; Press, Patt Dale, Elissa Leone

CAST

Ron Randell (Karl Richmond), Kelly Wood (Hilde Marner) or Janet Bell, David Knapp (Anton Korff), Richard Lupino (Edwards), George Vogel (Inspector Lomer), Tim Fahey (Julian Raynor)

A drama in two acts. The action takes place in the recent past in Paris.

Ken Howard Photo

THE PRODUCTION COMPANY THEATRE
Sunday, March 22, - April 13, 1981. (17 performances and 3 previews)
The Production Company (Norman Rene, Artistic Director; Caren Harder, Managing Director) presents:

RANDY NEWMAN'S
MAYBE I'M DOING IT WRONG

Music and Lyrics, Randy Newman; Conceived and Directed by Joan Micklin Silver; Musical Arrangements and Direction, Michael S. Roth; Choreography, Ara Fitzgerald; Set, Heidi Landesman; Costumes, Oleksa; Lighting, Debra J. Kletter; Production Manager, David L. Nathans; Stage Manager, Susi Mara; Press, Judy Jacksina, Glenna Freedman, Dolph Browning, Angela Wilson

CAST

Mark Linn-Baker   Deborah Rush
Patti Perkins   Treat Williams

MUSICAL NUMBERS: My Old Kentucky Home, Birmingham, Political Science, Jolly Coppers on Parade, Caroline, Maybe I'm Doing It Wrong, Simon Smith and the Amazing Dancing Bear, The Debutante's Ball, Love Story, Tickle Me, It's Money That I Love, God's Song (That's Why I Love Mankind), Sail Away, Yellow Man, Rider in the Rain, Rollin', You Can Leave Your Hat On, Old Man, Davy the Fat Boy, Marie, Short People, I'll Be Home, Dayton Ohio 1903

A musical in two parts.

Mark Linn-Baker, Deborah Rush

ORPHEUM THEATRE
Thursday, March 19, - June 21, 1981. (124 performances)
Bloolips Ltd., Mitchell Maxwell, Alan Schuster in association
with the Eastside Theatre Corporation present:

BLOOLIPS LUST IN SPACE

Conceived by Jon Taylor, Rex Lay and The Bloolips; Director, Bette
Bourne; General Manager, Stephen Wagner; Set and Costumes, The
Bloolips; Lighting, David K. H. Elliott; Stage Manager, Eve Har-
rington-Baxter; Company Manager/Press, Paul Matwiow

CAST

Bossy Bette, Gretel Feather, Lavinia Co-Op, Naughty Nickers, Diva
Dan, Precious Pearl

A "musical space epidemic" in two acts.

"Bloolips"

Maggie Soboil, Mary Alice

THEATER AT ST. PETER'S CHURCH
Sunday, March 22,-29, 1981. (10 performances)
Lucille Lortel and Haila Stoddard in association with The Common at St. Peter's Church present The White Barn Theatre
production of:

GLASSHOUSE

By Fatima Dike; Director, Rina Yerushalmi; Set, Wynn P. Thomas;
Costumes, Susan Hilferty; Lighting, Robby Monk; Assistant Director, Meyer Baron; Original Music, Don Elliott; General Manager,
Vincent Curcio; Company Manager, Ben Sprecher; Assistant to Producers, Doris Elliott; House Manager, Ronald Venable; Stage Managers, Meyer Baron, Cheryl Lynn Bruce; Press, John Springer, Meg
Gordean, Suzanne Salter, Jeffrey Wise

CAST

Mary Alice (Phumla Hlophe), Maggie Soboil (Linda Black), Jack
Scavella (Drummer), Understudies: Cheryl Lynn Bruce (Phumla),
Jocelyn Johnson (Linda)

A drama in two acts. The action takes place in 1976 in Constantia,
a suburb of Cape Town, South Africa

Martha Swope Photo

PERRY STREET THEATRE
Sunday, March 22,-29, 1981. (7 performances and 23 previews)
Steven Steinlauf presents:

FORTY-DEUCE

By Alan Bowne; Director, Sheldon Larry; Set, Dan Leigh; Lighting,
Craig Miller; Costumes, Gary Lisz; Production Associate, Anne
Thomson; General Management, Albert Poland; Company Man-
ager, Erik Murkoff; Production Assistant, Ethan Silverman; Stage
Manager, Michael Ritchie; Press, Judy Jacksina, Glenna Freedman,
Dolph Browning, Angela Wilson

CAST

W. M. Hunt (Roper), Timothy Mathias (John Anthony), Barry
Miller (Ricky), John Pankow (Blow), Willie Reale (Crank), John
Leitz (Augie), Thomas Waites (Mitchell)

A drama in 2 acts and 4 scenes. The action takes place at the
present time in a dingy Times Square hotel room overlooking Eighth
Avenue in Manhattan.

Bob Kiss Photo

John Pankow, Barry Miller

Richard Maxfield, S. Proctor Gray,
Elizabeth de Charay

STAGE 15
Thursday, March 26, - April 26, 1981. (20 performances)

RUSSIAN ROULETTE

By Alan A. Gabor; English adaptation by Mario D. Fenyo; Director, Alan A. Gabor; Set, Joe Varga; Lighting, Scott Pinkney; Costumes, Alan Gabor; Stage Manager, George Morelli; Art Work, Joseph Turoczy

CAST

Elizabeth DeCharay, Alan A. Gabor, Richard Maxfield, S. Proctor Gray, Fred Engel

A play in two acts. The action takes place at the present time in a New York City brownstone.

Peter Cunningham Photo

HORACE MANN THEATRE

Monday, March 30, - April 16, 1981. (25 performances)
The Center for Theatre Studies at Columbia University (Andrew B. Harris, Producer) presents:

SUDDENLY LAST SUMMER

By Tennessee Williams; Director, Bruce Levitt; Designed by Quentin Thomas; Technical Director, Michael Valentino; Sound, Jon Welstead; Assistant to Director, Elizabeth Diamond, Maryellen Kernaghan; Assistant to Producer, Mickie Cruz; Assistant Designer, Caline Thomas; Costume Coordinator, Carolyn Baehr; Stage Managers, Carol Brown, Fred Shaw; Press, Shirley Herz, Jan Greenberg, Sam Rudy, Peter Cromarty

CAST

Dina Merrill (Mrs. Venable), Jerry Whiddon (Dr. Cukrowicz), Elizabeth Korn (Miss Foxhill), Letha Elliott (Mrs. Holly), Rod McLucas (George Holly), Kathleen Helmer (Catharine Holly), Betty Pelzer (Sister Pelzer)

A drama performed without intermission. The action takes place on the veranda and patio of a mansion in the Garden District of New Orleans during the fall of 1935.

Peter Krupenye Photo

Jerry Whiddon, Dina Merrill

WONDERHORSE THEATRE

Wednesday, April 1 - 18, 1981 (17 performances)
New World Theatre (Jane Stanton, Artistic Director) presents:

HALF-LIFE

By Julian Mitchell; Director, Jane Stanton; Set, Bob Phillips; Lighting, Jeffery L. Robbins; Costumes, Amanda J. Klein; Company Manager, Andrew Krawetz; Technical Adviser, Eric Cornwell; Assistant to Director, Sydnee Blake; Technical Director, Stephen Caldwell; Sound, Richard Loyd; Stage Managers, D. King Rodger, Thomas Whalen; Press, Max Eisen, Francine L. Trevens

CAST

Michael Dorkin (Jones), Evan Thompson (Sir Noel Cunliffe), Paul Milikin (Francis Mallock), Martha Farrar (Helen Mallock), Robert Walsh (Mike Clayton), Charles Maggiore (Lord Rupert Carter), Trinity Thompson (Barbara Burney), Ann Burr (Prue Hoggart)

A play in three acts. The action takes place on midsummer eve in 1976 in the garden of Sir Noel Cunliffe's country house in Wiltshire.

Esther Bubley Photo

Paul Milikin, Michael Dorkin, Robert Walsh,
Charles Maggiore, Evan Thompson

Sylvia Miles

PLAYHOUSE THEATRE II
Monday, April 13,-19, 1981. (8 performances and 13 previews)
Steven A. Greenberg presents:

IT'S ME, SYLVIA!

Book and Lyrics, Sylvia Miles; Music, Galt MacDermot; Director, Arthur Sherman; Set, Eugene Lee; Lighting, Roger Morgan; Costumes, Clifford Capone; Musical Director, Galt MacDermot; Executive Producer, Jeffrey Madrick; Associate Producer, Liska March; Accompanist, Vince Morton; General Manager, Weiler/Miller, Barbara Carrellas; Assistant to Director, Suzanne Wren; Stage Managers, Carmine R. Pontilena, John M. Flood; Press, Shirley Herz, Jan Greenberg, Sam Rudy, Peter Cromarty

CAST

Sylvia Miles

A one-woman show performed in two parts. The action takes place in Sylvia's apartment from the fall of 1979 through the spring of 1980.

Bert Andrews Photo

CIRCLE IN THE SQUARE DOWNTOWN
Monday, April 13,-18, 1981. (6 performances and 19 previews)
Mark R. Gordon presents:

THE BUDDY SYSTEM

By Jonathan Feldman; Director, Edward Berkeley; Setting, Dan Leigh; Costumes, Hilary Rosenfeld; Lighting, Fred Buchholz; Sound, Paul Garrity; Associate Producer, Sally Darling; General Manager, Albert Poland; Company Manager, Peter Schneider; Production Assistant, Nora Peck; Production Associate, Paul Berdann; Stage Managers, Julia Gillett, Patrick Burke; Press, Solters/Roskin/Friedman, Becky Flora, David LeShay, Cindy Valk

CAST

Keith Gordon (Stu Fisher), Victor Bevine (Sam Carrino), Ralph Bruneau (Howie Guttman), Ron Fassler (Bruce "Duck" Tischenkal), Christopher Gartin (Bobby Horan), John Rothman (Doug Schlesinger), David Wohl (Arthur "Gruely" Gruelbacher)

A comedy in two acts. The action takes place at Camp Chipahawa in Maine during the summer of 1963.

Susan Cook Photo

David Wohl, Ralph Bruneau, Christopher Gartin, Ron Fassler

Ned Eisenberg, Richard Hayes, Bradford Bancroft

AMDA STUDIO I
Friday, April 17, - May 4, 1981. (14 performances)
New York Theatre Studio (Richard V. Romagnoli, Artistic Director; Cheryl Faraone, Managing Director) presents:

REDBACK

By Denis Spedaliere; Director, Richard V. Romagnoli; Set, Loy Arcenas; Lighting, John Hickey; Sound, Gary Massey; Costumes, Gayle Everhart; Production Coordinator, Sally Burnett; Original Music, James Petosa; Fight Choreographer, Grant Stewart; Technical Director, Dennis Runge; Stage Managers, Moss Hassell, Joanna Ward; Press, Burnham/Callaghan, Ed Callaghan

CAST

Timothy Askew (Father), Harry Bennett (Cop/Watch Cap), Bradford Bancroft (Cliff), Ned Eisenberg (Vance), Richard Hayes (Joe), James Paradise (The Dominican), Gary Pollard (Foreman), Gina Richards (Linda), Ivette Richards (Whore/Dominican Woman), Angela Sargeant (Cheryl), Basil Wilson (Sonny), Hookers, Pimps, Hispanics: Jeffrey K. Gordon, Michael Slattery, Sally Burnett

A "futuristic drama" in two acts. The action takes place over a period of three days during the summer of 1988.

Jack Neubeck Photo

THE COLONNADES
Wednesday, April 22, - May 10, 1981. (16 performances)
A New Space Stage presents:

PRINCIPALLY PINTER/SLIGHTLY SATIE

Conceived and Directed by Thaddeus Motyka; Music Director, John Evans; Set, Wade Giampa; Costumes, James Nadeaux; Lighting, Judy Rasmuson; Production Supervisor, Patricia Saphier; Technical Director, Greg Criscuolo; Stage Managers, Patricia Saphier, Caryn Broth; Press, Fred Hoot

CAST

Diane Armistead, Viveca Parker, Virgil Roberson, Michael Scarborough, Armin Shimerman, Molly Stark

PROGRAMME: Les Chemins de l'Amour, Request Stop, Choral Inappetissant, Black and White, Sonatine Bureaucratique, Applicant, Sur un Casque, Trouble in the Works, Chanson du Chat, That's Your Trouble, Cadence Obligee, Last to Go, Le Yachting, That's All, Tendrement, Interview, La Diva de l'Empire, Corcovado, Special Offer, Dialogue for Three, Valse to Eric Satie, Night

An "entertainment with music" performed without intermission.

Roger Greenawalt Photo

Molly Stark, Armin Shimerman,
Diane Armistead

Helen Eckard

ALL SOUL'S HALL
Friday, April 24, - May 11, 1981. (12 performances)
The All Soul's Players present:

CARNIVAL

Music and Lyrics, Bob Merrill; Book, Michael Stewart; Staged by Jeffery K. Neill; Music Director, Wendell Kindberg; Associate Music Director, Joyce Hitchcock; Set, Tran William Rhodes; Costumes Charles W. Roeder; Lighting, Mark Turney; Assistant to Director Suzanne Kaszynski; Producers, Howard Van Der Meulen, Henry Levinson, Pat Sheffield; Technical Director, Charles Simpson; Stage Managers, Pat Sheffield, Faith Knowlton; Press, Peter Sauerbrey Carol Kram, Jean Turney

CAST

Helen Eckard (Lili), Paul F. Hewitt (Paul), Ken Seiter (Marco) Linda Lipson (Rosalie), Tran William Rhodes (Jacquot), Hank Levinson (B. B. Schlegal), Ken Woodard (Grobert), Terry Beringer (Bluebird Girl), Michael Berglund (Roustabout), George Bouley (Roustabout), Kim Dunke (Gloria Zuwicki), Bonnie MacSaveny (Gladys Zuwicki), Kimberly Maddock (Bluebird Girl), Antoine McCoy (Strongman/Roustabout), Dan McCoy (Roustabout) Kathy Flynn McGrath (Bluebird Girl), Sheryl A. Martin (Bluebird Girl), John J. Nagle (Roustabout), Jane Wasser (Olga), Barbara Whitman (Greta)

A musical in two acts.

Alvin Levine Photo

GREEK ORTHODOX CHURCH
Friday, May 1,-17, 1981. (20 previews)
Rene Savich presents:

LOU

By Gayle Stahlhuth from the writings of Louisa May Alcott; Director, Richard Harden; Set, Vicki Paul; Costumes, Hillary Sherred; Lighting and Sound, Rob E. Holland; Press, Judy Jacksina, Glenna Freedman, Angela Wilson, Dolph Browning; Stage Manager, Rob E. Holland; Production Assistant, Carolyn Bengston

CAST

Gayle Stahlhuth

A one-woman show in two parts. The action takes place in Boston during the fall of 1871.

Len Kaltman Photo

Gayle Stahlhuth

SOUTH STREET THEATRE
Monday, May 11,-23, 1981. (28 performances)
Jay Garon presents:

AH, MEN

By Paul Shyre; Director, Mr. Shyre; Scenery and Costumes, Eldon Elder; Lighting, John Gisondi; Associate Producer, Larry Carpenter; Production Assistant, Gary Sullivan; Stage Manager, Peter Jablonski; Press, Max Eisen, Francine L. Trevens

CAST

Jane White   Curt Dawson
Jack Betts   Stephen Lang
Standbys: Jane Bergere, Wayne Maxwell

An "entertainment on the male experience" with music performed without intermission.

MUSICAL NUMBERS: Ah Men, Man Is for the Woman Made, When After You Pass My Door, My First, The Last Minute Waltz, Truck Stop, Illusions, Daddy Blues

Stephanie Saia Photo

**Stephen Lang, Curt Dawson,
Jack Betts, Jane White**

Bryan Clark

TYSON STUDIO THEATRE
Tuesday, May 12,-31, 1981. (16 performances and 2 previews)
Empire Stage Players present:

SPORTS CZAR

By Donald J. Rothschild; Director, Pat Robertson; Scenery, Victor Cappecce; Lighting, Andrea Wilson; Costumes, Denise Galonsky; Sound, Raymond Benson; Producer, Peter Pope; Company Manager, Ellowyn Castle; Art Director, Pamela Cunningham; Technical Director, Mark Scott; Production Assistants, Jillian Henree, Judy Thomas; Stage Managers, Kelly Carty, Larry Rhodes; Press, Fred Hoot

CAST

Bryan Clark (Chuck Parker), Alan Storck (Stan Elliot), Charles Maggiore (Paul Lucas), Susanna Clemm (Gina Larsen), Joe White (Rolly), Rita Montone (Sharon Parker), James Pickens, Jr. (Marshal Hunt), Patrick Taylor (Kurt Sterling)

A play in 2 acts and 4 scenes. The action takes place in Coach Parker's office during the final week of the season.

Pamela Cunningham Photo

PLAYHOUSE THEATRE
Wednesday, May 13,-31, 1981. (22 performances and 1 preview)
Arthur Cantor and Greer Garson present:

ST. MARK'S GOSPEL

A solo performance by Alec McCowen; Lighting, Leo B. Meyer; General Manager, Harvey Elliott; Company Manager, Arthur Cantor; Production Assistants, Ken Bryant, Marilyn Rosenberg; Stage Manager, Larry Bussard; Press, Arthur Cantor, Arthur Solomon

Performed in two parts.

Alec McCowen

Elizabeth Ward, Lois Diane Hicks (background)

THEATRE EAST
Thursday, May 14,-30, 1981. (20 performances)
Tom Taldone presents the friends repertory company production of:

THE ROPE DANCERS

By Morton Wishengrad; Director, Mitch Weiss; Set, Richard Berg; Lights, J. Peter Culver; Costumes, Margo LaZaro; Music, Mitch Weiss; Stage Managers, Dean Hill, Kitty Glenn, Bertin Rowser; Assistant Director, Kathy Bonomi; Assistant to Producer, Dean Capaccio; Press, Howard Atlee, Jim Baldassare

CAST

James Greene (James Hyland), Lois Diane Hicks (Margaret Hyland), Kerri Lee (Clementine), James Goodwin Rice (Dr. Jacobson), Stewart Schwartz (Moving Man/Lameshnik), Barbara Spiegel (Mrs. Farrow), Elizabeth Ward (Lizzie Hyland)

A drama in 2 acts and 4 scenes. The action takes place sometime after the turn of the century in the two-room flat of Margaret Hyland on the fifth floor of a New York tenement.

Carol Rosegg Photo

WESTSIDE ARTS THEATRE
Thursday, May 14, 1981
Ray Gaspard in association with Chris Silva, Stephen Dailey and Will Dailey present:

I CAN'T KEEP RUNNING IN PLACE

Book, Music and Lyrics by Barbara Schottenfeld; Director, Susan Einhorn; Set, Ursula Belden; Costumes, Christina Weppner; Lighting, Victor En Yu Tan; Choreography, Baayork Lee; Musical Supervision, John McKinney; Musical Director, Robert Hirschhorn; Assistant Choreographer, Dennis Grimaldi; Orchestrations, Barbara Schottenfeld; General Managers, Chris Silva, Stephen Dailey, Will Dailey; Company Manager, Michael Thomas Lord; Technical Director, Michael Gallagher; Assistant to Director, Page Burkholder; Stage Managers, Meryl Schaffer, Christine Anderson; Press, Jeffrey Richards, Robert Ganshaw, Ben Morse, C. George Willard, Helen Stern, Ted Killmer, Stanley Evans, Richard Humleker

CAST

Marcia Rodd (Michelle), Helen Gallagher (Beth), Mary Donnet (Mandy), Joy Franz (Eileen), Jennie Ventriss (Gwen), Bev Larson (Sherry), Evalyn Baron (Alice)

MUSICAL NUMBERS: I'm Glad I'm Here, Don't Say Yes If You Want to Say No, I Can't Keep Running in Place, I'm on My Own, More of Me to Love, I Live Alone, I Can Count on You, Penis Envy, Get the Answer Now, What If We. . . ., Almosts Maybes and Perhaps, Where Will I Be Next Wednesday Night?

A musical in 2 acts and 4 scenes. The action takes place at the present time in a loft somewhere in SoHo during a six week workshop from late winter to early spring in New York.

Carol Rosegg Photo

**Top Right: Joy Franz, Bev Larson,
Helen Gallagher, Jennie Ventriss**

**Mary Donnet (front), Jennie Ventriss, Helen
Gallagher, Joy Franz, Marcia Rodd, Evalyn
Baron, Bev Larson**

WESTSIDE MAINSTAGE
Thursday, May 14, - June 7, 1981. (20 performances)
Re-opened Friday, June 12, 1981 at the Cherry Lane Theatre.
Penumbra Productions (Mike Houlihan, Executive Producer;
John Tilliner, Artistic Director) presents:

ENTERTAINING MR. SLOANE

By Joe Orton; Director, John Tillinger; Hairstylist, Leon Gagliardi;
Wardrobe, Anne King; Set, Mark Haack; Lighting, David Weiss;
Costumes, Bill Walker; Stage Managers, Kevin Mangan, Mike Boak;
Press, Fred Nathan, Eileen McMahon

CAST

Barbara Bryne (Kath), Maxwell Caulfield (Sloane), Gwyllum Evans
(Kemp), Joseph Maher (Ed)

A drama in three acts. The action takes place at the present time
in the home of Kath and her father Kemp.

George Connolly Photo

Joseph Maher, Maxwell Caulfield
Top: Barbara Bryne, Maxwell Caulfield

THEATRE DE LYS
Monday, May 18, 1981–
Michel Stuart and Harvey J. Klaris in association with Michel
Kleinman Productions present:

CLOUD 9

By Caryl Churchill; Director, Tommy Tune; Sets, Lawrence Miller;
Costumes, Michel Stuart, Gene London; Lighting, Marcia Madeira;
Title Song and Incidental Music, Maury Yeston; Sound, Warren
Hogan; Hairstylist, Michael Gottfried; General Management, Mari-
lyn S. Miller, Berenice Weiler, Barbara Carrellas, Marshall Purdy;
Management Assistant, Mitchell Lemsky; Technical Coordinator,
Tom Shilhanek; Wardrobe, Timothy Dunleavy; Speech Consultant,
Elizabeth Smith; Music Director, Maury Yeston; Stage Managers,
Murray Gitlin, Michael Morris, Martin Shakar; Press, Judy Jack-
sina, Glenna Freedman, Dolph Browning, Angela Wilson; Associate
Producer, Mark Beigelman.

CAST

Don Amendolia (Joshua/Cathy/Soldier), Veronica Castang
(Maud/Lin), Zeljko Ivanek (Betty/Gerry), Jeffrey Jones (Clive/Ed-
ward), E. Katherine Kerr (Ellen/Mrs. Saunders/Betty), Nicolas
Surovy (Harry/Martin), Concetta Tomei (Edward/Victoria), Understudies: Michael Morris, Martin Shakar, Barbara Berg

A comedy in two acts. The action takes place in Africa in 1880
and in London in 1980.

Peter Cunningham Photo

Right Center: Jeffrey Jones,
Nicolas Surovy

Katherine Kerr, Zeljko Ivanek,
Veronica Castang

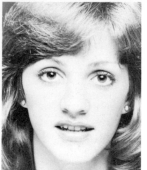

ON STAGE
Sunday, May 24, - July 5, 1981. (37 performances)
Barbara Darwall and John Montagnese in association with Talent to Amuse present:

OH COWARD!

Words and Music, Noel Coward; Devised and Directed by Roderick Cook; Musical Director, Russell Walden; Lighting, F. Mitchell Dana; Costumes, Jack McGroder; Musical Staging, Clarence Teeters; Company Manager, Robert P. Montagnese; Business Adviser, Sally Campbell; Stage Manager, D. King Rodger; Press, Becky Flora

CAST

Terri Klausner   Dalton Cathey
Russ Thacker   Kay Walbye

A musical revue using the words and music of Noel Coward and performed in two acts.

Marc Raboy Photo

Left: Russ Thacker, Terri Klausner

INTAR HISPANIC AMERICAN THEATRE
Thursday, May 28, - July 5, 1981. (24 performances)
INTAR/International Arts Relations (Max Ferra, Artistic Director; Vrancyne de St. Amand, Managing Director) presents:

LIFE IS A DREAM

By Pedro Calderon de La Barca; Adapted and Directed by Maria Irene Fornes; Music, George Quincy; Set, Christina Weppner; Costumes, Molly Maginnis; Lighting, Joe Ray; Pianist/Vocal Coach, Mary Rodgers; Stage Managers, John N. Concannon, Andres Santana; Press, Clarence Allsopp

CAST

Margaret Harrington (Rosaura), Manuel Martinez (Clarin), Dain Chandler (Segismund), Shirley Lemmon (Angel), Abe Wald (Clotaldo), Christofer De Oni (Astolfo), Ellen Blake (Estrella), Cliff Seidman (Basilio)

A drama in 3 acts and 8 scenes.

Rafael Llerena Photo

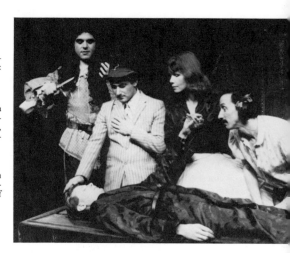

Christofer De Oni, Abe Wald, Margaret Harrington, Manuel Martinez, Cliff Seidman

TOWN HALL
Saturday, January 31–February 15, 1981 (35 performances)
The Paper Bag Players present:

HOT FEET

Written and Directed by Judith Martin; Music and Lyrics, Donald Ashwander; Costumes and Props, Judith Martin; Administrator, Judith Liss; Associate, Edith Harnik; Press, Scanlon, Inc.; Stage Manager, David Bradford

COMPANY

Judith Martin   Irving Burton
Donald Ashwander   Buck Hobbs
                        Jan Maxwell

Paper Bag Players

SULLIVAN STREET PLAYHOUSE
Opened Tuesday, May 3, 1970.*
Lore Noto presents:

THE FANTASTICKS

Book and Lyrics, Tom Jones; Suggested by Edmond Rostand's "Les Romanesques"; Music, Harvey Schmidt; Director, Word Baker; Original Musical Direction and Arrangements, Julian Stein; Designed by Ed Wittstein; Associate Producers, Sheldon Baron, Dorothy Olim, Robert Alan Gold; Assistant Producers, Bill Mills, Thad Noto; Production Assistant, John Krug; Original Cast Album by MGM Records

CAST

The Narrator, El Gallo .... Sal Prevenza†1
The Girl............................ Carole-Ann Scott†2
The Boy............................ Christopher Seppe†3
The Boy's Father .... Lore Noto†4
The Girl's Father .... Sy Travers†5
The Old Actor.......................... Bryan Hull†6
The Man Who Dies/The Indian........... Robert R. Oliver†7
The Mute............................ Glenn Davish†8
At the piano .... Jimmy Roberts
At the harp .... Andre C. Tarantiles

UNDERSTUDIES: Glenn Davish (Narrator/Boy), Joan Wiest (The Girl), Sy Travers (The Boy's Father)
MUSICAL NUMBERS: Overture, Try to Remember, Much More, Metaphor, Never Say No, It Depends on What You Pay, Soon It's Gonna Rain, Rape Ballet, Happy Ending, This Plum Is Too Ripe, I Can See It, Plant a Radish, Round and Round, They were You.

A musical in two acts.

Press; Anthony Noto
Stage Managers: Tom Brittingham, Glenn Davish

* Still playing May 31, 1981. For original production, see THEATRE WORLD Vol. 16.
† During its 20 year run, the following have appeared in the various parts: 1. Jerry Orbach, Gene Rupert, Bert Convy, John Cunningham, Don Stewart, David Cryer, Keith Charles, John Boni, Jack Metter, George Ogee, Tom Urich, Jack Crowder, Nils Hedrick, Robert Goss, Joe Bellomo, Michael Tartel, Donald Billett, Martin Vidnovic, David Rexroad, David Snell, Hall Robinson, Chapman Roberts, David Brummell, Roger Alan Brown, Joseph Galiano, Douglas Clark, Richard Muenz, Joseph Galiano, George Lee Andrews, 2. Rita Gardner, Carla Huston, Liza Stuart, Eileen Fulton, Alice Cannon, Royce Lenella, B. J. Ward, Leta Anderson, Carole Demas, Anne Kaye, Carolyn Mignini, Virginia Gregory, Marty Morris, Sharon Werner, Leilani Johnson, Sarah Rice, Cheryl Horne, Betsy Joslyn, Kathy Vestuto, Kathy Morath, Amy Niles, Debbi McLeod, Joan Wiest, Marty Morris, 3. Kenneth Nelson, Gino Conforti, Jack Blackton, Paul Giovanni, Ty McConnell, Richard Rothbard, Gary Krawford, Bob Spencer, Erik Howell, Steve Skiles, Craig Cornellia, Sam Ratcliffe, Jimmy Dodge, Geoffrey Taylor, Michael Glenn-Smith, Phil Killian, Richard Lincoln, Bruce Cryer, Ralph Bruneau, Jeff Knight, 4. William Larsen, Donald Babcock, George Riddle, Charles Blackburn, Richard A. Kennerson, David Sabin, Philip Baker Hall, Edward Garrabrandt, Lore Noto, Kenneth Kimmins, Tom Lacy, Jay Hampton, Dick Latassa, Richard Kinter, Ray Steward, Hansford Rowe, Ed Penn, Charles Goff, Charles Welch, Lore Noto, 5. Hugh Thomas, David Vaughan, Charles Blackburn, Charles Goff, John High, Maurice Edwards, John J. Martin, Ray Stewart, Conzalo Madruga, Ken Parker, Jerry Russak, Arthur Anderson, David Vogal, John Martin, John High, Sy Travers, Jack Schmidt, Byron Grant, 6. Thomas Bruce (Tom Jones), Stanley Jay, Jay Hampton, John Heffernan, Ed Call, Lowry Miller, Gary Nairns, Curt Williams, F. Murray Abraham, Hugh Alexander, Justin Gray, Ron Prather, Frank Geraci, Donald Babcock, Seamus O'Brien, Donald Babcock, George Riddle, Russell Lieb, Elliot Levine, Robert Molnar, 7. George Curley, Robert Worms, Don Pomes, Richard A. Kennerson, Jay Hampton, Curt Williams, Tom Lacy, Ed Garrabrandt, Richard Kuss, Peter Blaxill, Samuel As-said, William McIntyre, James Cook, Donald Babcock, James Cook, Bill Preston, James Cook, Liam O'Begley, James Cook, 8. Blair Stauffer, Richard Thayer, Jake Dengel, James Cook, Frank Geraci, Richard Barrie, Ron Prather, Les Shenkel, Robert Crest, Robert Brigham, Tom Flagg, John Thomas Waite, Douglas Clark, Alan Hemingway

Van Williams Photos

(1980–81 replacements not submitted)

Sy Travers, Christopher Seppe, Carole-Ann Scott, Lore Noto

ASTOR PLACE THEATRE

Opened Monday, April 28, 1980.*
Sweet Olive, Inc., Maryellen Flynn, Bonnie Weeks present:

A COUPLA WHITE CHICKS
SITTING AROUND TALKING

By John Ford Noonan; Director, Dorothy Lyman; Set, Charles Cosler; Costumes, Gary Lisz; Lighting, F. Mitchell Dana; Original Songs, Loudon Wainwright III; General Management, Marilyn S. Miller, Berenice Weiler; Manager, Barbara Carrellas; Wardrobe, Benjamin Wilson; Stage Managers, Sherry Cohen, Donna Daley; Press, Judy Jacksina, Glenna Freedman, Angela Wilson, Dolph Browning.

CAST

Hannah Mae Bindler . . . . Eileen Brennan†1
Maude Mix . . . . Susan Sarandon†2

A comedy in two acts. The action takes place at the present time in early June at 19 Charlemagne Lane in the town of Fox Hollow in a secluded corner of northern Westchester County, N.Y.

* Closed May 17, 1981 after 440 performances and 9 previews.
† Succeeded by: 1. Dixie Carter, Louise Lasser, Donna Daley, Susan Tyrrell, Carrie Snodgress, 2. Dorothy Lyman, Jobeth Williams, Anne Archer, Candy Clark.

Stephanie Saia Photos

**Sylvia Williams, Thais Clark,
Bruce Strickland, Topsy Chapman**

VILLAGE GATE/UPSTAIRS

Opened Monday, June 11, 1979.*
James Adams Vaccaro and Jimmy Wisner in association with Ciro A. Gamboni present:

SCRAMBLED FEET

By John Driver, Jeffrey Haddow; Musical Direction and Arrangements, Jimmy Wisner; Director, John Driver; Scenery, Ernest Allen Smith; Costumes, Kenneth M. Yount; Lighting, Robert F. Strohmeier; Assistant Musical Director-Additional Arrangements, Roger Neil; Wardrobe, Paula Davis

CAST

Evalyn Baron†1, John Driver†2, Jeffrey Haddow†3, Roger Neil†4

ACT I: Going to the Theatre, P. T. Playwrighting Kit, Makin' the Rounds, Answering Machine, Agent, Composer Tango, No Small Roles, Stanislaw, Only One Dance, Good Connections, Olympics, Theatre Party Ladies

ACT II: Guru, Party Doll, Love in the Wings, Huns/British, Could Have Been, Sham Dancing, Improv/EDT, Have You Ever Been on Stage?, Advice to Producers, Happy Family

General Manager: Leonard A. Mulhern
Press: Jeffrey Richards, Ben Morse
Stage Manager: Sari E. Weisman

* Closed June 7, 1981 after 831 performances.
† Succeeded by: 1. Susan Edwards, Faith Prince, K. K. Preece, 2. Mitchell Greenberg, Jonathan Hadary, Scott Robertson, 3. Jeffrey Haddow, Steve Liebman, 4. Jim Walton, Roger Neil, Jim Walton.

Peter Cunningham Photos

Anne Archer, Susan Tyrrell

VILLAGE GATE/DOWNSTAIRS

Opened Monday, October 22, 1979.*
Art D'Lugoff, Burt D'Lugoff, Jerry Wexler in association with Shari Upbin present:

ONE MO' TIME

Conceived and Directed by Vernel Bagneris; Additional Staging, Dean Irby; Musical arrangements, Lars Edegran, Orange Kellin; Music performed by the New Orleans Blue Serenaders; Costumes, Joann Clevenger; Scenery, Elwin Charles Terrel II; Lighting, Joanna Schielke; Sound, Seltzer; Production Consultant, Pepsi Bethel; Assistant to Producers, George Harvey; Wardrobe, Elise Garber; Original Cast Album by Warner Brothers Records

CAST

Sylvia "Kuumba" Williams (Bertha Williams), Thais Clark (Ma Reed), Topsy Chapman (Thelma), Vernel Bagneris (Papa Du) succeeded by Bruce Strickland, John Stell (Theatre Owner)

UNDERSTUDIES: Peggy Alston (Ma Reed/Thelma), Michael Pierre Dean (Papa Du), Denise Rogers (Bertha), Albert Poland (Theatre Owner)

Bertha Williams and her touring company are in the Lyric Theatre in New Orleans, La., to perform "One Mo' Time" in 1926. Performed with one intermission.

General Manager: Albert Poland
Company Manager: Pamela Hare

Press: Solters/Roskin/Friedman, Milly Schoenbaum, Kevin Patterson

*Still playing May 31, 1981.

Bert Andrews/David LeShay Photos

**Mitchell Greenberg, K. K. Preece,
Jim Walton, Steve Liebman**

THE ACTORS STUDIO

June 1, 1980–May 31, 1981

President/Artistic Director, Lee Strasberg; Vice President, Eli Wallach; Secretary, Liska March; Treasurer, Carl Schaeffer; Board of Directors, Elia Kazan, Al Pacino, Martin Balsam, Ellen Burstyn, Arthur Penn, Sydney Pollack, Mark Rydell, Anna Strasberg, Shelley Winters

PRODUCTIONS AND CASTS

THE SECRET THIGHS OF NEW ENGLAND WOMEN by Jan Paetow; Director, Patrick Brafford. CAST: Robert Fitch, Gayle Greene, Dianne Hull, Rusti Moon, Rory O'Moore, Martin Shakar, Madeleine Thornton-Sherwood

JOEY NO-TALK by Richard Vetere; Director, John Camera. CAST: Joseph Maruzzo, Frank Geraci, Frank Nastasi, Vincent Russo, Adrienne Wallace, Linda Gillen

IT'S ME MARIE by Marica Haufrecht; Directors, Robert LuPone, Myra Turley. CAST: Marcia Haufrecht

WARSAW OPERA by Nancy Heiken; Director, Peter Flood; Coordinator, Lily Parker. CAST: Francis Fisher, Michael Haspiel, Richard Kuss, Lucille Patton, Peter Phillips, Sam Schact, Joe Tobin, Mimi Turque, Allen Hahn, Fisher Stevens, Brian Schachter, Ivonne Coll, David Evans, Kathleen Fahrner, Mimi Friedman, Kilian Ganly, Mark Humphrey, Joe Hunt, Greta Kaufman, Paul Lueken, Jan Praver, Cyndi Raftus, Richard Rochester, Minna Rose, Jana Schneider, Elliot Swift, John Wendall

SECOND-STORY SUNLIGHT by Bruce Serlen; Director, June Rovenger. CAST: Martin Shakar, Ann Hennessey, Corinne Neuhateau, Bret Morgan, Patricia Adshead, John Bennes

ON BLISS STREET IN SUNNYSIDE written and directed by Marcia Haufrecht. CAST: Irene Dailey, Jackie Knapp, Ric Lavin, Murray Moston, Eulalie Noble

THE SECRET THIGHS OF NEW ENGLAND WOMEN by Jan Paetow; Director, Patrick Brafford. CAST: Robert Fitch, Gayle Greene, Denise Lute, Rusti Moon, Rory O'Moore, Sam Schacht, Madeleine Thornton-Sherwood

Denise Lute, Robert Fitch, Rory O'Moore, Sam Schact, Gayle Greene, Rusti Moon, Madeleine Thornton-Sherwood Above: Thornton-Sherwood, Fitch in "Secret Thighs . . ."

AMAS REPERTORY THEATRE

Founder/Artistic Director, Rosetta LeNoire; Business Manager, Gary Halcott; Administrator, Jerry Lapidus; Children's Theatre Coordinator, Karen Jackson; Administrative Director, Marshall B. Purdy

PRODUCTIONS AND CASTS

WE LOVE YOU ALWAYS by Rosetta LeNoire, Clyde Williams; Musical Direction/Staging, Clyde Williams; Assistant Musical Director, David Davis; Stage Managers, Thom Yarnal Eva Lopez. CAST: Bob Brooker, Joey Ginza, Debbie Liguori, Jackie Miles, Barbara Purdy, Charlie Rodriguez, Andrew Tabbat, Diane Wilson

THE PEANUT MAN, GEORGE WASHINGTON CARVER by Melvin Hasman; Director, Reggie Life; Choreography, Andy Torres; Musical Director, William Gregg Hunter; Production Manager, Thom Yarnal; Stage Manager, Richard Douglass. CAST: Nora Cole, Sharon K. Brooks, Jean Cheek, Barbara Warren-Cooke, Steve R. Fertig, Kevin Gruden, Mel Johnson, Jr., Cliff Terry, Marsha Perry, Lance Roberts, Judy Soto, Christopher Stewart, Leon Summers, Jr.

MAMA, I WANT TO SING with Book and Lyrics by Vy Higginsen; Additional Lyrics, Ken Wydro; Director, Duane L. Jones. CAST: Vanessa Bell, Steven Bland, Joe Breedlove, Richard Dow, Ann Duquesnay, Sheila Ellis, Leo Elmore, Andrew Friarson, Helena D. Garcia, Crystal Johnson, Tony Lawrence, Robert Melvin, Eboyn Jo-Ann Pinkney, Charlie Serrano, Ursuline Kairson, Tyrone Williams, Diane Wilson

MO' TEA, MISS ANN? with Book and Lyrics by Bebe Coker; Music, Leander Morris; Direction-Choreography, Denny Shearer. CAST: Jimmy Almistad, Suzanne Buffington, Jay Aubrey Jones, Joy Kelly, Boncellia Lewis, Charles Muckle, Herb Quebec, Zoe Walker, Juanita Walsh, Carmiletta Wiggins, Alonzo G. Reid, Sundy Leigh Leake

THE CRYSTAL TREE with Book and Lyrics by Doris Julian; Music, Luther Henderson; Director, Billie Allen; Choreographer, Walter Raines. CAST: Albert S. Bennett, T. Renee Crutcher, Jean Du Shon, Val Eley, Leon Summers, Jr., Grenoldo Frazier, Dolores Garcia, Ira Hawkins, Norman Matlock, Andre Morgan, Christine Spencer, Vanessa Thornton, Marta Vidal

Suzanne Buffington, Zoe Walker, Juanita Walsh, Charles Muckle in "Mo' Tea, Miss Ann?" Left Center: Susan Beaubian, Mel Johnson, Leon Summers in "The Peanut Man"

Robert Sheehan Photos

AMERICAN JEWISH THEATRE

92nd Street YM-YWHA
September 27, 1980–June 7, 1981

Artistic Director, Stanley Brechner; Managing Director, Michael Bavar; Technical Director, Mitchell Yacknowitz; Directors, Dan Held, Allan Pierce, Kent Paul; Sets, Tony Castrigno, Christopher Cade, Quentin Thomas; Costumes, Karen Hummel, Christopher Cade, Kathy Blake, Quentin Thomas; Lighting, Helen Gatling, Christopher Shriver, Quentin Thomas; Sound, Andy Bloor; Stage Managers, Joe Erdey, Paula Mayo, Doug Laidlaw, Jennifer Borge, Bill Rubidge, Robert Owens, David Vallery; Press, Lois Cohn, Mark Glickman; Musical Director, Don Jones

PRODUCTIONS AND CASTS

THE TENTH MAN by Paddy Chayefsky, with Sol Frieder, Albert S. Bennett, Milton Lansky, Victor Jacoby, Norman Golden, Lou Miranda, Lydia Leeds, Art Burns, Victor Ritz, Robert Vogel, Bill Collins, Joel Rooks, Ed Breen
CAPELLA by David Boorstin, Israel Horovitz, with Sol Frieder, James McDonnell, Daniel Rebekenner, Marion McCorry, Carol Rich, Marsha Hagen
FROM THE MEMOIRS OF PONTIUS PILATE by Eric Bentley, with Bruce Altman, Arthur Burns, Terry Christgau, Bill Gold, David Kieserman, Con Roche, Jerry Rutkowski, Zvee Scooler, Albert Sinkys, Albert Verdesco
THE CAINE MUTINY COURT MARTIAL by Herman Wouk, with Arthur Burns, James Handy, Barbara Held, Lorraine Brunetti, Frank Anderson, Jonathan Bogart, Andrew Daniel, Tom O'Leary, Charles Korn, Michael T. Folie, Steve Hartov, John C. Cook, Jason Kuschner, Lee Moore, Albert Sinkys, Virgil Roberson, Kevin Browne, Gilbert Cole, Vincent Neil, Gordon G. Jones, Brad Bellamy
BRECHT ON BRECHT by George Tabori, with Thomas A. Carlin, Annie Combs, Christopher Cull, Martha Schlamme

Gerry Goodstein/Brian Jontow Photos

Right: Bill Gold, Zvee Scooler, Terry Christgau in "From the Memoirs of Pontius Pilate" Below: Annie Coombs, Chris Cull, Martha Schlamme, Thomas Carlin in "Brecht on Brecht" Top: Norman Golden, Joel Rooks in "The Tenth Man"

Kevin Kaloostian, Dale Fuller, Jean Barbour, Charles Barney, Joseph Citta, Paul Curtis

AMERICAN MIME THEATRE

New York, N.Y.
Twenty-ninth Year
Founder/Director, Paul J. Curtis; Administrator, Jean Barbour; Counsel, Joel S. Charleston

COMPANY

Jean Barbour
Charles Barney
Joseph Citta
Paul Curtis

Dale Fuller
Kevin Kaloostian
Erica Sarzin
Mr. Bones

REPERTORY: The Lovers, The Scarecrow, Dreams, Hurly-Burly, Evolution, Sludge, Six

AMERICAN PLACE THEATRE

Seventeenth Season

Director, Wynn Handman; Associate Director, Julia Miles; Literary Adviser, Bonnie Marranca; General Manager, Joanna Vedder; Technical Director, Russell Stevens; Wardrobe, Kathleen L. Fredericks; Assistant Director, Richard Schiff; Production Assistants, Tom Epps, Larry Woodbridge; Press, Jeffrey Richards Associates

AMERICAN PLACE THEATRE

Sunday, June 1–November 9, 1980 (30 performances)
SIM, or "One Night with a Lady Undertaker from Texas" written and directed by William Osborn; Set, Mr. Osborn; Lighting and Sound, Kathleen McCutcheon; Stage Manager, John Bill Jones.

CAST: Mary Bozeman.

A solo performance in two acts. The action takes place at the present time on the back porch of Mrs. Elma Beale Beck in Yoakum, Texas.

Thursday, June 5,-15, 1980. (13 performances and 8 previews)
American Place Theatre presents:

KILLINGS ON THE LAST LINE

By Lavonne Mueller; Director, Dorothy Silver; Set, Henry Millman; Costumes, Mimi Maxmen; Lighting, Annie Wrightson; Production Assistants, Nina Berstein, Sara Jamison, Todd Liebler, Rory Anderson; Wardrobe, Kathleen L. Fredericks; Sound, Nancy Harrington; Stage Managers, W. Scott Allison, Mary R. Lockhart; Music, Dennis Bacigalupi

CAST

Ellen Barkin (Starkey), Sandy Martin (Mrs. Starkey), Verona Barnes (Juba), Rosanna Carter (Quashie), Joan MacIntosh (Ellis), Alice Drummond (Betty), Marilyn Hamlin (Hidelman), Marian Primont (Day Tripper), Pat McNamara (Elmhurst), Kathleen Chalfant (Mavis)

The action takes place in a Chicago factory during 1979, The Year of the Child.

Friday, October 17 to November 9, 1980 (28 performances)
THE IMPOSSIBLE H. L. MENCKEN, The Bad Boy of Baltimore, by and with John Rothman; Director, Scott Redman; Set, Michael Molly; Musical Direction, Michael Minard; Lighting, James F. Ingalls; Costume, William Ivey Long; Dance Movement, Art Bridgeman; Stage Manager, W. Scott Allison; Bartender, Jack Gremli

The life and words of Henry Louis Mencken presented in two parts.

Saturday, November 15, 1980–
AFTER THE REVOLUTION by Nadja Tesich; Director, Joyce Aaron; Set, Christina Weppner; Lighting, Frances Aronson; Costumes, Sally J. Lesser, Kathleen Smith. CAST: Lily Knight, Karen Ludwig, John Nesci, Will Patton, Joe Ponazecki, Ebbe Roe Smith, Lydia Stryk

Sunday, January 11,-25, 1981. (12 performances and 8 previews)

MEMORY OF WHITENESS

By Richard Hamburger; Director, Robert Gainer; Set, Lighting, Costumes, Fred Kolouch; Associate Costume Design, Erica Hollmann; Sound, Michael Canick; General Manager, Joanna Vedder; Technical Director, Russell Stevens; Press, Jeffrey Richards, Virginia Snow, Helen Stern, Ted Killmer

CAST

Bernard Duffy (Ben), Katherine Squire (Grandma), Lois Markle (Agnes), David Brooks (Leon), Donna Davis (Sherry), Rusty Jacobs (Boy)

Performed without intermission.

Stephanie Saia Photo

Top Right: David Brooks, Lois Markle in "Memory of Whiteness" Below: Paul Dooley in "The Amazin' Casey Stengel"

AMERICAN PLACE THEATRE

Thursday, February 19, - March 22, 1981. (33 performances and 7 previews)

STILL LIFE

Written and Directed by Emily Mann; Setting and Costumes, Tom Lynch; Lighting, Annie Wrightson; Assistant Director, Judy Dennis; Song, Holly Near; Technical Director, Scott Allison; Stage Managers, Joseph S. Kubala, Rachel Milder, Larry Woodbridge; Press, Jeffrey Richards Associates

CAST

John Spencer (Mark), Mary McDonnell (Cheryl), Timothy Near (Nadine)

Performed without intermission. For the most part, these are the people's own words as told to Emily Mann during the summer of 1978.

Thursday, April 9, - May 10, 1981. (33 performances)

THE AMAZIN' CASEY STENGEL

Or "Can't Anybody Here Speak This Game?" by Michael Zettler, Shelly Altman; Director, Stephen Zuckerman; Sets, Tom Schwinn; Lighting, Robby Monk; Costumes, Christina Weppner; Organist, Marcy Stein; Voices, Stephen Zettler; Production Associate, Larry Woodbridge; Sound, Michael Weferling; Production Assistant, Russell Waldman; Stage Manager, W. Scott Allison; General Manager, Joanna Vedder; Press, Jeffrey Richards, Robert Ganshaw, Helen Stern, Ted Killmer

CAST

Paul Dooley

Performed with one intermission.

Martha Holmes Photo

AMERICAN RENAISSANCE THEATER

Artistic Director, Robert Elston; Associate Director, Elizabeth Perry; Assistant Director, Susan Reed; Executive Secretary, Carole Warner; Lighting, David Simpson; Sound, Ed Atchison

June 12–29, 1980 (12 performances)
DID YOU SEE THE ELEPHANT? by Elizabeth Perry; Director, Anita Khanzadian; Set, Christopher Nolan; Costumes, Maura Clifford; Stage Manager, Larry Neumann. CAST: Molly Adams, Bonnie Deroski, Derrel Edwards, Wendy Finnegan, Mimi Huntington, Kyle-Scott Jackson, John Jennings, Elizabeth Perry, Francis Reilly

June 26 to July 17, 1980 (7 performances)
APPLESAUCE, cabaret performances, with Jered Holmes, Bambi Linn, Susan Reed, Sue Renee Bernstein, Judith Lesley, Barbara Gilbert, Claudette Sutherland

July 28–30, 1980 (3 performances)
THREE ONE-ACT PLAYS: "Say Goodbye to Hollywood" by Marion Levine, with Louis Vuolo, Stephanie Musnick, Robert John Keiber, Mimi Huntington, Sharron Shayne; "Joe" by Richard Lewine, with Louis Vuolo, Robert John Keiber; "Recitations on a Man Named Claude" by Steven Hart, with John Bacher, Deborah Genninger, Michael Bahr, Edwin Scott Klein, Steve Reicher, John Moraitis

October 2 to November 2, 1980 (20 performances)
DO YOU STILL BELIEVE THE RUMOR by Jeffrey Knox; Director, Robert Elston; Set, Harold Seeley; Costumes, Alice Carey; Stage Manager, Margaret Janney. CAST: Scott Jarvis, Robert C. Hartman, Peter Walker, Susan Reed, Anita Keel, Robert John Keiber

December 4 to 7, 1980 (4 performances)
JUDITH LESLEY IN CONCERT

January 5 to 10, 1981 (4 performances)
WOMEN OF IRELAND in poetry and song, performed by Bambi Linn and Susan Reed

February 5 to March 1, 1981 (20 performances)
SWEETHEARTS by Ted Nemeth; Director, Robert Elston; Set and Costumes, Susan Reed; Sound, Alex Simmons. CAST: Brian Muirhill, Michael Bahr, Will Osborne, Ned Farster, Sharron Shayne, John Bacher, Mary Rocco, Walter Leyden, Molly Adams

March 26 to April 19, 1981 (20 performances)
THREE ONE-ACT PLAYS by Joseph Hart; Director, Lynn M. Thomson; Set, Don Jensen; Costumes, Marianne Gutknecht; Lighting, Ray Swaggerty; Sound, Gary Fassler, Craig Ferraro; Stage Manager, Jaclyn Ferraro. CAST: "Rookies" with Ben Bettenbender, Sally Dunn; "Hit and Run" with Paul Austin, Ellwoodson Williams; "Hall of Fame" with Brandwell Teuscher

Robert Elston Photos

Right Ben Bettenbender, Sally Dunn in "Triple Play" Above: Anita Keal, Robert Keiber, Peter Walker, Susan Reed, Scott Jarvis, Robert Hartman in "Do You Still Believe the Rumor?" Top: Bonnie Deroski, Elizabeth Perry, Wendy Finnegan in "Did You See the Elephant?"

ARK THEATRE COMPANY

Founders, Donald Marcus, Lisa Milligan; Directors, Donald Marcus, Lisa Milligan, Bruce Daniel; Development/Press, Mary Keil

PRODUCTIONS AND CASTS.

May 29 through June 22, 1980 (16 performances)
WAY OF SNOW created by Julie Taymor in collaboration with the company; Director, Miss Taymor; Lighting, Bruce Daniel; Set, Bruce Daniel, Julie Taymor; Costumes, Rachelle Bornstein. CAST: Peter Baird, John S. Leandowski, Wes Sanders, Kate Schmitt, Louise Smith, Debra Wise, Roger Babb, Rachelle Bornstein, Dan Erkkila, Genji Ito, Michael Sirotta

October 23 through November 23, 1980 (20 performances)
STARMITES by Barry Keating; Staged by Charles Karchmer; Supervised by Barry Keating; Choreography, Edmond Kresley; Musical Direction, James McElwaine; Sets, Nina Moser; Lighting, Karen Singleton; Costumes, Bosha Johnson; Electronic Score, Adrian Lo; Stage Managers, Priscilla Boyd, Robert Morrow, Raymond Benkoczy. CAST: Chuck Richie, Wendy Jo Belcher, Camille, Fisher Stevens, Toby Parker, Ron Golding, Perry Arthur, Russ Kupfrian, Michael McCurry, Johanna Albrecht, Martha Horstman, Susan Shanline, Karen McIntyre, Gloria Sauve, Debby Sheward

January 27 through February 8, 1981 (12 performances)
SALT SPEAKS by Roger Babb, Rachelle Bornstein, John Fleming, Dan Levy, Graham Paul, Louise Smith; Director, Roger Babb; Designed by the company; Stage Manager, Margaret Hahn. CAST: Graham Paul, Louise Smith, Rachelle Bornstein, John Fleming

May 14 through June 7, 1981 (16 performances)
TROUBLE by Marisa Gioffre; Director, Charles I. Karchmer; Set, John Falabella; Lighting, Richard Lund; Costumes, Nina Moser; Stage Managers, David Oberon, Charles Goodman. CAST: Paul Vincent, Theresa Saldana, Lisa Ellex, Kay Michaels, Alice Spivak, John Jiler, Martita Palmer, Stefano Loverso

Edward J. Chanda Photos

Paul Vincent, Theresa Saldana, Alice Spivak in "Trouble"

BAM THEATER COMPANY

David Jones, Artistic Director
Associate Director, Arthur Penn; Managing Director, Charles Dillingham; Associate Manager, Suzanne Sato; Production Supervisor, Arthur Karp; Props, Sharon Seymour; Wardrobe, Robert Sniecinski; Stage Managers, Susie Cordon, Ray Gin, Laura deBuys, Ron Durbian, William L. McMullen; Press, Rima Corben, Ellen Lampert

BROOKLYN ACADEMY OF MUSIC

Sunday, January 1, - March 29, 1981. (14 performances in repertory)

A MIDSUMMER NIGHT'S DREAM

By William Shakespeare; Director, David Jones; Set and Costumes, Santo Loquasto; Lighting, F. Mitchell Dana; Assistant Director, Emily Mann; Composer, Bruce Coughlin; Choreographer, Cheryl McFadden; Hairstylist, Paul Huntley; Stage Managers, Susie Cordon, Laura deBuys, William L. McMullen

CAST

James Harper (Theseus), Cheryl Yvonne Jones (Hippolyta), Dominic Chianese (Egeus), Beth McDonald (Hermia), Joe Morton (Lysander), Don Scardino (Demetrius), Laura Esterman (Helena), C. B. Anderson (Philostrate), Attendants: Tracy Griswold, Robert Rutland, Ben Halley, Jr., Jerome Dempsey (Peter Quince), Gerry Bamman (Nick Bottom), Frank Maraden (Francis Flute), Richard Jamieson (Tom Snout), MichaelJohn McGann (Robin Starveling), Randle Mell (Snug), Brian Murray (Oberon), Sheila Allen (Titania), Ted Sod (Puck), Olivia Virgil Harper (First Fairy), Kristin Rudrud (Peaseblossom), Keith Moore (Cobweb), Priscilla Shanks (Moth), Scott Richards (Mustardseed), Oberon's Attendants: Tracy Griswold, Ben Halley, Jr., Robert Rutland

Performed with one intermission.

Ken Howard Photo

Sheila Allen, Brian Murray Top: Beth McDonald,
Joe Morton, Don Scardino, Laura Esterman
in "A Midsummer Night's Dream"

BAM/HELEN OWEN CAREY PLAYHOUSE

Thursday, January 22, - February 26, 1981. (14 performances in repertory)
BAM Theater Company presents:

THE RECRUITING OFFICER

By George Farquhar; Director, Laird Williamson; Set, Robert Blackman; Costumes, Dunya Ramicova; Lighting, F. Mitchell Dana; Composer, John McKinney; Hairstylist, Paul Huntley; Stage Managers, Ray Gin, Ron Durbian; Press, Rima Corben, Ellen Lampert

CAST

Joe Morton (Kite), Ted Sod (Tycho), Keith Moore (Cartwheel), James Harper (Harvester), Brian Murray (Capt. Plume), Frank Maraden (Worthy), Laura Esterman (Melinda), Laurie Kennedy (Silvia), Cheryl Yvonne Jones (Lucy), Jerome Dempsey (Mr. Balance), Tracy Griswold (Steward), Don Scardino (Thomas Appletree), Randle Mell (Costar Pearmain), Beth McDonald (Rose), MichaelJohn McGann (Bullock), Richard Jamieson (Capt. Brazen), Gerry Bamman (Thomas), Ben Halley, Jr. (Pluck), Sam Gray (Constable), Dominic Chianese (Mr. Scale), C. B. Anderson (Mr. Scruple), Keith Moore (Watch), William L. McMullen (Watch), Scott Richards (Servant), James Harper (1st Recruit), Priscilla Shanks (His Wife), Robert Rutland (2nd Recruit), Kristin Rudrud (His wife, a whore), Children: Timaree Larson, Jason Lillard, Lynn Robinson, David Smith

A play in two acts. The action takes place in Shrewsbury in Shropshire during the late summer of 1704.

Ken Howard Photo

Richard Jamieson, Laurie Kennedy, Brian Murray
Above: Brian Murray, Laurie Kennedy

BAM/PLAYHOUSE

Thursday, March 12, - April 5, 1981. (28 performances in repertory)

THE WILD DUCK

By Henrik Ibsen; A new version by Thomas Babe from a translation by Erik J. Friis; Director, Arthur Penn; Set, John Lee Beatty; Costumes, Carol Oditz; Lighting, F. Mitchell Dana; Wigs and Hairstyles, Paul Huntley; Stage Managers, Susie Cordon, Laura deBuys; Press, Ellen Lampert, Dominique Alfandre

CAST

Michael Gross (Gregers Werle), Sam Gray (Werle), Sheila Allen (Mrs. Sorby), Randle Mell (Graberg), Frank Maraden (Hjalmar Ekdal), Joan Pape (Gina Ekdal), Tenney Walsh (Hedvig Ekdal), Dominic Chianese (Old Ekdal), Gerry Bamman (Dr. Relling), Ben Halley, Jr. (Molvik), Richard Jamieson (Petterson), James Harper (Jensen), Keith Moore, William L. McMullen (Waiters), Jerome Dempsey (Bergman), Seth Allen (Kasperson), Joe Morton (Naval Officer), Robert Rutland (Flor), Guests: C. B. Anderson, Tracy Griswold, MichaelJohn McGann, Scott Richards, Ted Sod

Performed in five scenes with one intermission. The action takes place in Werle's home and in Hjalmar Ekdal's home.

Ken Howard Photo

**Tenney Walsh, Frank Maraden, Joan Pape
in "The Wild Duck"**

**Vic Polizos, Seth Allen, Don Scardino
in "Jungle of Cities"**

BAM/PLAYHOUSE

Thursday, April 16, - May 3, 1981. (23 performances in repertory)
BAM Theater Company presents:

JUNGLE OF CITIES

By Bertolt Brecht; Literal Translation, Douglas Arthur; New Version, Richard Nelson; Director, David Jones; Set, John Jensen; Costumes, Susan Hilferty; Lighting, F. Mitchell Dana; Composer, Norman L. Berman; Wigs and Hairstyles, Paul Huntley; Stage Managers, Ray Gin, Ron Durbian, William L. McMullen; Press, Ellen Lampert, Dominique Alfandre

CAST

Seth Allen (Shlink), Vic Polizos (Skinny), Frank Maraden (J. Finnay, The Worm), James Harper (Collie Couch, the Baboon), Kristin Rudrud (Schlink's Secretary), C. B. Anderson (Owner of Library), Keith Moore (Salvation Army Officer), Tracy Griswold (Salvation Army Drummer), Olivia Virgil Harper, Kristin Rudrud (Salvation Army Girls), Scott Richards (Waiter), Robert Rutland (Chuck), Ted Sod (Snub-nosed Man), Tracy Griswold (Man from Garga's block), Don Scardino (George Garga), Sam Gray (His Father), Joan Pape (His Mother), Beth McDonald (His Sister), Priscilla Shanks (His Girlfriend), MichaelJohn McGann (Pat Manky)

A drama in two acts. The action takes place in Chicago during 1912.

Ken Howard Photo

BAM/LEPERCQ SPACE

Thursday, April 23, - May 10, 1981. (24 performances in repertory)

OEDIPUS THE KING

By Sophocles; New version by Stephen Berg and Diskin Clay; Director, Emily Mann; Set, Ming Cho Lee; Costumes, Jennifer von Mayrhauser; Lighting, Arden Fingerhut; Composer, Bill Vanaver; Stage Managers, Susie Cordon, Laura deBuys; Press, Ellen Lampert, Dominique Alfandre

CAST

Joe Morton (Oedipus), Ben Halley, Jr. (Priest), Richard Jamieson (Kreon), Laura Esterman (Peasant Woman), Cheryl Yvonne Jones (Young Woman), Gedde Watanabe (Young Man), Gerry Bamman (Leader), Michael Gross (Teiresias), Monathan Manzo (Boy), Sheila Allen (Jocasta), Randle Mell (Servant), Jerome Dempsey (Messenger), Dominic Chianese (Shepherd), Erika Larson (Antigone), Timaree (Ismene)

A drama performed without intermissions.

Ken Howard Photo

**Richard Jamieson, Joe Morton
in "Oedipus the King"**

CIRCLE REPERTORY COMPANY

Marshall W. Mason, Artistic Director
Twelfth Season
Producing Director, Porter Van Zandt; Dramaturg, Milan Stitt;
Literary Manager, B. Rodney Marriott; Business Manager, Paul
Daniels; Assistant to Mr. Mason, John Bard Manulis; Production
Manager, Alice Galloway; Wardrobe, Joan E. Weiss; Stage Managers, Jody Boese, Fred Reinglas, Annette Hallberg; Press, Richard
Frankel, Glenna L. Clay, Jane Brandmeir

CIRCLE REPERTORY THEATRE

Tuesday, July 29, - September 14, 1980. (34 performances and
7 previews in repertory with "The Woolgatherer")
Circle Repertory Company by arrangement with Globe Enterprises presents:

MACREADY!

Written by Frank Barrie; Based on the Diaries of William Charles
Macready (1793–1873); Director, Donald MacKechnie

CAST

Frank Barrie

A celebration of the actor performed with one intermission.

Gerry Goodstein Photo

Frank Barrie as Macready

Robert MacNaughton, Timothy Shelton
in "The Diviners"

CIRCLE REPERTORY THEATRE

Thursday, October 16 - November 20, 1980. (41 performances
and 9 previews.)

THE DIVINERS

By Jim Leonard, Jr.; Director, Tom Evans; Set, John Lee Beatty;
Lighting, Arden Fingerhut; Costumes, Jennifer von Mayrhauser;
Production Manager, Alice Galloway; Stage Managers, James M.
Arnemann, Rosemary Sykes

CAST

Jacqueline Brookes (Norma), Mollie Collison (Goldie), Jack Davidson (Basil), John Dossett (Dewey), Laura Hughes (Darlene), Robert
MacNaughton (Buddy), Lisa Pelikan (Jennie Mae), Timothy Shelton (Showers), Ben Siegler (Melvin), Elizabeth Sturges (Luella),
James Ray Weeks (Ferris)

A drama in two acts. The action takes place during the early
1930's in the homes, fields, and public gathering places of the mythical southern Indiana town of Zion, population 40.

Gerry Goodstein Photo

CIRCLE REPERTORY THEATRE

Friday, December 12, 1980 - February 1, 1981. (27 performances and 6 previews) in repertory with "The Beaver Coat")

TWELFTH NIGHT

By William Shakespeare; Director, David Mamet; Assistant Director, Judy Dennis; Set, Fred Kolouch; Costumes, Clifford Capone;
Lighting, Dennis Parichy; Fight Director, Peter Nels; Musical Director, Sara Sugihara; Stage Manager, Daniel Morris

CAST

Jay O. Sanders (Orsino), Rob Gomes (Curio), David Pillard (Valentine), Lindsay Crouse (Viola), Burke Pearson (Sea Captain/Priest),
Michael Lerner (Sir Toby Belch), Marcell Rosenblatt (Maria,) Jake
Dengel (Sir Andrew Aguecheek), Colin Stinton (Feste), Marshall W.
Mason (Malvolio), Trish Hawkins (Olivia), Robert LuPone (Antonio), W. H. Macy (Sebastian), Charles T. Harper (Fabian), Ken
Kliban (Officer)

A comedy performed with one intermission. The action takes
place in a city in Illyria and the nearby seacoast.

Gerry Goodstein Photo

Lindsay Crouse, Marshall W. Mason
in "Twelfth Night"

113

CIRCLE REPERTORY THEATRE

Sunday, January 11, - February 1, 1981. (14 performances and 21 previews in repertory with "Twelfth Night")

THE BEAVER COAT

By Gerhart Hauptmann; Translated by Michael Feingold; Director, John Bishop; Assistant Director, Geoffrey Schlaes; Sets, Fred Kolouch; Costumes, Clifford Capone; Lighting, Dennis Parichy; Stage Managers, Daniel Morris, Andrea Naier

CAST

Tanya Berezin (Frau Wolf), Carol Wade (Leontine Wolf), Ken Kliban (Julius Wolf), Jane Fleiss (Adelaide Wolf), Tom Brennan (Volkov), Charles T. Harper (Motes), Marcell Rosenblatt (Frau Motes), Burke Pearson succeeded by William Severs (Mitteldorf), Michael Ayr succeeded by Burke Pearson (Judge Wehrhahn), Colin Stinton (Glasenapp), Jake Dengel (Kreuger), W. H. Macy (Dr. Fleischer), Eben Davidson (Philip)

A comedy in two acts. The action takes place on the outskirts of Berlin about 1890.

Gerry Goodstein Photo

Right: W. H. Macy, Eben Davidson, Tanya Berezin

William Hurt, Lindsay Crouse

CIRCLE REPERTORY THEATRE

Thursday, February 26, - April 12, 1981. (53 performances and 8 previews)

CHILDE BYRON

By Romulus Linney; Director, Marshall W. Mason; Set, David Potts, Costumes, Michael Warren Powell; Lights, Dennis Parichy; Fight Director, Peter Nels; Sound, Bruce Kaiser, Chuck London; Visuals, Daniel Irvine; Stage Manager, Alice Galloway; Press, Richard Frankel, Jane Brandmeir; Music, Hector Berlioz

CAST

Lindsay Crouse (Ada), succeeded by Debra Mooney, John Dossett (Boy), Stephanie Gordon (Woman), William Hurt (Byron), Stephanie Musnick (Young Woman), Richard Seff (The Man), Timothy Shelton (Young Man), Patricia Wettig (Girl)

A drama in two acts. The action takes place on Nov. 27, 1852 in London in the bedroom of Augusta Ada, Countess of Lovelace, Lord Byron's only legitimate child.

Gerry Goodstein Photo

CIRCLE REPERTORY THEATRE

Thursday, April 23, - May 24, 1981. (38 performances)

IN CONNECTICUT

By Roy London; Directors, Daniel Irvien, Marshall W. Mason; Set, David Potts; Costumes, Joan E. Weiss; Lighting, Dennis Parichy; Sound, Chuck London; Music, Michael Valenti; Production Manager, Alice Galloway; Stage Managers, Alice Galloway, M. A. Howard, Jody Boese, Fred Reinglas; Press, Richard Frankel, Jane Brandmeir

CAST

Rosemary Prinz (Candy Schull), Lisa Emery (Irene Call), Jeff McCracken (Louis), Shelby Buford, Jr. (Federico DiPinto), Henrietta Bagley (Giannina DiPinto), Robert LuPone (Andrew Call), Sharon Madden (Valerie Call), Rob Gomes (Maxie)

A play in two acts. The action takes place at the present time in New Preston, Connecticut.

Gerry Goodstein Photo

Rosemary Prinz, Jeff McCracken, Sharon Madden

CSC/CLASSIC STAGE COMPANY

Fourteenth Season
October 16, 1980–May 17, 1981

Artistic Director, Christopher Martin; Executive Director, Dennis Turner; General Manager, Alberto Torre; Administrative/Press Director, Stephen J. Holland; Designers, Terry A. Bennett, Pamela Howard, Isabell Ring; Music Composition/Direction, Noble Shropshire; Technical Director/Lighting, Seth Price; Stage Managers, Ryan Kelly, Catherine Rust, David Snizek, Randall Wheatley, Timothy Barrett

COMPANY

Timothy Barrett, Jonathan Bolt, John Mackay, Christopher Martin, Mary Eileen O'Donnell, Catherine Rust, Noble Shropshire, David Snizek, Tom Spiller, Robert Stattel, Karen Sunde, Eric Tavaris, Randall Wheatley, Walter Williamson

PRODUCTIONS

The Oedipus Cycle by Sophocles, translated by Paul Roche: Oedipus Rex (57 performances), Oedipus at Colonus (37 performances), Antigone (55 performances), Gilles de Rais (Bluebeard) by Roger Planchon, translated and adapted by John Burgess (33 performances); George Buchner's two plays, Woyzeck, and Leonce and Lena were presented together for 30 performances.

Gerry Goodstein Photos

**Right: Christopher Martin, Robert Stattel
in "Gilles de Rais"**

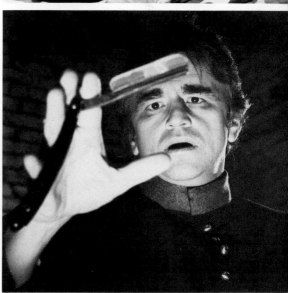

Robert Stattel, Karen Sunde in "Oedipus at Colonus" Above: Christopher Martin, Eric Tavaris in "Antigone"

Robert Stattel in "Woyzeck" Above: Eric Tavaris, Noble Shropshire in "Leonce and Lena" 115

EQUITY LIBRARY THEATRE

George Wojtasik, Managing Director
Lynn Montgomery, Production Director
Thirty-eighth Season

Business Manager, Tony Nicosia, Jr.; Office Manager/Audience Development, Debra Waxman; Assistant to Production Director, Wendy Orshan; Technical Directors, John Patterson Reed, Deborah Alix Martin; Costumiere, Kate E. Rogers; Staff Assistant Musical Director, Henry Aronson; Sound, Hal Schuler; Press, Lewis Harmon, Sol Jacobson; Photographer, Gary Wheeler

MASTER THEATRE

Thursday, September 25, - October 12, 1980. (18 performances)
Equity Library Theatre presents:

THE DEVIL'S DISCIPLE

By George Bernard Shaw; Director, Robert Barton; Set, Joseph A. Varga; Lighting, Ned Hallick; Costumes, Daria Wheatley; Stage Managers, K. Siobhan Phelan, David Michael Kenney, Jonathan D. Secor

CAST

Bob Cooper, Jr. (Uncle Titus), J. F. Curtin (Fifer), Margaret Dawson (Mrs. Titus), Herbert Du Val (Gen. Burgoyne), Barry Ford (Rev. Anderson), Edward Emerson French (Brudenell/Chaplain), Bonnie Horan (Mrs. Dudgeon), Donald R. Klecak (Sergeant), Richard Leighton (Richard Dudgeon), David Lipman (Judge Hawkins), Peter McRobbie (Maj. Swindon), Carol Potter (Judith), Joan Shangold (Essie), Warren Sweeney (Christopher Dudgeon), Maxine Taylor-Morris (Annie Dudgeon), Gerald Walling (Uncle William), Keith Lynch (Drummer), Soldiers: Tom Burnett, John Daggan, Scott Dainton, Daniel Graham, Norman Katz, Stephen Runske

Scott Bylund, Jonathan Kestly, Connie Coit
in "A Funny Thing Happened ..."

MASTER THEATRE

Thursday, December 4,-21, 1980. (22 performances)
Equity Library Theatre presents:

KIND LADY

By Edward Chodorov; Adapted from story by Hugh Walpole; Director, Carol Thompson; Set, John MacGregor; Lighting, Susan A. White; Costumes, Mary I. Whitehead; Sound, Hal Schuler; Props, Donna Brueger; Wardrobe, Ali Davis; Dialect Coach, Christopher Wells; Movement Consultant, Jill Beck; Stage Managers, Mark Schorr, Bonnie L. Becker, Dede Miller

CAST

Deborah Allison (Phyllis Glenning), Fran Anthony (Mrs. Edwards), Ward Asquith (Doctor), Helen Lloyd Breed (Rose), Richard Fancy (Henry Abbott), Susan Frazer (Ada), John Hallow (Mr. Edwards), Andi Henig (Aggie), Paul Hoover (Rosenberg), James Jenner (Peter Santard), Emily Kipp (Lucy), Charmian Sorbello (Mary Herries), Kevin Sullivan (Foster)

A drama in 3 acts and 4 scenes with a prologue and epilogue. The action takes place in the living room of Mary Herries' home in Montagu Square, London, in the 1930's.

Richard Leighton
in "The Devil's Disciple"

MASTER THEATRE

Thursday, October 30, - November 23, 1980. (32 performances)
Equity Library Theatre presents:

A FUNNY THING HAPPENED ON THE WAY TO THE FORUM

Music and Lyrics, Stephen Sondheim; Book, Larry Gelbart, Burt Shevelove; Director, Cash Baxter; Musical Director, Robert McNamee; Choreographer, Michael Perrier; Scenery, James Morgan; Costumes, Lewis Rampino; Lighting, Mark DiQuinzio; Stage Managers, Debra A. Acquavella, Travis DeCastro, Lisa Salomon

CAST

Janet Aldridge (Geminae Twin), Joel Anderson (Protean), Michelle Berman (Tintinabula), Scott Bylund (Hero), Connie Coit (Philia), Christopher Coucill (Miles Gloriosus), Marcia-Anne Dobres (Vibrata), Carolyn Friday (Domina), Bo Gerard (Protean), Lloyd Hubbard (Erronius), Charles Hudson (Lycus), Jonathan Kestly (Pseudolus), Frank Kosik (Protean), Wendy Laws (Geminae Twin), Andrea Lee (Panacea), Art Ostrin (Senex), Patricia Roark (Gymnasia), Geoffrey Webb (Hysterium)

MUSICAL NUMBERS: Comedy Tonight, Love I Hear, Free, House of Marcus Lycus, Lovely, Pretty Little Picture, Everybody Ought to Have a Maid, I'm Calm, Impossible, Bring Me My Bride, That Dirty Old Man, That'll Show Him, Dirge, Comedy Tonight

A musical in two acts. The action takes place on a spring day two hundred years before the Christian era on a street in Rome in front of the houses of Lycus, Senex and Erronius.

Gary Wheeler Photo

Fran Anthony, Charmian Sorbello, John Hallow,
Richard Fancy in "Kind Lady"

MASTER THEATRE

Thursday, January 8, - February 1, 1981. (30 performances)
Equity Library Theatre presents:

GODSPELL

Conceived by John-Michael Tebelak; Music and New Lyrics, Stephen Schwartz; Director, William Koch; Set, John Scheffler; Lighting, Paul Mathiesen; Musical Direction, Gregory Martindale; Costumes, James Delaney Collum; Production Assistant, Adam Phillips; Stage Managers, Dickson Lane, Patricia Finn McManamy, Janet Callahan

CAST

Alynne Amkraut, Scott Bakula, Elizabeth Bruzzese, Liz Callaway, Michael J. Duran, Jason Graae, Bev Larson, Kevin Rogers, Andy Roth, Laurine Towler

MUSICAL NUMBERS: Prologue, Prepare Ye, Save the People, Day by Day, Learn Your Lessons Well, Bless the Lord, All for the Best, All Good Gifts, Light of the World, Turn Back Oh Man, Alas for You, By My Side, We Beseech Thee, On the Willows, Finale

A musical in two acts.

Scott Bakula in "Godspell"

MASTER THEATRE

Thursday, February 12, - March 1, 1981. (24 performances)
Equity Library Theatre presents

DEATH TAKES A HOLIDAY

By Alberto Casella; Rewritten by Walter Ferris; Director, Michael Diamond; Set, Daniel H. Ettinger; Costumes, Mary L. Hayes; Lighting, Sean Murphy; Original Music, Bill Bly, Martin Verdrager; Assistant to Director, Carol Ann Klein; Stage Managers, Patricia Halpop, David W. Pratt, Trey Hunt; Press, Lewis Harmon, Sol Jacobson

CAST

Francis Barnard (Baron Cesarea), John Bergstrom (Shadow), I. Mary Carter (Princess), Peter Efthymiou (Corrado), Lucinda Jenney (Rhoda), Ron Johnston (Duke), Ron Keith (Major Whitread), Vivien Landau (Stephanie), Debra Lass (Cora), Samuel Maupin (Eric Fenton), Mary Portser (Grazia), Duke Potter (Fedele), Chris Weatherhead (Alda)

A drama in 2 acts and 3 scenes. The action takes place in the villa of Duke Lambert during August.

Left: John Bergstrom, Lucinda Jenney

MASTER THEATRE

Thursday, March 12, - April 5, 1981. (30 performances)
Equity Library Theatre presents:

ANYTHING GOES

Music and Lyrics, Cole Porter; Book, Guy Bolton, P. G. Wodehouse, Howard Lindsay, Russel Crouse; Director, Richard Michaels; Musical Staging, Karin Baker; Musical Direction and Vocal Arrangements, Rick Lewis; Set, Rob Hamilton; Lighting, Phil Monat; Costumes, Jack McGroder; Stage Managers, Ross Michaels, D. Kyria Krezel, Lisa Salomon, Hannah Murray; Wardrobe, Mary Lou Rios; Props, Peter Dominic, Laura Zelasnick; Sound, Hal Schuler; Press, Lewis Harmon, Sol Jacobson

CAST

Colleen Ashton (Virtue), Clayton Berry (Sir Evelyn), Andrea Cohen, Dolly Colby, Barbara Passolt (Debutantes), E. Lawford Cole (Whitney), Lee H. Doyle (Captain), Scott Evans (Sailor/Dance Captain), Michele Franks (Charity), Jim Gemmell (Cameraman/Ching), Gail Johnston (Hope), Nora Mae Lynd (Cruise Director), Eileen McCabe (Mrs. Harcourt), Cynthia Meryl (Reno Sweeney), Bob Morrisey (Billy Crocker), Jan Neuberger (Bonnie), Douglas Newton (Steward), John Remme (Moonface), Richard A. Starr (Bishop/Ling), Barbara Warren-Cooke (Chastity), David C. Wright (Purser)

MUSICAL NUMBERS: You're the Top, Bon Voyage, It's Delovely, Heaven Hop, Friendship, I Get a Kick Out of You, Anything Goes, Public Enemy Number One, Let's Step Out, Let's Misbehave, Blow Gabriel Blow, All Through the Night, Be Like the Bluebird, Take Me Back to Manhattan, Finale

A musical comedy in 2 acts and 11 scenes. The action takes place aboard an ocean liner during its voyage from New York to England in 1934.

John Remme, Cynthia Meryl, Bob Morrisey in "Anything Goes"

117

MASTER THEATRE

Thursday, April 16, - May 3, 1981. (22 performances)
Equity Library Theatre presents:

THE MISER

By Moliere; Translated and Directed by Earl McCarroll; Music and Lyrics, Robert Johanson; Musical Direction, Craig Lee; Set, Michael Anania; Lighting, Jason Kantrowitz; Costumes, Mary Thomasine Harkins; Musical Arrangements, David Evans; Wardrobe, Alin Millo; Stage Managers, Bo Metzler, Roger Kent Brechner, Arlene Mantek; Press, Lewis Harmon, Sol Jacobson

CAST

Stockman Barner (Maitre Simon/Seigneur Anselme), Claudine Cassan (Mariane), Martha Danielle (Elise), Joel Fredrickson (Brindavoine), Lyle Kanouse (Jacques), Alan Kass (Harpagon), Lola Powers (Frosine), Daniel Stewart (Cleante), Valerie Toth (La Merluche), Carol Trigg (Dame Claude), Martin Van Treuren (La Fleche), Robert Yacko (Valere)

MUSICAL NUMBERS: Money Minuet, If You Only Knew Love, My Money, Mariane, I Am Frosine, Separate Thoughts, Light the Candles, Revenge, When a Man Loves a Woman, Hallelu

A comedy with music in two acts. The action takes place during the 17th Century in the garden of M. Harpagon in Paris.

MASTER THEATRE

Thursday, May 14,-June 7, 1981. (36 performances)
Equity Library Theatre presents:

RAISIN

Book, Robert Nemiroff, Charlotte Zaltzberg; Based on Lorraine Hansberry's "A Raisin in the Sun"; Music, Judd Woldin; Lyrics, Robert Brittan; Director, Helaine Head; Musical Supervision/Choral and Vocal Arrangements, Chapman Roberts; Choreography, Al Perryman; Conductor/Pianist, Jim Cantin; Musical Direction/-Piano Arrangements, Fred Gripper; Assistant Director, C. Townsend Olcott II: Set, John Kenny; Lighting, Shirley Prendergast; Costumes, John Harris, Jr.; Production Assistant, Richard Dow; Stage Managers, Bob Hallman, Peggy Imbrie; Press, Lewis Harmon, Sol Jacobson

CAST

Nate Barnett (Walter Lee Younger), Claude Brooks (Travis' Friend/Drummer), David Love Calloway (Travis Younger), Jamil Garland (Pastor), Mel Haynes (Karl Linder), Rhetta Hughes (Ruth Younger), Robert Jason (Joseph Asagai), Joe Lynn (Bobo Jones), Saundra McClain (Mrs. Johnson), Claudia McNeil (Lena Younger), Cleo Quitman (Pastor's Wife), Ronald E. Richardson (Willie Harris), Deborah Lynn Sharpe (Beneatha), Ensemble: Charles A. Anderson, Claude Brooks, Cynthia S. Ellis, Lawrence Hamilton, Donna Patrice Ingram, Mary Leake, Sundy Leigh Leake, Bary Phillips, Lacy Darryl Phillips, Cleo Quitman, DeeDee Smith, Barron Truman, Inda E. Young

MUSICAL NUMBERS: Man Say, Whose Little Angry Man, Runnin' to Meet the Man, A Whole Lotta Sunlight, Booze, Alaiyo, Sweet Time, You Done Right, He Come Down, It's a Deal, Sidewalk Tree, Not Anymore, Measure Valleys

A musical in 2 acts and 14 scenes. The action takes place in Chicago's Southside during the 1950's.

Lola Powers, Alan Kass
in "The Miser"

EQUITY LIBRARY THEATRE
INFORMAL SERIES

Managing Director, George Wojtasik; Informal Series Producer, Debra Waxman; Production Coordinator, Wendy Orshan; Technical Director, Deborah Alix Martin

LINCOLN CENTER LIBRARY & MUSEUM

September 15, 16, 17, 1980 (3 performances)
SAVE THAT SONG FOR ME with music and lyrics/musical direction by Dennis Andreopoulos; Choreographer, Larry Hyman; Production Consultant, Steven Rivellino; Stage Manager, W. Scott Allison; Lighting, Scott A. Hunsberger; Costume Coordinator, Kevin Rayn. CAST: Helena Andreyko, Michael Crouch, Liza Gennaro, William Daniel Grey, Cass Morgan, E. G. Roberts, Zoe Walker

October 20, 21, 22, 1980 (3 performances)
A MAN BETWEEN TWILIGHTS conceived and edited by Kevin Edward Kennedy; Based on life and writings of James Agee; Music, Christopher Kennedy; Director, Kathlyn Chambers; Musical Direction, Jacqueline Schweitzer; Lighting, Stephen Finn; Costumes, Michael Ford Welch; Choreography, Eileen Thomas; Stage Managers, Nora Peck, Corinna Harmon. CAST: Suzanne Ford, Douglas Jones, Deborah Strang

November 17, 18, 19, 1980 (3 performances)
SARA by Michael Brady; Director, Richard Bruno; Costumes, Suzanne Schwartzer; Set, Edward Radonic; Lighting, Karen Arrajj; Producer, Tony Nicosia; Stage Manager, Jerome Hoffman. CAST: Catherine Bruno, Ellen Kaplan, Olivia Virgil Harper, Jennifer Johanos, Gregory Johnson, James McDonnell, Cindy Rosenthal, Russell Bonanno

December 8, 9, 10, 1980 (3 performances)
ACTORS by Geoffry Brown; Director, Elowyn Castle; Costumes, Claudia Brown; Music, Richard Feldman, Aralee Hambro; Stage Managers, Dan Zittel, Lee Jeffers. CAST: Thomas Wagner, Geoffrey Wade, Bob McDonald, David Anthony, David Garwood, John Fanning, James Bartz, Don Hampton, Regina O'Malley, Wendy Nute, Elaine Hyman

January 19, 20, 21, 1981 (3 performances)
A BIT OF OLD IRELAND: (Four One-Act Irish Plays) The Meadow Gate, Michelin, The Bogie Man by Lady Gregory, The Tinker's Wedding by J. M. Synge; Directors, Elowyn Castle, John Fanning; Costumes, Gayle Everhart; Sound, Allen Paley; Technical Coordinator, Judy Snyder; Stage Manager, Murphy Terrell. CAST: Conan Carroll, Mary Reid Horan, Lori Lynott, Michael Meyerson, J. Patrick O'Sullivan

February 2, 3, 4, 1981 (3 performances)
MOLNAR IN THE AFTERNOON: (Two One-Act Plays by Ferenc Molnar) Still Life, An Actor From Vienna; Director, Philip B. Epstein; Lighting, Andrea Randall; Stage Manager, Ruth E. Kramer. CAST: Carrie Zivetz, Albert Owens, Tee Scatuorchio, Bob J. Mitchell, Thomas H. Costello

March 16, 17, 18, 1981 (3 performances)
BUT SHIRLEY FAIRWEATHER! with music by Stephen Brown, lyrics by Paul Gaston, book by Deirdre Barber; Director, Peg Zitko; Assistant Director, Craig Leitner; Costumes, Kathy McGrath; Lighting, Mio Rodriguez. CAST: Kate Ingram, Kevin Paul, Ronald Owen, Peg Zitko, Susan Glaze, Diane Maggio, Dennis Bateman

(No photos submitted)

Rhetta Hughes, Nate Barnett
in "Raisin"

Louise Claps, Douglas Overtoom, Jackie
Rady in "Ape over Broadway"

HENRY STREET SETTLEMENT'S NEW FEDERAL THEATRE

Producers, Woodie King, Jr., Steve Tennen; Executive Director, Dr.
Miathan Allen; Administrative Director, Barbara Tate; Production
Coordinators, Dwight R. B. Cook, Maggie Grynastyl; Production
Manager, Robert Edmonds; Technical Directors, Vito Perri, Bonnie
Becker; Press, Warren Knowlton, Howard Atlee, Hilary Becker

HARRY DeJUR PLAYHOUSE
Friday, July 18, 1980—
BRANCHES FROM THE SAME TREE by Marjorie Eliot; Direc-
tor, Arthur French; Set, Wynn Thomas; Costumes, Judy Dearing;
Lighting, Sandra Ross. CAST: Verona Barnes (Carrie), Arthur W.
French III (Sonny), Vickie Thomas (Mable), Louise Stubbs (Mama),
David Downing (Ben), Joe Fields (Willie), Yolanda Karr (Anna),
Maxwell Glanville (Joe), Clebert Ford (Arthur)
　　Thursday, January 1–18, 1981 (12 performances)
THE TRIAL OF DR. BECK by Hughes Allison; Director, Phillip
Lindsay; Set, Robert Edmonds; Costumes, Carlo Thomas; Lights,
Larry Johnson. CAST: Don Paul (Clerk), Neil Napolitan (Judge),
Carl Pistilli (D.A.), Alkis Papuchis (Dr. Hicks), Herb Downer (Coll-
ings), Dennis Tate (Fields), Hollis Granville (Patrolman), George
Riddle (Inspector), Reuben Green (Dr. Beck), Dina Paisner (Ella),
Lawrence James (George), Minnie Gentry (Lulu), Janice Jenkins
(Hilda), Paul Knowles (Brooks), Donald Wait Keyes (Dr. Sims),
LaTanya Richardson (Carrie), Elizabeth Van Dyke (Elenore),
Juanita Bethea (Ruth), John Delph (Herman), Colleen Gaughan
(Mary), George Curley (George), Frank Vento (Guard), Roni Unger
(Stenographer), Andre Worthy (Reporter)

LOUIS ABRONS ARTS FOR LIVING CENTER
　　Saturday, January 10–February 1, 1981 (11 performances)
THINGS OF THE HEART: MARIAN ANDERSON'S STORY
by Shauneille Perry; Director, Denise Hamilton; Set, Llewellyn Har-
rison; Costumes, Judy Dearing; Lights, Leo Gambacorta. CAST:
Victoria Howard (Marian Anderson), Franz Jones (Actor I), Hy
Mencher (Actor III), Lucy Holland (Actress II), Addison Greene
(Actor II), Celestine Heard (Actress III), Robert Grossman (Actor
IV), Marina Stefan (Actress IV)
　　Friday, March 20–April 18, 1981 (17 performances)
THE DANCE AND THE RAILROAD by David Henry Hwang;
Director, John Lone; Sculpture, Andrea Zakin; Costumes, Judy
Dearing; Lights, Grant Orenstein; Stage Manager, Alice Jankowiak.
CAST: John Lone, Tzi Ma, Glenn Kubota (alternate)
　　Friday, March 27–April 12, 1981 (12 performances)
WIDOWS by Mfundi Vundla; Director, Vantile E. Whitfield; Set,
Llewellyn Harrison; Costumes, Judy Dearing; Lights, Leo Gam-
bacorta. CAST: Victoria Howard (Sindi), Pamela Poitier (Thabi-
tha), Tina Sattin (Zala)
　　Friday, April 24–May 31, 1981 (23 performances)
NO by Alexis DeVeaux; Director, Glenda Dickerson; Costumes,
Rise Collins, Glenda Dickerson; Set, Robert Edmonds; Lights, Mar-
shall Williams. CAST: Cheryl Lynn Bruce, Rise Collins, Yvette
Erwin, Gwendolen Hardwick, Judith Alexa Jackson, Andre Liguori,
Marilyn Nicole Worrell

Bert Andrews Photos

**Top Right: Carl Pistilli, LaTanya Richardson,
Reuben Green in "Trial of Dr. Beck" Below: Cynthia
Belgrave, Robert Silver, Morgan Freeman in
"The Connection"**

THE FANTASY FACTORY

Staff: Bill Vitale, Ed Kuczewski, Donna Lee Betz, Marcos Oksen-
hendler, Joyce Griffen, Charles Moore, Milly Russell, Theodore Sod,
Sara Bannin, Victor Mayo
　　November 21 through December 14, 1980 (16 performances)
APE OVER BROADWAY with book by Andrew Herz, music by
Steve Ross, lyrics and direction by Bill Vitale, choreography and
musical staging by Robert Speller, musical direction by Jim Sim-
mons, arrangements, Frederick S. Roffman, Set by Elmon Webb and
Virginia Dancy, lighting by Alex Palacios, costumes by Angeline
Thomas, Connie Caes; Stage Managers, Linda Baldwin, Joe
Keneally; Director, Bill Vitale. CAST: Dave Barnes, Patricia Berg,
Louise Claps, James Coleman, Judy Elliott, Jerome Foster, Stephen
Foster, Joe Garran, Mark Lebowitz, Douglas Overtoom, Jackie
Rady, Holly Ronick, Rouviere Santana, Jesse Stokes, Louis Zippi
　　May 15 through June 7, 1981 (12 performances)
FABRICATIONS by Mijo Johnson; Songs and Music, Bill Vitale;
Director, James Coleman; Musical Direction, Frank Lindquist; Set,
Tamas Banovich; Lighting, Alex Palacios; Stage Manager, Ken
Bridges. CAST: Louise Claps, Joyce Griffen, Ed Kuczewski

Marian Kelner/John Michael Cox, Jr. Photos

**Victoria Howard, Addison Greene
in "Things of the Heart"**

HUDSON GUILD THEATRE

David Kerry Heefner, Producing Director
Judson Barteaux, Managing Director
Casting/Literary Assistant, Iris Edith Bond; Workshops Director, Geraldine Teagarden; Production Manager, Peter Wrenn-Meleck; Production Stage Manager, Buzz Cohen; Photographer, Ken Howard; Press, Jeffrey Richards, Robert Ganshaw

HUDSON GUILD THEATRE
Wednesday, September 17, - October 19, 1980. (35 performances)

SUMMER

By Hugh Leonard; Director, Brian Murray; Setting, Steven Rubin; Costumes, Jane Greenwood; Lighting, Dennis Parichy; Production Assistant, Don Buschmann; Production Associate, Mitch Erickson; Wardrobe, Jan Shoebridge

CAST

David Canary (Richard), Swoosie Kurtz (Trina), Victor Bevine (Michael), Thomas A. Carlin (Stormy), Charlotte Moore (Jan), Mia Dillon (Lou), James Greene (Jess), Pauline Flanagan (Myra)

A play in two acts. The action takes place on a hillside overlooking Dublin, Ireland, on a summer Sunday in 1968, and a summer Sunday in 1974.

Ken Howard Photo

James Greene, Swoosie Kurtz, Charlotte Moore,
David Canary in "Summer"

Robertson Smith, Daniel Gerroll, John
Pankow, Gene O'Neill in "Slab Boys"

HUDSON GUILD THEATRE
Wednesday, November 19, - December 21, 1980. (35 performances)

THE SLAB BOYS

By John Byrne; Director, Peter Maloney; Setting, James Leonard Joy; Costumes, Elizabeth Covey; Lighting, Jeff Davis; Production Assistant, Elizabeth Bachman; Dialect Consultant, Cynthia Mace; Press, Jeffrey Richards, Robert Ganshaw

CAST

Gene O'Neill (Spanky Farrell), John Pankow (Hector McKenzie), Daniel Gerroll (Phil McCann), Richmond Hoxie (Jack Hogg), Bo Smith (Alan Downie), Ian Trigger (Willie Curry), Helena Carroll (Sadie), Noreen Tobin (Lucille Bentley)

A drama in two acts. The action takes place in the "Slab Room" of a carpet factory near Glasgow, Scotland, on a Friday in 1957.

Ken Howard Photos

HUDSON GUILD THEATRE
Wednesday, January 14, - February 15, 1981. (34 performances)

WAITING FOR THE PARADE

"Scenes of Women on the Home Front"; By John Murrell; Director, David Kerry Keefner; Setting and Costumes, Christina Weppner; Lighting, Robby Monk; Production Assistant, Joseph Keneally; Sound, Tom Gould; Dance Consultant, John Montgomery; Wardrobe and Props, Clark Taylor

CAST

Mia Dillon (Eve), Roxanne Hart (Catherine), Jo Henderson (Marta), Marti Maraden (Janet), Marge Redmond (Margaret)

A drama in two acts. The action takes place in Calgary, Alberta, Canada, from 1939 to 1945.

Ken Howard Photo

Roxanne Hart, Marge Redmond,
Marti Maraden, Mia Dillon

HUDSON GUILD THEATRE

Wednesday, March 4, - April 5, 1981. (30 performances)

KNUCKLE

By David Hare; Director, Geoffrey Sherman; Setting and Lighting, Paul Wonsek; Costumes, Denise Romano; Production Assistant, Carol Klein; Wardrobe and Props, Clark Taylor; Press, Jeffrey Richards, Robert Ganshaw

CAST

Fran Brill (Jenny Wilbur), Donald R. Klecak (Barman/Storeman/-Policeman/Porter), Daniel Gerroll (Curly Delafield), Alice Drummond (Grace Dunning), Gwyllum Evans (Patrick Delafield), Peter Jolly (Max/Voice of Lomax)

A drama in 2 acts and 16 scenes. The action takes place during September of 1974 in Guildford, Surrey, England.

Ken Howard Photo

Right: Fran Brill, Daniel Gerroll
Below: Daniel Gerroll, Peter Jolly
Right Center: Gerroll, Brill

NED AND JACK

By Sheldon Rosen; Director, Colleen Dewhurst; Setting, James Leonard Joy; Costumes, David Murin; Lighting, Robby Monk; Production Assistant, Carol Klein; Stage Manager, Buzz Cohen; Press, Jeffrey Richards, Robert Ganshaw

CAST

Dwight Schultz (Edward "Ned" Sheldon), Barbara Caruso (Ethel Barrymore), Peter Michael Goetz (John "Jack" Barrymore)

A play in two acts. The action takes place in Ned Sheldon's New York penthouse apartment after midnight on November 17, 1922.

Ken Howard Photo

Peter Michael Goetz, Barbara Caruso,
Dwight Schultz in "Ned and Jack"

JEWISH REPERTORY THEATRE

Sixth Season

Artistic Director, Ran Avni; Managing Director, Linda Evans; Literary Adviser, Edward M. Cohen; Chairman of the Board, Alfred L. Plant; Visual Consultant, Samuel Leve

EMANU-EL MIDTOWN YM-YWHA

June 10–29, 1980 (11 performances). Returned July 26, 1980
"36" by Norman Lessing; Director, Marc Daniels; Set, Jay Klein; Costumes, Jessica Fasman, Lights, William Hladik; Stage Manager, Evelyn Tuths. CAST: Charles; Carshon, Richard DeFabees, Joe Ponazecki, Sherry Rooney, Mark Weston, William Wise

October 15–November 16, 1980 (24 performances)
ME AND MOLLY by Gertrude Berg; Director, Edward M. Cohen; Set, Geoffrey Hall; Costumes, Jessica Fasman; Lights, Dan Kinsley; Stage Managers, Brian Manning, Harry Isaacs. CAST: Brian Manning, Harry Issacs, Denise Schultz, Julie Garfield, Herman O. Arbeit, Ira Katz, Ann Spettell, Gerry Lou, Sheldon Silver, Richard Niles, Alan Brandt, Nancy Barr

December 3, 1980–January 4, 1981 (24 performances)
SUCCESS STORY by John Howard Lawson; Director, Lynn Polan; Set, Jeffrey Schneider; Costumes, Julie Zabel; Lights, Adam Gross; Stage Manager, Myra Taylor. CAST: Ellen Abramowitz, Robert Coe, Ron DeMarco, David Faulkner, Frank Geraci, Nancy Kawalek, Catherine Lacy, Michael Albert Mantel, Brandwell Teuscher, Diane Zaremba

January 31, – February 26, 1981 (24 performances)
THE BIRTHDAY PARTY by Harold Pinter; Director, Anthony McKay; Set, Brian Martin; Costumes, Madeleine Cohen; Assistant Director, Patricia Jenkins; Lighting, Carol Sealey; Stage Manager, Harry Isaacs. CAST: Jerry Matz, Dermot McNamara, Ruth Miller, Vic Polizos, Susan Sandler, Loudon Wainwright

March 21–April 16, 1981 (24 performances)
MARYA by Isaac Babel; English version, Michael Glenny, Harold Shukman; Adapted by Christopher Hampton; Director, Patricia Lawler; Set, Adalberto Ortiz; Costumes, Linda Vigdor; Lights, Adam Gross; Stage Managers, Tresa Davidson, Mitchell Maglio. CAST: Licia Colombi, Valerie Gunderson, Howard Pinhasik, Sarah Joseph, Norman Katz, Tom Leo, Agnes Leicester, Rob McKay, Rosemary McNamara, Leslie Middlebrook, Joe Muzikar, Brad Russell, Frank Stoegerer, Kevin Sullivan, Robin Tagliente, David Vogel

May 16–June 11, 1981 (24 performances)
INCIDENT AT VICHY by Arthur Miller; Director, Ran Avni; Set, Adalberto Ortiz; Costumes, Edi Giguere; Lights, Carol Sealy; Assistant Director, Patricia Jenkins; Stage Managers, Jeffrey Norberry, Mitchell Maglio. CAST: Frank Anderson, Ward Asquith, Erick Avari, William Brenner, Robin Chadwick, Nicholas B. Daddazio, Robert Davis, Mark Fleischman, Donald J. Hoffman, Donald Ilko, Robert Kaufman, Michael Albert Mantel, Bernie Rachelle, Fred Sanders, Hal Studer

Right: Rosemary MacNamara, David Vogel in "Marya"
Above: Michael Albert Mantel in "Success Story"
Top: Frank Anderson, Hal Studer in "Incident at Vichy"

Chuck Portz, Horace Foster
in "Railroad Bill"

LABOR THEATER

Fifth Season

Artistic Director, C. R. Portz; Executive Producer, Bette Craig; Assistant to Producer, Nancy Langer; Music Coordinator, Martin Burman; Press, Ed Felder; Sets and Lighting, Tom Smith-Stalians; Costumes, K. L. Fredericks; Stage Managers, Karen Adelman, Kathi Levitan; Production Assistants, Rose Ann Romano, Natasha Williams

ST. PETER'S HALL

January 14–February 8, 1981 (24 performances)
RAILROAD BILL by C. R. Portz; Director, Mr. Portz; Musical Direction, Martin Burman. CAST: Chuck Portz (Caldwell), Horace Foster, Jr. (Railroad Bill), James Edward Foster (Homer), Preston Boyd (Mitchell), Bruce Willis (Sheriff), Gussie Harris (Widow), Martin Burman (Passenger)

February 18–March 8, 1981 (19 performances)
LEFT OUT LADY by John McGrath; Adapted by C. R. Portz; Music, Mark Brown; Director, C. R. Portz; Musical Direction, Martin Burman. CAST: Robin Bady, Nick Bennett, Bette Craig, Ellen McLaughlin, Socorro Santiago, Paul Schulze, Guy Sherman, John D. Swain, Natasha Williams

Ed Snider/Images Unlimited Photos

LIGHT OPERA OF MANHATTAN

June 1, 1980–May 31, 1981
Twelfth Season

Producer-Director, William Mount-Burke; Associate Director, Raymond Allen; Chairman of the Board, Dr. Milton Hopkins; Choreographer, Jerry Gotham; Assistant Musical Director/Pianist, Brian Molloy; Assistant Conductor/Organist, Stanley German; Assistant to Mr. Mount-Burke, Robert Hultman; General Manager, Barbara Marsh; Administrator, Charles Startup; Librarian, Rhanda Elizabeth Spotton; Costumes, James Nadeaux; Wardrobe, Penny Babel, Jodi Denn; Press; Jean Dalrymple, Peggy Friedman; Stage Manager, Jerry Gotham

COMPANY

Raymond Allen, Robert Barker, Joyce Bolton, Jon Brothers, Elizabeth Burgess-Harr, Cathy Cosgrove, Kathleen Cuvelier, Clem Egan, Dennis English, Bruce Gould, Lloyd Harris, Ed Harrison, G. Michael Harvey, Karen Hartman, Joanne Jamieson, Mary Jennings, Ann Kirschner, Eleanore Knapp, Ethelmae Mason, Georgia McEver, Bruce McKillip, Cole Mobley, James Nadeaux, Tom Olmstead, Stephen O'Mara, Vashek Pazdera, Richard Perry, Gary Pitts, Gary Ridley, Irma Rodgers, Cheryl Savitt, Craig Schulman, Rhanda Elizabeth Spotten, Mary Lee Rubens, Nancy Temple, J. J. Weber

PRODUCTIONS

The Pirates of Penzance, The Mikado, Iolanthe, HMS Pinafore, Trial by Jury, The Zoo, Cox and Box, Naughty Marietta, The Merry Widow, The Vagabond King, The Desert Song, Babes in Toyland, The Gondoliers, Patience, The Student Prince

Joseph Tenga Photos

Right: Karen Hartman, Robert Barker in "The Zoo"
Below: Raymond Allen, Craig Schulman, Cheryl
Savitt in "Pinafore" Right: Gary Pitts, Cheryl
Savitt in "Trial by Jury"

Eleanore Knapp, Lloyd Harris
in "The Student Prince"

Raymond Allen in "Babes
in Toyland"

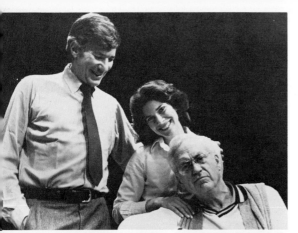

Richard Woods, Kathrin King Segal
in "A Pair of Hearts"

MANHATTAN PUNCH LINE

October 2, 1980–June 14, 1981

Artistic Director, Steve Kaplan; Executive Director, Mitch McGuire; Executive Assistant, Josie Lawrence; Production Coordinator, Terry Christgau; Press, Reva Cooper; Literary Manager, Brian Ross; Dramaturg, Victor Gluck; Musical Consultant, Kathrin King Segal; Design Consultants, Tony Castrigno, Francis L. Sabino; Sound, Robert Armin

MANHATTAN PUNCH LINE

October 2–26, 1980 (16 performances)
THE MALE ANIMAL by Elliot Nugent, James Thurber; Director, John Gerstad; Stage Manager, Jim McGivney; Lighting, George Gilsbach. CAST: Ronda Hansome (Cleota), Carole Monferdini (Ellen), Mitch McGuire (Tommy), Charlotte Booker (Patricia), Sam Green (Wally), Robert McFarland (Dean Damon), Bill Rutkoski (Michael), Frank Elmore (Joe), S. Barkley Murray (Blanche), Regis Bowman (Ed), Alice Rosengard (Myrtle), Tom Reiff (Nutsy)

November 6–30, 1980 (16 performances)
CLOSE RELATIONS by Leslie Weiner; Director, Leslie Weiner; Set and Costumes, Ernest Allen Smith; Lights, Robert F. Strohmeir; Stage Manager, William Blair. CAST: Henderson Forsythe (Harry), Laurie Heineman (Mary), Michael Tolan (Ernie).

December 11, 1980–January 5, 1981 (16 performances)
THE FRONT PAGE by Ben Hecht, Charles MacArthur; Director, Steve Kaplan; Lighting, Gregory Chabay; Costumes, Frank Piazza; Assistant Director, W. B. Rubidge; Stage Manager, Sharon Fenwald. CAST: Doug Baldwin (Endicott), Thomas Lenz (Schwartz), Gordon G. Jones (Murphy), Brendan Conway (Wilson), Dave Washburn (McCue), Brad Bellamy (Kruger), Harold Shepard (Bensinger), Ales Rowe (Mrs. Schlosser), John Ahlin (Eichorn), Domenick Jack Irrera (Diamond Louis), Patrick Husted (Hildy), Mary E. Baird (Jennie), Rea Rosno (Mollie), Lee H. Doyle (Sheriff), Carol Potter (Peggy), Eleanor Cody Gould (Mrs. Grant), David Berry (Mayor), Robert Tennehouse (Pincus), Mike Champagne (Williams), Jay Devlin (Walter), Bruce Pachtman (Carl), Alex Neel (Frank), James McGivney (Policeman), Dave Herman (Policeman), David Staskowski (Sailor), Daniel Smith (Skipper)

February 5–March 1, 1981 (16 performances)
THE PREVALENCE OF MRS. SEAL by Otis Bigelow; Director, Jason Buza; Set, Bob Phillips; Costumes, Karen Hummel; Sound, Frank Vince; Lighting, Mal Sturchio; Choreography, Erica Eigenberg; Technical Director, David Staskowski; Stage Manager, Michael Spellman. CAST: Matthew Lewis (Graves), Nancy Donohue (Mrs. Pilgrim), Humphrey David (Murdstone), Stephen Ahern (Harry), Beth Austin (Belinda), Richard Council (Smith), I. M. Hobson (Porteous), Tony Cummings (Igor), Frances Sternhagen (Mrs. Seal).

March 12–April 5, 1981 (16 performances)
THE COMEDY OF ERRORS by William Shakespeare; Director, Paul Schneider; Set, Geoffrey Hall; Stage Managers, Patrick D'Antonio, Warren Berger, Anne Sawyer. CAST: Warrington Winters (Egeon), Win Atkins (Solinus), Robert Therrien (Jailer), James Strafford (Merchant), Eric Conger (Antipholus of Syracuse), John Guerrasio (Dromio of Syracuse), Robert Dorfman (Dromio of Ephesus), Carol Potter (Adriana), Amanda Carlin (Luciana), Tom Rolfing (Antipholus of Ephesus), Steven Worth (Balthazar), Gordon Ahlstom (Officer), Joel Bernstein (Angelo), Bob McFarland (2nd Merchant), Alice Rosengard (Courtesan). Jim Fitzpatrick (Pinch), Victoria Boothby (Priestess)

April 16–May 10, 1981 (16 performances)
ENGAGED by W. S. Gilbert; Director, Jerry Heymann; Set, Barry Axtell; Costumes, Mary L. Hayes; Stage Managers, Fran R. Rosenthal, Julye Calder; Lighting, Mark Diquinzio. CAST: Michael Deep (Pianist), Mike Moran (Angus), Margaret R. Pine (Maggie), Cynthia Hopkins (Mrs. MacFarlane), Arthur Erickson (Belvawney), Kate Weiman (Miss Trenerne), Tom Costello (Symperson), Larry Pine (Cheviot), Joel Simon (McGillicuddy), Beth Austin (Minnie), Abigail Costello (Parker), James Strafford, Robert Therrien (Groomsmen)

May 21–June 14, 1981 (16 performances)
A PAIR OF HEARTS by Monte Merrick; Director, Steve Kaplan; Set, Barry Axtell; Lighting, Susan A. White; Costumes, Gayle Everhart; Sound, Robert Armin; Stage Manager, Hannah Murray. CAST: Leslie Frances William (Peg), Nancy Linehan (Margie), Mitch McGuire (Ben), Julio Robin Pollack (Mike), Mary Baird (Babs), Kathrin King Segal (Lolly), Richard Woods (Hal), Steven Worth (Luke)

Cathryn Williams Photos

Left Center: Mitch McGuire, Bill Rutkoski
in "The Male Animal" Above: Nancy Donohue, I. M.
Hobson, Richard Council, Humphrey Davis, Frances
Sternhagen in "The Prevalence of Mrs. Seal" Top:
Michael Tolan, Laurie Heineman, Henderson
Forsythe in "Close Relations"

MANHATTAN THEATRE CLUB

Ninth Season

Artistic Director, Lynne Meadow; Managing Director, Barry Grove; General Manager, Connie L. Alexis; Development, Barbara Benisch, Patricia Cox, W. Alexander Fraser, Denise Cooper, Gary Murphy; Assistants to Directors, Michael Bush, Jillson Knowles; Literary Manager, Jonathan Alper; Musical Consultant, Murray Horwitz; Directors for Writers in Performance, Janet Sternburg, Jana Harris; Production Manager, Paul Fitzmaurice; Technical Director, Brian Lago; Props, Debra Schutt; House Manager, Linda Hempling; Press, Susan L. Schulman, Sandi Kimmel

MANHATTAN THEATRE CLUB/DOWNSTAGE
Wednesday, October 22, - November 30, 1980. (45 performances)

VIKINGS

By Steve Metcalfe; Director, Lynne Meadow; Associate Director, George Mead; Set, Tony Straiges; Costumes, Linda Fisher; Lighting, F. Mitchell Dana; Wardrobe, Terilyn Brown; Stage Managers, Virginia Hunter, Richard Patrick-Warner

CAST

Tom Atkins (Peter Larsen), William Swetland (Yens Larsen), Boyd Gaines (Gunnar Larsen), Sheila Allen (Betsy Simmons), Standby for Gunnar: Richard Patrick-Warner

A drama in two acts. The action takes place in and around the home of the Laren family.

Gerry Goodstein Photo

MANHATTAN THEATRE CLUB/UPSTAGE
Opened Tuesday, December 9, 1980.*
Manhattan Theatre Club (Lynne Meadow, Artistic Director; Barry Grove, Managing Director) presents:

CRIMES OF THE HEART

By Beth Henley; Director, Melvin Bernhardt; Set, John Lee Beatty; Costumes, Patricia McGourty; Lighting, Dennis Parichy; Assistant to Director, Gregory Johnson; Hairstylist, Hal Truesdale; Wardrobe, Julia H. Weitzman; Production Assistant, Katharine Stewart; Technical Director, Brian Lago

CAST

Lenny MaGrath	Lizbeth MacKay
Chick Boyle	Julie Nesbitt
Doc Porter	Stephen Burleigh
Meg MaGrath	Mary Beth Hurt
Babe Botrelle	Mia Dillon
Barnette Lloyd	Peter MacNicol

A comedy/drama in three acts. The action takes place in Hazlehurst, Mississippi, in 1974, five years after Hurricane Camille.

Production Manager: Paul Fitzmaurice
Stage Managers: James Pentecost, David Caine
Press: Susan L. Schulman, Sandi Kimmel

*Closed January 11, 1981 after 32 performances. Winner of 1981 Pulitzer Prize, and New York Drama Critics Circle citation for Best New American Play.

Gerry Goodstein Photos

**Tom Atkins, Boyd Gaines,
William Swetland in "Vikings"**

MANHATTAN THEATRE CLUB/UPSTAGE
Tuesday, October 28, - November 30, 1980. (35 performances)

ONE TIGER TO A HILL

By Sharon Pollock; Director, Thomas Bullard; Set, David Potts; Costumes, Judy Dearing; Lighting, F. Mitchell Dana; Casting Director, Mary Colquhoun; Dialect Coach, Tim Monich; Fight Director, Jake Turner; Stage Manager, Loretta Robertson

CAST

Dann Florek (Cecil Stocker), John Getz (Everett Chalmers), Jane Hoffman (Lena Benz), Larry Joshua (Gillie MacDermott), Alan Mixon (George McGowen), Vic Polizos (Carl Hanzuk), Michael Tucker (Frank Soholuk), Denzel Washington (Tommy Paul), Margaret Whitton (Dede Walker)

A drama in two acts. The action takes place at the present time in a maximum security penitentiary in Western Canada.

Gerry Goodstein Photo

**Left: Michael Turner, Larry Joshua, Denzel
Washington, John Getz**

**Mary Beth Hurt, Lizbeth Mackay, Mia Dillon
in "Crimes of the Heart"**

125

MANHATTAN THEATRE CLUB/DOWNSTAGE
  Tuesday, December 16, 1980 - January 25, 1981. (46 performances

AMERICAN DAYS

By Stephen Poliakoff; Director, Jacques Levy; Set, Andrew Jackness; Costumes, Kenneth M. Yount; Lighting, Dennis Parichy; Music, Urban Blight; Musical Supervisor, Stanley Walden; Hairstylists, Charles LoPresto, Pamela Lorelli, Patrik Moreton; Dialect Coach, Gordon Jacoby; Wardrobe, Julia H. Weitzman; Production Assistants, Mari S. Schatz, Debra A. Acquavella; Stage Managers, Edward R. Fitzgerald, Wendy Chapin; Press, Susan L. Schulman, Winnie Sampson, Sandi Kimmel

CAST

Anna Levine (Tallulah), John Snyder (Gary), Alexander Spencer (Ian), Pippa Pearthree (Lorraine), John Shea (Don Sherman), David Blue (Murray), Ed Setrakian (Voice of Conroy), Standbys: Jane Hickey, Todd Waring

A play in two acts. The action takes place at the present time in the studios of an international record company in London.

Gerry Goodstein Photo

**Anna Levine, John Snyder, John Shea,
Pippa Pearthree in "American Days"**

**Dale Soules, Pamela Blair, Chip Zien,
Janie Sell, Gibby Brand, Merwin Goldsmith**

MANHATTAN THEATRE CLUB/UPSTAGE
  Wednesday, February 11, - March 1, 1981.

REAL LIFE FUNNIES

From Stan Mack's Comic Strip; Reported verbatim by Stan Mack; Adapted by Howard Ashman; Songs, Alan Menken; Based on an idea by Lawrence Kraman; Director, Howard Ashman; Choreography, Douglas Norwick; Arrangements and Musical Direction, Larry Hochman; Lighting, Frances Aronson; Assistant to Director, Jim Stern; Wardrobe, Julia H. Weitzman; Production Assistants, Arlene Mantek, Jane MacPherson; Stage Managers, Paul Mills Holmes, Betsy Nicholson

CAST

Pamela Blair, Gibby Brand, Merwin Goldsmith, Janie Sell, Dale Soules, Chip Zien

MUSICAL NUMBERS AND SKETCHES: Real Life Funnies, Is It Art?, I Love Your Brains, Pleasantly Plump, Lifted, Someday, People Collecting Things, Ah Men, Every Thursday Night, Divorce Has Brought Us Together, The Way of My Father, Someone to Come Home with Me Tonight

Performed without an intermission.

Gerry Goodstein Photo

MANHATTAN THEATRE CLUB/DOWNSTAGE
  Tuesday, February 24, - March 22, 1981. (48 performances)

CLOSE OF PLAY

By Simon Gray; Director, Lynne Meadows; Set, John Lee Beatty; Costumes, Jennifer von Mayrhauser; Lighting, Dennis Parichy; Stage Managers, Edward R. Fitzgerald, Kate Stewart; Production Assistant, Robert Nolan; Wardrobe, Julia H. Weitzman; Music Adaptation, Robert Dennis; Sound, Ken Bowser; Dialect Coach, Gordon Jacoby; Assistant to Director, Jennifer McCray; Wigs, Paul Huntley; Press, Susan L. Schulman, Sandi Kimmel

CAST

Veronica Castang (Marianne), Pauline Flanagan (Daisy), John Horton (Henry), John Christopher Jones (Benedict), Caroline Lagerfelt (Margaret), Lynn Milgrim (Jenny), William Roerick (Jasper), Alexander Winter (Matthew)

A drama in two acts. The action takes place in the home of Professor Jasper Spencer. The game of cricket may be played over a period of several days. The "close of play" is a term referring to the standing score at the end of one day's play, but never to the concluding day's play.

Gerry Goodstein Photo

**William Roerick, Caroline Lagerfelt,
John Horton in "Close of Play"**

MANHATTAN THEATRE CLUB
IN-THE-WORKS/UPSTAGE

Tuesday, March 17–29, 1981 (14 performances)
AFTER ALL by Vincent Canby; Director, Douglas Hughes; Set, David Emmons; Costumes, Christa Scholtz; Lighting, Dawn Chiang; Stage Manager, Jason LaPadura. CAST: George Guidall, Lois Smith

Tuesday, March 31 –April 12, 1981 (14 performances)
THE CHISHOLM TRAIL WENT THROUGH HERE by Brady Sewell; Director, Steven Schachter; Set, David Emmons; Costumes, Christa Scholtz; Lighting, Dawn Chiang; Stage Manager, Kate Hancock. CAST: Helen Stenborg (Mae), William Converse-Roberts (Bryan), Kristen Palmieri (JoBeth), William Russ (Buck), John Goodman (Jack), Jean DeBaer (Belle), Robert Desiderio (Malcolm), Ed VanNuys (Grady), Shannon John (Peggy), Paula Trueman (Josie), Ellen Tobie (Eileen)

Tuesday, April 14–26, 1981 (14 performances)
A CALL FROM THE EAST by Ruth Prawer Jhabvala; Director, John Tillinger; Set, David Emmons; Costumes, Christa Scholtz; Lighting, Dawn Chiang; Stage Manager, Kate Stewart. CAST: Dana Ivey (Isabel), W. H. Macy (Leopold), John Vickery (Rev. Rushbrooke), Lisa Banes (Margaret), Veronica Castang (Florence), Theodore Sorel (Swami)

Tuesday, April 28–May 10, 1981 (14 performances)
SCENES FROM LA VIE DE BOHEME by Anthony Giardina; Director, Douglas Hughes; Set, David Emmons; Costumes, Christa Scholtz; Lighting, Dawn Chiang; Stage Manager, Jason LaPadura. CAST: John Christopher Jones (Jacob), Michael Kaufman (Paul), Rick Lieberman (Malcolm), Marcell Rosenblatt (Deanna), Al Corley (John), Mia Dillon (Una), Mike Brennan (Man with Una), Frank Nastasi (Dimme), Robin Karfo (Joria)

Gerry Goodstein Photos

Right: Helen Stenborg, Paula Trueman in "The Chisholm Trail . . ." Below: Lois Smith, George Guidall in "After All"

Al Corley, Michael Kaufman, Robin Karfo, John Christopher Jones in "Scenes from La Vie de Boheme"

Theodore Sorel, Lisa Banes in "A Call from the East"

MANHATTAN THEATRE CLUB/DOWNSTAGE
Tuesday, April 7, - May 17, 1981. (48 performances)

TRANSLATIONS

By Brian Friel; Director, Joe Dowling; Set, Kate Edmunds; Costumes, David Murin; Lighting, David F. Segal; Production Assistant, Jeanne Nicolosi; Stage Managers, Loretta Robertson, Eileen Haring; Press, Susan L. Schulman, Sandi Kimmel

CAST

Stephen Burleigh (Owen), Jarlath Conroy (Manus), Jake Dengel (Jimmy Jack), Daniel Gerroll (Yolland), Barnard Hughes (Hugh), Valerie Mahaffey (Sarah), Sam McMurray (Doalty), Ellen Parker (Maire), George Taylor (Capt. Lancey), Lauren Thompson (Bridget)

A drama in three acts. The action takes place during 1833 in a hedge-school in the townland of Baile Beag/Ballybeg, an Irish-speaking community in County Donegal.

Gerry Goodstein Photo

Barnard Hughes, Sam McMurray, Valerie Mahaffey, Lauren Thompson, and above with company of "Translations"

MUSIC-THEATRE GROUP/ LENOX ARTS CENTER

Producing Directors, Lyn Austin, Margo Lion; Associate Producer, Diane Wondisford; General Manager, Thomas Whelan

THE CUBICULO
Wednesday, June 11–29, 1980 (18 performances)
WAS IT GOOD FOR YOU? by Susan Rice; Suggested by original material by Edward Koren; Director, Susan Rice; Set and Lighting, Lenny Cowles; Costumes, Whitney Blausen; Score, Amy Rubin; Stage Manager, Reid Pierce; Producers, Music-Theatre Group/- Lenox Arts Center, Margo Lion, Lyn Austin, Cameron Thompson. CAST: Sam Schacht (Man), Alexandra Borrie (Woman)
Wednesday, November 12–December 7, 1980 (24 performances)
ELIZABETH DEAD by George Trow; Director, Martha Clarke; Composed by Robert Dennis; Set and Costume, Lawrence Casey; Lighting, William Armstrong; Stage Manager, Diane Wondisford. CAST: Linda Hunt
Wednesday, April 22–May 10, 1981 (18 performances)
DISROBING THE BRIDE by Harry Kondoleon; Director, Mr. Kondoleon; Music, Gary S. Fagin; Set and Lighting, Loren Sherman; Costumes, Ann Emonts; Stage Manager, Elizabeth Rothberg. CAST: Ellen Greene, Caroline Kava, Mary Beth Lerner

Stephanie Saia Photos

128

Sam Schacht, Alexandra Borrie in "Was It Good for You?"

Left Center: Caroline Kava, Mary Beth Lerner, Ellen Greene in "Disrobing the Bride"
Above: Linda Hunt in "Elizabeth Dead"

THE MEAT & POTATOES COMPANY
Fifth Season

Artistic Director, Neal Weaver; Production Manager, Ann Folke; Administrative Director/Press, Jane Dwyer; Technical Consultant, Terry H. Wells; General Manager, Bonnie Arquilla

ALVINA KRAUSE THEATRE

June 5–29, 1980 (16 performances)
THE DOUBLE INCONSTANCY by Pierre Carlet de Chamblain de Marivaux; Translated by Oscar Mandel; Direction and Design, Neal Weaver; Lighting, Herbert Fogelson; Stage Manager, Elliott Landen. CAST: Donald Nardini (Prince), Alvin Railey (Lord Lumley), David Schmitt (Trivet), Dustyn Taylor (Lisette), Karli Dwyer (Lady-in-waiting), Christopher Karczmar (Robin), Elliott Landen (Footman), Sally Mercer (Sylvia), Sarah Hall (Flaminia).

July 10–August 3, 1980 (16 performances)
WAR GAMES by Neal Weaver; Direction and set, Neal Weaver; Stage Manager, Garwood. CAST: W. H. Macy (John), Marilyn Moynihan (Mrs. Moylan), Alvin Railey (Ted), Elliott Landen (Gen. Flagstad), Maxine Taylor-Morris (Anastasia), Dustyn Taylor (Sandra)

September 11–October 5, 1980 (16 performances)
THE RELAPSE by Sir John Vanbrugh; Director, Neal Weaver; Set, James Roberts; Music, William Grueneberg; Stage Manager, Julie Connason. CAST: Toni Brown (Nurse), David Coxx (Foretop), James Crabtree (Clumsy), Anne Deauville (Abigail), Garwood (Old Coupler) William Grueneberg (Lory), Archie Harrison (Friendly), David Keats (Waterman), Scott Klavan (Worthy) succeeded by K. C. Kizziah, Barbara Knowles (Amanda), Elliott Landen (Bull), David Lane (Page), Vyvyan Pinches (Foppington), Terri Price (Berinthia), Greg Schaffert (Shoemaker), David Schmitt (Loveless), David Sederholm (Fashion) succeeded by Paul DeBoy, Dustyn Taylor (Miss Hoyden)

October 16–November 16, 1980 (20 performances)
THE TAVERN by George M. Cohan; Director, Barbara Knowles; Set, Bob Burns; Sound, Paul Garrity; Costumes, Archie Harrison; Stage Manager, Jonathan Lipscomb. CAST: Paul DeBoy (Tom) succeeded by David Cooper-Wall, Michael Gilles (Tony) succeeded by Philip Mansfield, Diane Heles (Virginia), Neal Jones (Zach), David Keats (Ezra), Richard Lette (Stevens) succeeded by Robert Zukerman, Howard McMaster (Sheriff), John Meyer (Lamson), Tessa M. Mills (Mrs. Lamson), Vyvyan Pinches (Vagabond), Terri Price (Violet), John Tyson (Willum), Alex Wexler (Joshua), Warrington Winters (Freeman), Bonnie Wiseman (Sally)

November 28–December 21, 1980 (16 performances)
THE PHILANDERER by George Bernard Shaw; Direction and Set, Neal Weaver; Stage Manager, Gary Hebbel. CAST: Stephen Ahern (Paramore), K. C. Kizziah (Charteris), Elliott Landen (Craven), Barbara Leto (Grace), Jack McLaughlin (Cuthbertson), Terri Price (Julia), Dustyn Taylor (Sylvia), Alex Wexler (Page) succeeded by Larry Hough

January 8–February 1, 1981 (16 performances)
THE IMPORTANCE OF BEING EARNEST by Oscar Wilde; Direction and Set, Neal Weaver; Stage Manager, Rachelle Minkoff. CAST: Stephen Ahern (Jack) succeeded by Kirk Wolfinger, Lisa Cosman (Miss Prism), Colin Leslie Fox (Chasuble), Nancy Hammill (Gwendolen), David Keats (Lane) Elissa Napolin (Cecily), Maxine Taylor-Morris (Lady Bracknell) succeeded by Frances Ford, Lee Brockman Welch (Algernon), Steve Winfield (Merriman)

February 19–March 15, 1981 (16 performances)
THE PILLARS OF SOCIETY by Henrik Ibsen; Director, Neal Weaver; Set, Michael Morrows; Costume Coordinator, Terri Price; Lighting, Herbert Fogelson; Stage Managers, Evan Senreich, Tom Starace. CAST: Toni Genfan Brown (Mrs. Holt), Lisa Cosman (Mrs. Lynge), Jack L. Davis (Johan), Herbert DuVal (Karsten), Michelle Giannini (Betty), Adam Kilgour (Aune), Nancy Killmer (Lona), Martin Kleino (Jacob), Elliott Landen (Rummel), Tessa M. Mills (Mrs. Rummel), Anthony Moore (Rorlund) Michael Genger (Olaf), Hugh Karraker (Kraap) succeeded by Michael Morrows, Donald Pace (Hilmar), Terri Price (Martha), Janeice Scarbrough (Dina), Evan Senreich (Vigeland), Tom Starace (Sandstad)

March 26–April 19, 1981 (20 performances)
ICEBOUND by Owen Davis; Director, W. H. Macy; Set, Donald Beckman; Costumes, Erica Hollmann; Music, James Barry; Lighting, Tom Smith-Stalians; Stage Managers, Garwood, Michael Pritchard; Technical Director, Mark Haack. CAST: Sherry H. Arell (Hannah), Toni Genfan Brown (Sadie), James Barry (Ben), Jayne Chamberlin (Ella), Herbert DuVal (Bradford), Hugh Karraker (Jim), Carla Macy (Nettie), Joel Parsons (Henry), Jesse Sheppard (Orin), Mary Shortkroff (Jane), Jennifer Sullivan (Emma)

Bottom Right: Alvin Railey, W. H. Macy, Dustyn Taylor in "War Games" Above: Mary Shortkroff, Herbert DuVal in "Icebound" Top: Barbara Knowles, David Schmitt in "The Relapse"

May 7–31, 1981 (16 performances)
TROILUS AND CRESSIDA by William Shakespeare; Direction and Design, Neal Weaver; Costumes, Georgeanne Ventura, Lisa Cosman. CAST: Stephen Ahern (Thersites), Scott Bergs (Antenor), Russell Bonanno (Nestor), Frank Ciraci (Menelaus), Malachy Cleary (Troilus), Jack DiMonte (Diomedes), Herbert DuVal (Ulysses) succeeded by K. C. Kizziah, Cameron Foord (Helen), Joseph Jamrog (Ajax), Scott Klavan (Hector), Ken Kliban (Achilles), Chip Lamb (Aeneas), Elliott Landen (Agamemnon), Elissa Napolin (Cressida), Perry Norton (Cassandra), Kevin Osborne (Alexander), Harry Spillman (Pandarus), Don Taylor (Paris), Eric R. Thomas (Helenus), Robert Thurston (Priam), Jonathan Trumper (Patroclus)

Herbert Fogelson Photos

129

NEGRO ENSEMBLE COMPANY

Thirteenth Season

Artistic Director, Douglas Turner Ward; Managing Director, Gerald S. Krone; General Manager, Leon B. Denmark; Assistant, William Edwards; Playwright in Residence, Steve Carter; Executive Assistant, Deborah McGee; Administrative Assistant, Yvette Erwin; Theatre Management, Dorothy Olim Associates; Technical Director, Rodney J. Lucas; Stage Manager, Femi Sarah Heggie; Production Assistant, Brendajoy Griffin; Wardrobe, Arniece McWilliams; Choreographic Consultant, Dyane Harvey; Press, Howard Atlee, Tom Trenkle, Jim Baldassare

THEATRE FOUR

Tuesday, September 30–November 9, 1980 (48 performances)
THE SIXTEENTH ROUND by Samm-Art Williams; Director, Horacena J. Taylor; Set, Felix E. Cochren; Costumes, Judy Dearing; Lighting, Shirley Prendergast; Stage Manager, Clinton Turner Davis. CAST: Paul Benjamin (Jesse), Rosalind Cash (Marsha), Roscoe Orman (Lemar). A drama in two acts and five scenes. The action takes place in North Philadelphia in the apartment of Marsha and Jesse Taft at the present time.

Tuesday, November 25, 1980–January 4, 1981 (48 performances)
ZOOMAN AND THE SIGN by Charles Fuller; Director, Douglas Turner Ward; Set, Rodney J. Lucas; Lighting, Shirley Prendergast; Costumes, Judy Dearing; Stage Manager, Clinton Turner Davis. CAST: Alvin Alexis (Victor Tate), Mary Alice (Rachel Tate), Ray Aranha (Reuben Tate), Terrance Terry Ellis (Russell), Giancarlo Esposito (Zooman), Frances Foster (Ash), Carl Gordon (Emmett Tate), Steven A. Jones (Donald Jackson), Carol Lynn Maillard (Grace), Understudy: Phylicia Ayers-Allen. A drama in two acts. The action takes place at the present time in Philadelphia, Pennsylvania, in the Tate home and the street outside.

Tuesday, January 27–March 8, 1981 (48 performances)
WEEP NOT FOR ME by Gus Edwards; Director, Douglas Turner Ward; Set, Wynn Thomas; Lighting, William H. Grant III; Costumes, Judy Dearing; Stage Manager, Clinton Turner Davis. CAST: Ethel Ayler (Lillian), Bill Cobbs (Jake), Seret Scott (Crissie), Elain Graham (Deanie), Chuck Patterson (Willy), Phylicia Ayers-Allen (Janet), Robert Gossett (Mel), Brian Evaret Chandler (Henry), Sarallen (Sylvie), A play in 2 acts and 7 scenes. The action takes place now or in the very near future in an apartment in the South Bronx section of New York City.

Saturday, April 4–May 3, 1981 (36 performances)
IN AN UPSTATE MOTEL by Larry Neal; Director, Paul Carter Harrison; Set, Edward Burbridge; Sound, Regge Life; Lighting, Shirley Prendergast; Costumes, Judy Dearing; Stage Manager, Femi Sarah Heggie. CAST: Phylicia Ayers-Allen (Female Shadow), Carl Gordon (Male Shadow), Donna Bailey (Queenie), Charles Henry Patterson (Duke). A play in two acts. The action takes place in an upstate New York motel now and then.

Friday, May 8–June 14, 1981 (45 performances)
HOME by Samm-Art Williams; Director, Douglas Turner Ward; Set, Felix E. Cochren; Costumes, Alvin B. Perry; Lighting, William H. Grant III; Stage Manager, Clinton Turner Davis. CAST: Samuel L. Jackson (Cephus), L. Scott Caldwell (Woman One/Pattie Mae), Michele Shay (Woman Two). A play performed without intermission. The action takes place from the late 1950's to the present.

Bert Andrews Photos

Right Center: Roscoe Orman, Rosalind Cash, Paul Benjamin in "The 16th Round" Above: Elain Graham, Phylicia Ayers-Allen, Seret Scott, Bill Cobbs in "Weep Not for Me" Top: Giancarlo Esposito, Ray Aranha, Carl Gordon, Mary Alice in "Zooman and the Sign"

Carl Gordon, Donna Bailey, Phylicia Ayers-Allen, Charles Henry Patterson in "In an Upstate Motel"

NEW DRAMATISTS INC.

October 15, 1980–June 26, 1981
President, Zilla Lippmann; Executive Director, Thomas G. Dunn; Program Director, David Juaire; Literary Services Director, David Copelin; Projects Coordinator, Joy Blacksmith; Technical Director, Harvey Wilson

STAGED READINGS

KETCHUP by John Patrick Shanley; Director, Susan Gregg, with Jeffrey Anderson-Gunter, Joseph Montalbo, Tony Shultz, Jan Buttram, Carol Ann Mansell, Richard Sale, Atsumi Sakato, Joseph Mason, Charles Michael Wright, Tom Bade, Michael Morin

MY SISTER IN THIS HOUSE by Wendy Kesselman; Director, Iverna Lockpez, with Sofia Landon, Patricia Charbonneau, Rebecca Schull, Brenda Currin, Annemarie Hollander, John Peilmeier, Mark Hofmaier, Valerie von Volz

THESE DAYS THE WATCHMEN SLEEP by Karl Evans; Director, Stephan Maro, with Herbert Rubens, Joseph Giardina, Dan Lauria, Michael Hardstark, George Pollack, Phyllis Somerville, Nancy Weems, Nancy New, Willie Reale, Brian Zoldessy

SHIRLEY BASIN by Jack Gilhooley; Director, Robert Siegler, with Theresa Karanik, Erika Petersen, Ken Costigan, Peg Murray, Jane Cronin, Phyllis Somerville, Anna Minot, Gail Kellstrom, John Homa, Channing Chase

LA VISIONARIA by Renaldo Eugenio Ferradas; Director, John Henry Davis, with Dennis Parker, Dan Lauria, Paul Farin, Valerie von Volz, Rebecca Schull, Jaime Tirelli, Tom Bade, Martin Zone

GORILLA by John Patrick Shanley; Director, Susan Gregg, with James Maxwell, Phyllis Somerville, Bruce Somerville, Tom Bade, Michael Morin, John Guerrasio, Erin Blackwell, Charles Michael Wright, Vickie Bradbury, Carol Ann Mansell, Oona Short, Gail Kellstrom, Mary Louise Burke, Peter Phillips

BRIGITTE BERGER by Stanley Taikeff; Director, Thomas Gruenewald, with Anita Keal, Ron Siebert, Larry Joshua, Jeffrey Anderson-Gunter, Kathy Danzer, Paul Nevens, Valerie von Volz, Marcella Andre

THE WAR BRIDES by Terri Wagener; Director, Elaine Kanas, with Frances Fisher, Sara Jessica Parker, Libby Boone, Catherine Wolf, Sloane Shelton, Cara Duff-MacCormick, Ellen Parker

EVE OF ALL SAINTS by Syl Jones; Director, Susan Gregg, with Jack R. Marks, Victoria Boothby, Theresa Karanik, Victor Slezak, Ivonne Coll, Tim Donoghue, Michael Horan

ABOUT SPONTANEOUS COMBUSTION by Sherry Kramer; Director, Pat Carmichael, with Susan Merson, Dolores Kenan, Eddie Jones, Cleve Roller, David Strathairn, Lisa Sloane

SNOW IN THE VIRGIN ISLANDS by Marisha Chamberlain; Director, Richard Dow, with Damien Leake, Theresa Karanik

QUARTET by Peter Dee; Director, John Henry Davis, with Cynthia Neer, Jonathan Bolt, Theresa Karanik, Eddie Jones

LOVE MINUS by Mary Gallagher; Director, Morgan Sloane, with Stephanie Murphy, Brian Keeler, Stephen Schnetzer, Christine Lavren, Roy Sorrells

RED STORM FLOWER by John Patrick Shanley; Director, Susan Gregg, with Cara Duff-MacCormick, Corey Parker, Douglas Jones

JASS by John Pielmeier; Director, Susan Gregg, with Anne Pitoniak, Phyllis Somerville, Irene O'Brien, Mia Dillon, Lamya Derval, Kent Rizley, James Maxwell, Tony Shultz, Eddie Jones, Millege Mosley, Erik Ferguson, Frankie R. Faison

Barbara Beck Photos

**Cara Duff-MacCormick, Corey Parker
in "Red Storm Flower"**

**L. Scott Caldwell, Samuel L. Jackson
in "Home" (Negro Ensemble Co.)**

**Phyllis Somerville, Irene O'Brien, John Pielmeier,
Ann Pitoniak, Tony Shultz, James Maxwell in "Jass"**

NEW YORK SHAKESPEARE FESTIVAL PUBLIC THEATER

Joseph Papp, Producer

General Manager, Robert Kamlot; Company Managers, Roger Gindi, Rheba Flegelman; Assistant to General Manager, Richard Berg; Play Department, Gail Merrifield; Casting, Rosemarie Tichler; Assistants to Producer, Louise Edmonson, Timothy Chandler; Production Manager, Andrew Mihok; Technical Director, Mervyn Haines, Jr.; Prop Master, Joe Toland; Costume Shopmaster, Milo Morrow; Audio Master, Bill Dreisbach; Press, Merle Debuskey, Richard Kornberg, Ed Bullins; Production Supervisor, Jason Steven Cohen

PUBLIC/MARTINSON HALL

Sunday, June 8, - July 13, 1980. (42 performances and 14 previews)

Joseph Papp presents:

F. O. B.
(Fresh Off the Boat)

By David Henry Hwang; Director, Mako; Musical Direction, Lucia Hwong; Scenery, Akira Yoshimura, James E. Mayo; Costumes, Susan Hum; Battle Sequence choreographed by John Lone; Lighting, Victor En Yu Tan; Assistant Director, David Oyama; Wardrobe, Tim Buckley; Props, Jane Hubbard; Production Assistant, Peter Chiang; Stage Managers, Greg Fauss, Ruth Kreshka

CAST

Willy Corpus (Onstage Stage Manager 2), Lucia Hwong (Voice of Radio DJ/Musical Director), Calvin Jung (Dale), John Lone (Steve), Tzi Ma (Onstage Stage Manager 1), Ginny Yang (Grace)

A drama in two acts. The action takes place at the present time in the backroom of a small Chinese restaurant in Torrance, California.

Susan Cook Photo

**Right: John Lone, Ginny Yang, Calvin Jung
(also Top Right)**

PUBLIC/OTHER STAGE

Thursday, September 25, - October 4, 1980. (30 performances) New York Shakespeare Festival (Joseph Papp, Producer) presents:

GIRLS, GIRLS, GIRLS

By Marilyn Suzanne Miller; Director, Bob Balaban; Music and Music Direction, Cheryl Hardwick; Lyrics, Marilyn Suzanne Miller; Choreography, Graciela Daniele; Scenery, Akira Yoshimura; Costumes, Karen Roston; Lighting, Arden Fingerhut; Associate Set Designer, James E. Mayo; Assistant to Director, Janine Dreyer; Wardrobe, Dawn Johnson; Props, Jane Hubbard; Sound, Amy Steindler; Stage Managers, Ruth Kreshka, Dan Moran

CAST

Valri Bromfield (Woman in Jeans), Frances Conroy (Woman in Skirt), Anne DeSalvo (Woman in Jeans), Judith Ivey (Woman in Overalls)

MUSICAL NUMBERS: Opening, The Betty Song, High School, Vicki Lawrence, Punk, Frances' Ballad, Lovers, Credit Card, Divorce, Planet of No Thigh Bulge, Street Lady, Man/Woman, Val's Ballad

A musical performed without intermission.

Susan Cook Photo

**Valri Bromfield, Judith Ivey,
Anne DeSalvo, Frances Conroy**

PUBLIC/NEWMAN THEATER

Tuesday, November 11, - December 14, 1980. (40 performances and 24 previews)
Joseph Papp presents:

THE SEA GULL

By Anton Chekhov; Adapted by Jean-Claude van Itallie; Director, Andrei Serban; Music, Elizabeth Swados; Arranged by the composer and Lee Curreri; Scenery, Michael H. Yeargan; Costumes, Jane Greenwood; Lighting, Jennifer Tipton; Production Supervisor, Jason Steven Cohen; Production Assistant, Page Burkholder; Stage Managers, Richard Jakiel, Susan Green; General Manager, Robert Kamlot; Press, Merle Debuskey, Richard Kornberg, John Howlett, Ed Bullins

CAST

Rosemary Harris (Arkadina), Christopher Walken (Trigorin), F. Murray Abraham (Dorn), Michael Butler (Yakov), Kathryn Dowling (Nina), Michael Egan (Shamraev), George Hall (Sorin), Pamela Payton-Wright (Masha), Richard Russell Ramos (Medvedenko), Brent Spiner (Konstantin Treplev), Joyce Van Patten (Pauline), Janni Brenn (Cook), Gayle Harbor (Maid), Fritz Sperberg (Watchman)

UNDERSTUDIES: Annette Hunt (Arkadina), Michael Butler (Treplev), John Straub (Sorin/Dorn), Gayle Harbor (Nina), Ken Costigan (Shamraev), Janni Brenn (Masha/Pauline), Fritz Sperberg (Trigorin/Medvedenko/Yakov)

A drama in four acts performed with two intermissions. The action takes place on Sorin's country estate.

Martha Swope Photos

George Hall, Kathryn Dowling, Rosemary Harris,
F. Murray Abraham Left: Dowling, Christopher Walken
Top: Rosemary Harris, Christopher Walken

PUBLIC/OTHER STAGE

Tuesday, November 18, 1980 - March 1, 1981. (96 performances)
Joseph Papp presents a Mabou Mines production of:

DEAD END KIDS

A History of Nuclear Power Conceived and Directed by Joanne Akalaitis; Assistant Director, Chas Cowing; Technical Director, B. St. John Schofield; Set, Robert Israel, Joanne Akalaitis; Lighting, Beverly Emmons; Costumes, Sally Rosen; Choreography, Mary Overlie, Gail Conrad, Michael Smith; Film, David Hardy; Music, Philip Glass, Hector Berlioz, Ronnie & The Pomonas, The Four Sargents, Ramsey Lewis; Press, Merle Debuskey, Richard Kornberg, John Howlett

COMPANY

David Brisbin, Scotty Snyder, John Fistow, Michael Kuhling, Greg Mehrten, Terry O'Reilly, Juliet Glass, Zachary Glass, B. St. John Schofield, Chas Cowing, Ellen McElduff, Ruth Maleczech, George Bartenieff, Jerry Mayer

Carol Rosegg Photo

Ellen McElduff, David Brisbin

PUBLIC/ANSPACHER THEATER

Tuesday, December 9, 1980 - January 24, 1981. (45 performances)
Joseph Papp presents:

ALICE IN CONCERT

Music and Lyrics, Elizabeth Swados; Based on Lewis Carroll's "Alice in Wonderland" and "Through the Looking Glass"; Director, Joseph Papp; Choreography, Graciela Daniele; Conductor, Miss Swados; Vocal Arrangements, Carolyn Dutton; Setting, Michael H. Yeargan; Lighting, Arden Fingerhut; Costumes, Theoni V. Aldredge; Production Assistant, Page Burkholder; Stage Managers, Richard Jakiel, Susan Green; Production Supervisor, Jason Steven Cohen

CAST

Meryl Streep (Alice), Betty Aberlin, Stuart Baker-Bergen, Richard Cox, Sheila Dabney, Rodney Hudson, Michael Jeter, Charles Lanyer, Mark Linn-Baker, Kathryn Morath, Amanda Plummer, Deborah Rush, Understudies: Deborah Rush, Kathryn Morath, David Patrick Kelly, Pi Douglass

MUSICAL NUMBERS: What There Is, The Rabbit's Excuse, Down Down Down, Drink Me, Goodby Feet, The Rabbit's House, Bill's Lament, Caterpillar's Advice, Beautiful Soup, Wow Wow Wow, Pretty Piggy, Cheshire Puss, If You Knew Time, No Room No Room, Starting Out Again, White Roses Red, Alphabet, Red Queen, Never Play Croquet, Mock Turtle Lament, Lobster Quadrille, Eating Mushrooms, Child of Pure Unclouded Brow, Jabberwocky, Bird Song, Humpty Dumpty, Tweedledum and Tweedledee, The Walrus and the Carpenter, White Queen, White Knight, An Aged Aged Man, The Examination, The Lion and the Unicorn, Queen Alice, What Is a Letter

A musical in two acts.

Martha Swope Photo

Meryl Streep, Rodney Hudson

Tommy Lee Jones, Peter Boyle

PUBLIC/MARTINSON HALL

Wednesday, December 10, 1980 - January 11, 1981. (52 performances)
Joseph Papp presents:

TRUE WEST

By Sam Shepard; Director, Robert Woodruff; Set, David Gropman; Costumes, William Ivey Long; Lighting, Beverly Emmons; Sound, Amy Steindler; Wardrobe, Russell Duke; Props, Random Gott; Stage Managers, Ruth Kreshka, Jane Hubbard; Press, Merle Debuskey, Richard Kornberg, John Howlett, Ed Bullins; Production Supervisor, Jason Steven Cohen

CAST

Peter Boyle (Lee), Tommy Lee Jones (Austin), Louis Zorich (Saul Kimmer), Georgine Hall (Mom), Understudies: Dan Moran (Austin/Saul), William Andrews (Lee), Regina David (Mom)

A drama in two acts.

Martha Swope Photo

PUBLIC/NEWMAN THEATER

Tuesday, January 20, - February 22, 1981. (40 performances)
Joseph Papp and the Ontological-Hysteric Theatre present:

PENGUIN TOUQUET

Written, Directed and Musically Scored by Richard Foreman; Scenery, Heidi Landesman, Richard Foreman; Costumes, Carol Oditz; Lighting, Pat Collins; Sound, Daniel M. Schreier; Wardrobe, Dawn Johnson; Stage Managers, Michael Chambers, Loretta Robertson; Press, Merle Debuskey, Richard Kornberg, John Howlett; Production Supervisor, Jason Steven Cohen

CAST

Kate Manheim (Agatha), David Warrilow (Psychiatrist), Diane Venora (The Other (Same) Woman), Gretel Cummings (Grand Dame), Brenda Currin (Tourist), Raymond J. Barry (Dangerous Man), Shelly Desai (Waiter in Turban), Eric Loeb (Waiter Who Plays Cymbals), Robert Schlee (Tumbling Waiter), Jeffrey Alan Chandler (Waiter Who Drops Big Tray)

Performed without intermission.

Carol Rosegg Photo

Kate Manheim, David Warrilow

PUBLIC/LuESTHER HALL
Sunday, February 15,-22, 1981. (46 performances)
Joseph Papp presents the Dodger Theater production of:

MARY STUART

By Wolfgang Hildesheimer; English version by Christopher Holmes; Director, Des McAnuff; Scenery, Jim Blayburgh; Costumes, Patricia McGourty; Lighting, Fred Buchholz; Stage Managers, Bill McComb, Wendy Chapin; Production Supervisor, Jason Steven Cohen; Assistant to Director, Betsy Shevey; Dialect Consultant, Elizabeth Smith; Fights, B. H. Barry; Wardrobe, Anita Ellis, Saidah Nelson

CAST

John Bottom (Raoul), Cecile Callan (Anne), Philip Casnoff (John), Roy Cooper (Executioner), Ron Faber (Symmons), Herb Foster (Paulet), George Hall (Kent), George Lloyd (Didier), Stephen Markle (Gervais), Roberta Maxwell (Mary Stuart), Brad O'Hare (Andrew), Wyman Pendleton (Dean), Rebecca Schull (Jane), Donald Vanhorn (Mate), Todd Waring (Guard), Understudies: Rebecca Schull (Mary), Johanna Lesiter (Jane/Anne), Jack R. Marks, Todd Waring

Performed without intermission.

Susan Cook Photo

Roberta Maxwell and company

Joseph Chaikin

PUBLIC/NEWMAN THEATER
Sunday, March 8,-22, 1981. (18 performances)
Joseph Papp presents:

TEXTS

By Samuel Beckett; Adapted by Joseph Chaikin and Steven Kent; Director, Steven Kent; Scenery, Gerald Bloom; Costumes, Mary Brecht; Lighting, Craig Miller; Production Supervisor, Jason Steven Cohen; Stage Manager, Ruth Kreshka; Press, Merle Debuskey, Richard Kornberg, John Howlett; Assistant to Director, Steven Reisner

CAST

Joseph Chaikin

A solo performance without intermission. Adapted from Samuel Beckett's "Texts for Nothing" and "How It Is."

Nathaniel Tileston Photo

PUBLIC/LuESTHER HALL
Saturday, April 4, - June 14, 1981. (72 performances)
Joseph Papp presents:

THE HAGGADAH

By Elizabeth Swados; Adapted and Directed by the composer; Narration Adapted from texts by Elie Wiesel; Scenery, Costumes, Puppetry, Masks, Julie Taymor; Lighting, Arden Fingerhut; Production Supervisor, Jason Steven Cohen; Arrangements and Final Chorale, Carolyn Dutton; Stage Managers, Richard Jakiel, Gretchen Green; Production Assistant, Tony Papp; Press, Merle Debuskey, Richard Kornberg, John Howlett, Ed Bullins

CAST

Richard Allen, Anthony B. Asbury, Shami Chaikin, Craig Chang, Victor Cook, Sheila Dabney, Jossie de Guzman, Michael Edward-Stevens, Onni Johnson, Sally Kate, Esther Levy, Larry Marshall, Steven Memel, Martin Robinson, David Schechter, Peter Schlosser, Zvee Scooler, Ira Siff, Louise Smith, Kerry Stubbs

A Passover Cantata performed without intermission

Martha Swope Photo

"The Haggadah"

PUBLIC/NEWMAN THEATER
Tuesday, April 14,-26, 1981. (12 performances)
Joseph Papp presents The Acting Company (John Houseman, Producing Artistic Director; Michael Kahn, Alan Schneider, Artistic Directors; Margot Harley, Executive Producer) in:

IL CAMPIELLO:
A VENETIAN COMEDY

By Carlo Goldoni; Adapted by Richard Nelson; Director, Liviu Ciulei; Literal Translation, Erica Gastelli; Sets, Radu Boruzescu; Costumes, Miruna Boruzescu; Lighting, Dennis Parichy; Musical Director, Bruce Adolphe; Choreography, Anna Sokolow; Assistant to Director, Christopher J. Markle; Press, Fred Nathan, Eileen McMahon

CAST

Pamela Myberg (Gasparina), Michele-Denise Woods (Donna Katherine Panchiana), Lori Putnam (Lucietta), Lynn Chausow (Donna Pasqua Polegana), Johann Carlo (Gnese), Laura Smyth (Orsola), Brian Reddy (Zorzetto), Robert Lovitz (Anzoletto), Richard Howard (The Count), Casey Biggs (Fabrizio), Jeffrey M. Rubin (Sansuga), Paul Walker (Urchin), Townspeople: Becky Borczon, Kevin McGuire, Richard S. Iglewski, Alan Silver

A comedy in two acts. The action takes place in Venice in 1756.

WAITING FOR GODOT

By Samuel Beckett; Director, Alan Schneider; Set, Radu Boruzescu; Costumes, Miruna Boruzescu; Lighting, Dennis Parichy; Assistant to Director, Randolph Foerster

CAST

Richard S. Iglewski (Estragon), Richard Howard (Vladimir), Paul Walker (Lucky), Keith David (Pozzo), Johann Carlo (Boy)

A comedy in two acts.

A MIDSUMMER NIGHT'S DREAM

By William Shakespeare; Director, David Chambers; Sets, Heidi Landesman; Lighting, Dennis Parichy; Costumes, Carol Oditz; Assistant to Director, Christopher J. Markle; Music Composed and Directed by Ken Guilmartin; Electronic Music Design, Pril Smiley; Movement, Kathryn Posin

CAST

Lynn Chausow (Hermia), Casey Biggs (Lysander), Robert Lovitz (Demetrius), Pamela Nyberg (Helena), Alan Silver (Peter Quince), Brian Reddy (Snug), Richard S. Iglewski (Nick Bottom), Paul Walker (Francis Flute), Jeffrey M. Rubin (Egeus/Tom Snout), Richard Howard (Philostrate/Puck), Kevin McGuire (Robin Starveling), Keith David (Theseus/Oberon), Michelle-Denise Woods (Hippolyta/Titania), Lori Putnam (Cobweb), Johann Carlo (1st Fairy/Peaseblossom), Becky Borczon (Mustardseed)

Martha Swope Photos

Top Right: "Il Campiello"
Below: "Waiting for Godot"
Bottom: "A Midsummer Night's Dream"

NO SMOKING PLAYHOUSE

June 6, 1980–May 24, 1981

Artistic Director, Norman Thomas Marshall; Associate Directors, George Wolf Reily, John Von Hartz; Press, Anne Einhorn, Adam Redfield

June 6–29, 1980

TWELFTH NIGHT by William Shakespeare; Director, George Wolf Reily; Costumes, Rita Robbins; Set, Llewellyn Harrison; Music, Steve Cohen; Lighting, Ron Katz; Assistant Director, Christin Cockerton; Stage Manager, Brad Ruekberg; Props, Lauren Lumley; Technical Director, R. J. Robbins. CAST: Maggie Miller (Olivia), Chet Carlin (Malvolio), Christine Cockerton (Gentlewoman), Lauren Lumley (Gentlewoman), Bert Kruse (Antonio), Scott Ference (Sebastian), Sanford Rockwerk (Fabian), D. A. G. Burgos (Troubadour), Rob Pherson (Rosino), Neil Wycoff (Valentine), Mark Krone (Curio), Bill Brooks (Lord), Eden Lee Murray (Viola), Tim McLaughlin (Captain), Malcolm Gray (Sir Toby), Joan B. Waters (Maria), Raleigh Miller (Sir Andrew), Adam Redfield (Feste)

July 17–August 24, 1980

ENTER MIDSUMMER WITH A FLOURISH: A festival of One-Act Plays; Sets, Nicholas Vizzini; Lighting, Linda Thurmond; Sound, George Jacobs; Stage Managers, Sheila Mathews, Michael Craig, Louis Scarborough, Lefty Olivier. CAST: Alan Bruun, Mary Connoly, Joe Correa, Gary Cox, Frank Girardeau, Malcolm Gray, Allen Lane, Tom Leo, Lauren Lumley, Norman Thomas Marshall, Jill Meadow, Eve Meckler, Eden Lee Murray, Annie O'Sullivan, George Wolf Reily, Susan Shanline, Jyll Stein, Patrick Sullivan, Sturgis Warner, J. B. Waters. PLAYS: *Kitchen Interlude* by Charles Pulaski, directed by Norman Thomas Marshall; *Cracked Canines* by Lucas Myers, directed by Norman Thomas Marshall; *Middle Man Out* by Dick Riley, directed by Granville Burgess; *The Shepherd's Tale* by Joseph Matthewson, directed by Fay Bright; *Remission* by Richard Dremer, directed by Joe Correa; *It Would End in Divorce* by Charles Pulaski, directed by Eden Lee Murray; *Dreams of Dirty Wisdom* by William Schimmell, directed by Norman Thomas Marshall; *Timberlines* by Jeanine O'Reilly, directed by George Wolf Reily; *I Talk to Myself* by William Redfield, directed by Adam Redfield; *The Telephone Call* by Dick Parker; *The Disciple* by Robert Sommerfeld, directed by George Allison Elmer; *Wrong Number* by Tony Giordano, directed by Paul Davis; *Louise* by Walter Corwin, directed by Ken Buckshi; *Sweet Cowslip's Grace* by George Hammer, directed by David Fitelson; *Did You Go to PS 43?* by Michael Schulman, directed by Nina Giovannitti.

January 15–February 8, 1981

DANGEROUS CORNER by J. B. Priestley; Director, Marvin Einhorn; Set, William Rothfuss; Lighting, Nicholas Vizzini; Costumes, Van Ramsey; Stage Manager, Julie Garfinkel. CAST: Susan Willis (Maud), Maggie Miller (Olwen), Alan Bluestone (Robert), Marina Posvar (Freda), Jim McConnell (Gordon), Carrick Glenn (Betty), George Wolf Reily (Charles)

March 21–April 12, 1981

HAMLET by William Shakespeare; Director, George Wolf Reily; Set, Nicholas Vizzini; Lighting, George Allison Elmer; Costumes, Van Ramsey; Music, Steve Cohen; Stage Manager, Sheila Mathews. CAST: Ted Bardy (Lucianus), Alan Bluestone (Osric), Douglas Capozzalo (Francisco), Chet Carlin (Claudius), Malcolm Gray (Polonius), Marvin Einhorn (Ghost), Bert Kruse (Laertes), Marc Krone (Rosencrantz), Richard Litt (Bernardo), Eden Lee Murray (Ophelia), Marina Posvar (Gertrude), Adam Redfield (Hamlet), Ted Reinert (Guildenstern), Sylvester Rich (Horatio), Lorraine Thompson (Understudy), Neil Wycoff (Priest)

April 30–May 24, 1981

SWEET/SOUR by Sebastian Stuart; Director, Norman Thomas Marshall; Set, R. Patrick Sullivan; Costumes, Van Ramsey; Lighting, Leslie Ann Kilian; Technical Director, Nicholas Vizzini; Stage Manager, Phillip Davis. CAST: Richard Spore (Charles), Marc Krone (Jeffrey), Reggie Robinson (Ezzard), Tom Matsusaka (Chu), Ruthie Rosenfeld (Bag Lady), Natalie Ross (Ann), Marina Posvar (Betty), Carrick Glenn (Claire), Fran Carlon (Paula)

Marvin Einhorn Photos

Top Right: Maggie Miller, Chet Carlin in "Twelfth Night" Below: Adam Redfield as Hamlet

Marina Posvar, George Wolf Reily in "Dangerous Corner"

137

OPEN SPACE THEATRE EXPERIMENT

Artistic Director, Lynn Michaels; Administrative Director, Harry A. Baum; Technical Director, Rick Shannin; Sound, David Nunemaker; Press, Bruce Cohen

June 5–28, 1980 (19 performances)
THE SANCTUARY LAMP *(American Premiere)* by Thomas Murphy; Directed by Mr. Murphy; Set, Gregory William Bolton; Lighting, Carol B. Sealey; Costumes, Ealine R. Mason; Stage Manager, Elizabeth Rothberg. CAST: Hazen Gifford (Harry), Mary Garripoli (Maudie), Peter Rogan (Francisco), Wally Peterson (Monsignor), Sue Sheehy (Old Woman)

October 16–November 9, 1980 (16 performances)
THE TOOTH OF CRIME by Sam Shepard; Director, Lawrence Sacharow; Music, Ric Cherwin; Sets, Geoffrey P. Hall; Lights, Nat Cohen; Costumes, Geoffrey; Choreography, Jay Norman; Stage Manager, Lisa di Franza. CAST: Eivind Harum (Hoss), Deirdre O'Connell (Becky-Lou), Davidson Lloyd (Star-Man), John Nesei (Galactic Jack), Mary Tepper (Cheyenne), Moishe Rosenfeld (Doc), Elena Nicholas (Referee), Christopher McCann (Crow)

February 19–March 22, 1981 (20 performances)
A DREAM PLAY by August Strindberg; Translated by Elizabeth Sprigge; Director, Susan Einhorn; Set, Ursula Belden; Lighting, Victor En Yu Tan; Costumes, Linda Vigdor; Composer, Skip LaPlante; Dramaturg/Adapter, Elinor Fuchs; Stage Manager, Bill Kavanagh. CAST: Susan Stevens (Agnes), Michael Arkin (Glazer), Charles Shaw-Robinson (Officer), Diane Tarleton (Kristin), Paul Peeling (Father), Bonnie Brewster (Lina), Martin Treat (Lawyer), Bruce Somerville (Poet)

April 9–May 3, 1981 (16 performances)
WHERE HAVE ALL THE DREAMERS GONE? *(American Premiere)* by Melba Thomas; Director, Don Price; Set, Barry Axtell; Lights, Susan A. White; Costumes, Mary Whitehead; Stage Managers, Leonie Fletcher, Brian Chavanne. CAST: Marilyn Berry (Richard's Mother), Hugh Byrnes (Harry), Ernesto Gonzalez (Don Juan), Ron Johnston (Freud), Merle Louise (Mira), Fred Morsell (Richard), Natalie Priest (Mira's Mother), Grace Roberts (Phyllis), Robin Thomas (Charles Boyer), Yvonne Warden (God)

May 14–June 14, 1981 (20 performances)
A COLLIER'S FRIDAY NIGHT by D. H. Lawrence *(American Premiere)*; Director, John Beary; Set, Jack Chandler; Lighting, Tom Hennes; Costumes, Carol H. Beule; Backdrops, Sarah Oliphant; Music, Daniel Werts; Stage Managers, Andrew King, Kathy Jennings. CAST: Robin Howard (Mrs. Lambert), Susan Stevens (Nellie), Cecile Callan (Gertie), Tom Brennan (Lambert), Stephen Eldredge (Ernest), Ron Keith (Barker), Martin Treat (Carlin), Ryn Hodes (Maggie), Maura Ellyn (Beatrice)

Carol Rosegg Photos

Top Right: Eivind Harum, John Nesci
in "The Tooth of the Crime"
Below: Tom Brennan, Robin Howard
in "A Collier's Friday Night"

Hazen Gifford, Mary Garripoli
in "The Sanctuary Lamp"

Fred Morsell, Merle Louise
in "Where Have All the Dreamers Gone?"

PHOENIX THEATRE

T. Edward Hambleton, Managing Director
Steven Robman, Artistic Director
Twenty-eighth Season
General Manager, Lynne M. Kemen; Casting Director, Bonnie G. Timmermann; Literary Manager, Anne Cattaneo; Development, Eleanor Eastman, Sheryl Eisenberg, J. Martha Sturgeon, Beverly Pelzner; Administrative Assistant, Eric A. Segal; Press, Susan L. Schulman

MARYMOUNT MANHATTAN THEATRE
Monday, October 13, - November 2, 1980. (24 performances and 6 previews)
The Phoenix Theatre presents:

BONJOUR, LA, BONJOUR

By Michel Tremblay; Translated by John Van Burek, Bill Glassco; Director, Steven Robman; Scenery, Marjorie Kellogg; Costumes, Jennifer von Mayrhauser; Lighting, Ronald M. Bundt; Production Manager, Donna Lieberman; Wardrobe, Sheila A. Andersen; Stage Managers, J. Thomas Vivian, Kathleen Marsters

CAST

Veronica Castang (Lucienne), Judith Drake (Denise), Cara Duff-MacCormick (Monique), Mary Fogarty (Charlotte), William Katt (Serge), Beverly May (Albertine), Fred Stuthman (Gabriel), Dianne Wiest (Nicole)

A drama without intermission. The action takes place in Montreal, Canada.

Martha Swope Photos

William Katt, Cara Duff-MacCormick
Top: William Katt, Beverly May, Mary
Fogarty, Fred Stuthman, Dianne Wiest

Sigourney Weaver, Jim Borrelli, Kate
McGregor-Stewart, Stephen Collins
Above: Collins, Weaver

MARYMOUNT MANHATTAN THEATRE
Thursday, January 1,-25, 1981. (24 performances and 6 previews)

BEYOND THERAPY

By Christopher Durang; Director, Jerry Zaks; Set, Karen Schultz; Costumes, Jennifer von Mayrhauser; Lighting, Richard Nelson; Sound, David Rapkin; Production Manager, Donna Lieberman; Assistant to Director, Patricia Swartz; Wardrobe, Barbara Perkins; Props, Nina Sheffy; Stage Manager, Mary Michele Miner; Press, Susan L. Schulman, Sandi Kimmel

CAST

Jim Borrelli (Dr. Stuart Framingham), Stephen Collins (Bruce), Jack Gilpin (Bob), Conan McCarty (Andrew), Kate McGregor-Stewart (Mrs. Charlotte Wallace), Nick Stannard (Paul Rennard), Sigourney Weaver (Prudence)

A comedy in 2 acts and 10 scenes. The action takes place at the present time.

Martha Swope Photo

MARYMOUNT MANHATTAN THEATRE
Monday, February 2,-15, 1981. (16 performances and 5 previews)
The Phoenix Theatre presents:

THE CAPTIVITY OF PIXIE SHEDMAN

By Romulus Linney; Director, John Pasquin; Set, Robert Blackman; Costumes, Linda Fisher; Lighting, Jennifer Tipton; Sound, David Rapkin; Dialect Consultant, Timothy Monich; Production Manager, Donna Lieberman; Wardrobe, Terilyn Brown; Production Assistants, Stacy Fleisher, Kathleen Mellor; Stage Managers, J. Thomas Vivian, Kathleen Marsters; Press, Susan L. Schulman, Sandi Kimmel

CAST

William Carden (Bertram Shedman), Penelope Allen (Pixie Shedman), Ron Randell (Col. Bertram Shedman), Jon DeVries (Doc Bertram Shedman), Leon Russom (Doc Bertram Shedman, Jr.), Sarah Navin (Sandy Shedman)

A drama in two acts. The action takes place in a studio on the top floor of an old apartment hotel in New York City.

Martha Swope Photo

Top Right: William Carden, Penelope Allen, Sarah Navin Below: Penelope Allen, Jon DeVries

Michele Shay, Carl Lumbly

MARYMOUNT MANHATTAN THEATRE
Monday, March 30, - April 19, 1981. (24 performances and 5 previews)
The Phoenix Theatre presents:

MEETINGS

By Mustapha Matura; Director, Gerald Gutierrez; Scenery, John Kasarda; Costumes, Karen Miller; Lighting, Spencer Mosse; Sound, David Rapkin; Dialect Consultant, Beverly Wideman; Production Manager, Donna Lieberman; Production Assistant, Stacey Fleischer; General Manager, Lynne M. Kemen; Stage Managers, J. Thomas Vivian, Kathleen Marsters; Press, Susan L. Schulman, Sandi Kimmel

CAST

Carl Lumbly (Hugh), Michele Shay (Jean), Seret Scott (Elsa)

A drama in two acts. The action takes place at the present time in the home of Carl and Jean in a suburb of Port of Spain, capital of Trinidad, West Indies.

Martha Swope Photo

MARYMOUNT MANHATTAN THEATRE

Thursday, May 28, - June 28, 1981. (37 performances)
The Phoenix Theatre presents:

ISN'T IT ROMANTIC

By Wendy Wasserstein; Director, Steven Robman; Scenery, Marjorie Bradley Kellogg; Costumes, Jennifer von Mayrhauser; Lighting, Spencer Mosse; Sound, David Rapkin; Movement Consultant, Nora Peterson; Production Manager, Donna Lieberman; Stage Managers, J. Thomas Vivian, Kathleen Marsters; Press, Susan L. Schulman, Sandi Kimmel

CAST

Barbara Baxley (Lillian Cornwall), Alma Cuervo (Janie Blumberg), Bob Gunton (Paul Stuart), Jane Hoffman (Tasha Blumberg), Laurie Kennedy (Harriet Cornwall), Fritz Kupfer (Vladimir/Salvatore), Bernie Passeltiner (Simon Blumberg), Peter Riegert (Marty Sterling)

A comedy in two acts. The action takes place at the present time.

Martha Swope Photo

Bob Gunton, Laurie Kennedy, Peter Riegert, Alma Cuervo in "Isn't It Romantic?"

THE PRODUCTION COMPANY

Artistic Director, Norman Rene; Managing Director, Caren Harder; Production Manager, David L. Nathans; Sets, Jane Thurn; Lighting, Debra J. Kletter; Wardrobe, Eileen Nober; Stage Manager, David L. Nathans; Press, Judy Jacksina, Glenna Freedman, Dolph Browning, Angela Wilson

Wednesday, January 14–February 8, 1981
TIED BY THE LEG by Georges Feydeau *(American Premiere)*; Translated, Adapted and Directed by Ted Bank; Set, Jane Thurn; Costumes, John Carver Sullivan; Lighting, Gregory C. MacPherson. CAST: Deborah Allison (Viviane), Walter Atamaniuk (General), Diane Heles (Firmine), Diane Kamp (Lucette), Stephen D. Keener (de Chenneviette), Lilene Mansell (Marcelline), Rica Martens (Mme. Duverger), Anderson Matthews (Bouzin), Michael Pace (de Fontanet), Frank Tully (Priest), Jake Turner (Bois-D'Enghien)

Sardi Klein Photo

Friday, March 13–April 5, 1981
SCENES AND REVELATIONS by Elan Garonzik; Director, Sheldon Epps; Set, Jane Thurn; Costumes, Jeanette Oleksa; Lighting, William Armstrong. CAST: Sofia Landon, Marilyn McIntyre, Caitlin O'Heaney, Valerie Mahaffey, Stephen Burleigh, Richard Merrell, Nicholas Saunders

Jeff Crespi Photo

Saturday, May 16–June 7, 1981 (25 performances and 3 previews)
MISSING PERSONS by Craig Lucas; Director, Norman Rene; Set, John Falabella; Costumes, Oleksa; Lighting, Debra Kletter; Incidental Music, E. Martin Perry; Production Manager, David Nathans; Stage Manager, Trey Hunt. CAST: Richard Backus (Hat), Helen Harrelson (Addie), Christopher Marcantel (Steve), Antonia Rey (Gemma), Margo Skinner (Joan), Ryan Sperry (Young Hat), Daniel Von Bargen (Tucker). A play in two acts. The action takes place during October of 1978 in Northeastern Pennsylvania.

Richard Backus, Margo Skinner in "Missing Persons" Above: Jake Turner, Diane Kamp in "Tied by the Leg"

PLAYWRIGHTS HORIZONS

Tenth Season

Producing Director, Robert Moss; Managing Director, Robin J. Gold; Artistic Director, Andre Bishop; Production Supervisor, Dorothy J. Maffei; Business Manager, Eric Overmyer; Playwrights-in-Residence, Richard Lees, Ron Whyte; Technical Director, Bill Camp; Costumer, Pat Paine; Props, Laura Heller; Press, Bob Ullman

STUDIO THEATRE

Tuesday, June 3–28, 1980 (20 performances)
FABLES FOR FRIENDS by Mark O'Donnell; Director, Douglas Hughes; Set, Joe Mibilia; Costumes, Steven Birnbaum; Lighting, Frederick Buchholz; Composer/Pianist, Peter Homans. CAST: Mia Dillon, Anthony Heald, Robert Joy, Ann McDonough, Patricia Richardson, Jay O. Sanders

MAINSTAGE THEATRE

Saturday, November 22, 1980–April 12, 1981 (176 performances)

COMING ATTRACTIONS

By Ted Tally; Director, Andre Ernotte; Music, Jack Feldman; Lyrics, Bruce Sussman, Jack Feldman; Scenery, Andrew Jackness; Costumes, Ann Emonts; Lighting, Paul Gallo; Sound, Alex McIntyre; Orchestrations, Arnold Gross; Production Consultant, Bonnie G. Timmermann; Musical Staging, Theodore Pappas; Stage Managers, Fredric H. Orner, Dan Strickler, Judith Ann Chew.

CAST

Christine Baranski (Miss America) succeeded by Carolyn Casanave, Larry Block (Manny Alter), Griffin Dunn (Lonnie Wayne Burke) succeeded by Michael McCormick, June Gable (Teri Sterling), Jonathan Hadary (Sammy Dazzle), Dan Strickler (Publisher), Allan Wasserman (Biff Braddock), Understudies: Randy Graff, John Lefkowitz

Performed without intermission.

Thursday, February 19–March 7, 1981 (15 performances)
SUMMER FRIENDS by Mel Marvin, Stephanie Cotsirilos; Production Consultants, Gerald Gutierrez, Dorothy J. Maffei; Lighting, David N. Weiss. CAST: Stephanie Cotsirilos
Wednesday, April 1–May 16, 1981 (42 performances)
Moved to Mainstage May 20, 1981
MARCH OF THE FALSETTOS by William Finn; Director, James Lapine; Set, Douglas Stein; Lighting, Frances Aronson; Costumes, Maureen Connor; Musical Director, Michael Starobin; Production Manager, William M. Camp; Technical Director, Bob Bertrand; Stage Managers, Johnna Murray, Steve Rockwell

CAST

Stephen Bogardus (Whizzer), Alison Fraser (Trina), James Kushner (Jason), Michael Rupert (Marvin), Chip Zien (Mendel)

A musical performed without intermission. The action takes place at the present time.

Susan Cook Photo

Top Right: Christine Baranski, Griffin Dunne in "Coming Attractions" Below: Michael Rupert, Alison Fraser, James Kushner, Chip Zien, Stephen Bogardus in "March of the Falsettos"

QUEENS THEATRE-IN-THE-PARK

Saturday, November 8–30, 1980 (23 performances)

SHE LOVES ME by Joe Masteroff, Jerry Bock, Sheldon Harnick; Director, Gerald Gutierrez; Set, David Potts; Costumes, Karen Miller; Lighting, David Elliot; Musical Staging, Theodore Pappas. CAST: Walter Bobbie, Sophie Schwab, Mary Barber, John Corenswet, Gwyllum Evans, Clay James, Don Kehr, Leslie Michelle Laurer, Andrea Martin, Suzanne M. Murphy, Scott Robertson, Susan Rosenstock, Richard Ryder, Alan Schack, Mimi Sherwin, Roy K. Stevens

Saturday, December 6–28, 1980 (23 performances)

THE GENTLE PEOPLE by Irwin Shaw; Director, Robert Moss; Set, John Kasarda; Lighting, David Segal; Costumes, Nan Cibula. CAST: Edward O'Neill, Nana Tucker, Lee Wallace, James Carruther, Marilyn Chris, Richard Frank, Mitchell Jason, Lola Pashalinski, Paul Stolarsky, Robert Wayne

Saturday, April 11,–May 3, 1981 (22 performances)

HEAT OF RE-ENTRY by Abraham Tetenbaum; Director, Lev Shekhtman; Set, Joseph A. Varga; Costumes, Karen Miller; Lighting, Annie Wrightson; Original Music, Norman L. Berman. CAST: Ellen Gould, Richard Grusin, Charlotte Jones, Keith McDermott

Saturday, May 9–31, 1981 (23 performances)

SLEUTH by Anthony Shaffer; Director, Robert Moss; Set, William M. Camp; Costumes, Patricia Paine; Lighting, David N. Weiss; Original Music, Michael Lee Stockler. CAST: James Cahill, Charles Shaw-Robinson

Susan Cook Photos

Walter Bobbie, Mary Barber in "She Loves Me"

QUAIGH THEATRE

Artistic Director, Will Lieberson; Managing Director, Dey Gosse; Assistant to Mr. Lieberson, Isabella Schwartz; Administrative Consultant, Susanne Braham; Production Coordinators, Richard Young, Paul Griffin; Artistic Consultants, Albert Brower, David Simon; Press, Max Eisen, Maria Soma, Francine L. Trevens.

Monday, October 17–November 15, 1980 (17 performances)
DULCY by Marc Connelly; Director, Clinton Atkinson; Set, Ken Molamon; Lighting, John Hickey; Stage Manager, Bo Metzler; Props, Stephanie Broos. CAST: Ben Lemon (Parker), Dennis Helfend (Henry), Michael Waldron (Gordon),Harry Bennett (Tom), Kathy Morath (Dulcy), George Cavey (Schuyler), James Harder (Forbes), K. T. Bauman (Mrs. Forbes), Annie Laurita (Amelia), David Dannenbaum (Vincent), William Sevedge, Jr. (Blair)

Saturday, November 27–December 29, 1980 (20 performances)
THE BUTTERFINGERS ANGEL, MARY AND JOSEPH, HEROD THE NUT AND THE SLAUGHTER OF TWELVE HIT CAROLS IN A PEAR TREE by William Gibson; Director, Francine L. Trevens; Assistant, James R. Smith; Set, Bob Phillips; Costumes, Johnetta Lever; Musical Director, Nathan Hurwitz; Choreography, Frank Hatchett; Lighting, Marie Barrett; Stage Manager, Pamela Edington. CAST: J. Scott William (Butterfinger Angel), Paul Haggard (Joseph), April Kelly (Child), Melissa Thea (Donkey), Karen Liswood (Tree), Dori Salois (Mary), Cleve Roller (1st Woman), Justine Buck (Sheep), Kim Plumridge (Girl), Shamus Murphy (Herod), Stephen Berenson (1st King), Michael Leslie (3rd King), Brian Kosnik (2nd King), Waltrudis Mathes (Choir)

Sunday, December 14–28, 1980 (10 performances)
THE RETURN OF P. T. BARNUM by Kricker James; Director, Ernest McCarty; Assistant Director/Stage Manager, Lys Hopper; Lights, Melissa Thea; Costumes, Diane Margaret Lent; Sound, George Jacobs. CAST: Kricker James (Barnum)

Wednesday, March 11–April 15, 1981 (20 performances)
DARKNESS AT NOON by Sidney Kingsley; Director, Will Lieberson; Set, Stephen Caldwell; Lights, E. St. John Villard; Costumes, Elizabeth Lynch; Stage Managers, Lysbeth Hopper, Katherine Cuba; Sound, Frank J. Palazzi, George Jacobs. CAST: Thom Coon (Guard), Mark O'Banks (Guard), Frank Biancamano (Rubashov), John Dorish (Illich), Brian Strickland (Guard), Frank Dwyer (402), Carl Trone (302), Kricker James (202), Susan Monts (Luba), Patrick Egan (Gletkin), Brian Strickland (Trooper), Gisli Jonsson (Richard), Katherine Cuba (Nazi Girl), Leslie Goldstein (Ivanoff), Paul Hart (Bogriv), Richard Dahlia (Hritsch), Terence Cartwright (Albert), Vincent Hank (Luigi), Karl Perry (Pablo), Angus MacDonald (Andre), Mary Beth Pape (Secretary), Lysbeth Hopper (Secretary)

Monday, April 10–May 3, 1981 (20 performances)
A NICKEL FOR PICASSO by Elliott Caplin; Director, Gary Bowen; Set, John Dollinger; Costumes, Elizabeth Lynch; Lights, Jeffrey McRoberts; Stage Manager, Lawrence Berrick. CAST: Neil Bernstein (Mark), Suzanne Toren (Martha), John Michalski (Philip), Albie Polinsky (Mark at 7), Steven Gelborn (Uncle Eddie), Mary Ellen Murphy (Aunt Esther), Elaine Grollman (Mrs. Warsaw), Rea Rosno (Pat)

John Dorish, Susan Monts in "Darkness at Noon" Top: James Harder, Kathy Morath, Michael Waldron in "Dulcy"

RICHARD MORSE MIME THEATRE

Friday, October 3–December 21, 1980
OFF CENTER directed by Rasa Allan, with Patty Ashley, Philip Burton, Barbara Knight, David McGee, Richard Morse

Friday, October 31–December 20, 1980
MIDNIGHT MIME conceived and directed by Anastasia Nicole and Gabriel Barre, with Kenneth Michels, Richard Morse, Anastasia Nicole, Michael Shaffer

Saturday, November 29, 1980
NOVEMBER 29, 1980 with Rasa Allan, Patty Ashley, Gabriel Barre, Philip Burton, Barbara Knight, David McGee, Kenneth Michels, Richard Morse, Anastasia Nicole

Wednesday, December 24, 1980–January 4, 1981
THE BLUEBIRD by Anastasia Nicole, with Roberto Badillo, Julie Bolt, Tom Candela, Kenneth Michels, Richard Morse, Anastasia Nicole, Christine Smeysters

Saturday, September 13, 1980–January 1, 1981
CARRIED AWAY by Anastasia Nicole, directed by Rasa Allan, with Tom Candela, Barbara Knight, Mark Keeler, Kenneth Michels, Anastasia Nicole, Shepard Sobel

Wednesday, December 24, 1980–January 18, 1981
WHOOOSH conceived and directed by Rasa Allan, with Patty Ashley, Barbara Knight, David McGee, Kenneth Michels

Friday, February 6–April 12, 1981
MAN IN MOTION a one-man show conceived, directed and performed by Richard Morse.

Richard Morse Mime Company

ROUNDABOUT THEATRE

Gene Feist, Michael Fried, Producing Directors
Fifteenth Season

Business Manager, Patricia A. Yost; Audience Development, Gary A. Kamprath; Administrative Assistant, Amelia Mercurio; Production Manager, Philip Giller; Sound, Philip Campanella; Production Assistants, D.C.A. Associates, Jim Robertson, T. J. Turgeon, Victoria Grecki, Claudia Brown; Press, Susan Bloch Associates, Adrian Bryan-Brown

ROUNDABOUT STAGE ONE
Friday, June 6, - October 26, 1980. (148 performances)
Roundabout Theatre Presents:

LOOK BACK IN ANGER

By John Osborne; Director, Ted Craig; Set, Roger Mooney; Lighting, Dennis Parichy; Costumes, A. Christina Giannini; Musical Supervision, Philip Campanella; Stage Manager, Martha R. Jacobs; Press, Susan Bloch, Adrian Bryan-Brown

CAST

Malcolm McDowell (Jimmy Porter), Lisa Banes (Alison Porter), Robert Burr (Colonel Redfern), Fran Brill (Helena Charles), Raymond Hardie, (Cliff Lewis), Understudy: Jeff Abbott

A drama in three acts and five scenes. The action takes place at the present time in the Porters one-room flat in a large town in the Midlands, England.

Martha Swope Photo

Right: Lisa Banes, Malcolm McDowell
Top: Fran Brill, Malcolm McDowell,
Raymond Hardie, Lisa Banes

Ralph Clanton, David Haller, Remak Ramsay

Tuesday, September 16, 1980 - January 25, 1981 (152 performances) *

THE WINSLOW BOY

By Terence Rattigan; Director, Douglas Seale; Set, Roger Mooney; Costumes, A. Christina Giannini; Lighting, Norman Coates; Sound, Philip Campanella; Assistant to Director, Mitzi Metzl-Pazer; Stage Manager, Michael S. Mantel

CAST

Remak Ramsay (Sir Robert Morton), Ralph Clanton (Arthur Winslow), Barbara Colton (Violet), David Haller (Ronnie Winslow), James Higgins (Desmond Curry), Elizabeth Owens (Grace Wilson), Giulia Pagano (Catherine Winslow), Lee Toombs (Dickie Winslow), Michael Tylo (John Watherstone)

A drama in 2 acts and 4 scenes. The action takes place in the drawing-room of a house in Kensington, and extends over two years of a period preceding the war of 1914-1918.

* After closing, company went on tour.

Martha Swope Photo

Left Center: (standing) James Higgins, Elizabeth Owens, Remak Ramsay, Lee Toombs, Michael Tylo, Ann McMillan, (seated) David Haller, Ralph Clanton, Giulia Pagano

ROUNDABOUT STAGE ONE
    Tuesday, October 14–26, 1980 (16 performances)
STREETSONGS by and with Geraldine Fitzgerald; Director, Richard Maltby, Jr.; Musical Direction, Stanley Wietrzychowski; Arrangements, Stanley Wietrzychowski, Philip Campanella; Vocal Direction, Andy Thomas Anselmo; Lighting, Robert F. Strohmeier; Costumes, Bill Walker; Stage Manager, M. R. Jacobs

ROUNDABOUT STAGE ONE
    Tuesday, October 28–November 23, 1980 (32 performances)
HERE ARE LADIES performed by Siobhan McKenna portraying the women of Joyce, Shaw, O'Casey, Yeats, Synge and Stephens; Lighting, Norman Coates; Production Associate, Claire Cahill; Stage Manager, M. R. Jacobs

Geraldine Fitzgerald

Siobhan McKenna
Left: Ronald Drake, Philip Bosco, Paul Sparer,
Arlene Francis in "Don Juan in Hell"

ROUNDABOUT STAGE ONE
    Tuesday, November 25, 1980 - January 28, 1981. (76 performances)

DON JUAN IN HELL

By George Bernard Shaw; Director, George Keathley; Set, Roger Mooney; Lighting, Robert F. Strohmeier; Costumes, A. Christina Giannini; Musical Supervision, Philip Campanella; Stage Manager, M. R. Jacobs; Press, Susan Bloch, Adrian Bryan-Brown, Ellen Zeisler

CAST

Arlene Francis (Dona Ana), Paul Sparer (Don Juan), Ronald Drake (The Commandant), Philip Bosco (The Devil)

Performed with one intermission.

Martha Swope Photo

**Philip Bosco, Arlene Francis,
Ronald Drake, Paul Sparer**

ROUNDABOUT STAGE TWO
Tuesday, January 27–February 22, 1981 (32 performances)
FACES OF LOVE performed by Carol Teitel; Set, Roger Mooney;
Costume, Jane Greenwood; Lighting, Pat Kelly; Sound, Philip Campanella; Stage Manager, T. J. Turgeon

Right: Carol Teitel

Nicol Williamson, Andrea Weber

ROUNDABOUT STAGE ONE
Tuesday, February 3, - April 5, 1981. (73 performances)

INADMISSIBLE EVIDENCE

By John Osborne; Director, Anthony Page; Set, Roger Mooney;
Costumes, Mimi Maxmen; Lighting, Arden Fingerhut; Sound, Philip Campanella; Stage Managers, Martha R. Jacobs, Morton Milder;
Press, Susan Bloch, Adrian Bryan-Brown

CAST

Nicol Williamson (Bill Maitland), Philip Bosco (Hudson), Elaine
Bromka (Shirley), Barbara Caruso (Mrs. Garnsey), Christine Estabrook (Joy), Anthony Heald (Jones), Jeanne Ruskin (Liz), Andrea
Weber (Jane Maitland)

A drama in two acts. The action takes place during the early
1960's in Bill Maitland's legal office in London, England.

Martha Swope Photos

Nicol Williamson, Christine Estabrook
Above: Philip Bosco, Williamson

ROUNDABOUT STAGE TWO

Tuesday, March 3, - June 14, 1981. (119 performances)
Re-opened Friday, June 19, 1981 at the Century Theatre.

A TASTE OF HONEY

By Shelagh Delaney; Director, Tony Tanner; Set, Roger Mooney;
Costumes, A. Christina Giannini; Lighting, Robert W. Mogel;
Sound, Philip Campanella; Assistant to Director, Mitzi Metzl-
Pazer; Press, Susan Bloch, Adrian Bryan-Brown

CAST

Valerie French (Helen), Amanda Plummer (Jo), John Carroll (Peter), Tom Wright (The Boy), Keith Reddin (Geoffery)

A play in two acts. The action takes place in Salford, Lancashire,
England.

Donna Svennevik Photo

**Right: John Carroll, Valerie French, Amanda
Plummer, Tom Wright, Keith Reddin Below:
Amanda Plummer, Valerie French**

ROUNDABOUT STAGE ONE

Tuesday, April 14, - June 14, 1981. (51 performances and 24
previews)

HEDDA GABLER

By Henrik Ibsen; Adapted by Christopher Hampton; Director, Mi-
chael Kahn; Set, Lawrence King, Michael Yeargan; Costumes, Jane
Greenwood; Lighting, Dennis Parichy; Sound, Eric Rissler Thayer;
Wigs and Hairstyles, Paul Huntley; Stage Managers, M. R. Jacobs,
Morton Milder; Press, Susan Bloch, Adrian Bryan-Brown

CAST

Katherine Squire (Aunt Julia), Barbara Lester (Berte), Harris Yulin
(George Tesman) succeeded by Theodore Sorel, Susannah York
(Hedda Gabler) succeeded by Jeanne Ruskin, Roxanne Hart (Mrs.
Elvsted), Philip Bosco (Judge Brack), Paul Shenar (Eilert Lovborg)

A drama in 2 acts and four scenes. The action takes place in
Tesman's villa in the fashionable quarter of town.

Donna Sevennevik Photo

Susannah York, Roxanne Hart

Above: Susannah York, Paul Shenar

147

THE SECOND STAGE

Robyn Goodman, Carole Rothman
Artistic Directors

Assistant to Artistic Directors, Drew Farber; Director Audience Development, Linda Gaunt; Management, Pentacle Management, Mara Greenberg, Ivan Sygoda; Technical Consultant, John Patterson Reed; Photographer, Stephanie Saia; Press, Richard Kornberg

THE SECOND STAGE
Sunday, December 7,-20, 1980. (15 performances)

HOW I GOT THAT STORY

By Amlin Gray; Director, Carole Rothman; Set, Patricia Woodbridge; Lighting, Victor En Yu Tan; Costumes, Susan Denison; Sound, Gary Harris; Dance Sequence, Harry Streep III; Production Supervisor, Ada H. Citron; Production Assistant, Christine Sinclair; Technical Director, Rob Hamilton; Sound, Bob Kahan; Wardrobe, Nurit Bochner; Stage Managers, Clifford M. Schwartz, Lindy Rollo; Press, Richard Kornberg

CAST

The Reporter............................... Daniel Stern
The Historical Event .... Bob Gunton

A play in two acts.

Stephanie Saia Photo

Bob Gunton, Daniel Stern

SECOND STAGE
Sunday, February 22, - March 1, 1981. (15 performances)
The Second Stage presents:

IN TROUSERS

By William Finn; Director, Judith Swift; Choreography, Sharon Kinney; Orchestrations and Musical Direction, Michael Starobin; Set, Nancy Winters; Lighting, Victor En Yu Tan; Costumes, Karen D. Miller; Audio-Visual Consultant, Gary Harris; Stage Managers, Belle Baxter, Connie Cloyed McDonnell; Technical Director, Rob Hamilton; Wardrobe, Meredith January; Production Supervisor, Ada H. Citron; Press, Richard Kornberg, Peter Sanders; Co-Choreographer, Marta Renzi

CAST

Jay O. Sanders (Marvin), Kate Dezina (His Wife), Alaina Reed (His Teacher/Miss Goldberg), Karen Jablons (His High School Sweetheart)

MUSICAL NUMBERS: I Can't Sleep, A Helluva Day, How Marvin Eats His Breakfast, My High School Sweetheart, Set Those Sails, I Swear I Won't Ever Again, Rit Tit Tat, I Am Wearing a Hat, Marvin's Giddy Seizures, A Breakfast over Sugar, I'm Breaking Down, Whizzer Brown, The Rape of Miss Goldberg, Mommy Dear Has Dropped Dead in Her Sleep, Nausea Before the Game, Love Me for What I Am, How America Got Its Name, Marvin Takes a Victory Shower, Another Sleepless Night, Goodnight

Performed without an intermission

Stephanie Saia Photo

Karen Jablons, Jay O. Sanders,
Kate Dezina, Alaina Reed

THE SECOND STAGE
Friday, April 17, - May 10, 1981. (25 performances)

FISHING

By Michael Weller; Director, Amy Saltz; Scenery and Lighting, Neil Peter Jampolis; Costumes, Judy Dearing; Sound, Gary Harris; Technical Director, Rob Hamilton; Music, Kirk Stambler, Dean Restum; Special Movement Consultant, Randy Kovitz; Stage Managers, Davis S. Rosenak, P'nenah Goldstein, Chris Sinclair; Press, Richard Kornberg

CAST

Richard Cox (Rob), Robyn Goodman (Mary-Ellen), Daniel Hugh-Kelly (Bill), Penelope Milford (Shelley), Timothy Phillips (Dane), Ralph Roberts (Riley), John Spencer (Rory)

A comedy-drama in two acts. The action takes place at the present time somewhere on the coast of the Pacific Northwest during 24 hours.

Stephanie Saia Photo

Richard Cox, Penelope Milford,
Robyn Goodman

SEPARATE THEATRE COMPANY
James Harter, Artistic Director

JAN HUS CHURCH
Thursday, July 31–August 23, 1980 (12 performances)
TWO BY MOLIERE directed by James Harter; Costumes, Penny Howell; Stage Manager, Lawrence W. Bakaitis. THE FLYING DOCTOR with Charles Iorio, Rebekah Oakes, Eileen Desmond, Neil Shovlin, Rory Lance, James Caulfield, SGANARELLE with Charles Iorio, Rebekah Oakes, Neil Shovlin, Rory Lance, James Caulfield, Deborah Fuchs
Friday, August 29–September 21, 1980 (11 performances)
DON JUAN IN HELL by George Bernard Shaw; Director, Lawrence W. Bakaitis. CAST: Donna Drewes (Dona Ana), James Harter (Don Juan), David Lipman (Statue), Lee Owens (Devil)
Thursday, October 9–25, 1980 (11 performances)
WINNER TAKE ALL? written and directed by James Harter; Assistant Director, Lawrence W. Bakaitis; Stage Manager, Nancy Raffman. CAST: Sheila Browne (Laura), James Caulfield (George), Diane Cypkin (Caroline), Donna Drewes (Sally), Bambi Elizabeth Everson (Irina), Charles Iorio (Mike, Sr.), Lee Owens (Mike, Jr.), Neil Shovlin (Perry), Bill Tatum (Gary)

Eileen Desmond, Rebekah Oakes, Neil
Shovlin, Charles Iorio, Rory Lance,
James Caulfield in "Sganarelle"
(Separate Theatre Company)

Penelope Milford, Robyn Goodman
in "Fishing" (Second Stage)

SPECTRUM THEATRE

Artistic Director, Benno Haehnel; Administrative Director, Ted Baird; Associate Producer, Leda Gelles; Special Projects, Anita Cooper, Walter Scholz; Press, Therry Frey
Friday, February 6–March 8, 1981 (20 performances)
THE PLAYBOY OF THE WESTERN WORLD by John Millington Synge; Director, Chet Doherty; Costumes, Susan Johnston. CAST: Albert Amateau, Carol Bivens, Anita Cooper, Ted Cronin, Robert Davis, Pat Doheny, Ethan Dufault, Bump Heeter, Henry House, Kathleen Kellaigh, Janice Lathen, Gwynn Press, Marty Roppelt, Stanley Sayer
Wednesday, March 18–April 12, 1981 (20 performances)
THE TRIAL OF THE CATONSVILLE NINE by Daniel Berrigan; Director, Walter Scholz; Costumes, Laura Gelles; Lighting, Richard Harmon; Set, Kevin Golden; Sound, George Jacobs; Stage Manager, Diane Greenberg. CAST: Steve Abbruscato, Neal Ashmun, Steven Burch, Carla Charny, Joseph Culliton, Carolyn Halpert, Esther Jenkins, Stephan Maro, Ruth Nerken, Herbert Rubens, James Secrest, Jane Staab
Thursday, April 30–May 31, 1981 (20 performances)
GLORY! HALLELUJAH! by A. M. Barlow; Director, Benno Haehnel. CAST: David Abbott, Denise Bessette, Laraine Brennan, Rebecca Darke, Leonard DiPierri, Christian Doherty, David Dulow, Ethan Dufault, Rusty Jacobs, Janice Lathen, George Lloyd, Peter Lownds, Kevin Mahon, Stephan Maro, Tom McKinnon, Christopher Murray, Scott Palmer, Steve Pesola, Margo Regan, Stanley Sayer, Sara Stead, Guy Stroman
Thursday, May 14–June 14, 1981 (20 performances)
GETHSEMANE SPRINGS by Harvey Perr; Director, Alan Mokler; Set and Lighting, Dennis Size; Costumes, Jesse Harris. CAST: Ruth Bauers, David Bickford, Lawrence Gewirtz, Dean Kyburz, Karen Ludwig, Russell Leib, Lola Pashalinski, Nada Rowand, Howard Lee Sherman, Doris Gramovot

(No photos submitted)

TAYMON WELSH THEATRE CO.

First Season

Founders, Donald Montgomery, Suzanne Shelley, Hiram Taylor, Leslie Welles; General Manager, Margay Whitlock; Executive Adviser, Toni Tinkelman; Stage Managers, Paul Flannery, Georganne Rogers; Press, Judy Jacksina, Glenna Freedman, Angela Wilson, Dolph Browning

COMPANY

Valerie Armstrong, Barbara Bonilla, Michael G. Byrnes, Edward Earle, Brian Evers, Paul Heffler, Joanne Jacaruso, Rick Johnston, Mari Jones, Roger Kozol, Michael Landrum, Michael Lanza, Bobo Lewis, Donald Montgomery, Jake Packard, Diane Pearson, Alex Semple, Suzanne Shelley, David Swatling, Hiram Taylor, Toni Tinkelman, Liza Vann, Gretchen Walther, Leslie Welles, Carol Wenz

PRODUCTIONS

Teasers by Hiram Taylor, Fifth Avenue by Hiram Taylor, Villa Serena by Rick Johnston, Bumps and Grinds by Hiram Taylor; Sets, Donald Montgomery; Costumes, Carol Wenz; Lighting, Daniel D. Dashman

Donald Montgomery Photos

David Swatling, Joanne Jacaruso
in "Fifth Avenue" Top: Diane Pearson,
Mari Jones, Roger Kozel in "Teasers"

THEATRE OFF PARK

Producing Director, Patricia Flynn Peate; Managing Director, Jay Nellmann Stephens; Production Manager, Tamara Block; Press, Elsie Adler; Sound, Anton Stayduhar; Stage Managers, Tamara Block, Brooke Allen; General Manager, Prudence Hill
Wednesday, January 7–24, 1981
FAITH HEALER by Brian Friel; Director, Jamie Brown; Set, Richard Dorfman, Lisa Devlin; Costumes, Lynda L. Salsbury; Lighting, Richard Dorfman. CAST: William Knight (Frank), Mary Fogarty (Grace), Lium O'Begley (Teddy)
Wednesday, February 11–28, 1981
TO BE YOUNG, GIFTED AND BLACK by Lorraine Hansberry; Director, Lynnie Godfrey; Set, Bob Provenza; Costumes, Henri Saavedra; Lighting, Michael M. Bergfeld; Stage Manager, D. C. Rosenberg. CAST: Carolyn Byrd, Jill Dalton, Michele Harrell, Todd Jackson, Elizabeth McGovern, Elton Richardson, Anna Deavere Smith, Ellen Tobie, Jeff Zinn
Wednesday, April 1–25, 1981
RIVERS RETURN by Robert Corpora; Director, Mr. Corpora; Set, John Kasarda; Costumes, Henri Saavedra; Lighting, Leslie Spohn; Stage Manager, Linda Becket. CAST: Meg Mundy (Celia), John Beal (Jim), Olga Druce (Anna)
Wednesday, May 13–June 6, 1981
WOMEN IN TUNE conceived and directed by Aubrey Cooke; Musical Direction/Arrangements, Betsy Maxwell; Set, Terry Ariano; Choreography, Todd Rinehart; Lighting, John Senter; Costumes, Henri Saavedra; Stage Manager, Tom Heppler. CAST: Rosalyn Rahn, LuAnn Barry, Alynne Amkraut, Hal Maxwell, Stuart Zagnit

Tom Schworer Photos

John Beal, Meg Mundy
in "Rivers Return"

Top Left: Hal Maxwell, LuAnn Barry, Stuart Zignat in "Women in Tune" Below: Liam O'Begley, William Knight, Mary Fogarty in "Faith Healer"

THEATER FOR THE NEW CITY

Artistic Directors/Producers, George Bartenieff, Crystal Field; Administrative Assistant, Linda Chapman; General Manager, Steven Miller; Press, Howard Atlee, Jim Baldassare

Saturday, August 2–September 14, 1980 (12 performances)
THE GREATEST MYSTERY OF OIL by Crystal Field, George Bartenieff; Director, Miss Field; Music, Mark Hardwick; Musical Director, Rob Felstein; Set, Anthony Angel, Tommy Pace; Costumes, Edmund Felix, Manouchehr Hasini; Sound, Gary Harris; Stage Manager, Patty Contaxis. CAST: Amber, Alexander Bartenieff, George Bartenieff, Ken Buckshi, Joseph C. Davies, John DeTommaso, Christine Dubensky, Sajada Fakar, Crystal Field, Juliet Garson, Steven Greechie, Malcolm Horton, Kenneth Johnson, Tino Juarez, Stephen Landsman, Paxton Little, Carmen Mathis, Margaret Miller, Vince Monzo, Sharon Myers, Peter Neiburg, Sandra Nieves, Claudia Orenstein, Michael Ortiz, Bernita Robinson, Tracy Sherman, Dalita Shimzey, Melissa Thies, Betsy Wingfield

Thursday, February 19–March 8, 1981 (12 performances)
BUTTERFACES by Leonard Melfi; Director, Crystal Field; Set, Lance Miller; Lights, Joanna Schielke; Sound, Paul Garrity; Costumes, Edmund Felix; Stage Managers, Sam Buccio, Jim Shelley. CAST: John Carroll (Byron), Alexander Bartenieff (Lucks), Maggie Burke (Gloria), Ed Crowley (Tex), Hope Stansbury (Landra), Brenda Morgan (Jolly), Julia Barr (Jessica), John Albano (Ezra) Robin Klauber (Ingena)

Thursday, April 23–May 10, 1981 (12 performances)
A MIDNIGHT MOON AT THE GREASY SPOON by Miguel Pinero; Director, Steve Reed; Set, Reagan Cook; Lights/Sound, Terry Alan Smith; Costumes, Maura Clifford; Assistant Director/-Choreographer, Ron Vigneau; Stage Manager, Kate Mennone. CAST: Harvey Pierce (Joe), Art Kempf (Gerry), Warrington Winters (Fred), James Klawin (Jimbo), Geretta, Roma Maffia (Hookers), Israel Juarbe (Nightlife), Raymond Sumpf (Lockhart), Barbara Wild (Junkie), Alexis Mylonas (Nico), George Buck (Cop), Joan Turetzky (Zulma), Clarenze F. Jarmon (Jake)

Wednesday, May 13–June 7, 1981
FARMYARD by Franz Xaver Kroetz; Translated by Michael Roloff in collaboration with Jack Gelber; Director, Lawrence Sacharow; Set, Abe Lubelski; Lights, Naomi Berger; Costumes, Deborah Benson; Stage Manager, Gordon Kupperstein. CAST: Tom Noonan (Sepp), Pamela Pascoe (Beppi), Joel Rooks (Farmer), Anita Keal (Wife)

Thursday, May 7–31, 1981
ZALOOMINATIONS a program of one-man shows by Paul Zaloom

Thursday, May 28, 1981–
THE MEEHANS by Sam Pottle (Music) and Charles Choset (Book/Lyrics); Director, Peter Napolitano; Choreographer, Ronald Dabney; Musical Director, Ernest Lehrer; Arranger, Richard Fiocca; Stage Manager, Ana Pettit. CAST: Donna Pelc, Howard Pinhasik, Richard Alpers, David Berk, Jesse Cline, Charles Del Vecchio, Gary DiMauro, Joe Duquette, John Gallogly, Jesse L. Stokes, Bonnie Horan, Kathi McGunnigle, Debbie Petrino, Frank Torren

Top Right: Brenda Morgan, Julia Barr, Hope Lansbury, Maggie Burke in "4 in a Dressing Room" Below: Paul Zaloom

Art Kempf, Joan Turetzky, Harvey
Pierce in "Midnight Moon. . . ."

Kenneth Johnson (top), George Bartenieff,
John DeTommaso in "Greatest Mystery of Oil"

UNION SQUARE THEATRE

September 21–December 31, 1980
Fifth Season
Founder-Artistic Director, Avadne Giannini; Producing Director,
Lee Pucklis; Associate to Directors, William E. Mack; Business
Manager, Cinda Gilliland; Press, Linda Harris; Stage Manager,
Scott Ross; Technical Director, Rob Hamilton

PRODUCTIONS AND CASTS

WORKING by Studs Terkel; Director, Evadne Giannini. CAST:
Terry Annwn, Shake Carlson, Lawrence Hamilton, Melanie Hen-
derson, Jacqueline Knapp, Tom Kopache, Stephen Lang, Bill New-
man, Fran Salisbury, Sophie Schwab
FESTIVAL FINALE by Francis X. Duffy; Directors, Evadne Gian-
nini, William E. Mack. CAST: Jeff Birchfield, Jean Cheek, Mike
Davis, Francis X. Duffy, Penny England, Ellen Foreman, Mark
Gardner, Lucia Hamilton, Cheryl Henderson, Andrea Hunt, Frank
Kane, Dai Kornberg, Maxine Lefkowitz, Kevin Osborne, Martha
Roth, David Schall, Scott Valentine, Marta Vidal, David Walker,
James Wilson
DOWN IN THE VALLEY with music by Kurt Weill; Libretto,
Arnold Sundgaard; Director, Mark Tyler; Musical Director, J. Har-
ris Wooten; Choreography, Roslyn Biskin; Set, Mark Tyler; Light-
ing, William E. Mack; Costumes, Evadne Giannini; Stage Manager,
Julann Rosa. CAST: Rick Hamlin (Brack), Maureen Curtin (Jen-
nie), Albert Hansen (Thomas), Raymond Armstrong (Leader), Vin-
cent Gerardi (Preacher), Patrick Chicalese (Peters), Calvert
DeForest (Jeannie's Father), Chuck Fisher (A Man), Sylvia Moss,
Julann Rosa (Two Women), Raymond Armstrong, Ada Di Donna,
Vincent Gerardi, Albert Hansen, Kathleen Miles, Sylvia (Chorus)
A CHILD'S CHRISTMAS IN WALES by Dylan Thomas;
Adapted by Joan White and Evadne Giannini; Director, Joan White;
Designers, Rob Hamilton, Ellen Oshins; Technical Director, Wil-
liam E. Mack; Stage Manager, Linda Harris. CAST: Noel Koran,
Robert York (The Boy)

Mack & Mack Photo

Fran Salisbury
in "Working"

WPA THEATRE

Producing Director, Kyle Renick; Artistic Director, Howard Ashman; Resident Designer/Technical Director, Edward T. Gianfrancesco; Business Manager, Michael Kartzmer; Literary Adviser,
Darlene Kaplan; Press, Faith Geer

PRODUCTIONS AND CASTS

April 25–May 18, 1980 (16 performances)
JACOB'S LADDER by Barbara Graham; Director, Caymichael
Patten; Costumes, Zoe Brown; Lighting, Craig Evans; Stage Man-
ager, Paul Mills Holmes. CAST: George Bamford (Will), Fran Brill
(Leona), Adam Stolarsky (Jacob), Mary Diveny (Annie), Peter
Friedman (Peter)
June 5–29, 1980 (16 performances)
ALBUM by David Rimmer; Director, Joan Micklin Silver; Set,
David Potts; Costumes, Susan Denison; Stage Manager, Sarah Whi-
tham. CAST: Ann Richards (Peggy), Jan Leslie Harding (Trish),
Kevin Bacon (Billy), Keith Gordon (Boo)
October 3–26, 1980 (20 performances)
PUT THEM ALL TOGETHER by Anne Commire; Director,
Howard Ashman; Costumes, Marcia Cox; Stage Managers, Paul
Mills Holmes, Leslie Moore. CAST: Alma Cuervo (Maggie), Jean
DeBaer (Kate), Adam Stolarsky (David), Bonnie-Campbell Britton
(Cashier), Suzanne Collins (Mrs. Garritson), Michael Gross
(Tucker), Bryan Clark (Dr. Frisch)
February 19–March 15, 1981 (20 performances)
THE FREAK by Granville Wyche Burgess; Director, Stephen
Zuckerman; Lighting, Richard Winkler; Stage Manager, John N.
Concannon. CAST: James Rebhorn (Dr. Ketchum), Peter J. Saputo
(Charlie), William R. Riker (Squire Cayce), Polly Draper (Gertrude
Cayce), Dann Florek (Edgar Cayce), David James Forsyth (Dr.
Quigley), Richard Patrick-Warner (Dr. Barber), Rod Houts (Dr.
Shepherd)
April 2–26, 1981 (20 performances)
THE TRADING POST by Larry Ketron; Director, R. Stuart
White; Costumes, Susan Denison; Stage Manager, Paul Mills
Holmes. CAST: Jane Cronin (Claudia), Conrad McLaren (Wallace),
Burke Pearson (Louis), David Morse (Jim), Kristin Griffith (Kather-
ine), Betsy Aidem (Shelby)
April 30–May 17, 1981 (15 performances)
BODY MAGIC by and with Michael Grando; A program of pan-
tomime; Set, Edward T. Gianfrancesco; Lighting, Craig Evans;
Stage Manager, Philip Kerzner

Chip Goebert Photos

Burke Pearson, David Morse
in "The Trading Post"

Left Center: Alma Cuervo, Michael Gross,
Jean DeBaer in "Put Them All Together"

YORK PLAYERS COMPANY

Janet Hayes Walker, Artistic Director
Twelfth Season

CHURCH OF THE HEAVENLY REST
November 14–30, 1980 (12 performances)
RELATIVELY SPEAKING by Alan Ayckbourn; Director, Christopher Murney; Set, James Morgan; Costumes, Konnie Kittrell Berner; Lighting/Sound, David Gotwald; Technical Director, Sally Smith; Stage Manager, Molly Grose. CAST: Joel Leffert (Greg), Nancy Nichols (Ginny), William Cain (Philip), Janet Hayes (Sheila)
January 23–February 1, 1981 (10 performances)
FACADE with poems by Edith Sitwell; Music, William Walton; Scenery, James E. Morgan; Costumes, Konnie Kittrell Berner; Lighting, David Gotwald; Technical Director, Sally Smith; Stage Manager, Molly Grose; Choreography, Cal del Pozo; Musical Director, Eric Stern; Director, Fran Soeder. CAST: Kermit Brown, Mayla McKeehan, Rosemary McNamara, Kevin Sweeney, Timothy Wahrer, Sara Wiedt
March 20–April 12, 1981 (21 performances)
A LITTLE NIGHT MUSIC by Stephen Sondheim; Book, Hugh Wheeler; Set, James Morgan; Lighting, David Gotwald; Costumes, Sydney Brooks; Sound, Joseph D. Sukaskas; Technical Director, Sally Smith; Stage Manager, Molly Grose; Music Director, Eric Stern; Choreographer, Helen Butleroff; Director, Fran Soeder. CAST: Terry Baughan (Mrs. Segstrom), Helen Lloyd Breed (Mme. Armfeldt), Barbara Broughton (Charlotte), Melissa Ann Green (Osa), Kenneth Kantor (Carl), Jane Krakowski (Fredrika), Mary Lynne Metternich (Desiree), Kathryn Morath (Anne), Diane Pennington (Petra), Keith Rice (Henrik), Robert Sanders (Frid), Gordon Stanley (Erlanson), Jay Stuart (Fredrik), Gail Titunik (Mrs. Anderssen), M. Lynne Wieneke (Mrs. Nordstrom), Don Woodman (Lindquist)
May 22–30, 1981 (8 performances)
THE LADY'S NOT FOR BURNING by Christopher Fry; Director, Janet Hayes Walker; Set, James Morgan; Costumes, Holly E. Hynes; Lighting, David Gotwald; Stage Manager, Molly Grose. CAST: Joe Aiello (Humphrey), Joseph Culliton (Mendip), James Duff (Nicholas), Carol Mayo Jenkins (Jennet), Frank Lowe (Chaplain), John Rainer (Edward), Julie Ramaker (Jennet), Robert Sanders (Richard), Molly Scates (Alizon), Joan Shepard (Margaret), Sam Stoneburner (Hebbie), Evan Thompson (Skipps)

Right: Sara Wiedt, Kermit Brown in "Facade"
Top: Nancy Nichols, William Cain
in "Relatively Speaking"

Jane Krakowski, Helen Lloyd Breed
in "A Little Night Music"

Joseph Culliton, Carol Mayo Jenkins
in "The Lady's Not for Burning"

ALBERT EINSTEIN:
The Practical Bohemian

Written by Ed Metzger, Laya Geiff; Director, Laya Geiff; Artistic Coordinator, Sully Boyar; Presented by MC Square Productions; Began tour November 1979, and still touring May 31, 1981.

CAST

ED METZGER
as
Albert Einstein

A solo performance portraying the character and ideas of Albert Einstein in two acts: The Years in Europe, The Years in America.

Ed Metzger as Albert Einstein

ANNIE

Book, Thomas Meehan; Music, Charles Strouse; Lyrics, Martin Charnin; Director, Mr. Charnin; Musical Numbers and Choreography, Peter Gennaro; Sets, David Mitchell; Costumes, Theoni V. Aldredge; Lighting, Judy Rasmuson; Musical Direction, Glen Clugston; Dance Arrangements, Peter Howard; Orchestrations, Philip J. Lang, Producers, Mike Nichols, Irwin Meyer, Stephen R. Friedman, Lewis Allen, Peter Crane, Alvin Nederlander Associates, JFK Center, Icarus Productions; Stage Manager, Robert J. McNally III; Press, David Powers, Barbara Carroll; Opened Thursday, March 23, 1978 at O'Keefe Center, Toronto, Canada, and still touring May 31, 1981.

CAST

Annie	Mary K. Lombardi†1
Oliver Warbucks	Norwood Smith
Miss Hannigan	Ruth Kobart
Grace Farrell	Ellen Martin†2
Rooster Hannigan	Bob Morrisey†3
FDR	Stephen Everett†4
Lily	Jacalyn Switzer†5
July	Laura Myers†6
Tessie	Rachael Antill
Pepper	Courtney Stevens†7
Duffy	Melanie Martin†8
Kate	Dana Tapper†9
Molly	Kristi Coombs†10
Sandy	Himself
Bundles McCloskey/Ickes	Jim Brett
Dog Catcher/Bert Healy/Hull	James Todkill
Dog Catcher/Jimmy Johnson/Guard	Edmond Dante
Lt. Ward/Justice Brandeis	Charles Cagle
Sophie/Cecile/Ronnie Boylan	Linda Rios†11
Drake	John Anania
Mrs. Pugh/Connie Boylan	Laurel Cronin†12
Mrs. Greer/Page/Perkins	Kathleen Marsh†13
Annette/Bonnie Boylan	Kerry Hill†14
Fred McCracken/Howe	Randall Robbins†15

MUSICAL NUMBERS: See Broadway Calendar, page 60. For original NY production, see THEATRE WORLD, Vol. 33.

† Succeeded by: 1. Theda Stemler, Louanne, 2. Martha Whitehead, 3. Michael Calkins, 4. Randall Robbins, 5. Pamela Matteson, 6. Vicky Todd, 7. Megan Welch, Tammy Kauffman, 8. Kia Joy Goodwin, 9. Laura Kerr, Kim Davis, 10. Danyle Heffernan, 11. Janet Yetka, 12. Fern Radov, 13. Lynne Winterstelter, 14. Kerry Casserly, 15. John-Charles Kelly

Martha Swope Photos

Norwood Smith, Louanne, Sandy

Left Center: Ruth Kobart
and orphans

ANNIE

For additional credits, see preceding listing; Musical Direction, Milton Greene; Company Manager, Mark Andrews; Stage Managers, Bryan Young; Sam Stickler, L. A. Lavin, Sam Burgess; Associate Conductor, Allan Alper; Press, David Powers, Barbara Carroll, Stanley Kaminsky; Opened Thursday, June 22, 1978 at the Curran Theatre in San Francisco, Ca., and still touring May 31, 1981.

CAST

Molly	Michele DeCuir†1
Pepper	Lork Kickliter†2
Duffy	Stacey Morze†3
July	Stephanie Ann Levy†4
Tessie	Simone Francis†5
Kate	Nicole Francis†6
Annie	Marisa Morell†7
Miss Hannigan	Jane Connell
Bundles McCloskey/Ickes	David Green†8
Dog Catcher/Fred McCracken/Guard	Chuck Bergman†9
Dog Catcher/Bert Healy/Hull	Frank O'Brien†10
Sandy	Himself†11
Lt. Ward/Morganthau/Brandeis	John J. Fox†12
Sophie/Mrs. Pugh/Perkins	Toni Lamond†13
Grace Farrell	Lisa Robinson†14
Drake	Jack Collins†15
Mrs. Greer/Connie Boylan	Lisa Robinson†16
Cecile/Bonnie Boylan	Carol Secretan†17
Annette/Ronnie Boylan	Frances Asher†18
Oliver Warbucks	Reid Shelton
Rooster Hannigan	Tom Offt
Lily	Linda Lauter†19
Jimmy Johnson/Howe	Walter Niehenke†20
FDR	Tom Hatten†21
A Star to Be	Carol Secretan†22
Kaltenborn's Voice/Ickes	Leslie Feagan
Ensemble Alternates	Eric Richardson, Laurel van der Linde

MUSICAL NUMBERS: See Broadway Calendar, page 60. For original production, see THEATRE WORLD, Vol. 33.

† Succeeded by: Regina Meredith, 2. Wendy Finnegan, 3. Jennifer Maillet, 4. Denise Meredith, 5. Arlene Kulis, 6. Alyssa Jayne Milano, 7. Kristi Coombs, 8. Leslie Feagan, 9. John LaMotta, 10. Roy Hausen, 11. Buttercup, 12. Edmund Gaynes, 13. Maralyn Nell, 14. Krista Neumann, 15. Chuck Bergman, 16. Sigrid Heath, 17. Janet Aldrich, 18. Kathryn Skatula, 19. Maggy Gorrill, 20. Jon Rider, 21. Allan Wikman, 22. Janet Aldrich

Martha Swope Photos

Maggy Gorrill, Jane Connell, Tom Offt
Top: Reid Shelton, Kristi Coombs

ANNIE

For additional credits, see preceding listings; Musical Director, Arthur Greene; Assistant Conductor, Steve Oirich; Stage Managers; Kathleen A. Sullivan, David Clive, Janyce Ann Wagner, Chip Neufeld, J. B. Adams; Company Manager, Don Joslyn; Press, David Powers, Barbara Carroll, Jim Kerber

CAST

Molly	Ellyn Gale†1
Pepper	Patti Gilbert†2
July	Theda Stemler†3
Tessie	Melissa Betancourt†4
Kate	Mollie Hall†5
Annie	Rosanne Sorrentino†6
Miss Hannigan	Patricia Drylie†7
Bundles McCloskey/Ickes	Dick Decareau†8
Jimmy Johnson/Howe	William McCalry†9
Dog Catcher/Bert Healy/Honor Guard	David Ardao†10
Sandy	Himself†11
Lt. Ward/McCracken/Hull/Brandeis	Charles Rule†12
Sophie/Annette/Ronnie Boylan/Perkins	Kim Creswell†13
Grace Farrell	Deborah Jean Templin†14
Drake/Morganthau	David Wasson†15
Mrs. Pugh/NBC Page	Jill Harwood
Mrs. Greer/Connie Boylan	Sara Fidler†16
Cecile/Bonnie Boylan	Jill Bosworth†17
Oliver Warbucks	Harve Presnell
Rooster Hannigan	Michael Leeds†18
Lily	Katharine Buffaloe†19
Duffy	Stephanie Wellings†20
FDR	Jack Denton

UNDERSTUDIES: David Barron (Warbucks), Jill Harwood (Miss Hannigan), Kathleen Kollar (Annie), Elizabeth Stiles (Grace), Travis DeCastro (Rooster), Barbara Richardson (Lily), J. B. Adams (FDR), Alternates: J. B. Adams, Gail Pearson

For musical numbers, see Broadway Calendar, page 60.

† Succeeded by: 1. Senta Moses, 2. Deborah Webster, 3. Kathleen Kollar, 4. Sarah Navin, 5. Alyson Kirk, 6. Bridget Walsh, 7. Kathleen Freeman, 8. Robert Calvert, 9. Travis DeCastro, 10. Charles Goff, 11. Moose, 12. Ronald Highley, 13. Ann Heinricher, 14. Lauren Mitchell, 15. David Barron, 16. Elizabeth Stiles, 17. Barbara Richardson, 18. Dennis Parlato, 19. Wendy Kimball, Colleen Simon

Martha Swope Photos

David Barron, Jack Denton,
Harve Presnell, Bridget Walsh

BARNUM

Music, Cy Coleman; Lyrics, Michael Stewart; Book, Mark Bramble; Directed and Staged by Joe Layton; Assistant to Director, Edward Kresley; Scenery, David Mitchell; Costumes, Theoni V. Aldredge; Lighting, Craig Miller; Sound, Otts Munderloh; Orchestrations, Hershy Kay; Vocal Arrangements, Cy Coleman; Music Director, Robert Billig; Circus Training by The Big Apple Circus/The NY School for Circus Arts; Production Supervisor, Mary Porter Hall; Hairstylists, Ted Azar, Christine Domenech, Ann Miles; Technical Supervisor, Peter Feller; Props, Thomas Loughlin; Wardrobe, Warren Morrill, John Corbo; Management Assistants, Michael Gill, Marsha Best; General Management, James Walsh; Stage Managers, Warren Crane, Kate Pollock, Steve Wappel; Company Manager, John Corkill; Press, David Powers, Barbara Carroll; Assistant to Producers, Erik P. Sletteland; Producers, Judy Gordon, Cy Coleman, Maurice & Lois F. Rosenfield, Irvin Feld, Kenneth Feld; Opened Tuesday, May 12, 1981 at Saenger Performing Arts Center, New Orleans, La.

Stacy Keach as Barnum

CAST

Phineas Taylor Barnum	Stacy Keach
Chairy Barnum	Dee Hoty
Ringmaster/James A. Bailey	Gabriel Barre
Jenny Lind	Catherine Gaines
Joice Heth	Terri White
Tom Thumb	Bobby Lee
Lady Aerialist	Diane Abrams
One-Man Band/Edgar Templeton	Paul Browne
Baton Twirler	Darlene Cory
Sherwood Stratton/Wilton	Richard Gervais
Julius Goldschmidt/Humbert Morrissey	Steve Hall
Lady Bricklayer	K. Leslie
Lady Plate Balancer	Stephanie Nash
Amos Scudder	Andrew Hill Newman
Whitefaced Clown	Michael Oster
Acrobat Extraordinaire	Malcolm Perry
Chester Lyman	Melvin Roberts
Highwire Lady	Andrea Wright

Swing Ensemble: Betty Ann LaRusso, Gordon Weiss, Bo Gerard, Leslie Wing

MUSICAL NUMBERS: See Broadway Calendar, page 61.

A musical in two acts. The action takes place all over America and the major capitals of the world from 1835 through 1880.

Martha Swope Photos

Alexis Smith, Larry Hovis (top), William Hardy, Barbara Marineau, Marilyn Johnson

THE BEST LITTLE WHOREHOUSE IN TEXAS

Book, Larry L. King, Peter Masterson; Music and Lyrics, Carol Hall; Directors, Peter Masterson, Tommy Tune; Musical Numbers Staged by Tommy Tune; Sets, Marjorie Kelloff; Lighting, Beverly Emmons; Costumes, Gary Jones; Musical Supervision/Direction/Vocal Arrangements, Robert Billig; Hairstylists, Michael Gottfried, Kelvin Trahan; Props, Michael Durnin, Sr.; Wardrobe, Ellen Anton; Sound, William Weingart; Assistant Choreographer, Jerry Yoder; General Managers, Jack Schlissel, Jay Kingwill, Jeff Chernoff; Company Manager, Jo Rosner; Stage Managers, Jack Welles, Ric Barrett, Joe Gillie; Press, Jeffrey Richards Associates, Warren Knowlton, Marjorie Ornston, Diane Ornston; Presented by Universal Pictures; Opened Tuesday, Oct. 2, 1979 at the Shubert Theatre in Boston, Ma. Closed Jan. 11, 1981 at Pantages Theatre, Los Angeles, Ca. For original Broadway production, see THEATRE WORLD Vol. 35.

CAST

Narrator	Bradley Clayton King
Girls	Valerie Leigh Bixler, Dolly Colby, Ruth Gottschall, Ruth Lucas, Amy Miller, Deborah Magid, Karen Tamburrelli, Mimi Bessette
Cowboys	Don Bernhardt, Beau Allen, Davis Gaines
Farmer/Dogette	Andy Parker
Shy Kid/Aggie/Reporter/Camerman	Jeff Calhoun
Miss Wulla Jean/Beatrice	Roxie Lucas
Traveling Salesman/Scruggs/Brewster/Governor	Tom Avera
Slick Dude/Leroy Sliney/Co-Dog	Jeffry George
Choir	Joe Hart, Ruth Gottschall, Robert Moyer, Deborah Magid
Angel	Rebecca Ann Seay
Shy	Valerie Austyn
Jewel	Marilyn J. Johnson
Mona Stangley	Alexis Smith
Her Girls	Linda Lou (Valerie Leigh Bixler), Dawn (Mimi Bessette), Ginger (Ruth Gottschall), Beatrice (Roxie Lucas), Taddy Jo (Dolly Colby), Ruby Rae (Amy Miller), Eloise (Karen Tamburrelli), Durla (Deborah Magid)
Melvin P. Thorpe	Larry Hovis
Sheriff Ed Earl Dodd	William Hardy
Mayor Rufus Poindexter/Senator Wingwoah	Joseph Warren
Edsel Mackey	Robert Moyer
Doatsey Mae/Reporter	Barbara Marineau
Governor's Aide	Davis Gaines
Aggies	Beau Allen, Robert Hendrickson, Andy Parker, Don Bernhardt, Jeffry George, Davis Gaines, Jeff Calhoun, Joe Hart
Alternates	Joe Gillie, Pamela Pilkenton

MUSICAL NUMBERS: see Broadway Calendar, page 62.

Ilene Jones Photo

THE BEST LITTLE WHOREHOUSE IN TEXAS

For additional credits, see preceding listing; Associate Musical Director, Art Yelton; Company Manager, Jean Rocco; Press, Molly Smyth; Stage Managers, Roger Allan Raby, J. Marvin Crosland, Sidney Rojo, Paul Hope; Props, Leon B. Chenier, Jr.; Wardrobe, Pal Padilla; Hairstylist, Sally Harper; Presented by Stevie Phillips in association with Universal Pictures; Opened Monday, June 9, 1980 at Civic Auditorium, Jacksonville, Fl., and still touring May 31, 1981.

CAST

Six Easy Pieces . . . . Tony Booth (Narrator), Jimmy Powell, Kerry Demeria, Eddie Nation, Bob White, Art Yelton
Cowboy/Leroy Sliney/Aggie . . . . Brian Mounsey
Cowboy/Aggie/Strutter . . . . Neil Badders
Farmer/Ukranian Aggie/Governor's Aide . . . . . . Ricky Carlson
Shy Kid/Specialty Dancer/Thorpe Singer . . . . Gregg Murphy
Miss Wulla Jean/Ginger . . . . Sidney Rojo
Salesman/Scruggs/Chip Brewster . . . . Ed Geldart
Slick Dude/Co-Dog/Aggie . . . . Thomas Hulsey
Angel/Angelette . . . . Francie Mendenhall succeeded by
Yvonne McCord
Shy . . . . Allison Marich
Jewel . . . . Jackie Teamer
Miss Mona Stangley . . . . June Terry
Her Girls . . . . . Susan Shofner (Linda Lou), Jan Alford (Dawn),
Ann Faulkner (Ginger), Hilary Fields (Beatrice), Suzanne Smith
(Taddy Jo), Maggie Johnson (Ruby Rae), Theresa
Nelson (Eloise), Jennie Welch (Durla)
Melvin P. Thorpe . . . . Kevin Cooney
Sheriff Ed Earl Dodd . . . . Richard Kennedy succeeded by
William Larsen
Cameraman/Aggie/Choir . . . . Gary Bankston
Mayor Poindexter/Senator Wingwoah . . . . J. Nick Walker
Edsel Mackey . . . . Jim Goode
Doatsey Mae/Singer/Reporter . . . . Peggy Byers
Angelette Imogene Charlene/Eloise . . . . Theresa Nelson
Angelettes . . . . Susan Shofner, Jennie Welch, Ann Faulkner,
Maggie Johnson, Yvonne McCord
Governor . . . . David Doty
Aggies . . . . Richard Wyatt, Steve Marland, Gregg Murphy
Alternate Dancers . . . . Angie Wheeler, Paul Hope

MUSICAL NUMBERS: see Broadway Calendar, page 62.

William Larsen, June Terry

THE BEST LITTLE WHOREHOUSE IN TEXAS

Book, Larry L. King, Peter Masterson; Music and Lyrics, Carol Hall; Directors, Peter Masterson, Tommy Tune; Musical Numbers, Mr. Tune; Associate Choreographer, Thommie Walsh; Costumes, Ann Roth; Sets, Lawrence Miller; Lighting, Beverly Emmons; Sound, Abe Jacob; Hair and Wig Stylists, Lamara Jackson, Peter Bonsignore; Producers, Stevie Phillips, Universal Pictures, Bonnie Champion, Danny Kreitzberg; General Management, American Theatre Productions; Production Supervisor, Paul Phillips; Company Manager, Peter H. Russell; Musical Director, Guy Strobel; Wardrobe, Jerry A. Wolf; Stage Managers, Michael J. Frank, Grant Brown, Marian Reed; Press, Jeffrey Richards Associates, Fred Weterick; Opened Monday, Nov. 17, 1980 at Playhouse, Wilmington, De.; Still touring May 31, 1981. For original Broadway production, see THEATRE WORLD Vol. 35.

CAST

Edsel the Fiddler . . . . Ernie Reed
Girls . . . . Gena Scriva, Wendy Laws, Charmion Clark,
Susan Hartley
Cowboys . . . . Guy Strobel, Joel Anderson, William Ryall
Farmer/Melvin P. Thorpe/Chip Brewster . . Steven Earl-Edwards
Shy Kid/Thorpe Singer . . . . Joey Morris
Miss Wulla Jean . . . . Marian Reed
Traveling Salesman/C. J. Scruggs/Governor . . . . Robert Weil
Slick Dude/Soundman/Reporter . . . . Eric Aaron
Choir . . . . Susan Beaubian, Alan Bruun, Jan Buttram,
Kristie Hannum, Mark Reina, William Ryall, Guy Strobel,
Vincent Vogt
Angel/Imogene Charlene . . . . Jenny Lee Wax
Shy . . . . Martha Gehman
Jewel . . . . Susan Baubian
Mona Stangley . . . . Francie Mendenhall
Her Girls . . . . Linda Lou (Wendy Laws),
Dawn (Gena Scriva), Ginger (Charmion Clark), Beatrice (Kristie
Hannum), Ruby Rae (Susan Hartley), Eloise (Marcia
Ann Dobres)
Leroy Sliney/Thorpe Singer/Photographer . . . . Alan Bruun
Dogettes . . . . Joel Anderson, Joey Morris, William Ryall
Sheriff Ed Earl Dodd . . . . Christopher Wynkoop
Mayor Rufus Poindexter/Senator Wingwoah . . . . . Page Johnson
Doatsey Mae/Thorpe Singer/Reporter . . . . Jan Buttram
TV Announcer . . . . Larry L. King
Aggies . . . . Joel Anderson, William Ryall, Joe Morris,
Guy Strobel, Alan Bruun, Mark Reina, Eric Aaron (Specialty),
Vincent Vogt
Governor's Aides . . . . William Ryall, Vincent Vogt
Understudies . . . . . . Jan Buttram (Mona), Page Johnson (Sheriff)

MUSICAL NUMBERS: see Broadway Calendar, page 62.

A musical in two acts. The action takes place in the State of Texas during the fall of 1973.

Page Johnson
Above: Angelettes

Francie Mendenhall

BURLESQUE U. S. A.

Entire Production Conceived, Directed and Choreographed by Barry Ashton; Costumes, Ashton-Kochmann; Lighting, David Carpenter; Scenery, Tom Meleck; Musical Conductor, Jon Charles; Production Supervisor, William Ross; Burlesque Consultant, Bobby Faye; Production Coordinator, Deborah Oppenheimer; Assistant Choreographer, Dana Landers; Stage Managers, William David Carpenter, Lisa Harbach, Kathy J. Faul; Presented by Michael Brandman in association with Martin Kummer and William Ross; Opened Wednesday, June 3, 1980, at the Lyric Theatre, Kansas City, Mo., and still touring May 31, 1981.

CAST

Red Buttons, Robert Alda, Miss Tempest Storm, Patrick, Joey Faye, Lee Meredith, Josip Elic, Claude Mathis, Gina Bon Bon, Judy Faye, Karen Arp, Linda Snider, Gary Snider, April Maitland, Silki St. James

ACT I: Introducing, Girls of the World, The Audition, Exotic, Pork Chops, Powder My Back, The Transformer, Party Crasher, The Dodger, Ten Terrific Girls
ACT II: Forty-Second Street, Sam You Made the Pants Too Long, Feature, Floogle Street, Super Star of Burlesque, The Stand In, Say Something Nice about America

Joanna Miles Photo

Robert Alda, Tempest Storm, Red Buttons

CAMELOT

For staff and credits, see Broadway Calendar, page   . Associate Producers, Steve Herman, Jon Cutler; Manager, Carl Sawyer; General Manager, Arthur Anagnostou; Assistant Company Manager, Kathleen Turner; Assistant Conductor, Philip Parnes; Stage Managers, Jonathan Weiss, Cathy Rice; Press, Seymour Krawitz, Patricia McLean Krawitz, Martin Shwartz, Joel W. Dein; Opened Tuesday, Aug. 26, 1980 in Chicago's Arie Crown Theatre, and still touring May 31, 1981.

CAST

Arthur	Richard Burton†1
Sir Sagramore	Andy McAvin
Merlyn/Friar	James Valentine
Guenevere	Christine Ebersole†2
Sir Dinidan	William Parry
Nimue	Jeanne Caryl
Lancelot Du Lac	Richard Muenz
Mordred	Robert Fox
Dap	Robert Molnar
Lady Anne	Nora Brennan
Lady Sybil	Deborah Magid†3
Sir Lionel	William James
King Pellinore	Paxton Whitehead†4
Horrid	Bob†5
Sir Lionel's Squire	Davis Gaines†6
Sir Sagramore's Squire	Steve Soborn†7
Sir Dinidan's Squire	Herndon Lackey†8
Tom	Thor Fields
Knights of the Investiture	Ken Henley, Gary Jaketic, Jack Starkey, Ronald Bennett Stratton
Friar	Michael James Fisher

KNIGHTS, LORDS & LADIES: Nora Brennan, Bjarne Buchtrup, Jeanne Caryl, Melanie Clements, Stephanie Conlow, John Deyle, Debra Dickinson, Cecil Fulfer, Lisa Ann Grant, Ken Henley, Gary Jaketic, William James, Peter Kapetan, Kelby Kirk, Dale Kristien, Lorrainte Lazarus, Kevin Marcum, Craig Mason, Andy McAvin, Laura McCarthy, Robert Molnar, Randy Morgan, Steve Osborn, Patrice Pickering, Nancy Rieth, Patrick Rogers, Deborah Roshe, D. Paul Shannon, Jack Starkey, Ronald Bennett Stratton, Sally Ann Swarm, Sally Williams, Alternates: Ellyn Arons, Richard Maxon UNDERSTUDIES: William Parry (Arthur/Lancelot), Debra Dickinson (Guenevere), Gary Jaketic (Lancelot), James Valentine (Pellinore), Andy McAvin (Mordred), Robert Molnar (Merlyn), Sally Williams (Nimue), D. Paul Shannon/Craig Mason (Dinidan), John Deyle (Lionel), Craig Mason (Sagramore), Kevin Marcum (Dap), Patrick Rogers (Tom)
MUSICAL NUMBERS: see Broadway Calendar, page 14.
† Succeeded by: 1. William Parry, Richard Harris, 2. Meg Bussert, 3. Patrice Pickering, 4. Barry Ingham, 5. Daisy, 6. Steve Osborn, 7. Randy Morgan, 8. Craig Mason

Martha Swope Photos

Meg Bussert, Richard Muenz, Richard Harris

Left Center: Christine Ebersole, Richard Burton

CHILDREN OF A LESSER GOD

By Mark Medoff; Director, Gordon Davidson; Set, David Jenkins; Costumes, Nancy Potts; Lighting, Tharon Musser; Producers, Emanuel Azenberg, The Shubert Organization, Dasha Epstein, Ron Dante, William P. Wingate, Kenneth Brecher; General Managers, Jose Vega, Jane Robison, Linda Cohen; Wardrobe, G. Scarbough; Stage Managers, Mark Wright, Sally Greenhut, Robert Daniels; Press, Bill Evans, Harry Davies, Bruce Cohen, Leslie Anderson; Opened Friday, Nov. 21, 1980 at Parker Playhouse, Ft. Lauderdale, Fl., and still touring May 31, 1981. For original Broadway production, see THEATRE WORLD, Vol. 36.

CAST

Sarah Norman	Linda Bove
James Leeds	Peter Evans
Orin Dennis	Richard Kendall
Mr. Franklin	Ken Letner
Mrs. Norman	Stanja Lowe
Lydia	Nanci Kendall
Edna Klein	Deanna Dunagan

STANDBYS: Freda C. Norman (Sarah), Rico Peterson (James), Jackie Roth Kinner (Lydia), Robert Daniels (Orin), Jo Ferwell (Edna/Mrs. Norman)

A drama in two acts.

Martha Swope Photos

Peter Evans, Linda Bove

DANCIN'

A "musical entertainment" conceived, directed and choreographed by Bob Fosse; Re-created by Gail Benedict; For additional credits, see Broadway Calendar, page . Presented by Tom Mallow, James Janek; Musical Director, Jack Jeffers; Production Supervisor, Richard Martini; Wardrobe, Joel Miller, Rebecca Denson; Hairstylists, Romaine Greene, Rhonda Esposito; Company Manager, Peter H. Russell; Stage Managers, Mark S. Krause, Luis Montero, Germaine Edwards; Press, Max Eisen, Barbara Glenn; Opened Tuesday, July 29, 1980 in the Performing Arts Center, Milwaukee, Ws., and closed Dec. 23, 1980 in St. Petersburg, Fl. For original Bdwy Production, see THEATRE WORLD Vol. 34.

CAST

Douglas Bates, Pamela Jean Blasetti, William H. Brown, Jr., Maggie Caponio, Nita Chyree, Jim Corti, Ronald Dunham, Germaine Edwards, Janet L. Hubert, Diane Laurenson, Allison Renee Manson, Peggy Parten, Jamie Patterson, Roumel Reaux, Willie Rosario, Linda Smith, Thomas Tofel, Cynthia Watts
MUSICAL NUMBERS: see Broadway Calendar, page 65.

Martha Swope Photo

Left: "Dancin" company

GERTRUDE STEIN GERTRUDE STEIN GERTRUDE STEIN

By Marty Martin; Director, Milton Moss; Set, Anne Gibson; Costume, Garland Riddle; Lighting, Ruth Roberts; Stage Manager, Ellen Zalk; Business Manager, Burton Greenhouse; Technical Director, David Laudra; Press, Janice S. Morgan; Opened Oct. 3, 1980 at Arena Stage, Washington, DC, and still touring May 31, 1981.

CAST

PAT CARROLL
as
Gertrude Stein
A solo performance in two acts. The action takes place during 1938 in Miss Stein's apartment at 27 Rue de Fleuris in Paris, France.
Gerry Goodstein Photo

Pat Carroll as Gertrude Stein

THE ELEPHANT MAN

By Bernard Pomerance; Director, Jack Hofsiss; Set, David Jenkins; Costumes, Julie Weiss; Lighting, Beverly Emmons; Associate Producers, Ray Larsen, Ted Snowdon; Production Supervisor, Roger Franklin; Company Manager, Paul Holland; Wardrobe, Byron Brice; Assistant to Director, Ethan Silverman; Production Assistant, Jean doPico; Production Coordinator, Scott Steele; Wigs, Paul Huntley; Musical Arrangements, David Heiss; Stage Managers, Robert Bruce Holley, Margaret Hatch, Mary Dierson; Press, Solters/Roskin/Friedman, Joshua Ellis, Becky Flora, David LeShay, Cindy Valk; Presented by Richmond Crinkley, Elizabeth I. McCann, Nelle Nugent; Opened Monday, Nov. 26, 1979 in the Mechanic Theatre, Baltimore, Md., and closed March 8, 1981 in the Orpheum, Minneapolis, Mn. For original NY production, see THEATRE WORLD, Vol. 35.

CAST

Frederick Treves/Belgian Policeman	Ken Ruta†1
Carr Gomm/Conductor	Richard Neilson†2
Ross/Bishop How/Snork	Danny Sewell†3
John Merrick	Philip Anglim†4
Pinhead Manager/Policeman/Will/Lord John	Jeffrey Jones†5
Pinhead/Miss Sandwich/Princess Alexandra	Etain O'Malley†6
Mrs. Kendal/Pinhead	Penny Fuller†7
Orderly	Michael O. Smith†8
Cellist	Richard Sher†9

A drama in two acts and ten scenes. The action takes place in London between 1886 and 1890.

† Succeeded by: 1. Ralph Williams, 2. Dennis Lipscomb, 3. Thomas Toner, 4. David Bowie, Jeff Hayenga, 5. Dennis Lipscomb, Thomas Apple, 6. Jeannette Landis, 7. Concetta Tomei, 8. Kensyn Crouch, Thomas Apple, Robert Bruce Holley, 9. David Heiss, Neal LoMonaco, Anthony Pirollo.

Susan Cook/Ron Scherl Photos

Jeff Hayenga, Concetta Tomei
Top: Richard Neilson, Philip Anglim,
Ken Ruta

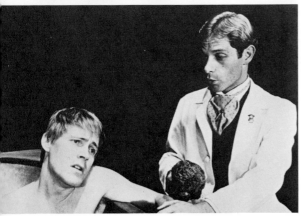

Courtney Burr, Kenneth Garner

THE ELEPHANT MAN

By Bernard Pomerance; Director, Brent Peek; Set, David Jenkins; Costumes, Julie Weiss; Lighting, Beverly Emmons; Production Supervisor, Richard Martini; Musical Arrangements, David Heiss; General Manager, James Janek; Company Manager, Jay Brooks; Wardrobe, Donna Peck; Props, Robert Michael; Stage Managers, Leanna Lenhart, Gregory Nicholas; Press, Max Eisen, Sandra Manley, Eileen McMahon, Merlin Group; Opened Saturday, Oct. 4, 1980 at the Ocean State Center, Providence, RI, and still touring May 31 1981. For original NY production, see THEATRE WORLD, Vol. 35.

CAST

Frederick Treves/Belgian Policeman	Kenneth Garner
Carr Gomm/Conductor	Larry Swanson
Ross/Bishop How/Snork	K. Lype O'Dell
John Merrick	Courtney Burr
Pinhead Manager/Policeman/Will/Lord John	Peter Bartlett
Pinhead/Miss Sandwich/Princess Alexandra	Judith Calder
Mrs. Kendal/Pinhead	Joan Grant
Orderly	Michael Russell
Cellist	Larry J. Rawdon

UNDERSTUDIES: Peter Bartlett (Merrick/Treves), Michael Russell (Gomm/Conductor/Ross/Bishop/Lord John), Judith Calder (Mrs. Kendal/Pinhead), Connie Roderick (Pinhead/Sandwich/Princess)

Susan Cook Photos

Left Center: Courtney Burr, Joan Grant

EVITA

Lyrics, Tim Rice; Music, Andrew Lloyd Webber; Director, Harold Prince; Choreography, Larry Fuller; General Management, Howard Haines; Company Manager, David Wyler; Assistant Musical Director, Bill Elton; Wardrobe, Dorothy Priest; Hairstylists, Richard Allen, Bob Brophy, Richard Matson; Production Assistant, Wilfy Hausam; For additional credits, see Broadway Calendar; Stage Managers, Jack Sims, John H. Lowe III, Mark A. Lipschutz, Kenneth W. Urmston; Props, Fred Belosic; Press, Mary Bryant, Judi Davidson, Barbra Desatnik; Opened Sunday, Jan 13, 1980 at the Shubert Theatre, Los Angeles, Ca., and still playing May 31, 1981. For original NY production, see THEATRE WORLD, Vol. 36.

CAST

Eva	Loni Ackerman, Derin Altay (matinees)†1
Che	Scott Holmes
Peron	Jon Cypher
Magaldi	Sal Mistretta†2
Peron's Mistress	Kelli James

PEOPLE OF ARGENTINA: Leslie Bisno, Angela Maria Blasi, Tim Bowman, Mark Bradford, Richard Byron, Jenean Chandler, Harold W. Clousing, Sheri Cowart, Nikki D'Amico, Barbara Dobkin, Karen Elise-Brown, Barry Gorbar, David Gold, Julia Hannibal, Mark Harryman, Barbara Hartman, Mary Ann Hay, Robin-Ann Kay, Ed Kerrigan, Kathleen King, Larry Merritt, Sha Newman, Vincent Pirillo, Darlene Romano, David Romano, Michael Alan Ross, Wayne Scherzer, Sharon J. Scott, Jerry Scurlock, Bruce Senesac, Timothy Smith, Roger Spivy, Dan Tullis, Jr., Kenneth W. Urmston, Brian Whitaker, Michel Woolworth, Karen Yarmat, Dena Sue Gilmore, Melanie Hyatt, Danny Mortenson, Evan Richards
UNDERSTUDIES: Sheri Cowart (Eva), Tim Bowman (Che), Brian Whitaker (Peron), Larry Merritt (Magaldi), Sharon J. Scott (Mistress)
† Succeeded by: 1. Florence Lacy, 2. Mark Syers
MUSICAL NUMBERS: see Broadway Calendar, page 69.

Martha Swope Photos

Jon Cypher, Loni Ackerman
Top: Loni Ackerman, Sal Mistretta

EVITA

Musical Supervisor, Paul Gemignani; Musical Director, Jack Gaughan; General Management, Howard Haines; Company Manager, Robert P. Bron; Assistant Musical Director, Pam Drews; Wardrobe, Adelaide Laurino, Frank Marblo; Hairstylists, Richard Allen, Lake Watson; Production Assistants, Charles Christensen, Patrick Fitzpatrick; Stage Managers, Thomas M. Guerra, Christine Lawton, Jayne Turner; Press, Mary Bryant, Margie Korshak, Philip Rinaldi; For additional credits, see Broadway Calendar; Opened Tuesday, Sept. 30, 1980 at the Shubert Theatre, Chicago, Il., and still playing May 31, 1981. For original NY production, see THEATRE WORLD, Vol. 36.

CAST

Eva	Valerie Perri, Joy Lober (matinees)
Che	John Herrera
Peron	Robb Alton
Peron's Mistress	Cynthia Simpson†
Magaldi	Peter Marinos

PEOPLE OF ARGENTINA: Arminae Azarian, Riselle Bain, Dennis Callahan, Anthony V. Crivello, David Dannehl, Larry Devon, Gregg Edelman, Michael Ehlers, John Eskola, Elaine Freedman, Tracy Friedman, Michael Hansen, James Harms, Lois Hayes, Robert Heitzinger, Didi Hitt, Rudy Hogenmiller, Ken Land, Deborah Lasday, Mark Lazore, Joy Lober, Michael Lofton, Paula Markovitz, Giselle Montanez, Susan Lubeck Oken, David Perkovich, Lisa Peters, Ivson Polk, Candice Prior, Mary-Robin Roth, Roger H. Rouillier, Paul Solen, Richard Stafford, Bruce Taylor, Joanie Winter, John Leslie Wolfe, David Hopkins, Brandon Lower, Bridgett McCarthy, Matthew Moran
UNDERSTUDIES: Riselle Bain (Eva), Anthony V. Crivello (Che), John Leslie Wolfe (Peron), David Dannehl (Magaldi), Susan Lubeck Oken (Mistress)
MUSICAL NUMBERS: See Broadway Calendar, page 69.
† Succeeded by Jamie Dawn Gangi

Martha Swope Photos

Valerie Perri (L), Robb Alton (R)

Left Center: Peter Marinos, Valerie Perri, John Herrera

I OUGHT TO BE IN PICTURES

By Neil Simon; Director, Herbert Ross; Re-staged by Frank Marino; Scenery, David Jenkins; Costumes, Nancy Potts; Lighting, Tharon Musser; Production Supervisor, James Riley; General Manager, Jose Vega; Technical Supervisor, Arthur Sicardi; Wardrobe, Judith Giles; Props, Jan Marasak; Presented by Zev Bufman Entertainment Inc.; Company Manager, L. Liberatore; Stage Managers, Richard Evans, James Bronson; Press, Charles Cinnamon, Bill Evans, Harry Davies, Leslie Anderson-Lynch; Opened Friday, Nov. 28, 1980 in Bayfront Center, St. Petersburg, FL, and closed May 31, 1981 at National Theatre, Washington, DC. For original NY production, see THEATRE WORLD Vol. 36.

CAST

Libby .... Alexa Kenin
Steffy...................................... Patricia Harty
Herb.. Bill Macy

UNDERSTUDIES: Chev Rodgers (Herb), Mimi Bensinger (Steffy), Amy Epstein (Libby)

A comedy in two acts. The action takes place at the present time in Herb's home in West Hollywood, California.

Martha Swope Photos

MY FAIR LADY

Book and Lyrics, Alan Jay Lerner; Music, Frederick Loewe; Director, Patrick Garland; Musical Staging and Choreography, Crandall Diehl; Based on original by Hanya Holm; Book based on "Pygmalion" by George Bernard Shaw; Sets, Oliver Smith; Costumes, Cecil Beaton; Lighting, Ken Billington; Costumes Supervision, John David Ridge; Sound, John McClure; Conductor, Robert Kreis; Musical Arrangements, Robert Russell Bennett, Philip Lang; Musical Director, Franz Allers; Presented by Don Gregory and Mike Merrick; Associate Producers, Steve Herman, Jon Cutler; Executive Director, Jay Levy; Manager, Marshall Young; Assistant to Producers, Ruthann M. Barshop; Assistant to Director, Harold DeFelice; Assistant to Choreographer, Scott Harris; Props, Dennis Randolph; Wardrobe, Mary Beth Regan, Carla Lawrence; Hairstylists, Angela Gari, Dale Brownell; Production Assistants, Kathryn Frawley, Amy Young; Wigs, Paul Huntley; Stage Managers, Jack Welles, William Weaver, Paul Schneeberger, Scott Harris; Press, Seymour Krawitz, Martin Shwartz, Patricia McLean Krawitz, Joel W. Dein; Opened Sunday, Sept. 14, 1980 at the Saenger Performing Arts Center, New Orleans, La., and still playing May 31, 1981. For original NY production, see THEATRE WORLD, Vol. 12.

CAST

Buskers............ Eric Alderfer, Alan Gilbert, Lisa Guignard
Mrs. Eynsford-Hill .... Harriet Medin
Eliza Doolittle............................ Cheryl Kennedy
Freddy Eynsford-Hill .... Nicholas Wyman
Colonel Pickering .... Jack Gwillim
Henry Higgins........................... Rex Harrison
Selsey Man/Harry/Ambassador .... Ben Wrigley
Hoxton Man/Jamie.................... Clifford Fearl
Bystander................................ Joseph Billone
Another Bystander/Cockney .... Ned Coulter
First Cockney/Footman................ John Caleb
Fourth Cockney .... Jeffrey Calder
Bartender/Major-Domo .... David Cale Johnson
Alfred P. Doolittle...................... Milo O'Shea
Mrs. Pearce............................ Marian Baer
Mrs. Hopkins/Lady Boxington .... Mary O'Brien
Butler.................................. Frank Bouley
Servants .... Jeralyn Glass, David Miles, Ellen McLain, Judith Thiergaard
Mrs. Higgins .... Cathleen Nesbitt
Chauffeur/Constable.................... Alan Gilbert
Footman/Bartender .... Ned Peterson
Lord Boxington....................... Richard Ammon
Flower Girl .... Karen Toto
Zoltan Karpathy .... Jack Sevier
Queen of Transylvania .... Svetlana McLee Grody
Mrs. Higgins' Maid .... Elizabeth Worthington

SINGERS: Frank Bouley, Jeffrey Calder, John Caleb, Ned Coulter, Diana Lynne Drew, Julie Ann Fogt, Terri Gervais, Jeralyn Glass, David Cale Johnson, Michael McGifford, Ellen McLain, David Miles, Mary O'Brien, Ned Peterson, Nancy Ringham, Judith Thiergaard
DANCERS: Eric Alderfer, Richard Ammon, Joseph Billone, Arlene Columbo, Ron Crofoot, Raul Gallyot, Alan Gilbert, Svetlana McLee Grody, Lisa Guignard, Scott Harris, Lynn Keeton, Gail Lohla, James Boyd Parker, Karen Paskow, Karen Toto, Elizabeth Worthington, Alternates: Scott Harris, Karen Paskow
STANDBYS & UNDERSTUDIES: Michael Allinson (Henry), Kitty Sullivan (Eliza), Clifford Fearl (Pickering), Ben Wrigley (Doolittle), Harriet Medin (Mrs. Higgins), Mary O'Brien (Mrs. Pearce), Jeffrey Calder (Freddy), Jack Sevier (Harry), Frank Bouley (Karpathy/Jamie)
MUSICAL NUMBERS: Street Entertainers, Why Can't the English?, Wouldn't It Be Loverly?, With a Little Bit of Luck, I'm an Ordinary Man, Just You Wait, The Rain in Spain, I Could Have Danced All Night, Ascot Gavotte, On the Street Where You Live, The Embassy Waltz, You Did It, Show Me, Get Me to the Church on Time, A Hymn to Him, Without You, I've Grown Accustomed to Her Face

A musical in 2 acts and 18 scenes.

Martha Swope Photos

Top Left: Bill Macy, Alexa Kenin, Patricia Harty in "I Ought to Be in Pictures"

**Cheryl Kennedy, Jack Gwillim, Rex Harrison
Above: Kennedy, Harrison, Cathleen Nesbitt**

NATIONAL SHAKESPEARE COMPANY
Eighteenth Year

Artistic Director, Philip Meister; Administrative Director, Albert Schoemann; Tour Director, Michael Hirsch; Scenery, Bob Phillips; Costumes, Amanda Klein, Sharon Hollinger; Lighting, Angus Moss; Company Manager, Carole Roberts; Technical Director, Dale Keever; Press/Assistant Tour Director, Stephen C. Hayes; Stage Manager, Peter Powell; Opened Sunday, Sept. 28, 1980 in Wilkes Barre, Pa., and closed May 15, 1981 in Cincinnati, Ohio.

PRODUCTIONS

THE COMEDY OF ERRORS by William Shakespeare; Staged by Kirk Wolfinger from original direction of Sue Lawless. CAST: Norris Browne (Jailer/Balthazar/Emilia), Dale Keever (Solinus), Peter Whitehouse (Egeon/2nd Merchant), Michael Sullivan (1st Merchant/Officer), Will Leckie (Antipholus of Syracuse), Louis Fischer (Dromio of Syracuse), Carole Roberts (Luce), Catherine Thorpe (Adriana), Kethleen Henderson (Luciana), Pat Kennerly (Antipholus of Ephesus), Lary Ohlsen (Dromio of Ephesus), Mykael O'Sruitheain (Angelo)
ROMEO AND JULIET by William Shakespeare; Directed by Mario Siletti. CAST: Will Leckie (Escalus/Apothecary), Peter Whitehouse (Peter), Mykael O'Sruitheain (Sampson/Friar Lawrence), Pat Kennerly (Paris), Louis Fischer (Tybalt), Norris Browne (Benvolio), Lary Ohlson (Montague/Mercutio), Dale Keever (Capulet), Catherine Thorpe (Lady Capulet), Carole Roberts (Nurse), Michael Sullivan (Romeo), Elizabeth Kelly (Juliet)
RICHARD III by William Shakespeare; Directed by Mario Siletti. CAST: Norris Browne (Edward IV/Tyrrel/Lord Mayor/Executioner), Louis Fischer (Catesby/Murderer #2), Elizabeth Kelly (Lady Anne Neville/Richard Duke of York), Dale Keever (Duke of Buckingham), Lary Ohlson (Murderer #1/Lord Stanley/Prince of Wales), Mykael O'Sruitheain (Duke of Gloucester/Richard III), Pat Kennerly (Earl Richmond/Lord Rivers), Will Leckie (Duke of Clarence/Lord Hastings), Carole Roberts (Queen Margaret), Peter Whitehouse (Sir Robert Barkenbury/Bishop/Mayor), Catherine Thorpe (Queen Elizabeth), Michael Sullivan (Marquess of Dorset)

Mykael O'Sruitheain, Elizabeth Kelly in "Richard III"
Top: Michael Sullivan, Kelly in "Romeo and Juliet"

NATIONAL THEATRE OF THE DEAF
David Hays, Artistic Director
Thirteenth Year

General Manager, David Relyea; Tour and Publicity Director, Mack Scism; Press Assistant, Laine Dyer; Training Program, Andy Vasnick; Actors Advocate, Elizabeth House; Opened Friday, Sept. 26, 1980 and closed May 27, 1981.

PRODUCTIONS

THE ILIAD, PLAY BY PLAY adapted by Shanny Mow; Director, Edmund Waterstreet; Set, David Hays; Costumes, Fred Voelpel; Lighting, Stephen Howe; Consultant, Michael Posnick; Half-time Show staged by William Rhys. CAST: Carole Addabbo (Athena), Carol Lee Aquiline (Hera), Charles Baird (Agamemnon), Adrian Blue (Patroclus/Priam), Sandi Inches (Aphrodite), Mark Kindschi (Calchas), Mike Lamitola (Menelaus), Charles Michael Roper (Hector), Howie Seago (Achilles) succeeded by Edmund Waterstreet, and Paul Johnston, Jean St. Clair (Thetis), Jody Steiner (Commentator Sophia), Andy Vasnick (Commentator Nick), Nat Wilson (Odysseus/Paris)
FOUR FABLES by James Thurber; Director, Edmund Waterstreet; A CHILD'S CHRISTMAS IN WALES by Dylan Thomas; Director, Bernard Bragg; Scenery, David Hays; Costumes, Fred Voelpel, Herta Joslin; Stage Manager, Betty Beekman. CAST: Charles Baird, Adrian Blue, Sandi Inches, Charles Michael Roper, Jody Steiner
OF THIS WORLD written and directed by Richard Lewis; Music, Ben Strout; Settings, Charles Baird; Costumes, Fred Voelpel, Herta Joslin; Stage Manager, Stephen Howe. CAST: Carole Addabbo, Mark Kindschi, Mike Lamitola, Jean St. Clair, Howie Seago (succeeded by Shanny Mow)
HERE WE ARE by Dorothy Parker; Director, Mark Scism; THE BEAR by Anton Chekhov; Director, Shanny Mow; BEDTIME STORY by Jean O'Casey; Director, Shanny Mow; Costumes, Herta Joslin; Stage Manager, Debbie Bosworth. CAST: Carol Lee Aquiline, Nat Wilson

Carol Lee Aquiline Above: Nat Wilson,
Adrian Blue, Howie Seago in "The Iliand"

OKLAHOMA!

Music, Richard Rodgers; Book and Lyrics, Oscar Hammerstein 2nd; Based on "Green Grow the Lilacs" by Lynn Riggs; Director, William Hammerstein; Choreography, Agnes de Mille; Re-created by David Evans; Kansas City Choreography, Miriam Nelson; Scenery, Michael J. Hotopp, Paul De Pass; Costumes, Bill Hargate; Lighting, Thomas Skelton; Musical Direction, Jay Blackton; General Manager, Theatre Now, Inc. (William Court Cohen, Edward H. Davis, Norman E. Rothstein, Ralph Roseman); Associate General Manager, Charlotte Wilcox; Company Manager, Hans Hortig; Props, Val Medina; Wardrobe, Sydney Smith; Assistant Conductor, Scott Oakley; Assistant to Director, Linda Shiers; Production Supervisor, James Riley; Stage Managers, Jay B. Jacobson, Jeanne Fornadel, Dennis D. Driskill; Presented by Zev Bufman in association with Donald C. Carter; Press, Fred Nathan, Eileen McMahon, Nora Peck; Opened Monday, Dec. 29, 1980 at Civic Auditorium, Jacksonville, FL, and still touring May 31, 1981. For original NY/revival, see THEATRE WORLD, Vol. 36.

CAST

Aunt Eller	Mary Boucher
Curly	William Mallory
Laurey	Christine Andreas†1
Ike Skidmore	Dennis D. Driskill
Slim	Ralph Bard
Will Parker	Lara Teeter
Jud Fry	Richard Leighton
Ado Annie Carnes	Paige O'Hara
Ali Hakim	Bruce Adler
Gertie Cummings	Catherine Campbell
Andrew Carnes	Philip Rash
Cord Elam	Robertson Carricart

Dream Ballet:

Laurey	Louise Hickey†2
Curly	Michael Ragan†3
Jud	Michael Howell Deane
The Child	Judy Epstein
Jud's Postcards	Patti Ross†4, Kristina Koebel†5, Susan Whelan

SINGERS: Ralph Bard, Carol Burt, Catherine Campbell, Robertson Carricart, Dennis D. Driskill, Lorraine Foreman, Bobby Grayson, John Kildahl, Joel T. Myers, Philip Rash, Phyllis Van Houten, Barbara Walsh
DANCERS: Paul Cavin, Michael Howell Deane, Judy Epstein, Marshall Hagins, Louise Hickey, Marguerite Hickey, Kristina Koebel, Bobby Longbottom, Michael Page, Michele Pigliavento, Michael Ragan, Patti Ross, Kevin Ryan, Robert Sullivan, Cynthia Thole, Susan Whelan, Swing Dancers: Marc Hunter, Suzie Jary
MUSICAL NUMBERS: Oh What a Beautiful Mornin', The Surrey with the Fringe on Top, Kansas City, I Cain't Say No, Many a New Day, People Will Say We're in Love, Pore Jud Is Daid, Lonely Room, Out of My Dreams, Laurey Makes Up Her Mind Ballet, The Farmer and the Cowman, All er Nuthin', Oklahoma, Finale

A musical in 2 acts and 6 scenes. The action takes place in Indian territory (now Oklahoma) just after the turn of the century.
† Succeeded by: 1. Jeannine Taylor, 2, Bronwyn Thomas, Jeff Fahey, 4. Elena Malfitano, 5. Jan Ilene Miller

Ray Fisher Photos

William Mallory, Christine Andreas (C)
and company in "Oklahoma"

PETER PAN

Lyrics, Carolyn Leigh; Music, Moose Charlap; Based on play by James M. Barrie; Direction and Choreography, Rob Iscove; Musical and Vocal Direction, Jack Lee; Production Supervisor, Ron Field; Additional Lyrics, Betty Comden, Adolph Green; Additional Music, Jule Styne; Orchestrations, Ralph Burns; Dance Arrangements, Wally Harper, David Krane; Scenery, Peter Wolf; Costumes, Bill Hargate; Lighting, Thomas Skelton; Hairstylist, Werner Sherer; Sound, Richard Fitzgerald; Laser Effects, Laser Media; Flying by Peter Foy; General Manager, Theatre Now; Company Manager, Michael Kasdan; Associate Director, John Calvert; Artistic Supervisor, Bonnie Walker; Associate Conductor, Jean Browne; Props, Liam Herbert; Wardrobe, Patricia Britton; Stage Managers, Barbara-Mae Phillips, David Rubinstein, Nelson K. Wilson, Penny Peters McGuire; Presented by Zev Bufman and James M. Nederlander in association with Jack Molthen, Spencer Tandy, J. Ronald Horowitz; Press, Solters/Roskin/Friedman, Joshua Ellis, David LeShay, Cindy Valk; Opened Wednesday, April 15, 1981 at the Municipal Opera House, Boston, Ma., and still touring May 31, 1981. For original NY revival, see THEATRE WORLD, Vol. 36.

CAST

Wendy/Jane	Marsha Kramer
John	Matt McGrath
Liza	Anne McVey
Michael	Johnny Morgal
Nana	James Cook
Mrs. Darling	Adrienne Angel
Mr. Darling/Captain Hook	Christopher Hewett
Peter Pan	Sandy Dennis
Lion	Jim Wolfe
Turtle/Crocodile	Robert Kellet
Kangaroo	Robert Brubach
Ostrich	C. J. McCaffrey
Tootles	Michael Emery
Nibs	Dennis Courtney
Slightly	Hans Krown
Twins	Edgar Glascott, Jim Wagg
Curly	Michael Estes
Noodler	J. C. Sheets
Smee	Oscar Stokes
Tiger Lily	Robin Cleaver
Starkey	Jon Vandertholen
Cecco	Al De Cristo
Jukes	Anthony Hoylen
Mullins	Bill Mulliken
Wendy Grown-up	Karen Luschar

PIRATES: James Cook, Al De Cristo, Anthony Hoylen, Bill Mulliken, Charles Rule, J. C. Sheets, Jon Vandertholen
INDIANS: Robert Brubach, Robert Kellet, Karen Luschar, C. J. McCaffrey, Anne McVey, Roger Preston Smith, Brian Sutherland, Jim Wolfe
UNDERSTUDIES: Charles Rule (Hook/Darling), Anne McVey (Mrs. Darling), Chris Vecchione (Wendy/Jane/Lost Boys), Bill Mulliken (Smee), Nelson K. Wilson (Nana), Penny Peters McGuire (Liza), Dance Alternates: Penny Peters McGuire, Greg Minahan
MUSICAL NUMBERS: Tender Shepherd, I've Got to Crow, Neverland, I'm Flying, Morning in Neverland, Pirate March, A Princely Scheme, Indians, Wendy, Another Princely Scheme, I Won't Grow Up, Mysterious Lady, Ugg-a-Wugg, Distant Melody, Hook's Waltz, The Battle, Finale

A musical in 3 acts and 9 scenes. The action takes place in the nursery of the Darling home, in Neverland, and on the Jolly Roger.

Christopher Hewett, Sandy Duncan
in "Peter Pan"

Martha Swope Photos

SUGAR BABIES

Conceived by Ralph G. Allen, Harry Rigby; Sketches, Ralph G. Allen based on traditional material; Music, Jimmy McHugh; Lyrics, Dorothy Fields, Al Dubin; Additional Music and Lyrics, Arthur Malvin, Hugh Martin and Ralph Blane, Larry Brown and Irwin Levine; Staged, Choreographed and Supervised by Ernest Flatt; Sketches Directed by Rudy Tronto; Scenery and Costumes, Raoul Pene du Bois; Lighting, Gilbert V. Hemsley, Jr.; Vocal Arrangements, Arthur Malvin, Hugh Martin, Ralph Blane; Musical Director, Patrick Holland; Orchestrations, Dick Hyman; Dance Music Arrangements, Arnold Gross; Assistant Choreographer, Toni Kaye; Scenic Supervisor, Fred Kolouch; Producers, Terry Allen Kramer, Harry Rigby in association with Columbia Pictures; Associate Producers, Jack Schlissel, Frank Montalvo; General Management, Jack Schlissel, Jay Kingwell; Production Manager, Alan Wasser; Company Manager, John Scott; Props, Cheri Herbert; Wardrobe, Kathe Long; Hair and Wigs, Stephen LoVullo; Assistant Conductor, Terry LaBolt; Production Assistant, William Braden; Assistant to Producers, Susie Murphy; Stage Managers, Pat Tolson, Jay B. Jacobson, Charles Reif; Press, Henry Luhrman Associates, Fred Weterick; Opened Tuesday, Aug. 12, 1980 in Dallas, Tx, and closed Nov. 1, 1980 at the Colonial Theatre in Boston, Ma. For original NY production, see THEATRE WORLD, Vol. 36.

Carol Channing, Robert Morse
in "Sugar Babies"

CAST

Carol	Carol Channing
Jay	Jay Stuart
Maxie	Maxie Furman
Billy	William Linton
Bobby	Robert Morse
Sally	Sally Benoit
Leonard	Leonard Wolen
Chaz	Chaz Chase
Gene DeTroy and the Marquis Chimps	
Gaiety Quartet	David Brownlee, Sterling Clark,

Ken Miller, Douglas Newton, Edward Pfeiffer (Alternate)

SUGAR BABIES: Carol Ann Basch, Julie Collins, Katherine Lynne Condit, Kimberly Ann Dean, Laurie Diamond, Candy Durkin, Melanie Montana, Kate Murtagh, Regina Newsome, Tracy Poulter, Joan Powers, Rusty Riegelman, Cynthia Thole, Evelyn Watson, Laura Lynn MacLeod (Alternate)

SONGS AND SKETCHES: A Good Old Burlesque Show, Let Me Be Your Sugar Baby, Meet Me 'Round the Corner, I Want a Girl, Servant Trouble, My Handyman, Baby of the Year, Be A Little Sweet to Me, Scenes from Domestic Life, Feathered Fantasy, Little Red Schoolhouse, Early Sophie, The Broken Arms Hotel, A Moving Love Song, I Can't Believe You're in Love with Me, Foolish Fables, Ellis Island Love Story, World's Greatest Knife Thrower, Bon Appetit, Special Added Attraction, Candy Butcher, Girls and Garters, Court of Last Retort, Strip Tease, In a Greek Garden, Cautionary Tales, Tropical Madness, Our Divine Diva, McHugh Medley, Old Glory

A "burlesque musical" in two acts.

Martha Swope Photos

Angela Lansbury, George Hearn
in "Sweeney Todd"

SWEENEY TODD
The Demon Barber of Fleet Street

Music and Lyrics, Stephen Sondheim; Book Hugh Wheeler; Based on a version of "Sweeney Todd" by Christopher Bond; Director, Harold Prince; Dance and Movement, Larry Fuller; Scenery, Eugene Lee; Costumes, Franne Lee; Lighting, Ken Billington; Orchestrations, Jonathan Tunick; Musical Supervisor, Paul Gemignani; Musical Conductor, Jim Coleman; Assistant to Director, Ruth Mitchell; Assistant to Producers, Jerry Sirchia; Presented by Richard Barr and Charles Woodward; General Management, R. Tyler Gatchell, Jr., Peter Neufeld; Associate, Doug Baker; Company Manager, James G. Mennen; Sound, Jack Mann; Wigs, Lynn Quiyou; Associate Musical Conductor, Randolph Mauldin; Technical Director, Arthur Siccardi; Wardrobe, Adelaide Laurino; Stage Managers, Arthur Masella, Frank Hartenstein, Patrick O'Leary, Stephen G. Hults; Press, Mary Bryant, Patt Dale, Philip Rinaldi; Opened Saturday, Oct. 25, 1980 in JFK Center Opera House, Washington, DC, and still touring May 31, 1981. For original NY production, see THEATRE WORLD Vol. 35.

CAST

Anthony Hope	Cris Groenendaal
Sweeney Todd	George Hearn
Beggar Woman	Angelina Reaux†
Mrs. Lovett	Angela Lansbury, Denise Lor (matinees)
Judge Turpin	Edmund Lyndeck
The Beadle	Calvin Remsberg
Johanna	Betsy Joslin
Tobias Ragg	Ken Jennings
Pirelli	Sal Mistretta
Jonas Fogg	Michael Kalinyen

COMPANY: Walter Charles, Roy Gioconda, Skip Harris, Terry Iten, Michael Kalinyen, Spain Logue, Carolyn Marlow, Duane Morris, Patricia Parker, Meredith Rawlins, Stuart Redfield, Dee Etta Rowe, Carrie Solomon, Joseph Warner, Swings: Cheryl Mae Stewart, James Edward Justiss, Stephen G. Hults

UNDERSTUDIES: Walter Charles (Sweeney), Denise Lor (Mrs. Lovett), Spain Logue (Anthony), Carrie Solomon (Johanna), Michael Kalinyen (Beadle), Joseph Warner (Judge), Skip Harris (Tobias), Roy Gioconda (Pirelli), Carolyn Marlow (Beggar)

MUSICAL NUMBERS: Ballad of Sweeney Todd, No Place Like London, The Barber and His Wife, Worst Pies in London, Poor Thing, My Friends, Green Finch and Linnet Bird, Ah Miss, Johanna, Pirelli's Miracle Elixir, The Contest, Wait, Kiss Me, Ladies in Their Sensitivities, Quartet, Pretty Women, Epiphany, A Little Priest, God That's Good!, Not While I'm Around, City on Fire!, Final Sequence

A musical in two acts. The action takes place during the 19th Century in London on Fleet Street and environs.
† Succeeded by Pamela McLernon, Sara Woods

Martha Swope Photos

THEY'RE PLAYING OUR SONG

Book, Neil Simon; Music, Marvin Hamlisch; Lyrics, Carole Bayer Sager; Director, Robert Moore; Musical Numbers Staged by Patricia Birch; Scenery and Projections, Douglas W. Schmidt; Costumes, Ann Roth; Lighting, Tharon Musser; Music Director, Jack Everly; Music Supervisor, Fran Liebergall; Orchestrations, Ralph Burns, Richard Hazard, Gene Page; Presented by Emanuel Azenberg; General Manager, Jose Vega; Associate Manager, Maurice Schaded; Company Manager, Mitchell Brower; Production Supervisor, Philip Cusack; Production Coordinator, Robert D. Currie; Assistant to Director, George Rondo; Assistant to Choreographer, Lani Sundsten; Tom Morse; Associate Conductor, Jon Olson; Wardrobe, Ellen Anton; Hairstylist, Burt Pitcher; Props, Bob Curry; Assistant to Producer, Leslie Butler; Stage Managers, Peter B. Mumford, James Bernardi, John Everson; Press, Bill Evans, Harry Davies, Claudia McAllister, Leslie Anderson; Opened Tuesday, Dec. 11, 1979 at the Shubert Theatre, Chicago, Il, and still touring May 31, 1981. For original NY production, see THEATRE WORLD Vol. 35.

CAST

Vernon Gersch .... Victor Garber
Sonia Walsk................................ Ellen Greene†1
Voices of Vernon.. Kenneth Bryan, Clint Clifford, Bubba Rambo
Voices of Sonia ... Ivy Austin, Andrea Green†2, Cheryl Howard
Voice of Phil, the engineer..................... Orrin Reiley

UNDERSTUDIES: Orrin Reiley (Vernon), Lauren Mitchell (Sonia), Clint Clifford (Vernon/Phil), Connie Gould (Sonia), Swing Singer/Dancers: Connie Gould, David Brent Hickox, Lauren Mitchell
MUSICAL NUMBERS: see Broadway Calendar, page 74.

A musical in 2 acts and 13 scenes. The action takes place at the present time.
† Succeeded by: 1. Marsha Skaggs, 2. Teresa Puente

Martha Swope Photos

THEY'RE PLAYING OUR SONG

Book, Neil Simon; Music, Marvin Hamlisch; Lyrics, Carole Bayer Sager; Director, Philip Cusack; Musical Numbers Staged by Patricia Birch; Scenery, Douglas W. Schmidt; Costumes, Ann Roth; Lighting, Tharon Musser; Musical Director, Albert L. Fiorello, Jr.; Music Supervisor, Fran Liebergall; Orchestrations, Larry Blank; Sound, Tom Morse; Presented by Tom Mallow in association with James Janek; Hair and Wig Designs, David Brian Brown; Assistant Conductor, O. T. Myers; Wardrobe, Linda Berry; Props, Bill Craven; General Manager, James Janek; Production Supervisor, Richard Martini; Company Manager, Jay Brooks; Stage Managers, Charles Collins, Luis Montero, George-Paul Fortuna; Press, Max Eisen, Barbara Glenn; Opened Monday, January 19, 1981 in The Playhouse, Wilmington, De., and still touring May 31, 1981. For original NY production, see THEATRE WORLD Vol. 35.

CAST

Vernon Gersch .... John Hammil†
Sonia Walsk................................. Lorna Luft
Voices of Sonia . Lynne Lamberis, Gail Oscar, Peggy A. Stamper
Voices of Vernon........... George-Paul Fortuna, Paul Mack, Michael Mitz
Voice of Phil, the engineer.............. George-Paul Fortuna

UNDERSTUDIES: George-Paul Fortuna (Vernon), Gail Oscar (Sonia), Paul Mack (Phil), Swing Singers/Dancers: Roy Miller, Renee Glicker
MUSICAL NUMBERS: See Broadway Calendar, page 74.
† Succeeded by Richard Ryder

Gerry Goodstein Photos

Gloria DeHaven, Van Johnson
in "Tribute"

Lorna Luft, Richard Ryder
Top: Victor Garber, Marsha Skaggs
in "They're Playing Our Song"

TRIBUTE

By Bernard Slade; Director, Arthur Storch; Set, William Ritman; Costumes, Lowell Detweiler; Lighting, Tharon Musser; Presented by Morton Gottlieb; Associate Producers, Ben Rosenberg, Warren Crane; Wardrobe, Kevin Woodworth; Props, John Bernabei; Hairstylist, Michael Robinson; General Manager, Ben Rosenberg; Company Manager, Kim Sellon; Stage Managers, Kenneth Porter, Scott Allen, Jeffery Brocklin; Press, Solters/Roskin/Friedman, Milly Schoenbaum, Warren Knowlton; Opened Monday, Sept. 22, 1980 at the Hanna Theatre, Cleveland, Oh, and closed Nov. 9, 1980 at the Blackstone Theatre, Chicago, Il. For original NY production, see THEATRE WORLD, Vol. 35.

CAST

Lou Daniels................................ Alan Manson
Dr. Gladys Petrelli......................... Joyce Krempel
Scottie Templeton .... Van Johnson
Sally Haines............................... Laura Beattie
Maggie Stratton........................... Gloria DeHaven
Jud Templeton............................. Timothy Askew
Hilary.................................... Peggy Cosgrave
Mrs. Everhardt............................ Anne Dodge
STANDBYS AND UNDERSTUDIES: Norman Beim (Scottie/Lou), Patricia Wheel (Gladys/Hilary/Mrs. Everhardt), Jeffery Brocklin (Jud), Marie Ferguson (Sally)

A comedy in 2 acts and 7 scenes. The action takes place at the present time in the living room of a New York townhouse, and on the stage of a New York theatre.

Martha Swope Photos

THE WEST SIDE WALTZ

By Ernest Thompson; Director, Noel Willman; Setting, Ben Edwards; Costumes, Jane Greenwood; Lighting, Thomas Skelton; Music Supervised and Arranged by David Krane; Presented by Robert Whitehead and Roger L. Stevens in association with Center Theatre Group-Ahmanson; General Manager, Oscar E. Olesen; Company Manager, David Hedges; Piano Consultant, and Teacher, Laura Fratti; Violin Teacher and Consultant, Elvira Morgenstern, Louis Gabowitz; Hairstylist, Charles La France; Assistants to Producers, Doris Blum, Jean Bankier; Production Assistant, Sally Lapiduss; Sound, James Cliney; Wardrobe, James McGaha; Stage Managers, Ben Strobach, Valentine Mayer; Press, Seymour Krawitz, Gertrude Bromberg; Opened Monday, Dec. 22, 1980 at the Spreckels Theatre, San Diego, Ca., and closed June 7, 1981 at the Fifth Avenue Theatre, Seattle, Wa.

CAST

Cara Varnum	Dorothy Loudon
Serge Barrescu	David Margulies
Margaret Mary Elderdice	Katharine Hepburn
Robin Bird	Regina Baff
Glen Dabrinsky	Don Howard

STANDBYS AND UNDERSTUDIES: Ludi Claire (Dorothy Loudon), Pat Santino (Serge/Glen), Lynn Weaver (Regina)

A comedy in 2 acts and 6 scenes. The action takes place in the living-room of a West Side, New York City, apartment.

Katharine Hepburn, Dorothy Loudon
in "West Side Waltz"

WHOSE LIFE IS IT ANYWAY?

By Brian Clark; Director, Michael Lindsay-Hogg; Set, Alan Tagg; Costumes, Pearl Somner; Lighting, Tharon Musser; Presented by Emanuel Azenberg, James M. Nederlander and Ray Cooney; General Managers, Jose Vega, Max Allentuck; Company Manager, Noel Gilmore; Technical Supervisor, Arthur Siccardi; Sound, Thomas Morse; Wardrobe, Ursula Jones; Props, Richard Johnson, Jr.; Assistant to Producers, Leslie Butler; Stage Managers, Cathy B. Blaser, Joanna Malley; Press, Bill Evans, Judi Davidson, Dan Kephart, Leslie Anderson-Lynch; Opened Firday, Aug. 15, 1980 at the Wilshire Theatre, Los Angeles, Ca., and closed Feb. 14, 1981 at the Morris Mechanic Theatre, Baltimore, Md. For original NY production, see THEATRE WORLD, Vol. 35.

CAST

Ken Harrison	Laurence Luckinbill[1]
Nurse Anderson	Catherine Gaffigan[2]
Mary Jo Sadler	Suzanna Hay[3]
John	Kim Sullivan
Dr. Claire Scott	Lucie Arnaz[4]
Dr. Michael Emerson	Brooks Rogers[5]
Mrs. Boyle	Carol Fox[6]
Philip Hill	Joseph McCaren[7]
Dr. Paul Jacobs	Lawrence C. Lott[8]
Dr. Robert Barr	Christopher Nelson[9]
Andrew Eden	Ben Kapen[10]
Judge Wyler	Arnold Moss[11]
Peter Kershaw	Dillon Evans

UNDERSTUDIES: Mary Boucher (Nurse/Mrs. Boyle/Dr. Barr), Lawrence C. Lott (Hill), Ellen Tobie (Scott), Ben Kapen (Judge/Emerson), Christopher Nelson (John/Jacobs/Eden), Lynne Kadish (Nurse/Mrs. Boyle/Dr. Barr)

A comedy in two acts. The action takes place at the present time in a hospital in England.
† Succeeded by: 1. Lucie Arnaz, Brian Bedford, 2. Delphi Lawrence, 3. Lynne Kadish, 4. Lawrence Luckinbill, 5. Leon Charles, 6. Kate Fitzmaurice, 7. Stephen G. Arlen, 8. Kenneth Danziger, 9. Lawrence C. Lott, 10. Ben Kapen, 11. Gordon Chater

Jay Thompson Photos

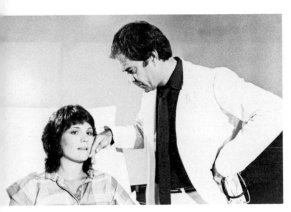

Lucie Arnaz, Laurence Luckinbill
in "Whose Life Is It Anyway?

THE WINSLOW BOY

By Terence Rattigan; Director, Douglas Seale; Set, Roger Mooney; Costumes, A. Christina Giannini, Jane Greenwood; Lighting, Martin Aronstein; Sound, Philip Campanella; Presented by Roundabout Theatre Co. (Gene Feist, Michael Fried, Producing Directors); General Manager, Paul Berkowsky; Company Manager, Jerry Livengood; Stage Managers, Pat Tolson, Michael S. Mantel; Press, Susan Bloch Associates; Opened Tuesday, Feb. 3, 1981 at Fifth Avenue Theatre, Seattle, Wa., and closed May 23, 1981 at the Eisenhower Theatre, JFK Center, Washington, DC. For original NY production THEATRE WORLD, Vol. 4.

CAST

Ronnie Winslow	David Haller
Violet	Ann MacMillan
Arthur Winslow	Ralph Clanton
Grace Winslow	Elizabeth Owens
Dickie Winslow	Lee Toombs
Catherine Winslow	Giulia Pagano
John Watherstone	Michael Tylo
Desmond Curry	James Higgins
Sir Robert Morton	Remak Ramsay

A drama in 2 acts and 4 scenes. The action takes place in the drawing-room of a house in Kensington, England, and extends over two years of a period preceding the war of 1914–1918.

Martha Swope Photos

Michael Tylo, Remak Ramsay, Giulia
Pagano in "The Winslow Boy"

PRODUCTIONS THAT OPENED AND CLOSED BEFORE SCHEDULED BROADWAY PREMIERES

ONE NIGHT STAND

Music, Jule Styne; Book and Lyrics, Herb Gardner; Director, John Dexter; Choreography, Peter Gennaro; Scenery, Robin Wagner; Costumes, Patricia Zipprodt; Lighting, Andy Phillips; Orchestrations, Philip J. Lang; Dance Arrangements, Marvin Laird; Music Director, Eric Stern; Hairstylists, Patrik D. Moreton, Michael Kriston; Production Assistant, Phil Seward; Musical Coordinator, Earl Shendell; Assistant to Choreographer, Dee Erickson; Assistant to Director, Vivian Martin; Production Coordinator, Jerry Harris; Sound, Otts Munderloh; General Management, Richard Horner Associates; Company Manager, Malcolm Allen; Stage Managers, Nicholas Russiyan, Robert O'Rourke, Michael Petro; Presented by Joseph Kipness, Lester Osterman, Joan Cullman, James M. Nederlander, Alfred Taubman; Press, Seymour Krawitz, Patricia McLean Krawitz, Martin Shwartz, Joel W. Dein. Opened Monday, Oct. 20, 1980 at the Nederlander Theatre, NYC, and closed there Oct. 25, 1980 after 8 previews.

CAST

Charlie .... Charles Kimbrough
Stage Manager...................... Thomas Barbour
Sid................................... Charles Levin
Gerry .... Paul Binotto
Nat/Sol's Voice........................ Brandon Maggart
Eddie .... Jack Weston
Young Eddie .... Steven Boockvor
Amanda................................ Catherine Cox
Assistant Stage Manager .... Michael Petro
Suzies .... Kerry Casserly, Cheryl Clark, Ida Gilliams,
       Sonja Stuart, Terri Treas, Kathryn Ann Wright
Margie .... Kate Mostel
Young Charlie......... William Morrison, Christopher Balcom
Molly .... Terri Treas
Leo/Barclay............................ John Mineo

STANDBYS & UNDERSTUDIES: Jeff Keller (Charlie), Bette Henritze (Margie), Daniel Goldfeld (Nat), Michael Petro (Sid), Brandon Maggart (Eddie), Michael T. W. (Young Charlie), Gina Martin (Suzies), Jim Litten (Young Eddie/Leo/Barclay)
MUSICAL NUMBERS: Everybody Loves Me, There Was a Time (Part I), A Little Travelin' Music, Go Out Big, Some Day Soon, For You, I Am Writing a Love Song, Gettin' Some, Somebody Stole My Kazoo, We Used to Talk Once, The "Now" Dance, Long Way from Home, Too Old to Be So Young, There Was a Time (Part II), Here Comes Never

A musical in two acts. The action takes place at the present time on the bare stage of the Nederlander Theatre between bookings from 8 to 10:30 P.M.

Martha Swope Photos

Jack Weston, Charles Kimbrough
Top: Jack Weston

THE STITCH IN TIME

By Marc Connelly; Director, Larry Forde; Set, Bob Guerra; Costumes, Carrie Robbins; Lighting, John Gleason; Special Effects, Charlie Reynolds; Musical Arranger, Marian McPartland; Presented by Leonard Finger; Production Assistant, Allan Haines; General Manager, Theatre Now, Inc.; Stage Managers, Arlene Grayson, David Piel; Press, Henry Luhrman, Bill Miller, Terry M. Lilly, Kevin P. McAnarney. Opened at the ANTA Theatre Monday, Dec. 29, 1980 and closed there January 6, 1981.

CAST

Genevieve Holster........................ Amanda Plummer
Patrolman Malloy........................... Joseph Jamrog
Intern.................................... Kurt Johnson
Dr. Conrad Zuckhauser...................... George Hall
Ormond Tracy.............................. John Gallogly
Henry Yenberry .... John Hammond
Caroline Lou Bingham...................... Polly Draper
Capt. Benjamin Worth.................. Stephen C. Bradbury
Dr. Lucius Bingham......................... Wesley Addy
Prof. Lindsey Holster...................... Thomas Ruisinger
Gwen Holster .... Carol Teitel
Colonel Lenhart .... Joseph Jamrog
Major Miller/An Actor .... Ray Dooley
Miss Winston............................. Annette Miller
Mr. Archer .... Richard Stack

A comedy in two acts. The action takes place during commencement week at a university in the middle west.
(No photos available)

John Hammond

SARAH IN AMERICA

By Ruth Wolff; Director, Robert Helpmann; Scenery, William Ritman; Costumes, Theoni Aldredge; Lighting, Richard Nelson; Spe-
cial Effects, Chic Silber; Visuals, Lucie Grosvenor; Musical
Direction, John Lanchbery; Assistant to Director, Cecelia Gilchriest; Production Assistants, Alexandra Isles, Stephen Nasuta; Props,
Liam Herbert, Michael Gallagher; Technical Supervisor, Jeremiah
J. Harris; General Manager, Theatre Now, Inc., Charlotte Wilcox;
Company Manager, Robb Lady; Stage Managers, Mitchell Erickson, Richard Delahanty; Press, Jeffrey Richards, C. George Willard,
Robert Ganshaw, Ben Morse, Helen Stern, Ted Killmer; Presented
by JFK Center for the Performing Arts (Roger L. Stevens, Chair-
man; Marta Istomin, Artistic Director), Washington, DC: Opened
Friday, Jan. 23, 1981 at the American Shakespeare Theatre, Strat-
ford, CT, and closed March 7, 1981 at the JFK Center/Eisenhower
Theater.

CAST

Sarah Bernhardt . . . . Lilli Palmer
Marianne . . . . Georgia Southcotte
Understudy: Patricia Fay (Marianne)

A play in 2 acts and 4 scenes. The action takes place during Miss
Bernhardt's American tours from 1880 to 1918.

Martha Swope Photos

Lilli Palmer as Sarah Bernhardt

**Jack Aranson, June Hovoc
in "Jitters"**

A REEL AMERICAN HERO

Book, Judy GeBauer, Burt Vinocur; Music, Gordon Kent, Stephanie
Peters; Lyrics, Gerald Hillman, Stephanie Peters; Director, Nancy
Tribush Hillman; Choreography, George Bunt; Scenery and Light-
ing, Harry Silverglat Darrow; Costumes, Carol Wenz; Lighting,
Giles Hogya; Orchestrations and Vocal Arrangements, Gordon
Kent; Musical Direction and Dance Arrangements, Roger Neil;
Presented by Gerald Paul Hillman; General Management, Maria Di
Dia, James Fiore; Hairstylist, Ellise Garber; Assistant to Director,
Ruth Carlin; Assistant to Producer, Karin Ferber; Sound, Neal
Schatz; Wardrobe, Ellise Garber, Marcie Belton; Stage Managers,
Bruce Kagel, Claudia Burk; Press, Bruce Cohen. Opened March 25,
1981 in the New Rialto Theatre, NYC, and closed there March 29,
1981 after 5 previews.

CAST

Ruby. . . . . Vidya Kaur
Louie . . . . Peter Newman
Chorine . . . . Roxanna White
Dick . . . . Jess Richards
Lili . . . . Hillary Bailey

MUSICAL NUMBERS: I Want to Be Somebody, What's Gone
Wrong, Garter Song, Lili Is a Lady with a Suitcase up Her Sleeve,
Ratta Tat Tat, Sugar Daddy Blues, Dance with Me, You Mustn't
Eat People, Monster Medley, Show White My Daughter, Tempus
Fugit, The Movie Game of Make Believe, Chan Ballet, The
Gunfighter, My Sargeant Doesn't Look Like Big John Wayne, Fly
Eagle Fly, I'll Be Waitin', Here's a Love Song, Hero Time, Finale

A musical in two acts.

Carol Rosegg Photo

JITTERS

By David French; Director, Bill Glassco; Set, John Lee Beatty;
Costumes, Robert Wojewodski; Lighting, Jamie Gallagher; Produc-
tion Assistants, Ken Bryant, Marilyn Rosenberg; Wardrobe, Kevin
Woodworth; Props, Tom Ciaccio; Producers, Arthur Cantor, Greer
Garson; Associate Producer/General Manager, Harvey Elliott;
Company Manager, Kim Sellon; Stage Managers, Scott Allen, Ste-
phen G. Hults; Press, Arthur Cantor Associates, Karen Gromis.
Opened Tuesday, March 17, 1981 in the Walnut Street Theatre,
Philadelphia, Pa., and closed there March 29, 1981.

CAST

Jessica Logan. . . . . June Havoc
Philip Mastorakis . . . . George Sperdakos
Tom Kent . . . . Joel Polis
George Ellsworth . . . . Jim Jansen
Patrick Flanagan. . . . . Jack Aranson
Nick . . . . William Garden
Susi. . . . . Mary Pat Gleason
Peggy . . . . Helena Power
Robert Ross. . . . . Dennis Boutsikaris

A comedy in three acts. The action takes place at the present time
in a small theatre in Toronto, Canada, during dress rehearsal, opening night, and the day after.

Martha Swope Photo

**Jess Richards (C), Roxanna White, Peter Newman,
Hillary Bailey, Vidya Kaur**

PROFESSIONAL RESIDENT COMPANIES

(Failure to meet deadline necessitated several omissions)

ACT: A CONTEMPORARY THEATRE

Seattle, Washington
June 1, 1980–May 31, 1981
Sixteenth Season

PRODUCTIONS AND CASTS

CATHOLICS by Brian Moore *(World Premier);* Director, Gergory A. Falls; Set, Shelley Henze Schermer; Costumes, Sally Richardson; Lighting, Phil Schermer. CAST: David White (Tomas O'Malley), Tony Amendola (Br. Kevin), John Aylward (Fr. Walter), Rod Pilloud (Br. Seamus), Robert John Zenk (Br. Seamus), Richard Marlin Tutor (Br. Martin), Maury Cooper (Fr. Matthew), Bernard Frawley (Fr. Manus), Peter Kelley (Fr. Donald), Glenn Mazen (Br. Paul), John Procaccino (Fr. Kinsella)

ARTICHOKE by Joanna McClelland Glass; Director, M. Burke Walker; Set, Scott Weldin; Costumes, Susan Tsu; Lighting, Frank Simons. CAST: Maury Cooper (Jake), Glenn Mazen (Archie), Lynda Myles (Margaret), Ted D'Arms (Walter), Joan Shangold (Lily), Ben Tone (Gramps), Clayton Corzatte (Gibson)

WINGS by Arthur Kopit; Director, John Dillon; Set, Bill Raoul; Costumes, Susan Tsu; Lighting, Phil Schermer; Sound, Joseph Seserko. CAST: Eve Roberts (Emily), Tony Amendola (Doctor), Robert John Zenk (Doctor), Calliandra Austin (Nurse), Nina Wishengrad (Nurse), Katherine Ferrand (Amy), John Procaccino (Billy), Glenn Mazen (Brownstein), Marjorie Nelson (Mrs. Timmins)

BURIED CHILD by Sam Shepard; Director, Robert Loper; Set, Scott Weldin; Costumes, Julie James; Lighting, Donna Grout. CAST: Ben Tone (Dodge), Marjorie Nelson (Halie), Ted D'Arms (Tilden), Mark Jenkins (Bradley), R. Hamilton Wright (Vince), Nina Wishengrad (Shelly), Clive Rosengren (Fr. Dewis)

STARTING HERE, STARTING NOW by Richard Maltby, Jr. and David Shire; Director/Choreographer, Judith Haskell; Costumes, Laura Crow; Set, Shelly Henze Schermer; Lighting, Paul W. Bryan; Musical Director, Stan Keen. CAST: Gwen Arment, Nancy Callman, Robert Manzari

A CHRISTMAS CAROL by Charles Dickens; Adapted by Gregory A. Falls; Music, Robert MacDougall. CAST: John Gilbert, Richard Riehle, David Mong, Edward Baran, Jim Royce, Christopher Marks, Rosheen Dunne, Gayle Bellows, Amy Steltz, R. A. Farrell, Nina Wishengrad, Bradley Stam, Elizabeth Rukavina, Suzy Hunt, Daniel Daily

CUSTER by Robert E. Ingham; Director, John Kauffman; Set, Shelley Henze Schermer; Costumes, Julie James; Lighting, Phil Schermer. CAST: William Ferriter (Custer), Ted D'Arms (Benteen), Nesbitt Blaisdell (Reno), Brenda Hubbard (1st Woman), Elizabeth Rukavina (2nd Woman), R. A. Farrell (Lt. Harrington), Allen Nause (Myles), Rod Pilloud (George), David Hunter Koch (Man with carbine), Understudies: Maureen Kilmurry, Daniel Daily, David Mong

Chris Bennion Photos

Jeffrey Prather, Edwin McDonough,
Maeve McGuire in "The Elephant Man"

Eve Roberts, Katherine Ferrand in "Wings"
Top: Clayton Corzatte, Lynda Myles in "Artichoke"

ALASKA REPERTORY THEATRE

Anchorage/Fairbanks, Alaska
January 20–May 17, 1981
Fifth Season

Artistic Director, Robert J. Farley; Producing Director, Paul Brown; Administrative Director, Mark Somers; Production Manager, Bennett E. Taber; Technical Director, Gary C. Field; Press, John Webb, Elaine Rick, Nancy Campbell

PRODUCTIONS AND CASTS

WILL ROGERS' U.S.A. adapted by Paul Shyre; Director, Robert J. Farley; Set and Costumes, Timothy Ames; Lighting, Hugh Hall; Stage Manager, Dan Sedgwick. CAST: Sid Conrad

ON GOLDEN POND by Ernest Thompson; Director, Clayton Corzatte; Set, Karen Gjelsteen; Costumes, Nanrose Buchman; Lighting, Michael Stauffer; Sound, Steven Bennett; Stage Manager, Ann Mathews. CAST: Shirley Bryan, Mitchell Edmonds, Michael Johnson, Tanny McDonald, Michael Santo, William Swetland

THE ELEPHANT MAN by Bernard Pomerance; Director, Robert J. Farley; Set and Lighting, Robert W. Zentis; Costumes, Michael Olich; Sound, Steven Bennett; Stage Manager, Ryan Kelly. CAST: Kermit Brown, John Clarkson, James Hotchkiss, Edwin J. McDonough, Maeve McGuire, Karen McLaughlin, Jeffrey L. Prather, Michael Santo, Luan Schooler, Robert Tornfelt

A MIDSUMMER NIGHT'S DREAM by William Shakespeare; Director, Walton Jones; Set, Kathleen Armstrong; Costumes, William Ivey Long; Lighting, James D. Sale; Sound, Steven Bennett; Wigs and Hairstyles, Paul Huntley; Musical Director, Richard Stillman; Choreography and Movement, Laurie Boyd; Stage Manager, Ann Mathews. CAST: John Ahearn, Deborah Bauman, Laurie Boyd, Bill Buell, James Burton, Jeff David, Harry Frazier, Daniel Frichman, Sharon Harrison, James Hotchkiss, Nancy Houfek, Pirie MacDonald, Ann McDonough, Joe Meek, Kathleen Melvin, John W. Morrow, Jr., E. E. Norris, John Pielmeier, William Preston, Ralph Redpath, Diane Salinger, Luan Schooler, Joan Shangold, Richard Stillman, Matthew Brown, John Heginbotham, Perrin Morse, Justin Vaughn

Jim Lavrakas Photos

ACTORS THEATRE OF LOUISVILLE

Louisville, Kentucky
September 24, 1980–May 24, 1981
Seventeenth Season

Producing Director, Jon Jory; Administrative Director, Alexander Speer; Associate Director, Trish Pugh; Press, Jenan Dorman, Mina S. Davis; Literary Manager, Elizabeth King; Business Manager, Patricia A. Brennan; Assistant to Producing Director, L. Susan Rowland; Technical Director, Tom Rupp; Directors, John Bettenbender, Larry Deckel, Radha Delamarter, Michael Hankins, Elizabeth Ives, Ken Jenkins, Jon Jory, Victor Jory, Frazier Marsh, Marsha Norman, Adale O'Brien, Amy Saltz, B. J. Whiting; Fight Director, David L. Boushey, Gary Sloan; Choreographer, Margaret Castleman-Schwartz; Designers: Sets, Hugh Landwehr, Paul Owen, Karen Schulz, Hal Tine, Joseph A. Varga; Costumes, Paul Owen, Kurt Wilhelm; Lighting, Geoffrey T. Cunningham, Jeff Hill, Paul Owen; Sound, John North; Props, Sam Garst, Sandra Strawn; Stage Managers, Tom Aberger, Steven D. Albrezzi, Richard A. Cunningham, Benita Hofstetter, Bob Hornung, Frazier Marsh, Susanna Meyer

COMPANY

Herman O. Arbeit, Andy Backer, Helen Baldwin, Ellen Barber, Jean Barker, Kathy Bates, Robert Blackburn, Michael Bologna, Kent Broadhurst, Bob Burrus, Timothy Busfield, William Cain, John C. Capodice, Susan Cash, Patricia Charbonneau, Christopher W. Cooper, Stephen Cowie, Stephen Daley, Andrew Davis, Beth Dixon, Lee Anne Fahey, Frances Foster, Ray Fry, Lisa Goodman, Laura Hicks, Katharine Houghton, Pat Hume, Ken Jenkins, Robert Judd, Brian Keeler, K. C. Kelly, Michael Kevin, Elwood Klaphaak, George Kimmel, Susan Kingsley, Charles Kissinger, Gerald Lancaster, David Lively, Terrence Markovich, Vaughn McBride, William McNulty, Julie Nesbitt, Adale O'Brien, Marianne Owen, Anne Pitoniak, Peggity Price, Cecelia Riddett, Brian Rose, Christine Rose, Robert Schenkkan, Patricia Sherick, Howard Lee Sherman, Michael Sokoloff, Danton Stone, Dierk Toporzysek, Diane Thompson, Steve Wise

PRODUCTIONS

Sea Marks, Terra Nova, A Christmas Carol, Sly Fox, On Golden Pond, Black Coffee, Artichoke, Bus Stop, Getting Out, The Autobiography of a Pearl Diver and *Premieres* of Semi-Precious Things, Final Placement, Chocolate Cake, Just Horrible, Morning Call, Propinquity, Chug, The Most Trusted Man in America, Let's Us, Generations, Early Times, Future Tense, Extremities, A Full Length Portrait of America, My Sister in This House, Swop

David S. Talbott Photos

Kathy Bates, Susan Kingsley
in "Chocolate Cake"

ALLIANCE THEATRE COMPANY

Atlanta, Georgia
October 15, 1980–May 23, 1981

Managing Director, Bernard Havard; Artistic Director, Fred Chappell; Associate Director, Charles Abbott; Administrative Director, Gully Stanford; Sets, John Doepp, Philipp Jung, Mark Morton, Michael Stauffer, W. Joseph Stell; Lighting, John Doepp, William B. Duncan, Michael Orris Watson; Costumes, Thom Coates, David Robinson; Stage Managers, D. Wayne Hughes, Charles Otte, Allen Hughes; Press, Mark Arnold

PRODUCTIONS AND CASTS

A HISTORY OF THE AMERICAN FILM by Christopher Durang; Music, Mel Marvin. CAST: Ivar Brogger, Nancy Clay, Lynn Fitzpatrick, Charlie Hensley, Jack Hoffman, Joseph Kelly, Rick Khan, Judy Langford, Robert Lund, Megan McFarland, Court Miller, Jean Smart, Chondra Wolle
THE KING AND I by Richard Rodgers and Oscar Hammerstein II. CAST: David Pendleton, Linda Stephens, Edward Ball, Terry Beaver, Kay Daphne, Freda Foh Shen, Scott Isert, Michael Licata, Robert C. Torri, Sharon Caplan, Phil DiPietro, Dennis Durrett-Smith, Neva Leigh Edrington, Nancy Farrar, Tim Garrett, Barbara Hancock, Diane Hedrick, Yvette Johnson, Joseph Kelly, Stefanie Kornegay, Judy Langford, Suzanne Loebus, Heidi Longwith, Sharrone Mitchell, Jay Patterson, Lynn Safrit, Don Spalding, Lynn Thompson, Steve Laventini, Mary Wells
ON GOLDEN POND by Ernest Thompson. CAST: Harry Ellerbe, Mary Nell Santacroce, Spencer Cox, Al Hamacher, Jack Hoffman, Antony Newfield, Chondra Wolle
SLY FOX by Larry Gelbart; Based on "Volpone" by Ben Jonson. CAST: William Hutt, Kevin Barrows, Hall Bennett, Chester Clark, Nancy Jane Clay, Chris Curran, Adrian Elder, Anne Gartlan, Al Hamacher, Charlie Hensley, Woody Romoff, Reno Roop, Coleman White
ANTONY AND CLEOPATRA by William Shakespeare. CAST: Jane Alexander, Edward J. Moore, Donzaleigh A. Abernathy, Hal Bennett, Chester Clark, Doug Dillingham, James Eckhouse, Adrian Elder, Lynn Fitzpatrick, Skip Foster, David Gale, Al Hamacher, Jon Hayden, David Head, Judy Langford, David McCann, Jay McMillan, Anthony Newfield, Jim Peck, Marshall Rosenblum, Coleman White, Kent Whipple
HONEY by Jim Peck (*World Premiere*). CAST: George Ellis, Charlie Gonzalez, David Head, Judy Langford, Larry Larson, Lynn Mitchell, Marshall Rosenblum
THE ACTORS by Lezley Havard (*World Premiere*). CAST: Charles Abbott, David Wasman
NOT JUST KIDSTUFF created by the company (*World Premiere*); Conceived and Adapted by Liza Nelson, Charles Abbott; Music Composed and Directed by Michael Fauss; Lyrics and Additional Dialogue, Charles Abbott; Based on the writings of Georgia school children. CAST: Joe Collins, Nancy Farrar, Charlie Gonzales, Jeroy Hannah, Pat Harding, Jan Maris, David Rifkin, Don Spalding, James Stovall

Charles Rafshoon Photos

Jane Alexander, Edward J. Moore
in "Antony and Cleopatra"

AMERICAN CONSERVATORY THEATRE

San Francisco, California
October 11, 1980–May 31, 1981
Fifteenth Season

General Director, William Ball; Executive Producer, James B. McKenzie; Executive Director, Edward Hastings; Stage Directors, William Ball, Allen Fletcher, David Hammond, Edward Hastings, Elizabeth Huddle, Nagle Jackson, Tom Moore, Jack O'Brien, Jerry Turner, Laird Williamson, Eugene Barcone, John C. Fletcher, Janice Garcia, James Haire, John Kauffman, Larry Russell; Production Managers, John A. Woods, John Brown; Production Coordinator, James Sulanowski; Production Assistant, Bradford Clark; Costumes, Walter Watson; Lighting, Wendy Heffner; Music, Todd Barton, Larry Delinger, Richard Hindman, Lee Hoiby, Conard Susa; Sets, Robert Blackman, William Bloodgood, Ralph Funicello, Richard Hay, Kent Homchick, Richard Seger; Costumes, Martha Burke, Robert Fletcher, Robert Morgan, Michael Olich, Carrie Robbins; Lighting, Richard Devin, F. Mitchell Dana, Dirk Epperson, James Sale, Duane Schuler; Sound, Randy Bobo, Alfred Tetzner; Stage Managers, James Haire, James L. Burke, Eugene Barcone, David Hyslop, Cornelia Twitchell, Karen Van Zandt, Michael Poe, Christina Shu-Hwa Yao; Costumes and Wigs, Warren Caton; Props, Oliver C. Olsen; Wardrobe, Deborah Capen, Donald Long-Hurst; General Manager, Benjamin Moore; Press, Jim Kerber, Richard D. Carreon

COMPANY

Joseph Bird, Raye Birk, Joy Carlin, Mimi Carr, Penelope Court, Barbara Dirickson, Peter Donat, Dana Elcar, John C. Fletcher, Julia Fletcher, Janice Garcia, Mark Harelik, Thomas Harrison, Lawrence Hecht, Jill Hill, Elizabeth Huddle, John Hutton, Johanna Jackson, Byron Jennings, Nicholas Kaledin, Lauren R. Klein, Anne Lawder, Dakin Matthews, Matt McKenzie, William McKereghan, DeAnn Mears, Delores Mitchell, Mark Murphey, Thomas Oglesby, Frank Ottiwell, William Paterson, Stacy Ray, Ray Reinhardt, Frank Savino, Garland J. Simpson, Sally Smythe, Deborah Sussel, Sydney Walker, Marrian Walters, Marshall Watson, Isiah Whitlock, Jr., Bruce Williams, Michael Winters, Paul Bates, William Brown, Bess Brown, Martin Curland, Patra Dawe, Mariano DiMarco, Gina Ferrall, Emily Heebner, Ed Hobson, Stephen Johnson, Jane Jones, Robert Krimmer, Gary Logan, Mary Loquvam, Terrence O'Brien, Greg Patterson, Robert Pescovitz, Wendi Radford, Kate Redway, Daniel Renner, Randall Richard, Gretchen Rumbaugh, Melissa Stern, Carl Turner, Stefan Windroth, Paul Yeuell

PRODUCTIONS

Much Ado about Nothing, Ghosts, Hay Fever, Tiger at the Gates, A Christmas Carol, Night and Day, Another Part of the Forest, The Rivals, The Three Sisters, The Little Foxes

DeAnn Mears, Mark Harelik
in "Night and Day"

AMERICAN REPERTORY THEATRE

Cambridge, Massachusetts
Second Season

Artistic Director, Robert Brustein; Managing Director, Robert J. Orchard; Literary Director, Michael Kustow; Production Manager, Jonathan Miller; Financial Director, Sam Guckenheimer; Technical Director, Donald Soule; Sets, Tom Lynch, Michael H. Yeargan, Adrianne Lobel, Tony Straiges, Kate Edmunds, Andrew Jackness; Costumes, Dunya Ramicova, Adrianne Lobel, Rita Ryack, Nancy Thun, Zack Brown; Lighting, James F. Ingalls, William Armstrong, Paul Dallo; Musical Directors, Daniel Stepner, Gary Fagin, Stephen Drury; Choreographic Associate; Carmen de Lavallade; Stage Managers, Thomas DiMauro, Thomas R. Bruce, Shannon J. Sumpter; Press, Jan Geidt

PRODUCTIONS AND CASTS

AS YOU LIKE IT by William Shakespeare; Director, Andrei Belgrader. CAST: Jeremy Geidt, William McGlinn, Harry S. Murphy, Thomas Derrah, Tony Shalhoub, Stephen Rowe, Gerry Bamman, Richard Spore, Eric Elice, Cherry Jones, Karen MacDonald, Cynthia Darlow, Elizabeth Norment, Geraldine Librandi
A MIDSUMMER NIGHT'S DREAM by William Shakespeare; Director, Alvin Epstein. CAST: Harry S. Murphy, Karen MacDonald, John S. Drabik, Cynthia Darlow, Stephen Rowe, Eric Elice, Cherry Jones, Jeremy Geidt, John Bottoms, Richard Grusin, John McAndrew, Chris Clemenson, William McGlinn, Thomas Derrah, Tony Shalhoub, Kenneth Ryan, Carmen de Lavallade, Richard Spore
TWO BY BRECHT AND WEILL: (translated by Michael Feingold) "The Berlin Requiem" directed by Travis Preston with Robert Honeysucker, David Ripley, Kim Scown. "The Seven Deadly Sins" directed by Alvin Epstein, with Ellen Greene, Carmen de Lavallade, Kim Scown, Mark Jackson, Robert Honeysucker, David Ripley, Harry S. Murphy, Eric Elice, Tony Shalhoub, William McGlinn, Thomas Derrah, Cynthia Darlow, Karen MacDonald
LULU by Frank Wedekind; Adapted by Michael Feingold; Director, Lee Breuer. CAST: Catherine Slade, Frederick Neumann, Eric Elice, Richard Spore, Kenneth Ryan, Jeremy Geidt, Thomas Derrah, Carmen de Lavallade, Stephen Rowe, Tony Shalhoub, William McGlinn, Karen MacDonald, Cynthia Darlow, Harry S. Murphy
HAS "WASHINGTON" LEGS? (American Premiere) by Charles Wood; Director, Michael Kustow. CAST: Stephen Rowe, Tony Shalhoub, Richard Spore, Eric Elice, Kenneth Ryan, Thomas Derrah, William McGlinn, Frederick Neumann, Karen MacDonald, Jeremy Geidt, Harry S. Murphy
THE MARRIAGE OF FIGARO by Beaumarchais; Translated and Adapted by Mark Leib; Director, Alvin Epstein. CAST: Harry S. Murphy, Cheryl Giannini, Tony Shalhoub, Karen MacDonald, Barbara Orson, Albert J. Duclos, Linda Atkinson, George Martin, William McGlinn, Thomas Derrah
GROWNUPS (World Premiere) by Jules Feiffer; Director, John Madden. CAST: Barbara Orson, George Martin, Karen MacDonald, Bob Dishy, Cheryl Giannini, Jennifer Dundas

Richard Feldman Photos

Carmen de Lavallade (C), Ellen Greene (R)
in "Two by Brecht and Weill"

AMERICAN THEATRE ARTS

Hollywood, California
Artistic Director, Don Eitner; Managing Director, Jim Bennett; Administrator, Nancy Jeris; Art Director, James J. Agazzi; Head of Production, Robert Smitherman; Production Coordinator, Barbara Levy; Directors, Joseph Ruskin, James J. Agazzi, Don Eitner, Dianne Haak, Bette Ferber, Kip Niven; Press, Robbie Trombetta

PRODUCTIONS AND CASTS

DAYS IN THE DARK LIGHT *(World Premiere)* by James W. Kearns. CAST: Richard Bull, Barbara Collentine, Maureen McIlroy, Sara Shearer
NUDE WITH VIOLIN by Noel Coward. CAST: Robert Garrison, Robbie Trombetta, Howard Adler, Jeanie Van Dam, Cathryn Perdue, Gary Graves, Margo Speer, Daniel Grace, Tanya George, Nancy Jeris, Gary Spatz, Kevin Spillane, Nicholas Shaffer
RICHARD'S CORK LEG by Brendan Behan. CAST: Sara Shearer, Jodi Thelen, Rob Donohue, Martin Donovan, Dave Casey, Georgie Huntington, Gerald Anderson, Dave Casey, Richard Harris, Lee Rossignol
OUT OF THE CROCODILE *(American Premiere)* by Giles Cooper. CAST: Robert Garrison, Sara DeWitt, Mary Bomba, John Terry Bell, Michele Gazzaniga, Paula Heller, Margo Speer
WINESBURG, OHIO by Sherwood Anderson, dramatized by Christopher Sergel. CAST: Nancy Jeris, Robert Sampson, Barry Bartle, Arlee Suddeth, Nora Morgan Eckstein, Kay Worthington, Dave Casey, John McKinney, Daniel Grace, Rick Moffitt, Martin Donovan, Frank Groby, Christopher Sampson, Niche Saboda

Barry Bartle Photos

Nancy Jeris, Gary Spatz
in "Nude with Violin"

ARENA STAGE

Washington, D.C.
October 17, 1980–June 14, 1981
Thirtieth Year
Producing Director, Zelda Fichandler; Executive Director, Thomas C. Fichandler; Associate Producer, Nancy Quinn; Associate Director, Douglas C. Wager; Technical Director, Henry R. Gorfein; Administrative Director, JoAnn M. Overholt; Press, Richard Bryant; Stage Directors, Howard Ashman, Vernel Bagneris, Martin Fried, Mary Kyte, Ron Lagomarsino, Gene Lesser, Robert Prosky, Richard Russell Ramos, Douglas C. Wager; Sets, Karl Eigsti, Marjorie Kellogg, Adrianne Lobel, Tom Lynch, Lance Pennington, Tony Straiges; Costumes, Nan Cibula, JoAnn Clevenger, Sandra Yen Fong, Mary Ann Powell, Marjorie Slaiman; Lighting, Arden Fingerhut, Allen Lee Hughes, Hugh Lester, William Mintzer, Nancy Schertler; Composers, Tim Eyermann, Alan Menken, Jack Eric Williams; Stage Managers, Peter Dowling, Suzanne Fry, Meredith Hatch

COMPANY

Stanley Anderson, Richard Bauer, Leslie Cass, Terrence Currier, Kevin Donovan, Mark Hammer, Charles Janasz, Annalee Jefferies, Christina Moore, Robert Prosky, David Toney, Robert W. Westenberg, Halo Wines, and *Guest Actors:* Peggy Alston, Barbara Andres, William Andrews, Christopher Bauer, Lady B. J., Gary Lee Blumsack, Charles K. Bortell, Avery Brooks, Michael Butler, Carol Clarke, Frederick Coffin, Suzanne Costallos, Allison Daneberg, Stephanie Daneberg, Randy Danson, Roger DeKoven, Richard deLaubenfels, John Elko, Brad Eney, Kimberly Farr, Henry Fonte, Jeffery Gordon, Ernest Graves, Castulo Guerra, Dorothea Hammond, Darrell Harris, Michael Hartford, Tom Hull, Lois Kelso Hunt, Gerry Kasarda, Mikel Lambert, Katherine Leask, Robert Lesko, Don Liberto, Steve Liebman, Cam Magee, James W. Mannon, Lisa Lynne Mathis, Kate McDarby, Kim Merrill, Barbara Montgomery, John Edward Mueller, Rita Nachtmann, John Neville-Andrews, Joe Palmieri, Addison Powell, John Proksy, Theresa Rakov, Sean Roberts, Marshall Robinson, David P. Samson, Kitty D. Samson, William G. Schilling, Scott Schofield, Robert Shampain, Trevor R. Spradlin, James Sterner, James Tolkan, John Madden Towey, Raquel Valadez, Stratton Walling, Eric Weitz, Jack Eric Williams, Frederick Todd Wilson, Ron Wyche

PRODUCTIONS

Galileo by Bertolt Brecht, One Mo' Time by Vernel Bagneris, The Man Who Came to Dinner by George S. Kaufman and Moss Hart, The Suicide by Nikolai Erdman, Cold Storage by Ronald Ribman, American Buffalo by David Mamet, God Bless You Mr. Rosewater by Kurt Vonnegut with book and lyrics by Howard Ashman and music by Alan Menken with additional lyrics by Dennis Green *World Premieres* of Disability by Ron Whyte, and The Child by Anthony Giordina, *American Premieres* of Kean by Jean-Paul Sartre, Pantomime by Derek Walcott. Special Events: The Flying Karamazov Brothers, Pat Carroll as Gertrude Stein, Stephen Wade in Banjo Dancing

George de Vincent/Joe B. Mann Photos

Mark Hammer, Annalee Jefferies in "The Man
Who Came to Dinner" Above: "The Suicide"

173

ASOLO STATE THEATER

Sarasota, Florida
June 1, 1980–May 31, 1981
Twenty-first Year

Executive Director, Richard G. Fallon; Managing Director, David S. Levenson; Artistic Director, Robert Strane; Literary Manager, Eberle Thomas; Musical Director, John Franceschina; Manager, Thomas Veeder; Press, Edith N. Anson; Sets, Sandro LaFerla, Holmes Easley, Bennet Averyt, John Ezell, Robert Darling, Franco Colavecchia; Costumes, Catherine King, Flozanne John, Sally A. Kos, Vicki S. Holden; Lighting, Martin Petlock; Stage Managers, Marian Wallace, Stephanie Moss, Dolly Meenan; Technical Director, Victor Meyrich.

COMPANY

Peter Burnell, Bernerd Engel, Deborah Fezelle, David S. Howard, Jeffrey Bryan King, Denise Koch, Theodore May, Monique Morgan, Robert Murch, Bette Oliver, Robert Strane, Isa Thomas, Bradford Wallace, Robert Elliott, Lawrence Gallegos, James Hunt, Ruth Kidder, Douglas R. Nielsen, Edward Stevlingson, William Van Hunter, Cynthia Wells, Ronald Wendschuh, David Gaines, Mark Jacoby, Patricia Masters, Kathy Morath, Chris Wheeler, Susannah Berryman, Raye Blakemore, Tara Buckley, Marnie Carmichael, James Hunt, James Daniels, Paul Dewey, Helen Halsey, Mark Hirschfield, Alan Kimberly, Clardy Malugen, Paul Singleton, Charles Bennison, Charles Cronk, Robert Ferguson, Jeanann Glassford, Marc H. Glick, Elizabeth Harrell, Michael Hodgson, Arthur Glen Hughes, Robert Kratky, Robin Llewellyn, Lowry Marshall, Peter Massey, Jon Michaelsen, Mark Rosenwinkel, Connie Rotunda, Elizabeth Streiff, Deborah Allen, Carolyn Bowes, Laurence Daggett, Ray Frewen, Leo Garcia, Richard Grubbs, Daniel Hagen, Neil Herlands, Jay Keye, Graves Mark Kiley, Phil Lombardo, Vicki March, Carol McCann, Mark Mikesell, Jane Rosinski, Sharon Taylor, Carlos Valdes-Dapena.

PRODUCTIONS

Man and Superman, Idiot's Delight, The Warrens of Virginia, Stand-Off at Beaver and Pine, On Golden Pond, The Beggar's Opera, Terra Nova, The Song Is Kern!, and *World Premiere* of Transcendental Love

Gary W. Sweetman Photos

Bradford Wallace, Peter Burnell
in "Man and Superman"

BARTER THEATRE

Abingdon, Virginia
April 7, 1980–April 11, 1981
Forty-eighth Season

Artistic Director/Producer, Rex Partington; Business Manager, Pearl Hayter; Press, Lou Flanigan; Associate Artistic Consultant, Owen Phillips; Directors, Patricia Carmichael, John Going, Pamela Hunt, James Kirkland, Ada Brown Mather, Jeff Meredith, John Olon, Rex Partington; Sets, Bennet Averyt, C. L. Hundley, Galen M. Logsdon; Costumes, Nancy Atkinson, Carol Blevins, C. L. Hundley, Sigrid Insull, Rachel Kurland, Galen M. Logsdon; Lighting, Bennet Averyt, Tony Partington, Karen Wenderoff; Musical Director, Marvin Jones; Stage Managers, Holley Jack Horner, Champe Leary, Tony Partington.

PRODUCTIONS AND CASTS

MISALLIANCE by George Bernard Shaw. CAST: Michael Guido, Cleo Holladay, William Mahone, Robert McNamara, Frederikke Meisiter, David Ossian, Rex Partington, Peggity Price, William Tost
THE ODYSSEY by Gregory A. Falls and Kurt Beattie. CAST: Duane Boyer, Tina James, Alan Kootsher, Michael McArthur, Charles Muckle, Shaw Purnell, Allen Schoer, Patrick Turner
THE IMPORTANCE OF BEING EARNEST by Oscar Wilde. CAST: Rusty Fawcett, Ted Houck, Alan Kootsher, Carolyn Olga Kruse, BettyAnn Leeseberg, Lily Lodge, Owen Phillips, Shaw Purnell, Richard Tabor, Patrick Turner
THE ROYAL FAMILY by George S. Kaufman and Edna Ferber, AH WILDERNESS! by Eugene O'Neill, THE DESPERATE HOURS by Joseph Hayes in repertory. CAST: Leta Bonynge, Russell Gold, Cleo Holladay, Roger Kozol, Bruce McPherson, Fillmore McPherson IV, Paul Merrill, Cynthia Parva, Tony Partington, Shaw Purnell, Carol Ann Runion, Luke Rebecca Taylor, Donna Thatcher, Haynes Tuell, Patrick Turner, Bruce Van Cott, Richard Voigts, Charles Michael Wright
THE HEIRESS by Ruth and Augustus Goetz. CAST: Eunice Anderson, Joseph Culliton, Libby Hisey, Cleo Holladay, Marion Hunter, Olivia Negron, Rex Partington, Tony Partington, Piper Smith
BLITHE SPIRIT by Noel Coward. CAST: Leigh Burch, Jolene Fodor, Cleo Holladay, Olivia Negron, Ralph Redpath, Piper Smith, Richard Voights
BERLIN TO BROADWAY WITH KURT WEILL performed by Alan Marks, Deborah Moldow, Barbara Niles, Curt Williams
RIVERWIND by John Jennings. CAST: Gregory Colan, Roger Fawcett, Marion Hunter, Deborah Moldow, Barbara Niles, Patty O'Brien, David Vogel
STARTING HERE, STARTING NOW by Richard Maltby, Jr. and David Shire. CAST: Deborah Moldow, Barbara Niles, Jean-Paul Richard
THE FANTASTICKS by Tom Jones and Harvey Schmidt. CAST: Jonathan Ball, Kenton Benedict, Jeff Burchfield, Lessie Burnum, Alan Hemingway, Donald Norris, Kevin O'Leary, Tony Partington
HOME OF THE BRAVE by Arthur Laurents. CAST: Mike Champagne, Ray Hill, Daniel Oreskes, Con Roche, Richard Tabor, Gerald Walling

Bill Adams/John Cornelius Photos

"The Fantasticks"
Above: "The Royal Family"

174

BODY POLITIC

Chicago, Illinois
May 1, 1980–June 7, 1981

Artistic Director, James D. O'Reilly; Managing Director, Sharon Phillips; Marketing Director, Warner Crocker; Business Manager, Gretchen Althen; Assistant Artistic Director/Literary Manager, Terry McCabe; Stage Manager, John Scavone

PRODUCTIONS AND CASTS

THE CLUB by Eve Merriam; Director, Michael Maggio; Choreography, Tracy Friedman; Set and Lights, Maher Ahmad; Costumes, Christa Scholtz; Stage Manager, John P. Kenny. CAST: Tracy Friedman, Eileen Manganaro, Mary Cobb, Linda Lorelle, Iris Liberman, Jill Shellabarger, June Shellene
BURIED CHILD by Sam Shepard; Director, Greg Kandel; Set, Maher Ahmad; Costumes, Marsha Kowal; Stage Manager, Myra Bowie. CAST: Nathan Davis, Marji Bank, Bob Swan, Richard Lavin, Jonathan Fuller, Ina Jaffe, Jim Keith
MARTIN LUTHER: APOSTLE OF DEFIANCE by John Kirk; Director, Dennis Zacek; Set, J. William Ruyle; Costumes, Douglas J. Koertge; Stage Manager, Kathy Kirk. CAST: Cal Pritner
COMING ATTRACTIONS by Jerry Haslmaier and Shelly Goldstein; Director, Kate Benton; Set, Sara Berg; Stage Manager, Steve Lippman. CAST: Shelly Goldstein, Sara Berg, Sandy Snyder, Barbara Howard, Christina Noonan
TWELFTH NIGHT by William Shakespeare; Directors, Pauline Brailsford, Susan Dafoe; Set, Lynn Ziehe; Costumes, Nan Zabriskie; Lights, Gary Heitz; Composer, Dan Tucker; Stage Manager, Lynn Ziehe. CAST: Marsha Bernstein, Lia McCoo, Brendan Phillips, Julie Sandor, Ray Rodriguez, Jeffrey Hutchinson, Douglas McBride, Razz Jenkins, Larry Brandenburg, Laura Innes, Stan Winiarski, Jill Holden, Gerry Becker, Tom Mula, Jay Ellen Hand, William J. Norris, Richard Kuhlman, Tucker Smith, David Westgor, Vince Viverito, Patrick Billingsley
TIES by Jeffrey Sweet; Director, Dennis Zacek; Set, Rick Paul; Costumes, Marsha Kowal; Stage Manager, Galen Ramsey. CAST: Roger Mueller, Jack Wallace, Ann Goldman, Rob Knepper, Tim Halligan, Greg Vinkler, Rita Kreger, Bill Appelbaum, Harry Ross
THE SEA HORSE by Edward J. Moore; Director, James O'Reilly; Set, Nels Anderson; Costumes, Elizabeth Passman; Lights, Gary Heitz; Stage Manager, John Scavone. CAST: Elizabeth Jacobs, Michael Lloyd

**Michael Lloyd, Elizabeth Jacobs
in "The Sea Horse"**

BONFILS THEATRE

Denver, Colorado
October 8, 1980–June 27, 1981

Producer, Henry E. Lowenstein; Production Manager, Ted Ross; Technical Director, Sean Woodburn; Press, Rebecca Toma, Steve Gould

PRODUCTIONS AND CASTS

NEW FACES OF 1980 *(World Premiere)* conceived and written by John Kluge and Bev Newcomb; Music and Lyrics, Milton Larsen, Richard M. Sherman, Beverly Mango; Director, Bev Newcomb; Choreography, Claudia Newcomb; Set, John Ross; Costumes, Becky Thompson, Stage Manager, Gary Miller. CAST: Paul Attardi, William Croy, B. J. Gibbons, Lori Lewis, Margaret Stenzel, Darline White
PIANO BAR by Doris Willens, Rob Fremont; Director, Robert Wells; Set, John Ross; Costumes, Carol Ramsdell; Props, Jack Prather. CAST: B. J. Gibbons, Paul Attardi, Stephen Nye, Ben Detterman, Kaby Birdsall
SLY FOX by Larry Gelbart; Director, Robert Wells; Set, John Ross; Stage Manager, Debra Barr. CAST: Christian Schoon, Wayne Cote, Wallace Vander Jagt, Jack Silcott, Douglas E. O'Brien, Bill Berry, Les Miller, Jeffrey Harms, Nita Froelich, Debra A. Brickhaus, Ken Lange, Dale Stewart, Kristie Taylor, Daymond Schweer, Larry Sapp
GUYS AND DOLLS by Frank Loesser, Jo Swerling, Abe Burrows; Director, Buddy Butler; Musical Direction, David Lee Roberts; Choreography, Cleo Parker Robinson; Costumes, Carol Ramsdell. CAST: Hayward Doyle, Jr., Mark Whalin, Valerie Pallai, Sheilah Wilkins, Bob Ingram, Jr., Zane Gray, Carl Finley, Vincent C. Robinson, Lisa A. Rose, Steven James, Helen Singer, Ed Battle
ISADORA DUNCAN SLEEPS WITH THE RUSSIAN NAVY by Jeff Wanshel; Director, Robert Wells. CAST: Roderic R. Kaats, Jay Blodgett, Alice A. Vaughn, Kevin Hart, Michael Duran, LuAnn Buckstein, Jeffrey Hess, Jamie Heinlein, Diane Gail Davies, Ken Milder
THE GLASS MENAGERIE by Tennessee Williams; Director, Bev Newcomb. CAST: Ruth Seeber, John MacKay, Glenna Kelly, Claudia Newcomb, Richard M. Coomer
SAME TIME, NEXT YEAR by Bernard Slade; Director, Bev Newcomb. CAST: Norman Jones, Mary Jo Moore
PAUL ROBESON by Phillip Hayes Dean; Director, Buddy Butler. CAST: Bob Ingram, Jr., Raymond Ross, E. Hayward Hobbs, Vincent Hardy
GREASE by Jim Jacobs, Warren Casey; Director Robert Wells. CAST: Helen Singer, Martha Newlin, Jonathan Wilhoft, Patti Williams, Marty Rapp, Cindy Schlager-Stubbs, Gary Pugh, Daymond Schweer, Jeffrey Harms, Hilary Klyn, R. J. Harris, Jennifer Sue Yarter, Kimberly G. Howard, Rich Beall, Urban Sanchez, Kay Carrillo, Jim Podhaisky
THE FANTASTICKS by Tom Jones and Harvey Schmidt; Director, Bev Newcomb. CAST: Terry McDonald, Ruthann Curry, Timothy Albo, Richard Chauncey, Tom Hughes, Albert Turner, Stuart Whitmore, Jeffrey Hess

Henry E. Lowenstein Photos

**Mary Jo Moore, Norman Jones
in "Same Time, Next Year"**

CALDWELL PLAYHOUSE

Boca Raton, Florida
November 18, 1980–May 3, 1981
Premiere Season
Artistic and Managing Director, Michael Hall; Scenic Design, Frank Bennett; Costume Design, Bridget Bartlett, Frank Bennett; Lighting Design, Jas Myers; Press, Patricia Burdett

PRODUCTIONS AND CASTS

YOU CAN'T TAKE IT WITH YOU with W. C. "Mutt" Burton, Mimi Honce, Viki Boyle, Peter Haig, Barbara Bradshaw, Gary Nathanson, Freda Kavanagh, Steven Bakker, Susan Hatfield, Rex King, Jannis Johnson, J. Robert Dietz, Ed Hinkle, Ann Sams, Ralph Redpath, Gerry Dedera, Kenneth Kay, Jim Carl
TEN LITTLE INDIANS with Barbara Bradshaw, Ralph Redpath, Patrick Beatey, Susan Hatfield, Peter Haig, Viki Boyle, Charles Cragin, Gary Nathanson, Ed Hinkle, Gerry Dedera, Steven Bakker
PICNIC with Susan Hatfield, Terrence O'Hara, Maggie Baird, Ralph Redpath, Susan Riskin, A. D. Cover, Virginia Mattis, Rica Martens, Gerry Dedera, Viki Boyle, Eilene Pierson
THE RELUCTANT DEBUTANTE with Julia Meade, Caroline Meade, Miller Lide, Erica Martens, Ellen Adamson, James Judy, Timothy Lewis

Linda Bannister Photos

Top Right: W. C. "Mutt" Burton, Barbara Bradshaw and company in "You Can't Take It with You"
Center: Caroline Meade, Julia Meade in "The Reluctant Debutante"
Bottom: Susan Hatfield, Terrence O'Hara in "Picnic"

Martha Nell Hardy in "Tamsen Donner"

CAROLINA REGIONAL THEATRE

Chapel Hill, North Carolina
September 19, 1980–May 2, 1981
Artistic Director, Martha Nell Hardy; General Manager, John E. Blizzard; Business Manager, B. Sue Boase; Resident Director, Norman E. Ussery

PRODUCTIONS AND CASTS

TAMSEN DONNER: A WOMAN'S JOURNEY with Martha Nell Hardy
SAINTS AND SINNERS with Lloyd Borstelmann, Walter Smith
TENNESSEE'S WALTZ with Marion Fitz-Simons, William M. Hardy, Carol Leigh Ponder, Lisa Whalin, Benny Key
THE JOHNNY BULL by Kathleen Betsko with B. Sue Boase, Cynthia Wood, John Whitty, Jerry Rogers, Carol Leigh Ponder
SHELTER by Karyn Traut with Carol Leigh Ponder, Marti Wilkerson, Gil Nelson, Ian McDowell, Peter Hardy, Jill Jackson, Erin McGinn, Bruce Ballard, Lisa Wright, Ellen McQueen
MESMER by Richard James with James Slaughter, William Hardy, Mark Stundenmind, Bruce Evers, Carol Leigh Ponder, Erin McGinn, Steve Tilson, Mike Rowan, Cynthia Wood, David Williamson

Thomas Fuldner Photos

CENTER STAGE

Baltimore, Maryland
September 19, 1980–June 14, 1981
Second Season

Artistic Director, Stan Wojewodski, Jr.; Managing Director, Peter W. Culman; Associate Artistic Director, Jackson Phippin; Press, Sally Livingston; Stage Managers, Amanda Megden, Barbara Abel; Technical Director, Jeff Muskovin; Lighting, Bonnie Ann Brown; Costumes, Lesley Skannal; Props, Richard Goodwin; Sound, Lewis Erskine

PRODUCTIONS AND CASTS

THE FRONT PAGE by Ben Hecht and Charles MacArthur; Director, Stan Wojewodski, Jr.; Set, Barry Robison. CAST: Zeke Zaccaro, Ray Dooley, John Martinuzzi, James Rebhorn, Walter Pearthree, Paul Peeling, Daniel Szelag, Rosemary Gaffney, Andrew Clark, Mark Margolis, Terrance O'Quinn, Barbara Hipkiss, Diana Stagner, Lance Davis, Patricia Kalember, Anne Sargent, Paul C. Thomas, J. S. Johnson, John Pielmeier, Richard Kneeland, Ted Schneider, William Jensen, Lonzo Davis, Ed Klein

AGNES OF GOD by John Pielmeier; Director, Stan Wojewodski, Jr.; Set, Hugh Landwehr; Costumes, Dona Granata; Lighting, Spencer Mosse. CAST: Jo Henderson, Anne Pitoniak, Tania Myren

THE DUENNA By Richard Brinsley Sheridan; Adapted and Composed by Lance Mulcahy *(World Premiere)*; Director, Garland Wright; Set and Costumes, Desmond Heelev; Lighting, Frances Aronson; Musical Director, Michael Ward; Choreographer, Randolyn Zinn. CAST: Lance Davis, Henry J. Jordan, Brent Barrett, Mary Elizabeth Mastrantonio, Lu Leonard, Gordon Connell, Betsy Beard, Joel Kramer

A MAN FOR ALL SEASONS by Robert Bolt; Director, Geoffrey Sherman; Set, Paul Wonsek; Costumes, Robert Wojewodski; Lighting, Arden Fingerhut. CAST: Patrick Cronin, Robert Burr, Robert Spencer, William Duff-Griffin, Sylvia Short, Denise Koch, Wil Love, Michael Thompson, Clement Fowler, Rick Duet, James McDonnell, Terrance O'Quinn, Rosemary Knower, William Verderber

SALLY'S GONE, SHE LEFT HER NAME by Russell David *(World Premiere)*; Director, Stan Wojewodski, Jr.; Set, Hugh Landwehr; Costumes, Linda Fisher. CAST: Elizabeth Franz, Talia Balsam, Federick Coffin, Paul McCrane, Peggy Cosgrave, Gerald J. Quimby

INHERIT THE WIND by Jerome Lawrence and Robert E. Lee; Director, Jackson Phippin; Set, Hugh Landwehr, Richard Goodwin; Costumes, Tiny Ossmam. CAST: Julian Fleisher, Hannah Treitel, Denise Koch, Walter Pearthree, James McDonnell, Vivienne Shub, Ken Hayward, Walt MacPherson, John Henry Cox, Scott Elliott, Robert Burr, Hilmar Sallee, Irving Engleman, Jacqueline Britton, Fred Rasmussen, William Jensen, Daniel Corcoran, Zachary Knower, Sarah Hart, Melissa Moran, Tom Quinn, Nancy Kay Uffner, Rosemary Knower, Bob Horen, Beth Vaughan, Michael Thompson, Robert Gerringer, Patricia Falkenhain, Joseph Snair, Dan Cuddy, Daniel Szelag, Paul Ballard, Michael Barrett, Rosemary Polen, Robert Pastene, J. S. Johnson, William Duff-Griffin, Bruce Godfrey, John Edmunds, Chuck Spoler

HOME AGAIN KATHLEEN by Thomas Babe with Frederick Coffin, Susan Sharkey, Carol Jean Lewis, Peg Murray, Kathy McKenna, Suzanne Stone, Lance Davis, Rick Duet

SACRED PLACES by Kermit Frazier with Suzanne Stone and Jay Fernandez

BACK TO BACK by Al Brown with Jay Fernandez and Paul McCrane

CAPTIVE RITES by Irene Oppenheim with Brenda Wehle, John McMartin, Hansford Rowe, Denise Koch, Terrance O'Quinn

THE STUDY by Sophy Burnham with Brenda Wehle, James McDonnell, Denise Koch, Katherine Squire, Hansford Rowe

THE WIND-UP TOYS by Sylvia Regan with Terrance O'Quinn, Denise Koch, John McMartin, David Marshall Grant, William Duff-Griffin, Rosemary Knower, Hansford Rowe, Laurinda Barrett, Katherine Squire, Brenda Wehle, Edie Kauffmann, Michael Thompson, James McDonnell, Ben Masters, Paula Marmon

THE FURTHER ADVENTURES OF SALLY by Russell Davis with David Marshall Grant, Ben Masters, Laurinda Barrett

THE WOODS by David Mamet with Cristine Rose, Graham Beckel

THE WOOLGATHERER by William Mastrosimone with Dennis Boutsikaris, Pat Karpen

Richard Anderson Photos

**Top Right: Joel Kramer, Lu Leonard
in "The Duenna" Below: Robert Pastene,
Robert Gerringer in "Inherit the Wind"
Center: "The Duenna"**

**Paul McCrane, Talia Balsam
in "Sally's Gone . . ."**

CENTER THEATRE GROUP/ AHMANSON THEATRE

Los Angeles, California
October 3, 1980–May 23, 1981
Fourteenth Season

Artistic Director, Robert Fryer; Managing Director, Michael Grossman; Associate Artistic Director, James H. Hansen; Press, Rupert Allan, James H. Hansen, Michelle McGrath; Administrative Coordinator, Joyce Zaccaro; Production Administrator, Ralph Beaumont; Stage Managers, Bill Holland, Patrick Watkins; Technical Supervisor, Robert Routolo; Sound, William Young; Wardrobe, Eddie Dodds

PRODUCTIONS AND CASTS

HOLIDAY by Philip Barry; Director, Robert Allan Ackerman; Set, John Lee Beatty; Costumes, Robert Wojewodski; Lighting, Arden Fingerhut; Production Associate, Robert Linden. CAST: Marisa Berenson (Julia), Ivor Barry (Henry), Colby Chester (Charles), Kevin Kline (Johnny), Sally Kellerman (Seton), Carole Kean (Laura), Nicholas Hormann (Nick), Marya Small (Susan), Understudies: Terrence O'Connor, Colby Chester, Ivor Barry, Phoebe Pfeiffer, Tom McKitterick, Patrick Watkins

THE CRUCIFER OF BLOOD by Paul Giovanni; Director, Mr. Giovanni; Sets, John Wulp; Costumes, Noel Taylor; Lighting, David Hersey; Effects, Bran Ferren; Production Associate, Robert Linden. CAST: Dwight Schultz (Maj. Ross), Alan Coates (Capt. St. Claire), Christopher Curry (Small), Ian Abercrombie (Hindu/Inspector), Tuck Milligan (Afghan/Birdy), J. Christopher O'Connor (Mohammedan), Charlton Heston (Sherlock Holmes), Jeremy Brett (Dr. Watson), Suzanne Lederer (Irene), Ronald Dennis (Tonga), Liu Han T'Seng (Chinaman), Richard Denison (Policeman), C. Edward Pogue (Sailor), Understudies: Michael Ensign, Richard Denison, Sally Klein, C. Edward Pogue, J. Christopher O'Connor, Christopher Canaan

THE WEST SIDE WALTZ by Ernest Thompson. See National Touring Companies, page 167.

MARY STUART by Friedrich Schiller; Translated and adapted by Joe McClinton; Director, Jack O'Brien; Sets and Costumes, Sam Kirkpatrick; Lighting, John McLain; Music, Conrad Susa; Sound Roger Gans; Production Supervisor, Thomas Hall. CAST: Robert Cornthwaite (Paulet), Richard Denison (Drury), Neva Patterson (Hannah), Marsha Mason (Mary Stuart), Stephen McHattie (Mortimer), Thomas Hill (Baron Burleigh), Gary Dontzig (Davison), John-Frederick Jones (Earl of Kent), Michael Learned (Elizabeth I), Robert Foxworth (Earl of Leicester), William Schallert (Earl of Shrewsbury), John Allison (Count L'Aubespine), Stefan Fischer (Count Bellievre), Paul Haber (Page), Phoebe Pfeiffer (Barbara), Craig Dudley (O'Kelly), Ian Abercrombie (Melvil), Amy Levitt (Margaret Curl), Attendants: Vaughn Armstrong, Don Bilotti, Joseph Cappelli, Michael Sullivan, Standbys: Amy Levitt, Paddi Edwards, Vaughn Armstrong, Don Bilotti, Joseph Cappelli, Richard Denison, Craig Dudley, Paul Haber, John-Frederick Jones, Phoebe Pfeiffer, Liam Sullivan, Michael Sullivan

Jay Thompson Photos

Right: Craig Dudley, Stephen McHattie
in "Mary Stuart" Above: Ian Abercrombie,
Jeremy Brett, Charlton Heston in "Crucifer
of Blood" Top: Marisa Berenson, Sally Kellerman,
Maurice Evans, Kevin Kline in "Holiday"

Katharine Hepburn
in "West Side Waltz"

Neva Patterson, William Schallert, Marsha Mason,
Michael Learned, Robert Foxworth in "Mary Stuart"

CENTER THEATRE GROUP/ MARK TAPER FORUM

Los Angeles, California
August 14, 1980–July 26, 1981
Fourteenth Season

Artistic Director/Producer, Gordon Davidson; Managing Director, William P. Wingate; Associate Artistic Director, Kenneth Brecher; Director Improvisational Theatre Project, John Dennis; Staff Producer for Laboratory Programs, Madeline Puzo; Press, Nancy Hereford, Anthony Sherwood, Karen Kruzich; Literary Manager, Russell Vandenbroucke; Director Writer Development, Joseph Morgenstern; Staff Producer for ITP, Philip Himberg; Designer, Tharon Musser; Technical Director, Robert Routolo; Production Administrator, Don Winton; Stage Managers, Frank Bayer, Bud Coffey, Nikos Kafkalis, Bonnie Panson, Don Winton, Paul Gustie, Linda Intaschi, Jonathan Barlow Lee, James T. McDermott

PRODUCTIONS AND CASTS

THE LADY AND THE CLARINET *(World Premiere)* by Michael Cristofer; Director, Gordon Davidson; Music, Leonard Rosenman; Lyrics, Alan and Marilyn Bergman; Set, John Lee Beatty; Costumes, Carrie F. Robbins; Lighting, John Gleason, CAST: Rose Gregorio (Luba), Kevin Geer (Paul), David Spielberg (Jack), Josef Sommer (George), Bill Lamden (The Clarinet)

BILLY BISHOP GOES TO WAR by John Gray in collaboration with Eric Peterson; Director, John Gray; Set, David Gropman; Lighting, Jennifer Tipton. CAST: Eric Peterson (Billy Bishop), John Gray (Narrator/Pianist)

A CHRISTMAS CAROL adapted from Charles Dickens' novel by Doris Baizley; Director, Frank Condon; Sets and Costumes, Charles Berliner; Lighting, Tom Ruzika; Music, Susan Seamans Harvey; Choreography, Walter Kennedy. CAST: Bruce French (Scrooge), Socorro Valdez (Tiny Tim), Ralph Steadman (Marley), Tony Papenfuss (Bob Cratchit), Chequita Jackson (Mrs. Crachit), Michael Knight (Fred), Deborah Tilton (Fred's Wife), Don J. Boughton (Fezziwig), Donna Fuller (Mrs. Fezziwig), Julianna Fjeld (Ghost of Christmas Present), John Salazar (Christmas Present II), Victoria Thatcher (Ghost of Christmas Future), Stuart K. Robinson (Christmas Present III)

HOAGY, BIX AND WOLFGANG BEETHOVEN BUNKHAUS *(American Premiere)* a jazz play by Adrian Mitchell; Based on "The Stardust Road" by Hoagy Carmichael; Director, Steven Robman; Set, Tony Walton; Costumes, Dona Granata; Lighting, Tharon Musser, Musical Direction and Arrangements, Richard M. Sudhalter. CAST: David Frishberg (Pianist), Larry Cedar (Hoagy Carmichael), Amanda McBroom (Betty), Neva Small (Meg), Harry Groener (Bix Beiderbecke), Philip Baker Hall (Photographer, Pete Costas), Richard M., Sudhalter (Cornet), F. William Parker (Mr. Beiderbecke/Engineer/Paul Whiteman), Bruce French (Wolfgang Beethoven Bunkhaus)

TINTYPES conceived by Mary Kyte with Mel Melvin and Gary Pearle; See Broadway Calendar, page

TWO PLAYS IN REPERTORY: Scenery, Douglas W. Schmidt; Costumes, John Conklin; Lighting, Martin Aronstein; Music, Catherine MacDonald, Fight and Dance Choreography, Anthony DeLongis; Production Coordinator, Frank Bayer

CHEKHOV IN YALTA by John Driver and Jeffrey Haddow; Directed by Ellis Rabb and Gordon Davidson. CAST: Lois Foraker (Fyokla), Robin Gammell (Anton Chekhov), Keene Curtis (Maxim Gorky), James R. Winker (Ivan Alexeivich Bunin), Marian Mercer (Masha Chekhov), Penny Fuller (Olga Leonardova Knipper), Dana Elcar (Vladimir Nemirovich-Danchenko), Andra Akers (Lilina Stanislavski), Michael Bond (Luzhki), Jeffrey Combs (Moskvin), Rene Auberjonois (Konstantin Sergeievich Stanislavski), Douglas Blair, Edward Fabry (Peasants)

TWELFTH NIGHT by William Shakespeare; Directed by Ellis Rabb and Diana Maddox. CAST: Robin Gammell (Orsino), Edward Fabry (Curio), Kario Salem (Valentine), Penny Fuller (Viola), Michael Bond (Sea Captain), Dana Elcar (Sir Toby Belch), Lois Foraker (Maria), James R. Winker (Sir Andrew Aguecheek), Keene Curtis (Feste), Marian Mercer or Andra Akers (Olivia), Rene Auberjonois (Malvolio), Douglas Blair (Antonio), Craig Zehms (Sebastian), Jeffrey Combs (Fabian), Zale Kessler (Priest)

Right Center: Robin Gammell, Rene Auberjonois in "Chekhov in Yalta" Above: Bruce Frendh, Harry Groener, Larry Cedar in "Hoagy, Bix and Wolfgang ..." Top: Bill Lamden, Rose Gregorio in "The Lady and the Clarinet"

FORUM LABORATORY

TONGUES by Sam Shepard and Joseph Chaikin; Director, Robert Woodruff; Costumes, Mary Brecht; Lighting, Beverly Emmons; Music, Sam Shepard; Performed by Skip LaPlante. CAST: Joseph Chaikin

THE LAST YIDDISH POET created by A Traveling Jewish Theatre; Written by Naomi Newman Pollack, Albert Greenberg, Corey Fischer; Director, Miss Pollack; Set and Lighting, Tom Clover; Musical Direction, Albert Greenberg; Masks, Corey Fischer. CAST: Corey Fischer, Albert Greenberg

APEWATCH by Elaine Osio; Director, G. W. Bailey; Set, Keith Gonzales; Lighting, Brian Gale; Costumes, Sherry Thompson; Sound, Chris Fielder. CAST: Carol Williard (Lisa), Dean Santoro (Richard), Linda Carlson (Karen), Andy Wood (Christopher)

STARS IN YOUR EYES conceived by Oz Scott and Ron Abel; Director, Oz Scott; Music, Ron Abel; Lyrics, Ron Abel, Bob Garrett; Additional Lyrics, Robin Blair, Warren Ham, Marilyn Pasekoff; Choreography and Musical Staging, Murphy Cross, Newton Winters. CAST: Ron Abel, Nathan Cook, Nedra Dixon, Kara Grannum, Elizabeth Lamers, Jaison Walker

A PRELUDE TO DEATH IN VENICE by Lee Breuer; A Mabou Mines Project with SISTER SUZIE CINEMA

Jay Thompson Photos

CINCINNATI PLAYHOUSE

Cincinnati, Ohio
October 7, 1980–July 12, 1981

Producing Director, Michael Murray; Managing Director, Robert W. Tolan; Directors, Michael Murray, Michael Hankins, Edward Berkeley, Amy Saltz, Jacques Cartier, John Going; Musical Director, Boyd Staplin; Choreographer, David Holdgreiwe; Sets, Neil Peter Jampolis, Karen Schultz, Joseph A. Varga, Patricia Woodbridge, Jonathan Arkin, David Jenkins, Karl Eigsti, William Schroder; Costumes, Jennifer van Mayrhauser, Rebecca Senske, Caley Summers, Ann Firestone, Jeanne Button, Elizabeth Palmer, William Schroder; Lighting, Neil Peter Jampolis, Jay Depenbrock, Spencer Mosse, F. Mitchell Dana; Press, Jerri Roberts; Stage Managers, Patricia Ann Speelman, G. Roger Abell; Business Manager, Kathy Mohylsky.

PRODUCTIONS AND CASTS

COMPULSION with John Beran, Ken Bright, Donald Christopher, Yolanda Delgado, James Eckhouse, Richard Fitch, Richard Hayes, Mickey Zale Heller, Bill Hurlbut, Virginia Hut, J. Douglas James, Eileen Letchworth, Leslie Meeker, Ken Myles, Jay Patterson, Richard Pruitt, Constance Ray, Michael M. Ryan, James Secrest, Robert Shrewsbury, Neil Sims, David Upson, Nona Waldeck, David Wiles, John Wylie
BURIED CHILD with Donald Christopher, James Eckhouse, Virginia Hut, Eileen Letchworth, Jay Patterson, Michael M. Ryan, John Wylie
THE MAN WHO CAME TO DINNER with Donna Adams, Kip Baker, Shirl Bernheim, Ken Bright, Lanni Carvel, Suzanne Granfield, Mickey Zale Heller, John High, Bob Horen, Bill Hurlbut, J. Douglas James, Dorothy Lancaster, Ralph C. Lewis, Jillian Lindig, Leslie Meeker, Monica Merryman, Vance Mizelle, Philip Polito, Gary Pollard, Constance Ray, Robert Shrewsbury, David Upson, David Wohl
LOOSE ENDS with Kitty Mei-Mei Chen, Sandy Faison, Ed Hyland, Pat Karpen, J. Courtlandt Miller, Jay Patterson, Gary Pollard, Reno Roop, Sally Sockwell, John Spencer
SERENADING LOUIE with Jim DeMarse, Edmond Genest, Jill O'Hara, Lynn Ritchie
THE SCHOOL FOR SCANDAL with Louis Beachner, Arthur Bergel, Thomas Carson, Robertson Dean, John Emes, Bill Hurlbut, Amy Ingersoll, Jeffry Kilgore, Joyce Krempel, Gwendolyn Lewis, Ralph C. Lewis, Ellen Lee Margulies, J. Courtlandt Miller, Jana Robbins, Neil Sims, Paul C. Thomas, David Upson, Nona Waldeck
A VIEW FROM THE BRIDGE with Alan Ansara, Tom Caruso, Tony Darnell-Davis, Yolanda Delgado, Richard Fitch, Tony Hoty, Bill Hurlbut, Bram Lewis, Ralph C. Lewis, Tom Mardirosian, Diane Martella, Richard Pruitt, Steven J. Schulz, Jackie Walsh
THE GIN GAME with Anne Pitoniak, John Wylie
TINTYPES with Tom Flagg, Beth Fowler, David Green, Mary Louise, Tanny McDonald

Sandy Underwood Photos

Left Center: "School for Scandal" Above: "The Man Who Came to Dinner" Top: "Compulsion"

**Sandy Faison, Kitty Mei-Mei Chen
in "Loose Ends"**

**Anne Pitoniak, John Wylie
in "The Gin Game"**

CLEVELAND PLAY HOUSE

Cleveland, Ohio
September 16, 1980–May 17, 1981
Sixty-fifth Season

Director, Richard Oberlin; Acting Associate Director, Kenneth Albers; General Manager, Janet Wade; Business Manager, Nelson Isekeit; Dramaturg, Peter Sander; Production Manager, James Irwin; Scenic Director, Richard Gould; Press, Edwin P. Rapport; Administrative Assistant, Linda M. Steffancin; Directors, Kenneth Albers, Paul Lee, Evie McElroy, Richard Oberlin, William Rhys, Peter Sander, Lynne Gannaway, Michael Maggio, Larry Tarrant; Sets, Richard Gould, James Irwin, Estelle Painter, Charles Berliner, Gary Eckhart, Wayne Merritt, Paul Rodgers; Costumes, Estelle Painter; Choreographer, Susan Epstein Irwin; Props, Jamie Reich; Music Consultant, David Gooding; Stage Managers, Anthony Berg, Jan Crean, Annette Jops, Michael Stanley

COMPANY

Mary Adams-Smith, Kenneth Albers, Norm Berman, Sharon Bicknell, Allan Byrne, Candice M. Cain, Elisabeth Farwell, Paul A. Floriano, June Gibbons, Richard Halverson, Joseph G. Jefferson, James P. Kisicki, Joe D. Lauck, Allen Leatherman, Paul Lee, Morgan Lund, Harper Jane McAdoo, Evie McElroy, Judy Nevits, Richard Oberlin, Si Osborne, Herbert Mark Parker, Carolyn Reed, William Rhys, James Richards, Gary Smith, Cassandra Swanson, Wayne S. Turney, Mary Jane Wells, *Guest Artists:* Catherine Albers, Pat Carroll, David Frazier, George Gould, Jack Ryland, Katherine Squire, Dudley Swetland, Stephen Wade

PRODUCTIONS

Banjo Dancing by Stephen Wade, Watch on the Rhine by Lillian Hellman, Indulgences in the Louisville Harem by John Orlock, Filumena by Eduardo de Filippo, adapted by Willis Hall and Keith Waterhouse, A Christmas Carol by Charles Dickens, adapted by Doris Baizley, Bedroom Farce by Alan Ayckbourn, Emigrants by Slawomir Mrozek, translated by Peter Sander, Strider: The Story of a Horse by Mark Rozovsky, adapted by Robert Kalfin and Steve Brown, Children of Darkness by Edwin Justus Mayer, Gertrude Stein by Marty Martin, On Golden Pond by Ernest Thompson, A Funny Thing Happened on the Way to the Forum by Bert Shevelove, Larry Gelbart, Stephen Sondheim, How I Got That Story by Amlin Gray

Michael Edwards Photos

Top Left: Carolyn Reed, Joe Lauck
in "Children of Darkness" Below:
William Rhys in "Strider . . ."

THE CRICKET THEATRE

Minneapolis, Minnesota
October 24, 1980–June 13, 1981

Managing Director, Cynthia Mayeda; Artistic Director, Lou Salerni; Guest Director, Howard Dallin; Press, Lee Eddison; Literary Manager/Dramatug, John Orlock; Assistant Managing Director, Diane Knust; Administrative Assistant, Rebecca Bringgold; Sets and Costumes, Vera Polovko-Mednikov; Lighting, Michael Vennerstrom; Stage Managers, Charlotte Green, Beth Azemore, Norbert Een; Technical Director, Bob Davis; Props, Colin Tugwell

PRODUCTIONS AND CASTS

BLUES *(World Premiere)* by Kirk Ristau; Director, Lou Salerni; Composer and Musical Director, Hal Atkinson. CAST: Naomi Hatfield, Tia Mann, Amy Buchwald, Denise Ellis, Robert Mailand
SIGHTLINES *(World Premiere)* by Mark Eisman; Director, Howard Dallin. CAST: Robert Breuler, Allison Giglio
TACTICS FOR NON-MILITARY BODIES *(World Premiere)* by John Orlock; Director, Lou Salerni. CAST: Robert Mailand, Robert Breuler, Barbara Reid, Camille Gifford, James Martin
NORTHERN LIGHTS *(World Premiere)* by Erik Brogger; Director, Howard Dallin. CAST: John Lewin, Robert Mailand, David Wohl, Clive Rosengren, Binky Wood, Barbara Reid, James Harris, Chris Forth
THE DARK AT THE TOP OF THE STAIRS by William Inge; Director, Lou Salerni. CAST: Camille Gifford, Robert Mailand, Donald Goff, Amy Buchwald, Chris Forth, John Lewin, Shirley Venard Diercks, Dale Goff, Stephen DiMenna
TALLEY'S FOLLY by Lanford Wilson; Director, Howard Dallin. CAST: Michael Laskin, Karen Landry
SIDE BY SIDE BY SONDHEIM by Stephen Sondheim; Director, Lou Salerni; Musical Director, Jimmy Martin; Choreographer, Lewis Whitlock. CAST: Richard Allison, Susan Long, Dolores Noah, Dave Moore

Patrick Boemer Photos

Denise Ellis in "Blues"

DELAWARE THEATRE COMPANY

Wilmington, Delaware
December 11, 1980–March 7, 1981

Artistic Director, Cleveland Morris; Producing Director, Peter DeLaurier; Technical Director, Howard Paul Beals, Jr.; Stage Manager, Michael Petro; Press, D'Arcy Webb; Sets, Dennis Size, Thomas Schraeder, Howard P. Beals, Jr.; Lighting, Rachel Budin, Thomas Schraeder; Costumes, Paige Southard, April Briggs; Sound, Alan Gardner

PRODUCTIONS AND CASTS

A CHRISTMAS CAROL by Charles Dickens; Adapted by Peter DeLaurier; Director, Bohdan Senkow. CAST: Avrom Berel, David Pichette, David Hopson, Ceal Phelan, Rhiannon Shute, Anne Eder, Peter Rosacker, Donn Giammarco, Michael Manning, Mary Ann Rizzo, John Janney, Thomas Quinlan
THE LITTLE HUT by Andre Roussin; Adapted by Nancy Mitford; Director, Cleveland Morris. CAST: David Hopson, Carolyn Olga Kruse, Sam Blackwell, Robert B. Kessler, Peter Free
BUS STOP by William Inge; Director, Cleveland Morris. CAST: Anne Eder, Ceal Phelan, Drury Pifer, Carolyn Olga Kruse, Jack Axelrod, David Baffone, Chaz Denny, Hollis Huston
THE AMERICAN DREAM by Edward Albee and DOING A GOOD ONE FOR THE RED MAN by Mark Medoff; Director, Sam Blackwell. CAST: Beverly Jense, Michael Metzel, Chaz Denny, Ceal Phelan, Molly McGhee

David Owen/Richard Carter Photos

Beverly Jensen, Michael Metzel, Molly McGhee in "The American Dream"

DENVER CENTER THEATRE COMPANY

Denver, Colorado
November 21, 1980–April 18, 1981
Second Season

Artistic Director, Edward Payson Call; Managing Director, Sarah Lawless; Production Manager, Peter Davis; Assistant to Artistic Director, Walter Schoen; Stage Directors, Edward Payson Call, Jerome Kilty, Stuart Vaughan, Kenneth Welsh, Laird Williamson; Assistant Directors, Mark Cuddy, Peter Hackett; Sets, Robert Blackman, Lowell Detweiler, Sam Fleming, Merrily Ann Murray; Lighting, Pamela Cooper, Donald Darnutzer, Dirk Epperson, Robert Jared, Danny Ionazzi, Duane Schuler; Music, Brice Odland, Larry Delinger; Sound, Bruce Odland, Choreographer, Carolyn Dyer; Fight Choreography, Tony Simotes; Musical Director, P. Kevin Kennedy; Stage Managers, Kent Conrad, Mary Hunter, Douglas Pagliotti, Preston Lovell Terry; Literary Manager, Christopher Kirkland; Company Manager, Karyn Browne; Business Manager, Tim Shields; Press, Sharon Griggins, Eleanor Glover, Mary Nelson

REPERTORY COMPANY

Gregg Almquist, Mary Benson, Tony Carpenter, Gregory Cole, Maury Cooper, Tandy Cronyn, James Doescher, Andrea Edwards, Julian Gamble, Paul Hebron, Gregg Henry, Todd Jamieson, Raymond Lang, James Lawless, Darrie Lawrence, Judy Leavell, Rod Loomis, Loraine M. F. Masterton, John Napierala, James Newcomb, Catherine O'Connell, Pamela O'Conner, Nigel Parr, James Read, Linda Robinson, Mercedes Ruehl, Kym Schwartz, Brockman Seawell, Earl Sennett, Tucker Shaw, Connor Smith, Tom Spackman, Miles Stasica, Susan-Joan Stefan, Theodore Stevens, Bret Torbeck, Edward Vogels, Bill Walters, Jerry Webb, Amelia White
PRODUCTIONS IN REPERTORY: Henry IV Part I by William Shakespeare, Under Milk Wood by Dylan Thomas, Misalliance by George Bernard Shaw, Medea by Euripides (adapted by Robinson Jeffers), Loot by Joe Orton
ADDITIONAL PRODUCTIONS:
WINGS by Arthur Kopit, with Robert H. Gingrich, Darrie Lawrence, Gary J. Mazzu, Midge Montgomery, Patricia Moren, John Napierala, Earl Sennett, Joan St. Onge, Geoffrey Wade, Sandy Walper, Amelica White, Lee Brock, Lance Ashton Fishbein, Kevin Hart, R. Aaron Lincoln, Joseph C. McDonald, Marion Copeland Mitchell, Patrick T. Peeples, Tyson Douglas Rand, Julie N. Sisk, Stan C. Soto, Becky Thompson, Brent Varner
HOW TO SUCCEED IN BUSINESS WITHOUT REALLY TRYING by Abe Burrows, Jack Weinstock, Willie Gilbert, Frank Loesser. CAST: Gregg Almquist, Tony Carpenter, Paul Hebron, Leslie Hicks, Todd Jamieson, Stephanie Juenger, James Lawless, Judy Leavell, James Newcomb, Catherine O'Connell, Jeffrey Reese, Alexana Ryer Rieth, Kym Schwartz, Keith Ashley Sellon, Connor Smith, Susan-Joan Stefan, Bill Walters, Jerry Webb, Perri Williamson, B. Paul Blount, Tracey Girdley, Lynda Hatfield, James Carl Manley, Terry McDonald, Al McFarland, Koni Murdock, Robin Nicholas, Todd Robinson, Jay Willick, Frederick Winship

John Youngblut Photos

Darrie Lawrence, Mercedes Ruehl in "Medea"
Above: Tandy Cronyn, Brockman Seawell, James Lawless in "Misalliance"

DETROIT REPERTORY THEATRE

Detroit, Michigan
November 6, 1980–June 28, 1981
Artistic Director, Bruce E. Millan; Executive Director, Robert Williams; Directors, Dee Andrus, Barbara Busby, Bruce E. Millan; Stage Managers, Dee Andrus, William Boswell; Sets and Lighting, Marylynn Kacir, Dick Smith; Costumer, Vida Darrell

PRODUCTIONS AND CASTS

CATSPLAY by Istvan Orkeny, with Dee Andrus (Ersi), Barbara Busby (Giza), Ruth Palmer (Paula), John Baird (Yanos), Monika Ziegler (Mousie), Robert Williams (Yoshka), Alisa Foster (Ilona), William Boswell (Victor), Barbara Henderson (Adelaide)
AMERICAN BUFFALO by David Mamet, with Robert Skrok (Bobby), Von H. Washington (Teach), Robert Williams (Donny)
PUNTILA AND MATTI, HIS HIRED MAN by Bertolt Brecht, with Dee Andrus, Jocelyn K. Ashford, William Boswell, Gregory Bowman, Barbara Busby, Darius L. Dudley, Dennis Dunne, Evelyn Green, Willie Hodge, Mark Murri, Robert Rucker, Ron Samuel, Robert Skrok, Robert Williams
BOSOMS AND NEGLECT by John Guare, with Ruth Allen Palmer (Henny), Barbara Busby (Deidre), Council Cargle (Scooper)

Bruce E. Millan Photos

Barbara Busby, Council Cargle
in "Bosoms and Neglect"
Top: Ruth Allen Palmer, William Boswell,
Dee Andrus in "Catsplay"

EAST WEST PLAYERS

Los Angeles, California
June 26, 1980–June 21, 1981
Artistic Director, Mako; Assistant Artistic Director, Alberto Isaac; Administrator, Janet Mitsui; Producers, Jim Ishida, Clyde Kusatsu; Administrative Assistant, Irma Escamilla; Production Assistant, Patricia Yasutake; Technical Director, Jerry Tondo; Sets, Woodward Romine, Jr., Rae Creevey, Jay Koiwai; Costumes, Rodney Kageyama, J. Maseras Pepito, Ellen Wakamatsu; Lighting, Rae Creevey, Bill Schaffner, Doreen Remo; Sound, Lucia Hwang; Musical Director, Glen Chin; Stage Managers, Irma Escamilla, Sheila Klein, Jerry S. Tondo, Dave Jacobs, Keone Young, Marcus Mukai, Elizabeth Reiko Kubota, Ellen Wakamatsu, Leigh Kim, Tamra McLeod, Doreen Remo; Press, Emily Kuroda, Betty Muramoto

PRODUCTIONS AND CASTS

HAPPY END by Bertolt Brecht, Kurt Weill. CAST: Clyde Kusatsu, Marcus K. Mukai, Glen Chin, Dom Magwili, Jim Ishida, Alberto Isaac, Shizuko Hoshi, Patti Yasutake, Rob Narita, Virginia Wing, Susan Haruye Ioka, Saachiko, Jerry S. Tondo, Nancy Omi, Deborah Nishimura, David Hirokane, Tom L. Atha, Dave Jacobs, Mimosa Iwamatsu, Sala Iwamatsu, Vincent Freeman
F.O.B. by David Henry Hwang. CAST: Keone Young, Kim Yumiko, John Lone, Susan Haruye, Merv Maruyama, Susan Haruye, J. Maseras Pepito, Alberto Isaac, Richard Narita, Emily Kuroda, Ellen Wakamatsu, Patti Yasutake, Doug Yasuda
HOKUSAI SKETCHBOOKS by Seiichi Yashiro. CAST: Mako, Clyde Kusatsu, Emily Kuroda, Petti Yasutake, Yuki Shimoda, Jim S. Ishida, Soon-Teck Oh, Keone Young, J. Maseras Pepito, Susan Haruye Ioka, Saachiko, Ellen Wakamatsu, David Hirokane, Merv Maruyama, Leigh Kim
GODSPELL by John Michael Tebelak, Stephan Schwartz. CAST: Tom L. Atha, Glen Chin, Tim Dang, Susan Haruye Ioka, Dian Kobayashi, Elizabeth R. Kubota, Dom Magwili, Marcus Mukai, Deborah Nishimura, Saachiko, Dave Jacobs, Marv Maruyama, Nancy Omi, Marilyn Tokuda, Jerry Tondo, Patti Yasutake

Emily Kuroda/James Wong Photos

John Lone, Kim Yumiko in "F.O.B."
Above: Emily Kuroda, Yuki Shimoda
in "Hokusai Sketchbooks"

FOLGER THEATRE GROUP

Washington, D.C.
September 30, 1980–August 2, 1981
Eleventh Season

Producer, Louis W. Scheeder; Associate Producer, Michael Sheehan; General Manager, Mary Ann deBarbieri; Production Manager, Michael Foley; Costumes, Bary Allen Odom; Technical Director, Bill Tesk; Props, Janet Windus; Sound, Jacky English; Company Manager, Ruth Lancaster; Assistant to Producers, Eileen Cowel, Valerie Hanlon; Music Consultant, William Penn; Wardrobe, Laura Barierre; Press, Paula Bond, Tracy Ann Christin

PRODUCTIONS AND CASTS

MEASURE FOR MEASURE by William Shakespeare; Director, Roger Hendricks Simon; Set, Ursula Belden. CAST: Justin Deas, David Little, Moultrie Patten, Donald Warfield, Floyd King, Eric Zwemer, James Williams, Jr., Brian Kale, Timothy O'Hare, Michael W. Howell, David Cromwell, John Neville-Andrews, Jim Beard, Brenda Curtis, Marion Lines, Lorraine Pollack, Cam Magee, Janice Fuller, Stuart Lerch, Jean Korey, Janet Stanford, David Nachmanoff, Elizabeth Hamilton, Kevin Kinley

MUSEUM by Tina Howe; Director, Leonard Peters; Set, Hugh Lester. CAST: Peter Dowling, Jim Brady, Larry Marshall, Richard Bey, Ralph Cosham, Patricia Triana, Ruby Holbrook, Kathleen Helmer, Deborah Weathers, Anne Stone, Robert Bonds, Paul Norwood, Larry Rosler, June Squibb, Nannette Rickert, Jack Landron, John Gilliss, Michael G. Chin, Tara Loewenstern, Ellen Newman

THE RIVALS by Richard Brinsley Sheridan; Director, Mikel Lambert; Set, Russell Metheny. CAST: Leonardo Cimino, Eric Zwemer, Ralph Cosham, David Cromwell, Moultrie Patten, Floyd King, Jim Beard, Mark Basile, June Hansen, Glynis Bell, Marion Lines, Anne Stone, Paul Norwood, Patricia Babb, Cam Magee, Bill Schlaht, Elizabeth Hamilton, Kevin Kinley

CROSSING NIAGARA (American Premiere) by Alonso Alegría; Translated from the Spanish by Mr. Alegría; Director, Louis W. Scheeder; Set, Hugh Lester. CAST: Michael Tolaydo (Blondin), Tobias Haller (Carlo)

LOVE'S LABOUR'S LOST by William Shakespeare; Director, Louis W. Scheeder; Set, Hugh Lester; Choreography, Virginia Freeman. CAST: Ralph Cosham, Michael Tolaydo, David Cromwell, Jim Beard, Leonardo Cimino, Paul Norwood, David Wano, James Williams, Jr., Albert Corbin, Eric Zengota, Michael Gabel, Earle Edgerton, Terry Hinz, Tobias Haller, Tom Aldridge, Marion Lines, Ellen Newman, Katherine Manning, Lorraine Pollack, Glynis Bell

HOW I GOT THAT STORY by Amlin Gray; Director, Carole Rothman; Set, Patricia Woodbridge; Sound, Gary Harris; Stage Managers, Martha Knight, Laura Burroughs. CAST: Don Scardino (The Reporter), Richard Kline (The Historical Event)

ROMEO AND JULIET by William Shakespeare; Director, Michael Tolaydo; Set, John Hodges. CAST: Leonardo Cimino, David Chandler, Paul Norwood, Ralph Cosham, Franchelle Stewart Dorn, Robert L. Burns, Patrick Clear, David Wano, James Williams, Jr. Earle Edgerton, Marion Lines, Margaret Whitton, Kenneth Meseroll, Glynis Bell, Tobias Haller, Terry Hinz, Jim Beard, Pamela Brown, Maureen McGinnis, David Cromwell, Dion Anderson, John Elko, Lorraine Pollack, Craig Wroe

Joan Marcus Photos

Robert L. Burns, Margaret Whitton in "Romeo and Juliet" Top: Don Scardino, Richard Kline in "How I Got That Story"

FORD'S THEATRE

Washington, D.C.
April 13, 1980–June 21, 1981
Tenth Season

Executive Producer, Frankie Hewitt; Managing Director, Maury Sutter; Development, Anne Fleming; Press, Patricia Humphrey, Nancy Lesser

PRODUCTIONS AND CASTS

JOSEPH AND THE AMAZING TECHNICOLOR DREAMCOAT by Andrew Lloyd Webber and Tim Rice. Cast and credits not submitted.

HOLY GHOSTS by Romulus Linney; Director, John Loven; Set, James F. Pyne, Jr.; Technical and Lighting Director, Norm Dodge; Musical Director, Charles McWilliams; Producing Director, Danny S. Fruchter; Stage Managers, Adrienne Neye, Mark Abram. CAST: Rodney W. Clark, Marcia Evers, Ralph Galen, Murphy Guyer, Bill Lewis, Bob Lohrmann, Catherine MacNeal, Michael McKee, Sean McKinley, Thomas Meigs, Walter Rhodes, Carol Rocamora, Mets Suber, Reenie Upchurch

STEPS IN TIME by The American Dance Machine; Supervised and Directed by Lee Theodore; Costumes, Beth Liss; Lighting, Curt Ostermann; Musical Direction, James Raitt. CAST: Janet Eilber, Denny Shearer, John Jones, Vicki Regan, Catherine Caplin, Kathleen Gutrick, Jack Perez, Darlene Kesner, Ralph Rodriguez, Eleonore Treiber, and Francois Szony

A CHRISTMAS CAROL by Charles Dickens; Adapted by Rae Allen, Timothy Near; Settings and Costumes, Christina Weppner; Lighting, John Gisondi; Musical Direction, Michael Howe; Associate Director, Judy Jurgaitis; Director, Rae Allen; Stage Manager, John Vivian. CAST: John Cullum, Ann Blessing, Conor Bohan, Jennifer Borge, Jonathan Dyas-Sysel, Nicholas Guest, Mary Irey, Judy Jurgaitis, Josie Lawrence, Daniel Levoff, Phillip Lewis, Paul Milikin, Greg Procaccino, David Pursely, Nancy Sellin, Coley Sohn, Douglas Stender, Kathy Vivian, Steven Worth

I'M GETTING MY ACT TOGETHER AND TAKING IT ON THE ROAD by Gretchen Cryer and Nancy Ford; Director, Amy Saltz; Musical Direction, George Broderick; Musical Supervision, John Franceschina; Choreography, Helen Kent; Set, Pat Woodbridge; Lighting, Patricia Simmons; Costumes, Carol Oditz; Stage Manager, James Brady. CAST: Ralph Byers (Joe), Louisa Flaningam (Heather), Linda Lang Ford (Cheryl), Louise Robinson (Alice), Paul Rosa (Jake)

John Cullum (C) as Scrooge in "A Christmas Carol"

Gordie Corbin/Judy Switt Photo

GEORGE STREET PLAYHOUSE

New Brunswick, N. J.
September 25, 1980 – May 2, 1981
Artistic Director, Eric Krebs; Managing Director, John Herochik;
Business Manager, Shana Higgins; Press, Gregory Hatala; Production Manager, Gary Kechely; Stage Managers, Cheri Bogdan, Maureen Heffernan; Technical Director, Gary W. Fassler; Props, Gene
Kish; Costumer, Linda Reynolds

PRODUCTIONS AND CASTS

DEATH OF A SALESMAN by Arthur Miller; Director, Paul Austin; Set, Daniel Proett. CAST: Dick Shepard, Gloria Cromwell,
Edmond Genest, Bill Cwikowski, Eric Loeb, Caron Buinis, Matthew
Lewis, Emmett Reeks, Dan Guggenheim, Linette Bishop, Stan
Schwartz, Barbara Summerville, Martha Haney
PARLAY *(World Premiere)* by David Richmond; Director, Bob
Hall; Set, Allen Cornell; Lighting, Cynthia J. Hawkins; Sound, Craig
Ferraro. CAST: Lou Bedford (Billy Curtis), Catherine Burns (Jess
McLaughlin), Tom Crawley (Blandford)
PURLIE by Gary Geld, Peter Udell, Ossie Davis, Philip Rose;
Director, Rick Khan; Set, Daniel Proett; Musical Director, Thom
Bridwell; Choreographer, Al Perryman; Lighting, Dan Stratman.
CAST: Jim Cyrus, Vickie D. Chappell, Venida Evans, Jeffery V.
Thompson, Paul O'Connor, Lenore Davis, Emmett Reeks, Amar,
Ron Blanco, William Bradley, Louise H. Gorham, Lawrence Hamilton, Dana Hollowell-Khan, Eugene Lee, Leah Randolph-Bridwell,
Sherri Smith-Richardson, Judy Tate, Brenda Thomas
VIADUCT *(World Premiere)* by Aleen Malcolm; Director, David
Kitchen; Set, Bob Phillips; Lighting, Natasha Katz. CAST: George
Taylor (George Sydney Biggins), Jennifer Sternberg (Dora Rose
Biggins), Eric Schurenberg (David George Charles Biggins), George
Falkenberry (Brian Walter Smith)
CANDIDA by George Bernard Shaw; Director, Bob Hall; Set, Daniel Stratman; Lighting, Gary W. Fassler; Sound, Tim McCusker.
CAST: Judith K. Hart, Bruce Probst, Paul Farin, Ronald Bishop,
Susanne Peter, Matt Callahan
TWO FOR THE SEESAW by William Gibson; Director, Maureen
Heffernan; Set, Gary W. Fassler; Lighting, Gary Kechely; Sound,
Tim McCusker. CAST: Victoria Paley, Bruce Probst

Robert Faulkner Photos

Richard Shepard, Edmond Genest, Bill
Cwikowski, Gloria Cromwell in "Death
of a Salesman" Top: Tom Crawley, Lou
Bedford, Catherine Burns in "Parlay"

Matt Callahan, Susanne Peters
in "Candida" (George Street)

GeVa THEATRE

Rochester, N. Y.
October 31, 1980 – April 19, 1981
Artistic Director, Gideon Y. Schein; Acting Managing Director,
Timothy C. Norland; Literary Director, Bruce E. Rodgers; Stage
Manager, Saylor Creswell; Technical Director, Tim Pickens; Costumes, Pamela Scofield; Scenery, Sharon Perlmutter, Daniel P. Boylan, Susan Hilferty, Desmond Heely, David Potts; Lighting, Dennis
Parichy, John Gisondi, Robert Jared, Annie Wrightson; Sound,
Chuck London; Choreographer, Gretchen Glover; Press, Jayne M.
Hustead, Steven R. Beste

PRODUCTIONS AND CASTS

TERRA NOVA by Ted Tally; Director, Ben Levit. CAST: David
Gale, Rand Bridges, Jeanne Ruskin, Michael Kolba, Curt Karibalis,
William Brenner, Matthew Kimbrough
HAY FEVER by Noel Coward; Director, Mark Harrison. CAST:
Zelijko Ivanek, Kristen Lowman, Bonnie Bowers, Jane Cronin,
Jonathan Moore, Tony Pasqualini, Terry Calloway, Dan Diggles,
Linda Kampley
SEA MARKS by Gardner McKay. CAST: Richard Zobel, Janni
Brenn
AGNES OF GOD by John Pielmeier; Director, Beth Dixon. CAST:
Brenda Wehle, Bette Henritze, Charlotte Booker
KEYSTONE by Lance Mulcahy, John McKellar, Dion McGregor;
Musical Director, Rick Jensen. CAST: Scott Bakula, Ann Morrison,
Linda Page Neelly, Lance Davis, Jason Graae, Douglas Walker,
Valerie Beaman, Susie Fenner, Caroline Kaiser, Thomas Sinclair
IN CONNECTICUT by Roy London; Directors, Marshall W. Mason, Daniel Irvine. CAST: Rosemary Prinz, Lisa Emery, Jeff
McCracken, Shelby Buford, Jr., Henrietta Bagley, Robert LuPone,
Sharon Madden, Nicholas Dunn

(No photos submitted)

185

HARTFORD STAGE COMPANY

Hartford, Connecticut
May 30, 1980 – July 5, 1981

Artistic Director, Mark Lamos; Managing Director, William Stewart; General Manager, William W. Monroe; Press, Kathleen Cahill; Business Manager, Norman E. Magnuson; Literary Manager, Mary B. Robinson; Administrative Assistant, Joanne Page; Executive Assistant, Patricia Quinn; Production Coordinator/Technical Director, Jack Conant; Stage Managers, J. J. Jefferson, Fred Hoskins; Costumes, Martha Christian, Cindy Emmet Smith; Wardrobe, Cynthia Demand; Props, Meg Young; Designers, Lowell Detweiler, Linda Fisher, Stephen Ross, Spencer Mosse, Fred Voelpel, Arden Fingerhut, John Conklin, Pat Collins, David Jenkins, John Lee Beatty, Jess Goldstein; Musical Direction, Bruce Coughlin, Amy Rubin; Choreographer, Nora Peterson

PRODUCTIONS AND CASTS

THE LADY FROM DUBUQUE by Edward Albee; Director, Paul Weidner. CAST: Sharon Madden, David Faulkner, Kate Kelly, Frederick Coffin, Henry J. Jordan, Elaine Bromka, Earle Hyman, Myra Carter
THE BEAUX' STRATAGEM by George Farquhar; Director, Mark Lamos. CAST: Ted McAdams, David Murphy, Bernard Frawley, Kathleen Doyle, Alan Coates, Tom Donaldson, Linda Thorson, Meg Wynn Owen, Nesbitt Blaisdell, Jeff Brooks, Deborah Taylor, Richard Warwick, James C. Burge, William Andrews, Diane Newman, Grace Keagy, Rick Duet, John Basinger, Timothy Landfield
EINSTEIN AND THE POLAR BEAR (World Premiere) by Tom Griffin; Director, J. Ranelli. CAST: John Wardwell (Andrew), Robert Nichols (Charlie), Pamela Blair (Diane), Terry O'Quinn (Bill), Marjorie Lovett (Helen), David Strathairn (Bobby)
CYMBELINE by William Shakespeare; Director, Mark Lamos. CAST: Davis Hall, Jerry Allan Jones, Barbara Bryne, Mary Layne, J. T. Walsh, Richard Mathews, Robert Cornthwaite, Steven Ryan, Mark Capri, Nafe Katter, Ted McAdams, Jean Smith, Bernard Frawley, Mary Munger, Gary Sloan, William Wright, Peter Davies, James Phipps, Mark Nelson, George Bowe, Jeff Dolan, James Hyland, Sean Kellner, Ross MacKenzie, Stephen Rust, Jeffrey Adams, Kevin Collins, Billy Meegan, Brant Pope, David Murphy
UNDISCOVERED COUNTRY (American Premiere) by Arthur Schnitzler; Adapted by Tom Stoppard; Director, Mark Lamos. CAST: Jennifer Harmon, Pan Riley, Ruby Holbrook, Mary Layne, James Phipps, Davis Hall, Keith Baxter, Mark Capri, Carol Fox Prescott, Nafe Katter, William Wright, Barbara Bryne, Stephen Rust, David Murphy, Ted McAdams, Bernard Frawley, Stefan Schnabel, Joan Parrish, Jerry Allan Jones, Diane MacDonald, Ian Drosdova, Peter Davies, Mary Munger, Meg Young, Mark Nelson, Sean Kellner, Adam Joseph Dexter, Christine Kluntz, Hannah Shapiro
IS THERE LIFE AFTER HIGH SCHOOL? (World Premiere) with book by Jeffrey Kindley; Music and Lyrics, Craig Carnelia; Director, Melvin Bernhardt. CAST: Raymond Baker, Susan Bigelow, Roger Chapman, Joel Colodner, David Patrick Kelly, Elizabeth Lathram, Michael McCormick, Maureen Silliman

Lanny Nagler Photos

David Patrick Kelly, Raymond Baker, Joel Colodner In "Is There Life after High School?" Top: Mary Layne, Keith Baxter in "Undiscovered Country"

HARTMAN THEATRE COMPANY

Stamford, Connecticut
February 11, to May 31, 1981
Sixth Season

Artistic Director, Edwin Sherin; Managing Director, Roger L. Meeker; Press, Joyce Schreiber, Allison Jaffe; Directors, Edwin Sherin, Michael Lessac, James Hammerstein; Sets, Marjorie Kellogg, Robert U. Taylor, John Falabella, Robin Wagner; Costumes, Marianna Elliott, Dona Granata, Walter Pickette, Jane Greenwood, David Charles, Ann Roth; Lighting, Roger Morgan, Marcia Madeira, Andy Phillips; Sound, Michael Jay, Gary Harris, Charles Gross; Stage Managers, Jay Adler, Amy Pell, Randy Becker, David N. Feight, Hope Chillington

PRODUCTIONS AND CASTS

SHOWDOWN AT THE ADOBE MOTEL (World Premiere) by Lanny Flaherty, with Henry Fonda, Cecilia Hart, Arthur E. Lund
MOLIERE IN SPITE OF HIMSELF by David Morgan, Michael Lessac, with Curtis Armstrong, Judith Barcroft, Nesbitt Blaisdell, Jacqueline Cassel, Richard Frank, Walker Hicklin, Marcia Hyde, Richard Kiley, Berit Lagerwall, James Maxwell, Debra Monk, Brian O'Mallon, Norman Snow, Charlie Stavola, Tom Tammi, Ralph Williams
MERTON OF THE MOVIES by George S. Kaufman, Marc Connelly, with Tom Bade, Joseph Bergmann, Marilyn Caskey, Lynn Cohen, Leonard Drum, Harry Groener, Linda Kamplay, Roger Kozol, Annette Kurek, George Maguire, Peter Pagan, Richard Peterson, Eric Uhler, Ray Zifo
SEMMELWEISS by Howard Sackler, with Sally Bagot, Leslie Barrett, Kathy Bates, John Blazo, Roberts Blossom, Ivar Brogger, Chet Carlin, Mel Cobb, John P. Connolly, Jeffrey DeMunn, Pamela Rose Kilburn, Susan Lynch, R. Bruce MacDonald, Michelle Maulucci, Jonathan Moore, Gabor Morea, Gordana Rashovich, Lee Richardson, Mary Lou Rosato, David Schramm, Sanford Seeger, Jack Wetherall, K. C. Wilson

Gerry Goodstein Photos

Henry Fonda, Art Lund in "Snowdown at the Adobe Motel"

INDIANA REPERTORY THEATRE

Indianapolis, Indiana
October 24, 1980 - May 17, 1981
Artistic Director, Tom Haas; Producing Director Benjamin Mordecai; Production Manager, Chris Armen; Stage Manager, Joel Grynheim; Technical Director, J. T. LaCourse; Costumes, Dana H. Tinsley; Props, Ruth Long; Business Manager, Steven R. Ross; Press, Jimmy Seacat

PRODUCTIONS AND CASTS

HOAGY, BIX, AND WOLFGANG BEETHOVEN BUNKHAUS *(American Premiere)* by Adrian Mitchell; Director, Tam Haas; Musical Director, Richard M. Sudhalter; Set and Costumes, Steve Rubin; Choreography, Lynnette Schisla; Lighting, Jeff Davis. CAST: Jamey Sheridan (Hoagy), Phyllis Somerville (Betty), Linda Daugherty (Meg), Armin Shimerman (Bix), Bernard Kates (Costas), Gregory Salata (Monk), Frank Kopyc (Whiteman/Beiderbecke)
A CHRISTMAS CAROL by Charles Dickens; Adapted and Directed by Tom Haas; Sets, Karen Schulz; Costumes, Susan Hilferty; Music, Thomas Jordan. CAST: Scott Wentworth (Narrator), Robert Boyle (Crachit), Bernard Kates (Scrooge), Warren T. Slinkard II (Tiny Tim), and David Adamson, Tom Bade, Jack Couch, Judith Elaine, Priscilla Lindsay, Lowry Miller, Tom Myler, Robbie Newell, Mary Ed Porter, Rae Randall, Patricia Sherick, Anne Atkins, Laura L. Bailey, Jessica Lee Funches, Matthew Galvin, Ruby Harvey, Brent S. Hendon, August Leagre, David Mayes, Noble Melton, Gregor Paslawsky, Stephen Preusse, Matt W. Stuckey
ROCKET TO THE MOON by Clifford Odets; Director, Eric Steiner; Sets, David Potts; Costumes, Rachel Kurland. CAST: Kevin O'Connor, Carole Monferdini, Katie Grant, Zeke Zaccaro, Bernard Kates, Scott Wentworth, Stephen Mendillo
TREATS by Christopher Hampton; Director, William Peters; Sets, Heidi Landesman; Costumes, Nan Cibula. CAST: Priscilla Lindsay, William Perley, Scott Wentworth
THE FAILURE TO ZIGZAG by John B. Ferzacca; Director, Tom Haas; Sets, Kate Edmunds; Costumes, Leon Brauner. CAST: Stan Birnbaum, John Daggan, Richard Council, Bernard Kates, Victor Arnold, Gregory Chase, Richard Voigts, Edward Cannan, Joel Swetow, Michael Margulis, Larry Welch, Dallas Greer, Christopher McCann, Andrew Davis, Ernest Abuba, Steve Pudenz, Jon R. Bailey, Tony Cerola, Craig Gaylor, John K. Hedges, Donald Lang, Steven Laughn, Joseph Hayes Lilley, Rockey Mitchell, Kurt S. Owens, Gregor Paslawsky
AH, WILDERNESS! by Eugene O'Neill; Director, David Rotenberg. CAST: John Carpenter, Bette Henritze, John Daggan, Stephen Preusse, Sallyanne Tackus, Joe Wright, Bernard Kates, Maxine Taylor-Morris, Steve Pudenz, Cynthia Judge, Barry O'Donnell, Priscilla Lindsay, Anne Atkins, Edward Cannan, Stephen Gabis
World Premieres of Oedipus at the Holy Place by Robert Montgomery, Live Tonight: Emma Goldman by Michael Dixon, Coming of Age by Barbara Field, Murder in the Cabaret by Tom Haas

Dan Francis Photos

**Clifton James, Thomas Waites,
Al Pacino in "American Buffalo"**

**Scott Wentworth, Priscilla Lindsay,
William Perley in "Treats"**

LONG WHARF THEATRE

New Haven, Connecticut
October 4, 1980 – June 14, 1981
Sixteenth Season
Artistic Director, Arvin Brown; Executive Director, M. Edgar Rosenblum; Press, Jill McGuire, Dennis Powers, Stage Directors, Arvin Brown, John Tillinger, Donald Howarth, Kenneth Frankel, Barry Davis, Bill Ludel; Sets, John Jensen, Marjorie Kellogg, Donald Howarth, Steven Rubin, Hugh Landwehr, David Gropman, Karl Eigsti; Costumes, Bill Walker, J. Allen Highfill, Rachel Kurland; Lighting, Daniel Clayman, Ronald Wallace, Jamie Gallagher, Judy Rasmuson; Stage Managers, Anne Keefe, Christopher Greene, James Harker, Robin Kevrick

PRODUCTIONS AND CASTS

AMERICAN BUFFALO by David Mamet, with Clifton James, Thomas Waites, Al Pacino
SOLOMON'S CHILD *(World Premiere)* by Tom Dulack; Director, John Tillinger. CAST: Steven Gilborn (Allan), Rochelle Oliver (Vera), Ellis "Skeeter" Williams (Joe), Tom Nardini (Sam), Michael O'Keefe (Shelley), Peter Michael Goetz (Balthazar), Deborah Hedwall (Naomi), Joyce Ebert (Liz), James Seymour (State Trooper)
WAITING FOR GODOT by Samuel Beckett, with Winston Ntshona, John Kani, Peter Piccolo, Bill Flynn, Silamour Philander
THE ADMIRABLE CRICHTON by James Barrie, with John McMartin, John Rothman, Douglas Parker, John Tillinger, Ruth Kidder, Emery Battis, Lisa Banes, Alice Playten, Nancy Boykin, Robin Groves, Paddy Croft, Jane Tamarkin
CLOSE TIES by Elizabeth Diggs, with Margaret Barker, Donald Symington, Joyce Ebert, Laralu Smith, Alexandra Borrie, Deborah Hedwall, Jeff Rohde, Mark Blum
ROMEO AND JULIET by William Shakespeare, with Thomas Hulce, Mary Beth Hurt, Dana Mills, Douglas Parker, Jose Santana, Adam LeFevre, Peter Gallagher, Gary Sloan, Robert Blackburn, Fredi Olster, Robert Beseda, William Barry, Rose Marie Himes, John Tillotson, Aideen O'Kelly, Jack Wetherall, Emery Battis, Paul F. Ugalde, Richard Mathews, Daniel McGuire, Curtis Borg
BODIES *(American Premiere)* by James Saunders; Director, Kenneth Frankel. CAST: Carolyn Seymour (Anne), Meg Wynn Owen (Helen), Roger Newman (David), Kenneth Haigh (Mervyn)
A LIFE by Hugh Leonard, with William Swetland, Shirley Bryan, Peg Murray, Monique Fowler, Eric Tull, Timothy Busfield, Emery Battis, Anne O'Sullivan
National Tours of:
THE LION IN WINTER by James Goldman, with Rex Robbins, Donna Snow, Henry Stram, Scott Walters, David Combs, Barbara Sohmers, Peter Webster
PRIVATE LIVES by Noel Coward, with Donna Snow, Rex Robbins, Dugg Smith, Barbara Sohmers, Bara-Cristen Hansen

William B. Carter/Gerry Goodstein Photos

187

MANITOBA THEATRE CENTRE

Winnipeg, Canada
October 23, 1980 – May 16, 1981

Artistic Director, Richard Ouzounian; General Manager, Zdzislaw R. Bajon; Press, Patricia Elsworth; Production Manager, Jack Timlock; Technical Director, Ron Kresky; Stage Directors, John Gray, Sharon Pollock, Malcolm Black, Richard Ouzounian, Guy Sprung, David Schurmann, Gordon McCall; Sets and Costumes, David Gropman, Guido Tondino, Phillip Silver, Evan Ayotte, Lawrence Schafer, Barbra Matis, William Chesney, Arthur Penson, Gavin Semple, Phillip Clarkson; Choreography, Jacques Lemay; Fight Director, Jean-Pierre Fournier; Musical Director, Peter Yakimovich

PRODUCTIONS AND CASTS

BILLY BISHOP GOES TO WAR by John Gray, with Cedric Smith, Ross Douglas
BETRAYAL by Harold Pinter, with Michael Ball, John Innes, Leueen Willoughby, Peter Smith
JITTERS by David French, with Janis Dunning, David Gillies, Eric House, Edward Ledson, George Merner, Jennifer Phipps, James Rankin, Nicholas Rice, Rebecca Toolan
MACBETH by William Shakespeare, with Michael Ball, John Innes, Leueen Willoughby, Guy Bannerman, Keith Dinicol, Lorne Kennedy, Jonathan Barrett, Jean-Pierre Fournier, Fran Gebhard, Gordon McCall, Brent Fidler, Martha Little, Peter Smith, Gavin Wise
BALCONVILLE by David Fennario, with Jean Archambault, Yolande Circe, Danielle Filion, Marc Gelinas, Patricia Hamilton, Peter MacNeill, Robert Parson, Gilles Tordjman
BENT by Martin Sherman, with Lorne Kennedy, Benedict Campbell, Adam Henderson, Alf Silver, Neal Rempel, Timothy Lee, Gordon McCall, Harvey Harding, John Innes
GREASE by Jim Jacobs and Warren Casey with Jay Brazeau, Judy Cook, Tracy Dahl, Nancy Drake, Janis Dunning, Michelle Fisk, Kimble Hall, Terry Harford, Edward Ledson, Pamela Macdonald, Cheryl MacInnis, Shane McPherson, Max Reimer, Jim White, Martin Williams
THE ELEPHANT MAN by Bernard Pomerance, with Michael Donaghue, Richard Vincent-Hurst, John Innes, Carolyn Jones, Lorne Kennedy, David Schurmann, Rebecca Toolan
1837: THE FARMERS' REVOLT by Rick Salutin and Theatre Passe Muraille, with Tom Anniko, Alexe Duncan, Robb Paterson, Brian Paul, Chick Reid
AS YOU LIKE IT by William Shakespeare, with Tom Anniko, Jonathan Barrett, Barbara Budd, John-Pierre Fournier, Greg George, Janice Greene, Ben Henderson, Richard Vincent-Hurst, John Innes, Lorne Kennedy, Gerald Loewen, Gordon McCall, Robb Paterson, Brian Paul, Paula Schappert, David Schurmann, Goldie Semple, Alf Silver, John Wojda

Gerry Kopelow Photos

John Innes, John Wojda in "As You Like It"
Top: Janis Dunning, Judy Cook, Tracy
Dahl in "Grease"

MEADOW BROOK THEATRE

Rochester, Michigan
October 9, 1980 – May 17, 1981

Artistic-General Director, Terence Kilburn; Assistant General Director/Tour Director, Frank F. Bollinger; Directors, Terence Kilburn, Edward Kaye-Martin, Charles Nolte, Cash Baxter; Sets, Peter-William Hicks, Barry Griffith; Lighting, Barry Griffith, Larry A. Reed. Reid G. Johnson, Daniel Jaffe; Stage Managers, Rachael Lindhart, Thomas Spence; Production Manager, Peter-William Hicks; Technical Director, Barry Griffith; Sound, Kim Kaufman; Costume Coordinator, Mary Lynn Bonnell; Wardrobe, Jill Patterson, Elaine Sutherland; Props, Charles Beal; Press, Jane U. Mosher

PRODUCTIONS AND CASTS

THIEVES CARNIVAL with Barbara Berge, Lou Brockway, Terry Carpenter, A. D. Cover, Donald W. Dailey, Harry Ellerbe, Donald Ewer, Mark Halpin, Thomas Hansen, Robert Jones, Gary Ed Mach, Terence Marinan, Bob Murdy, Melanie Resnick, Polly Rowles, Allan Stevens, Elaine Sutherland, Karen Swantek, Stefani Van Meter, Patricia Verellen
OUR TOWN with Jeanne Arnold, Peter Brandon, Craig Collicott, A. D. Cover, Donald W. Dailey, Andrew Dunn, Donald Ewer, Stanley Flood, Fiona Hale, Krystyn Loucks, Judith McIntyre, Tom Mahard, Marianne Muellerleile, Bob Murdy, Steven L. Schultz, Jr., T. J. Scott, Ron Seka
THE IMAGINARY INVALID with Lou Brockway, A. D. Cover, Donald Ewer, George Gitto, Mary Pat Gleason, Henson Keys, David Kroll, Ray Lonergan, Lynn Mansbach, Judith McIntyre, Marianne Muellerleile, Bob Murdy
DON JUAN IN HELL with Barbara Berge, Donald Ewer, George Gitto, Michael Lipton
ARSENIC AND OLD LACE with Jeanne Arnold, Jean Barker, Kathryn Breech, Carleton Carpenter, Craig Collicott, J. L. Dahlmann, Donald W. Dailey, Janthan Freeman, David Green, Todd Hissong, Phillip Locker, Tom Mahard
ANOTHER PART OF THE FOREST with Jean Ashley, Bethany Carpenter, Virginia Hut, J. Douglas James, Rhomeyn Johnson, Phillip Locker, Alma Parks, Cynthia Parva, Michael M. Ryan, Ron Seka, Steve Wise
BUS STOP with J. L. Dahlmann, Faye Haun, Mark Margolis, Marianne Muerllerleile, Jim Oyster, Michael Patterson, Cyd Quilling, Ron Seka
STARTING HERE STARTING NOW with Mary Gutzi, Barbara Heuman, Michael Scott, Robert McNamee

Dick Hunt Photos

Jeanne Arnold, Jean Baxter, Carleton Carpenter,
Jonathan Freeman, Tom Mahard in "Arsenic & Old Lace"
Above: Peter Brandon, Stanley Flood, Judith
McIntyre in "Our Town"

McCARTER THEATRE COMPANY

Princeton, N.J.

September 30, 1980 – April 11, 1981

Artistic Director, Nagle Jackson; Managing Director, Alison Harris; Production Manager, Rafe Scheinblum; Technical Director, Ross Hamilton; Costumer, Robin Hirsch; Wardrobe, Martha Dye; Props, Abigail Fitzgibbons; Assistant to Directors, Lois Newhart; Business Manager, C. G. Brian Thomas; Press, Linda S. Kinsey, Veronica Brady; Stage Managers, Francis X. Kuhn, Trey Altemose, Kendall Crolius; Sets, Daniel Boylen, Brian Martin, Michael Miller, John Jensen, Karen Eisler

PRODUCTIONS AND CASTS

THE TAMING OF THE SHREW by William Shakespeare; Director, William Woodman. CAST: Marci Rigsby, Jeffrey Farrington, Richard Risso, Karl Light, Gary Roberts, Tom Robbins, G Wood, Leslie Geraci, Greg Thornton, Harriet Hall, Hubert Kelly, John Mansfield, Bruce Somerville, Robert Lanchester, Jay Doyle
A CHRISTMAS CAROL by Charles Dickens; Adapted and Directed by Nagle Jackson. CAST: G Wood, Robert Lanchester, Gary Roberts, Bruce Somerville, John Mansfield, Jay Doyle, Libby Boone, Richard Risso, Chris Hanlin, Greg Thornton, Harriet Hall, Karl Light, Bruce Coleman, Tom Robbins, Leslie Geraci, Michele Colodney, Ehrin Harrison, Marci Rigsby, Cynthia J. Babler, T. J. Cluff, Rebecca Jackson, Seth Herzog, Rebecca Gantwerk, Clarke McFarlane, Harriet Hall, Libby Boone, Karl Light
CUSTER by Robert Ingham; Director, Nagle Jackson. CAST: Barry Boys, Richard Risso, Katherine McGrath, John Mansfield, Greg Thornton, G Wood, Gary Roberts, Thomas Nahrwold
THE PLAY'S THE THING by Ferenc Molnar; Adapted by P. G. Wodehouse. CAST: Jay Doyle, Robert Lanchester, Gary Roberts, Katherine McGrath, Barry Boys, Greg Thornton, Richard Risso
PUTTING ON THE DOG by Deloss Brown; Director, Robert Lanchester, CAST: Richard Risso, Derry Light, Jay Doyle, Susan Jonas, Gary Roberts, G Wood, Greg Thornton
GERTRUDE STEIN GERTRUDE STEIN GERTRUDE STEIN with Pat Carroll

Cliff Moore/William Faulkner Photos

Richard Risso (C) and cast in "Moby Dick Rehearsed" Top: Jay Doyle, Derry Light in "Putting on the Dog"

Gilbert Price in "Julius Caesar"
Above: Anne Kerry, William Leach
in "Cyrano de Bergerac"

MILWAUKEE REPERTORY THEATER

Milwaukee, Wisconsin

September 12, 1980–May 17, 1981

Artistic Director, John Dillon; Directors, Sharon Ott, Richard Cottrell; Sets, William Eckart, Karl Eigsti, Hugh Landwehr, Laura Maurer; Lighting, Rachel Budin, Dawn Chiang, Arden Fingerhut, Spencer Mosse; Costumes, Colleen Muscha, Jo Peters, Susan Tsu; Music Director, Edmund Assaly; Sound, David R. Bednar; Composers, Donald St. Pierre, Mark Van Hecke; Production Managers, Gregory S. Murphy, Varney Knapp, Burt J. Patalano; Stage Managers, Robert Goodman, Robin Rumpf; Wardrobe, Carol Jean Horaitis, Mary Piering; Props, Sandy Struth; Managing Director, Sara O'Connor; Business Manager, Peggy Haessler Rose; Press, Susan Medak, Diane S. Nahabedian

COMPANY

Paul Bentzen, Tom Berenger, Lisa Brailoff, Janni Brenn, Ritch Brinkley, Candace Broecker, Alan Brooks, Emma Campbell, Robert Colston, Peggy Cowles, Leland Crooke, Gregory T. Daniel, Montgomery Davis, Dottie Dee, Ellen Dolan, Geoff Garland, Susan Gordon-Clarke, William Hall, Jr., Dana Hart, Eric Hill, Anne Kerry, Mark Kuechle, Jack Hyrieleison, Sonja Lanzener, William Leach, Ella Mae Lentz, Paul Meacham, Daniel Mooney, Marjorie Nelson, James Pickering, Rose Pickering, Ralitza Popcheva, C. C. H. Pounder, Gilbert Price, Victor Raider-Wexler, Margaret Ritchie, Ruth Schudson, Henry Strozier, Michael Tezla, Maggie Thatcher, Jack Wallace, Terry Weber, Gail Baumann, Rachel Borouchoff, Mark Bucher, Caroline K. Calicchio, Rebecca Fishel, Jeff Scot Gendelman, Edward Lee Kelly, Max Manthey, Luz Montez, Ellen Hill, David Rommel, Richard J. Weber

PRODUCTIONS

Cyrano de Bergerac by Edmond Rostand, Mother Courage by Bertolt Brecht, Children of a Lesser God by Mark Medoff, Julius Caesar by William Shakespeare, A Streetcar Named Desire by Tennessee Williams, and *World Premieres* of The Christmas Eve Murder by Daniel Stein, Giants in the Earth by Amlin Gray, Fridays by Andrew Johns, Outlanders by Amlin Gray, The Double by Amlin Gray, The 80's by Tom Cole, the Immense Walk of the Late-Season Traveler by Tom Cole, The Years of the Whirlwind by Daniel Stein

Mark Avery Photos

MISSOURI REPERTORY COMPANY

Kansas City, Missouri

Executive Director, Patricia McIlrath; Business Manager, Daniel P. Baker, Administrative Associate, Iona Henderson; Assistant to Director, Maxine Sifers; Production Manager, Ronald Schaeffer; Press, Patricia A. Moore, Rendall Himes; Directors, James Assad, Francis J. Cullinan, George Hamlin, John Reich; Dramaturg, Felicia Hardison Londre; Technical Director, Douglas C. Taylor; Sound, Steven W. Vrba; Sets, Franco Colavecchia, John Ezell, James Leonard Joy, Carolyn L. Ross; Lighting, Joseph Appelt, Arden Fingerhut; Costumes, Vincent Scassellati, Baker S. Smith; Musical Director, Molly Jessup Alley; Stage Managers, Terrence Dwyer, Joyce McBroom, Don Tomei, Jim Birdsall; Props, John Sadler; Wardrobe, Victoria Marshall

COMPANY

Donna M. Arand, Ellen Baker, Peter Bakely, Jim Birdsall, Bryan Burch-Worch, Carolgene Burd, John Caywood, Montie Chambers, Rosanna E. Coppedge, Jerome Collamore, Cynthia Dozier, Glenna Forde, Steven Gefroh, Richard Gustin, Timothy S. Hancock, Samuel Marcelo Hernandez, Devin Paul Hofeditz, Barbara Houston, Jennifer Houston, Robin Humphrey, Bryan Janssen, Rosemary John, Robert Lewis Karlin, Martin Kelly, Kristina Kemper, Gerry Kinerk, George Kuhn, Bruce D. Lecuru, Patti McGill, Patrick McKay, William Metzo, Ryan Morgan, Nancy Nichols, Woody Owen, Richard Primeaux, Bruce Roach, Mark Robbins, Elizabeth Rubino, Susan K. Selvey, Peg Small, Raymond E. Smith, Deborah Stauber, Ronetta Wallman, Patricia Hamarstrom Williams, Jennifer Winn, Donald Woods

PRODUCTIONS

Lady Audley's Secret by Francis J. Cullinan; Adapted from the novel by Mary Elizabeth Braddon and William Suter, The Night of the Iguana by Tennessee Williams, Wings by Arthur Kopit, A Perfect Gentleman by Herbert Appleman

(No photos submitted)

**T. G. Finkbinder
in "American Polar"
(New Playwrights)**

**Cornelia Ravenal, Nick Olcott, Tonette
Hartman in "Dear Desperate"**

NEW PLAYWRIGHTS' THEATRE

Washington, D. C.
October 15, 1980 – June 28, 1981

Founder-Producing Director, Harry M. Bagdasian; Managing Director, Mary Ann Karinch; Literary Manager/Dramaturg, Lloyd Rose; Press, Daniel Browne; Production Manager, Martin Guttenplan; Technical Director, Greg Basdavanos; Stage Manager, Pat Cochran; Assistant to Managing Director, Lisa Sommers; Production Assistant, Jan Simmons-Killibrew

PRODUCTIONS AND CASTS

THE AMSTERDAM AVENUE THEATER PRESENTS DIRECT FROM DEATH ROW THE SCOTTSBORO BOYS *(World Premiere)* with book, music and lyrics by Mark Stein; Director, Harry M. Bagdasian. CAST: Walt Lockman, Kelly Kennedy, Ron Canada, Caron Tate, Jerome Huggins, Joseph E. Killibrew, Benjamin Wright, Michael Mack

AMERICAN POLAR *(World Premiere)* by John Alan Spoler; Director, Lloyd Rose. CAST: Stu Lerch, Carlos Brocas, Martin Goldsmith, Stephen Zazanis, Kevin Murray, Eric Zengota, Gary Alan Shelton, Ernie Meier, Mark Brutsche, Reed Harvey, T. G. Finkbinder

DEAR DESPERATE *(World Premiere)* by Tim Grundmann; Director, Harry M. Bagdasian. CAST: Wayne Anderson, Tonette Hartmen, Tanis Roach, Barbara Rappaport, Frank Edwards, Nick Olcott, Michael Willis, Amelia Estin, James Festa, Porter Koontz, Cornelia Ravenal, Steve Skardon, Valerie Stanislawcyzk, Mark Donahue, Richard Tappen, Mary Saloschin

A FESTIVAL OF ONE ACT PLAYS: "The Waiting" by Ken Greenman, with Hank Jackelen, Anne Stone, Anne Wittman, Jon Helmrich, Daniel Browne, Ernie Meiei; "Our Lady of the Depot" by J. Stafford, with Ethel H. Minor, Michael Willis, J. R. Dusenberry, Joe Glenn, Manolo Santalla; "Tomorrow Is Another Day" by Peter Perhonis, with Seymour M. Horowitz, Barbara Rappaport, Cal Hoffman, James Marilley; "Fourplay" by Ross McLean, with Cliff Jewell, Malane Siegrist, Stephen Zazanis, Janet Stanford; "Mash Note to an Old Codger" by Toni Press, with David Foster, Paula Marmon, Helen Oney, Jenette Dovell Fuschini, Julie Herz; "Tuba Solo" by Michael Lynch, with Jeff Albert, Maureen Downing; "The Diviners" by Jim Leonard, Jr., with Jenny Brown, Dianne Couves, Joe Glenn, Hank Jackelen, Ernie Meier, Boyce William Miller, Jr., Paul Preston, Barbara Rappaport, Mary Saloschin, Kathleen Weber, Michael Willis

Doc Dougherty Photos

**Left Center: "The Amsterdam Avenue Theater
Presents Direct from Death Row the Scottsboro Boys"**

PENNSYLVANIA STAGE COMPANY

Allentown, Pennsylvania
September 24, 1980 – April 12, 1981
Fourth Season

Producing Director, Gregory S. Hurst; Managing Director, Jeff Gordon; Directors, Ron Lagomarsino, Gregory S. Hurst, Sue Lawless, Susan Kerner; Sets, Raymond C. Recht, Quentin Thomas, Vittorio Capecce, Ronald Plazcek, Curtis Dretsch, Kevin Wiley; Costumes, Ann Emonts, Sigrid Insull, Elizabeth Palmer, Elizabeth Covey, Lisa Micheels, Thomas Keller; Lights, Candice Dunn, Quentin Thomas, Betsy Adams, Thomas Barrow, Curtis Dretsch; Stage Managers, Steve Adler, Patricia Noto; Technical Director, Kevin Wiley; Press, Sharon P. Bernstein

PRODUCTIONS AND CASTS

A FLEA IN HER EAR by Georges Feydeau, with Ray Xifo, Beth Leavel, Scott Severance, Michael Tomlinson, Diane Kamp, Linda Lee Johnson, Michael Connolly, Theodore May, Rocco Sisto, Dea Guidobono, Joel Kramer, Elise Dewsberry, Peter Palmer, Ric Stoneback

PRIVATE LIVES by Noel Coward, with Katherine Bruce, Ian Stuart, Drew Keil, Jennifer Bassey, Tracee Patterson, Jeanne Saulnier

THAT CHAMPIONSHIP SEASON by Jason Miller, with Gary Holcombe, John Ramsey, John Madden Towey, John Capodice, Gerald Richards

THE TAMING OF THE SHREW by William Shakespeare, with Stanton Cunningham, Stanley Flood, John Madden Towey, Geoff Garland, Patricia O'Donnell, Scott Severence, Tracee Patterson, Mark Castillo, Arnaldo Santana, Robert Boyle, Jeanne Saulnier, Beth Leavel, Peter Palmer, Danielle Newberry, Michael Goldberg, Ric Stoneback

FEATHERTOP (World Premiere) by Bruce Peyton; Music and Lyrics, Skip Kennon; Director, Gregory S. Hurst. CAST: Alexandra Korey, George Maguire, Jared Matesky, Sue Ann Gershenson, James Van Treuren, Ralph Bruneau

GREAT EXPECTATIONS (World Premiere) by Drew Kalter; Music and Lyrics, Jeremiah Murray; Choreography, Diana Baffa-Brill. CAST: James Fleetwood, Gian-Carlo Vellutino, Jack Davison, Sara Woods, Ric Stoneback, Scot Severence, Michael Goldberg, Whitney Webster, J. R. Horne, Victoria Boothby, Robert Hayman, Richard White, Tricia O'Connell, Dennis Warning, Catherine Gaines, Tracee Patterson, Stanton Cunningham, Beth Leavel, Stephen Hope, Barbara Marineau, Alice Morgan, Patricia Ludd

Gregory M. Fota Photos

"Great Expectations"
Top: Theodore May, Linda Lee Johnson,
Michael Connolly in "A Flea in Her Ear"

PHILADELPHIA DRAMA GUILD

Philadelphia, Pennsylvania
October 17, 1980 – May 10, 1981

Artistic Director, Irene Lewis; Managing Director, Gregory Poggi; Press, Roy A. Snyder; Business Manager, Timothy W. Brennan; Stage Managers, Pat DeRousie, Joe Watson, David Farrell; Sets, Hugh Landwehr, Karen Schulz, Peter Wingate; Costumes, David Murin, Linda Fisher, Dona Granata, Jess Goldstein; Lighting, Arden Fingerhut, Paul Gallo, Pat Collins, Neil Peter Jampolis; Directors, Irene Lewis, Tony Giordano, John Going; Music, Gerald Busby

PRODUCTIONS AND CASTS

WATCH ON THE RHINE by Lillian Hellman, with Vivienne Shub, Carmen Mathews, Everett Ensley, Robert Black, Jennifer Harmon, George Morfogen, Tana Hicken, Jim Summers, Andy Wang, Jocelyn Scott, Richard Kavanaugh

A DAY IN THE DEATH OF JOE EGG by Peter Nichols, with Munson Hicks, Tana Hicken, Janelle Miller, Dale Hodges, Daniel Szelag, Beverly May, Danielle Harris, Kimberly Imperiale, Chris Lane, Harvey Price

PHILADELPHIA, HERE I COME! by Brian Friel, with Virginia Downing, John Christopher Jones, Boyd Gaines, Thomas Barbour, Kate Kelly, Laurence Hugo, John Leighton, Julia Curry, Hank deLuca, Richard Marr, Terry Hinz, Andrew Davis, Stephen Gabis, Gwyllum Evans

THE FRONT PAGE by Ben Hecht and Charles MacArthur, with Tom McCarthy, Michael Barone, Edward L. O'Neill, Josh Burton, Richard Portnow, John Loven, David O. Petersen, Rosemary Gaffney, John Ahlin, Rik Colitti, Geoffrey Pierson, Alden Redgrave, Tana Hicken, J. R. Horne, Carolyn Hurlburt, Mary Fogarty, Jack Bittner, Sam Kressen, Jeff Brooks, Milton Selzer, Marvin Gendelman, Ethan Selzer

OLD WORLD by Aleksei Arbuzov, translated by Ariadne Nicolaeff, with Donald Davis, Helen Burns

Gerry Goodstein Photos

Milton Selzer, Rik Colitti, Geoffrey Pierson
in "The Front Page" Above: Donald Davis, Helen
Burns in "Old World"

PiTTSBURGH PLAYHOUSE THEATRE CENTER

Pittsburgh, Pennsylvania
September 18, 1980 – June 1, 1981

General Director, Mark Lewis; Producer, James O. Prescott; Production Manager, Alan Forino; Administrative Director, Mary Turner; Technical Director, Mary Margaret Sesak; Press, Maura Minteer, James Miller, Thomas Hischak; Assistants to General Director, Joseph McGoldrick, Carole Berger; Assistant to Producer, Catherine Hischak; Costumes, Mary Turner, Don DiFonso, Juli Bohn; Sets, Eileen Garrigan, Mary Burt; Lighting, Alan Forino, Jennifer Ford; Directors, Raymond Laine, James O. Prescott, Thomas Hischak, Robert Spanabel, William Leech, Ron Tassone, Don Wadsworth, Jill Wadsworth

COMPANY

Nancy Chesney, Raymond Laine, Maura Minteer, James O. Prescott, Hugh A. Rose, Robert Spanabel, Don Wadsworth, Kate Young, and *Guest Artists* Carol DePaul, Eleanor Glockner, Betty Gillette, Catherine Hischak, Tim Kirby, Frank Klingensmith, K. V. Mellott, Ray Nikolaison, Jean Pascal, Jeff Paul, Richard Rauh, William Thunhurst

PRODUCTIONS

Deathtrap by Ira Levin, Side by Side by Sondheim by Stephen Sondheim, That Championship Season by Jason Miller, Twelfth Night by William Shakespeare, Chapter Two by Neil Simon, No Place to Be Somebody by Charles Gordone, The Robber Bridegroom, The Rivals by Richard Sheridan, Royal Gambit by Hermann Gressieker, Children's Theatre: Rumpelstiltskin, A Christmas Carol, Aladdin, The Indian Captive, Cinderella

Kelly Crawford Photos

LaChele Carl, Eileen Seeley in "The Rivals"
Top: Hugh Rose in "Deathtrap"

PITTSBURGH PUBLIC THEATER

Pittsburgh, Pennsylvania
September 11, 1980–August 9, 1981
Sixth Season

Artistic Director, Ben Shaktman; Executive Director, Howard J. Millman; Stage Managers, Roy W. Backes, Jere W. Lamp; Press, Helene Morrow, Karen Long; Directors, Amy Saltz, Ben Shaktman, Peter Wexler, Stephen Kanee, J. Ranelli, Judith Haskell, Eberle Thomas, Woodie King, Jr.

PRODUCTIONS AND CASTS

I'M GETTING MY ACT TOGETHER AND TAKING IT ON THE ROAD by Gretchen Cryer and Nancy Ford, with Allan Carlsen, Louisa Flaningam, Linda Langford, Louise Robinson, Paul Rosa

DEATH OF A SALESMAN by Arthur Miller, with Tama Bodenrader, John Carpenter, Debra Gordon, James Handy, James Hunt, Katherine Knowles, Gregory Lehane, John Perkins, Dan Peters, Dorothy Stinnette, David Stocker, Joan L. Varnum, George Vogel

TERRA NOVA by Ted Tally, with Berkeley Harris, Shaine Marinson, Gary McGurk, Jack Ryland, Edward Seamon, Steven Sutherland, John C. Vennema

TANGLES *(World Premiere)* by Robert Litz; Director, Ben Shaktman; Set, David Emmons; Costumes, David Toser. CAST: Dawn Davis, Terry Layman, Monica Merryman, Amy Van Nostrand, Stephan Mark Weyte

THE TWO GENTLEMEN OF VERONA by William Shakespeare, with Beth Andrachick, Marty Bayhan, Robert Blackburn, Cindy Blaha, Santa DiLavore, John Hall, Eric Hoffmann, Jack Honor, Floyd King, James Lieb, Julia MacKenzie, Anderson Matthews, Jodie Lynne McClintock, Kevin O'Rourke, Tia Melissa Riebling, Bruce Rodgers, Emily Salvo, Nick Salvo, Eric Schurenberg, James Selby, Michele Seyler, Tom Spinella

THE LIFE OF GALILEO by Bertolt Brecht, with Joan Ammon, Beth Andrachick, Curtis Armstrong, Dori Arnold, Lamont Arnold, David Berman, Robert Beseda, Lachele Carl, Deirdre-Leigh Cramer, Ray Dooley, Michael Egan, Frank Geraci, Wilson (Kim) Hutton, Peter Kybart, Nancy Mette, Ken Milchick, Ruth Miller, Pamela Norris, Kevin O'Leary, Lazaro Perez, Christopher Potter, Jack Price, James Rogers, Richard Stack, Mark Thompson, James Tolkan

STREETSONGS with Geraldine Fitzgerald in her solo performance.

WORKSHOP PRODUCTIONS of Campaign Relief by Judith Haskell, O. Henry's Christmas by Thomas Edward West, Appear and Show Cause by Stephen Taylor

Dawn Davis, Stephan Mark in "Tangles"
Above: David Stocker, John Carpenter,
James Hunt in "Death of a Salesman"

192

Adam Weinhold Photos

PLAYERS STATE THEATRE

Coconut Grove, Florida
October 17, 1980 – April 26, 1981
Fourth Season
Artistic and Producing Director, Dr. David Robert Kanter; Managing Director, G. David Black; General Manager, Barry Steinman; Company Manager, Christi Sanchez; Press, Susan Westfall, Robert Holtzman, Jim Whicker; Directors, David Robert Kanter, Michael Montel; Stage Managers, Dennis A. Blackledge, Rafael V. Blanco, Debbie Ann Thompson, Susan Inge Wood; Sets, H. Paul Mazer, Lyle Baskin, Kenneth N. Kurtz; Costumes, Maria Marrero; Lighting, Andrea Wilson, Jean E. Shorrock, H. Paul Mazer, Kenneth N. Kurtz; Fight Director, B. H. Barry

PRODUCTIONS AND CASTS

GEMINI by Albert Innaurato, with Peter Ivanov, Rose Anna Mineo, J. Cameron, James E. Mosiej, Robert Riesel, Roz Simmons
HAMLET by William Shakespeare, with Craig Dudley (Hamlet), Richard Ashford, Ralph Wakefield, Tim Crowther, Claude-Albert Saucier, Jack Trevor, Thomas Buckland, Peter Ivanov, Raul Melo, Eileen Russell, Mary E. Teahan, Miller Lide, Thomas A. Stewart, William Metzo, Isa Thomas, J. Cameron, Jack Trevor, Kathy Lee, Raul Melo, Don Stout
A CHRISTMAS CAROL by Charles Dickens, adapted by David Robert Kanter, with Richard Ashford, Harold Bergman, Thomas Buckland, J. Cameron, Adam Finkle, Anne Gilliam, Peter Ivanov, Lamont Johnson, Bob Kanter, Miller Lide, Marilyn Nix, Joseph H. Reed, Eileen Russell, Thomas A. Stewart, Don Stout, Kevin Kiley, Mary E. Teahan, Jack Trevor, Ralph Wakefield, Debbie Boyar, Heidi Kanter, Karin Kanter, Marla Schaffel, Kyle Temple, Jeff Korson, Danny Matis
GETTING OUT by Marsha Norman, with Megan McTavish, J. Cameron, William Fuller, Max Howard, Ralph Wakefield, John Archie, Anne Gilliam, Barbara Bernoudy, Ralph Wakefield, Joe Horvath, Harold Bergman, Margo Martindale
1959 PINK THUNDERBIRD by James McLure: Laundry and Bourbon with Ann Crumb, Margo Martindale, Susan Pitts, Lone Star with Steve Vandegriek, Gregory Grove, Max Howard
AGNES OF GOD by John Pielmeier, with Barbara Bradshaw, Anne Gilliam, J. Cameron
GO BACK FOR MURDER by Agatha Christie, with Stephen Temperley, Ronald Shelley, Barbara Bradshaw, Ralph Wakefield, William Meisle, Tom McDermott, Brenda Curtis, Anne Gilliam, J. Cameron, Peter Brandon

Adam Markowitz Photos

Max Howard, Megan McTavish
in "Getting Out"
Top: Craig Dudley as Hamlet

David Rosenbaum, Laura Copland
in "Talley's Folly"

PORTLAND STAGE COMPANY

Portland, Maine
October 18, 1980 – May 17, 1981
Artistic Director, Charles Towers; Managing Director, Richard Ostreicher; Business Manager, Patricia Egan; Technical Director, Steven J. Sysko, Jr.; Stage Manager, Teresa Elwert; Directors, Charles Towers, Jamie Brown, David A. Penhale, Evadne Giannini, John Stix; Sets, John Doepp, Lisa Devlin, Charles Kading, A. Christina Giannini; Costumes, Lynda L. Salsbury, A. Christina Giannini; Lighting, Charles Towers, Steven J. Sysko, Jr., John Doepp, Robert Strohmeier; Sound, Chuck London, Andrew Luft, John North; Choreography, Allan Sobek; Musical Director, Alan Smallwood

PRODUCTIONS AND CASTS

SORROWS OF STEPHEN by Peter Parnell, with Lesley Anderson, Tom Anderson, Michael Garfield, Sally Hadley, Jock MacDonald, Ellen Parks, Laurie Gay Spencer, Rebecca Wells, Joseph Wilkins
FAITH HEALER by Brian Friel, with Lium O'Begley, Mary Fogarty, William Knight
A CHILD'S CHRISTMAS by Charles Dickens, developed by the company, with Tom Anderson, Mike Burns, Millard Fillmore, Richard Greene, Dana Hardwick, Stacie Harvey, Jock MacDonald, Adam Porter
OLD TIMES by Harold Pinter, with Jan Granger, Natalie Hurst, David A. Penhale
TALLEY'S FOLLY by Lanford Wilson, with Laura Copland, David Rosenbaum
ISLAND by Peter Link, Joe Bravaco, Larry Rosler, with Terry Burrell, Cass Morgan, Byron Utley, Christopher Wells
SEA MARKS by Gardner McKay, with John Getz, Kate Kelley

Julie Coxe Photos

Left Center: Ellen Parks, Michael
Garfield in "Sorrows of Stephen"

REPERTORY THEATRE OF ST. LOUIS

St. Louis, Missouri
September 5, 1980 – April 19, 1981
Formerly Loretto-Hilton Repertory Theatre; Artistic Director, Wallace Chappell; Managing Director, Michael P. Pitek III; Assistant, Kim Bozark; Press, Sarah Beaman Jones, Doyle Reynolds; Production Manager, Steven Woolf; Technical Directors, Max De Volder, John Dorsey; Company Manager, Joyce Volker Ruebel; Stage Managers, Glenn Dunn, Margaret Stuart-Ramsey; Production Assistants, Lamira Hopkins, Tom Martin; Sets, Carolyn L. Ross, Tim Jozwick, Gary Barten; Props, John Roslevich, Jr.; Costumes, Dorothy Marshall, Alison Todd; Wardrobe, Jane Stein; Lighting, Peter E. Sargent; Sound, Robert Wotawa

PRODUCTIONS AND CASTS

In repertory: OTHELLO, A MIDSUMMER NIGHT'S DREAM by William Shakespeare, with Brendan Burke, Marie Elizabeth Chambers, Wallace Chappell, Alan Clarey, Bert Coleman, John Cothran, Skip Foster, William Grivna, Stephen Henderson, Eric Hill, Lynn Ann Leveridge, Kristan Linklater, Pamela R. Moore, Beverly Ostroska, Gavin Reed, Ian Trigger, Paul Winfield
EVE by Larry Fineberg; Director, Craig Anderson; Score and Conductor, Norman L. Berman. CAST: Jan Miner, Hansford Rowe, Dan Desmond, Louis Zorich, Susie Bradley
SWEET PRINCE (World Premiere) by A. E. Hotchner; Director, Wallace K. Chappell. CAST: James Luisi (Judd), Gavin Reed (J. C.), Elizabeth Burr (Deedie), Brian Worley (Schultz)
A CHRISTMAS CAROL by Charles Dickens; Adapted by Addie Walsh; Director, Michael P. Pitek III; Music Terrence Sherman. CAST: Michael Genovese, Dana Mills, Joneal Joplin, Chris Limber, Brendan Burke, Alan Clarey, Susan Maloy Wall, Donald Moore, Ron Bommer, Stephen M. Henderson, Julia Callahan, Barry Signorelli, Anne Woodward, Christopher Nickel, Jack Reidelberger, Jonathan Gillard, Marie Chambers, Brenda Varda, Gil McCauley, Julie Beard, Jimmy Peterson, Gian Cavallini, Suzanne Drebes, Sherri Boonshaft, Jim Geison, Lance Ashline, Megan Sargent, Michelle Morgan
HAPPY ENDING (World Premiere) by Dennis de Brito; Director, Clyde Ventura. CAST: Hal England (Ira), Paul Winfield (Calvin), Beth Baur (Carrie), Brett Somers (Beth), Don Keefer (Ryan), Leigh Hamilton (Barbara), Gertrude Jeannette (Isabel), Faye Butler (Leu)
RICHARD III by William Shakespeare; Director, Wallace Chappell; CAST: Brendan Burke, Jack Reidelberger, Christopher Nickel, Joneal Joplin, Philip Kerr, Ernie Sabella, Skip Foster, Alan Clarey, Jon Westholm, Donald C. Moore, Richard Pilcher, Wayne Salomon, Robert John Metcalf, John Cothran, Jr., Randy Kleffner, Hayden Hicks, Maxwell Beaver, Julia Jonathan, Kristin Linklater, Judith Tillman, Marie Chambers, Ron Bommer, Anthony J. DeStefanis, Gary Glasgow, Rick Lewis, Peter Rybolt, Robert Standley, David Whitehead
TALLEY'S FOLLY by Lanford Wilson; Director, Michael P. Pitek III. CAST: Lloyd Battista, Donna Davis
THE ISLAND by Athol Fugard, John Kani, Winston Ntshona; Director, Jim O'Connor. CAST: John Cothran, Jr., Stephen McKinley Henderson
AMERICAN SOAP (World Premiere) by Ron Mark; Director, Wallace Chappel. CAST: Jonathan Gillard (Joe), Susan Maloy Wall (Amy)
A LIFE IN THE THEATRE by David Mamet; Director, Steven Woolf. CAST: Brendan Burke, Stephan Cowan

Michael Eastman Photos

Helen Harrelson, Jan Miner, Toni
Darnay in "Ladies in Retirement"

Hal England, Paul Winfield, Brett Somers,
Beth Baur in "Happy Ending" Top: Jan
Miner in "Eve"

ROYAL POINCIANA PLAYHOUSE

Palm Beach, Florida
January 12, – March 21, 1981
Twenty-fourth Season
Producer, Herbert A. Bargeon, Jr.; Associate Producer, Iggie Wolfington; Consultant, Terry Lorden; General Manager, Albert P. Schwarz; Press, Susan Kennedy; Sets, Vittorio Capecce; Lighting, Andrea Wilson; Props, Trueman Kelley; Production Coordinator, Joseph Hill; Stage Managers, Alan Fox, Robert Townsend, Joseph Kavanagh, Roger Shea, Peter Flint, James Arneman, Jamie Jo Reynolds, Elliott Woodruff, Esther Cohen; Directors, Philip Polito, John Going, Larry Arrick, Tony Tanner, Morton DaCosta, Michael Montel, George Mead, Brian Murray, Wayne Bryan

PRODUCTIONS AND CASTS

COLE devised by Benny Green and Alan Strachan, with Sherry Mathis, David Holliday, T. J. Boyle, Lola Powers, Rosalyn Rahn, Patrick Quinn
CHILDREN by A. R. Gurney, Jr., with Jan Sterling, Steve Simpson, Monica Merryman, Gisela Caldwell
BETRAYAL by Harold Pinter, with Robert Drivas, April Shawhan, Michael Zaslow
A BEDFULL OF FOREIGNERS by David Freeman, with Tony Tanner, Barbara Berge, Marshall Borden, John Michalski, Elaine Rinehart, Jack Schmidt, Sharon Watroba
OLD WORLD by Aleksei Arbuzov, translated by Ariadne Nicolaeff, with Alexander Scourby, Lori March
I OUGHT TO BE IN PICTURES by Neil Simon, with Gabe Dell, Deborah Offner, Carol Mayo Jenkins
VIKINGS by Steve Metcalfe, with Ron Harper, William Cain, Bill Randolph, Lois Markle
SUMMER by Hugh Leonard, with Thomas A. Carlin, Mia Dillon, James Greene, Charlotte Moore, Brian Murray, Ciaran O'Reilly, April Shawhan, Sloane Shelton
LADIES IN RETIREMENT by Edward Percy and Reginald Denham, with Jan Miner, Helen Harrelson, Toni Darnay, Marie Paxton, Dorothy Blackburn, Leta Anderson, William Sadler
TINTYPES by Mary Kyte, Mel Marvin, Gary Pearle, with Stephen Berger, Marie King, Faith Prince, David Pursley, Lillias White

Anita Feldman Photos

SEATTLE REPERTORY THEATRE

Seattle, Washington
October 22, 1980 – May 24, 1981

Consulting Artistic Director, John Hirsch; Producing Director, Peter Donnelly; Resident Director, Daniel Sullivan; Associate Director, Robert Egan; Production Coordinator, Vito Zingarelli; Technical Director, Robert Scales; Administrative Director, Jeff Bentley; Business Manager, Mareno Wilkinson; Press, Marta Mellinger, Marnie Andrews, Kate Dwyer; Stage Directors, John Hirsch, John Kaufman, Daniel Sullivan, M. Burke Walker, Judith Haskell; Sets, Richard Belcher, Cameron Porteous, Robert A. Dahlstrom, James Leonard Joy, Ralph Funicello; Costumes, Kurt Wilhelm, Laura Crow, Andrew R. Marlay; Lighting, David F. Segal, Jeffrey Dallas, Robert Dahlstrom, Richard Devin, Richard Nelson, Robert Scales; Stage Managers, Milt Commons, Marc Rush, Michael F. Wolfe, Paul Shaw; Sound, Daniel Birnbaum; Musical Director, Stan Keen

PRODUCTIONS AND CASTS

STRIDER, THE STORY OF A HORSE adapted from Tolstoy's story by Robert Kalfin, Steve Brown, with Biff McGuire, George Sperdakos, Jeffrey L. Prather, John Procaccino, Daniel Noel, Michael Flynn, Robert Loper, Katherine Ferrand, Chad Henry, Steve Sneed, Stuart Wynn, Felix Winters, R. A. Farrell, Nina Wishengrad, Margit Moe, Mara Scott-Wood, Cheryl Whitener
THE GRAND HUNT (American Premiere) by Gyula Hernady, adapted by Suzanne Grossmann, with Gillie Fenwick, Jack Medley, Al Kozlik, Andrew Gillies, Terence Kelly, Warren Craig Huartson, Roland Hewgill, Peter Hutt, Carole Shelley, Jan Triska, Carl Sander, Ronn Sarosiak
AH, WILDERNESS! by Eugene O'Neill, with Biff McGuire, Anne Gerety, Jeffery L. Prather, L. Michael Craig, Karen Kay Cody, Jeff Covell, Thomas Hill, Constance Dix, Glenn Mazen, Susan Greenhill, Malcolm Hillgartner, Cheri Sorenson, Mary Walworth, J. V. Bradley, Barry M. Press
BORN YESTERDAY by Garson Kanin, with Jill Klein, John Procaccino, Allen Nause, Carl Sander, Eugene Hughes, Ric Mancini, Jerry Harper, Nora McLellan, Lowry Miller, Jane Bray, Don Matt, Glenn Mazen, Susan Ludlow, J. V. Bradley
THE DANCE OF DEATH by August Strindberg, with Robert Lansing, Eve Roberts, Leon Russom, Kathryn Mesney, Richard Hawkins
TINTYPES by Mary Kyte, Mel Marvin, Gary Pearle, with Stephen Berger, Marie King, Janet Powell, Faith Prince, David Pursley

Greg and Dorothy Gilbert Photos

Michael Craig, Susan Greenhill
in "Ah, Wilderness!" Top: Biff
McGuire (L) in "Strider . . ."

Nomi Mitty, Clarke Gordon
in "Screwball"

SOUTH COAST REPERTORY

Costa Mesa, California
September 23, 1980 – July 5, 1981

Artistic Directors, David Emmes, Martin Benson; Business Director, Tom Spray; Press, John Mouledoux, Michael Bigelow Dixon, Steve Winget; Directors Assistant, Jo Ann Palmieri; Production Coordinator, Martin Benson; Technical Director, Leo Collin; Costumes, Dwight Richard Odle; Lighting, Tom Ruzika; Props, Michael Beech; Wardrobe, Nancy J. Hamann; Production Assistants, Mimi Apfel, Tony Grillo, Jay Rabins; Stage Managers, Bill Venom, Julie Haber, Linda L. Kimball; Directors, Martin Benson, David Emmes, John Going, John-David Keller, David Ostwald, Lee Shallat; Composer, Joel Kabakov; Designers, Michael Devine, Mark Donnelly, Cliff Faulkner, Cameron Harvey, Merrily Ann Murray, Dwight Richard Odle, Tom Ruzika, William Schroeder, Susan Tuohy

COMPANY

Wayne Alexander, George Archambeault, Ronald Boussom, Steve DeNaut, Richard Doyle, John Ellington, Patricia Fraser, James Gallery, Wayne Grace, Noreen Hennessy, Karen Hensel, Patti Johns, John-Frederick Jones, John-David Keller, Art Koustik, Hal Landon, Jr., Charles Lanyer, Anni Long; Martha McFarland, Jonathan McMurtry, Sylvia Meredith, Ron Michaelson, Steve Patterson, Irene Roseen, Sarah Rush, Lee Shallat, Howard Shangraw, Ann Siena-Schwartz, Caroline Smith, James Staley, James Staskel, Kristoffer Tabori, Jeffrey Tambor, Don Tuche, Penelope Windust

PRODUCTIONS

MAINSTAGE: Hotel Paradiso by Georges Feydeau and Maurice Desvallieres, The Glass Menagerie by Tennessee Williams, A Christmas Carol by Charles Dickens, adapted by Jerry Patch, The Elephant Man by Bernard Pomerance, The Merchant of Venice by William Shakespeare, Childe Byron by Romulus Linney, Anything Goes! by Cole Porter
SECOND STAGE: American Buffalo by David Mamet, Bosoms and Neglect by John Guare, Screwball (World Premiere) by Lawrence Schneiderman, Ashes by David Rudkin, Chevaliere (World Premiere) by David Trainer

Left Center: John Wylie, William Needles,
Stephen Russell in "Merchant of Venice"   **195**

STAGEWEST

West Springfield, Massachusetts
October 16, 1980 – May 10, 1981
Producing Director, Stephen E. Hays; Managing Director, Robert
A. Rosenbaum; Press, Sheldon Wold, Debora Lichtenberg; Production Manager, Paul J. Horton; Directors, Ted Weiant, Geoffrey
Sherman, Pamela Hunt, Richard Gershman, Robert Brewer, Harold
Scott, Stephen E. Hays; Designers, Joseph Long, Deborah Shaw,
Ned Hallick, Thomas Cariello, Jan Morrison, Robby Monk, John
Ferenchek Brancale, Anne Thaxter Watson, Paul J. Horton, Brian
R. Jackins, Frank J. Boros, Elizabeth Covey, Barry Arnold, Richmond Hoxie; Stage Managers, Ken Denison, Thomas J. Rees; Choreographer, Pamela Hunt

PRODUCTIONS AND CASTS

THE DIARY OF ANNE FRANK by Frances Goodrich, Albert
Hackett, with Joseph Costa, Deborah Stenard, Jean Richards, Ron
Johnston, Jeremy Gilbert, Patricia Mertens, Christiane McKenna,
Emily Phillips, David Hyatt, Arnold Stang
ON GOLDEN POND by Ernest Thompson, with Conrad
McLaren, Georgia Southcotte, Ron Johnston, Jean Richards, Brad
Steinberg, David Hyatt
DAMES AT SEA by George Haimsohn, Robin Miller, Jim Wise,
with Barbara Niles, Suzanne Dawson, Don Bradford, Virginia Seidel, Kevin Daly, Tod Miller, Don Bradford
AGNES OF GOD by John Pielmeier, with Tana Hicken, Gloria
Cromwell, Monique Fowler
A MOON FOR THE MISBEGOTTEN by Eugene O'Neill, with
Karen Shallo, Jamie Cass, Mike Miller, Donald Gantry, D. Peter
Moore
OTHELLO by William Shakespeare, with John Martinuzzi, Richard DeFabees, Donald Christopher, Donald Molter, Leon Morenzie,
Peter Burnell, Lee Croghan, Dexter Witherell, D. Peter Moore, Jeff
Dolan, Robert Campbell, Anne Kerry, Gannon McHale, Christian
Gironda, Margery Shaw, Susanne Marley, Michael Cote, Anthony
Petrucelli, Mark Matthews Michael F. Finnerty
13 RUE DE L'AMOUR by Mawby Green, Ed Feilbert from play
by Georges Feydeau, with John Martinuzzi, Karen Shallo, Charles
Antalosky, Deborah Stenard, Richard DeFabees, Peter Burnell, Jety
Herlick, Gannon McHale, Michael Cote, Mark Matthews

Alan Epstein Photos

**Charles Antalosky, Richard DeFabees in "13 Rue de
l'Amour" Top: Tana Hicken, Monique Fowler, Gloria
Cromwell in "Agnes of God"**

STUDIO ARENA THEATRE

Buffalo, N. Y.
September 26, 1980 – May 23, 1981
Sixteenth Season
Artistic Director, David Frank; Managing Director, Barry Hoffman; Executive Assistant, Carol A. Kolis; Dramaturg/Assistant to
Directors, Kathryn Long; Press, Blossom Cohan, Cindy Laughlin;
Business Manager, Mark Crotty; Stage Managers, Robert C. Mingus, Ross Haarstad, Laurel A. Simons; Technical Director, John T.
Baun; Costumes, Sayuri Nina Pinckard; Wardrobe, Susan Kuss,
Props, David C. Woolard; Sound, Rick Menke; Directors, Jack
O'Brian, Davey Marlin-Jones, David Frank, Lawrence Kornfeld;
Designers, John Arnone, Sayuri N. Pinckard, Paul Wonsek, Mischa
Petrow, Hal Tine, Robert Morgan; Lighting, John McLain, James
H. Gage, Paul Wonsek, Joe Pacitti, Robby Monk, Frances Aronson

PRODUCTIONS AND CASTS

LADY OF THE DIAMOND by Mark Berman, with Christine
Baranski, Robert Spencer, Robert Darnell, Victor Arnold, John
Goodman, Terry Alexander, Joel Polis, Lynn Cohen, Timothy Meyers, Mark Missert, Carl Schurr, Philip Knoerzer, Brian DeMarco
ONE FLEW OVER THE CUCKOO'S NEST by Dale Wasserman,
with Darrell Sandeen, Terry Alexander, Eugene Key, Margaret
Winn, Lorna Hill, Jack Collard, Joel Polis, David Fendrick, Timothy Meyers, Robert Spencer, Donald Grant, Robert Darnell, Carl
Schurr, Robert Wallace, Mickey Hartnett, Jan Maris
CURSE OF THE STARVING CLASS by Sam Shepard, with Stephan Lang, Angela Paton, Gretchen West, Carl Schurr, Eddie Jones,
Robert Darnell, Timothy Meyers, Robert Darnell
WRITE ME A MURDER by Frederick Knott, with Robin Chadwick, Joan Croydon, Robert Schenkkan, Timothy Meyers, Cara
Duff-MacCormick, David Lamb, Ross Haarstad, Henry Sadoff
AH, WILDERNESS! by Eugene O'Neill, with Margaret Massman,
Fritz Kohl, Glen Shannon, Carl Schurr, Alice White, Joan Matthiessen, Robert Darnell, Jack Collard, Richard Seer, Timothy Meyers, Elise Pearlman, Gordon Clapp, Mickey Hartnett, David Noll,
Ric Shaffer, Deborah Taylor
LOOT by Joe Orton, with Carl Schurr, Linda Thorson, Richard
Seer, Gordon Thomson, Robert Darnell, Timothy Meyers
TALLEY'S FOLLY by Lanford Wilson, with Robert Darnell,
Christine Baranski

Phototech/Irene Haupt Photos

**Robert Darnell, Christine Baranski in "Talley's
Folly" Above: Richard Seer (C) in "Ah, Wilderness!"**

SYRACUSE STAGE

Syracuse, N. Y.
November 14, 1980 – May 24, 1981

Producing Director, Arthur Storch; Managing Director, James A Clark; Business Manager, Betty Starr; Press, Kay O. Hoone, Shirley Lockwood, Barbara Beckos; Dramaturg, Tom Walsh; Production Manager, Bob Davidson; Costumer, Anne Shanto; Props, Diann Fay; Technical Director, Brett J. Thomas; Sound, David Schnirman; Designers, John Doepp, Hal Tine, Timothy Galvin, Bill Schroder, James Berton Harris, Carr Garnett, Anne Shabto, Nanzi Adzima; Directors, Arthur Storch, Larry Alford, Peter Maloney, Judith Haskell, Terry Schreiber

PRODUCTIONS AND CASTS

THE COMEDY OF ERRORS by William Shakespeare, with Neville Aurelius, Kensyn Crouch, Jack Hollander, Marcus Smythe, Kenin M. Shumway, Jerry Beal, David Goldstein, Lerie Peter Callender, Yolande Bavan, Balery Daemke, Mary Stout, Gerard Moses, Madeleine leRoux, William Preston, Mary Gautheir, Ron Reed, Al Rodriguez, Steve Simon, Kevin Berdini, Michael Carrington, Armand Paganelli, Margaret Saraco, Gwyneth Whyte, Barbara Baptiste, Pam Trevisani
DAMES AT SEA by George Haimsohn, Robin Miller, Jim Wise, with Dorothy Stanley, Jan Neuberger, Richard Sabellico, Eydie Alyson, Richard Casper, Mark Martino
PARADISE IS CLOSING DOWN (American Premiere) by Pieter-Dirk Uys, with le Clanche du Rand, Valery Daemke, Basil Wallace, Donna Haley
GOODNIGHT, GRANDPA by Walter Landau, with John Carpenter, Joe DeSantis, Fyvush Finkel, Sylvia Harman, Estelle Kemler, Richard Kevlin-Bell, Earl Sydnor, Maxine Taylor-Morris, Penelope Willis
FOR COLORED GIRLS WHO HAVED CONSIDERED SUICIDE/WHEN THE RAINBOW IS ENUF by Ntozake Shange, with Celestine DeSaussure, Sharita Hunt, Venida Evans, Leona Johnson, Denise Washington, Arlene Quiyou, Gwyneth Whyte
A DOLL'S HOUSE by Henrik Ibsen, with Erika Petersen, Joan Kendall, Kenneth Gray, Andrea Masters, Craig Kuehl, Gerard Moses, Michael Haight, Jeffery Woodard, Courtney Woodard

Bob Lorenz/Mainstreet Photos

Estelle Kemler, Joe DeSantis, (background)
Richard Kevlin-Bell, Penny Willis in
"Goodnight, Grandpa" Top: Yolande Bavan (C)
in "Comedy of Errors"

TENNESSEE WILLIAMS FINE ARTS CENTER

Key West, Florida
January 28 to March 8, 1981

Artistic Director, William Prosser; Business Manager/Press, Julianna Fields; Costumes, Jeff Hendry, Nancy Weintraub; Sets, Michael Orris Watson, John Kavelin, John Merriman; Lighting, Michael Orris Watson, John Toia, John Merriman; Sound, Stewart Shaw; Technical Director, John Merriman; Props, Lucile Kravitz; Stage Manager, John Toia; Directors, William Prosser, Joseph Stockdale, Stuart Howard; Assistant to Director, Warren Keyes

PRODUCTIONS AND CASTS

THE TEMPEST by William Shakespeare, with David Schramm, Mary Ewald, Michael Mulligan, Harry Richard, Warren Keyes, Roddy Brown, William Simington, Kirk Condyles, Paul Corman, Philip Bratnober, George Gugleotti, Scott Rhyne, Roxana Stuart, Paula Rose, Diana Haegelin, Bertram Prosser, Jennifer Belland, Lori Gamble, Penny Mollot, Lori Russ, Alison Young, Dixon Johnson, Brandon Kulik, Mathew Skelly, William Woehrle
THE LITTLE FOXES by Lillian Hellman, with Alyce Webb, Clarence Thomas, Marjorie Lovett, David Schramm, Warren Keyes, Roxana Stuart, Philip Bratnober, William Simington, Mary Ewald, Scott Rhyne
HAY FEVER by Noel Coward, with Roxana Stuart, Paul Corman, Diana Haegelin, Marjorie Lovett, William Simington, Scott Rhyne, Lisa McMillan, Philip Bratnober, Mary Ewald
THE NIGHT OF THE IGUANA by Tennessee Williams, with Joey Ruiz, Lisa McMillan, Luis Miguel Urizar, Douglas Stender, Carlton Fuller, Paula Rose, Scott Rhyne, Judy Miller, Warren Keyes, Iris Acker, Roxana Stuart, Mary Ewald, William Simington, Philip Bratnober

Douglas Stender, Roxana Stuart in "Night of the
Iguana" Above: Stuart, Lisa McMillan, William
Simington, Paul Corman in "Hay Fever"

THEATRE PROJECT COMPANY

St. Louis, Missouri
October 31, 1980 – April 26, 1981
Artistic Director, Fontaine Syer; General Manager, Christine E. Smith; Associate Director, Wayne Salomon; Technical Director, Deidre A. Taylor; Business Manager, Diane Holt; Directors, Wayne Salomon, Courtney Flanagan, William Grivna; Sets, Bill Schmiel, Hunter Breyer, Carol Billings, Suzanne Sessions; Costumes, Jane Alois Stein, Linda Bosomworth, Nancy Kay Webb; Lighting, Deirdre A. Taylor; Composer, Charles Rose; Stage Managers, Lee Patton Hasegawa, Amy Loui, Sue Greenberg, Dave Novak

COMPANY

John Contini, John Grassilli, Brian Hohlfeld, Courtney Flanagen, Jim Michael, David Novak, Bobby Miller, Lee Patton Hasegawa, Doyle Reynolds, Wayne Salomon, Fontaine Syer, Sharon Spence, Jerome Vogel

PRODUCTIONS

Catch-22 by Joseph Heller, Treasure Island adapted from the novel by Timothy Mason, Loose Ends by Michael Weller, Cat on a Hot Tin Roof by Tennessee Williams, A Taste of Honey by Shelagh Delaney, The Tempest by William Shakespeare

Sue Greenberg/Jerry McAdams Photos

Joe Hanrahan, Jerome Vogel, Gerry Becker
in "Loose Ends" Top: Fontaine Syer, Bobby
Miller in "Cat on a Hot Tin Roof"

TRINITY SQUARE REPERTORY COMPANY

Providence, Rhode Island
June 3, 1980 – May 31, 1981
Eighteenth Season
Director, Adrian Hall; Managing Director, E. Timothy Langan; General Manager, Michael Ducharme; Press, Scotti DiDonato; Sets, Eugene Lee, Robert D. Soule; Lighting, John F. Custer; Costumes, William Lane; Directors, Adrian Hall, Larry Arrick, George Martin, Richard Kneeland, Peter Gerety, Melanie Jones, William Radka, Philip Minor, James Howard Laurence; Stage Managers, Maureen F. Gibson, Rebecca Linn, Joseph Kavanagh

COMPANY

William R. Begley, Barbara Blossom, Bree, Dan Butler, Cait Calvo, Vince Ceglie, Timothy Crowe, Sylvia Davis, Gary de Lena, Maurice Dolbier, Bettie Endrizzi, Peter Gerety, Bradford Gottlin, Tom Griffin, Ed Hall, Richard Jenkins, David C. Jones, Melanie Jones, Richard Kavanaugh, David Kennett, Richard Kneeland, Howard London, James Howard Laurence, Mina Manente, George Martin, Ruth Maynard, Tim McDonough, Derek Meader, Daniel Nagrin, Barbara Orson, Susan Payne, Lenka Peterson, Ford Rainey, Arthur Roberts, Hilmar Sallee, Anne Scurria, April Shawhan, Vivienne Shub, Margo Skinner, Norman Smith, Myra Turley, Amy Van Nostrand, Daniel Von Bargen, Rose Weaver

PRODUCTIONS

El Grande de Coca-Cola, An Almost Perfect Person, Deathtrap, Arsenic and Old Lace, Betrayal, On Golden Pond, A Christmas Carol, The Iceman Cometh, Inherit the Wind, How I Got That Story, Whose Life Is It Anyway?, and the *World Premiere* of "The Whales of August" by David Berry

Constance Brown/Bob Emerson Photos

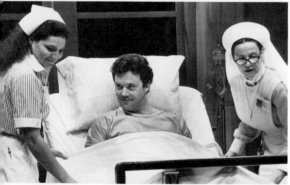

Myra Turley, Gary DeLena, Richard Kneeland,
Amy Van Nostrand in "El Grande de Coca Cola"

Top Left: Timothy Crowe, Mina Manente in "Deathtrap"
Below: Anne Scurria, Richard Kavanaugh, Barbara
Blossom in "Whose Life Is It Anyway?"

VIRGINIA MUSEUM THEATRE

Richmond, Virginia
September 26, 1980 – April 18, 1981
Twenty-sixth Season

Artistic Director, Tom Markus; Administrative Director, Baylor Landrum; Business Manager, Al Aucella; Press, David Griffith, Don Dale; Company Manager, Phil Crosby; Production Manager, Terry Burgler; Technical Director, Le Hook; Directors, Tom Markus, Darwin Knight, Terry Burgler, Jane Page, Russell Treyz; Sets, Charles Caldwell, Joseph A. Varga, Howard Cummings, Daniel Bishop; Costumes, Richard Hieronymus, Andrew B. Marlay, Linda Bradley, Moppy Vogely; Lighting, Richard Moore, Lynne Hartman; Sound, Richard Moore; Musical Direction, Harrison Fisher, Robert J. Bruyr; Choreographer, Hy Conrad; Stage Managers, Doug Flinchum, Jane Page, Jay Nellman, Terry Burgler

PRODUCTIONS AND CASTS

DEATHTRAP by Ira Levin, with Michael Lipton, Michael Scott, Nicola Sheara, Jean Sincere, Edward Stevlingson
GODSPELL by Stephen Schwartz, John-Michael Tebelak, with Constance Boardman, Randy Brenner, Zelie N. Daniels, Debrah Ann Holland, Jeff Johnson, Warren Kelley, Carl Blackwell Lester, Lynn Stafford, Becky Woodley, Sally Woodson
SIZWE BANSI IS DEAD by Athol Fugard, John Kani, Winston Ntshona, with Lou Ferguson, William Jay
THE FOURPOSTER by Jan de Hartog, with Kathleen Bishop, James Secrest
THE SEA HORSE by Edward J. Moore, with Judith Drake, David Gale
A MIDSUMMER NIGHT'S DREAM by William Shakespeare, with Charles Antalosky, Yolande Bavan, Andrew Bloom, Constance Boardman, Randy Brenner, Jeff Brooks, Hy Conrad, Jane Cromi, Phil Crosby, Yolanda Delgado, William Denis, Maury Erickson, Robert Foley, Jerry Guarino, Robert Jackson, Jean Lowes, Peter Murphy, Ange Pate, Michael Plunkett, William Preston, Mary Elizabeth Stewart, Paul S. Tomayko, Robert Walsh
GHOSTS by Henrik Ibsen (Rolf Fjelde translation), with William Denis, George Ede, Betty Leighton, Mary Lowry, Michael McKenzie
HAPPY DAYS by Samuel Beckett, with James W. Parker, Anne Sheldon
SOMETHING'S AFOOT by James McDonald, David Vos, Robert Gerlach, Ed Linderman, with Kevin Daly, William Denis, Patricia Falkenhain, Laura Gardner, Una Harrison, John High, Frederic Major, Susan Marchand, Vance Mizelle, Harold Shepard

"Godspell" Top: Michael Lipton,
Edward Stevlingson in "Deathtrap"

VIRGINIA STAGE COMPANY

Norfolk, Virginia
October 16, 1980–April 19, 1981
Second Season

Producing Director, Patrick Tovatt; Press, Carollynn Yurejefcic; Business Manager, Niki Thompson; Company Manager, Randy Adams; Directors, Patrick Tovatt, Israel Hicks, Jackson Phippin; Musical Director, John Lewis; Choreographer, Yvonne Rossen; Production Manager, Joe Ragey; Designers, Joe Ragey, Carrie Curtis, Bonnie Ann Brown, Peter Gould, Tiny Ossman; Stage Managers, J. P. Elins, Sarah Cornelia; Technical Director, David T. Whitmore; Props, Michelle Ritchie

PRODUCTIONS AND CASTS

ON GOLDEN POND by Ernest Thompson, with William Newman, Margaret Thomson, Fredric Major, Natalie Ross, Michael Joyner, Dennis Predovic
MRS. WARREN'S PROFESSION by George Bernard Shaw, with Kermit Brown, Meredith Ludwig, Natalie Ross, Bob Burrus, William Youmans, Fredric Major
CLASSIC COMICS by Moliere, with William Youmans, Linda Cook, Rocco Sisto, Bob Burrus, J. S. Johnson, Meredith Ludwig, Kermit Brown, Parlan McGaw, Robin M. Baker, Gary Henry
BURIED CHILD by Sam Shepard, with Bob Burrus, Fiona Hale, Rocco Sisto, John Henry Cox, William Youmans, Lind Cook, J. S. Johnson
THE INCREDIBLE MURDER OF CARDINAL TOSCA by Alden Nowlan, Walter Learning, with John Henry Cox, Fiona Hale, Rocco Sisto, Jeff Ware, Kirtan Coan, Jay Oney, John Ebner, Theodore May, Bob Burrus, Daniel Szelag, Parlan McGaw, Gary Henry, Steve Conway, David Marcia
LU ANN HAMPTON LAVERTY OBERLANDER by Preston Jones, with Kirtan Koan, Theodore May, Fiona Hale, Jeff Ware, Jay Oney, J. S. Johnson, Stephen Brown, Bob Burrus, John Henry Cox, Roy Cockrum, Julie Kelly
HOT GROG! by Jim Wann, Bland Simpson, with Roger Howell, Michele Dagavarian, Michael Hartman, Lanny Flaherty, Natalie Mosco, Steve Rankin, Ron Taylor, Mel Johnson, Jr., Richard Bowne, Deborah Stern, John Lewis, Sue Hadjopoulos

Meredith Ludwig/Robert K. Ander, Jr. Photos

Linda Cook, Meredith Ludwig in "Classic Comics"
Above: Bob Burrus in "Buried Child"

YALE REPERTORY THEATRE

New Haven, Connecticut
October 1, 1980 – May 16, 1981

Artistic Director, Lloyd Richards; Managing Director, Edward Martenson; Production Manager, Bronislaw J. Sammler; Sets, Michael H. Yeargan, Kevin Rupnik, Raymond M. Kluga, Karen Schulz, Steve Saklad; Costumes, Dunya Ramicova, Martha Kelly, Steve Saklad, Douglas O. Stein, Raymond M. Kluga, Rusty Magee; Lighting, William B. Warfel, John Tissot, David Noling, Michael H. Baumgarten, Timothy J. Hunter, Rick Butler; Stage Managers, Frank S. Torok, H. Lloyd Carbaugh, Shannon J. Sumpter, Neal Ann Stephens; Directors, Walton Jones, John Madden, Bill Ludel, Lloyd Richards, Jonas Jurasas; Press, Deborah J. Weiner

PRODUCTIONS AND CASTS

BOESMAN AND LENA by Athol Fugard, with Novella Nelson, Zakes Mokae, Brent Jennings

THE SUICIDE by Nikolai Erdman, with Joe Grifasi, Jane Kaczmarek, Merle Louise, Jerome Dempsey, Sasha von Scherler, James Cahill, Judith Roberts, David Alan Grier, Fred Melamend, J. T. Walsh, Katherine Borowitz, Dominic Chianese, Jeff Ginsberg, Becky London, Eve Gordon, Mitchell Lichtenstein, William Mesnik, Jeff Natter, Kathleen Reiter

TWELFTH NIGHT by William Shakespeare, with Phillip Casnoff, David Prittie, Edward Rudney, Michael Coerver, Reid Nelson, Jon Krupp, Brad O'Haire, William Newman, Seth Allen, John Ferraro, Ellen Parker, Kate Burton, Joan Pape, Becky London, Peter Jolly, Douglas Simes

WINTERSET: four new American plays: "Domestic Issues" by Corinee Jacker, with Nicolas Surovy, Gina Franz, Daniel Gold, Marcia Jean Kurtz, Ellen Yarker, Dann Florek; "Rococo" by Harry Kondoleon, with Madeleine le Roux, Jayne Haynes, Eve Gordon, Frances McDormand, Gary Basaraba, Jeff Ginsberg; "Sally and Marsha" by Sybille Pearson, with Frances Conroy, Robin Bartlett; "The Resurrection of Lady Lester" by Oyamo, with Darryl Croxton, David Alan Grier, Clarence Felder, Reg E. Cathey, Zakiah Barksdale Hakim, Isabell Monk, Cecilia Rubino, Scott Rickey Wheeler

HEDDA GABLER by Henrik Ibsen, with Jean-Pierre Stewart, Dianne Wiest, Sylvia O'Brien, Katherine Borowitz, James Earl Jones, John Glover, Regina David

THE MAGNIFICENT CUCKOLD by Fernand Crommelynck, with Jana Schneider, Becky London, Laurel Cronin, Eve Gordon, Earl Hindman, Richard Levine, Vytautas Ruginis, Richard Jenkins, Yusef Bulos, William Mesnik, Bern Sundstedt, Gary Basaraba, David Berman, Jeff Ginsberg, Kathleen Reiter, Melissa Smith, Scott Rickey Wheeler, David Wiles

AN ATTEMPT AT FLYING (American Premiere) by Yordan Radichkov; translated by Bogdan B. Athanassov; Directed by Mladen Kiselov; Music, Vasil Kazandgiev. CAST: Kurt Knudson, Michael Morgan, Clement Fowler, David Alan Grier, Jeffrey Alan Chandler, Stephen Rowe, David Sabin, Mitchell Lichtenstein, Jeff Natter, Zakes Mokae, Steven Hendrickson, Paul Espel, John Harnagel, Matt Sussman

W. B. Carter/Gerry Goodstein Photos

Right: Gina Franz, Nicolas Surovy in "Domestic Issues" Above: Philip Casnoff, Kate Burton in "Twelfth Night" Top: James Earl Jones, Dianne Wiest in "Hedda Gabler"

Jerome Dempsey, Joe Grifasi, Sasha von Scherler in "The Suicide"

Stephen Rowe, David Alan Grier in "An Attempt at Flying"

ALABAMA SHAKESPEARE FESTIVAL

Anniston, Alabama
Ninth Season

Martin L. Platt, Artistic Director; Michael Maso, Managing Director; Josephine E. Ayers, Executive Producer; Directors, Martin L. Platt, Russell Treyz; Sets, Michael Stauffer; Costumes, Lynne C. Emmert, Susan E. Mickey; Lighting, Michael Stauffer, Lauren Miller; Stage Manager, Ann Mathews; Musical Director, Joe Collins; Fight Choreographer, James Donadio; Props, Kathleen Brancato; Technical Director, Jeff McKay; Company Manager, Alexine Saunders

COMPANY

Carol Allin, Richard Andrew, Charles Antalosky, Karen Beauder, Kathy Brinton, Morris Brown, Robert Browning, A. D. Cover, Bruce Cromer, Joe DeBevc, James Donadio, Shannon Eubanks, Michelle Farr, Ellen Fiske, Sherre Galpert, Thomas Gibson, Rod Harter, Carol Haynes, Byron Hays, William Hollinde, Daniel Izzo, Peter Jack, Tom Key, Lauren Koslow, Terry Layman, Paul LeBlanc, Richard Levine, Jeff McCarthy, Jane Moore, Owen Page, Kerry Phillips, Philip Pleasants, Tom Reidy, Richard Ruskell, Anne Sandoe, Sam Sandoe, Mary Nell Santacroce, Dan Teal, James Thorp

PRODUCTIONS

(in repertory)

Romeo and Juliet, Tartuffe, The Two Gentlemen of Verona, The Importance of Being Earnest, Cymbeline

Michael Doege Photos

**Right: Bruce Comer in "Two Gentlemen
of Verona" Top: Philip Pleasants,
Shanon Eubanks, Charles Antalosky
in "Tartuffe"**

AMERICAN SHAKESPEARE THEATRE

Stratford, Connecticut
August 5-30, 1980
Twenty-fifth Year

President, Konrad Matthaei; Executive Director, Richard E. Bader; Comptroller, Charles Parker; Executive Assistants, Barbara Sirois, Donna Krasiejko; Technical Coordinator, Joe Patria; Props, Mario Fedeli; Director, Andre Ernotte; Set, Bill Stabile; Costumes, Ann Emonts; Lighting, Marc B. Weiss; Movement, Theodore Pappas; Stage Managers, Stephen Nasuta, Dianne Trulock, Hamilton Martin; Production Assistant, Jamie Clark; Company Manager, Robert Sheftic; Press, Richard Pheneger, Tom Holehan, Anne Montarro, Fred Sailer, Margaret Viola

CAST
RICHARD III by William Shakespeare

Michael Moriarty (Richard), Richard Seer (Tyrrel), Philip Casnoff (Clarence), Cyril Mallett (Brackenbury), Geoffrey Horne (Hastings), Denise Bessette (Lady Anne), Peter Von Berg (Bearer/Messenger), Georgine Hall (Richard's Mother), Robin Bartlett (Queen Elizabeth), Jay McCormack (Rivers), Viveca Lindfors (Queen Margaret), David Huffman (Buckingham), Eric Tull (Catesby), Bruce Kronenberg (Tailor), Vic Polizos (Ratcliff), Burke Pearson (King Edward), Gordon Chater (Stanley), Jason Scott (Prince Edward), Robert York (Young York), Donald Linahan (Bishop), David Tabor (Lord Mayor), Michael O'Hare (Richmond), Anna Galiena (Mistress Shore), Joe Zaloom (Concert Master/Pianist), Albert Malafronte (Lovel), Dancers: Mona Elgh, Kim Noor, Susan Stroman, Citizens/Soldiers/Musicians: Bill Applegate, Arnie Mazer, Peter Efthymiou

Jack Buxbaum/Robert Rienzi Photos

**Michael Moriarty, Viveca Lindfors
in "Richard III"**

CALIFORNIA SHAKESPEAREAN FESTIVAL

Visalia, California
June 27, - August 17, 1980
Second Season

Founder-Executive Director, David Fox-Brenton; Artistic Director, Mark Lamos; Managing Director, Alan Levey; Press, Chuck Carson; Design, John Conklin; Lighting, Pat Collins; Music, Hiram Titus; Sound, Roger Gans; Choreography and Direction, Mark Lamos; Assistant Director, Susanne L. Faull; Production Manager, Thomas Hall; Stage Managers, Thomas Hall, David Hay; Technical Director, John B. Forbes

COMPANY

Robert Beltran, Barry Boys, Jeffrey Combs, Robert Cornthwaite, Kim DeLong, Joe DeSalvio, Sarah-Jane Gwillim, Arthur Hanket, Will Huddleston, John-Fredrick Jones, Philip Kerr, Mary Layne, Heather MacDonald, Tony Plana, Judith Roberts, Benjamin Stewart, Nicolas Surovy, Sheriden Thomas, Harley Venton, Marchus Weishaus, G. Wood, Ginger Allen, Lisa Carlyle, Susan Miller, Wendi Radford, Garry Corgiat, Martin Curland, Kevin Leslie, Alan Litsey, Todd Mandel, Joel Mullenix, Tony Plana, Ron Salvador, Darrold Strubbe, Harley Venton, Tony Weber

PRODUCTIONS: Hamlet, A Midsummer Night's Dream

Micha Langer Photos

**Left: Mary Lane, Nicolas Surovy
in "Hamlet" Top: Nicolas Surovy,
Judith Roberts in "Hamlet"**

Arthur Hanket, Heather MacDonald, Mary
Layne, Jeffrey Combs in "Midsummer Night's Dream"

"A Midsummer Night's Dream"
(also above)

CHAMPLAIN SHAKESPEARE FESTIVAL

Burlington, Vermont
July 9, - August 23, 1980
Twenty-second Season

Producer-Director, Edward J. Feidner; Associate Producer-Director, Jennifer A. Cover; Stage Manager, Robert Lovell; Costumes, Mary Brownlow Huessy; Sets, Raymond Huessy; Lighting, Robert Little; Business Manager, Heidi Racht; Press, Rosemarie F. Eldridge; Music Director, Liz McGlinchey; Technical Director, Steven J. Sysko; Props, Lynn Barnicle.

COMPANY

Bill Christ, Paul D'Amato, Bradley A. Fox, Stacey Gladstone, Kate Goldborough, Cynthia Gould, Daniel Hagen, David Hall, Corky Hanger, Ron King, Edward Lindsay, Lissa Malley, Christopher Merrill, Robert Michalak, Patrick Moore, Brian Anthony Nelson, Jennifer O'Rourke, Martin Pizzuti, Vincent Rossano, Laurie Gay Spencer, Jim Tabakin, Eben Young, Mary Bradley, Billy Schubert, David Halley, Ursula Owre, Kristi McCormack, Heather Andrews, David Curtis

PRODUCTIONS

As You Like It, A Midsummer Night's Dream, Pericles

Heidi Racht/Alan Campbell Photos

**Left: Dan Hagen, Jennifer O'Rourke
in "Pericles" Top: Dan Hagen, Paul
D'Amato, Ron King in "A Midsummer
Night's Dream"**

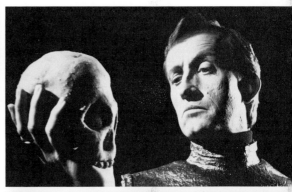

COLORADO SHAKESPEARE FESTIVAL

Boulder, Colorado
July 18–August 18, 1980
Twenty-third Season

Producing Director, Daniel S. P. Yang; Stage Directors, Daniel S. P. Yang, Jack Clay, Gavin Cameron-Webb; Costumes, Deborah Bays, David A. Busse, Marla Jurglanis; Technical Director, Charles E. Erven; Sets, Charles E. Erven, Norvid Jenkins Roos; Lighting, Robert Harris; Props, Bruce Jackson, Jr.; Production Manager, C. V. Bennett; Technical Director/Designer, Stancil Campbell; Stage Managers, Jane Page, Lucinda Gray; Composer and Musical Director, Cecil S. Effinger; Choreographer, Marilyn Cohen; Makeup/-Hairstylist, Joyce Degenfelder; Press, Nan B. Pirnack, Beverly Shaw

COMPANY

Dylan Baker, Tim Batson, Annette Bening, Christopher Boozer, Thomas Buckland, Rob Bundy, Shirley Carnahan, Judith Dickerson, Margaret Donaghy, James Finnegan, Larry Friedlander, Clare-Marie Guthrie, Lizabeth Hinton, Dennis P. Jans, Kjeld Erik Lyth, Michael Mancuso, Alan Stephen Masters, Anita Maynard, Kirk McCrea, Michael McKenzie, Randy Moore, David Morden, Paul Mullins, Patrick O'Connell, Christopher Erin Rock, Tom Rowan, Margie Shaw, Jane Shepard, Philip C. Sneed, David Stocker, Scott Swartsfager, Marshall Watson, Charles Wilcox, Will York

PRODUCTIONS: Love's Labour's Lost, Hamlet, Henry V

Jerry Stowall Photos

**James Finnegan, Anita Maynard in "Henry V"
Above: Randy Moore as Hamlet**

203

GLOBE PLAYHOUSE

Los Angeles, California
June 1, 1980, - May 24, 1981

President/Producer/Director, R. Thad Taylor; Executive Vice President, John D. Uhley; Stage Directors, David Schmalz, Lane Davies, John Flynn, Robert Machray, Simon MacCorkindale; Sets, Keith Hein, Tim Glavin, Steve Homsy; Costumes, Deborah Lowry, Jean Craig, Pam Grossman, Gretchen Spiess, Doreen Sachartoff; Lighting, Paulie Jenkins, Jane Dutra, Richard Niederberg, Ilya Mindlin, Mark Wood; Sound, Steve Munsie, John Garrick; Stage Managers, Debbie Chinn, Carol Tillman, Carl Moebus, Leslie Jordan, Lucy Pollak, Ilya Mindlin, Deena Booth, Steve Munsie, Norma Bowles; Choreographers, Roger Holzberg, Mary Michele, Michael Ross-Oddo; Composers, John Garrick, Jim Kessinger

PRODUCTIONS AND CASTS

COMEDY OF ERRORS with Rob Monroe, Don Altman, Jesse Ehrlich, Coe Kincade, John Boyle, Douglas Bruce, Paul Barber, Ron Woods, Peter Barbour, Pamela Brown, Kate Sarchet, Pamela Armstrong, James Dalesandro, Mark Burke, Frederick Ponzlow, Marilyn Dodds Frank, Joan Crosby

A MIDSUMMER NIGHT'S DREAM with Cathy Allyn, David Allyn, Teaka Allyn, John Sterling Arnold, Kriya Bon, Eugene Brezany, Ann Bronston, Beaumont Bruestle, Kimberly Eney, Jay D. Howard, Sydney Hibbert, Charles Hutchins, Dorene Ludwig, Mary Monaghan, Marcia Moran, Jim Nassiri, Mark Palko, Michael Ross-Oddo, Marc Silver, Douglas J. Stevenson, Steve Stuart, Larry Vigus, Kate Zentall

JULIUS CAESAR with David Asher, Charles Berendt, Michael Blackburn, William T. Blake, Deena Booth, Ann Bronston, Randall Brady, Michael W. Busa, Robert Curtin, Craig L. Dalton, Lane Davies, Steve Eoff, Allistair Findlay, John Garrick, Miranda Garrison, Mark Grover, Mark Hamlet, Ray Holland, Patrick Lee Houser, Enrique Perezarce Kandre, Paul Kawecki, John Lowry Lamb, Peter McDonald, Jan Munroe, Felix Navarro, Michael Ross-Oddo, Steve Osborn, Suzanne Peters, Ed Peterson, Ed Rombola, Anthony Scott, John Simpson, Tracey Thompson

THE TAMING OF THE SHREW with Karen Austin, Stephen A. J. Barbarich, Joe Barnaba, Michael Blackburn, Beaumont Bruestle, Erin Donovan, Julia Duffy, Jack Fisher, John Garrick, Mark Grover, Patrick Lee Houser, Kathy Johnston, Charles Hutchins, Rhonda Lewis, Carl Moebus, Peter McDonald, Felix Navarro, Glenn Rosenberg, Brent Shaphren, Marc Silver, Jon Stuart, B. J. Turner

THE MERCHANT OF VENICE with Greg Bell, Charles Berendt, J. P. Burns, Frank L. Bush, Shawna Culotta, Robert Factor, Michael Frost, William Gamble, Gloria Gifford, G. Adam Gifford, David Himes, Scott Jacoby, Perry King, Walter Klenhard, Christy Marx, Madora McKenzie, Sam Nudell, Rose Marie Perfect, Linda Purl, Mara Purl, Richard Rorke, Bradley C. Slaight, Marc Weishaus, Douglas Werner, Sarajane Robinson, Zai St. John

Photos by Sealy

Perry King, Linda Purl in "The Merchant of Venice" Above: Steve Stuart, Karen Austin in "Taming of the Shrew" Top: Robert Curtin, Charles Berendt in "Julius Caesar"

GREAT LAKES SHAKESPEARE FESTIVAL

Lakewood, Ohio
July 10, - September 28, 1980
Nineteenth Season

Artistic Director, Vincent Dowling; General Manager, Mary Bill; President, Henry M. Metcalf; Directors, Vincent Dowling, Robert Ellenstein, Michael Egan, Donald MacKechnie, Edward Stern; Designers, John Exell, Robert Schmidt, Mary-Anne Aston, Richard Donnelly, Linda Vidgor, Jonathon K. Duff, Kirk Bookman, Susan J. Christensen; Stage Managers, Olwen O'Herlihy, Ed Oster, Jason LaPadura; Technical Director, Richard Archer; Wardrobe, Diane B. Dalton; Props, Mary K. Stone; Sound, Thomas B. Dean; Assistant to Artistic Director, John Love; Dramaturg, Deborah Wood

COMPANY

Emery Battis, Nancy Boykin, Madylon Branstetter, John Q. Bruce, Jed Cooper, Clayton Corbin, Bairbre Dowling, Patricia Doyle, David Ellenstein, Robert Ellenstein, Robert Elliott, Bernard Kates, Bruce Matley, Sarah Nall, John Milligan, Si Osborne, Gavan O'Herlihy, Daniel Tamm, Thomas Waites, Barbara Haas, Lori Bezahler, Larry Ciferno, Steve Coulter, Jeanne Elser, Robert Kokai, Raymond Kurdziel, Wendy Lardin, Linda Meyers, Herbert Parker, Jim Reardon, Peter Robinson, Glenn de Roziere, Erika Schickel

PRODUCTIONS

Henry IV Part I by William Shakespeare, Charley's Aunt by Brandon Thomas, Hughie by Eugene O'Neill, Comedy of Errors by William Shakespeare, Titus Andronicus by William Shakespeare, and *World Premiere* of My Lady Luck by James A. Brown

Karabinus & Associates Photos

Right: Madylon Branstetter, Emery Battis in "Titus Andronicus" Top: Bruce Matley, Robert Elliott, Nancy Boykin in "The Comedy of Errors"

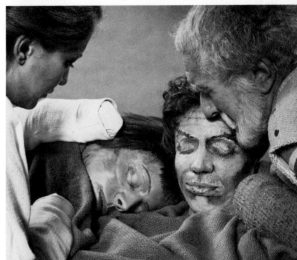

Vincent Dowling in "My Lady Luck"

Thomas Waites, Bernard Kates in "Henry IV Part I"

NEW JERSEY SHAKESPEARE FESTIVAL

Madison, N. J.
June 24, - December 28, 1980
Sixteenth Season

Artistic Director, Paul Barry; Associate Director/Press, Ellen Barry; Managing Director, Ed Cimbala; Stage Managers, James Wood, Richard S. Delahanty, Richard Dorfman, David Bosboom; Directors, Paul Barry, Dan Held, Samuel Maupin; Sets, Peter B. Harrison; Costumes, Kathleen Balke, Ann Emonts, Alice S. Hughes; Lighting, Richard Dorfman, David Bosboom; Musical Director, Deborah Martin; Press, Debra Waxman

COMPANY

Ellen Barry, Paul Barry, Victoria Boothby, Catherine Byers, Dimo Condos, Ron Coralian, Richard Graham, Robert Grossman, Davis Hall, Elizabeth Horowitz, David S. Howard, Eve Johnson, Warren Kliewer, Susanne Marley, Dana Mills, Don Perkins, William Perley, William Pitts, William Preston, Phillip Pruneau, Bill Roberts, Margery Shaw, Geddeth Smith, Jane Staab, David Tabor, Callan White, Diane Elisabeth Adams, Mitchell H. Baskin, Kathleen Beck, William Bensen, Edward Boerner, Robert Campbell, Pamela Cravens, John D'Amico, Jr., Jeffrey R. Dolan, Patricia Driscoll, Peter Engel, Paul B. Fenner, Anita Finlay, Julia Spencer Fleming, Helene Anne Fluhr, Patricia Flynn, Carol Furbay, Carol Ann Gatlin, Anne Giroux, Michael Goldstein, Mark Grannon, Lee Grober, Jennifer Haggin, Jennifer Hiers, Alexander Holsinger, Joy Jartman, Ellen Judith Kramer, Reeze La Londe, Kenneth Lask, Spencer Leuenberger, Gregg Loughridge, Guylaine Loriquer, Nancy Martin, Robert Martini, Lise Ann McMillan, Richard Mishaan, Mark Monaco, Carol Moreland, Walter W. Morrison, John Nichols, Linda Parsons Otto, Ingrid Price, Gregory Ragle, Richard Randall, Elisa Robin, Raymond Rizzo, Stephen Rogers, Stephen Rust, Ken Scherer, Steven Schlosser, Charles M. Simon, Jr., Jonathan Smedley, Joseph Lawrence Spiegel, Barbara Stefan, Nancy Sumner, Larry Vorsteg, Barbara Weiss, Elizabeth Whitehouse, Nancy Yeldezian

PRODUCTIONS

Comedy of Errors and Macbeth by William Shakespeare, Volpone by Ben Jonson, The Caretaker by Harold Pinter, Waltz of the Toreadors by Jean Anouilh, Knock Knock by Jules Feiffer, A Christmas Carol adapted from Charles Dickens by Paul Barry

Jerry Dalia Photos

Right: (standing) William Perley, Dana Mills, (seated) William Pitts, Davis Hall in "Comedy of Errors" Top: Paul Barry, Callan White in "Macbeth"

Phillip Pruneau, Davis Hall in "The Caretaker"

Ellen Barry, David Tabor, David Howard, William Pitts in "Knock Knock"

OREGON SHAKESPEARE FESTIVAL

Ashland, Oregon
February 26, - November 1, 1980
Forty-fifth Season

Producing Director, Jerry Turner; General Manager, William W. Patton; President of the Board, Stephen W. Ryder; Directors, Dennis Bigelow, Jon Cranney, Richard Allan Edwards, Luther James, Michael Kevin, James Moll, Pat Patton, Jerry Turner, James Edmondson, Audrey Stanley; Designers, Robert Blackman, William Bloodgood, Jeannie Davidson, Deborah M. Dryden, Richard L. Hay, Jesse Hollis, Michael Olich, Richard V. Parks, Robert Peterson, Richard Riddell, Christopher Sackett; Music Director/Composer, Todd Barton; Fight Director, David L. Boushey; Choreographers, Thomas A. Scales, Carl Wittman; Stage Managers, Peter W. Allen, David W. Brock, Lee Alan Byron, Michael D. Wise, Mary Steinmetz; Technical Directors, R. Duncan MacKenzie, Jeff Robbins

COMPANY

Linda Alper, Denis Arndt, James Avery, Traber Burns, James Carpenter, Mimi Carr, Casey Childs, Phyllis Courtney, Philip Davidson, Leonardo Defilippis, Cameron Dokey, Stuart Duckworth, Paul Duke, James Edmondson, Malinke Elliott, Richard Elmore, Michael T. Folie, Bill Geisslinger, Peter D. Giffin, Stephen J. Godwin, Bruce T. Gooch, Annette Helde, Robert Hirschboeck, J. Wesley Huston, Maureen Kilmurry, Barry Kraft, Ron Lindblom, John Norwalk, Jeanne Paulsen, Lawrence Paulsen, Rex Rabold, Robert M. Reid, Richard Riehle, Thomas A. Scales, John Shepard, Patricia Slover, Sally Smythe, Walter Stroud, Joan Stuart-Morris, Bill ter-Kuile, Kirk Thornton, Mary Turner, Tom Weiner, Cal Winn, Jeffrey Woolf

PRODUCTIONS

The Philadelphia Story by Philip Barry, Ring Round the Moon by Jean Anouilh, adapted by Christopher Fry, As You Like It by William Shakespeare, Coriolanus by William Shakespeare, Of Mice and Men by John Steinbeck, Seascape by Edward Albee, Sizwe Bansi Is Dead by Athol Fugard, John Kani and Winston Ntshona, Juno and the Paycock by Sean O'Casey, Lone Star/Laundry and Bourbon by James McLure, The Merry Wives of Windsor by William Shakespeare, Richard II by William Shakespeare, Love's Labour's Lost by William Shakespeare

Hank Kranzler Photos

Right: Margaret Rubin, Phyllis Courtney,
Cal Winn in "Merry Wives of Windsor"
Top: Cameron Dokey, John Shepard
in "As You Like It"

Philip Davidson, Joan Stuart-Morris
in "Love's Labour's Lost"

Bruce Gooch, Denis Arndt, James
Avery in "Coriolanus"

NATIONAL SHAKESPEARE FESTIVAL

San Diego, California
June 10–September 14, 1980
Thirty-first Season

Producing Director, Craig Noel; General Manager, Robert McGlade; Press, Bill Eaton; Technical Director, Stephen Roll; Stage Directors, Jack O'Brien, Craig Noel, Jerome Kilty; Costumes, Robert Morgan, Peggy Kellner, Deborah Dryden; Lighting, Sean Murphy; Composer, Conrad Susa; Dramaturg, Diana Maddox; Sound, Roger Gans; Props, James Gill; Fight Master, Anthony DeLongis; Stage Managers, William S. O'Brien, Peter Hackett

COMPANY

Meredith Alexander, Kim Bennett, Susan Chapman, Eric Christmas, Fredric Cook, Tandy Cronyn, Lane Davies, Richard Dix, John Dragon, Tovah Feldshuh, Lillian Garrett-Bonner, Jeff Scot Gendelman, Christopher Patrick Graham, Mary Gerber, Benjamin Hendrickson, Todd Jamieson, Jerry Allan Jones, Mark Kincaid, Michael Lueders, Jonathan McMurtry, Dag Paul MacLeod, Norman Maxwell, Jonathan Miller, John H. Napierala, Miki Outland, Steve Peterson, Harvey Solin, Ken Starcevic, Tom Stechschulte, Jill Tanner, Don Tuche, Lesley Vogel, James R. Winker, Rob Zimmerman

PRODUCTIONS

Two Gentlemen of Verona directed by Craig Noel, Romeo and Juliet directed by Jack O'Brien, Love's Labour's Lost directed by Jerome Kilty

Clifford Baker Photos

Right: Tovah Feldshuh, Jill Tanner
in "Romeo and Juliet" Top: Benjamin
Hendrickson, James R. Winker
in "Romeo and Juliet"

Jill Tanner, James R. Winker
in "Love's Labour's Lost"

Lillian Garrett-Bonner, Tovah Feldshuh
in "Two Gentlemen of Verona"

STRATFORD FESTIVAL OF CANADA

Stratford, Ontario, Canada
June 9 to November 8, 1980
Twenty-eighth Season

Artistic Director, Robin Phillips; Literary Manager, Urjo Kareda; Associate Directors, William Hutt, Peter Moss; Director of Production, Thomas Hooker; Media Development, Harvey Chusid; Treasurer, Gary Thomas; Head of Design, Daphne Dare; Production Manager, Peter Roberts; Technical Director, Kent McKay; Music Director, Berthold Carriere; Press, Anne Selby, Leonard McHardy; Music Administrator, Arthur Lang; Company Manager, Barry MacGregor; Stage Managers, Nora Polley, Vincent Berns, Bruce Blakemore, Martin Bragg, Colleen Stephenson, Michael Benoit, Laurie Freeman, Michael Shamata, Ann Stuart; Education Coordinator, Shelagh Hewitt; Archivist, Dan Ladell; Directors, Robin Phillips, Brian Bedford, Pam Brighton, Martha Henry, Jeff Hyslop, Urjo Kareda, Peter Moss, Gregory Peterson, Mel Shapiro; Designers, Daphne Dare, Susan Benson, Ann Curtis, Michael Eagan, Desmond Heeley, Sue LePage, Janice Lindsay, Robin Fraser Pay, John Pennoyer, Phillip Silver; Lighting, Michael Whitfield, Gil Wechsler, Harry Frehner; Composers, Berthold Carriere, Louis Applebaum, Gabriel Charpentier, Jonathan C. Holtzman, Norman Symonds.

COMPANY

Scott Baker, Rodger Barton, Rod Beattie, Stephen Beamish, Brian Bedford, Robert Benson, Christopher Blake, Mervyn Blake, Dwayne Brenna, Norman Browning, Barbara Budd, Graeme Campbell, Brent Carver, Patrick Christopher, David Clark, Patricia Collins, Patricia Conolly, William Copeland, Lloy Coutts, Hume Cronyn, Richard Curnock, John Cutts, Katia de Pena, David Dunbar, Maurice E. Evans, Janet Feindel, Carol Forte, Edda Gaborek, Pat Galloway, Sophie Gascon, Maurice Good, Donna Goodhand, Lewis Gordon, Janice Greene, Lynne Griffin, Luce Guilbeault, Jeffrey Guyton, Amelia Hall, David Harris, Max Helpmann, Martha Henry, Sten Hornborg, William Hutt, Keith James, Alicia Jeffery, Ray Jewers, Geordie Johnson, Lorne Kennedy, Joel Kenyon, Robert LaChance, Diana Leblanc, William Merton Malmo, Barry MacGregor, Roberta Maxwell, F. Braun McAsh, Robert McClure, Richard McMillan, Jim McQueen, Richard Monette, Marylu Moyer, Elizabeth Murphy, Sean T. O'Hara, Stephen Ouimette, Irene Pauzer, Nicholas Pennell, Jennifer Phipps, Douglas Rain, Kate Reid, Astrid Roch, Michael Ross, Stephen Russell, Booth Savage, Mary Savidge, Goldie Semple, Errol Slue, Maggie Smith, Wesley Stevens, Jessica Tandy, Michael Totzke, Reg Tupper, Davena Turvey, Peter Ustinov, Barry VanElen, Bruce Vavrina, Paul Wagar, Cathy Wallace, Gregory Wanless, Peggy Watson, William Webster, Jack Wetherall, John Wojda, Elizas Zarou.

PRODUCTIONS

William Shakespeare's Twelfth Night, Henry V, Titus Andronicus, Much Ado About Nothing, Henry VI (an adaptation), King Lear; The Beggar's Opera by John Gay, Virginia by Edna O'Brien, The Servant of Two Masters by Carlo Goldoni (adapted by Tom Cone), The Gin Game by D. L. Coburn, Bosoms and Neglect by John Guare, Brief Lives by Patrick Garland, Foxfire by Susan Cooper and Hume Cronyn, The Seagull by Anton Chekhov (adapted by John Murrell), Long Day's Journey into Night by Eugene O'Neill.

Robert C. Ragsdale Photos

Right Center: Richard Monette as Henry V
Above: Kate Reid, Barry MacGregor, Patrick
Christopher, Richard McMillan, Brian Bedford
in "Twelfth Night" Top: Diana LeBlanc,
Maggie Smith, Keith James, Max Helpmann
in "Much Ado about Nothing"

Jessica Tandy, Hume Cronyn
in "Foxfire"

209

PULITZER PRIZE PRODUCTIONS

1918–Why Marry?, **1919**–No award, **1920**–Beyond the Horizon, **1921**–Miss Lulu Bett, **1922**–Anna Christie, **1923**–Icebound, **1924**–Hell-Bent fer Heaven, **1925**–They Knew What They Wanted, **1926**–Craig's Wife, **1927**–In Abraham's Bosom, **1928**–Strange Interlude, **1929**–Street Scene, **1930**–The Green Pastures, **1931**–Alison's House, **1932**–Of Thee I Sing, **1933**–Both Your Houses, **1934**–Men in White, **1935**–The Old Maid, **1936**–Idiot's Delight, **1937**–You Can't Take It with You, **1938**–Our Town, **1939**–Abe Lincoln in Illinois, **1940**–The Time of Your Life, **1941**–There Shall Be No Night, **1942**–No award, **1943**–The Skin of Our Teeth, **1944**–No award, **1945**–Harvey, **1946**–State of the Union, **1947**–No award, **1948**–A Streetcar Named Desire, **1949**–Death of a Salesman, **1950**–South Pacific, **1951**–No award, **1952**–The Shrike, **1953**–Picnic, **1954**–The Teahouse of the August Moon, **1955**–Cat on a Hot Tin Roof, **1956**–The Diary of Anne Frank, **1957**–Long Day's Journey into Night, **1958**–Look Homeward, Angel, **1959**–J. B., **1960**–Fiorello!, **1961**–All the Way Home, **1962**– How to Succeed in Business without Really Trying, **1963**–No award, **1964**–No award, **1965**–The Subject Was Roses, **1966**–No award, **1967**–A Delicate Balance, **1968**–No award, **1969**–The Great White Hope, **1970**–No Place to Be Somebody, **1971**–The Effect of Gamma Rays on Man-in-the-Moon Marigolds, **1972**–No award, **1973**–That Championship Season, **1974**–No award, **1975**–Seascape, **1976**–A Chorus Line, **1977**–The Shadow Box, **1978**–The Gin Game, **1979**–Buried Child, **1980**–Talley's Folly, **1981**–Crimes of the Heart

NEW YORK DRAMA CRITICS CIRCLE AWARDS

1936–Winterset, **1937**–High Tor, **1938**–Of Mice and Men, Shadow and Substance, **1939**–The White Steed, **1940**–The Time of Your Life, **1941**–Watch on the Rhine, The Corn is Green, **1942**–Blithe Spirit, **1943**–The Patriots, **1944**–Jacobowsky and the Colonel, **1945**–The Glass Menagerie, **1946**–Carousel, **1947**–All My Sons, No Exit, Brigadoon, **1948**–A Streetcar Named Desire, The Winslow Boy, **1949**–Death of a Salesman, The Madwoman of Chaillot, South Pacific, **1950**–The Member of the Wedding, The Cocktail Party, The Consul, **1951**–Darkness at Noon, The Lady's Not for Burning, Guys and Dolls, **1952**–I Am a Camera, Venus Observed, Pal Joey, **1953**–Picnic, The Love of Four Colonels, Wonderful Town, **1954**–Teahouse of the August Moon, Ondine, The Golden Apple, **1955**–Cat on a Hot Tin Roof, Witness for the Prosecution, The Saint of Bleecker Street, **1956**–The Diary of Anne Frank, Tiger at the Gates, My Fair Lady, **1957**–Long Day's Journey into Night, The Waltz of the Toreadors, The Most Happy Fella, **1958**–Look Homeward Angel, Look Back in Anger, The Music Man, **1959**–A Raisin in the Sun, The Visit, La Plume de Ma Tante, **1960**–Toys in the Attic, Five Finger Exercise, Fiorello!, **1961**–All the Way Home, A Taste of Honey, Carnival, **1962**–Night of the Iguana, A Man for All Seasons, How to Succeed in Business without Really Trying, **1963**–Who's Afraid of Virginia Woolf?, **1964**–Luther; Hello, Dolly!, **1965**–The Subject Was Roses, Fiddler on the Roof, **1966**–The Persecution and Assassination of Marat as Performed by the Inmates of the Asylum of Charenton under the Direction of the Marquis de Sade, Man of La Mancha, **1967**–The Homecoming, Cabaret, **1968**–Rosencrantz and Guildenstern Are Dead, Your Own Thing, **1969**–The Great White Hope, 1776, **1970**–The Effect of Gamma Rays on Man-in-the-Moon Marigolds, Borstal Boy, Company, **1971**–Home, Follies, The House of Blue Leaves, **1972**–That Championship Season, Two Gentlemen of Verona, **1973**–The Hot 1 Baltimore, The Changing Room, A Little Night Music, **1974**–The Contractor, Short Eyes, Candide, **1975**–Equus, The Taking of Miss Janie, A Chorus Line, **1976**–Travesties, Streamers, Pacific Overtures, **1977**–Otherwise Engaged, American Buffalo, Annie, **1978**–Da, Ain't Misbehavin', **1979**–The Elephant Man, Sweeney Todd, **1980**–Talley's Folly, Evita, Betrayal, **1981**–Crimes of the Heart, A Lesson from Aloes, Special Citations to Lena Horne, The Pirates of Penzance

AMERICAN THEATRE WING
ANTOINETTE PERRY (TONY) AWARD PRODUCTIONS

1948–Mister Roberts, **1949**–Death of a Salesman, Kiss Me, Kate, **1950**–The Cocktail Party, South Pacific, **1951**–The Rose Tattoo, Guys and Dolls, **1952**–The Fourposter, The King and I, **1953**–The Crucible, Wonderful Town, **1954**–The Teahouse of the August Moon, Kismet, **1955**–The Desperate Hours, The Pajama Game, **1956**–The Diary of Anne Frank, Damn Yankees, **1957**–Long Day's Journey into Night, My Fair Lady, **1958**–Sunrise at Campobello, The Music Man, **1959**–J. B., Redhead, **1960**–The Miracle Worker, Fiorello! tied with The Sound of Music, **1961**–Becket, Bye Bye Birdie, **1962**–A Man for All Seasons, How to Succeed in Business without Really Trying, **1963**–Who's Afraid of Virginia Woolf?, A Funny Thing Happened on the Way to the Forum, **1964**–Luther, Hello Dolly!, **1965**–The Subject Was Roses, Fiddler on the Roof, **1966**–The Persecution and Assassination of Marat as Performed by the Inmates of the Asylum of Charenton under the Direction of the Marquis de Sade, Man of La Mancha, **1967**–The Homecoming, Cabaret, **1968**–Rosencrantz and Guildenstern Are Dead, Hallelujah Baby!, **1969**–The Great White Hope, 1776, **1970**–Borstal Boy, Applause, **1971**–Sleuth, Company, **1972**–Sticks and Bones, Two Gentlemen of Verona, **1973**–That Championship Season, A Little Night Music, **1974**–The River Niger, Raisin, **1975**–Equus, The Wiz, **1976**–Travesties, A Chorus Line, **1977**–The Shadow Box, Annie, **1978**–Da, Ain't Misbehavin', Dracula, **1979**–The Elephant Man, Sweeney Todd, **1980**–Children of a Lesser God, Evita, Morning's at Seven, **1981**–Amadeus, 42nd Street, The Pirates of Penzance

BRIAN BACKER
of "The Floating Light Bulb"

LISA BANES
of "Look Back in Anger"

MEG BUSSERT
of "The Music Man"

MICHAEL ALLAN DAVIS
of "Broadway Follies"

GIANCARLO ESPOSITO
of "Zooman and the Sign"

PHYLLIS HYMAN
of "Sophisticated Ladies"

CYNTHIA NIXON
of "The Philadelphia Story"

DANIEL GERROLL
of "Slab Boys"

AMANDA PLUMMER
of "A Taste of Honey"

ADAM REDFIELD
of "A Life"

WANDA RICHERT
of "42nd Street"

REX SMITH
of "The Pirates of Penzance"

213

THEATRE WORLD AWARDS PARTY: Thursday, May 28, 1981. Top: Christopher Walken, Estelle Parsons, John Rubinstein, Tammy Grimes, Gregory Hines; Danny Aiello; George Grizzard, Patricia Elliott, James Mitchell, Anita Gillette Below: Fay Sappington, John Willis; Brian Backer, Gloria Foster; Mayor Edward Koch; Michael Davis; Third Row: Elizabeth Taylor, Maureen Stapleton; Giancarlo Esposito; Cynthia Nixon; Wanda Richert, Christopher Walken Bottom Row: Liza Redfield (for Adam Redfield); Rex Smith, Estelle Parsons; Gregory Hines, Phyllis Hyman; Tammy Grimes, Amanda Plummer

J. M. Viade, Van Williams Photos

Top: Anita Gillette, Michael Fried (for Lisa Banes); Meg Bussert; Daniel Gerroll; Elizabeth Taylor, Maureen Stapleton, Mayor Edward Koch; Below: Lee Roy Reams, Wanda Richert; Fran Brill, Kevin Conway; Fritz Weaver; Maxwell Caulfield, Juliet Mills; Third Row: Joan Copeland, Radie Harris, Rosemary Murphy, Christopher Walken, Natalie Schaefer; Patricia Elliott; Daniel Gerroll, Dennis Christopher; Bottom: Charles Repole, Maureen O'Sullivan, Russ Thacker, Suellen Estey; Colleen Dewhurst; Johnny Ray, Lisa Kirk, Juliette Koka

J. M. Viade, Van Williams Photos

| Harry Belafonte | Nell Carter | Charlton Heston | Maureen Stapleton | Anthony Perkins |

PREVIOUS THEATRE WORLD AWARD WINNERS

1944–45: Betty Comden, Richard Davis, Richard Hart, Judy Holliday, Charles Lang, Bambi Linn, John Lund, Donald Murphy, Nancy Noland, Margaret Phillips, John Raitt

1945–46: Barbara Bel Geddes, Marlon Brando, Bill Callahan, Wendell Corey, Paul Douglas, Mary James, Burt Lancaster, Patricia Marshall, Beatrice Pearson

1946–47: Keith Andes, Marion Bell, Peter Cookson, Ann Crowley, Ellen Hanley, John Jordan, George Keane, Dorothea MacFarland, James Mitchell, Patricia Neal, David Wayne

1947–48: Valerie Bettis, Edward Bryce, Whitfield Connor, Mark Dawson, June Lockhart, Estelle Loring, Peggy Maley, Ralph Meeker, Meg Mundy, Douglass Watson, James Whitmore, Patrice Wymore

1948–49: Tod Andrews, Doe Avedon, Jean Carson, Carol Channing, Richard Derr, Julie Harris, Mary McCarty, Allyn Ann McLerie, Cameron Mitchell, Gene Nelson, Byron Palmer, Bob Scheerer

1949–50: Nancy Andrews, Phil Arthur, Barbara Brady, Lydia Clarke, Priscilla Gillette, Don Hanmer, Marcia Henderson, Charlton Heston, Rick Jason, Grace Kelly, Charles Nolte, Roger Price

1950–51: Barbara Ashley, Isabel Bigley, Martin Brooks, Richard Burton, Pat Crowley, James Daly, Cloris Leachman, Russell Nype, Jack Palance, William Smothers, Maureen Stapleton, Marcia Van Dyke, Eli Wallach

1951–52: Tony Bavaar, Patricia Benoit, Peter Conlow, Virginia de Luce, Ronny Graham, Audrey Hepburn, Diana Herbert, Conrad Janis, Dick Kallman, Charles Proctor, Eric Sinclair, Kim Stanley, Marian Winters, Helen Wood

1952–53: Edie Adams, Rosemary Harris, Eileen Heckart, Peter Kelley, John Kerr, Richard Kiley, Gloria Marlowe, Penelope Munday, Paul Newman, Sheree North, Geraldine Page, John Stewart, Ray Stricklyn, Gwen Verdon

1953–54: Orson Bean, Harry Belafonte, James Dean, Joan Diener, Ben Gazzara, Carol Haney, Jonathan Lucas, Kay Medford, Scott Merrill, Elizabeth Montgomery, Leo Penn, Eva Marie Saint

1954–55: Julie Andrews, Jacqueline Brookes, Shirl Conway, Barbara Cook, David Daniels, Mary Fickett, Page Johnson, Loretta Leversee, Jack Lord, Dennis Patrick, Anthony Perkins, Christopher Plummer

1955–56: Diane Cilento, Dick Davalos, Anthony Franciosa, Andy Griffith, Laurence Harvey, David Hedison, Earle Hyman, Susan Johnson, John Michael King, Jayne Mansfield, Sarah Marshall, Gaby Rodgers, Susan Strasberg, Fritz Weaver

1956–57: Peggy Cass, Sydney Chaplin, Sylvia Daneel, Bradford Dillman, Peter Donat, George Grizzard, Carol Lynley, Peter Palmer, Jason Robards, Cliff Robertson, Pippa Scott, Inga Swenson

1957–58: Anne Bancroft, Warren Berlinger, Colleen Dewhurst, Richard Easton, Tim Everett, Eddie Hodges, Joan Hovis, Carol Lawrence, Jacqueline McKeever, Wynne Miller, Robert Morse, George C. Scott

1958–59: Lou Antonio, Ina Balin, Richard Cross, Tammy Grimes, Larry Hagman, Dolores Hart, Roger Mollien, France Nuyen, Susan Oliver, Ben Piazza, Paul Roebling, William Shatner, Pat Suzuki, Rip Torn

1959–60: Warren Beatty, Eileen Brennan, Carol Burnett, Patty Duke, Jane Fonda, Anita Gillette, Elisa Loti, Donald Madden, George Maharis, John McMartin, Lauri Peters, Dick Van Dyke

1960–61: Joyce Bulifant, Dennis Cooney, Sandy Dennis, Nancy Dussault, Robert Goulet, Joan Hackett, June Harding, Ron Husmann, James MacArthur, Bruce Yarnell

1961–62: Elizabeth Ashley, Keith Baxter, Peter Fonda, Don Galloway, Sean Garrison, Barbara Harris, James Earl Jones, Janet Margolin, Karen Morrow, Robert Redford, John Stride, Brenda Vaccaro

1962–63: Alan Arkin, Stuart Damon, Melinda Dillon, Robert Drivas, Bob Gentry, Dorothy Loudon, Brandon Maggart, Julienne Marie, Liza Minnelli, Estelle Parsons, Diana Sands, Swen Swenson

1963–64: Alan Alda, Gloria Bleezarde, Imelda De Martin, Claude Giraud, Ketty Lester, Barbara Loden, Lawrence Pressman, Gilbert Price, Philip Proctor, John Tracy, Jennifer West

1964–65: Carolyn Coates, Joyce Jillson, Linda Lavin, Luba Lisa, Michael O'Sullivan, Joanna Pettet, Beah Richards, Jaime Sanchez, Victor Spinetti, Nicolas Surovy, Robert Walker, Clarence Williams III

1965–66: Zoe Caldwell, David Carradine, John Cullum, John Davidson, Faye Dunaway, Gloria Foster, Robert Hooks, Jerry Lanning, Richard Mulligan, April Shawhan, Sandra Smith, Lesley Ann Warren

1966–67: Bonnie Bedelia, Richard Benjamin, Dustin Hoffman, Terry Kiser, Reva Rose, Robert Salvio, Sheila Smith, Connie Stevens, Pamela Tiffin, Leslie Uggams, Jon Voight, Christopher Walken

1967–68: David Birney, Pamela Burrell, Jordan Christopher, Jack Crowder (Thalmus Rasulala), Sandy Duncan, Julie Gregg, Stephen Joyce, Bernadette Peters, Alice Playten, Michael Rupert, Brenda Smiley, Russ Thacker

1968–69: Jane Alexander, David Cryer, Blythe Danner, Ed Evanko, Ken Howard, Lauren Jones, Ron Leibman, Marian Mercer, Jill O'Hara, Ron O'Neal, Al Pacino, Marlene Warfield

1969–70: Susan Browning, Donny Burks, Catherine Burns, Len Cariou, Bonnie Franklin, David Holliday, Katharine Houghton, Melba Moore, David Rounds, Lewis J. Stadlen, Kristoffer Tabori, Fredricka Weber

1970–71: Clifton Davis, Michael Douglas, Julie Garfield, Martha Henry, James Naughton, Tricia O'Neil, Kipp Osborne, Roger Rathburn, Ayn Ruymen, Jennifer Salt, Joan Van Ark, Walter Willison

1971–72: Jonelle Allen, Maureen Anderman, William Atherton, Richard Backus, Adrienne Barbeau, Cara Duff-MacCormick, Robert Foxworth, Elaine Joyce, Jess Richards, Ben Vereen, Beatrice Winde, James Woods

1972–73: D'Jamin Bartlett, Patricia Elliott, James Farentino, Brian Farrell, Victor Garber, Kelly Garrett, Mari Gorman, Laurence Guittard, Trish Hawkins, Monte Markham, John Rubinstein, Jennifer Warren, Alexander H. Cohen (Special Award)

1973–74: Mark Baker, Maureen Brennan, Ralph Carter, Thom Christopher, John Driver, Conchata Ferrell, Ernestine Jackson, Michael Moriarty, Joe Morton, Ann Reinking, Janie Sell, Mary Woronov, Sammy Cahn (Special Award)

1974–75: Peter Burnell, Zan Charisse, Lola Falana, Peter Firth, Dorian Harewood, Joel Higgins, Marcia McClain, Linda Miller, Marti Rolph, John Sheridan, Scott Stevensen, Donna Theodore, Equity Library Theatre (Special Award)

1975–76: Danny Aiello, Christine Andreas, Dixie Carter, Tovah Feldshuh, Chip Garnett, Richard Kelton, Vivian Reed, Charles Repole, Virginia Seidel, Daniel Seltzer, John V. Shea, Meryl Streep, A Chorus Line (Special Award)

1976–77: Trazana Beverley, Michael Cristofer, Joe Fields, Joanna Gleason, Cecilia Hart, John Heard, Gloria Hodes, Juliette Koka, Andrea McArdle, Ken Page, Jonathan Pryce, Chick Vennera, Eva LeGallienne (Special Award)

1977–78: Vasili Bogazianos, Nell Carter, Carlin Glynn, Christopher Goutman, William Hurt, Judy Kaye, Florence Lacy, Armelia McQueen, Gordana Rashovich, Bo Rucker, Richard Seer, Colin Stinton, Joseph Papp (Special Award)

1978–79: Philip Anglim, Lucie Arnaz, Gregory Hines, Ken Jennings, Michael Jeter, Laurie Kennedy, Susan Kingsley, Christine Lahti, Edward James Olmos, Kathleen Quinlan, Sarah Rice, Max Wright, Marshall W. Mason (Special Award)

1979–80: Maxwell Caulfield, Leslie Denniston, Boyd Gaines, Richard Gere, Harry Groener, Stephen James, Susan Kellermann, Dinah Manoff, Lonny Price, Marianne Tatum, Anne Twomey, Dianne Wiest, Mickey Rooney (Special Award)

1980–81: Brian Backer, Lisa Banes, Meg Bussert, Michael Allan Davis, Giancarlo Esposito, Daniel Gerroll, Phyllis Hyman, Cynthia Nixon, Amanda Plummer, Adam Redfield, Wanda Richert, Rex Smith, Elizabeth Taylor (Special Award)

Alynne Amkraut

C. B. Anderson

Myra Anderson

Joel Anderson

Patricia Angelin

BIOGRAPHICAL DATA ON THIS SEASON'S CASTS

ABBOTT, ANDREA. Born Feb. 1, 1951 in Alliance, Nb. Graduate Temple Buell Col. Debut 1980 OB in "Period of Adjustment."

ABERLIN, BETTY. Born Dec. 30, 1942 in NYC. Graduate Bennington College. Debut OB 1954 in "Sandhog," followed by "Upstairs at the Downstairs," "I'm Getting My Act Together," "Alice in Concert," Bdwy 1964 in "Cafe Crown."

ABRAHAM, F. MURRAY. Born Oct. 24, 1939 in Pittsburgh, PA. Attended UTex. OB bow 1967 in "The Fantasticks," followed by "An Opening in the Trees," "Fourteenth Dictator," "Young Abe Lincoln," "Tonight in Living Color," "Adaptation," "Survival of St. Joan," "The Dog Ran Away," "Fables," "Richard III," "Little Murders," "Scuba Duba," "Where Has Tommy Flowers Gone?," "Miracle Play," "Blessing," "Sexual Perversity in Chicago," "Landscape of the Body," "The Master and Margarita," "Biting the Apple," "The Seagull," Bdwy in "The Man in the Glass Booth" (1968), "6 Rms Riv Vu," "Bad Habits," "The Ritz," "Legend," "Teibele and Her Demon."

ABRAMS, NORMAN. Born July 21, 1943 in Brooklyn, NY. Graduate Oklahoma U. Bdwy debut 1974 in "Scapino," followed by "Lolita," OB in "Scapino," BAM Theatre Co's "Devil's Disciple," "The Play's the Thing," and "Julius Caesar."

ABUBA, ERNEST. Born Aug. 25, 1947 in Honolulu, HI. Attended Southwestern Col. Bdwy debut 1976 in "Pacific Overtures," followed by "Loose Ends," OB in "Sunrise," "Monkey Music."

ACKROYD, DAVID. Born May 30, 1940 in Orange, NJ. Graduate Bucknell, Yale. Bdwy debut 1971 in "Unlikely Heroes," followed by "Full Circle," "Hamlet," "Hide and Seek," "Children of a Lesser God," OB in "Isadora Duncan Sleeps with the Russian Navy."

ADAMS, JOSEPH. Born Feb. 4, 1956 in Concord, CA. Debut 1980 in ELT's "Romeo and Juliet," Bdwy 1981 in "The Survivor."

ADAMS, MOLLY. Born in Portchester, NY. Graduate Smith Col. Debut OB 1973 in "Older People," followed by "Hot l Baltimore," "The Unicorn in Captivity," "Did You See the Elephant," "Sweethearts," Bdwy 1979 in "Bedroom Farce," followed by "The Father."

ADAMSON, DAVID. Born Nov. 30, 1944 in Winona MN. Graduate UNI and UNC. Debut 1980 OB in "Kohlhass," followed by "Sister Aimee."

ADDY, WESLEY. Born Aug. 4, 1913 in Omaha, NE. Attended UCLA. Bdwy debut 1935 in "Panic," followed by "How Beautiful with Shoes," "Hamlet," "Richard II," "Henry IV," "Summer Night," "Romeo and Juliet," "Twelfth Night," "Antigone," "Candida," "Another Part of the Forest," "Galileo," "Leading Lady," "The Traitor," "The Enchanted," "King Lear," "The Strong Are Lonely," "First Gentleman," "South Pacific," "A Stitch in Time," OB in "A Month in the Country," "Candida," "Ghosts," "John Brown's Body," "Curtains."

AHEARN, DAN. Born Aug. 7, 1948 in Washington, DC. Attended, Carnegie Mellon. Debut OB 1981 in "Woyzeck."

AIDEM, BETSY SUE. Born Oct. 28, 1957 in Eastmeadow, NY. Graduate NYU. Debut 1981 OB in "The Trading Post."

AIELLO, DANNY. Born June 20, 1935 in NYC. Bdwy debut 1975 in "Lampost Reunion" for which he received a Theatre World Award, followed by "Wheelbarrow Closers," "Gemini," "Knockout," "The Floating Light Bulb."

AKERS, ANDRA. Born Sept. 16, 1946 in NYC. Attended Sarah Lawrence Col. Bdwy debut 1970 in "Charley's Aunt," followed by "Perfectly Frank," OB in "Wanted."

ALDREDGE, TOM. Born Feb. 28, 1928 in Dayton, OH. Attended Dayton U., Goodman Theatre. Bdwy bow 1959 in "The Nervous Set," followed by "UTBU," "Slapstick Tragedy," "Everything in the Garden," "Indians," "Engagement Baby," "How the Other Half Loves," "Sticks and Bones," "Where's Charley?," "Leaf People," "Rex," "Vieux Carre," "St. Joan," "Stages," "On Green Pond," "The Little Foxes," OB in "The Tempest," "Between Two Thieves," "Henry V," "The Premise," "Love's Labour's Lost," "Troilus and Cressida," "Butter and Egg Man," "Ergo," "Boys in the Band," "Twelfth Night," "Colette," "Hamlet," "The Orphan," "King Lear," "Iceman Cometh."

ALDRIDGE, JANET. Born Oct. 16, 1956 in Hinsdale, IL. Graduate UMiami. Off-Bdwy debut 1980 in "A Funny Thing Happened on the Way to the Forum."

ALEXANDER, COLETTE. Born Dec. 2, 1951 in Brooklyn, NY. Bdwy debut 1981 in "Lolita."

ALEXANDRINE, DRU. Born Apr. 23, 1950 in Cheshire, Eng. Attended Royal Ballet School. Bdwy debut 1973 in "Pajama Game," followed by "My Fair Lady," "Onward Victoria."

ALEXIS, ALVIN. Born July 5 in NYC. Debut 1976 OB in "In the Wine Time," followed by "Rear Column," "Class Enemy," "Zooman and the Sign."

ALICE, MARY. Born Dec. 3, 1941 in Indianola, MS. Debut OB 1967 in "Trials of Brother Jero," followed by "The Strong Breed," "Duplex," "Thoughts," "Miss Julie," "House Party," "Terraces," "Heaven and Hell's Agreement," "In the Deepest Part of Sleep," "Cockfight," "Julius Caesar," "Nongogo," "Second Thoughts," "Spell #7," "Zooman and The Sign," "Glasshouse," Bdwy 1971 in "No Place to Be Somebody."

ALLEN, BEAU. Born Mar. 2, 1950 in Wilmington, DE. Graduate Tufts U. Bdwy debut 1972 in "Jesus Christ Superstar," followed by "Two Gentlemen of Verona," "Best Little Whorehouse in Texas."

ALLEN, G. BRANDON. Born Dec. 27, 1952 in NYC. Graduate Queens Col, AMDA. Bdwy debut 1981 in "The Five O'Clock Girl."

ALLEN, SETH. Born July 13, 1941 in Brooklyn, NY. Attended Musical Theatre Acad. OB in "Viet Rock," "Futz," "Hair," "Candaules Commissioner," "Mary Stuart," "Narrow Road to the Deep North," "More Than You Deserve," "Split Lip," "The Misanthrope," "Hard Sell," "The Wild Duck," "Jungle of Cities," Bdwy 1972 in "Jesus Christ Superstar."

ALLEN, SHEILA. Born Oct. 22, 1932 in Chard, Somerset, Eng. RADA Graduate. Debut with Royal Shakespeare Co.'s 1975 season at BAM. With BAM Theatre Co. in "Winter's Tale," "The Barbarians," "The Wedding," "A Midsummer Night's Dream," "The Wild Duck," "Oedipus the King," "Vikings."

ALTAY, DERIN. Born Nov. 10, 1954 in Chicago, IL. Attended Goodman School, AmCons. Broadway debut in "Evita."

AMENDOLIA, DON. Born Feb. 1, 1945 in Woodbury, NJ. Attended Glassboro State Col., AADA. Debut 1966 OB in "Until the Monkey Comes," followed by "Park," "Cloud 9."

AMKRAUT, ALYNNE. Born July 3, 1953 in Amityville, NY. Graduate Syracuse U. Debut OB 1981 in "Godspell," followed by "Women in Tune."

ANDERMAN, MAUREEN. Born Oct. 26, 1946 in Detroit, MI. Graduate UMich. Bdwy debut 1970 in "Othello," followed by "Moonchildren" for which she received a Theatre World Award, "An Evening with Richard Nixon . . . ," "The Last of Mrs. Lincoln," "Seascape," "Who's Afraid of Virginia Woolf?" "A History of the American Film," "The Lady from Dubuque," "The Man Who Came to Dinner," OB in "Hamlet," "Elusive Angel," "Out of Our Father's House," "Sunday Runners," "Macbeth."

ANDERSON, C. B. Born June 18, 1939 in Nashville, TN. Attended UGa. Debut 1980 with BAM Theatre Co. in "The Winter's Tale," followed by "Johnny on a Spot," "The Recruiting Officer," "The Wild Duck," "Jungle of Cities," "Court of Miracles."

ANDERSON, JOEL. Born Nov. 19, 1955 in San Diego, CA. Graduate UUtah. Debut 1980 OB in "A Funny Thing Happened on the Way to the Forum."

ANDERSON, MYRA. Born May 12, 1949 in Detroit MI. Graduate UMich., NYU. Debut 1979 OB in "The Shirt," followed by "Margaret's Bed," "The Butterfingers Angel."

ANDERSON, PAUL. Born in Boston, MA. Attended Middlebury Col., Fordham U., AADA. Bdwy debut 1944 in "Decision," followed by "Mary Rose," "Playboy of the Western World," "Minnie and Mrs. Williams," CC's "The Devil's Disciple," "She Stoops to Conquer," "The Corn Is Green" and "The Heiress," OB in "Les Blancs!"

ANDREAS, CHRISTINE. Born Oct. 1, 1951 in Camden, NJ. Bdwy debut 1975 in "Angel Street," followed by "My Fair Lady" for which she received a Theatre World Award, "Oklahoma" (1979), OB in "Disgustingly Rich," "Rhapsody in Gershwin."

ANDRES, BARBARA. Born Feb. 11, 1939 in NYC. Catholic U. graduate. Bdwy debut 1969 in "Jimmy," followed by "The Boy Friend," "Rodgers and Hart," "Rex," "On Golden Pond," "One Act Play Festival," OB in "Threepenny Opera," "Landscape of the Body," "Harold Arlen's Cabaret."

ANDRINI, KATHY. Born May 17, 1958 in San Francisco, CA. Bdwy debut 1979 in "The 1940's Radio Hour," followed by OB "Trixie True."

ANGELIN, PATRICIA. Born in LaCrosse, WI, Mar. 9, 1954. Graduate PennStateU. Debut 1980 OB in "The Glass Menagerie."

ANGELOVICH, VIRGINIA MARY. Born Mar. 20, 1943 in Bridgeport, CT. Graduate Boston U. Debut OB 1980 in "Period of Adjustment."

Fran Anthony   Sal Anthony   Beth Austin   Ward Asquith   Mary E. Baird

ANGLIM, PHILIP. Born Feb. 11, 1953 in San Francisco, CA. Yale graduate. Debut OB and Bdwy 1979 in "The Elephant Man" for which he received a Theatre World Award, followed by "Macbeth," "Judgment." (OB).

ANTHONY, FRAN. Born July 18 in Brooklyn, NY. Graduate Queens Col. Debut OB 1953 in "Climate of Eden," followed by "Pappa Is Home," "Summer Brave," "The Warriors Husband," "Kind Lady."

ANTHONY, SAL. Born Apr. 2, 1956 in Paterson, NJ. Debut 1981 OB in "Black Elk Lives."

ANTON, WILLIAM. Born July 6, 1952 in Ross, CA. Graduate IlStateU, UCal. Debut 1980 OB in "The Glass Menagerie."

ARANAS, RAUL. Born Oct. 1, 1947 in Manila, Phil. Pace U. grad. Debut 1976 OB in "Savages," followed by Bdwy 1978 in "Loose Ends."

ARCHER, ANNE. Born in California. Debut 1981 OB in "A Coupla White Chicks Sitting Around Talking."

ARLT, LEWIS. Born Dec. 5, 1949 in Kingston, NY. Graduate Carnegie Tech. Bdwy debut 1975 in "Murder Among Friends," followed by "Piaf," OB in "War and Peace," "The Interview."

ARMAGNAC, GARY. Born Aug. 17, 1952 in New Jersey. Iona Col. grad. Debut 1981 OB in "A Taste of Honey."

ARMISTEAD, DIANE. Born May 26, 1936 in Canton, OH. Attended Wooster Col. Debut OB 1979 in "The Old Maid and the Thief," followed by Light Opera of Manhattan, "Principally Pinter/Slightly Satie."

ARNOLD, DULCIE. Born Nov. 20, 1949 in Neptune, NJ. Syracuse U. grad. Debut 1980 OB in "Last Summer at Bluefish Cove."

ARONIN, MICHAEL J. Born Nov. 5, 1944 in NYC. Bdwy debut 1979 in "Knockout," OB in "Marlon Brando Sat Here," followed by "Toyland."

ARONSON, JONATHAN. Born June 17, 1953 in Miami, FL. Attended Dade Col. AMDA. Bdwy debut 1979 in "Whoopee!" followed by "Sugar Babies," "Five O'Clock Girl," OB in "Tip-Toes."

ARTHUR, BEATRICE. Born May 13, 1926 in NYC. Attended New School. Bdwy debut 1955 in "Seventh Heaven," followed by "Nature's Way," "Fiddler on the Roof," "Mame," "The Floating Light Bulb," OB in "The Threepenny Opera," "Shoestring Revue," "Ulysses in Nighttown," "The Gay Divorce."

ARTHUR, CAROL. Born Aug. 4, 1935 in Hackensack, NJ. Attended AMDA. Bdwy debut 1964 in "High Spirits," followed by "Once Upon a Mattress," "Kicks and Co." "Oh, What a Lovely War!," "On the Town," "I Can Get It for You Wholesale," "Music Man."

ARTHUR, HELEN-JEAN. Born Nov. 2, 1933 in Chicago, IL. Graduate Beloit Col. Debut 1957 OB in "Othello," followed by "Twelve Pound Look," "Streets of New York," "Vera with Kate," "Declasse," Bdwy in "Send Me No Flowers," "Moon Beseiged," "Look Back in Anger."

ASBURY, CLEVE. Born Dec. 29, 1958 in Houston, TX. Attended L.A. Valley Col. Bdwy debut 1979 in "Peter Pan," followed by "West Side Story," "Bring Back Birdie."

ASHLEY, MARY ELLEN. Born June 11, 1938 in Long Island City, NY. Graduate Queens Col. Bdwy debut 1943 in "Innocent Voyage," followed by "By Appointment Only," "Annie Get Your Gun," "Yentl," OB in "Carousel," "Polly," "Panama Hattie," "Soft Touch," "Suddenly the Music Starts," "The Facts of Death."

ASKEW, TIMOTHY. Born Sept. 19, 1951 in Atlanta, GA. Graduate Emory U. Debut 1978 OB in "The Devil's Disciple," followed by "Jimmy the Veteran," "Redback."

ASQUITH, WARD. Born March 21 in Philadelphia, PA. Graduate UPa., Columbia. Bdwy 1979 in "After the Rise," followed by "Kind Lady," "Incident at Vichy."

ASTREDO, HUMBERT ALLEN. Born in San Francisco, CA. Attended SFU. Debut 1967 OB in "Arms and the Man," followed by "Fragments," "Murderous Angels," "Beach Children," "End of Summer," "Knuckle," "Grand Magic," "Big and Little," "The Jail Diary of Albie Sachs," Bdwy in "Les Blancs," "An Evening with Richard Nixon . . . ," "The Little Foxes."

ATHERTON, WILLIAM. Born July 30, 1947 in Orange, CT. Graduate Carnegie Tech. Debut 1971 OB in "House of Blue Leaves," followed by "The Basic Training of Pavlo Hummel," "Suggs" for which he received a Theatre World Award, "Rich and Famous," "The Passing Game," Bdwy in "The Sign in Sidney Brustein's Window" (1972), "Happy New Year," "The American Clock."

ATKINS, TOM. Born in Pittsburgh, Pa. Graduate Duquesne U, AADA. Bdwy debut 1967 in "The Unknown Soldier and His Wife," followed by "Cyrano," "Keep It in the Family," "Front Page," "The Changing Room," OB in "Whistle in the Dark," "Nobody Hears a Broken Drum," "Long Day's Journey into Night," "The Tempest," "Vikings."

ATKINSON, PEGGY. Born Oct. 1, 1943 in Brooklyn, NY. Attended Ithaca Col. Bdwy debut 1967 in "Fiddler on the Roof," followed by "Two Gentlemen of Verona," OB in "Boccaccio," "The Faggot," "One Free Smile," "One Cent Plain," "Hostage."

AUSTIN, BETH. Born May 23, 1952 in Philadelphia, PA. Graduate Point Park Col., Pittsburgh Playhouse. Debut 1977 OB in "Wonderful Town," followed by "The Prevalence of Mrs. Seal," "Engaged," Bdwy 1977 in "Sly Fox," followed by "Whoopee," "Onward Victoria."

AVALOS, LUIS. Born Sept. 2, 1946 in Havana, Cuba. Debut OB in "Never Jam Today," followed by "Rules for Running of Trains," LC's "Camino Real," "Beggar on Horseback," "Good Woman of Setzuan" and "Kool Aid," "The Architect and the Emperor," "As You Like It," "El Grande de Coca Cola," "Zoo Story," "Payment as Pledged," "Armenians," "Marco Polo," "Save Grand Central."

AVERA, TOM. Born Feb. 21, 1923 in Rocky Mount, NC. UNC grad. Bdwy debut 1944 in "One Touch of Venus," followed by "Carousel," "Oklahoma!," "Lo and Behold," "Marathon 33," "On the Town," "Best Little Whorehouse in Texas," "Woman of the Year."

AYR, MICHAEL. Born Sept. 8, 1953 in Great Falls, MT. Graduate SMU. Debut 1976 OB in "Mrs. Murray's Farm," followed by "The Farm," "Ulysses in Traction," "Lulu," "Cabin 12," "Stargazing," "The Deserter," "Hamlet," "Mary Stuart," "Save Grand Central," "The Beaver Coat," Bdwy 1980 in "Hide and Seek," "Piaf."

AZITO, TONY. Born July 18, 1948 in NYC. Attended Juilliard. Debut 1971 OB in "Red, White and Black," followed by "Players Project," "Secrets of the Citizens Correction Committee," "Threepenny Opera," Bdwy 1977 in "Happy End," followed by "Pirates of Penzance."

BABATUNDE, OBBA. Born in Jamaica, NY. Attended Brooklyn Col. Debut OB 1970 in "The Secret Place," followed by "Guys and Dolls," "On Toby Time," "The Breakout," "Scottsborough Boys," "Showdown Time," "Dream on Monkey Mt.," "Sheba," Bdwy in "Timbuktu," "Reggae," "It's So Nice to Be Civilized."

BACALL, LAUREN. Born Sept. 16, 1924 in NYC. Attended AADA. Bdwy debut 1942 in "Johnny 2 X 4," followed by "Goodbye Charlie," "Cactus Flower," "Applause," "Woman of the Year."

BACIGALUPI, DENNIS. Born July 14, 1956 in San Francisco, CA. Attended Juilliard. Debut 1978 OB in "King Lear," Bdwy, 1981 in "Frankenstein."

BACKER, BRIAN. Born Dec. 5, 1956 in NYC. Attended Neighborhood Playhouse. Bdwy debut 1981 in "The Floating Light Bulb" for which he received a Theatre World Award.

BACKUS, RICHARD. Born Mar. 28, 1945 in Goffstown, NH. Harvard graduate. Bdwy debut 1971 in "Butterflies Are Free," followed by "Promenade, All" for which he received a Theatre World Award, "Ah, Wilderness!," OB in "Studs Edsel," "Gimme Shelter," "Sorrows of Stephen," "Missing Persons."

BACON, KEVIN. Born July 8, 1958 in Philadelphia, PA. Debut 1978 OB in "Getting Out," followed by "Glad Tidings," "Album."

BADOLATO, DEAN. Born June 6, 1952 in Chicago, IL. Attended UIll. Bdwy debut 1978 in "A Chorus Line," followed by "Pirates of Penzance."

BAGDEN, RONALD. Born Dec. 26, 1953 in Philadelphia, PA. Graduate Temple U., RADA. Debut OB 1977 in "Oedipus Rex," followed by "Oh! What a Lovely War!," Bdwy 1980 in "Amadeus."

BAILEY, DENNIS. Born Apr. 12, 1953 in Grosse Pointe Woods, MI. UDetroit graduate. Debut 1977 OB in "House of Blue Leaves," Bdwy 1978 in "Gemini."

BAIRD, MARY E. Born June 26, 1947 in Berkeley, CA. Attended Chabot Col. Debut OB 1974 in "At Sea with Benchley, Kalmar & Ruby," followed by "Rubbers," "Peg O'My Heart," "Front Page."

BAKER, BLANCH. (nee Brocho Freyda Garf) Dec. 20, 1956 in NYC. Attended Wellesley Col. Bdwy debut 1981 in "Lolita."

BAKER, MARK. Born Oct. 2, 1946 in Cumberland, MD. Attended Wittenberg U., Carnegie-Mellon U., Neighborhood Playhouse, AADA. Bdwy debut 1972 in "Via Galactica," followed by "Candide" for which he received a Theatre World Award, "Habeas Corpus," OB in "Love Me, Love My Children," "A Midsummer Night's Dream," "From Rodgers and Hart with Love."

| Scott Baker | Joanne Baron | Tom Batten | Vanessa Bell | Stephen Berenson |

BAKER, SCOTT. Born May 30, 1948 in Tulsa, OK. Graduate UTulsa, Northwestern U. Debut 1973 OB in "Christmas Rappings," followed by "Love's Labour's Lost," "East Lynne," "Matinee Kids," Bdwy 1978 in "Oh! Calcutta!"

BALOU, BUDDY. Born in 1953 in Seattle, WA. Joined American Ballet Theatre in 1970, rising to soloist. Joined Dancers in 1977; "A Chorus Line" in 1980.

BANES, LISA. Born July 9, 1955 in Chagrin Falls, OH. Juilliard grad. Debut OB 1980 in "Elizabeth I," followed by "A Call from the East," "Look Back in Anger" for which she received a Theatre World Award.

BARANSKI, CHRISTINE. Born May 2, 1952 in Buffalo, NY. Graduate Juilliard Sch. Debut OB 1978 in "One Crack Out," followed by "Says I Says He," "The Trouble with Europe," "Coming Attractions," Bdwy 1980 in "Hide and Seek."

BARCROFT, JUDITH. Born July 6 in Washington, DC. Attended Northwestern, Stephens Col. Bdwy debut 1965 in "Mating Dance," followed by "Plaza Suite," "Dinner at 8," "The Elephant Man," OB in "M. Amilcar."

BARNER, STOCKMAN. Born July 26, 1921 in New London, CT. Graduate UIowa. Bdwy debut 1945 in "Othello," OB in "The Hollow," "Revenger's Tragedy," "The Miser"(ELT).

BARNES, VERONA. Born June 2, 1940 in Wilson, NC. Graduate Winston-Salem State Col. Bdwy debut 1968 in "The Great White Hope," followed by OB's "Sleep," "The Cherry Orchard," "House Party," "All God's Chillun," "Divine Comedy," "Milk of Paradise," "Branches from the Same Tree," "Killings on the Last Line."

BARON, EVALYN. Born Apr. 21, 1948 in Atlanta, GA. Graduate Northwestern, UMinn. Debut OB 1979 in "Scrambled Feet," followed by "Hijinks," "I Can't Keep Running in Place," Bdwy 1980 in "Fearless Frank."

BARON, JOANNE. Born Feb. 3, 1953 in New Haven, CT. Attended UConn., Neighborhood Playhouse. Has appeared OB in "Pops!," "Bah Humbug," "Baal."

BARRIE, FRANK. Born in England, Sept. 19, 1940. London U. grad. Bdwy debut 1967 with Bristol Old Vic in "Romeo and Juliet," "Hamlet" and "Measure for Measure." OB 1980 in "Macready!"

BARRON, HOLLY. Born Feb. 1, 1947 in Oakland, CA. Graduate UCBerkeley. Debut 1977 OB in "Cracks," followed by "Mecca," "Last Summer at Bluefish Cove."

BARROWS, DIANA. Born Jan. 23, 1966 in NYC. Bdwy debut 1975 in "Cat on a Hot Tin Roof," followed by "Panama Hattie" (ELT), "Annie."

BARRY, B CONSTANCE. Born Apr. 29, 1913 in NYC. Attended Hofstra, New School. Debut 1974 OB in "Blue Heaven," followed by "Dark of the Moon," "Native Son," "Passing Time," "All the Way Home" (ELT), "Naomi Court."

BARRY, RAYMOND J. Born Mar. 14, 1939 in Hempstead, NY. Graduate Brown U. Debut 1963 OB in "Man Is Man," followed by "Penguin Touquet," Bdwy 1975 in "The Leaf People."

BARTENIEFF, GEORGE. Born Jan. 24, 1933 in Berlin, Ger. Bdwy bow 1947 in "The Whole World Over," followed by "Venus Is," "All's Well That Ends Well," "Quotations from Chairman Mao Tse-Tung," "The Death of Bessie Smith," "Cop-Out," "Room Service," "Unlikely Heroes," OB in "Walking to Waldheim," "Memorandum," "The Increased Difficulty of Concentration," "Trelawny of the Wells," "Charley Chestnut Rides the IRT," "Radio (Wisdom): Sophia Part I," "Images of the Dead," "Dead End Kids."

BASSETT, STEVE. Born June 25, 1952 in Escondido, CA. Graduate Juilliard. Bdwy debut 1979 in "Deathtrap," OB in "Spring Awakening."

BATEMAN, BILL. Born Dec. 10 in Rock Island, IL. Graduate Augustana Col. Debut 1974 OB in "Anything Goes," followed by Bdwy (1978) in "Hello, Dolly!," "Bring Back Birdie."

BATTAGLIA, CARL. Born Jan. 29, 1955 in Brooklyn, NY. Debut 1981 OB in "Black Elk Lives."

BATTEN, TOM. Born in Oklahoma City, OK. Graduate USC. Bdwy debut 1961 in "How to Succeed in Business," followed by "Mame," "Gantry," "Mack and Mabel," "She Loves Me," "On the 20th Century," "Can-Can."

BATTLE, HINTON. Born Nov. 29, 1956 in Neubraecke, Ger. Joined Dance Theatre of Harlem. Bdwy debut 1975 in "The Wiz," followed by "Dancin'," "Sophisticated Ladies."

BAUMANN, K. T. Born Aug. 13, 1946 in The Bronx, NY. Attended Neighborhood Playhouse. Bdwy debut 1967 in "The Prime of Miss Jean Brodie," followed by "Penny Wars," "Hello, Dolly!" ('78), OB in "Lemon Sky," "Effect of Gamma Rays . . .," "Trelawny of the Wells," "Dulcy."

BAXLEY, BARBARA. Born Jan. 1, 1925 in Porterville, CA. Attended Pacific Col., Neighborhood Playhouse. Bdwy debut 1948 in "Private Lives," followed by "Out West of Eighth," "Peter Pan," "I Am a Camera," "Bus Stop," "Camino Real," "Frogs of Spring," "Oh, Men! Oh, Women!," "The Flowering Peach," "Period of Adjustment," "She Loves Me," "Three Sisters," "Plaza Suite," "Me Jack, You Jill," "Best Friend," OB in "Brecht on Brecht," "Measure for Measure," "To Be Young, Gifted and Black," "Oh, Pioneers," "Are You Now or Have You Ever . . .," "Isn't It Romantic."

BAXTER, KEITH. Born Apr. 29, 1935 in Newport, Wales. Graduate RADA. Bdwy debut 1961 in "A Man for All Seasons" for which he received a Theatre World Award, followed by "The Affair," "Avanti," "Sleuth," "A Meeting by the River," "Romantic Comedy," OB in "The Penultimate Problem of Sherlock Holmes."

BEACH, GARY. Born Oct. 10, 1947 in Alexandria, VA. Graduate NCSch. of Arts. Bdwy bow 1971 in "1776," followed by "Something's Afoot," "Moony Shapiro Songbook," "Annie," OB in "Smile, Smile, Smile," "What's a Nice Country Like You . . .," "Ionescapade," "By Strouse."

BEAL, JOHN. Born Aug. 13, 1909 in Joplin, Mo. Graduate UPa. Among his many credits are "Wild Waves," "Another Language," "She Loves Me Not," "Russet Mantle," "Soliloquy," "Miss Swan Expects," "Liberty Jones," "Voice of the Turtle," "Lend an Ear," "Teahouse of the August Moon," "Calculated Risk," "Billy," "Our Town" ('70), OB in "Wilder's Triple Bill," "To Be Young, Gifted and Black," "Candyapple," "Long Day's Journey into Night," "Rivers Return."

BEAN, ORSON. Born July 22, 1928 in Burlington, VT. Bdwy bow 1953 in "Men of Distinction," followed by "John Murray Anderson's Almanac" for which he received a Theatre World Award, "Will Success Spoil Rock Hunter?," "Nature's Way," "Mister Roberts" (CC), "Subways Are for Sleeping," "Say, Darling" (CC), "Never Too Late," "I Was Dancing," "Ilya Darling," OB in "Home Movies," "A Round with Ring," "Make Someone Happy," "I'm Getting My Act Together."

BEERS, FRANCINE. Born Nov. 26 in NYC. Attended Hunter Col., CCNY, HB Studio. Debut 1962 OB in "King of the Whole Damned World," followed by "Kiss Mama," "Monopoly," "Cakes with Wine," Bdwy in "Cafe Crown," "6 Rms Riv Vu," "The American Clock."

BELANGER, MICHAEL. Born Nov. 26, 1959 in Manchester, NH. Debut 1980 OB in "Friend of the Family."

BELGRAVE, CYNTHIA. Born in NYC. Graduate Boston U. Bdwy debut 1959 in "Raisin in the Sun," followed by "The Amen Corner," OB in "Take a Giant Step," "The Blacks," "Funny-house of a Negro," "Trials of Brother Jero," "Citizen Bezique," "Emma," "Making Peace," "Remembrance," "Jam," "The Connection."

BELL, BETSY. Born Apr. 24, 1930 in Boston, MA. Attended Bennington Col. Debut 1980 OB in "Period of Adjustment."

BELL, JOAN. Born Feb. 1, 1935 in Bombay, Ind. Studied at Sylvia Bryant Sch. Bdwy debut 1963 in "Something More," followed by "Applause," "Chicago," "Woman of the Year."

BELL, VANESSA. Born Mar. 20, 1957 in Toledo, OH. Graduate OhU. Bdwy debut 1981 in "Bring Back Birdie," followed by "El Bravo!"

BELLOMO, JOE. Born Apr. 12, 1938 in NYC. Attended Manhattan Sch. of Music. Bdwy bow 1960 in "New Girl in Town," followed by CC's "South Pacific" and "Guys and Dolls," OB in "Cindy," "Fantasticks."

BENDO, MARK. Born Jan. 28, 1964 in NYC. Studied with Lee Strasberg. Debut 1977 OB in "The Dream Watcher," followed by "All the Way Home," Bdwy in "On Golden Pond," (1979), "The Survivor."

BENJAMIN, P. J. Born Sept. 2, 1951 in Chicago, IL. Attended Loyola U., Columbia. Bdwy debut 1973 in "Pajama Game," followed by "Pippin," "Sarava," "Charlie and Algernon," "Sophisticated Ladies."

BENTLEY, JOHN. Born Jan. 31, 1940 in Jackson Heights, NY. Graduate AADA, attended USyracuse. Debut 1961 OB in "King of the Dark Chamber," followed by "As to the Meaning of Words," Bdwy in "Mike Downstairs," "Lysistrata," "The Selling of the President," "A Funny Thing Happened on the Way to the Forum" (1972), "West Side Story" (1980).

BERENSON, STEPHEN. Born Mar. 29, 1953 in NYC. Graduate Drake U. Debut 1978 OB in "Dead End," followed by "Men in White," "The Butterfingers Angel."

| Nancy Berg | Robert Bloodworth | Robin Boudreau | Robert Boyle | Kathi Boulé |

BEREZIN, TANYA. Born Mar. 25, 1941 in Philadelphia, PA. Attended boston U. Debut OB 1967 in "The Sandcastle," followed by "Three Sisters," "Great Nebula in Orion," "him," "Amazing Activity of Charlie Contrare," "Battle of Angels," "Mound Builders," "Serenading Louie," "My Life," "Brontosaurus," "Glorious Morning," "Mary Stuart," "The Beaver Coat."

BERG, NANCY. Born July 9, 1931 in Kenosha, WI. Attended Neighborhood Playhouse. Bdwy debut 1956 in "Mister Roberts" (City Center), followed OB in "Too Much Johnson," "Memo," "Admissions Chairman," "Everything in the Garden," "Toyland."

BERGSTROM, JOHN. Born July 23, 1941 in Kewanee, IL. Graduate InU. Debut 1975 OB in "And So to Bed," followed by "Death Takes a Holiday," Bdwy in "Caesar and Cleopatra" ('77).

BERK, DAVID. Born July 20, 1932 in NYC. Graduate Manhattan School of Music. Debut OB 1958 in "Eloise," followed by "Carnival" (CC), "So Long 174th Street," "Wonderful Town" (ELT), "Anyone Can Whistle," "The Meehans."

BERK, LARA. Born July 12, 1972 in Elizabeth, NJ. Debut 1980 OB in "Really Rosie."

BERMAN, SHELLEY. Born Feb. 3, 1925 in Chicago, IL. Attended Goodman Theatre. Bdwy debut 1961 in "A Family Affair," followed by "Insideoutsideandallaround Shelley Berman."

BERRY, CLAYTON. Born May 24, 1942 in Ft. Collins, CO. Graduate Boston U., UMn. Debut 1980 OB in "Table Settings," followed by "Anything Goes" (ELT).

BERTRAND, JACQUELINE. Born June 1, 1939 in Quebec, Can. Attended Neighborhood Playhouse, Actors Studio, LAMDA. Debut 1978 OB in "Unfinished Women," followed by "Dancing for the Kaiser," "Lulu," "War and Peace."

BESSETTE, DENISE. Born Aug. 25, 1954 in Midland, MI. Graduate Marymount Manhattan Col., RADA. Debut 1977 OB in "Freshwater/Evening at Bloomsbury," followed by "La Ronde," "Admirable Crichton," "War and Peace," "Glory! Hallelujah!"

BEVAN, ALISON. Born Nov. 20, 1959 in Cincinnati, OH. Attended NYU. Debut 1980 OB in "Trixie True, Teen Detective."

BIGHAM, CHARLENE. Born Dec. 29, 1950 in Giddings, TX. Graduate SMU. Debut 1981 OB in "Progress."

BISHOP, JOEY. (nee Joseph Gottlieb) Born Feb. 3, 1918 in The Bronx, NY. Bdwy debut 1981 in "Sugar Babies."

BLAIR, PAMELA. Born Dec. 5, 1949 in Arlington, VT. Attended Ntl. Acad. of Ballet. Made Bdwy debut in 1972 in "Promises, Promises," followed by "Sugar," "Seesaw," "Of Mice and Men," "Wild and Wonderful," "A Chorus Line," "The Best Little Whorehouse in Texas," "King of Hearts," OB in "Ballad of Boris K.," "Split," "Real Life Funnies."

BLAKE, TIFFANY. Born July 3, 1971 in Fresh Meadows, NY. Bdwy debut 1980 in "Annie."

BLOCH, SCOTTY. Born Jan. 28 in New Rochelle, NY. Attended AADA. Debut 1945 OB in "Craig's Wife," followed by "Lemon Sky," "Battering Ram," "Richard III," "In Celebration," "An Act of Kindness," "The Price," Bdwy in "Children of a Lesser God."

BLOCK, LARRY. Born Oct. 30, 1942 in NYC. Graduate URI. Bdwy bow 1966 in "Hail Scrawdyke," followed by "La Turista," "Eh?," "Fingernails Blue as Flowers," "Comedy of Errors," "Coming Attractions."

BLOODWORTH, ROBERT. Born Sept. 13, 1939 in Fayetteville, NC. Graduate UNC, AADA. Debut 1980 OB in "To Bury a Cousin."

BLOUNT, HELON. Born Jan. 15 in Big Spring, TX. Graduate UTx. Bdwy debut 1956 in "Most Happy Fella," followed by "How to Succeed in Business . . .," "Do I Hear a Waltz?" "Fig Leaves Are Falling," "Follies," "Very Good Eddie," "Musical Chairs," "Woman of the Year," OB in "Fly Blackbird," "Riverwind," "My Wife and I," "Curley McDimple," "A Quarter for the Ladies Room," "Snapshot."

BLUM, MARK. Born May 14, 1950 in Newark, NJ. Graduate UPa., UMinn. Debut 1976 OB in "The Cherry Orchard," followed by "Green Julia," "Say Goodnight, Gracie," "Table Settings."

BOBBIE, WALTER. Born Nov. 18, 1945 in Scranton, PA. Graduate UScranton, Catholic U. Bdwy bow 1971 in "Frank Merriwell," followed by "The Grass Harp," "Grease," "Tricks," "Going Up," "A History of the American Film," OB in "Drat!," "She Loves Me."

BODIN, DUANE. Born Dec. 31, 1932 in Duluth, MN. Bdwy debut 1961 in "Bye Bye Birdie," followed by "La Plume de Ma Tante," "Here's Love," "Fiddler on the Roof," "1776," "Sweeney Todd."

BOGARDUS, STEPHEN. Born Mar. 11, 1954 in Norfolk, VA. Princeton graduate. Bdwy debut 1980 in "West Side Story," OB in "March of the Falsettos."

BOND, JAY. Born Aug. 11, 1953 in Detroit, MI. Graduate Central MiU. Debut 1980 OB in "The Cocktail Party."

BORDO, ED. Born Mar. 3, 1931 in Cleveland, OH. Graduate Allegheny Col., LAMDA. Bdwy bow 1964 in "The Last Analysis," followed by "Inquest," "Zalmen or the Madness of God," "Annie," OB in "The Dragon," "Waiting for Godot," "Saved."

BORRELLI, JIM. Born Apr. 10, 1948 in Lawrence, MA. Graduate Boston Col. Debut 1971 OB in "Subject to Fits," followed by "Beyond Therapy," "Basic Training of Pavlo Hummel," "Bullpen," Bdwy in "Grease."

BOSCO, PHILIP. Born Sept. 26, 1930 in Jersey City, NJ. Graduate Catholic U. Credits: "Auntie Mame," "Rape of the Belt," "Ticket of Leave Man" (OB), "Donnybrook," "Man for All Seasons," "Mrs. Warren's Profession," with LCRep in "The Alchemist," "East Wind," "Galileo," "St. Joan," "Tiger at the Gate," "Cyrano," "King Lear," "A Great Career," "In the Matter of J. Robert Oppenheimer," "The Miser," "The Time of Your Life," "Camino Real," "Operation Sidewinder," "Amphitryon," "Enemy of the People," "Playboy of the Western World," "Good Woman of Setzuan," "Antigone," "Mary Stuart," "Narrow Road to the Deep North," "The Crucible," "Twelfth Night," "Enemies," "Plough and the Stars," "Merchant of Venice," and "A Streetcar Named Desire," "Henry V," "Threepenny Opera," "Streamers," "Stages," "St. Joan," "The Biko Inquest," "Man and Superman," "Whose Life Is It Anyway," "Major Barbara," "A Month in the Country," "Bacchae," "Hedda Gabler," "Don Juan in Hell," "Inadmissible Evidence."

BOSTICK, DAVID. Born Feb. 3, 1948 in El Paso, TX. Graduate UCLA, Columbia. Debut 1980 OB in "Naomi Court."

BOUDREAU, ROBIN. Born Nov. 7, in Pittsburgh, PA. Graduate NYU. Bdwy debut 1981 in "Pirates of Penzance."

BOULE, KATHRYN. Born Dec. 27 in Washington, DC. Graduate UMd. Debut 1977 OB in "Fiorello!," Bdwy "Annie" ('80).

BOUTSIKARIS, DENNIS. Born Dec. 21, 1952 in Newark, NJ. Graduate Hampshire Col. Debut 1975 OB in "Another Language," followed by "Funeral March for a One-Man Band," "All's Well That Ends Well," "A Day in the Life of the Czar," Bdwy in "Filumena," "Bent."

BOVA, JOSEPH. Born May 25 in Cleveland, OH. Graduate Northwestern U. Debut 1959 OB in "On the Town," followed by "Once upon a Mattress," "House of Blue Leaves," "Comedy," "The Beauty Part," "Taming of the Shrew," "Richard III," "Comedy of Errors," "Invitation to a Beheading," "Merry Wives of Windsor," "Henry V," "Streamers," Bdwy in "Rape of the Belt," "Irma La Douce," "Hot Spot," "The Chinese," "American Millionaire," "St. Joan," "42nd Street."

BOWIE, DAVID. Born Jan. 8, 1947 in London, Eng. Bdwy debut 1980 in "The Elephant Man."

BOYD, PRESTON. Born Feb. 14, 1949 in Minneapolis, MN. Graduate Western Wash.U. Debut 1981 OB in "Railroad Bill."

BOYD, TOM. Born Oct. 1 in Hamilton, Ont., Can. Bdwy debut 1962 in "How to Succeed in Business . . .," followed by "Walking Happy," "Irene," "Sugar Babies."

BOYLE, ROBERT. Born Mar. 28, 1950 in Patton, PA. Graduate Carnegie-Mellon U. Debut 1980 OB in "Merton of the Movies" followed by "Pericles."

BOZYK, REIZL (ROSE). Born May 13, 1914 in Poland. Star of many Yiddish productions before 1966 Bdwy debut in "Let's Sing Yiddish," followed by "Sing, Israel, Sing," "Mirele Efros," OB in "Light, Lively and Yiddish," "Rebecca, the Rabbi's Daughter," "Wish Me Mazel-Tov."

BRAND, GIBBEY. Born May 20, 1946 in NYC. Ithaca Col. graduate. Debut 1977 OB in "The Castaways," followed by "The Music Man" (JB), "Real Life Funnies."

BRASINGTON, ALAN. Born in Monticello, NY. Attended RADA. Bdway debut 1968 in "Pantagleize," followed by "The Misanthrope," "Cock-a-Doodle Dandy," "Hamlet," "A Patriot for Me," "Shakespeare's Cabaret," OB in "Sterling Silver."

| Ralph Braun | Helen Lloyd Breed | Tommy Breslin | Shelly Burch | Robert Burke |

BRAUN, RALPH. Born Aug. 20, 1946 in Milwaukee, WI. Graduate Carroll College, UVa. Bdwy debut 1974 in "Irene," followed by "The Music Man," "Copperfield," OB in "Pirates of Penzance," "Nathan the Wise," "The Specialist."

BREED, HELEN LLOYD. Born Jan. 27, 1911 in NYC. Debut 1956 OB in "Out of This World," followed by "Winners," "Exiles," "Something Unspoken," "You Never Can Tell," "Liliom," "The Hollow," "Chalk Garden," "Ring Round the Moon," "Richard II," "Kind Lady," "A Little Night Music."

BRENN, JANNI. Born Feb. 13 in Ft. Wayne, IN. Graduate Stanford, Columbia. Debut 1970 OB in "Mod Donna," followed by "Jungle of Cities," "Subject to Fits," "Kaddish," "On Mt. Chimbrazo," "Big and Little," "The Survivor," "The Master and Margarita," "The Seagull."

BRENNAN, MIKE. Born Feb. 4, 1948 in NYC. Fordham U. Graduate. Debut 1973 OB in "Arms and the Man," followed by "Gay Divorce," "Blues for Mr. Charlie," "Scenes from La Vie de Boheme."

BRENNAN, NORA. Born Dec. 1, 1953 in East Chicago, IN. Purdue graduate. Bdwy debut 1980 in "Camelot."

BRENNAN, TOM. Born Apr. 16, 1926 in Cleveland, OH. Graduate Oberlin, Western Reserve. Debut 1958 OB in "Synge Trilogy," followed by "Between Two Thieves," "Easter," "All in Love," "Under Milkwood," "An Evening with James Purdy," "Golden Six," "Pullman Car Hiawatha," "Are You Now or Have You . . .," "Diary of Anne Frank," "Milk of Paradise," "Trancendental Love," "The Beaver Coat."

BRESLIN, TOMMY. Born Mar. 24, 1946 in Norwich, CT. Attended Iona Col. OB in "For Love or Money," "Freedom is a Two-Edged Sword," "Who's Who, Baby?," "Beggar on Horseback" (LC), "Moon Walk," "Dear Oscar," Bdwy bow 1971 in "70 Girls 70," followed by "Good News," "Musical Chairs," "Can-Can."

BRILL, FRAN. Born Sept. 30, 1946 in PA. Attended Boston U. Bdwy debut 1969 in "Red, White and Maddox," OB in "What Every Woman Knows," "Scribes," "Look Back in Anger," "Knuckle."

BROADHURST, KENT. Born Feb. 4, 1940 in St. Louis, MO. Graduate UNe. Debut 1968 OB in "The Fourth Wall," followed by "Design for Living," "Marching Song."

BROGGER, IVAR. Born Jan. 10, 1947 in St. Paul, MN. Graduate UMn. Debut 1979 OB in "In the Jungle of Cities," followed by "Collected Works of Billy the Kid," Bdwy 1981 in "Macbeth."

BROMKA, ELAINE. Born Jan. 6 in Rochester, NY. Smith Col. graduate. Debut 1975 OB in "The Dybbuk," followed by "Naked," "Museum," "The Son," "Inadmissible Evidence."

BROOK, PAMELA. Born Jan. 21, 1947 in London, Ont., Can. Graduate UToronto, UMinn. Debut 1976 OB in "The Philanderer," Bdwy 1980 in "Goodbye Fidel," followed by "To Grandmother's House We Go."

BROOKES, JACQUELINE. Born July 24, 1930 in Montclair, NJ. Graduate UIowa, RADA. Bdwy debut 1955 in "Tiger at the Gates," followed by "Watercolor," "Abelard and Heloise," OB in "The Cretan Woman" for which she received a Theatre World Award, "The Clandestine Marriage," "Measure for Measure," "Duchess of Malfi," "Ivanov," "Six Characters in Search of an Author," "An Evening's Frost," "Come Slowly, Eden," "The Increased Difficulty of Concentration," "The Persians," "Sunday Dinner," "House of Blue Leaves," "A Meeting by the River," "Owners," "Hallelujah," "Dream of a Blacklisted Actor," "Knuckle," "Mama Sang the Blues," "Buried Child," "On Mt. Chimorazo," "Winter Dancers," "Hamlet," "Old Flames," "The Diviners."

BROOKS, DAVID. Born Sept. 24, 1917 in Portland, OR. Attended UWash., Curtis Inst. Bdwy debut 1944 in "Bloomer Girl," followed by "Brigadoon," "Mr. President," "Sunday Man," "Park," "Can-Can," OB in "The Last Analysis," "A Memory of Whiteness."

BROWN, JEB. Born Aug. 11, 1964 in NYC. Bdwy debut 1974 in "Cat on a Hot Tin Roof," followed by "Bring Back Birdie."

BROWN, KERMIT. Born Feb. 3, 1937 in Asheville, NC. Graduate Duke U. With APA in "War and Peace," "Judith," "Man and Superman," "The Show-Off," "Pantagleize," "The Cherry Orchard," OB in "The Millionairess," "Things," "Lulu," "Heartbreak House," "Glad Tidings," "Anyone Can Whistle," "Facade."

BROWN, LOREN. Born Dec. 15, 1952 in Kansas City, MO. Graduate Stanford, AADA. Debut 1978 OB in "The Grinding Machine," followed by Bdwy 1980 in "The Survivor."

BROWN, WALTER. Born Apr. 18, 1926 in Newark, NJ. Attended Bklyn Consv. Bdwy in "Porgy and Bess," "Fiorello!," "The Advocate," "Guys and Dolls," "South Pacific," "Kelly," "Hello, Dolly!," "Raisin," OB in "Sweethearts."

BROWNE, SHEILA. Born in 1947 in High Point, NC. Graduate Marymount Manhattan Col., Neighborhood Playhouse. Debut 1980 OB in "Winner Take All?"

BRUCE, SHELLEY. Born May 5, 1965 in Passaic, NJ. Debut OB 1973 in "The Children's Mass," Bdwy 1977 in "Annie."

BRUMMEL, DAVID. Born Nov. 1, 1942 in Brooklyn, NY. Bdwy debut 1973 in "The Pajama Game," followed by "Music Is," "Oklahoma!," OB in "Cole Porter," "The Fantasticks."

BRUNEAU, RALPH. Born Sept.22, 1952 in Phoenix, AZ. Graduate UNotre Dame. Debut 1974 OB in "The Fantasticks," followed by "Saints," "Suddenly the Music Starts," "On a Clear Day You Can See Forever," "King of the Schnorrers," "The Buddy System."

BRUNNER, HOWARD. Born Aug. 20, 1940 in Atlanta, GA. Attended Pasadena Playhouse, Actors Inst. Bdwy debut 1980 in "Children of a Lesser God."

BRUZZESE, ELIZABETH. Born Aug. 6, 1958 in New Brunswick, NJ. Attended Parsons Sch. Debut 1981 OB in "Godspell."

BRYAN, WAYNE. Born Aug. 13, 1947 in Compton, CA. Graduate UCal. Bdwy debut 1974 in "Good News," followed by "Rodgers and Hart," OB in "Tintypes."

BRYANT, DAVID. Born May 26, 1936 in Nashville, TN. Attended TnStateU. Bdwy debut 1972 in "Don't Play Us Cheap," followed by "Bubbling Brown Sugar," "Amadeus."

BRYDON, W. B. Born Sept. 20, 1933 in Newcastle, Eng. Debut 1962 OB in "The Long, the Short and the Tall," followed by "Live Like Pigs," "Sjt. Musgrave's Dance," "The Kitchen," "Come Slowly Eden," "The Unknown Soldier and His Wife," "Moon for the Misbegotten," "The Orphan," "Possession," Bdwy in "The Lincoln Mask," "Ulysses in Nighttown," "The Father."

BUCHALTER, JEAN. Born Oct. 4 in NYC. Graduate Fordham U. Debut 1963 OB in "Line of Least Existence," followed by "12 Days of Christmas," "Waltz of the Toreadors," "Ghosts," "The Confirmation," "Curtains."

BUCKLEY, BETTY. Born July 3, 1947 in Big Spring, TX. Graduate TCU. Bdwy debut 1969 in "1776," followed by "Pippin," OB in "Ballad of Johnny Pot," "What's a Nice Country Like You. . . .," "Circle of Sound," "I'm Gettin My Act Together. . . ?"

BUELL, BILL. Born Sept. 21, 1952 in Paipai, Taiwan. Attended Portland State. Debut 1972 OB in "Crazy Now," followed by "Declassee," Bdwy 1979 in "Once a Catholic."

BULOFF, JOSEPH. Born Dec. 6, 1907 in Wilno, Lith. Bdwy debut 1936 in "Don't Look Now," followed by "Call Me Ziggy," "To Quito and Back," "The Man from Cairo," "Morning Star," "Spring Again," "My Sister Eileen," "Oklahoma!," "The Whole World Over," "Once More with Feeling," "Fifth Season," "Moonbirds," "The Wall," OB in "Yoshkie Musikant," "The Price," "Chekhov Sketchbook."

BURCH, SHELLY. Born Mar. 19, 1960 in Tucson, AZ. Attended Carnegie-Mellon U. Bdwy debut 1978 in "Stop the World I Want to Get Off," followed by "Annie."

BURGE, GREGG. Born 1959 in NYC. Graduate Juilliard. Bdwy debut 1975 in "The Wiz," followed by "Sophisticated Ladies."

BURKE, ROBERT. Born July 25, 1948 in Portland, ME. Graduate Boston Col. Debut 1975 OB in "Prof. George," followed by "Shortchanged Review," "The Arbor," "Slab Boys."

BURKHARDT, GERRY. Born June 14, 1946 in Houston, TX. Attended Lon Morris Col. Bdwy debut 1968 in "Her First Roman," followed by "The Best Little Whorehouse in Texas."

BURKS, DONNY. Born in Martinsville, VA. Graduate St. John's U. Debut 1964 OB in "Dutchman," followed by "Billy Noname" for which he received a Theatre World Award, "Miracle Play," Bdwy in "Hair"('68), "The American Clock."

BURNEY, STEVE. Born Sept. 17, 1954 in Waco, TX. Graduate AADA. Bdwy debut 1980 in "Fearless Frank," followed by OB in "10 by 6."

BURNS, EILEEN. Born in Hartsdale, NY. Has appeared in "Native Son," "Christopher Blake," "Small Hours," "American Way," "The Women"('36), "Merrily We Roll Along," "Daughters of Atreus," "First Lady," "Mourning Becomes Electra," OB in "Albee Directs Albee," "Declassee."

| Robert Burr | Catherine Byers | Allan Carlsen | Claudine Cassan | Danny Carroll |

BURR, ROBERT. Born in Jersey City, NJ. Attended Colgate U. Has appeared in "The Cradle Will Rock," "Mr. Roberts," "Romeo and Juliet," "Picnic," "The Lovers," "Anniversary Waltz," "Top Man," "Remains to Be Seen," "The Wall," "Andersonville Trial," "A Shot in the Dark," "Man for All Seasons," "Luther," "Hamlet," "Bajour," "White Devil," "Royal Hunt of the Sun," "Dinner at 8," "King John," "Henry VI," "Love-Suicide at Schofield Barracks," "Wild and Wonderful," "Look Back in Anger" (OB), "The Philadelphia Story."

BURSKY, JAY. Born Mar. 27, 1954 in Cleveland, OH. Graduate Indiana U. OB and Bdwy debut 1978 in "The Best Little Whorehouse in Texas."

BURSTYN, ELLEN. Born Dec. 7, 1932 in Detroit, MI. Attended Actors Studio. Bdwy debut 1957 (as Ellen McRae) in "Fair Game," followed by "Same Time Next Year," OB in "Three Sisters," "Andromeda II."

BURTON, RICHARD. Born Nov. 10, 1925 in Pontrhydyfen, S. Wales. Attended Exeter Col., Oxford. Bdwy debut 1950 in "The Lady's Not for Burning" for which he received a Theatre World Award, followed by "Legend of Lovers," "Time Remembered," "Camelot" (1960 & 1980), "Hamlet," "Equus."

BUSSERT, MEG. Born Oct. 21, 1949 in Chicago, IL. Attended UIll., HB Studio. Bdwy debut 1980 in "The Music Man" for which she received a Theatre World Award, followed by "Brigadoon."

BUTTRAM, JAN. Born June 19, 1946 in Clarkesville, TX. Graduate NTex-State. Debut 1974 OB in "Fashion," followed by "Startup," Bdwy 1978 in "The Best Little Whorehouse in Texas."

BYERS, CATHERINE. Born Oct. 7 in Sioux City, IA. Graduate UIa, LAMDA. Bdwy debut 1971 in "The Philanthropist," followed by "Don't Call Back," "Equus," OB in "Petrified Forest," "All My Sons," "Murder in the Cathedral."

BYRNE, BARBARA. Born in London; Graduate RADA. NY debut 1981 OB in "Entertaining Mr. Sloane."

BYRNE, MARTHA. Born Dec. 23, 1969 in Ridgewood, NJ. Bdwy debut 1980 in "Annie."

CAHN, LARRY. Born Dec. 19, 1955 in Nassau, NY. Graduate Northwestern U. Bdwy debut 1980 in "The Music Man."

CAIN, WILLIAM B. Born May 27, 1931 in Tuscaloosa, AL. Graduate George Washington U, Catholic U. Debut 1962 OB in "Red Roses for Me," followed by "Jericho Jim Crow," "Henry V," "Antigone," "Relatively Speaking," Bdwy in "Wilson in the Promise Land," "Of the Fields, Lately."

CALLMAN, NANCY. Born Apr. 12, 1949 in Buffalo, NY. Graduate SUNY/-Binghamton, Manhattan School of Music. Bdwy debut 1976 in "1600 Pennsylvania Ave.," followed by "Sweeney Todd," OB in "Circa 1900," "Broadway a la Carte," "Hit Tunes from Flop Shows."

CANARY, DAVID H. Born Aug. 25 in Elwood, IN. Graduate UCin., Cincinnati Consv. Debut 1960 OB in "Kittywake Island," followed by "The Fantasticks," "The Father," "Hi, Paisano," "Summer." Bdwy in "Great Day in the Morning," "Happiest Girl in the World," "Clothes for a Summer Hotel."

CANNON, CATHERINE. Born Apr. 18, 1957 in Boston, MA. Graduate Sarah Lawrence Col. Debut OB 1980 in "Friend of the Family."

CARDEN, WILLIAM. Born Feb. 2, 1947 in NYC. Attended Lawrence U, Brandeis U. Debut 1974 OB in "Short Eyes," followed by "Leaving Home," "Back in the Race."

CAREY, DAVID. Born Nov. 16, 1945 in Brookline, MA. Graduate Boston U, Ohio U. Debut 1969 OB in "Oh, What a Wedding," followed by "Let's Sing Yiddish," "Dad Get Married," "Light, Lively and Yiddish," "Wedding in Shtetl," "Big Winna," "Rebecca, the Rabbi's Daughter," "Wish Me Mazel-Tov."

CARLIN, PAUL. Born Nov. 26, 1956 in The Bronx, NY. Graduate Allentown Col. Debut 1980 OB in "Milk of Paradise."

CARLIN, THOMAS A. Born Dec. 10, 1928 in Chicago, IL. Attended Loyola U, Catholic U. Credits include "Time Limit!," "Holiday for Lovers," "Man in the Dog Suit," "A Cook for Mr. General," "Great Day in the Morning," "A Thousand Clowns," "The Deputy," "Players," OB in "Thieves Carnival," "Brecht on Brecht," "Summer."

CARLSEN, ALLAN. Born Feb 7 in Chicago IL. Attended UPa. Bdwy debut 1974 in "The Freedom of the City," OB in "The Morning after Optimism," "Iphigenia in Aulis," "Peg O' My Heart," "Star Treatment," "Starry Night."

CARPENTER, CARLETON. Born July 10, 1926 in Bennington, VT. Attended Northwestern U. Bdwy bow 1944 in "Bright Boy," followed by "Career Angel," "Three to Make Ready," "Magic Touch," "John Murray Anderson's Almanac," "Hotel Paradiso," "Box of Watercolors," "Hello, Dolly!," OB in "Stage Affair," "Boys in the Band," "Dylan," "Greatest Fairy Story Ever Told," "Good Old Fashioned Revue," "Miss Stanwyck Is Still in Hiding," "Rocky Road."

CARPENTER, THELMA. Born Jan. 15, 1922 in Brooklyn, NY. Appeared on Bdwy in "Memphis Bound," "Inside U.S.A.," "Shuffle Along," "Ankles Aweigh," "Hello, Dolly!," OB in "Turns."

CARR, CATHERINE. Born May 25, 1956 in Ironton, MO. Graduate Oberlin Col., NYU. Bdwy debut 1980 in "Barnum."

CARRADINE, JOHN. Born Feb. 5, 1906 in NYC. Bdwy credits include "Duchess of Malfi," "Volpone," "Galileo," "Cup of Trembling," "Madwoman of Chaillot," "Frankenstein."

CARROLL, DANNY. Born May 30, 1940 in Maspeth, NY. Bdwy bow in 1957 in "The Music Man," followed by "Flora the Red Menace," "Funny Girl," "George M!," "Billy," "Ballroom," "42nd Street," OB in "Boys from Syracuse," "Babes in the Woods."

CARROLL, HELENA. Born in Glasgow, Scot. Attended Webster-Douglas Sch. U.S. debut with Dublin Players. Bdwy debut 1956 in "Separate Tables," followed by "Happy as Larry," "A Touch of the Poet," "Little Moon of Alban," "The Hostage," "Oliver!," "Pickwick," "Something Different," "Georgy," "Borstal Boy," OB in "Three Hand Reel," "Pictures in the Hallway," "Small Craft Warnings," "The Slab Boys."

CARSON, THOMAS LEE. Born May 27, 1939 in Iowa City, IO. Graduate UIo. Debut 1981 OB in "The Feuhrer Bunker."

CARTER, DIXIE. Born May 25, 1939 in McLemoresville, TN. Graduate Memphis State U. Debut 1963 OB in "The Winter's Tale," followed by "Carousel," "The Merry Widow," "The King and I," at LC, "Sextet," "Jesse and the Bandit Queen" for which she received a Theatre World Award, "Fathers and Sons," "A Coupla White Chicks . . .," "Taken in Marriage," Bdwy in "Pal Joey" (1976).

CARTER, I. MARY. Born Oct. 3, 1938 in Washington, DC. Debut 1969 OB in "The Glorious Ruler," followed by "Why Hanna's Skirt Won't Stay Down," "Two by John Noonan," "The White Devil," "A Touch of the Poet," "Gallows Humor," "Grass Harp," "Hadrian VII," "Death Takes a Holiday."

CARTER, NELL. Born Sept. 13 in Birmingham, AL. Bdwy debut 1971 in "Soon," followed by "Jesus Christ Superstar," "Dude," "Don't Bother Me, I Can't Cope," "Ain't Misbehavin'" for which she received a Theatre World Award, OB in "Iphigenia in Taurus," "Bury the Dead," "Fire in the Mindhouse," "The Dirtiest Show in Town," "Black Broadway," "Rhapsody in Gershwin."

CARTER, ROSANNA. Born Sept. 20 in Rolle Town, Bahamas. Attended NEC Workshop. OB in "Lament of Rasta Fari," "Burghers of Callais," "Scottsboro Boys," "Les Femmes Noires," "Killings on the Last Line," Bdwy 1980 in "The American Clock" followed by "Inacent Black."

CARUSO, BARBARA. Born in East Orange, NJ. Graduate Douglass Col, RADA. Debut 1969 OB in "The Millionairess," followed by "Picture of Dorian Gray," "Wars of the Roses," "Chez Nous," "Ride a Cock Horse," "Inadmissible Evidence," "Ned and Jack," Bdwy in "Night of the Iguana (1976)."

CARVER, MARY. Born May 3, 1924 in Los Angeles, CA. Graduate USC. Debut 1950 OB in "Bury the Dead," followed by "Rhinoceros," "Life of Galileo," Bdwy in "Out West of 8th," "Low and Behold," "The Shadow Box," "5th of July."

CARYL, JEANNE. (formerly Caryl Tenney and Carol Jeanne) Born July 11 in Thatcher, AZ. Bdwy debut 1968 in "I'm Solomon," followed by "Two by Two," "Desert Song," "Carmelina," "Snow White," "Camelot"('80).

CASH, ROSALIND. Born Dec. 31, 1938 in Atlantic City, NJ. Attended CCNY. Bdwy debut 1966 in "The Wayward Stork," followed by "Fiorello!," OB in "June-bug Graduates Tonight," "To Bury a Cousin," "Song of the Lusitanian Bogey," "Kongi's Harvest," "Ceremonies in Dark Old Men," "An Evening of One Acts," "Man Better Man," "The Harangues," "Day of Absence," "Brotherhood," "Charlie Was Here," "King Lear," "16th Round."

CASSAN, CLAUDINE. Born Jan. 7, 1954 in NYC. Attended SUNY. Debut 1979 OB in "It's So Nice to Be Civilized," followed by "The Miser."

CASSIDY, TIM. Born March 22, 1952 in Alliance, OH. Attended UCincinnati. Bdwy debut 1974 in "Good News," followed by "A Chorus Line."

| Maria Cellario | David Chandler | Vickie Chappell | Peter Coffield | Connie Coit |

CASTANG, VERONICA. Born Apr. 22 in London, Eng. Attended Sorbonne. Bdwy debut 1966 in "How's the World Treating You?," followed by "The National Health," "Whose Life Is It Anyway?," OB in "The Trigon," "Sjt. Musgrave's Dance," "Saved," "Water Hens," "Self-Accusation," "Kaspar," "Ionescapade," "Statements after and Arrest under the Immorality Act," "Ride a Cock Horse," "Banana Box," "Bonjour La Bonjour," "A Call from the East," "Close of Play," "Cloud 9."

CASTILLO, HELEN. Born Feb. 5, 1955 in Santurce, PR. Graduate UPR, Juilliard. Bdwy debut 1979 in "They're Playing Our Song."

CAULFIELD, MAXWELL. Born Nov. 23, 1959 in Glasgow, Scot. Debut OB 1979 in "Class Enemy" for which he received a Theatre World Award, followed by "Crimes and Dreams," "Entertaining Mr. Sloane."

CELLARIO, MARIA. Born June 19, 1948 in Buenos Aires, Arg. Graduate Ithaca Col. Bdwy debut 1975 in "The Royal Family," OB in "Fugue in a Nursery," "Declassee."

CHAIKIN, SHAMI. Born Apr. 21, 1931 in NYC. Debut 1966 OB in "America Hurrah," followed by "Serpent," "Terminal," "Mutation Show," "Viet Rock," "Mystery Play," "Electra," "The Dybbuk," "Endgame," "Bag Lady," "The Haggadah."

HALFANT, KATHLEEN. Born Jan. 14, 1945 in San Francisco, CA. Graduate Stanford U. Bdwy debut 1975 in "Dance with Me," followed by OB "Jules Feiffer's Hold Me," "Killings on the Last Line."

CHAMPAGNE, MICHAEL. Born Apr. 10, 1947 in New Bedford, MA. Graduate SMU, MSU. Debut 1975 OB in "The Lieutenant," followed by "Alinsky," "The Hostage."

CHANDLER, DAVID. Born Feb 3, 1950 in Danbury, CT. Oberlin Graduate. Bdwy debut 1980 in "The American Clock."

CHANDLER, JEFFREY ALAN. Born Sept 9 in Durham, NC. Graduate Carnegie-Mellon. Bdwy debut 1972 in "Elizabeth I," OB in "The People vs Ranchman," "Your Own Thing," "Penguin Touquet."

CHANSKY, DOROTHY. Born Feb. 16. Graduate Smith Col., Catholic U. Bdwy debut 1976 in "Oh! Calcutta!," OB in "The Broken Heart," "Dark of the Moon," "The Hostage," "Cain."

CHAPPELL, VICKIE D. Born Oct., 1957 in Wedowee, AL. Graduate TxChristianU. Bdwy debut 1980 in "It's So Nice to Be Civilized."

CHEN, KITTY. Born in Shanghai, China. Graduate Brown U. Debut 1972 OB in "A Maid's Tragedy," followed by "The King and I," "Rashomon," "And the Soul Shall Dance," "Peking Man," "Flowers and Household Gods."

CHIANESE, DOMINIC. Born Feb. 24, 1932 in NYC. Graduate Brooklyn Col. Debut 1952 OB with American Savoyards, followed by "Winterset," "Jacques Brel Is Alive . . .," "Ballad for a Firing Squad," "City Scene," "End of the War," "Passione," "Midsummer Night's Dream," "Recruiting Officer," "The Wild Duck," "Oedipus the King," Bdwy in "Oliver!," "Scratch," "The Water Engine," "Richard III."

CHILDRESS, YOLANDA. Born in East Rainelle, WVA. Graduate Westhampton Col., AADA. Debut 1965 OB in "Troubled Waters," Bdwy 1980 in "The Man Who Came to Dinner."

CHRISTIAN, ROBERT. Born Dec. 27, 1939 in Los Angeles. Attended UCLA. OB in "The Happening," "Hornblend," "Fortune and Men's Eyes," "Boys in the Band," "Behold! Cometh the Vanderkellans," "Mary Stuart," "Narrow Road to the Deep North," "Twelfth Night," "The Past is the Past," "Going Through Changes," "Black Sunlight," "Terraces," "Blood Knot," "Boesman and Lena," "Statements after and Arrest under the Immorality Act," "Julius Caesar," "Coriolanus," "Mother Courage," Bdwy in "We Bombed in New Haven," "Does a Tiger Wear a Necktie?," "An Evening with Richard Nixon," "All God's Chillun," "Piaf."

CHRISTOPHER, DENNIS. Born Dec. 2, 1954 in Philadelphia, PA. Attended Temple U. Debut 1974 OB in "Yentl, the Yeshiva Boy," Bdwy 1981 in "The Little Foxes."

CHRISTOPHER, RICHARD. Born Nov. 1, 1948 in Ft. Knox, KY. Graduate SWLaU. Bdwy debut 1973 in "Seesaw," followed by "King of Hearts," "Happy New Year," OB in "Three Musketeers," "The Jones Matter."

CHRISTOPHERSON, INDIRA STEFANIANNE. Born Dec. 6 in San Francisco, CA. Attended San Francisco State Col/San Mateo. Debut 1979 OB in "The Umbrellas of Cherbourg," followed by "Harry Ruby's Songs My Mother Never Sang."

CIESLA, DIANE. Born May 20, 1952 in Chicago, IL. Graduate Clarke Col. Debut 1980 OB in "Uncle Money," followed by "Afternoons in Vegas."

CILENTO, WAYNE. Born Aug. 25, 1949 in The Bronx, NY. Graduate SUNY Brockport. Bdwy in "Irene," "Rachel Lily Rosenbloom," "Seesaw," "A Chorus Line," "The Act," "Dancin'," "Perfectly Frank."

CLANTON, RALPH. Born Sept. 11, 1914 in Fresno, CA. Attended Pasadena Playhouse, Bdwy in "Victory Belles," "Macbeth," "Richard III," "Othello," "Lute Song," "Cyrano," "Antony and Cleopatra," "Design for a Stained Glass Window," "Taming of the Shrew," "The Burning Glass," "Vivat! Vivat Regina!," "The Last of Mrs. Lincoln," OB in "Ceremony of Innocence," "Endecott and the Red Cross," "The Philanderer," "New York Idea," "Three Sisters," "You Never Can Tell," "Candida," "The Winslow Boy."

CLARK, BRYAN E. Born Apr. 5, 1929 in Louisville, KY. Graduate Fordham U. Bdwy debut 1978 in "A History of the American Film," followed by "Bent," OB in "Winning Isn't Everything," "Put Them All Together."

CLARK, CHARMION. Born Sept. 12, 1952 in Cincinnati, OH. Graduate Jacksonville U. Debut 1980 OB in "The Phantom," followed by "No Strings."

CLARK, CHERYL. Born Dec. 7, 1950 in Boston, MA. Attended Ind. U., NYU. Bdwy debut 1972 in "Pippin," followed by "Chicago," "A Chorus Line."

CLARK, JOSH. Born Aug. 16, 1955 in Bethesda, MD. Attended NCSch. of Arts. Debut 1976 OB in "The Old Glory," followed by "Molly," "Just a Little Bit Less Than Normal," "Rear Column," Bdwy in "The Man Who Came to Dinner"(1980).

CLARK, PHILLIP. Born Aug. 12, 1941 in San Diego, CA. Attended USCal. Bdwy debut 1966 in "We Have Always Lived in the Castle," followed by "5th of July," OB in "The Boys in the Band."

CLARKE, MARIAN. Born July 21, 1941 in England. Graduate Middlebury Col. Debut 1965 OB in "Arms and the Man," followed by "Clarence," "Ashes," "Perfect Mollusc," "A Month in the Country," "The Story of the Gadsbys."

CLARY, ROY. Born Aug. 20, 1939 in Winnipeg, Can. Graduate OhStateU, Goodman School. Debut 1968 OB in "Love and Let Love," followed by "Triptych."

CLAUSON, WILLIAM. Born Dec. 30, 1948 in Newton, KS. Graduate Rutgers U. Debut 1977 OB in "The Private Ear," followed by "Knitters in the Sun."

CLEMENT, MARIS. Born July 11, 1950 in Philadelphia, PA. Graduate Rollins Col. Debut 1976 OB in "Noel and Cole," Bdwy in "On the 20th Century," "Copperfield."

CLEMENTE, RENE. Born July 2, 1950 in El Paso, TX. Graduate WestTxStateU. Bdwy debut 1977 in "A Chorus Line."

CLOSE, GLENN. Born May 19, 1947 in Greenwich, CT. Graduate William & Mary Col. Bdwy debut 1974 with Phoenix Co. in "Love for Love," "Member of the Wedding," and "Rules of the Game," followed by "Rex," "Crucifer of Blood," "Barnum," OB in "The Crazy Locomotive," "Uncommon Women and Others," "Wine Untouched," "The Winter Dancers."

COCO, JAMES. Born Mar. 21, 1930 in NYC. Debut 1956 OB in "Salome," followed by "Moon in the Yellow River," "Squat Betty/The Sponge Room," "That 5 A.M. Jazz," "Lovey," "The Basement," "Fragments," "Witness," "Next," "Monsters (The Transfiguration of Benno Blimpie)," Bdwy in "Hotel Paradiso," "Everybody Loves Opal," "Passage to India," "Arturo Ui," "The Devils," "Man of LaMancha," "The Astrakan Coat," "Here's Where I Belong," "Last of the Red Hot Lovers," "Wally's Cafe."

COE, JOHN. Born Oct. 19, 1925 in Hartford, CT. Graduate Boston U. Bdwy in "The Passion of Josef D," "Man in the Glass Booth," "La Strada," "Happy End," OB in "Marrying Maiden," "Thistle in My Bed," "John," "Wicked Cooks," "June Bug Graduates Tonight," "Drums in the Night," "America Hurrah," "Father Uxbridge Wants to Marry," "Nobody Hears a Broken Drum," "Dylan," "Screens," "The Kid," "Naomi Court."

COFFIELD, PETER. Born July 17, 1945 in Evanston, IL. Graduate Northwestern, U.Mich. Bdwy in "The Misanthrope," "Cock-a-Doodle Dandy," "Hamlet," "Abelard and Heloise," "Vivat! Vivat Regina!," "Merchant of Venice," "Tartuffe," "The Man Who Came to Dinner."

COHEN, LYNN. Born Aug. 10 in Kansas City, MO. Graduate NorthwesternU. Debut 1979 OB in "Don Juan Comes Back from the Wars," followed by "Getting Out," "The Arbor," "The Cat and the Canary," "Suddenly Last Summer."

COIT, CONNIE. Born Apr. 21, 1947 in Dallas, TX. Graduate SMU. Debut 1980 OB in "A Funny Thing Happened on the Way to the Forum"(ELT).

COLBY, CHRISTINE. Born Feb. 27 in Cincinnati, OH. Attended UCincinnati. Bdwy debut 1978 in "Dancin'."

Dolly Colby **Michael Cone** **Caris Corfman** **Clayton Corbin** **Lauren Craig**

COLBY, DOLLY. Born May 29, 1951 in Long Island City, NY. Attended Springfield Col. Debut OB 1978 in "Piano Bar," followed by "Silk Stockings," "Anything Goes."

COLE, KAY. Born Jan. 13, 1948 in Miami, FL. Bdwy debut 1961 in "Bye Bye Birdie," followed by "Stop the World I Want to Get Off," "Roar of the Greasepaint . . .," "Hair," "Jesus Christ Superstar," "Words and Music," "Chorus Line," OB in "The Cradle Will Rock," "Two If By Sea," "Rainbow," "White Nights," "Sgt. Pepper's Lonely Hearts Club Band."

COLL, IVONNE. Born Nov. 4, in Fajardo, PR. Attended UPR, LACC, HB Studio. Debut 1980 OB in "Spain 1980," followed by "Animals," Bdwy 1980 in "Goodbye Fidel."

COLLAMORE, JEROME. Born Sept. 25, 1891 in Boston, MA. Debut 1918 with Washington Square Players in "Salome," and subsequently in, among others, "Christopher Bean," "Hamlet," "Romeo and Juliet," "Kind Lady," "Androcles and the Lion," "George Washington Slept Here," "The Would-Be Gentleman," "Cheri," "Abraham Cochran," "That Hat," Bam Co.'s "New York Idea," "Trouping Since 1912."

COLLINS, RISE. Born Sept. 18, 1952 in Houston, TX. Graduate Carnegie-Mellon U. Bdwy debut 1976 in "For Colored Girls Who Have Considered Suicide, . . .," OB in "Pericles," "Incandescent Tones," "Blues in the Night," "No."

COLLINS, STEPHEN. Born Oct. 1, 1947 in Des Moines, IO. Graduate Amherst Col. Bdwy debut 1972 in "Moonchildren," followed by "No Sex, Please, We're British," "The Ritz," "Censored Scenes from King Kong," OB in "Twelfth Night," "More Than You Deserve," "Macbeth"(LC), "Last Days of British Honduras," BAM's "New York Idea," "Three Sisters" and "The Play's the Thing," "Beyond Therapy."

COLLINS, SUZANNE. Born in San Francisco, CA. Graduate USan Francisco. Debut 1975 OB in "Trelawny of the Wells," followed by "The Cherry Orchard," "The Art of Dining," "Put Them All Together."

COLTON, BARBARA. Born July 10, 1938 in NYC. Graduate Boston U. Debut 1980 OB in "The Winslow Boy."

CONE, MICHAEL. Born Oct. 7, 1952 in Fresno, CA. Graduate UWash. Bdwy debut 1980 in "Brigadoon."

CONNELL, DAVID. Born Nov. 24, 1935 in Cleveland, OH. Attended Kent State U. Bdwy bow 1968 in "The Great White Hope," followed by "Don't Play Us Cheap," OB in "Ballet Behind the Bridge," "Miracle Play," "Time Out of Time."

CONNELL, GORDON. Born Mar. 19, 1923 in Berkeley, CA. Graduate UCal., NYU. Bdwy bow 1961 in "Subways Are for Sleeping," followed by "Hello, Dolly!," "Lysistrata," OB in "Beggar's Opera," "The Butler Did It."

CONNER, BYRON. Born Dec. 5, 1953 in Gadsden, AL. Graduate Ithaca College. Debut 1978 OB in "The Taming of the Shrew," followed by "On a Clear Day," "Floradora."

CONNOLLY, MICHAEL. Born Sept 22, 1947 in Boston, MA. Graduate Fordham U. Bdwy debut 1977 in "Otherwise Engaged," followed by "Break a Leg," "Clothes for a Summer Hotel," "Copperfield," OB in "Hijinks."

CONROY, FRANCES. Born in 1953 in Monroe, GA. Attended Dickinson Col., Juilliard, Neighborhood Playhouse. Debut 1978 OB with the Acting Co. in "Mother Courage," "King Lear," "The Other Half," followed by "All's Well That Ends Well," "Othello," "Sorrows of Stephen," "Girls Girls Girls," Bdwy 1980 in "The Lady from Dubuque."

CONROY, JARLATH. Born Sept. 30, 1944 in Galway, IR. Attended RADA. Bdwy debut 1976 in "Comedians," followed by "The Elephant Man," "Macbeth," OB in "Translations."

COOK, JAMES. Born Mar. 7, 1937 in NYC. Attended AADA. OB in "The Fantasticks," "Goa," "Cyrano," "A Cry of Players," "King Lear," "Playboy of the Western World," "Good Woman of Setzuan," "Enemy of the People," "In the Matter of J. Robert Oppenheimer," "The Architect and the Emperor," "Arsenic and Old Lace," Bdwy in "The Great White Hope," "Wrong Way Light Bulb," "Peter Pan."

COOK, JILL. Born Feb. 25, 1954 in Plainfield, NJ. Bdwy debut 1971 in "On the Town," followed by "So Long, 174th Street," "Dancin'," "Best Little Whorehouse in Texas," "Perfectly Frank," OB in "Carnival," "Potholes."

COOK, RODERICK. Born 1932 in London. Attended Cambridge U. Bdwy debut 1961 in "Kean," followed by "Roar Like a Dove," "The Girl Who Came to Supper," "Noel Coward's Sweet Potato," "The Man Who Came to Dinner," "Woman of the Year," OB in "A Scent of Flowers," "Oh, Coward!"

COOPER, BOB, JR. Born Sept. 19, 1941 in Grand Rapids, MI. Graduate WesternMiU. Debut 1980 OB in "The Devil's Disciple," followed by "School for Scandal."

COOPER, JOHN. Born Apr. 27, 1956 in San Jose, CA. Attended San Diego StateU. Debut 1980 OB in "Period of Adjustment."

COOPER, MARILYN. Born Dec. 14, 1936 in NYC. Attended NYU. Appeared in "Mr. Wonderful," "West Side Story," "Brigadoon," "Gypsy," "I Can Get It for You Wholesale," "Hallelujah Baby!," "Golden Rainbow," "Mame," "A Teaspoon Every 4 Hours," "Two by Two," "On the Town," "Ballroom," "Woman of the Year," OB in "The Mad Show," "Look Me Up."

COOPER, ROY. Born Jan. 22, 1930 in London, Eng. Bdwy debut 1968 in "The Prime Of Miss Jean Brodie," followed by "Canterbury Tales," "St. Joan," OB in "A Month in the Country," "Mary Stuart."

COPELAND, JOAN. Born June 1, 1922 in NYC. Attended Brooklyn Col., AADA. Debut 1945 OB in "Romeo and Juliet," followed by "Othello," "Conversation Piece," "Delightful Season," "End of Summer," "The American Clock," Bdwy in "Sundown Beach," "Detective Story," "Not for Children," "Hatful of Fire," "Something More," "The Price," "Two by Two," "Pal Joey," "Checking Out," "The American Clock."

CORBIN, CLAYTON. Born May 4, 1928 in Tacoma, WA. Graduate UCLA. Debut 1954 OB in "Of Mice and Men," followed by "The Ivory Branch," "Land Beyond the River," "Dark of the Moon," "Raisin' Hell in the Sun," "The Blacks," "Telemachus Clay," "The Old Glory," "Prometheus Bound," "Black Elk Lives," Bdwy in "Mr. Johnson," "Toys in the Attic," "Royal Hunt of the Sun."

CORFMAN, CARIS. Born May 18, 1955 in Boston, MA. Graduate FlaStateU, Yale. Debut 1978 OB in "Wings," Bdwy 1980 in "Amadeus."

COSTALLOS, SUZANNE. Born Apr. 3, 1953 in NYC. Attended NYU, Boston Consv., Juilliard. Debut OB 1977 in "Play and Other Plays by Beckett," followed by "Elizabeth I," "The White Devil," "Hunting Scenes from Lower Bavaria."

COSTIGAN, KEN. Born Apr. 1, 1934 in NYC. Graduate Fordham U., Yale U. Debut 1960 OB in "Borak," followed by "King of the Dark Chamber," "The Hostage," "Next Time I'll Sing to You," "Curley McDimple," "The Runner Stumbles," "Peg o' My Heart," "The Show-Off," "Midsummer Night's Dream," "Diary of Anne Frank," "Knuckle Sandwich," "Seminary Murder," "Declassee," Bdwy 1962 in "Gideon."

COUNCIL, RICHARD. Born Oct. 1, 1947 in Tampa, FL. Graduate UFla. Debut 1973 OB in "Merchant of Venice," followed by "Ghost Dance," "Look, We've Come Through," "Arms and the Man," "Isadora Duncan Sleeps with the Russian Navy," "Arthur," "The Winter Dancer," "The Prevalence of Mrs. Seal," Bdwy in "The Royal Family" (1975), "Philadelphia Story."

COURTNEY, DENNIS. Born Apr. 30, 1958 in Detroit, MI. Attended Col. Conservatory of Music. Debut 1978 OB in "Coolest Cat in Town," Bdwy 1979 in "Peter Pan."

COWAN, EDIE. Born Apr. 14 in NYC. Graduate Butler U. Bdwy debut 1964 in "Funny Girl," followed by "Sherry," "Annie."

COX, CATHERINE. Born Dec. 13, 1950 in Toledo, OH. Wittenberg U. graduate. Bdwy debut 1976 in "Music Is," followed by "Whoopee!," "Oklahoma!," "Shakespeare's Cabaret," "Barnum," OB in "By Strouse."

COX, RICHARD. Born May 6, 1948 in NYC. Yale graduate. Debut 1970 OB in "Saved," followed by "Fuga," "Moonchildren," "Alice in Concert," "Fishing," Bdwy in "The Sign in Sidney Brustein's Window," "Platinum."

CRABTREE, DON. Born Aug. 21, 1928 in Borger, TX. Attended Actors Studio. Bdwy bow 1959 in "Destry Rides Again," followed by "Happiest Girl in the World," "Family Affair," "Unsinkable Molly Brown," "Sophie," "110 in the Shade," "Golden Boy," "Pousse Cafe," "Mahagonny" (OB), "The Best Little Whorehouse in Texas," "42nd Street."

CRAIG, BETSY. Born Jan. 5, 1952 in Hopewell, VA. Attended Berry Col. Bdwy debut 1980 in "Brigadoon."

CRAIG, DONALD. Born Aug. 14, 1941 in Abilene, TX. Graduate Hardin-Simmons Col., UTex. Debut 1975 OB in "Do I Hear a Waltz?" (ELT). Bdwy 1977 in "Annie."

CRAIG, LAUREN. Born May 11, 1951 in Chicago, IL. Attended HB Studio. Debut 1980 OB in "To Bury a Cousin," followed by "Last Summer at Bluefish Cove."

CREAGHAN, DENNIS. Born May 1, 1942 in London, Eng. Attended Hofstra U., HB Studio. Debut 1973 OB in "Hamlet," followed by "The Tempest," "Edward II," "The Servant," Bdwy 1979 in "The Elephant Man."

| Ed Crowley | Gretel Cummings | Philip Cusack | Diane Cypkin | Richard Davidson |

CROFOOT, LEONARD JOHN. Born Sept. 20, 1948 in Utica, NY. Bdwy debut 1968 in "The Happy Time," followed by "Come Summer," "Gigi," "Barnum," OB in "Circus," "Joseph and the Amazing Technicolor Dreamcoat."

CRONIN, JANE. Born Apr. 4, 1936 in Boston, MA. Attended Boston U. Bdwy debut 1965 in "Postmark Zero," OB in "Bald Soprano," "One Flew over the Cuckoo's Nest," "Hot 1 Baltimore," "The Gathering," "Catsplay," "The Violano Virtuoso," "Afternoons in Vegas," "The Frequency," "A Month in the Country," "The Trading Post."

CROSS, MURPHY. Born June 22, 1950 in Baltimore, MD. Graduate NCSch. of Arts. Debut 1972 OB in "Look Me Up," Bdwy in "Bubbling Brown Sugar," "Division Street."

CROUSE, LINDSAY. Born May 12, 1948 in NYC. Radcliffe graduate. Bdwy debut 1972 in "Much Ado About Nothing." OB in "The Foursome," "Fishing," "Long Day's Journey into Night," "Total Recall," "Father's Day," "Hamlet," "Reunion," "Twelfth Night," "Childe Byron."

CROWLEY, EDWARD. Born Sept. 5, 1926 in Lewiston, ME. Attended AADA. Bdwy debut 1958 in "Make a Million," followed by "Family Way," OB in "Admirable Bashville," "An Evening with GBS," "Once Around the Block," "I Want You," "Lion in Love," "Telemachus Clay," "Hair," "How to Steal an Election," "In the Matter of J. Robert Oppenheimer," "An Evening for Merlin Finch," "Dylan," "Val, Christie and Others," "Danton's Death," "Arthur," "Butterfaces."

CRYER, DAVID. Born Mar. 8, 1936 in Evanston, IL. Attended DePauw U. OB in "The Fantasticks," "Streets of New York," "Now Is the Time for All Good Men," "Whispers on the Wind," "The Making of Americans," "Portfolio Revue," Bdwy in "110 in the Shade," "Come Summer" for which he received a Theatre World Award, "1776," "Ari," "Leonard Bernstein's Mass," "Desert Song," "Evita."

CRYER, GRETCHEN. Born Oct. 17, 1935 in Indianapolis, IN. Graduate DePauw U. Bdwy in "Little Me," "110 in the Shade," OB in "Now Is the Time for All Good Men," "Gallery," "Circle of Sound," "I'm Getting My Act Together . . ."

CUERVO, ALMA. Born Aug. 13, in Tampa, FL. Graduated Tulane U., Yale U. Debut 1977 OB in "Uncommon Women and Others," followed by "A Foot in the Door," "Put Them All Together," "Isn't It Romantic," Bdwy in "Once in a Lifetime," "Bedroom Farce," "Censored Scenes from King Kong."

CULLUM, JOHN. Born Mar. 2, 1930 in Knoxville, TN. Graduate U. Tenn. Bdwy bow 1960 in "Camelot," followed by "Infidel Caesar," "The Rehearsal," "Hamlet," "On a Clear Day You Can See Forever" for which he received a Theatre World Award, "Man of LaMancha," "1776," "Vivat! Vivat Regina!," "Shenandoah," "Kings," "The Trip Back Down," "On the 20th Century," "Deathtrap," OB in "Three Hand Reel," "The Elizabethans," "Carousel," "In the Voodoo Parlor of Marie Leveau," "The King and I" (JB).

CUMMINGS, GRETEL. Born July 3, in Bolzano, Italy. Attended Antioch Col. Debut 1964 OB in "Home Movies," followed by "Two Camps by Koutoukas," "Penguin Touquet," Bdwy in "Inner City," "Lolita, My Love," "Stages," "Agammemnon."

CUNNINGHAM, JOHN. Born June 22, 1932 in Auburn, NY. Graduate of Yale and Dartmouth. OB in "Love Me Little," "Pimpernel," "The Fantasticks," "Love and Let Love," "The Bone Room," "Dancing in the Dark," "Father's Day," "Snapshot," Bdwy in Hot Spot," "Zorba," "Company," "1776," "Rose."

CURTIN, J. F. Born Nov. 6, 1955 in Islip, NY. Graduate SUNY. Debut 1980 OB in "Devil's Disciple."

CURTIS, KEENE. Born Feb. 15, 1925 in Salt Lake City, UT. Graduate UUtah. Bdwy bow 1949 in "Shop at Sly Corner," with APA in "School for Scandal," "The Tavern," "Anatole," "Scapin," "Right You Are," "Importance of Being Earnest," "Twelfth Night," "King Lear," "Seagull," "Lower Depths," "Man and Superman," "Judith," "War and Peace," "You Can't Take It With You," "Pantagleize," "Cherry Orchard," "Misanthrope," "Cocktail Party," "Cock-a-Doodle Dandy," and "Hamlet," "A Patriot for Me," "The Rothschilds," "Night Watch," "Via Galactica," "Annie," "Division Street," OB in "Colette," "Ride across Lake Constance."

CUSACK, PHILIP. Born May 10, 1934 in Boston, MA. Attended Emerson Col. Bdwy bow 1966 in " 3 Bags Full," followed by "God's Favorite," "The Good Doctor," "The Gingerbread Lady," "Children, Children," "Let Me Hear You Smile," "California Suite," "They're Playing Our Song," OB in "Boys in the Band."

CWIKOWSKI, BILL. Born Aug. 4, 1945 in Newark, NJ. Graduate Smith and Monmouth Col. Debut 1972 OB in "Charlie the Chicken," followed by "Summer Brave," "Desperate Hours," "Mandrogola," "Two By Noonan," "Soft Touch," "Innocent Pleasures," "3 from the Marathon," "Two Part Harmony."

CYPKIN, DIANE. Born Sept. 10, 1948 in Munich, Ger. Attended Brooklyn Col. Bdwy debut 1966 in "Let's Sing Yiddish," followed by "Papa Get Married," "Light, Lively and Yiddish," OB in "Yoshke Musikant," "Stempenyu," "Big Winner," "A Millionaire in Trouble," "Winner Take All?"

DABDOUB, JACK. Born Feb. 5 in New Orleans, LA. Graduate Tulane U. OB in "What's Up," "Time for the Gentle People," "The Peddler," "The Dodo Bird," "Annie Get Your Gun," Bdwy in "Paint Your Wagon," (1952), "My Darlin' Aida," "Happy Hunting," "Hot Spot," "Camelot," "Baker St.," "Anya," "Her First Roman," "Coco," "Man of LaMancha," "Brigadoon" ('80).

DAGGAN, JOHN. Born Apr. 18, 1954 in Camden, NJ. Graduate UNC. Debut 1980 OB in "The Devil's Disciple," followed by "Elmatha's Apology."

DALE, JIM. Born in 1936 in Rothwell, Eng. Debut 1974 OB with Young Vic Co. in "Taming of the Shrew," followed by "Scapino" that moved to Bdwy, "Barnum."

DALEY, DONNA. Born June 2, 1952 in Providence, RI. Graduate UBridgeport. Debut 1980 OB in "A Coupla White Chicks Sitting Around Talking."

DALY, CAROLINE. Born Jan. 10, 1968 in NYC. Bdwy debut 1980 in "Annie."

DALY, JOSEPH. Born Apr. 7, 1930 in Oakland, CA. Debut 1959 OB in "Dance of Death," followed by "Roots," "Sjt. Musgrave's Dance," "Viet Rock," "Dark of the Moon," "Shadow of a Gunman," "Hamlet," "The Ride across Lake Constance," "A Doll's House," "Native Bird," "Yeats Trio," "Mecca," "Marching to Georgia."

DANEK, MICHAEL. Born May 5, 1955 in Oxford, PA. Graduate Columbia Col. Bdwy debut 1978 "Hello, Dolly!" followed by "A Chorus Line," "Copperfield," "Woman of The Year," OB in "Big Bad Burlesque," "Dreams."

DANGLER, ANITA. Born Sept. 26 in NYC. Attended NYU. Bdwy debut 1956 in "Affair of Honor," followed by "The Hostage," "Right You Are," "You Can't Take It with You," "War and Peace," "Cyrano," "The Man Who Came to Dinner," OB in "Hamlet," "Comedy of Errors," "Trelawny of the Wells," "Isadora Duncan Sleeps with the Russian Navy."

DANNER, BLYTHE. Born in Philadelphia, PA. Graduate Bard Col. Debut 1966 OB in "The Infantry," followed by "Collision Course," "Summertree," "Up Eden," "Someone's Comin' Hungry," "Cyrano," "The Miser" for which he received a Theatre World Award, "Twelfth Night," "The NY Idea," Bdwy in "Butterflies Are Free," "Betrayal," "The Philadelphia Story."

DANSON, RANDY. Born Apr. 30, 1950 in Plainfield, NJ. Graduate Carnegie Mellon. Debut 1978 OB in "Gimme Shelter," followed by "Big and Little," "The Winter Dancers," "Time Steps," "Casualties."

DANTUONO, MICHAEL. Born July 30, 1942 in Providence, RI. Debut 1974 OB in "How to Get Rid of It," followed by "Maggie Flynn," Bdwy 1977 in "Caesar and Cleopatra," "Can-Can" ('81).

D'ARCY, MARY. Born in 1956 in Yardville, NJ. Graduate Glassboro State Col. Bdwy debut 1980 in "The Music Man," OB in "Florodora."

DARKE, REBECCA. Born Dec. 6, 1935 in Brooklyn, NY. OB in "Midnight Caller," "Who'll Save the Plowboy," "Undercover Man," "Party for Divorce," "A Piece of Blue Sky," "Hey Rube," "Glory! Hallelujah!," Bdwy 1977 in "Basic Training of Pavlo Hummel."

DARNAY, TONI. Born Aug. 11 in Chicago, IL. Attended Northwestern U. Debut 1942 OB in "Name Your Poison," followed by "When the Bough Breaks," "Nocturne in Daylight," "The Gold Watch," "Possibilities," "The Sound of Music," (JB), Bdwy in "Sadie Thompson" ('44), "Affair of Honor," "Life with Father," "The Women," "Molly," "The Heiress," "Vieux Carre."

DAVIDSON, JACK. Born July 17, 1936 in Worcester, MA. Graduate Boston U. Debut 1968 OB in "Moon for the Misbegotten," followed by "Big and Little," "The Battle of Angels," "Midsummer Night's Dream," "Hot 1 Baltimore," "A Tribute to Lili Lamont," "Ulysses in Traction," "Lulu," "Hey, Rube," "In the Recovery Lounge," "The Runner Stumbles," "Winter Signs," "Hamlet," "Mary Stuart," "Ruby Ruby Sam Sam," "The Diviners," "Marching to Georgia," Bdwy in "Capt. Brassbound's Conversion" (1972), "Anna Christie."

DAVIDSON, RICHARD M. Born May 10, 1940 in Hamilton, Ont., Can. Graduate UToronto, LAMDA. Debut 1978 OB in "The Beasts," followed by "The Bacchae," Bdwy in "The Survivor" ('81).

Curt Dawson	**Susan Davis**	**Carl Don**	**Bairbre Dowling**	**Richard Dow**

DAVIS, BRUCE ANTHONY. Born Mar. 4, 1959 in Dayton, OH. Attended Juilliard. Bdwy debut 1979 in "Dancin'."

DAVIS, DONNA. Born June 28, 1949 in Elkin, NC. Graduate UNC. Bdwy debut 1978 in "Angel," followed by "Filumena," OB in "Getting Out," "Radical Solutions," "The Mousetrap." "Elmatha's Apology," "Memory of Whiteness."

DAVIS, MICHAEL ALLEN. Born Aug. 23, 1953 in San Francisco, CA. Attended Clown Col. Bdwy debut 1981 in "Broadway Follies" for which he received a Theatre World Award, followed by "Sugar Babies."

DAVIS, SUSAN. Born Apr. 27, 1960 in Tulsa, OK. Debut 1980 OB in "And Other Songs," followed by "El Bravo," Bdwy 1980 in "Barnum."

DAVISON, BRUCE. Born June 28, 1946 in Philadelphia, PA. Graduate Penn State, NYU. Debut 1969 OB in "A Home Away From," followed by LCRep's "Tiger at the Gates," "A Cry of Players," "King Lear," Bdwy 1980 in "The Elephant Man."

DAWSON, CURT. Born Dec. 5, 1941 in Kansas. Graduate RADA. Debut 1968 OB in "Futz," followed by "Boys in the Band," "Not Now, Darling," "White Nights," "Enter a Free Man," "You Never Can Tell," "Dona Rosita," "The Penultimate Problem of Sherlock Holmes," "Ah, Men," Bdwy 1975 in "Absurd Person Singular."

DAWSON, SUZANNE. Born Jan. 19, 1951 in Montreal, Can. Attended Boston Consv. Debut 1980 OB in "Chase a Rainbow."

DeANGELIS, ROSEMARY. Born Apr. 26, 1933 in Brooklyn, NY. Graduate Fashion Inst. Debut 1959 OB in "Time of Vengeance," followed by "Between Two Thieves," "To Be Young, Gifted and Black," "In the Summerhouse," "Monsters," "Rocky Road."

de BANZIE, LOIS. Born May 4 in Glasgow, Scot. Bdwy debut 1966 in "Elizabeth the Queen," followed by "Da," "Morning's at 7," OB in "Little Murders," "Mary Stuart," "People Are Living There," "Ride Across Lake Constance," "The Divorce of Judy and Jane," "What the Butler Saw," "Man and Superman," "The Judas Applause."

DEERING, OLIVE. Born in The Bronx, NY. Attended Actors Studio. Bdwy debut 1932 in "Girls in Uniform," followed by "Growing Pains," "Searching the Sun," "Daughters of Atreus," "Richard II," "Medicine Show," "They Walk Alone," "Nathan the Wise," "Skydrift," "Front Page," "Dark Legend," "The Devil's Advocate," "Marathon '33," "Vieux Carre," OB in "Ceremony of Innocence," "Two by Tennessee," "Winter Chicken," "Two Character Play."

DeFABEES, RICHARD. Born Apr. 4, 1947 in Englewood, NJ. Graduate Georgetown U. Debut 1973 OB in "Creeps," followed by "Monsters (Sideshow)," "36," Bdwy in "The Skin of Our Teeth," "Whose Life Is It Anyway?"

DeFRANK, ROBERT. Born Nov. 29, 1945 in Baltimore, MD. Graduate Towson State, Essex Community Col. Debut 1977 OB in "The Crazy Locomotive," followed by "The Taming of the Shrew," "The Madman and the Nun," "The Good Parts," "We Won't Pay," "Variations on a Theme."

DELANY, DANA. Born Mar. 13, 1956 in NYC. Graduate Wesleyan U. Bdwy debut 1980 in "A Life."

DEMPSEY, JEROME. Born Mar. 1, 1929 in St. Paul, MN. Toledo U graduate. Bdwy bow 1959 in "West Side Story," followed by "The Deputy," "Spofford," "Room Service," "Love Suicide at Schofield Barracks," "Dracula," OB in "Cry of Players," "Year Boston Won the Pennant," "The Crucible," "Justice Box," "Trelawny of the Wells," "The Old Glory," "Six Characters in Search of an Author," "Threepenny Opera," BAM's "Johnny on the Spot," "The Barbarians," "He and She," "Midsummer Night's Dream," "The Recruiting Officer," "Oedipus the King," "The Wild Duck."

DeMUNN, JEFFREY P. Born Apr. 25, 1947 in Buffalo, NY. Graduate Union Col. Debut 1975 OB in "Augusta," followed by "A Prayer for My Daughter," "Modigliani," "Chekhov Sketchbook," Bdwy in "Comedians," "Bent."

DENGEL, JAKE. Born June 19, 1933 in Oshkosh, WI. Graduate Northwestern U. Debut OB in "The Fantasticks," followed by "Red Eye of Love," "Fortuna," "Abe Lincoln in Illinois," "Dr. Faustus," "An Evening with Garcia Lorca," "Shrinking Bride," "Where Do We Go from Here?", "Woyzeck," "Endgame," "Measure for Measure," "Ulysses in Traction," "Twelfth Night," "The Beaver Coat," Bdwy in "Royal Hunt of the Sun," "Cock-a-Doodle Dandy," "Hamlet," "The Changing Room."

DENNISTON, LESLIE. Born May 19, 1950 in San Francisco, CA. Attended HB Studio. Bdwy debut 1976 in "Shenandoah" followed by "Happy New Year," for which she received a Theatre World Award, "To Grandmother's House We Go," "Copperfield."

DEROSKI, BONNIE. Born June 8, 1961 in Neptune, NJ. Debut 1977 OB in "Landscape of the Body," followed by "New England Legend," "Did You See the Elephant?"

DeSAI, SHELLY. Born Dec. 3, 1935 in Bombay, India. Graduate Okla. State U. Debut 1968 OB in "The Indian Wants the Bronx," followed by "Babu," "Wonderful Year," "Jungle of Cities," "Gandhi," "Savages," "Cuchulain," "Penguin Touquet."

DeSAL, FRANK. Born Apr. 14, 1943 in White Plains, NY. Attended AmThWing. Credits include "110 in the Shade," "Marco Millions," "Sherry!," "Sweet Charity," "How Now, Dow Jones," "Fig Leaves Are Falling," "Bring Back Birdie," OB in "Anything Goes."

DeSALVO, ANNE. Born Apr. 3 In Philadelphia, PA. OB in "Iphigenia in Aulis," "Lovers and Other Strangers," "The First Warning," "Warringham Roof," "God Bless You, Mr. Rosewater," "Girls Girls Girls," Bdwy 1977 in "Gemini."

DeSHIELDS, ANDRE. Born Jan. 12, 1946 in Baltimore, MD. Graduate UWi. Bdwy debut 1973 in "Warp," followed by "Rachel Lily Rosenbloom," "The Wiz," "Ain't Misbehavin'," OB in "2008½," "Jazzbo Brown."

DESMOND, EILEEN. Born Dec. 26, 1950 in Kohler, WI. Attended Ripon Col., Wisc. State. Debut 1976 OB in "Master Psychologist," followed by "Footworks," "Hedda Gabler."

DeVITO, KARLA. Born in Oak Lawn, IL. Attended Loyola U. Debut 1974 OB in "El Grande de Coca Cola," followed by "Jubilee," "Midsummer Night's Dream," Bdwy 1981 in "The Pirates of Penzance."

DEVLIN, JAY. Born May 8, 1929 in Ft. Dodge, IA. OB in "The Mad Show," "Little Murders," "Unfair to Goliath," "Ballymurphy," "Front Page," Bdwy 1978 in "King of Hearts."

DILLON, MIA. Born July 9, 1955 in Colorado Springs, CO. Graduate Penn State U. Bdwy debut 1977 in "Equus," followed by "Da," "Once a Catholic," OB in "The Crucible," "Summer," "Waiting for the Parade," "Crimes of the Heart," "Fables for Friends," "Scenes from La Vie de Boheme."

DOBRES, MARCIA-ANNE. Born Sept. 21, 1953 in Philadelphia, PA. Attended American U. Debut 1980 OB in "A Funny Thing Happened on the Way to the Forum."

DON, CARL. Born Dec. 15, 1916 in Vitebsk, Russia. Attended Western Reserve U. Bdwy debut 1954 in "Anastasia," followed by "Romanoff and Juliet," "Dear Me, the Sky Is Falling," "The Relapse," "The Tenth Man," "Zalmen," "Wings," OB in "Richard III," "Twelfth Night," "Winterset," "Arms and the Man," "Between Two Thieves," "He Who Gets Slapped," "Jacobowsky and the Colonel," "Carnival," "The Possessed."

DONNELLY, DONAL. Born July 6, 1931 in Bradford, Eng. Bdwy debut 1966 in "Philadelphia, Here I Come," followed by "A Day in the Death of Joe Egg," "Sleuth," "The Faith Healer," "The Elephant Man," OB in "My Astonishing Self."

DONNET, MARY. Born July 18, 1953 in Englewood, NJ. Graduate Sarah Lawrence Col. Debut OB in "La Ronde," followed by "Come Back to the 5 & Dime, Jimmy Dean," "Late City Edition," "I Can't Keep Running in Place."

DONOHUE, NANCY. Born Nov. 2, 1938 in Orange, NJ. Graduate Ct. Col. Bdwy debut 1964 in "Never Too Late," followed by OB in "Canadian Gothic," "Prometheus Bound," "Little Eyolf," "The Runner Stumbles," "The Gathering," "The Prevalence of Mrs. Seal."

DOOLEY, PAUL. Born Feb. 22, 1928 in Parkersburg, WVA. Graduate UWVa. Bdwy debut in "The Odd Couple," OB in "Threepenny Opera," "Toinette," "Fallout," "Dr. Willy Nilly," "Second City," "Adaptation," "White House Murder Case," "Jules Feiffer's Hold Me," "The Amazin' Casey Stengel."

DOTRICE, ROY. Born May 26, 1925 in Guernsey, Channel Islands. Bdwy debut 1967 in "Brief Lives," a return engagement in 1974, "Mr. Lincoln" (1980), "A Life."

DOUGLASS, PI. Born in Sharon, CT. Attended Boston Consv. Bdwy debut 1969 in "Fig Leaves Are Falling," followed by "Hello, Dolly!," "Georgy," "Purlie," "Ari," "Jesus Christ Superstar," "The Selling of the President," "The Wiz," OB in "Of Thee I Sing," "Under Fire."

DOW, RICHARD A. Born Aug. 30, 1941 in Cambridge, MA. Graduate UPa. Debut 1970 OB in "The Dirtiest Show in Town," followed by "Baba Goya," "Nourish the Beast," "Hothouse," "Action," "International Stud," "Bird with Silver Feathers," "Lenz," "Mama, I Want to Sing."

DOWLING, BAIRBRE. Born Mar. 27, 1953 in Dublin, Ire. Debut 1979 OB in "Flying Blind," followed by "Murder in the Cathedral," Bdwy in "Da."

| Judith Drake | David Downing | Lisa Driscoll | Craig Dudley | Cynthia Ellis |

DOWNING, DAVID. Born July 21, 1943 in NYC. Bdwy debut 1975 in "Raisin," followed by "The River Niger," "The Cool World," OB in "Days of Absence," "Happy Ending," "Song of the Lusitanian Bogey," "Ceremonies in Dark Old Men," "Man Better Man," "The Harangues," "Brotherhood," "Perry's Mission," "Rosalee Pritchett," "Dream on Monkey Mt.," "Ride a Black Horse," "Ballet Behind the Bridge," "Please Don't Cry and Say No," "Richard III," "Branches from the Same Tree."

DOYLE, LEE H. Born Apr. 20, 1928 in Cleveland, OH. Attended Tokyo U. Debut 1965 OB in "By Jupiter," followed by "Threepenny Opera," "Here Come the Clowns," "Woyzeck," "Miss Stanwyck Is Still in Hiding," "The Front Page," "Anything Goes," Bdwy 1976 in "Going Up."

DRAKE, JUDITH. Born Feb. 9 in Tulsa, OK. Graduate UTulsa. Bdwy debut 1968 in "Hello, Dolly!," followed by "Lysistrata," OB in "The Guardsman," "My Great Dead Sister," "Bonjour La Bonjour."

DREYFUSS, RICHARD. Born in 1948 in Brooklyn, NY. Bdwy debut 1969 in "But Seriously," OB in "Line," "Julius Caesar," "Othello."

DRISCHELL, RALPH. Born Nov. 26, 1927 in Baldwin, NY. Attended Carnegie-Tech. Bdwy in "Rhinoceros," "All in Good Time," "Rosencrantz and Guildenstern Are Dead," "The Visit," "Chemin de Fer," "Ah, Wilderness," "Stages," "The American Clock," "The Survivor," OB in "Playboy of the Western World," "The Crucible," "The Balcony," "Time of Vengeance," "Barroom Monks," "Portrait of the Artist," "Abe Lincoln in Illinois," "The Caretaker," "A Slight Ache," "The Room," "The Year Boston Won the Pennant," "The Time of Your Life," "Camino Real," "Operation Sidewinder," "Beggar on Horseback," "Threepenny Opera."

DISCROLL, LISA. Born Aug. 1, 1956 in Highland Park, IL. Graduate Stephens Col. Debut 1980 OB in "Time and the Conways."

DRIVER, JOHN. Born Jan 16, 1947 in Erie, PA. Graduate Smith Col., Northwestern U. Debut OB 1972 in "One Flew over the Cuckoo's Nest," followed by "Scrambled Feet," Bdwy in "Grease," (1973), "Over Here" for which he received a Theatre World Award.

DRUMMOND, ALICE. Born May 21, 1929 in Pawtucket, RI. Attended Pembroke Col. Bdwy debut 1963 in "Ballad of the Sad Cafe," followed by "Malcolm," "The Chinese," "Thieves," "Summer Brave," "Some of My Best Friends," OB in "Royal Gambit," "Go Show Me a Dragon," "Sweet of You to Say So," "Gallows Humor," "American Dream," "Giants' Dance," "Carpenters," "Charles Abbot & Son," "God Says There Is No Peter Ott," "Enter a Free Man," "Memory of Two Mondays," "Secret Service," "Boy Meets Girl," "Savages," "Killings on the Last Line," "Knuckle."

DUDA, MATTHEW. Born June 23, 1969 in San Diego, CA. Bdwy debut 1980 in "Charlie and Algernon."

DUDLEY, CRAIG, Born Jan, 22, 1945 in Sheepshead Bay, NY. Graduate AADA, AmThWing. Debut 1970 OB in "Macbeth," followed by "Zou," "Othello," "War and Peace."

DUFF-MacCORMICK, CARA. Born Dec. 12 in Woodstock, Can. Attended AADA. Debut 1969 OB in "Love Your Crooked Neighbor," followed by "The Wager," "Macbeth," "A Musical Merchant of Venice," "Ladyhouse Blues," "The Philanderer," "Bonjour La Bonjour," Bdwy 1972 in "Moonchildren" for which she received a Theatre World Award, followed by "Out Cry," "Animals."

DUKAS, JAMES. Born June 6, 1926 in Portsmouth, OH. Graduate UWVa. Credits OB: "Man with the Golden Arm," "Brothers Karamazov," "Threepenny Opera," "Incident at Vichy," "After the Fall," "Every Place Is Newark," Bdwy in "The Last Analysis," "Nobody Loves an Albatross," "Don't Drink the Water," "The Visit," "A Patriot for Me."

DUNCAN, SANDY. Born Feb. 20, 1946 in Henderson, TX. Attended Len Morris Col. NY debut 1965 in CC's revivals of "The Music Man," "Carousel," "Finian's Rainbow," "Sound of Music," "Wonderful Town," and "Life with Father," OB in "Ceremony of Innocence" for which she received a Theatre World Award, "Your Own Thing," Bdwy in "Canterbury Tales" (1969), "Love Is a Time of Day," "The Boy Friend" (1970), "Peter Pan" (1979).

DUNNE, GRIFFIN. Born June 8, 1955 in NYC. Attended Neighborhood Playhouse. Debut 1980 OB in "Marie and Bruce," followed by "Coming Attractions."

DUQUETTE, JOE. Born Mar. 9, 1949 in Fall River, MA. Graduate SoutheastMaU. Debut OB 1980 in "The Meehans."

DURAN, MICHAEL J. Born Nov. 25, 1953 in Denver, CO. Graduate UCo. Debut 1981 OB in "Godspell" (ELT).

DWYER, FRANK. Born Feb. 1, 1945 in Kansas City, MO. Graduate NYU, SUNY. Debut 1970 OB in "Moby Dick," followed by "Hamlet," "Bacchai," "The Governor," "Imaginary Invalid," "Enemies," "Merchant of Venice," "A Streetcar Named Desire," "Darkness at Noon."

EARLE, EDWARD. Born Dec. 20, 1929 in Santa Barbara, CA. Graduate USC. Bdwy debut 1959 in "The Dark at the Top of the Stairs," followed by "Viva Madison Avenue," "Show Me Where the Good Times Are," "Roar of the Greasepaint," "Musical Chairs," "Charlie and Algernon."

EASTERBROOK, RANDALL. Born Jan. 15, 1951 in Peoria, IL. Graduate Northwestern U. Bdwy debut 1977 in "Hair," OB in "Hijinks."

EATON, BRUCE. Born Aug. 21, 1957 in Waltham, MA. Graduate AADA. Debut 1980 OB in "Friend of the Family."

eda-YOUNG, BARBARA. Born Jan 30, 1945 in Detroit, MI. Bdwy debut 1968 in "Lovers and Other Strangers," OB in "The Hawk," LCRep's "The Time of Your Life," "Camino Real," "Operation Sidewinder," "Kool Aid" and "A Streetcar Named Desire," "The Gathering," "The Terrorists," "Drinks before Dinner," "Shout Across the River," "After Stardrive."

EDE, GEORGE. Born Dec. 22, 1931 in San Francisco, CA. Bdwy debut 1969 in "A Flea in Her Ear," followed by "Three Sisters," "The Changing Room," "The Visit," "Chemin de Fer," "Holiday," "Love for Love," "Rules of the Game" "Member of the Wedding," "Lady from the Sea," "A Touch of the Poet," "Philadelphia Story," OB in "The Philanderer," "The American Clock."

EDENFIELD, DENNIS. Born July 23, 1946 in New Orleans, LA. Debut 1970 OB in "The Evil That Men Do," followed by "I Have Always Believed in Ghosts," "Nevertheless They Laugh," Bdwy in "Irene" ('73), "A Chorus Line,"

EDMEAD, WENDY. Born July 6, 1956 in NYC. Graduate NYCU. Bdwy debut 1974 in "The Wiz," followed by "Stop the World. . . .," "America."

EDWARDS, BRANDT. Born Mar. 22, 1947 in Holly Springs, MS. Graduate UMiss. NY debut off and on Bdwy 1975 in "A Chorus Line."

EDWARDS, SUSAN. Born Aug. 24, 1950 in Levittown, NY. Graduate Hofstra U. Bdwy debut 1976 in "Bubbling Brown Sugar," followed by "The Suicide," OB in "Jazz Babies," "The Boys from Syracuse" (ELT), "Scrambled Feet."

EGAN, MICHAEL. Born Aug. 24, 1926 in Washington, PA. Graduate Buckness U. Bdwy debut 1956 in "The Great Sebastians," followed by "Luther," "A Cry of Players," "The Incomparable Max," "The Ritz," OB in "The Real Inspector Hound," "Drums in the Night," "Duck Variations," "American Buffalo," "Waiting for Godot," "The Seagull," "One Act Play Festival."

ELLIN, DAVID. Born Jan. 10, 1925 in Montreal, Can. Attended AADA. Bdwy in "Swan Song," "West Side Story," "Education of Hyman Kaplan," "Light, Lively and Yiddish," OB in "Trees Die Standing," "Mirele Efros," "End of All Things Natural," "Yoshe Kalb," "Fiddler on the Roof" (JB), "Rebecca, the Rabbi's Daughter," "Wish Me Mazel-Tov."

ELLINGTON, MERCEDES. Born Feb. 9, 1939 in NYC. Juilliard graduate. Bdwy debut 1970 in "No, No, Nanette," followed by "The Grand Tour," "Happy New Year," "Black Broadway," OB in "Around the World," (JB), "An Evening of Jerome Kern," "Sophisticated Ladies."

ELLIOTT, PATRICIA. Born July 21, 1942 in Gunnison, CO. Graduate U. Colo., London Academy. Debut with LCRep 1968 in "King Lear," and "A Cry of Players," followed by "Henry V," "The Persians," "A Doll's House," "Hedda Gabler," "In case of Accident," "Water Hen," "Polly," "But Not for Me," "By Bernstein," "Prince of Homburg," "Artichokes," "Wine Untouched," Bdwy bow 1973 in "A Little Night Music" for which she received a Theatre World Award, followed by "The Shadow Box," "Tartuffe," "13 Rue de L'Amour," "The Elephant Man."

ELLIS, CYNTHIA S. Born Sept. 14, 1959 in Wilson, NC. Attended American U, AADA. Debut 1981 OB in "Raisin." (ELT).

ELLIS, SCOTT. Born Apr. 19, 1957 in Washington, DC. Attended Goodman Theatre. Bdwy debut in "Grease," followed by "Musical Chairs," OB in "Mrs. Dally Has a Lover," "Hijinks."

ELLIS, TERRANCE TERRY. Born Sept. 20, 1957 in Chicago, IL. Graduate UIl. Debut 1980 OB in "Zooman and the Sign."

ELSTON, ROBERT. Born May 29, 1934 in NYC. Graduate Hunter Col., CCNY. Bdwy debut 1958 in "Maybe Tuesday," followed by "Tall Story," "Golden Fleecing," "Spoon River Anthology," "You Know I Can't Hear You When. . . .," "Vivat! Vivat Regina!," OB in "Undercover Man," "Conditioned Reflex," "Archy and Mehitabel," "Notes from the Underground."

| Yvette Erwin | Michael Estes | Suellen Estey | Ralph Farrington | Cecilia Flores |

ENSSLEN, DICK. Born Dec. 19, 1926 in Reading, PA. Attended MTA. Bdwy debut 1964 in "Anyone Can Whistle," followed by "Bajour," "Education of Hyman Kaplan," "Canterbury Tales," "Desert Song," "I Remember Mama," "Annie."

ERWIN, BARBARA. Born June 30, 1937 in Boston, MA. Debut 1973 OB in "The Secret Life of Walter Mitty," followed by "Broadway," Bdwy in "Annie," "Ballroom," "Animals."

ERWIN, YVETTE. Born Feb. 14, 1959 in Washington, DC. Attended SUNY, NYU, HB Studio. Debut 1981 OB in "No."

ESPOSITO, GIANCARLO. Born Apr. 26, 1958 in Copenhagen, Den. Bdwy debut 1968 in "Maggie Flynn," followed by "The Me Nobody Knows," "Lost in the Stars," "Seesaw," OB in "Zooman and the Sign," for which he received a Theatre World Award.

ESTERMAN, LAURA. Born Apr. 12, in NYC. Attended Radcliffe, LAMDA. Debut 1969 OB in "The Time of Your Life" (LCR), followed by "Pig Pen," "The Carpenters," "Ghosts," "Waltz of the Toreadors," "Macbeth" (LC), "The Seagull," "Rubbers," "Yanks 3, Detroit 0," "Golden Boy," "Out of Our Father's House," "The Master and Margarita," "Chinchilla," "Dusa, Fish, Stas and Vi," "Midsummer Night's Dream," "The Recruiting Officer," "Oedipus the King," Bdwy 1974 "God's Favorite," "Teibele and Her Demon," "The Suicide."

ESTES, MICHAEL P. Born July 10, 1955 in St. Louis, MO. Attended Butler U. Debut 1978 OB in "Can-Can," followed by "Mary," Bdwy 1979 in "Peter Pan."

ESTEY, SUELLEN. Born Nov. 21 in Mason City, IA. Graduate Stephens Col., Northwestern U. Debut 1970 OB in "Some Other Time," followed by "June Moon," "Buy Bonds Buster," "Smile, Smile, Smile," "Carousel," "The Lullaby of Broadway," "I Can't Keep Running," Bdwy 1972 in "The Selling of the President," followed by "Barnum."

EVANKO, ED. Born in Winnipeg, Can. Studied at Bristol Old Vic. Bdwy debut 1969 in "Canterbury Tales" for which he received a Theatre World Award, followed by "Rex," "Knickerbocker Holiday," OB in "Love Me, Love My Children," "Leaves of Grass," "Rhapsody in Gershwin."

EVANS PETER. Born May 27, 1950 in Englewood, NJ. Graduate Yale, London Central School of Speech. Debut OB 1975 in "Life Class," followed by "Streamers," "A Life in the Theatre," "Don Juan Comes Back from the War," "The American Clock," Bdwy in "Night and Day" (1979).

EVERHART, REX. Born June 13, 1920 in Watseka, IL. Graduate UMo, NYU. Bdwy bow 1955 in "No Time for Sergeants," followed by "Tall Story," "Moonbirds," "Tenderloin," "A Matter of Position," "Rainy Day in Newark," "Skyscraper," "How Now Dow Jones," "1776," "The Iceman Cometh," "Chicago," "Working," "Woman of the Year."

FABER, RON. Born Feb. 16, 1933 in Milwaukee, WI. Graduate Marquette U. Debut OB 1959 in "An Enemy of the People," followed by "The Exception and the Rule," "America, Hurrah," "Ubu Cocu," "Terminal," "They Put Handcuffs on Flowers," "Dr. Selavy's Magic Theatre," "Troilus and Cressida," "The Beauty Part," "Woyzeck," "St. Joan of the Stockyards," "Jungle of Cities," "Scenes from Everyday Life," "Mary Stuart," Bdwy in "Medea" (1973), "First Monday in October."

FABIANI, JOEL. Born Sept, 28, 1936 in Watsonville, CA. Attended LaSierra, Actors Workshop. Debut 1963 OB in "Dark Corners," followed by "Ashes," "I'm Getting My Act Together. . . .," Bdwy in "Love for Love," "Beyond the Fringe," "Rules of the Game," "As to the Meaning of Words."

FANCY, RICHARD. Born Aug. 2, 1943 in Evanston, IL. Attended LAMDA. Debut 1973 OB in "The Creeps," followed by "Kind Lady," "Rites of Passage."

FARER, RHONDA. Born Oct. 19, 1951 in Colonia, NJ. Graduate Rider Col. Debut 1973 in "Rachel Lily Rosenbloom," followed by "They're Playing Our Song," OB in "The Dog Beneath the Skin."

FARRAR, MARTHA. Born Apr. 22, 1928 in Buffalo, NY. Graduate Smith Col. Bdwy debut 1953 in "A Pin to See the Peepshow," OB in "The Cretan Woman," "Easter," "Half-Life."

FARRINGTON, RALPH. Born Nov. 8, 1954 in Brooklyn, NY. Graduate SUNY/Purchase. Debut 1968 OB in "Finian's Rainbow," Bdwy in "Your Arms Too Short to Box with God," "The Wiz."

FASSLER, RON. Born Mar. 4, 1957 in NYC. Attended SUNY/Purchase. Bdwy debut 1980 in "Censored Scenes from King Kong," OB in "The Buddy System."

FERRY, DAVID. Born Sept. 6, 1951 in Owen Sound, Can. Attended Memorial U. Newfoundland. Bdwy debut 1980 in "A Life."

FIELDS, JOE. Born Jan. 23, 1935 in Uniontown, AL. Attended Karmu Th. Sch. Debut 1969 OB in "Ceremonies in Dark Old Men," followed by "Of Mice and Men," "As You Like It," "Branches from the Same Tree," Bdwy in "Ain't Supposed to Die a Natural Death" ('71), "The Basic Training of Pavlo Hummel" for which he received a Theatre World Award.

FIELDS, THOR. Born Sept. 19, 1968 in NYC. Bdwy debut 1978 in "The King and I," followed by OB's "Yo Yo," "A Month in the Country," "Camelot" (1980).

FISHER, DOUGLAS. Born July 9, 1934 in Brooklyn, NY. Attended St. John's U, AADA. Debut 1963 OB in "Best Foot Forward," followed by "Frere Jacques," "Devil's Disciple," "Accent on Youth," "Lost in the Stars," "Say, Darling," "Shoestring Revue," "Penthouse Legend," "Call Me Madam," "Marjorie Daw," "God Bless You, Mr. Rosewater," "Florodora."

FITCH, ROBERT. Born Apr. 29, 1934 in Santa Cruz, CA. Attended USanta Clara. Bdwy debut 1961 in "Tenderloin," followed by "Do Re Me," "My Fair Lady," "The Girl Who Came to Supper," "Flora the Red Menace," "Baker Street," "Sherry," "Mack and Mabel," "Henry Sweet Henry," "Mame," "Promises Promises," "Coco," "Lorelei," "Annie," OB in "Lend an Ear," "Half-Past Wednesday," "Anything Goes," "Crystal Heart," "Broadway Dandies," "One Cent Plain," "Sweet Thighs of New England Women."

FITZGERALD, FERN. Born Jan. 7, 1947 in Valley Stream, NY. Bdwy debut 1976 in "Chicago," followed by "A Chorus Line."

FITZGERALD, GERALDINE. Born Nov. 24, 1914 in Dublin, Ire. Bdwy debut 1938 in "Heartbreak House," followed by "Sons and Soldiers," "Doctor's Dilemma," "King Lear," "Hide and Seek," "Ah, Wilderness," "The Shadow Box," "A Touch of the Poet," OB in "Cave Dwellers," "Pigeons," "Long Day's Journey into Night," "Everyman and Roach," "Streetsongs."

FITZPATRICK, JIM. Born Nov. 26, 1950 in Omaha, NE. Attended UNeb. Debut 1977 OB in "Arsenic and Old Lace" (ELT), followed by "Merton of the Movies" (ELT), "Oh, Boy!", "Time and the Conways."

FITZPATRICK, KELLY. Born Dec. 31, 1937 in Mt. Kisco, NY. Graduate Hobart Col. Bdwy debut 1971 in "Abelard and Heloise," followed by OB in "The Trial of Denmark Vesey," "Oakville," "Mississippi Moonshine," "Trees in the Wind," "Hothouse," "True History of Squire Jonathan. . . .," "Knitters in the Sun."

FLAGG, FANNIE. Born Sept. 21, 1944 in Birmingham, AL. Attended Pittsburgh Playhouse. Debut 1963 OB in "Just for Opening," followed by "Patio/-Porch," "Come Back to the 5 & Dime, Jimmy Dean," Bdwy 1980 in "The Best Little Whorehouse in Texas."

FLAGG, TOM. Born Mar. 30, 1949 in Canton, OH. Attended Kent State U., AADA. Debut 1975 OB in "The Fantasticks," followed by "Give Me Liberty," "The Subject Was Roses," Bdwy in "Legend," "Shenandoah," "Players."

FLANAGAN, PAULINE. Born June 29, 1925 in Sligo, Ire. Debut 1958 OB in "Ulysses in Nighttown," followed by "Pictures in the Hallway," "Later," "Antigone," "The Crucible," "The Plough and the Stars," "Summer," "Close of Play," Bdwy in "God and Kate Murphy," "The Living Room," "The Innocents," "The Father."

FLEISCHMAN, MARK. Born Nov. 25, 1935 in Detroit, MI. Attended UMi. Bdwy debut 1955 in "Tonight in Samarkand," followed by "A Distant Bell," "The Royal Family," OB in "What Every Woman Knows," "Lute Song," "The Beautiful People," "Big Fish, Little Fish," "Incident at Vichy."

FLOREK, DAVE. Born May 19, 1953 in Dearborn, MI. Graduate Eastern MiU. Debut 1976 OB in "The Collection," followed by "Richard III," "Much Ado about Nothing," Bdwy 1980 in "Nuts."

FLORES, CECILIA. Born Sept. 6, 1949 in San Antonio, TX. Graduate Trinity U. Bdwy debut 1981 in "Animals."

FOGARTY, MARY. Born in Manchester, NH. Debut 1959 OB in "The Well of Saints," followed by "Shadow and Substance," "Nathan, the Wise," "Bonjour La Bonjour," Bdwy in "The National Health," "Watch on the Rhine" (1980), "Of the Fields Lately."

FORD, BARRY. Born Mar. 27, 1933 in Oakland, CA. Graduate CaStateU. Debut 1972 OB in "Ruddigore," followed by "The Devil's Disciple."

FORD, BETTE. Born in McKeesport, PA. Attended UMx. Bdwy debut 1952 in "First Lady," followed by "Pal Joey" ('52), "Romantic Comedy," OB in "Threepenny Opera."

Herb Foster

Diane Fratantoni

Robert Fox

Yvette Freeman

Bryant Fraser

FORD, CLEBERT. Born Jan. 29, 1932 in Brooklyn, NY. Graduate CCNY, Boston U. Bdwy debut 1960 in "The Cool World," followed by "Les Blancs," "Ain't Supposed to Die a Natural Death," "Via Galactica," "Bubbling Brown Sugar," "The Last Minstrel Show," OB in "Romeo and Juliet," "Antony and Cleopatra," "Ti-Jean and His Brothers," "The Blacks," "Ballad for Bimshire," "Daddy," "Gilbeau," "Coriolanus," "Before the Flood," "The Lion and the Jewel," "Branches from the Same Tree."

FORD, SUZANNE. Born Sept. 22, 1949 in Auburn, NY. Attended Ithaca Col., Eastman Sch. Debut 1973 OB in "Fashion," followed by "El Grande de Coca-Cola," "Tenderloin," "A Man Between Twilights."

FORSYTHE, HENDERSON. Born Sept. 11, 1917 in Macon, MO. Attended UIowa. OB in "The Iceman Cometh," "The Collection," "The Room," "A Slight Ache," "Happiness Cage," "Waiting for Godot," "In Case of Accident," "Not I" (LC), "An Evening with the Poet-Senator," "Museum," "How Far Is It to Babylon?," Bdwy in "The Cellar and the Well," "Miss LonelyHearts," "Who's Afraid of Virginia Woolf?," "Malcolm," "Right Honourable Gentleman," "Delicate Balance," "Birthday Party," "Harvey," "Engagement Baby," "Freedom of the City," "Texas Trilogy," "The Best Little Whorehouse in Texas."

FOSTER, FRANCES. Born June 11 in Yonkers, NY. Bdwy debut 1955 in "The Western Trees," followed by "Nobody Loves an Albatross," "Raisin in the Sun," "The River Niger," "First Breeze of Summer," OB in "Take a Giant Step," "Edge of the City," "Tammy and the Doctor," "The Crucible," "Happy Ending," "Day of Absence," "An Evening of One Acts," "Man Better Man," "Brotherhood," "Akokawe," "Rosalee Pritchett," "Sty of the Blind Pig," "Ballet Behind the Bridge," "Good Woman of Setzuan" (LC), "Behold! Cometh the Vanderkellans," "Orrin," "Boesman and Lena," "Do Lord Remember Me," "Nevis Mountain Dew," "Daughters of the Mock," "Big City Blues," "Zooman and the Sign."

FOSTER, GLORIA. Born Nov. 15, 1936 in Chicago, IL. Attended IllState U. Goodman Th. Debut 1963 OB in "In White America," followed by "Medea" for which she received a Theatre World Award, "Yerma," "A Hand Is on the Gate," "Black Visions," "The Cherry Orchard," "Agamemnon," "Coriolanus," "Mother Courage," "A Long Day's Journey into Night."

FOSTER, HERBERT. Born May 14, 1936 in Winnipeg, Can. Debut 1967 OB in "The Imaginary Invalid," "A Touch of the Poet," "Tonight at 8:30," "Papers," "Henry V," "Playboy of the Western World," "Good Woman of Setzuan," "Scenes from American Life," "Mary Stuart."

FOX, COLIN. Born Nov. 20, 1938 in Aldershot, Can. Attended UWestern Ontario. Bdwy debut 1968 in "Soldiers," OB in "The Importance of Being Earnest," "Declassee."

FOX, ROBERT. (Formerly Bacigalupi) Born Oct. 21, 1949 in San Francisco, CA. Juilliard graduate. Bdwy debut 1975 in "The Robber Bridegroom," followed by "Camelot," OB in "Edward II," "The Time of Your Life," "Mother Courage," "King Lear."

FRANCIS, ARLENE. Born Oct. 20, 1908 in Boston, MA. Attended Finch Col. Bdwy debut 1936 in "Horse Eats Hat," followed by "The Women," "All That Glitters," "Michael Drops In," "Journey to Jerusalem," "The Doughgirls," "The Overtons," "The French Touch," "Cup of Trembling," "My Name is Aquilon," "Metropole," "Little Blue Light," "Late Love," "Once More with Feeling," "Beekman Place," "Mrs. Dally," "Dinner at 8," "Gigi," "Don't Call Back," OB in "Don Juan in Hell."

FRANKFATHER, WILLIAM. Born Aug. 4, 1944 in Kermit, TX. Graduate NMexStateU., Stanford U. Bdwy debut 1980 in "Children of a Lesser God."

FRANKLIN, NANCY. Born in NYC. Debut 1959 OB in "Buffalo Skinner," followed by "Power of Darkness," "Oh, Dad, Poor Dad. . . .," "Theatre of Peretz," "Seven Days of Mourning," "Here Be Dragons," "Beach Children," "Safe Place," "Innocent Pleasures," "The Loves of Cass McGuire," Bdwy in "Never Live over a Pretzel Factory," "Happily Never After," "The White House," "Charlie and Algernon."

FRANZ, ELIZABETH. Born June 18, 1941 in Akron, OH. Attended AADA. Debut 1965 OB in "In White America," followed by "One Night Stands of a Noisy Passenger," "The Real Inspector Hound," "Augusta," "Yesterday Is Over," Bdwy in "Rosencrantz and Guildenstern Are Dead," "The Cherry Orchard."

FRANZ, JOY. Born in 1944 in Modesto, CA. Graduate UMo. Debut 1969 OB in "Of Thee I Sing," followed by "Jacques Brel Is Alive . . .," "Out of This World," "Curtains," "I Can't Keep Running in Place," Bdwy in "Sweet Charity," "Lysistrata," "A Little Night Music," "Pippin," "Musical Chairs."

FRASER, ALISON. Born July 8, 1955 in Natick, MA. Attended Carnegie-Mellon U., Boston Consv. Debut 1979 OB in "In Trousers," followed by "March of the Falsettos."

FRASER, BRYANT. Born Feb. 10, 1955 in Newark, NJ. Attended ForhamU. Bdwy debut 1962 in "Oliver" followed by "Poor Bitos," "Child's Play," "The Yearling," "Our Town" (1969), OB in "Vestigial Parts," "Love's Labour's Lost."

FRATANTONI, DIANE. Born Mar. 29, 1956 in Wilmington, DE. Bdwy debut 1979 in "A Chorus Line."

FREEMAN, AL, JR. Born Mar. 21, 1934 in San Antonio, TX. Attended CCLA. Bdwy in "The Long Dream" ('60), "Tiger, Tiger Burning Bright," "Living Premise," "Blues for Mr. Charlie," "Dozens," "Look to the Lilies," OB in "Slave," "Dutchman," "Trumpets of the Lord," "Medea," "The Great McDaddy," "One Crack Out," "A Long Day's Journey into Night."

FREEMAN, MORGAN. Born June 1, 1937 in Memphis, TN. Attended LACC. Bdwy bow 1967 in "Hello, Dolly!" followed by "The Mighty Gents," OB in "Ostrich Feathers," "Niggerlovers," "Exhibition," "Black Visions," "Cockfight," "White Pelicans," "Julius Caesar," "Coriolanus," "Mother Courage," "The Connection."

FREEMAN, YVETTE. Born Oct. 1, 1950 in Chester, PA. Graduate UDel. Debut 1976 OB in "Let My People Come," Bdwy 1979 in "Ain't Misbehavin'."

FRELICH, PHYLLIS. Born Feb. 29, 1944 in NDakota. Graduate Gallaudet Col. Bdwy debut 1970 in Ntl. Theatre of the Deaf's "Songs from Milkwood," followed by "Children of a Lesser God," OB in "Poets from the Inside."

FRENCH, ARTHUR. Born in NYC. Attended Brooklyn Col. Debut 1962 OB in "Raisin' Hell in the Sun," followed by "Ballad of Bimshire," "Day of Absence," "Happy Ending," "Jonah," "Black Girl," "Ceremonies in Dark Old Men," "An Evening of One Acts," "Man Better Man," "Brotherhood," "Perry's Mission," "Rosalee Pritchett," "Moonlight Arms," "Dark Tower," "Brownsville Raid," "Nevis Mt. Dew," "Julius Caesar," "Friends," "Court of Miracles," Bdwy in "Ain't Supposed to Die a Natural Death," "The Iceman Cometh," "All God's Chillun Got Wings."

FRENCH, ARTHUR W. III. Born Apr. 30, 1965 in NYC. Debut OB 1971 in "Black Girl," followed by "Branches from the Same Tree."

FRENCH, EDWARD EMERSON. Born Apr. 17, 1951 in Boston, MA. Attended HB Studio. Debut 1980 OB in "The Devil's Disciple."

FRENCH, VALERIE. Born in London, Eng. Bdwy debut 1965 in "Inadmissible Evidence," followed by "Help Stamp Out Marriage," "Mother Lover," "Children, Children," OB in "Tea Party," "Trelawny of the Wells," "Studs Edsel," "Henry V," "John Gabriel Borkman," "Fallen Angels," "A Taste of Honey."

FREY, LEONARD. Born Sept. 4, 1938 in Brooklyn, NY. Attended Cooper Union, Neighborhood Playhouse. OB in "Little Mary Sunshine," "Funny House of a Negro," "Coach with Six Insides," "Boys in the Band," "The Time of Your Life," "Beggar on Horseback," "People Are Living There," "Twelfth Night," "Troilus and Cressida," Bdwy in "Fiddler on the Roof," "The National Health," "Knock Knock," "Kurt Weill Cabaret," "The Man Who Came to Dinner."

FRIDAY, BETSY. Born Apr. 30, 1958 in Chapel Hill, NC. Graduate NC Sch. of Arts. Bdwy debut 1980 in "The Best Little Whorehouse in Texas," followed by "Bring Back Birdie."

FRIEDMAN, PETER. Born Apr. 24, 1949 in NYC. Debut 1971 OB in "James Joyce Memorial Liquid Theatre," followed by "Big and Little," Bdwy in "The Visit," "Chemin de Fer," "Love for Love," "Rules of the Game," "Piaf."

FULLER, JANICE. Born June 4 in Oakland, CA. Attended RADA. Debut OB 1975 in "Ice Age," followed by "A Night at the Black Pig," "Grand Magic," "Marching to Georgia."

GABLE, JUNE. Born June 5, 1945 in NYC. Carnegie Tech graduate. OB in "Macbird," "Jacques Brel Is Alive and Well . . .," "A Day in the Life of Just About Everyone," "Mod Donna," "Wanted," "Lady Audley's Secret," "Comedy of Errors," "Chinchilla," "Star Treatment," "Coming Attractions," Bdwy in "Candide" (1974).

GAEBLER, MARY. Born May 4, 1951 in Davenport, IA. Graduate UWi., Oxford U. Bdwy debut 1980 in "The Music Man."

GAINES, BOYD. Born May 11, 1953 in Atlanta, GA. Juilliard graduate. Debut 1978 OB in "Spring Awakening," followed by "A Month in the Country" for which he received a Theatre World Award, BAM Theatre Co.'s "Winter's Tale," "The Barbarians," and "Johnny On a Spot," "Vikings."

GALARNO, BILL. Born Mar. 1, 1938 in Saginaw, MI. Attended Pittsburgh Playhouse. Debut 1962 OB in "Nathan the Wise," followed by "Pantagleize," "The Sound of Music," "Candide."

GALLAGHER, HELEN. Born in 1926 in Brooklyn, NY. Bdwy debut 1947 in "Seven Lively Arts," followed by "Mr. Strauss Goes to Boston," "Billion Dollar Baby," "Brigadoon," "High Button Shoes," "Touch and Go," "Make a Wish," "Pal Joey," "Guys and Dolls," "Finian's Rainbow," "Oklahoma!," "Pajama Game," "Bus Stop," "Portofino," "Sweet Charity," "Mame," "Cry for Us All," "No, No, Nanette," "A Broadway Musical," OB in "Hothouse," "Tickles by Tucholsky," "The Misanthrope," "I Can't Keep Running in Place."

GALLOGLY, JOHN. Born Aug. 23, 1952 in Providence, RI. Attended UNotre Dame. Debut OB 1975 in "Gorky," followed by "The Gathering," "The Meehans," Bdwy in "Runaways," "The Utter Glory of Morrissey Hall," "A Stitch in Time."

GARBER, VICTOR. Born Mar. 16, 1949 in London, Can. Debut 1973 OB in "Ghosts" for which he received a Theatre World Award, followed by "Joe's Opera," "Cracks," Bdwy in "Tartuffe," "Deathtrap," "Sweeney Todd," "They're Playing Our Song."

GARFIELD, DAVID. Born Feb. 6, 1941 in Brooklyn, NY. Graduate Columbia, Cornell. OB in "Hang Down Your Head and Die," "The Government Inspector," "Old Ones," "Family Business," "Ralph Roister Doister," Bdwy in "Fiddler on the Roof," "Rothschilds."

GARFIELD, JULIE. Born Jan. 10, 1946 in Los Angeles, CA. Attended UWi., Neighborhood Playhouse. Debut 1969 OB in "honest-to-God Schnozzola," followed by "East Lynne," "The Sea," "Uncle Vanya" for which she received a Theatre World Award," "Me and Molly," "Chekhov Sketchbook," Bdwy in "The Good Doctor," "Death of a Salesman," "The Merchant."

GARLAND, JAMIL K. Born Oct. 19, 1951 in Shreveport, LA. Attended Laney Col., UCal. Bdwy debut 1980 in "Your Arms Too Short to Box with God," OB in "Macbeth," "Helen," "Miss Truth," "Raisin."

GARNETT, CHIP. Born May 8, 1953 in New Kensington, PA. Attended IndU. Debut 1973 OB in "Inner City," followed by "Rhapsody in Gershwin," Bdwy in "Candide," "Bubbling Brown Sugar" for which he received a Theatre World Award.

GARRETT, TOM. Born Mar. 1, 1949 in Panama City, FL. Graduate FlStateU. Bdwy debut 1978 in "Hello, Dolly!," followed by "The Music Man."

GARRICK, BEULAH. Born Jun 12, 1921 in Notthigham, Eng. Bdwy debut 1959 in "Shadow and Substance," followed by "Auntie Mame," "Juno," "Little Moon of Alban," "High Spirits," "The Hostage," "Funny Girl," "Lovers," "Abelard and Heloise," "Ulysses in Nighttown," "Copperfield," OB in "Little Boxes," "Berkeley Square," "Fallen Angels."

GARRISON, DAVID. Born June 30, 1952 in Long Branch, NJ. Graduate Boston U. Debut in "Joseph and the Amazing Technicolor Dreamcoat," followed by "Living at Home," Bdwy in "A History of the American Film," "A Day in Hollywood/A Night in the Ukraine."

GARTIN, CHRISTOPHER. Born Jan. 12, 1968 in NYC. Debut 1981 OB in "The Buddy System."

GARZA, TROY. Born Aug. 20, 1954 in Hollywood, CA. Attended RADA. Bdwy debut 1977 in "A Chorus Line," followed by "Got Tu Go Disco," OB in "Fourtune," "Paris Lights."

GAVON, IGORS. Born Nov. 14, 1937 in Latvia. Bdwy bow 1961 in "Carnival," followed by "Hello, Dolly!," "Marat/deSade," "Billy," "Sugar," "Mack and Mabel," "Musical Jubilee," "Strider," OB in "Your Own Thing," "Promenade," "Exchange," "Nevertheless They Laugh," "Polly," "The Boss," "Biography: A Game," "Murder in the Cathedral."

GEFFNER, DEBORAH. Born Aug. 26, 1952 in Pittsburgh, PA. Attended Juilliard, HB Studio. Debut 1978 OB in "Tenderloin," Bdwy in "Pal Joey," "A Chorus Line."

GELKE, BECKY. Born Feb. 17, 1953 in Ft. Knox, KY. Graduate Western Ky.U. Debut 1978 OB and Bdwy in "The Best Little Whorehouse in Texas."

GENEST, EDMOND. Born Oct. 27, 1943 in Boston, MA. Attended Suffolk U. Debut 1972 OB in "The Real Inspector Hound," Bdwy in "Dirty Linen/New-Found-Land," "Whose Life Is It Anyway?" "Onward Victoria."

GERACI, FRANK. Born Sept. 8, 1939 in Brooklyn, NY. Attended Yale, HB Studio. Debut 1961 OB in "Color of Darkness," followed by "Mr. Grossman," "Balm in Gilead," "The Fantasticks," "Tom Paine," "End of All Things Natural," "Union Street," "Uncle Vanya," "Success Story," Bdwy in "Love and Suicide at Schofield Barracks."

GERROLL, DANIEL. Born Oct. 16, 1951 in London, Eng. Attended Central Sch. of Speech. Debut 1980 OB in "The Slab Boys," followed by "Knuckle" and "Translations" for which he received a Theatre World Award.

GETER, JOHN. Born Sept. 22, 1957 in Wenoka, OK. Graduate Hanover Col. Debut 1980 OB in "The Diviners," Bdwy 1980 in "Gemini."

GHOSTLEY, ALICE. Born Aug. 14, 1926 in Eve, MO. Attended UOkla. Bdwy debut in "New Faces of 1952," followed by "Sandhog," "Livin' the Life," "Trouble in Tahiti," "Shangri-La," "Maybe Tuesday," "Thurber Carnival," "The Beauty Part," "The Sign in Sidney Brustein's Window," "Love Is a Ball," "Annie."

GIANNINI, CHERYL. Born June 15 in Monessen, PA. Bdwy debut 1980 in "The Suicide."

GIBSON, KAREN. Born Jan. 9 in Columbus, OH. Attended OhStateU. Debut 1975 OB in "The Three Musketeers," followed by Bdwy in "My Fair Lady" ('76), "On the 20th Century," "The Utter Glory of Morrissey Hall," "Onward Victoria."

GILBERT, RONNIE. Born Sept. 7 in NYC. Bdwy debut 1968 in "The Man in the Glass Booth," OB in "America Hurrah," "Hector the Heroic," "Hot Buttered Roll," "Viet Rock," "Tourists and Refugees."

GILL, TERI. Born July 16, 1954 in Long Island City, NY. Graduate USIU. Bdwy debut 1976 in "Going Up," followed by "Evita," OB in "Allegro."

GILLETTE, ANITA. Born Aug. 16, 1938 in Baltimore, MD. Debut 1960 OB in "Russell Patterson's Sketchbook" for which she received a Theatre World Award, followed by "Rich and Famous," Bdwy in "Carnival," "All American," "Mr. President," "Guys and Dolls," "Don't Drink the Water," "Cabaret," "Jimmy," "Chapter Two," "They're Playing Our Song."

GILPIN, JACK. Born May 31, 1951 in Boyce, VA. Harvard graduate. Debut 1976 OB in "Goodbye and Keep Cold," followed by "Shay," "The Soft Touch," "Beyond Therapy," Bdwy in "Lunch Hour" ('80).

GINTER, LINDSEY. Born Dec. 13, 1950 in Alameda, CA. Attended UPacific. Debut 1980 OB in "Hamlet," followed by "Mary Stuart," "A Tale Told."

GIOMBETTI, KAREN. Born May 24, 1955 in Scranton, PA. Graduate NYU. Debut 1978 in "Stop the World, I Want to Get Off," Bdwy 1979 in "The Most Happy Fella," "Woman of the Year."

GIRARDEAU, FRANK. Born Oct. 19, 1942 in Beaumont, TX. Attended Rider Col., HB Studio. Debut 1972 OB in "22 Years," followed by "The Soldier," "Hughie," "An American Story," "El Hermano."

GLANVILLE, MAXWELL. Born Feb. 11, 1918 in Antigua, BWI. Attended New School. Bdwy debut 1946 in "Walk Hard," followed by "Anna Lucasta," "How Long Till Summer," "Freight," "Autumn Garden," "Take a Giant Step," "Cat on a Hot Tin Roof," "Simply Heavenly," "Interlock," "Cool World," "The Shrike," "Golden Boy," "We Bombed in New Haven," "Zelda," OB in "The Blacks," "Nat Turner," "Simple," "Lady Day," "Penance," "Anna Lucasta," "Branches from the Same Tree."

GLOVER, JOHN. Born Aug. 7, 1944 in Kingston, NY. Attended Towson State Col. Debut 1969 OB in "A Scent of Flowers," followed by "Government Inspector," "Rebel Women," "Treats," Bdwy in "The Selling of the President," "Great God Brown," "Don Juan," "The Visit," "Chemin de Fer," "Holiday," "The Importance of Being Earnest," "Frankenstein."

GLYNN, CARLIN. Born Feb. 19, 1940 in Cleveland, OH. Attended Sophie Newcomb Col., Actors Studio. Debut 1959 OB in "Waltz of the Toreadors," followed by "Cassatt," Bdwy debut 1978 in "The Best Little Whorehouse in Texas" for which she received a Theatre World Award.

GODFREY, LYNNIE. Born Sept. 11, 1952 in NYC. Hunter Col. graduate. Debut 1976 OB in "I Paid My Dues," Bdwy 1978 in "Eubie!"

GOLD, JULIANNE. Born June 18, 1960 in Rochester, MN. Attended CaStateU. Bdwy debut 1980 in "Children of a Lesser God."

GOLD, RUSSELL. Born Oct. 23, 1917 in New Britain, CT. Attended Pasadena Playhouse, AmThWing. Bdwy debut 1948 in "Harvey," followed by "Romeo and Juliet," "Point of No Return," "Dear Charles," "Little Foxes," "Amadeus," OB in "Royal Gambit," "The Prodigal," "Rendezvous at Senlis," "Place for Chance," "Corruption in the Palace of Justice," "Winterset."

GOLDBLUM, JEFF. Born Oct. 22, 1952 in Pittsburgh, PA. Attended Neighborhood Playhouse. Debut 1971 on Bdwy in "Two Gentlemen of Verona," followed by "Moony Shapiro Songbook," OB in "El Grande de Coca-Cola," "Our Late Night," "City Sugar."

GOLDSMITH, MERWIN. Born Aug. 7, 1937 in Detroit, MI. Graduate UCLA, Old Vic. Bdwy debut 1970 in "Minnie's Boys," followed by "The Visit," "Chemin de Fer," "Rex," "Dirty Linen," "The 1940's Radio Show," OB in "Hamlet as a Happening," "Chickencoop Chinaman," "Wanted," "Comedy," "Rubbers," "Yankees 3, Detroit 0," "Trelawny of the Wells," "Chinchilla," "Real Life Funnies."

GOLDSTEIN, LESLIE. Born Jan. 22, 1940 in Newark, NJ. Graduate Newark Col. Debut 1976 OB in "Men in White," followed by "Native Bird," "Antigone," "The Lover," "Middle of the Night," "Second Avenue Rag," "Darkness at Noon," Bdwy 1979 in "Meeting by the River."

GOLONKA, ARLENE. Born Jan. 23, 1938 in Chicago, IL. Attended Goodman Theatre, Actors Studio. Bdwy debut 1958 in "Night Circus," followed by "Take Me Along," "Come Blow Your Horn," "Ready When You Are, C. B.," "One Flew Over the Cuckoo's Nest," "I Won't Dance," OB in "Ladies of the Alamo."

GOODMAN, JOHN. Born June 20, 1952 in St. Louis, MO. Graduate Southwest MoStateU. Debut 1978 OB in "A Midsummer Night's Dream," followed by "The Chisholm Trail."

GOODMAN, ROBYN. Born Aug. 24, 1947 in NYC. Graduate Brandeis U. Debut 1973 OB in "When You Comin' Back, Red Ryder?," followed by "Richard III," "Museum," "Bits and Pieces," "Fishing."

GOODRUM, JOHN MICHAEL. Born. Nov. 22, 1953 in Stuttgart, Ger. Graduate UMd. Debut 1980 OB in "Friend of the Family."

GORBEA, CARLOS. Born July 3, 1938 in Santurce, PR. Graduate Fordham U. Bdwy debut 1964 in "West Side Story," followed by "Fiddler on the Roof," "Cabaret," "Candide," "Evita," OB in "Time of Storm," "Theatre in the Street."

GORDON, CARL. Born Jan. 20, 1932 in Richmond, VA. Bdwy 1966 in "The Great White Hope," followed by "Ain't Supposed to Die a Natural Death," OB in "Day of Absence," "Happy Ending," "The Strong Breed," "Trials of Brother Jero," "Kongi's Harvest," "Welcome to Black River," "Shark," "Orrin and Sugar Mouth," "A Love Play," "The Great MacDaddy," "In an Upstate Motel," "Zooman and the Sign."

GORDON, KEITH. Born Feb. 3, 1961 in NYC. Debut 1976 OB in "Secrets of the Rich," followed by "A Traveling Companion," "Suckers," "Gimme Shelter," "Sunday Runners," "Album," "The Buddy System."

GORRILL, MAGGY. Born Feb. 19, 1952 in Long Island City, NY. Attended Barnard Col. Debut 1975 OB in "Diamond Studs," followed by Bdwy in "Dr. Jazz," "A Broadway Musical," "Peter Pan."

John Gallogly   **Teri Gill**   **Carl Gordon**   **Rebecca Guy**   **Cris Groenendaal**

GOSSETT, ROBERT. Born Mar. 3, 1954 in The Bronx, NY. Attended AADA. Debut 1973 OB in "One Flew over the Cuckoo's Nest," followed by "The Amen Corner," "Weep Not for Me."

GOTLIEB, BEN. Born June 27, 1954 in Kfar Saba, Israel. Attended RADA, CUNY/Brooklyn Col. Bdwy debut 1979 in "Dogg's Hamlet and Cahoot's Macbeth," OB in "Kohlhass," "Relatively Speaking."

GOTTLEIB, MATTHEW. Born Apr. 6, 1951 in Ann Arbor, MI. Graduate CaInstofArts. Debut 1980 OB in "Friend of the Family."

GOULD, ELEANOR CODY. Born in Bradford, PA. Attended Elkins Col., AADA where she became a teacher. Returned to stage 1975 OB in "Ice Age," followed by "The Front Page."

GOULD, ELLEN. Born Dec. 30, 1950 in Worcester, MA. Graduate Brandeis U, NYU. Debut 1979 OB in "Confessions of a Reformed Romantic," followed by "Gewandter Songs," "Three Irish No Plays," "Yeats Trio," "Heat of Reentry," Bdwy in "Macbeth" ('81).

GOULD, GORDON. Born May 4, 1930 in Chicago, IL. Yale Graduate. With APA in "Man and Superman," "War and Peace," "Judith," "Lower Depths," "Right You Are," "Scapin," "Impromptu at Versailles," "You Can't Take It With You," "The Hostage," "The Tavern," "A Midsummer Night's Dream," "Merchant of Venice," "Richard II," "Much Ado About Nothing," "Wild Duck," "The Show-Off," and "Pantagleize," "Strider," Bdwy in "Freedom of the City," "Amadeus."

GOULD, HAROLD. Born Dec. 10, 1923 in Schenectady, NY. Graduate SUNY, Cornell. Debut 1969 OB in "The Increased Difficulty of Concentration," followed by "Amphitryon," "House of Blue Leaves," "Touching Bottom," Bdwy 1981 in "Fools."

GOZ, HARRY. Born June 23, 1932 in St. Louis, MO. Attended St. Louis Inst. Debut 1957 in "Utopia Limited," followed by "Bajour," "Fiddler on the Roof," "Two by Two," "Prisoner of Second Avenue," OB in "To Bury a Cousin."

GRAAE, JASON. Born May 15, 1958 in Chicago, IL. Graduate Cincinnati Consv. Debut 1981 OB in "Godspell."

GRAHAM, DANIEL. Born July 2, 1948 in Tampa, FL. Graduate Pittsburgh Playhouse. Debut 1972 OB in "Sweet Feet," followed by "The Devil's Disciple."

GRAHAM, DONNA. Born Sept, 28, 1964 in Philadelphia, PA. Bdwy debut 1977 in "Annie."

GRAMMIS, ADAM. Born Dec. 8, 1947 in Allentown, PA. Graduate Kutztown State Col. Bdwy debut 1971 in "Wild and Wonderful," followed by "Shirley MacLaine Show," "A Chorus Line," OB in "Dance Continuum," "Joseph and the Amazing Technicolor Dreamcoat."

GRANGER, FARLEY. Born July 1, 1928 in San Jose, CA. Bdwy debut 1959 in "First Impressions," followed by "The Warm Peninsula," "Advise and Consent," CC's "The King and I" and "Brigadoon," "The Seagull," "The Crucible," "Deathtrap," OB in "The Carefree Tree," "A Month in the Country."

GRANT, BYRON. Born June 14, 1936 in Columbus, GA. Graduate Huntingdon Col., Southern Il.U., AMDA. Debut 1978 OB in "Gay Divorce," followed by "Sound of Music" (JB).

GRANT, DAVID MARSHALL. Born June 21, 1955 in New Haven, CT. Attended ConnCol., Yale. Debut OB 1978 in "Sganarelle," follwed by "Table Settings," Bdwy in "Bent" ('79), "The Survivor."

GRAY, SAM. Born July 18, 1923 in Chicago, Il. Graduate Columbia U. Bdwy debut 1955 in "Deadfall," followed by "Six Fingers in a Five Finger Glove," "Saturday, Sunday, Monday," "Golda," OB in "Ascent of F-6," "Family Portrait," "One Tiger on a Hill," "Shadow of Heroes," "The Recruiting Officer," "The Wild Duck," "Jungle of Cities."

GREENBERG, MITCHELL. Born Sept. 19, 1950 in Brooklyn, NY. Graduate Harpur Col., Neighborhood Playhouse. Debut 1979 OB in "Two Grown Men," followed by "Scrambled Feet," Bdwy in "A Day in Hollywood, A Night in the Ukraine." ('80), "Can-Can" ('81).

GREENE, ADDISON. Born Dec. 10 in Baltimore, MD. Debut 1981 OB in "Things of the Heart."

GREENE, ELLEN. Born Feb. 22 in NYC. Attended Ryder Col. Debut 1973 in "Rachel Lily Rosenbloom," followed OB by "In the Boom Boom Room," "Threepenny Opera," "The Nature and Purpose of the Universe," "Teeth 'n' Smiles," "The Sorrows of Stephen," "Disrobing the Bride."

GREENE, GAYLE. Born Jan. 22, 1948 in NYC. Graduate Carnegie Tech. Debut 1975 OB in "The Love Death Plays of William Inge," followed by "Secrets Thighs of New England Women," "The Incognita."

GREENE, JAMES. Born Dec. 1, 1926 in Lawrence, MA. Graduate Emerson Col. OB in "The Iceman Cometh," "American Gothic," "The King and the Duke," "The Hostage," "Plays for Bleecker Street," "Moon in the Yellow River," "Misalliance," "Government Inspector," "Baba Goya," LCRep 2 years, "You Can't Take It With You," "School for Scandal," "Wild Duck," "Right You Are," "The Show-Off," "Pantagleize," "Festival of Short Plays," "Nourish the Beast," "One Crack Out," "Artichoke," "Othello," "Salt Lake City Skyline," "Summer," "The Rope Dancers," Bdwy in "Romeo and Juliet," "Girl on the Via Flaminia," "Compulsion," "Inherit the Wind," "Shadow of a Gunman," "Andersonville Trial," "Night Life," "School for Wives," "Ring Round the Bathtub," "Great God Brown," "Don Juan."

GREENE, RICHARD. Born Jan. 8, 1946 in Miami, FL. Graduate FlAtlanticU. Debut 1971 OB in "Macbeth," followed by "Play Strindberg," "Mary Stuart," "The Crucible," "Family Business," Bdwy in "Romeo and Juliet" ('77), "The Survivor."

GRIFFITH, KRISTIN. Born Sept. 7, 1953 in Odessa, TX. Juilliard graduate. Bdwy debut 1976 in "A Texas Trilogy," OB in "Rib Cage," "Character Lines," "3 Friends/2 Rooms," "A Month in the Country," "Fables for Friends," "The Trading Post," "Marching to Georgia."

GRIMES, TAMMY. Born Jan. 30, 1934 in Lynn, MA. Attended Stephens Col., Neighborhood Playhouse. Debut 1956 OB in "The Littlest Revue," followed by "Clerambard," "Molly," "Trick," "Are You Now or Have You Ever Been," "Father's Day," "A Month in the Country," Bdwy in "Look After Lulu" (1959) for which she received a Theatre World Award, "The Unsinkable Molly Brown," "Rattle of a Simple Man," "High Spirits," "The Only Game in Town" "Private Lives," "Musical Jubilee," "California Suite," "Tartuffe," "42nd Street."

GROENENDAAL, CRIS. Born Feb. 17, 1948 in Erie, PA. Attended Allegheny Col., Exeter (Eng) U, HB Studio. Bdwy debut 1979 in "Sweeney Todd."

GROENER, HARRY. Born Sept. 10, 1951 in Augsburg, Ger. Graduate UWash. Bdwy debut 1979 in "Oklahoma!" for which he received a Theatre World Award.

GROSS, MICHAEL. Born in 1947 in Chicago, IL. UIll and Yale graduate. Debut 1978 OB in "Sganarelle," followed by "Othello," "Endgame," "The Wild Duck," "Oedipus the King," "Put Them All Together," Bdwy in "Bent." ('79,) "The Philadelphia Story."

GUARDINO, HARRY. Born Dec. 23, 1925 in NYC. Credits include "End as a Man," "A Hatful of Rain," "Natural Affection," "Anyone Can Whistle," "The Rose Tattoo"('66), "The Seven Descents of Myrtle," "Woman of the Year."

GUIDA, MARIA. Born May 1, 1953 in Jackson Heights, NY. Graduate NYU. Debut 1972 OB in "Bread and Roses," followed by "Fallen Angels," "Impromptu," "Dutchman," "Pirates of Penzance," Bdwy in "King of Hearts."

GUIDALL, GEORGE. Born June 7, 1938 in Plainfield, NJ. Attended UBuffalo, AADA. Bdwy debut 1969 in "Wrong Way Light Bulb," followed by "Cold Storage," OB in "Counsellor-at-Law," "Taming of the Shrew," "All's Well That Ends Well," "The Art of Dining," "Biography," "After All."

GUNTON, BOB. Born Nov. 15, 1945 in Santa Monica, CA. Attended UCal. Debut 1971 OB in "Who Am I?," followed by "The Kid," "Desperate Hours," "Tip-Toes," Bdwy in "Happy End" (1977), "Working," "King of Hearts," "Evita."

GURRY, ERIC. Born Dec. 14, 1966 in NYC. Debut 1980 OB in "Table Settings," followed by "The Floating Light Bulb."

GUSKIN, HAROLD. Born May 25, 1941 in Brooklyn, NY. Graduate Rutgers U, Ind. U. Debut 1980 OB in "Second Avenue Rag," followed by "Grand Street."

GUY, REBECCA. Born June 19, 1953 in Gary, IN. Graduate UEvansville, Juilliard. Debut 1978 OB in "Spring Awakening," followed by "Between Daylight and Boonville."

HADARY, JONATHAN. Born Oct. 11, 1948 in Chicago, IL. Attended Tufts U. Debut 1974 OB in "White Nights," followed by "El Grande de Coca-Cola," "Songs from Pins and Needles," "God Bless You, Mr. Rosewater," "Pushing 30," "Scrambled Feet," "Coming Attractions," Bdwy 1977 in "Gemini" (also OB).

HADDOW, JEFFREY. Born Oct. 8, 1947 in NYC. Northwestern U. graduate. Debut 1979 OB in "Scrambled Feet."

HALL, CHARLES. Born Nov. 12, 1951 in Frankfort, KY. Graduate Murray State U. Debut 1977 OB in "Molly's Dream," followed by "Sheridan Square," "The Doctor in Spite of Himself," Bdwy 1979 in "Snow White."

| Marilyn Hamlin | Ben Halley, Jr. | Niki Harris | James Harter | Carliss Hayden |

HALL, GEORGE. Born Nov. 19, 1916 in Toronto, Can. Attended Neighborhood Playhouse. Bdwy bow 1946 in "Call Me Mister," followed by "Lend an Ear," "Touch and Go," "Live Wire," "The Boy Friend," "There's a Girl in My Soup," "An Evening with Richard Nixon . . .," "We Interrupt This Program," "Man and Superman," "Bent," OB in "The Balcony," "Ernest in Love," "A Round with Ring," "Family Pieces," "Carousel," "The Case Against Roberta Guardino," "Mary Me! Marry Me!" "Arms and the Man," "The Old Glory," "Dancing for the Kaiser," "Casualties," "The Seagull," "A Stitch in Time," "Mary Stuart."

HALL, GRAYSON. Born in Philadelphia, PA. Attended Temple U. Debut 1953 OB in "Man and Superman," followed by "La Ronde," "Six Characters in Search of an Author," "The Balcony," "The Buskers," "The Love Nest," "Shout from the Rooftops," "The Last Analysis," "Friends and Relatives," "The Screens," "Secrets of the Citizens Correction Committee," "The Sea," "What Every Woman Knows," "Jack Gelber's New Play," "Happy End," Bdwy in "Subways Are for Sleeping," "Those That Play the Clowns," "Leaf People," "Happy End," "The Suicide."

HALLEY, BEN. JR. Born Aug. 6, 1951 in Harlen, NY. Graduate CCNY, Yale. Bdwy debut 1978 in "A History of the American Film," OB in "A Day in the Life of the Czar," "Midsummer Night's Dream," "The Recruiting Officer," "The Wild Duck," "Oedipus the King."

HALLOW, JOHN. Born Nov. 28, 1924 in NYC. Attended Neighborhood Playhouse. Bdwy bow 1954 in "Anastasia," followed by "Ross," "Visit to a Small Planet," "Foxy," "Oh, Dad, Poor Dad . . .," "Ben Franklin in Paris," "3 Bags Full," "Don't Drink the Water," "Hadrian VII," "Tough to Get Help," "Ballroom," "A New York Summer," "The Man Who Came to Dinner," OB in "Hamlet," "Do I Hear a Waltz?," "Kind Lady," "The Butler Did It."

HAMILL, MARK. Born Sept. 25, 1952 in Oakland, CA. Attended LACC. Bdwy debut 1981 in "The Elephant Man."

HAMILTON, ROGER. Born May 2, 1928 in San Diego, CA. Attended San Diego Col., RADA. OB in "Merchant of Venice," "Hamlet," "Live Like Pigs," "Hotel Passionato," "Sjt. Musgrave's Dance," Bdwy in "Someone Waiting," "Separate Tables," "Little Moon of Alban," "Luther," "The Deputy," "Rosencrantz and Guildenstern Are Dead," "The Rothschilds," "Pippin," "Happy New Year."

HAMLIN, MARILYN. Born Feb. 22, 1946 in West Frankfort, IL. Graduate Southern IIU. Bdwy debut 1970 in "Not Now Darling," OB in "The Master and Margerita," "Killings on the Last Line."

HAMMIL, JOHN. Born May 9, 1948 in NYC. Attended UCLA. Bdwy debut 1972 in "Purlie," followed by "Oh! Calcutta!," "Platinum," "They're Playing Our Song," OB in "El Grande de Coca-Cola," "Songs from the City Streets."

HAMMOND, MICHAEL. Born Apr. 30, 1951 in Clinton, IA. Graduate UIowa, LAMDA. Debut 1974 OB in "Pericles," followed by "The Merry Wives of Windsor," BAM Theatre Co.'s "A Winter's Tale," "Barbarians," "The Purging."

HANAN, STEPHEN. Born Jan. 7, 1947 in Washington, DC. Gaduate Harvard, LAMDA. Debut 1978 OB in "All's Well That Ends Well," followed by "Taming of the Shrew," Bdwy 1981 in "Pirates of Penzance."

HANKS, BARBARA. Born Sept. 1, 1951 in Salt Lake City, UT. Debut 1978 OB in "Gay Divorce," Bdwy 1979 in "Sugar Babies."

HARALDSON, MARIAN. Born Sept. 5, 1933 in Northwood, ND. Graduate St. Olaf Col. Bdwy debut 1959 in "First Impressions," followed by "The Unsinkable Molly Brown," "Mr. President," "Girl Who Came to Supper," "Merry Widow," "Walking Happy," "Dear World," "No, No, Nanette," "Lorelei," "Woman of the Year," OB in "Peace."

HARDING, JAN LESLIE. Born 1956 in Cambridge, MA. Graduate Boston U. Debut 1980 OB in "Album."

HARMAN, PAUL. Born July 29, 1952 in Mineola, NY. Graduate Tufts U. Bdwy debut 1980 in "It's So Nice to Be Civilized."

HARPER, CHARLES THOMAS. Born Mar. 29, 1949 in Carthage, NY. Graduate Webster Col. Debut 1975 OB in "Down by the River . . .," followed by "Holy Ghosts," "Hamlet," "Mary Stuart," "Twelfth Night," "The Beaver Coat."

HARPER, JAMES. Born Oct. 8, 1948 in Bell, CA. Attended Marin Col., Juilliard. Bdwy debut 1973 in "King Lear," followed by "The Robber Bridegroom," "The Time of Your Life," "Mother Courage," "Edward II," OB in "Midsummer Night's Dream," "Recruiting Officer," "The Wild Duck," "Jungle of Cities."

HARPER, ROBERT. Born May 19, 1951 in NYC. Graduate Rutgers U. Bdwy debut 1978 in "Once in a Lifetime," followed by "Inspector General," "The American Clock."

HARRELSON, HELEN. Born in Missouri; graduate Goodman Theatre. Bdwy debut 1950 in "The Cellar and the Well," followed by "Death of a Salesman," "Days in the Trees," "Romeo and Juliet," OB in "Our Town," "His and Hers," "House of Atreus," "He and She," "Missing Persons."

HARRINGTON, DELPHI. Born Aug. 26 in Chicago, IL. Northwestern U. graduate. Debut 1960 OB in "Country Scandal," followed by "Moon for the Misbegotten," "Baker's Dozen" "The Zykovs," "Character Lines," "Richie," Bdwy in "Thieves," "Everything in the Garden," "Romeo and Juliet," "Chapter 2."

HARRIS, NIKI. Born July 20, 1948 in Pittsburgh, PA. Graduate Duquesne U. Bdwy debut 1980 in "A Day in Hollywood/A Night in the Ukraine."

HARRIS, ROSEMARY. Born Sept. 19, 1930 in Ashby, Eng. Attended RADA. Bdwy debut 1952 in "Climate of Eden" for which she received a Theatre World Award, followed by "Troilus and Cressida," "Interlock," "The Disenchanted," "The Tumbler," APA's "The Tavern," "School for Scandal," "The Seagull," "The Importance of Being Earnest," "War and Peace," "Man and Superman," "Judith," and "You Can't Take It with You," "Lion in Winter," "Old Times," "Merchant of Venice," "A Streetcar Named Desire," "The Royal Family," OB in "The New York Idea," "Three Sisters," and "The Seagull."

HARRIS, STEVEN MICHAEL. (formerly Steven Michael) Born Aug. 31, 1957 in Fall River, MA. Attended Pasadena City Col., Clown Col. Bdwy debut 1980 in "Barnum."

HART, ROXANNE. Born in 1952 in Trenton, NJ. Attended Skidmore and Princeton U. Bdwy debut 1977 in "Equus," followed by "Loose Ends," OB in "Winter's Tale," "Johnny On a Spot," "The Purging," "Hedda Gabler," "Waiting for the Parade."

HARTER, JAMES. Born Nov. 8, 1945 in Bryan, OH. Graduate Pasadena Playhouse. Debut 1973 OB in "The Comedy of Errors," followed by "Doctor in the House," "Uncle Vanya," "The Miser," "Don Juan in Hell."

HARTMAN, ELEK. Born Apr. 26, 1922 in Canton, OH. Graduate Carnegie Tech, OB in "Where People Gather," "Goa," "Loyalties," "The Matchmaker," "Mirandolina," "Cassatt," Bdwy in "We Bombed in New Haven" (1968), "Angel."

HARUM, EIVIND. Born May 24, 1944 in Stavanger, Norway. Attended Utah State U. Credits include "Sophie," "Foxy," "Baker Street," "West Side Story" ('68), "A Chorus Line," "Woman of the Year."

HAUSMAN, ELAINE. Born June 8, 1949 in Sacramento, CA. Graduate UCA., Juilliard. Bdwy debut 1975 in "The Robber Bridegroom," followed by "Edward II," "The Time of Your Life," "Three Sisters," "Brigadoon."

HAVOC, JUNE. Born Nov. 8, 1916 in Seattle, WA. Bdwy debut 1936 in "Forbidden Melody," followed by "The Women," "Pal Joey," "Mexican Hayride," "Sadie Thompson," "The Ryan Girl," "Dunnigan's Daughter," "Dream Girl," "Affairs of State," "Infernal Machine," "Beaux Stratagem," "The Warm Peninsula," "Dinner at 8," "Habeas Corpus."

HAWKINS, TRISH. Born Oct. 30, 1945 in Hartford, CT. Attended Radcliffe, Neighborhood Playhouse. Debut OB 1970 in "Oh! Calcutta!" followed by "Iphigenia," "The Hot l Baltimore" for which she received a Theatre World Award, "him," "Come Back, Little Sheba," "Battle of Angels," "Mound Builders," "The Farm," "Ulysses in Traction," "Lulu," "Hogan's Folly," "Twelfth Night," Bdwy 1977 in "Some of My Best Friends," "Talley's Folly" (1979).

HAYDEN, CARLISSA. Born July 19, 1953 in Havana, Cuba. Attended New School. Debut 1977 OB in "Snowangel" followed by "The Boor," "Love Is a Many Splintered Thing," "Talk to Me Like the Rain," "Option."

HAYDON, JULIE. Born June 10, 1910 in Oak Park, IL. Attended Gordon Sch. Bdwy debut 1935 in "Bright Star," followed by "Shadow and Substance," "The Time of Your Life," "Magic," "Hello Out There," "The Patriots," "The Glass Menagerie," "Miracle in the Mountains," "Our Lan'," OB in "The Glass Menagerie" ('80).

HAYES, JANET. Born June 11 in Shanghai, China. Graduate NEConsv. of Music, Hunter Col. Bdwy debut 1954 in "The Golden Apple," followed by "Anyone Can Whistle," "Camelot," "Music Man," "Damn Yankees," OB in "Boys from Syracuse," "A Touch of the Poet," "Plain and Fancy," "Candide," "Rain," "The Subject Was Roses," "Relatively Speaking."

Mel Haynes

Cordis Heard

Dan Hedaya

Ann Hodapp

John Hillner

HAYNES, MEL. Born Feb. 18, 1921 in Brooklyn, NY. Debut 1958 OB in "The Trial of Dmitri Karamazov," followed by "Titus Andronicus," "Legend of Lovers," "Purple Canary," "Drums in the Night," "Sunset," "Raisin," Bdwy 1965 in "Diamond Orchid."

HAYNES, TIGER. Born Dec. 13, 1907 in St. Croix, VI. Bdwy bow 1956 in "New Faces," followed by "Finian's Rainbow," "Fade Out—Fade In," "The Pajama Game," "The Wiz," "A Broadway Musical," "Comin' Uptown," OB in "Turns."

HAYS, REX. Born June 17, 1946 in Hollywood, CA. Graduate San Jose State U., Brandeis U. Bdwy debut 1975 in "Dance With Me," followed by "Angel," "King of Hearts," "Evita," "Onward Victoria," "Woman of the Year."

HEALD, ANTHONY. Born Aug. 25, 1944 in New Rochelle, NY. Graduate MiStateU. Debut 1980 OB in "The Glass Menagerie."

HEARD, CELESTINE. Born Dec. 21, in Cleveland, OH. Graduate AADA. Debut 1972 OB in "Voices of the Third World," followed by "Things of the Heart."

HEARD, CORDIS. Born July 27, 1944 in Washington, DC. Graduate Chatham Col. Bdwy debut 1973 in "Warp," followed by "The Elephant Man," "Macbeth," OB in "Vanities," "City Junket."

HEARD, JOHN. Born Mar. 7, 1946 in Washington, DC. Graduate Clark U. Debut 1974 OB in "The Wager," followed by "Macbeth," "Hamlet," "Fishing," "G.R. Point" for which he received a Theatre World Award, "Creditors," "The Promise," "Othello," "Split," "Checkhov Sketchbook," Bdwy 1973 in "Warp."

HEARN, GEORGE. Born June 18, 1934 in St. Louis, MO. Graduate Southwestern Col. OB in "Macbeth," "Antony and Cleopatra," "As You Like It," "Richard III," "Merry Wives of Windsor," "Midsummer Night's Dream," "Hamlet," "Horseman, Pass By," Bdwy in "A Time for Singing," "The Changing Room," "An Almost Perfect Person," "I Remember Mama," "Watch on the Rhine," "Sweeney Todd."

HEDAYA, DAN. Born in Brooklyn, NY. Graduate Tufts Col. Debut 1974 OB in "The Last Days of British Honduras," followed by "Conjuring an Event," "Museum," "Scenes from Everyday Life," Bdwy 1977 in "Basic Training of Pavlo Hummel."

HEFFERNAN, JOHN. Born May 30, 1934 in NYC. Attended CCNY, Columbia, Boston U. Bdwy debut 1963 in "Luther," followed by "Tiny Alice," "Postmark Zero," "Woman Is My Idea," "Morning, Noon and Night," "Purlie," "Bad Habits," "Lady from the Sea," "Knock Knock," "Sly Fox," "The Suicide," OB in "The Judge," "Julius Caesar," "Great God Brown," "Lysistrata," "Peer Gynt," "Henry IV," "Taming of the Shrew," "She Stoops to Conquer," "The Plough and the Stars," "Octoroon," "Hamlet," "Androcles and the Lion," "A Man's a Man," "Winter's Tale," "Arms and the Man," "St. Joan" (LC), "Memorandum," "Invitation to a Beheading," "The Sea," "Shadow of a Gunman," BAM's "A Winter's Tale," "Johnny On a Spot" and "Barbarians."

HEIKIN, NANCY. Born Nov. 28, 1948 in Philadelphia, PA. Graduate Sarah Lawrence Col. Bdwy debut 1981 in "The Pirates of Penzance."

HELFEND, DENNIS. Born Mar. 15, 1939 in Los Angeles, CA. Debut 1968 OB in "The Mad Show," followed by "American Gothics," "Inn at Lydda," "Dulcy," Bdwy in "Man in the Glass Booth."

HELSLEY, CHUCK. Born Aug. 9, 1949 in Harrisburg, PA. Attended St. Mary's U. Debut 1978 OB in "The Biko Inquest," followed by "Curtains."

HEMSLEY, WINSTON DeWITT. Born May 21, 1947 in Brooklyn, NY. Bdwy debut 1965 in "Golden Boy," followed by "A Joyful Noise," "Hallelujah, Baby," "Hello, Dolly!," "Rockabye Hamlet," "A Chorus Line," "Eubie!," OB in "Buy Bonds Buster."

HENDERSON, JO. Born in Buffalo, NY. Attended WMiU. OB in "Camille," "Little Foxes," "An Evening with Merlin Finch," "29th Century Tar," "A Scent of Flowers," "Revival," "Dandelion Wine," "My Life," "Ladyhouse Blues," "Fallen Angels," "Waiting for the Parade," Bdwy 1981 in "Rose."

HENIG, ANDI. Born May 6 in Washington, DC. Attended Yale U. Debut 1978 OB in "One and One," followed by "Kind Lady" (ELT).

HENNESSEY, NINA. Born July 1, 1957 in Deven, CO. Graduate Barnard Col. Debut 1979 OB in "Sweet Mainstreet," followed by "Odyssey," "Close Enough for Jazz."

HENRY, SUZANNE. Born Aug. 6 1948 in Pittsburgh, PA. Attended Duquesne U. Debut 1981 OB in "Marry Me a Little."

HERRERA, JOHN. Born Sept. 21, 1955 in Havana, Cuba. Graduate Loyola U. Bdwy debut 1979 in "Grease," followed by "Evita," "Camelot."

HERRMANN, EDWARD. Born July 21, 1943 in Washington, DC. Graduate Bucknell U., LAMDA. Debut 1970 OB in "The Basic Training of Pavlo Hummel," followed by "Midsummer's Night Dream," Bdwy in "Moonchildren" ('72), "Mrs. Warren's Profession," "Philadelphia Story."

HEUCHLING, PETER. Born May 26, 1953 in Evanston, IL. Graduate UMiami. Debut 1974 OB in "oh Lady, Lady!" (ELT), Bdwy 1980 in "The Best Little Whorehouse in Texas."

HEWETT, CHRISTOPHER. Born Apr. 5 in England, attended Beaumont Col. Bdwy debut 1957 in "My Fair Lady," followed by "First Impressions," "Unsinkable Molly Brown," "Kean," "The Affair," "Hadrian VII," "Music Is," "Peter Pan" (1980), OB in "Tobias and the Angel," "Trelawny of the Wells," "Finian's Rainbow" (JB), "New Jerusalem."

HICKS, LOIS DIANE. Born Sept. 3, 1940 in Brooklyn, NY. Graduate NYCCC, AADA. Debut 1979 OB in "On A Clear Day You Can See Forever," followed by "Yank in Beverly Hills," "The Rope Dancers," "Marching to Georgia."

HIGGINS, JAMES. Born June 1, 1932 in Worksop, Eng. Graduate Cambridge U., Yale. Debut 1963 OB in "The Magistrate," followed by "Stevie," "The Winslow Boy," Bdwy in "The Zulu and the Zayda," "Whose Life Is It Anyway?"

HIKEN, GERALD. Born May 23, 1927 in Milwaukee, WI. Attended UWis. OB in "Cherry Orchard," "Seagull," "Good Woman of Setzuan," "The Misanthrope," "The Iceman Cometh," "The New Theatre," "Strider," Bdwy in "Lovers," "Cave Dwellers," "Nervous Set," "Fighting Cock," "49th Cousin," "Gideon," "Foxy," "Three Sisters," "Golda," "Strider," "Fools."

HILL, RUSSELL. Born July 8, 1947 in Boston, MA. Graduate Trinity U. OB in "Moon of the Caribbees," "Richelieu," "Story of the Gadsbys."

HILLNER, JOHN. Born Nov. 5, 1952 in Evanston, IL. Graduate Denison U. Debut 1977 OB in "Essential Shepard," followed by Bdwy 1979 in "They're Playing Our Song."

HILTON, MARGARET. Born July 20 in Marple, Cheshire, Eng. Graduate ULondon, LAMDA. Debut 1979 OB in "Molly," followed by "Stevie," "Come Back to the 5 & Dime, Jimmy Dean," Bdwy 1981 in "Rose."

HINES, GREGORY. Born Feb. 14, 1946 in NYC. Bdwy debut 1954 in "The Girl in Pink Tights," followed by "Eubie!" for which he received a Theatre World Award, "Comin' Uptown," "Black Broadway," "Sophisticated Ladies."

HINES, MIMI. Born July 17, 1933 in Vancouver, Can. Bdwy debut 1965 in "Funny Girl," OB in "From Rodgers and Hart with Love."

HINES, PATRICK. Born Mar. 17, 1930 in Burkesville, TX. Graduate TexU. Debut OB in 'Duchess of Malfi," followed by "Peer Gynt," "Henry IV," "Richard III," "Hot Grog," BAM's "A Winter's Tale," "Johnny on a Spot," "Barbarians" "The Wedding," Bdwy in "The Great God Brown," "Passage to India," "The Devils," "Cyrano," "The Iceman Cometh," "A Texas Trilogy," "Caesar and Cleopatra," "Amadeus."

HINGLE, PAT. Born July 19, 1923 in Denver, CO. Graduate UTx. Bdwy bow 1953 in "End as a Man," followed by "Festival," "Cat on a Hot Tin Roof," "Girls of Summer," "The Dark at the Top of the Stairs," "Deadly Game," "Strange Interlude," "Blues for Mr. Charlie," "A Girl Could Get Lucky," "The Glass Menagerie," "Johnny No Trump," "The Price," "Child's Play," "Selling of the President," "That Championship Season," "Lady from the Sea," "A Life."

HIRSCH, JUDD. Born Mar. 15, 1935 in NYC. Attended AADA. Bdwy debut 1966 in "Barefoot in the Park," followed by "Chapter Two," "Talley's Folly," OB in "On the Necessity of Being Polygamous," "Scuba Duba," "Mystery Play," "Hot l Baltimore," "Prodigal," "Knock Knock," "Life and/or Death," "Talley's Folly."

HODAPP, ANN. Born May 6, 1946 in Louisville, KY. Attended NYU. Debut 1968 OB in "You're a Good Man, Charlie Brown," followed by "A Round with Ring," "House of Leather," "Shoestring Revue," "God Bless Coney," "What's a Nice Country Like You . . .," "Oh, Lady! Lady!," "Housewives Cantata," "A Day in the Port Authority," "A Little Wine with Lunch," "Fiorello!," Bdwy 1980 in "Fearless Frank."

HOFFMAN, JANE. Born July 24, in Seattle, WA. Graduate UCal. Bdwy debut 1940 in "Tis of Thee," followed by "Crazy with the Heat," "Something for the Boys," "One Touch of Venus," "Calico Wedding," "Mermaids Singing," "Temporary Island," "Story for Strangers," "Two Blind Mice," "Rose Tattoo," "The Crucible," "Witness for the Prosecution," "Third Best Sport," "Rhinoceros," "Mother Courage and Her Children," "Fair Game for Lovers," "A Murderer Among Us," "Murder Among Friends," OB in "American Dream," "Sandbox," "Picnic on the Battlefield," "Theatre of the Absurd," "Child Buyer," "A Corner of the Bed," "Someone's Comin' Hungry," "Increased Difficulty of Concentration," "American Hamburger League," "Slow Memories," "Last Analysis," "Dear Oscar," "Hocus-Pocus," "Lessons," "The Art of Dining," "Second Avenue Rag," "One Tiger to a Hill," "Isn't It Romantic."

HOGAN, JONATHAN. Born June 13, 1951 in Chicago, IL. Graduate Goodman Theatre. Debut OB 1972 in "The Hot l Baltimore," followed by "Mound Builders," "Harry Outside," "Cabin 12," "5th of July," "Glorious Morning," "Innocent Thoughts, Harmless Intentions," "Sunday Runners," Bdwy in "Comedians" (1976). "Otherwise Engaged," "5th of July."

HOLBROOK, RUBY. Born Aug. 28, 1930 in St. John's, Nfld. Attended Denison U. Debut 1963 OB in "Abe Lincoln in Illinois," followed by "Hamlet," "James Joyce's Dubliners," "Measure for Measure," "The Farm," "Do You Still Believe the Rumor?," Bdwy 1979 in "Da."

HOLLAND, ANTHONY. Born Oct. 17, 1933 in Brooklyn, NY. Graduate UChicago. OB in "Venice Preserved," "Second City," "Victim of Duty," "New Tenant," "Dynamite Tonight," "Quare Fellow," "White House Murder Case," "Waiting for Godot," "Tales of the Hasidim," "Taming of the Shrew," "Diary of Anne Frank," Bdwy in "My Mother, My Father and Me," "We Bombed in New Haven," "Dreyfus in Rehearsal," "Leaf People," "Division Street."

HOLLIDAY, DAVID. Born Aug. 4, 1937 in Illinois. Attended Carthage Col. Bdwy debut 1968 in "Man of LaMancha," followed by "Coco" for which he received a Theatre World Award, "Music Is," "Perfectly Frank," OB in "Nevertheless They Laugh."

HOLMES, GEORGE. Born June 3, 1935 in London, Eng. Graduate ULondon. Debut 1978 OB in "The Changeling," followed by "Love from a Stranger," "The Hollow," "The Story of the Gadsbys."

HOMAN, JAMES. Born Apr. 26 in Kenosha, WI. Graduate UWi. Bdwy debut 1978 in "Hello, Dolly!," followed by "The Five O'Clock Girl."

HOOVER, PAUL. Born June 20, 1945 in Rockford, IL. Graduate Pikeville Col., Pittsburgh Sem. Debut 1980 OB in "Kind Lady."

HORAN, BONNIE. Born Aug. 20, 1928 in Dayton, TX. Graduate UHouston, UParis, George Washington U. Debut 1980 OB in "The Devil's Disciple," followed by "The Meehans."

HORNE, LENA. Born June 30, 1917 in Brooklyn, NY. Bdwy debut 1934 in "Dance with Your Gods," followed by "Jamaica," "Tony Bennett and Lena Horne Sing," "The Lady and Her Music."

HORVATH, JAMES. Born Aug. 14, 1954 in Chicago, IL. Graduate Triton Col., Butler U. Debut 1978 OB in "Can-Can," Bdwy 1981 in "Can-Can."

HORWITZ, MURRAY. Born Sept. 28, 1949 in Dayton, OH. Graduate Kenyon Col. Debut 1976 OB in "An Evening of Sholom Aleichem," followed by "Hard Sell."

HOSBEIN, JAMES. Born Sept. 24, 1946 in Benton Harbor, MI. Graduate UMich. Debut 1972 OB in "Dear Oscar," followed by "Darrel and Carol and Kenny and Jenny," Bdwy 1977 in "Annie."

HOSMER, GEORGE. Born Sept. 4, 1941 in Essex, NY. Attended USC, UMd, UHeidelberg, HB Studio. Debut 1970 OB in "I'm Getting My Act Together and Taking It On the Road."

HOTY, DEE. Born Aug. 16, 1952 in Lakewood, OH. Graduate Otterbein Col. Debut 1979 OB in "The Golden Apple," followed by "Ta-Dah!," Bdwy in "The Five O'Clock Girl," "Shakespeare's Cabaret."

HOTY, TONY. Born Sept. 29, 1949 in Lakewood, OH. Attended Ithaca Col., UWVa. Debut 1974 OB in "Godspell" (also Bdwy 1976), followed by "Joseph and the Amazing Technicolor Dreamcoat," "Robin Hood."

HOUTS, ROD. Born Dec. 15, 1906 in Warrensburg, MO. Graduate UMo., NYU, Goodman Theatre. Bdwy debut 1932 in "Lucrece," OB in "Gallery Gods," "The Miracle Worker," "Early Dark," "The Dybbuk," "A Far Country," "Three Sisters," "Exhausting the Possibilities," "The Freak."

HOXIE, RICHMOND. Born July 21, 1946 in NYC. Graduate Dartmouth Col., LAMDA. Debut 1975 OB in "Shaw for an Evening," followed by "The Family," "Justice," "Landscape with Waitress," "3 from the Marathon," "The Slab Boys."

HUDSON, CHARLES. Born Mar. 29, 1931 in Thorpsprings, TX. Attended AADA, AmThWing. Bdwy bow 1951 in "Billy Budd," followed OB in "Streets of New York," "Summer of Daisy Miller," "Great Scot!," "Any Resemblance to Persons Living or Dead," "Kaboom," "Antiques," "Funny Thing Happened on the Way to the Forum."

HUGHES, BARNARD. Born July 16, 1915 in Bedford Hills, NY. Attended Manhattan Col. OB in "Rosmersholm," "A Doll's House," "Hogan's Goat," "Lime," "Older People," "Hamlet," "Merry Wives of Windsor," "Pericles," "Three Sisters," "Translations," Bdwy in "The Ivy Green," "Dinosaur Wharf," "Teahouse of the August Moon" (CC), "A Majority of One," "Advise and Consent," "The Advocate," "Hamlet," "I Was Dancing," "Generation," "How Now, Dow Jones?," "Wrong Way Light Bulb," "Sheep On The Runway," "Abelard and Heloise," "Much Ado About Nothing," "Uncle Vanya," "The Good Doctor," "All Over Town," "Da."

HUGHES, LAURA. Born Jan. 28, 1959 in NYC. Graduate Neighborhood Playhouse. Debut 1980 OB in "The Diviners."

HUGILL, RANDY. Born in Olney, IL. Graduate UFl. Bdwy debut 1974 in "Lorelei," followed OB by "Follies," "Romance Is."

HULL, BRYAN. Born Sept. 12, 1937 in Amarillo, TX. Attended UNMex., Wayne State U. Bdwy debut 1976 in "Something's Afoot," OB in "The Fantasticks."

HUMES, BIBI. Born Sept. 16, 1956 in Bay Shore, NY. Graduate UNM, Bennington Col. Debut 1980 OB in "Really Rosie."

HUNT, W. M. Born Oct. 9 in St. Petersburg, Fl. Graduate UMi. Debut OB 1973 in "The Proposition," followed by "The Glorious Age," "Mary," "Fortydeuce."

HUNTER, KIM. Born NOv. 12, 1922 in Detroit, MI. Attended Actors Studio. Debut 1947 in "A Streetcar Named Desire," followed by "Darkness at Noon," "The Chase," "The Children's Hour," "The Tender Trap," "Write Me a Murder," "Weekend," "Penny Wars," "The Women," "To Grandmother's House We Go," OB in "Come Slowly, Eden," "All Is Bright," "The Cherry Orchard."

HURT, WILLIAM. Born Mar. 20, 1950 in Washington, DC. Graduate Tufts U., Juilliard. Debut 1976 OB in "Henry V," followed by "My Life," "Ulysses in Traction," "Lulu," "5th of July," "The Runner Stumbles," He received a 1978 Theatre World Award for his performances with Circle Repertory Theatre, followed by "Hamlet," "Mary Stuart," "Childe Byron."

HUSMANN, RON. Born June 30, 1937 in Rockford, IL. Attended Northwestern U. Bdwy in "Fiorello," "Greenwillow," "Tenderloin" for which he received a Theatre World Award, "All American," "Lovely Ladies, Kind Gentlemen," "On the Town," "Irene," "Can-Can" ('81), OB in "Look Where I'm At."

HUTTON, BETTY. Born Feb. 26, 1921 in Battle Creek, MI. Bdwy debut 1940 in "Two for the Show," followed by "Panama Hattie," solo performances at the Palace (1952 & 1953), "Fade In Fade Out," "Annie."

HYMAN, EARLE. Born Oct. 11, 1926 in Rocky Mount, NC. Attended New School, Theatre Wing. Bdwy debut 1943 in "Run, Little Chillun," followed by "Anna Lucasta," "Climate of Eden," "Merchant of Venice," "Othello," "Julius Caesar," "The Tempest," "No Time for Sergeants," "Mr. Johnson" for which he received a Theatre World Award, "St. Joan," "Hamlet," "Waiting for Godot," "Duchess of Malfi," "Les Blancs," "The Lady from Dubuque," OB in "The White Rose and the Red," "Worlds of Shakespeare," "Jonah," "Life and Times of J. Walter Smintheus," "Orrin," "Cherry Orchard," "House Party," "Carnival Dreams," "Agamemnon," "Othello," "Julius Caesar," "Coriolanus," "Remembrance," "Long Day's Journey into Night."

HYMAN, LARRY. Born Oct. 21, 1955 in Los Angeles, CA. Bdwy debut 1976 in "Rockabye Hamlet," followed by "Going Up," "Bring Back Birdie."

HYMAN, PHYLLIS. Born July 6, 1941 in Philadelphia, PA. Attended Morris Jr. Col. Bdwy debut 1981 in "Sophisticated Ladies" for which she received a Theatre World Award.

INGRAM, TAD. Born Sept. 11, 1948 in Pittsburgh, PA. Graduate Temple U, LAMDA. Debut OB 1979 in "Biography: A Game," followed by "The Possessed," Bdwy 1979 in "Strider."

INTROCASO, JOHN C. Born June 3, 1947 in Rutherford, NJ. Graduate St. Peter's Col. Debut 1979 OB in "The Sound of Music," followed by "Time and the Conways."

IRVING, GEORGE S. Born Nov. 1, 1922 in Springfield, MA. Attended Leland Powers Sch. Bdwy bow 1943 in "Oklahoma!," followed by "Call Me Mister," "Along 5th Ave.," "Two's Company," "Me and Juliet," "Can-Can," "Shinbone Alley," "Bells Are Ringing," "The Good Soup," "Tovarich," "A Murderer Among Us," "Alfie," "Anya," "Galileo," "4 on a Garden" "An Evening with Richard Nixon," "Irene," "Who's Who in Hell," "All Over Town," "So Long 174th St," "Once in a Lifetime," "I Remember Mama," "Copperfield," OB in "Up Eden."

IVANEK, ZELJKO. Born Aug. 15, 1957 in Ljubljana, Yugo. Graduate Yale U., LAMDA. Bdwy debut 1981 in "The Survivor," followed OB by "Cloud 9."

IVES, JANE. Born Nov. 6, 1949 in NYC. Attended Ct. Col. Debut 1981 OB in "Murder in the Cathedral."

IVEY, DANA. Born Aug. 12, 1941 in Atlanta, GA. Graduate Rollins Col., LAMDA. Bdwy debut 1981 in "Macbeth" (LC), OB in "A Call from the East."

IVEY, JUDITH. Born Sept. 4, 1951 in El Paso, TX. Graduate IllStateU. Bdwy debut 1979 in "Bedroom Farce," followed by "Piaf," OB in "Dusa, Fish, Stas and Vi," "Sunday Runners," "Girls Girls Girls."

JABLONS, KAREN. Born July 19, 1951 in Trenton, NJ. Juilliard graduate. Debut 1969 OB in "The Student Prince," followed by "Sound of Music," "Funny Girl," "Boys from Syracuse," "Sterling Silver," "People In Show Business Make Long Goodbyes," "In Trousers," Bdwy in "Ari," "Two Gentlemen of Verona," "Lorelei," "Where's Charley?," "A Chorus Line."

JACKSON, ERNESTINE. Born Sept. 18 in Corpus Christi, TX. Graduate Del Mar Col., Juilliard. Debut 1966 in "Show Boat" (LC), followed by "Finian's Rainbow," "Hello, Dolly!," "Applause," "Jesus Christ Superstar," "Tricks," "Raisin" for which she received a Theatre World Award, "Guys and Dolls," "Bacchae."

JACKSON, GLENDA. Born May 9, 1936 in Hoylake, Cheshire, Eng. Attended RADA. Bdwy debut 1965 in "Marat/Sade," followed by "Rose" 1981.

JACOBI, DEREK. Born Oct. 22, 1938 in Leytonstone, Eng. Graduate St. John's Col., Cambridge. Bdwy debut 1980 in "The Suicide."

JACOBS, RUSTY. Born July 10, 1967 in NYC. Debut OB 1979 in "Tripletale," followed Bdwy 1979 in "Peter Pan," OB in "Glory! Hallelujah!"

JACOBSON, JOANNE. Born Dec. 19, 1937 in Cambridge, MA. Graduate Barnard Col. Debut 1958 OB in "Don't Destroy Me," followed by "Naomi Court."

| James Horvath | Dee Hoty | Peter Iacangelo | Cheryl Y. Jones | Page Johnson |

JAKETIC, GARY. Born Apr. 24, 1953 in Cleveland, OH. Attended Carnegie-Mellon U. Bdwy debut 1980 in "Camelot."

JAMES, KRICKER. Born May 17, 1939 in Cleveland, OH. Graduate Denison U. Debut 1966 OB in "Winterset," followed by "Out of Control," "Rainbows for Sale," "The Firebugs," "Darkness at Noon," "The Humbug Man."

JAMES, JESSICA. Born Oct. 31, 1933 in Los Angeles, CA. Attended USC. Bdwy debut 1970 in "Company," followed by "Gemini," OB in "Nourish the Beast," "Hothouse," "Loss of Innocence," "Rebirth Celebration of the Human Race," "Silver Bee," "Gemini."

JAMES, STEPHEN. Born Feb. 2, 1952 in Mt. Vernon, OH. Princeton graduate. Debut 1977 OB in "Castaways," followed by "Greed Pond," Bdwy in "The 1940's Radio Hour" for which he received a Theatre World Award, "A Day in Hollywood/A Night in the Ukraine."

JAMES, WILLIAM. Born Apr. 29 in Jersey City, NJ. Graduate NJ State Teachers Col. Bdwy bow 1962 in "Camelot," followed by "Maggie Flynn," "Coco," "My Fair Lady" (CC & 1976), "Where's Charley?" (CC), "She Loves Me," "Camelot" ('80), OB in "Anything Goes," "Smith," "The Music Man" (JB).

JAMROG, JOSEPH. Born Dec. 21, 1932 in Flushing, NY. Graduate CCNY. Debut 1970 OB in "Nobody Hears a Broken Drum," followed by "Tango," "And Whose Little Boy Are You?," "When You Comin' Back, Red Ryder?," "Drums at Yale," "The Boy Friend," "Love Death Plays," "Too Much Johnson," "A Stitch in Time."

JANSEN, JIM. Born July 27, 1945 in Salt Lake City, Ut. Graduate UUt., NYU. Debut OB 1973 in "Moonchildren," followed by "Marco Polo Sings A Solo," "Chez Nous," "Taming of the Shrew," "God Bless You, Mr. Rosewater," Bdwy in "All Over Town" ('74), "Onward Victoria."

JARRETT, BELLA. Born Feb. 9, 1931 in Adairsville, GA. Graduate Wesleyan Col. Debut 1958 OB in "Waltz of the Toreadors," followed by "Hedda Gabler," "The Browning Version," "Cicero," "Pequod," "Welcome to Andromeda," Bdwy in "Once in a Lifetime" ('78), "Lolita."

JARRETT, JERRY. Born Sept. 9, 1918 in Brooklyn, NY. Attended New ThSch. Bdwy debut 1948 in "At War with the Army," followed by "Gentlemen Prefer Blondes," "Stalag 17," "Fiorello!," "Fiddler on the Roof," OB in "Waiting for Lefty," "Nat Turner," "Me Candido," "That 5 A.M. Jazz," "Valentine's Day," "Tickles by Tucholsky," "Jazzbo Brown."

JAUCHEM, ESQUIRE. Born Oct. 20, 1947 in Akron, OH. Graduate Defiance Col. Debut 1981 in "Macbeth" (LC).

JAY-ALEXANDER, RICHARD. Born May 24, 1953 in Syracuse, NY. Graduated S.IllU. Debut 1975 OB in "Boy Meets Boy," Bdwy 1979 in "Zoot Suit," followed by "Amadeus."

JEANMAIRE, ZIZI. Born Apr. 29, 1924 in Paris, Fr. Bdwy debut 1954 in "Girl in Pink Tights," followed by "Zizi," "The Bat," "Can-Can" ('81).

JECKO, TIMOTHY. Born Jan. 24, 1938 in Washington, DC. Yale graduate. Bdwy debut 1980 in "Annie."

JENKINS, CAROL MAYO. Born Nov. 24 in Knoxville, TN. Attended Vanderbilt U., UTn., London Central Sch. of Speech. Bdwy debut 1969 in "The Three Sisters," followed by "There's One in Every Marriage," "Kings," "First Monday in October," "The Suicide," OB in "Zinnia," "The Lady's Not for Burning."

JENNER, JAMES. Born Mar. 5, 1953 in Houston, TX. Attended UTx., LAMDA. Debut 1980 OB in "Kind Lady" (ELT).

JENNINGS, KEN. Born Oct. 10, 1947 in Jersey City, NJ. Graduate St. Peter's Col. Bdwy Debut 1975 in "All God's Chillun Got Wings," followed by "Sweeney Todd" for which he received a Theatre World Award.

JENNINGS, PAT. Born Feb. 20, 1950 in Louisville, KY. Graduate Southeastern LaU. OB in "U.S.A.," "This Property Is Condemned," "Patio/Porch," "But Can a Woman Alone."

JEROME, TIMOTHY. Born Dec. 29, 1943 in Los Angeles, CA. Graduate Ithaca Col. Bdwy debut 1969 in "Man of La Mancha," followed by "The Rothschilds," "Creation of the World and Other Business," "Moony Shapiro Songbook," OB in "Beggar's Opera," "Pretzels," "Civilization and Its Discontents."

JETER, MICHAEL. Born Aug. 26, 1952 in Lawrenceburg, TN. Graduate Memphis State U. Bdwy debut 1978 in "Once in a Lifetime," OB in "The Master and Margarita," "G. R. Point" for which he received a Theatre World Award, "Alice in Concert."

JOCHIM, KEITH. Born Jan. 26, 1942 in Chicago, IL. Graduate KsU. UMi. Debut 1968 OB in "Macbird," followed by "America Hurrah," "Salt Lake City Skyline," Bdwy 1981 in "Frankenstein."

JOHNSON, KURT. Born Oct. 5, 1952 in Pasadena, CA. Attended LACC, Occidental Col. Debut 1976 OB in "Follies," followed by "Walking Papers," "A Touch of Marble," Bdwy in "Rockaby Hamlet," "A Chorus Line," "A Stitch in Time."

JOHNSON, LORNA. Born Oct. 19, 1943 in PA. Graduate West Chester State Col. Debut 1979 OB in "The Last Days at the Dixie Girl Cafe," followed by "The Chronicle of Jane," "Between Daylight and Boonville."

JOHNSON, MEL JR. Born Apr. 16, 1949 in NYC. Graduate Hofstra U. Debut 1972 OB in "Hamlet," followed by "Love! Love! Love!" "Shakespeare's Cabaret," "The Peanut Man," Bdwy in "On the 20th Century," "Eubie!"

JOHNSON, ONNI. Born Mar. 16, 1949 in NYC. Graduate Brandeis U. Debut 1964 in "Unfinished Business," followed by "She Stoops to Conquer," "22 Years," "The Master and Margarita," "Haggedah," Bdwy in "Oh, Calcutta!"

JOHNSON, PAGE. Born Aug. 25, 1930 in Welch, WV. Graduate Ithaca Col. Bdwy bow 1951 in "Romeo and Juliet," followed by "Electra," "Oedipus," "Camino Real," "In April Once" for which he received a Theatre World Award, "Red Roses for Me," "The Lovers," "Equus," OB in "The Enchanted," "Guitar," "4 in 1," "Journey of the Fifth Horse," APA's "School for Scandal," "The Tavern," and "The Seagull," "Odd Couple," "Boys In The Band," "Medea," "Deathtrap," "Best Little Whorehouse in Texas."

JOHNSON, TINA. Born Oct. 27, 1951 in Wharton, TX. Graduate North Tx. State U. Debut 1979 OB in "Festival," Bdwy in "The Best Little Whorehouse in Texas."

JOHNSTON, GAIL. Born Aug. 8, 1943 in Far Rockaway, NY. Attended Hofstra Col., Hunter Col. Bdwy debut 1959 in "Juno," followed by Tenderloin," "Do Re Mi," OB in "Streets of New York," "Shoemaker's Holiday," "Out of This World," "Things Are Getting Better," "Anything Goes."

JONES, BAMBI. Born Apr. 14, 1961 in NYC. Debut 1969 OB in "An Evening of One Acts," followed by "Forty-Deuce!"

JONES, CHARLOTTE. Born Jan. 1 in Chicago, IL. Attended DePaul, Loyola U. Bdwy debut 1953 in "Camino Real," followed by "Buttrio Square," "Mame," "How Now Dow Jones," "Skin of Our Teeth," "A Matter of Gravity," OB in "False Confessions," "Sign of Jonah," "Girl on the Via Flaminia," "Red Roses for Me," "Night in Black Bottles," "Camino Real," "Plays for Bleecker St.," "Pigeons," "Great Scott!," "Sjt. Musgrave's Dance," "Papers," "Johnny Johnson," "Beggar's Opera," "200 Years of American Furniture," "Belle Femme," "Heat of Re-Entry."

JONES, CHERYL YVONNE. Born July 8, 1953 in Pittsburgh, PA. Graduate Carnegie-Tech. Debut 1977 in "Unfinished Women Cry in No Man's Land," followed by "So Nice They Named It Twice," "Measure for Measure," "Midsummer Night's Dream," "The Recruiting Officer," "Oedipus the King."

JONES, EDDIE. Born in Washington, PA. Debut 1960 OB in "Dead End," followed by "Curse of the Starving Class," "The Ruffian on the Stair," "An Act of Kindness," Bdwy in "That Championship Season" ('74), "Devour the Snow."

JONES, FRANZ. Born Nov. 11, 1951 in Washington, DC. Graduate TxChristianU. Debut 1974 OB in "Holocaust," followed by "Trade-Offs," "Brainwashed," "Pepperwine," "Things of the Heart."

JONES, GORDON G. Born Nov. 1, 1941 in Urania, LA. Graduate LaTech., UAr. Debut OB 1980 in "Room Service," followed by "The Front Page," "Cain Mutiny Court Martial," "Panhandle," "Caveat Emptor," "Progress."

JONES, JAMES EARL. Born Jan. 17, 1931 in Arkabutla, MS. Graduate MiU. OB in "The Pretender," "The Blacks," "Clandestine on the Morning Line," "The Apple," "Midsummer Night's Dream," "Moon on a Rainbow Shawl" for which he received a Theatre World Award, "P.S. 193," "Last Minstrel," "Love Nest," "Bloodknot," "Othello," "Baal," "Danton's Death," "Boesman and Lena," "Hamlet," "Cherry Orchard," Bdwy in "The Egghead," "Sunrise at Campobello," "The Cool World," "A Hand Is on the Gate," "The Great White Hope," "Les Blancs," "King Lear," "The Iceman Cometh," "Of Mice and Men," "Paul Robeson," "Lesson from Aloes."

JONES, JEFFREY. Born Sept. 28, 1947 in Buffalo, NY. Graduate Lawrence U., LAMDA. Debut 1973 OB in "Lotta," followed by "The Tempest," "Trelawny of the Wells," "Secret Service," "Boy Meets Girl," "Scribes," "Cloud 9."

JONES, JEN. Born Mar. 23, 1927 in Salt Lake City, UT. Attended UUt. Debut 1960 OB in "Drums under the Window," followed by "Long Voyage Home," "Diff'rent," "Creditors," "Look at Any Man," "I Knock at the Door," "Pictures in the Hallway," "Grab Bag," "Bo Bo," Bdwy in "Dr. Cook's Garden," "But Seriously," "Eccentricities of a Nightingale," "Music Man" ('80).

JONES, REED. Born June 30, 1953 in Portland, OR. Graduate USIU. Bdwy debut 1979 in "Peter Pan," followed by "West Side Story," "America."

Lawrence Joshua

Lynn Kearney

Paul Kandel

Nancy Killmer

Nicholas Kepros

JONES, TOM LEE. Born Sept. 15, 1946 in San Saba, TX. Harvard graduate. Bdwy debut 1969 in "A Patriot for Me," followed by "4 on a Garden," "Ulysses in Nighttown," OB in "Blue Boys," "True West."

JOSHUA, LAWRENCE. Born Feb. 12, 1954 in NYC. Debut OB 1979 in "Tooth of Crime," followed by "Sunday Runners in the Rain," "Middleman Out," "Kid Champion, "One Tiger to a Hill."

JOSLYN, BETSY. Born Apr. 19, 1954 in Staten Island, NY. Graduate Wagner Col. Debut 1976 OB in "The Fantasticks," Bdwy 1979 in "Sweeney Todd."

JOY, ROBERT. Born Aug. 17, 1951 in Montreal, Can. Graduate Nfd. Memorial U., Oxford U. Debut 1978 OB in "The Diary of Anne Frank," followed by "Fables for Friends."

JUDE, PATRICK, Born Feb. 25, 1951 in Jersey City, NJ. Bdwy debut 1972 in "Jesus Christ Superstar," followed by 1977 revival, "Got Tu Go Disco," "Charlie and Algernon," OB in "The Haggadah."

KAGAN, DIANE. Born in Maplewood, NJ. Graduate FlStateU. Debut 1963 OB in "Asylum," followed by "Days and Nights of Beebee Fenstermaker," "Death of the Well-Loved Boy," "Madam de Sade," "Blue Boys," "Alive and Well in Argentina," "Little Black Sheep," "The Family," "Ladyhouse Blues," "Scenes from the Everyday Life," Bdwy in "Chinese Prime Minister," "Never Too Late," "Any Wednesday," "Venus Is," "Tiger at the Gates," "Vieux Carre."

KALEMBER, PATRICIA. Born Dec. 30, 1956 in Schenectady, NY. Graduate InU. Debut 1981 OB in "The Butler Did It."

KAMP, DIANE. Born Aug. 7, 1948 in Oskaloosa, IA. Graduate Calvin Col., UMi. Debut 1978 OB in "The Other Half," followed by "King Lear," "Mother Courage," "Tied by the Leg."

KANDEL, PAUL. Born Feb. 15, 1951 in Queens, NYC. Graduate Harpur Col. Debut 1977 OB in "Nightclub Cantata," followed by "Two Grown Men," "Scrambled Feet."

KANSAS, JERI. Born Mar. 10, 1955 in Jersey City, NJ. Debut 1978 OB in "Gay Divorce," Bdwy 1979 in "Sugar Babies," followed by "42nd Street."

KANOUSE, LYLE. Born July 12, 1952 in Ft. Worth, TX. Graduate TxWesleyanCol., InU. Debut 1981 OB in "The Miser" (ELT).

KANTOR, KENNETH. Born Apr. 6, 1949 in The Bronx, NY. Graduate SUNY, Boston U. Debut 1974 OB in "Zorba," followed by "Kiss Me,Kate," "A Little Night Music," Bdwy in "The Grand Tour," "Brigadoon"('80).

KAPEN, BEN. Born July 2, 1928 in NYC. Graduate NYU. Bdwy debut 1968 in "The Happy Time," followed by "The Man in the Glass Booth," "Penny Wars," "Animals," OB in "No Trifling with Love," "Good News," "A Memory of Two Mondays," "They Knew What They Wanted," "Deli's Fable."

KAREL, CHUCK. Born Apr. 22, 1935 in Newark, NJ. Attended USCal. Bdwy debut 1962 in "Milk and Honey," followed by "Hello, Dolly!," "Golden Rainbow," "Dear World," OB in "Chase a Rainbow."

KARNILOVA, MARIA. Born Aug. 3, 1920 in Hartford, Ct. Bdwy debut 1938 in "Stars in Your Eyes," followed by "Call Me Mister," "High Button Shoes," "Two's Company," "Hollywood Pinafore," "Beggar's Opera," "Gypsy," "Miss Liberty," "Out of This World," "Bravo Giovanni," "Fiddler on the Roof"(1964 & 1981), "Zorba," "Gigi," "God's Favorite," "Bring Back Birdie," OB in "Kaleidoscope."

KASS, ALAN. Born Apr. 23, 1928 in Chicago, IL. Graduate CCNY. Bdwy bow 1968 in "Golden Rainbow," followed by "Sugar," OB in "Guitar," "Be Kind to People Week," "The Miser."

KATE, SALLY. Born May 29, 1970 in Philadelphia, PA. Debut 1981 in "The Haggadah."

KATT, WILLIAM. Born 1955 in Los Angeles, CA. Debut 1980 OB in "Bonjour, La Bonjour."

KAVA, CAROLINE. Born in Chicago, IL. Attended Neighborhood Playhouse. Debut 1975 OB in "Gorky," followed by "Threepenny Opera," "The Nature and Purpose of the Universe," "Disrobing the Bride," "Marching Song," Bdwy 1978 in "Stages."

KAWALEK, NANCY. Born Feb. 25, 1956 in Brooklyn, NY. Graduate Northwestern U. Bdwy debut 1979 in "Strider," OB in "Success Story."

KAYE, JUDY. Born Oct. 11, 1948 in Phoenix, AZ. Attended UCLA, Ariz. State U. Bdwy debut 1977 in "Grease," followed by "On the 20th Century" for which she received a Theatre World Award, "Moony Shapiro Songbook."

KAYE, TONI. Born Aug. 26, 1946 in Chicago, IL. Bdwy debut 1979 in "Sugar Babies."

KEACH, STACY. Born June 2, 1941 in Savannah, GA. Graduate UCal., Yale, LAMDA. Debut 1967 OB in "MacBird," followed by "Niggerlovers," "Henry IV," "Country Wife," "Hamlet," Bdwy in "Indians," "Deathtrap."

KEAGY, GRACE. Born Dec. 16 in Youngstown, OH. Attended New Eng. Consv. Debut 1974 OB in "Call Me Madam," Bdwy in "Goodtime Charley," "The Grand Tour," "Carmelina," "I Remember Mama," "Musical Chairs."

KEAL, ANITA. Born In Philadelphia, PA. Graduate SyracuseU. Debut 1956 OB in "Private Life of the Master Race," followed by "Brothers Karamazov," "Hedda Gabler," "Witches' Sabbath," "Six Characters in Search of an Author," "Yes, My Darling Daughter," "Speed Gets the Poppys," "You Didn't Have to Tell Me," "Val, Christie and Others," "Do You Still Believe the Rumor," "Farmyard."

KEARNEY, LYNN. Born Apr. 9, 1951 in Chicago, IL. Graduate NYU. Bdwy debut 1978 in "Annie," OB in "Captive Audiences."

KELLERMANN, SUSAN. Born July 4. Attended Neighborhood Playhouse. Bdwy debut 1979 in "Last Licks," for which she received a Theatre World Award, followed by "Whose Life Is It Anyway?," "Lunch Hour," OB in "Wine Untouched," "Crab Quadrille," "Country Club," "Cinque and the Jones Man."

KELLY, K. C. Born Nov. 12, 1952 in Baraboo, WI. Attended UWisc. Debut 1976 OB in "The Chicken Ranch," followed by Bdwy in "Romeo and Juliet,"(1977), "The Best Little Whorehouse in Texas."

KENNEDY, LAURIE. Born Feb. 14, 1948 in Hollywood, CA. Graduate Sarah Lawrence Col. Debut 1974 OB in "End of Summer," followed by "A Day in the Death of Joe Egg," "Ladyhouse Blues," "He and She," "The Recruiting Officer," "Isn't It Romantic," Bdwy in "Man and Superman,"(1978) for which she received a Theatre World Award, "Major Barbara."

KENNEDY, TARA. Born Aug. 8, 1971 in Yonkers, NY. Bdwy debut 1979 in "I Remember Mama," followed by "Annie."

KEPROS, NICHOLAS. Born Nov. 8, 1932 in Salt Lake City, UT. Graduate UUt., RADA. Debut 1958 OB in "The Golden Six," followed by "Wars of Roses," "Julius Caesar," "Hamlet," "Henry IV," "She Stoops to Conquer," "Peer Gynt," "Octaroon," "Endicott and the Red Cross," "The Judas Applause," "Irish Hebrew Lesson," "Judgement at Havana," "The Millionairess," "Androcles and the Lion," "The Redemptor," "Othello," Bdwy "St. Joan"(1968), "Amadeus."

KERT, LARRY. Born Dec. 5, 1934 in Los Angeles, CA. Attended LACC. Bdwy bow 1953 in "John Murray Anderson's Almanac," followed by "Ziegfeld Follies," "Mr. Wonderful," "Walk Tall," "Look, Ma, I'm Dancin'," "Tickets Please," "West Side Story," "A Family Affair," "Breakfast at Tiffany's," "Cabaret," "La Strada," "Company," "Two Gentlemen of Verona," "Music! Music!" "Musical Jubilee," "Side by Side by Sondheim," OB in "Changes," "From Rodgers and Hart with Love."

KESTLY, JONATHAN. Born Jan. 18, 1947 in Milwaukee, WI. Graduate UWi., Neighborhood Playhouse. Debut 1978 OB in "Can-Can," followed by "A Funny Thing Happened on the Way to the Forum."

KEYES, DANIEL. Born Mar. 6, 1914 in Concord, MA. Attended Harvard. Bdwy debut 1954 in "Remarkable Mr. Pennypacker," followed by "Bus Stop," "Only in America," "Christine," "First Love," "Take Her, She's Mine," "Baker Street," Dinner at 8," "I Never Sang for My Father," "Wrong Way Light Bulb," "A Place for Polly," "Scratch," "Rainbow Jones," "Angel," "Passione," OB in "Our Town," "Epitaph for George Dillon," "Plays for Bleecker St.," "Hooray! It's a Glorious Day!," "Six Characters in Search of an Author," "Sjt. Musgrave's Dance," "Arms and the Man," "Mourning Becomes Electra," "Salty Dog Saga," "Hot 1 Baltimore," "Artichoke."

KILLMER, NANCY. Born Dec. 16, 1936 in Homewood, IL. Graduate Northwestern U. Bdwy debut 1969 in "Coco," followed by "Goodtime Charley," "So Long, 174th Street," OB in "Exiles," "A Little Night Music," "Sweeney Todd," OB in "Exiles," "Mrs. Murray's Farm," "Pillars of Society."

Ginny King	Peter Kingsley	Annette Kurek	Brian Kosnik	Sofia Landon

KING, GINNY. Born May 12, 1957 in Atlanta, GA. Attended NCSch. of Arts. Bdwy debut 1980 in "42nd Street."

KINGSLEY, PETER. Born Aug. 14, 1945 in Mexico City, MX. Graduate Hamilton Col., LAMDA. Debut 1974 OB in "The Beauty Part," followed by "Purification," "Moliere in Spite of Himself," "Old Man Joseph and His Family," Bdwy 1980 in "Amadeus."

KINGSTON, KAYE. Born Sept.5, 1924 in Youngstown, OH. Graduate UChicago. Bdwy debut 1955 in "Catch a Star," followed by "Midsummer Night's Dream," "As You Like It," "Call It Virtue," "Tiger at the Gates," "The Trial," "Mating Dance," "Victims," "Gemini," OB in "An Absence of Light."

KIPP, EMILY. Born July 19 in NYC. Bdwy debut 1956 in "Auntie Mame," followed by "The Gazebo," "Sweet Bird of Youth," "Face of a Hero," "Midgie Purvis," "Freedom of the City," OB in "Kind Lady."

KIRKHAM, WILLI. Born Dec. 14, 1929 in Ponca City, OK. Attended OkCol for Women. Debut 1978 OB in "The Contessa of Mulberry St."

KIRSCH, CAROLYN. Born May 24, 1942 in Shreveport, LA. Bdwy debut 1963 in "How to Succeed....," followed by "Folies Bergere," "La Grosse Valise," "Skyscraper," "Breakfast at Tiffany's," "Sweet Charity," "Hallelujah, Baby!," "Dear World," "Promises, Promises," "Coco," "Ulysses in Nighttown," "A Chorus Line," OB in "Silk Stockings," Telecast."

KIRSCH, GARY. Born July 14, 1953 in Buffalo, NY. Graduate SUNY/Fredonia. Debut 1980 OB in "Annie Get Your Gun," Bdwy 1981 in "The Five O'Clock Girl."

KLECAK, DONALD R. Born Sept, 29, 1945 in Buffalo, N.Y. Attended UHouston. Debut 1980 OB in "The Devil's Disciple," followed by "Knuckle."

KLIBAN, KEN. Born July 26, 1943 in Norwalk, CT. Graduate UMiami, NYU. Bdwy debut 1967 in "War and Peace," followed OB in "Puppy Dog Tails," "Istanbul," "Persians," "Home," "Elizabeth the Queen," "Judith," "Man and Superman," "Boom Boom Room," "Ulysses in Traction," "Lulu," "The Beaver Coat," "Troilus and Cressida."

KLINE, KEVIN. Born Oct. 24, 1947 in St. Louis, MO. Graduate Ind. U, Juilliard. Debut 1970 OB in "Wars of Roses," followed by "School for Scandal," "Lower Depths," "The Hostage," "Women Beware Women," "Robber Bridegroom," "Edward II," "The Time of Your Life," "Beware the Jubjub Bird," "Dance on a Country Grave," Bdwy in "Three Sisters," "Measure for Measure," "Beggar's Opera," "Scapin," "On the 20th Century," "Loose Ends," "Pirates of Penzance."

KLUNIS, TOM. Born in San Francisco, CA. Bdwy debut 1961 in "Gideon," followed by "The Devils," "Henry V," "Romeo and Juliet," "St. Joan," "Hide and Seek," "Bacchae," OB in "The Immoralist," "Hamlet," "Arms and the Man," "Potting Shed," "Measure for Measure," "Romeo and Juliet," "The Balcony," "Our Town," "Man Who Never Died," "God is My Ram," "Rise Marlow," "Iphigenia in Aulis," "Still Life," "The Master and Margarita," "As You Like It," "The Winter Dancers."

KMECK, GEORGE. Born Aug. 4, 1949 in Jersey City, NJ. Attended Glassboro State Col. Bdwy debut 1981 in "Pirates of Penzance."

KNAPP, DAVID. Born Sept. 25, 1940 in San Diego, CA. Attended UVa., Columbia, Neighborhood Playhouse. Debut 1981 OB in "The Tantalus."

KNELL, DANE. Born Sept. 27, 1932 in Winthrop, MA. Bdwy debut 1952 in "See the Jaguar," OB in "Ulster," "Moon Dances," "Court of Miracles."

KNIGHT, LILY. Born Nov. 30, 1956 in Baltimore, MD. Graduate NYU. Debut 1980 OB in "After the Revolution."

NIGHT, WAYNE. Born Aug. 7, 1955 in NYC. Graduate UGa. Bdwy debut 1979 in "Gemini."

KOSNIK, BRIAN. Born Nov. 20, 1955 in Cleveland, OH. Graduate Goodman School. Debut 1980 OB in "Ricochet."

KOVITZ, RANDY. Born Sept. 28, 1955 in Arlington, VA. Graduate Carnegie-Mellon. Debut 1981 in "Macbeth"(LC).

KOZOL, ROGER. Born June 5, 1947 in Boston, MA. Graduate Harvard, Stanford. Debut 1974 OB in "Godspell," followed by "New Girl in Town," "Teasers."

KRAMER, JOEL. Born July 1, 1943 in The Bronx, NY. Graduate Queens Col., UMi. Debut 1963 OB in "St. Joan of the Stockyards," followed by "Playboy of the Western World," "Measure for Measure," "The Man Who Corrupted Hadleyburg," "Call Me Madam," "Castaways," "Esther," Bdwy 1981 in "Animals."

KUREK, ANNETTE. Born Feb. 6, 1950 in Chicago, IL. Graduate UWi. Debut 1976 OB in "The Hairy Ape," followed by "Isadora Duncan Sleeps with the Russian Navy," "Word of Mouth," "Coming Attractions," "The Fuehrer Bunker."

KURTZ, SWOOSIE. Born Sept. 6 in Omaha, NE. Attended USCal., LAMDA. Debut 1968 OB in "The Firebugs," followed by "The Effect of Gamma Rays. . . .," "Enter a Free Man," "Children," "Museum," "Uncommon Women and Others," "Wine Untouched," "Summer," Bdwy in "Ah, Wilderness" (1975), "Tartuffe," "A History of the American Film," "5th of July."

KUSHNER, JAMAS. Born Dec. 10, 1968 in NYC. Debut 1981 OB in "March of the Falsettos."

KUSS, RICHARD. Born July 17, 1927 in Astoria, NY. Attended Ithaca Col. Debut 1951 OB in "Mother Said No," followed by "A Maid's Tragedy," "Winning Isn't Everything," Bdwy in "J.B.," "Wait Until Dark," "Solitaire/Double Solitaire," "Golda," "Loves of Cass Mcguire," "Bacchae," "John Gabriel Borkman."

KYRIELEISON, JACK. Born May 6, 1950 in Washington, DC. Attended Clemson U., UMd. Debut 1979 OB in "The Sound of Music," followed by "Sister Aimee."

LAGERFELT, CAROLYN. Born Sept. 23 in Paris. Graduate AADA. Bdwy debut 1971 in "The Philanthropist," followed by "4 on a Garden," "Jockey Club Stakes," "The Constant Wife," "Otherwise Engaged," "Betrayal," OB in "Look Back in Anger," "Close of Play."

LAHTI, CHRISTINE. Born Apr. 4, 1950 in Detroit, MI. Graduate UMich., HB Studio. Debut 1979 OB in "The Woods" for which she received a Theatre World Award, Bdwy 1980 in "Loose Ends," followed by "Division Street."

LANDAU, VIVIEN. (formerly Tisa Barone) Born Jan. 31 in NYC. Graduate CCNY. Debut 1958 OB in "Clerambard," followed by "Once in a Lifetime," "The Golden Six," "Death Takes a Holiday."

LANDON, SOFIA. Born Jan. 24, 1949 in Montreal, Can. Attended Northwestern U. Debut 1971 OB in "Red, White and Black," followed by "Gypsy," "Missouri Legend," "Heartbreak House," "Peg O' My Heart," "Scenes and Revelations."

LANGE, ANN. Born June 24, 1953 in Pipestone, MN. Attended Carnegie-Mellon U. Debut 1979 OB in "Rat's Nest," followed by "Hunting Scenes from Lower Bavaria," Bdwy 1981 in "The Survivor."

LANG, STEPHEN. Born July 11, 1952 in NYC. Graduate Swarthmore Col. Debut 1975 OB in "Hamlet," followed by "Henry V," "Shadow of a Gunman," "A Winter's Tale," "Johnny on a Spot," "Barbarians," "Ah, Men," Bdwy 1977 in "St. Joan."

LANSBURY, ANGELA. Born Oct. 16, 1925 in London, Eng. Bdwy debut 1957 in "Hotel Paradiso," followed by "A Taste of Honey," "Anyone Can Whistle," "Mame," "Dear World," "Gypsy," "The King and I(1978), "Sweeney Todd."

LAPOTAIRE, JANE. Born Dec. 26, 1944 in Ipswich, Eng. Attended Old Vic School. Debut 1974 OB in "The Taming of the Shrew," Bdwy 1981 in "Piaf."

LARSON, LISBY. Born Oct. 23, 1951 in Washington, DC. Graduate UKs. Debut 1976 OB in "The Boys from Syracuse," Bdwy 1981 in "The Five O'Clock Girl."

LASKY, ZANE. Born Apr. 23, 1953 in NYC. Attended Manhattan Com. Col., HB Studio. Debut 1973 OB in "The Hot 1 Baltimore," followed by "The Prodigal," "Innocent Thoughts, Harmless Intentions," Bdwy 1974 in "All Over Town."

LASS, DEBRA. Born Mar. 31, 1953 in Mason City, IA. Graduate Va. Commonwealth U. Debut 1981 OB in "Death Takes a Holiday," followed by "Settlement," "Partners."

LASSER, LOUISE. Born in NYC. Attended Brandeis U. Bdwy debut 1962 in "I Can Get It for You Wholesale," followed by "Henry, Sweet Henry," The Chinese and Dr. Fish," "Thieves," OB in "The Third Ear," "Are You Now or Have You Ever Been," "Marie and Bruce," "A Coupla White Chicks."

LATHAN, BOBBI JO. Born Oct. 5, 1951 in Dallas, TX. Graduate NTex State U. Bdwy debut 1979 in "The Best Little Whorehouse in Texas."

LAUDICINO, DINO. Born Dec. 22, 1939 in Brooklyn, NY. Bdwy bow 1960 in "Christine," followed by "Rosencrantz and Guildenstern Are Dead," "Indians," "Scratch," "The Innocents," "Animals," OB in "King of the Dark Chamber, "Dollar."

LAUGHLIN, SHARON. Graduate UWa. Bdwy debut 1964 in "One by One," followed by "The Heiress," OB in "Henry IV," "Huui, Huui," "Mod Donna," "Subject to Fits," "The Minister's Black Veil," "Esther," "Rag Doll," "Four Friends," "Heartbreak House," "Marching Song," "Declassee."

LAURIA, DAN. Born Apr. 12, 1947 in Brooklyn, NY. Graduate SConnState, UConn. Debut 1978 OB in "Game Plan," followed by "All My Sons," "Marlon Brando Sat Here," "Home of the Brave."

LAZARUS, FRANK. Born May 4, 1939 in Cape Town, SAf. Graduate UCape Town. Bdwy debut 1980 in "A Day in Hollywood/A Night in the Ukraine."

LEARY, DAVID. Born Aug 8, 1939 in Brooklyn, NY. Attended CCNY. Debut 1969 OB in "Shoot Anything That Moves," followed by "Macbeth," "The Plough and the Stars," Bdwy in "The National Health," "Da," "The Lady from Dubuque," "Piaf."

LEE, ANDREA. Born Apr. 6, 1957 in Ohio. Attended Interlochen Arts Acad. Debut 1980 OB in "Oh, Boy!," followed by "A Funny Thing Happened on theWay to the Forum."

LEE, KAIULANI. Born Feb. 28, 1950 in Princeton, NJ. Attended American U. Bdwy debut 1975 in "Kennedy's Children," followed by "Macbeth," OB in "Ballad of the Sad Cafe," "Museum," "Safe House," "Othello."

LeGALLIENNE, EVA. Born Jan. 11, 1899 in London, Eng. Bdwy debut 1915 in "Mrs. Boltay's Daughters," followed by "Bunny," "Melody of Youth," "Mr. Lazarus," "Saturday to Monday," "Lord and Lady Algy," "Off Chance," "Lusmore," "Elsie Janis and Her Gang," "Not So Long Ago," "Liliom," "Sandro Botticelli," "The Rivals," "The Swan," "Assumption of Hannele," "LaVierge Folle," "Call of Life," "Master Builder," "John Gabriel Borkman," "Saturday Night," "Cradle Song," "Inheritors," "Good Hope," "First Stone," "Improvisations in June," "Hedda Gabler," "Would-Be Gentleman," "Cherry Orchard," "Peter Pan," "Sunny Morning," "Seagull," "Living Corpse," "Romeo and Juliet," "Siegfried," "Alison's House," "Camille," "Dear Jane," "Alice in Wonderland," "L'Aiglon," "Rosmersholm," "Women Have Their Way," "Prelude to Exile," "Mme. Capet," "Frank Fay's Music Hall," "Uncle Harry," "Therese," "Henry VIII," "What Every Woman Knows," "Ghosts," "The Corn Is Green," "Starcross Story," "Southwest Corner," "Mary Stuart," "Exit the King," "The Royal Family," "To Grandmother's House We Go."

LEIGHTON, JOHN. Born Dec. 30 on Staten Island, NY. Attended NYU, Columbia. Debut 1954 OB in "In Splendid Error," followed by "Juno and the Paycock," "A Christmas Carol," "Quare Fellow," "Brothers Karamazov," "Montserrat," "Othello," "Merchant of Venice," "Enter a Free Man," Bdwy 1980 in "Of the Fields Lately."

LeMASSENA, WILLIAM. Born May 23, 1916 in Glen Ridge, NJ. Attended NYU. Bdwy bow 1940 in "Taming of the Shrew," followed by "There Shall Be No Night," "The Pirate," "Hamlet," "Call Me Mister," "Inside U.S.A.," "I Know My Love," "Dream Girl," "Nina," "Ondine," "Fallen Angels," "Redhead," "Conquering Hero," "Beauty Part," "Come Summer," "Grin and Bare It," "All over Town," "A Texas Trilogy," "Deathtrap," OB in "The Coop," "Brigadoon," "Life with Father," "F. Jasmine Addams," "The Dodge Boys."

LEMMON, SHIRLEY. Born May 15, 1948 in Salt Lake City, UT. Graduate UtStateU. Bdwy debut 1971 in "Company," followed by "Smith," "Words and Music," OB in "2 by 5," "Life Is a Dream."

LEMON, BEN. Born May 21, 1955 in Tarrytown, NY. Graduate Brown U. Debut 1980 OB in "Dulcy."

LENOX, ADRIANE. Born Sept. 11, 1956 in Memphis, TN. Graduate Lambuth Col. Bdwy debut 1979 in "Ain't Misbehavin'."

LENZ, THOMAS. Born Jan. 29, 1951 in Madison, WI. Graduate St. Mary's Col. Debut 1975 OB in "Running of the Deer," followed by "Wild Cats," "Richard II," "Henry IV," "Marquis of Keith," "Madwoman of Chaillot," "Love's Labour's Lost," "The Front Page."

LEO, TOM. Born Nov. 28, 1936 in Teaneck, NJ. Graduate UToronto. Debut 1974 OB in "More Than You Deserve," followed by "Beethoven/Karl," "A Little Wine with Lunch," "The Matchmaker," "Marya."

LEON, JOSEPH. Born June 8, 1923 in NYC. Atended NYU, UCLA. Bdwy debut in 1950 in "Bell, Book and Candle," followed by "Seven Year Itch," "Pipe Dream," "Fair Game," "Gazebo," "Julia, Jake and Uncle Joe," "Beauty Part," "Merry Widow," "Henry, Sweet Henry," "Jimmy Shine," "All Over Town," "California Suite," "The Merchant," "Break a Leg," "Once a Catholic," "Fools," OB in "Come Share My House," "Dark Corners," "Interrogation of Havana," "Are You Now or Have You Ever Been," "Second Ave Rag."

LEPORSKA, ZOYA. Born Dec. 19, 1920 in Siberia. Bdwy debut 1953 in "Pajama Game," followed by "Damn Yankees," "New Girl in Town," "Sound of Music," "Bravo Giovanni," "On the Town," "Bring Back Birdie."

LESLIE, MICHAEL. Born Mar. 31, 1952 in Neptune, NJ. Graduate Rutgers, Cornell U. Bdwy debut 1977 in "Hair," OB in "Butterfingers Angel."

LESTER, BARBARA. Born Dec. 27, 1928 in London, Eng. Graduate Columbia U. Bdwy debut 1956 in "Protective Custody," followed by "Legend of Lizzie," "Luther," "Inadmissible Evidence," "Johnny-no-Trump," "Grin and Bare It," "Abelard and Heloise," "One in Every Marriage," "Butley," "Man and Superman," "The Faith Healer," OB in "Electra," "Queen after Death," "Summer of the 17th Doll," "Richard II," "Much Ado about Nothing," "One Way Pendulum" "Biography," "Heartbreak House," "Hedda Gabler."

LEVINE, ANNA KLUGER. Born Sept. 18, 1955 in NYC. Attended Actors Studio. Debut 1975 OB in "Kid Champion," followed by "Uncommon Women and Others," "City Sugar," "A Winter's Tale," "Johnny on a Spot," "The Wedding," "American Days."

LEWIS, JENIFER. Born Jan. 25, 1957 in St. Louis, MO. Graduate Webster College. Bdwy debut 1979 in "Eubie," followed by "Comin' Uptown," OB in "Sister Aimee."

LEWIS, MARCIA. Born Aug. 18, 1938 in Melrose, Ma. Attended UCin. OB in "Impudent Wolf," "Who's, Who, Baby?," "God Bless Coney," "Let Yourself Go," Bdwy in "The Time of Your Life," "Hello, Dolly!," "Annie."

LEWIS, R. J. Born July 30, 1955 in Morristown, NJ. Attended AADA. Bdwy debut 1981 in "Barnum."

LIEBERMAN, RICK. Born May 10, 1950 in NYC. Graduate CornellU. Debut 1979 OB in "Justice," followed by "Split," "Scenes from La Vie de Boheme."

LIND, JANE. Born Nov. 6, 1950 in Hump Back Bay, Perryville, AK. Attended NYU. Debut 1971 OB in "Black Elk Lives."

LINDSEY, GENE. Born Oct. 26, 1936 in Beaumont, TX. Graduate Baylor U. OB in "By Jupiter," "Gogo Loves You," "Bernstein's Theatre Songs," "Deer Park," "Troubles in Tahiti," "Columbus," "Ramblings," "Unsung Cole," "Trixie True," Bdwy in "My Daughter, Your Son," "Cactus Flower."

LINN, BAMBI. Born Apr. 26, 1926 in Brooklyn, NY. Bdwy debut 1943 in "Oklahoma!" followed by "Carousel" for which she received a Theatre World Award, "Alice in Wonderland," "Sally," "Great to Be Alive," "I Can Get It for You Wholesale," OB in "Women of Ireland."

LINTON, WILLIAM. Born Dec. 16, 1935 in Edinburgh, Scot. Attended Pasadena Playhouse. Bdwy debut 1960 in "Beg, Borrow or Steal," followed by "Wildcat," "Family Affair," OB in "DuBarry Was a Lady," "Bourgeois Gentleman."

LIPMAN, DAVID. Born May 12, 1938 in Brooklyn, NY. Graduate LIU, Bklyn Col. Debut 1973 OB in "Moonchildren," followed by "The Devil's Disciple," "Don Juan in Hell," Bdwy 1981 in "Fools."

LITHGOW, JOHN. Born Oct. 19, 1945 in Rochester, NY. Graduate Harvard U. Bdwy debut 1973 in "The Changing Room," followed by "My Fat Friend," "Comedians," "Anna Christie," "Once in a Lifetime," "Spokesong," "Bedroom Farce," "Division Street," OB in "Hamlet," "Trelawny of the Wells," "A Memory of Two Mondays," "Secret Service," "Boy Meets Girl," "Salt Lake City Skyline."

LLOYD, GEORGE. Born in Richmond, VA. Attended Carnegie Tech. Bdwy bow 1937 in "Julius Caesar," followed by "Shoemaker's Holiday," "The Fabulous Invalid," "One for the Money," "Hand in Glove," OB in "Glory! Hallelujah!," "Mary Stuart."

LOEB, ERIC. Born Apr. 26, 1943 in Berkeley, Ca. Graduate UWi. Bdwy debut 1975 in "Sweet Bird of Youth," followed by "The Water Engine," OB in "Penguin Touquet."

LONE, JOHN. Born in Hong Kong in 1952. Graduate AADA. Debut 1980 in "F.O.B.," followed by "The Dance and the Railroad."

LONG, JODI. Born in NYC. graduate SUNY/Purchase. Bdwy debut 1963 in "Nowhere to Go but Up," followed by "Loose Ends," "Bacchae," OB in "Fathers and Sons."

LOPEZ, PRISCILLA. Born Feb. 26, 1948 in The Bronx, NY. Bdwy debut 1966 in "Breakfast at Tiffany's," followed by "Henry, Sweet Henry," "Lysistrata," "Company," "Her First Roman," "The Boy Friend," "Pippin," "A Chorus Line," "A Day in Hollywood/A Night in the Ukraine," OB in "What's a Nice Country Like You...."

LOUDON, DOROTHY. Born Sept. 17, 1933 in Boston, MA. Attended Emerson Col., Syracuse U. Debut 1961 OB in "World of Jules Feiffer," Bdwy 1963 in "Nowhere to Go but Up," for which she received a Theatre World Award, followed by "Noel Coward's Sweet Potato," "Fig Leaves Are Falling," "Three Men on a Horse," "The Women," "Annie," "Ballroom."

LOWERY, MARCELLA. Born Apr. 27, 1945 in Jamaica, NY. Graduate Hunter Col. Debut 1967 OB in "Day of Absence," followed by "American Pastoral," "Ballet Behind the Bridge," "Jamimma," "A Recent Killing," "Miracle Play," "Welcome to Black River," "Anna Lucasta," Bdwy in "A Member of the Wedding" ('75), "Lolita."

LUCAS, CRAIG. Born April 30, 1951 in Atlanta, GA. Graduate Boston U. Debut 1974 OB in "Carousel" followed by "Marry Me a Little," Bdwy in "Shenandoah" (1975), "Rex," "On the 20th Century," "Sweeney Todd."

LUCAS, J. FRANK. Born in Houston, TX. Graduate TCU. Debut 1943 OB in "A Man's House," followed by "Coriolanus," "Edward II," "Trip to Bountiful," "Orpheus Descending," "Guitar," "Marcus in the High Grass," "Chocolates," "To Bury a Cousin," "One World at a Time," Bdwy in "Bad Habits," "The Best Little Whorehouse in Texas."

LUCKINBILL, LAURENCE. Born Nov. 21, 1938 in Ft. Smith, AR. Graduate UArk., Catholic U. Bdwy debut in "A Man for All Seasons," followed by "Beekman Place," "Poor Murderers," "The Shadow Box," "Chapter 2," "Past Tense," OB in "Oedipus Rex," "There's a Play Tonight," "Fantasticks," "Tartuffe," "Boys in the Band," "Horseman, Pass By," "Memory Bank," "What the Butler Saw," "A Meeting by the River," "Alpha Beta," "A Prayer for My Daughter," "Life of Galileo."

LUDWIG, KAREN. Born Oct. 9, 1942 in San Francisco, CA. Bdwy debut 1964 in "The Deputy," followed by "The Devils," "Bacchae," OB in "Trojan Women," "Red Cross," "Muzeeka," "Huui, Huui," "Our Last Night," "The Seagull," "Museum," "Nasty Rumors," "Daisy," "Gethsemene Springs," "After the Revolution."

238

Bobbi Jo Lathan	Rick Lieberman	Betty Lynd	Peter Marinos	Carol Maillard

LUDWIG, SALEM. Born July 31, 1915 in Brooklyn, NY. Attended Bklyn Col. Bdwy bow 1946 in "Miracle in the Mountains," followed by "Camino Real," "Enemy of the People," "All You Need is One Good Break," "Inherit the Wind," "Disenchanted," "Rhinoceros," "Three Sisters," "The Zulu and the Zayda," "Moonchildren," "The American Clock," OB in "Brothers Karamazov," "Victim," "Troublemaker," "Man of Destiny," "Night of the Dunce," "Corner of the Bed," "Awake and Sing," "Prodigal," "Babylon," "The Burnt Flowerbed," "The American Clock."

LUGENBEAL, CAROL. Born July 14, 1952 in Detroit, MI. Graduate U.S. International U. Bdwy debut 1974 in "Where's Charley?" followed by "On the 20th Century," "Evita."

LUM, ALVIN. Born May 28, 1931 in Honolulu, HI. Attended UHi. Debut 1969 OB in"In the Bar of a Tokyo Hotel," followed by "Pursuit of Happiness," "Monkey Music," "Flowers and Household Gods," Bdwy in "Lovely Ladies, Kind Gentlemen," "Two Gentlemen of Verona."

LUNA, BARBARA. Born Mar. 2 in NYC. Bdwy debut 1951 in "The King and I," followed by "West Side Story" (LC), "A Chorus Line."

LUPINO, RICHARD. Born Oct. 29, 1929 in Hollywood, CA. Attended LACC, RADA. Bdwy debut 1956 in "Major Barbara," followed by "Conduct Unbecoming," "Sherlock Holmes," OB in "The Tantalus."

LuPONE, PATTI. Born Apr. 21, 1949 in Northport, NY. Juilliard graduate. Debut 1972 OB in "School for Scandal, " followed by "Women Beware Women," "Next Time I'll Sing to You," "Beggar's Opera," "Scapin," "Robber Bridegroom," "Edward II," Bdwy in "The Water Engine" (1978), "Working," Evita."

LuPONE, ROBERT. Born July 29, 1946 in Brooklyn, NY. Juilliard graduate. Bdwy debut 1970 in "Minnie's Boys," followed by "Jesus Christ Superstar," "The Rothschilds," "Magic Show," "A Chorus Line," "St. Joan," OB in "Charlie Was Here," "Twelfth Night," "In Connecticut."

LYMAN, DOROTHY. Born Apr. 18, 1947 in Minneapolis, MN. Attended St. Lawrence Col. Debut OB in "America Hurrah," followed by "Pequod," "American Hamburger League," "Action," "Fefu and Her Friends," "Later," "A Coupla White Chicks."

LYND, BETTY. Born in Los Angeles, CA. Debut 1968 OB in "Rondelay," followed by "Love Me, Love My Children," Bdwy in "The Skin of Our Teeth" (1975), "A Chorus Line."

LYNDECK, EDMUND. Born Oct. 4, 1925 in Baton Rouge, LA. Graduate Montclair State Col., Fordham U. Bdwy debut 1969 in "1776," followed by "Sweeney Todd," OB in "The King and I" (JB), "Mandragola," "A Safe Place," "Amoureuse," "Piaf: A Remembrance."

MacINTOSH, JOAN E. Born Nov. 25, 1945 in NJ. Graduate Beaver Col., NYU. Debut OB 1969 in "Dionysus in '69" followed by "Makbeth," "The Beard," "Tooth of Crime," "Mother Courage," "Marilyn Project," "Seneca's Oedipus," "St. Joan of the Stockyards," "Wonderland in Concert," "Dispatches," "Endgame," "Killings on the Last Line," "Request Concert."

MacKAY, JOHN. Graduate CUNY. Bdwy debut 1960 in "Under the Yum-Yum Tree," followed by "A Gift of Time," "A Man for All Seasons," "The Lovers," "Borstal Boy," OB in "Oedipus Cycle," "Gilles de Rais."

MACY, WILLIAM "BILL". Born May 18, 1922 in Revere, MA. Graduate NYU. Bdwy debut 1959 in "Once More with Feeling," followed by "And Miss Reardon Drinks a Little," "The Roast," "I Ought to Be in Pictures," OB in "Threepenny Opera," "Machinal," "The Balcony," "America Hurrah," "Cannibals," "Guns of Carrar," "Oh! Calcutta!," "Awake and Sing."

MACY, W. H. Born Mar. 13, 1950 in Miami, FL. Graduate Goddard Col. Debut 1980 OB in "The Man in 605," followed by "Twelfth Night," "The Beaver Coat," "A Call from the East," "Sittin'," "Shoeshine."

MADDEN, SHARON. Born July 8, 1947 in St. Louis, MO. Debut 1975 OB in "Battle of Angels," followed by "The Hot l Baltimore," "Who Killed Richard Cory?," "Mrs. Murray's Farm," "The Passing of Corky Brewster," "Brontosaurus," "Ulysses in Traction," "Lulu," "In the Recovery Lounge," "In Connecticut."

MADDUX, JACKLYN. Born Apr. 8, 1951 in San Francisco, CA. Attended S.F.StateU. Debut 1979 OB in "The Art of Dining," followed by "But Can A Woman Alone."

MAGGIORE, CHARLES. Born Mar. 19, 1936 in Valley Stream, NY. Attended Bates Col., Adelphi U., Neighborhood Playhouse. Bdwy debut 1967 in "Spofford," followed by "Sly Fox," OB in "Six Characters in Search of an Author," "Rivals," The Iceman Cometh," "Othello," "The Elizabethans," "Three Musketeers," "Half-Life."

MAGID, DEBORAH. Born Dec. 19, 1954 in Cleveland, OH. Attended Cleveland Inst. of Music. Debut 1975 OB in "Waking Up to Beautiful Things," followed by "Anyone Can Whistle," Bdwy in "The King and I" (1978), "Camelot" (1980).

MAGUIRE, GEORGE. Born Dec. 4, 1946 in Wilmington, DE. Graduate UPa. Debut 1975 OB in "Polly," followed by "Follies," "Antigone," "Primary English Class," "Sound of Music" (JB), Bdwy 1980 in "Canterbury Tales."

MAHAFFEY, VALERIE. Born June 16, 1953 in Sumatra, Indonesia. Graduate UTx. Debut 1975 OB in "Father Uxbridge Wants to Marry," followed by "Bus Stop," "Black Tuesday," "Scenes and Revelations," "Translations," Bdwy in "Rex," "Dracula," "Fearless Frank."

MAHER, JOSEPH. Born Dec. 29, 1933 in Westport, Ire. Bdwy bow 1964 in "The Chinese Prime Minister," followed by "The Prime of Miss Jean Brodie," "Henry V," "There's One in Every Marriage," "Who's Who in Hell," "Days in the Trees," "Spokesong," "Night and Day," OB in "The Hostage," "Live Like Pigs," "Importance of Being Earnest," "Eh?" "Local Stigmatic," "Mary Stuart," "The Contractor," "Savages," "Entertaining Mr. Sloane."

MAHONE, JUANITA M. Born Sept. 12, 1952 in Boston, MA. Graduate Boston U. Debut 1975 OB in "Don't Bother Me, I Can't Cope," followed by "Birdland," "The Verandah," "Face of Love," "The Sun Always Shines for the Cool," "Antigone," "Single Room Occupancy."

MAILLARD, CAROL LYNN. Born Mar. 4, 1951 in Philadelphia, PA. Graduate Catholic U. Debut 1977 OB in "The Great MacDaddy," followed by "It's So Nice To Be Civilized," "A Photograph," "Under Fire," "Zooman and the Sign," Bdwy in "Eubie!" (1979), "It's So Nice to Be Civilized."

MANN, PJ. Born Apr. 9, 1953 in Pasadena, CA. Bdwy debut 1976 in "Home Sweet Homer," followed by "A Chorus Line," "Dancin'."

MARADEN, FRANK. Born Aug. 9, 1944 in Norfolk, VA. Graduate UMn., MichStateU. Debut 1980 OB with BAM Theatre Co. in "A Winter's Tale," "Johnny on a Spot," "Barbarians," "The Wedding," "Midsummer Night's Dream," "The Recruiting Officer," "The Wild Duck," "Jungle of Cities."

MARADEN, MARTI. Born June 22, 1945 in El Centro, CA. Attended UMn., MichStateU. Debut 1980 OB in "A Winter's Tale," followed by "Barbarians," "He and She," "Waiting for the Parade."

MARCH, ELLEN. Born Aug. 18, 1948 in Brooklyn, NY. Graduate AMDA. Debut 1967 OB in "Pins and Needles," Bdwy in "Grease," "Once in a Lifetime," "The Floating Light Bulb."

MARCH, WILLIAM. Born Apr. 3, 1951 in St. Paul, MN. Graduate NYU. Debut 1975 OB in "The Gift of the Magi," followed by "Heart's Desire."

MARCHAND, NANCY. Born June 19, 1928 in Buffalo, NY. Carnegie Tech graduate. Debut 1951 in "Taming of the Shrew" (CC), followed by "Merchant of Venice," "Much Ado about Nothing," "Three Bags Full," "After the Rain." LCRep's "The Alchemist," "Yerma," "Cyrano de Bergerac," "Mary Stuart," "Enemies" and "The Plough and the Stars," "40 Carats," "And Miss Reardon Drinks A Little," "Veronica's Room," "Morning's at 7," OB in "The Balcony," "Children," "Taken in Marriage."

MARCUS, DANIEL. Born May 26, 1955 in Redwood City, CA. Graduate Boston U. Bdwy debut 1981 in "The Pirates of Penzance."

MARIE, JULIENNE. Born in 1943 in Toledo, OH. Attended Juilliard. Has appeared in "The King and I," "Whoop-Up," "Gypsy," "Foxy," "Do I Hear a Waltz?," "Ballroom," "Charlie and Algernon," OB in "The Boys from Syracuse" for which she received a Theatre World Award, "Othello," "Comedy of Errors," "Trojan Women."

MARINOS, PETER. born Oct. 2, 1951 in Pontiac, MI. Graduate MiStateU. Bdwy debut 1976 in "Chicago," followed by "Evita."

MARKS, KENNETH. born Feb. 17, 1954 in Harwick, PA. Graduate UPa, Lehigh U. Debut 1978 OB in "Clara Bow Loves Gary Cooper," followed by "Canadian Gothic," "Time and the Conways."

MARSHALL, E. G. Born June 18, 1910 in Owatonna, MN. Bdwy debut 1938 in "Prelude to Glory," followed by "Jason," "The Skin of Our Teeth," "Petrified Forest," "Jacobowsky and the Colonel," "The Iceman Cometh," "Hope's the Thing," "Survivors," "The Crucible," "Red Roses for Me," "Waiting for Godot," "The Gang's All Here," "The Little Foxes," "Plaza Suite," "Nash at 9," "John Gabriel Borkman."

MARSHALL, LARRY. born Apr. 3, 1944 in Spartanburg, SC. Attended Fordham U., New Eng. Cons. Bdwy debut in "Hair," followed by "Two Gentlemen of Verona," "A Midsummer Night's Dream," "Rockabye Hamlet," "Porgy and Bess," "A Broadway Musical," "Comin' Uptown," OB in "Spell #7," "Jus' Like Livin'," "The Haggadah."

MARTENS, LORA JEANNE. Born in Glen Ellyn, IL. Graduate IlWesleyanU. Bdwy debut 1980 in "Onward Victoria," followed by "The Five O'Clock Girl."

MARTIN, ANDREA. Born Jan. 15, 1947 in Portland, ME. Graduate Emerson Col. Debut 1980 OB in "Hard Sell," followed by "The Sorrows of Stephen," "She Loves Me."

MARTIN, LUCY. Born Feb. 8, 1942 in NYC. Graduate Sweet Briar Col. Debut 1962 OB in "Electra," followed by "Happy as Larry," "The Trojan Women," "Iphigenia in Aulis," Bdwy in "Shelter" (1973), "Children of a Lesser God."

MARTIN, NICHOLAS. Born June 10, 1938 in Brooklyn, NY. Graduate Carnegie Tech. Bdwy in "The Wild Duck," "You Can't Take It with You," "Right You Are," "School for Scandal," "Pantagleize," "The Man Who Came to Dinner," OB in "The Millionairess."

MARTIN, SANDY. Born Mar. 3, 1949 in Philadelphia, PA. Debut 1980 OB in "What's So Beautiful about a Sunset over Prairie Avenue?," followed by "Killings on the Last Line."

MARTIN, W. T. Born Jan. 17, 1947 in Providence, RI. Attended Lafayette Col. Debut 1972 OB in "The Basic Training of Pavlo Hummel," followed by "Ghosts," "The Caretaker," "Are You Now or Have You Ever Been," "Fairy Tales of New York," "We Won't Pay," "Black Elk Lives."

MASIELL, JOE. Born Oct. 27, 1939 in Brooklyn in "Cindy" followed by "Jacques Brel Is Alive and . . .," "Sensations," "Leaves of Grass," "How to Get Rid of It," "A Matter of Time," "Tickles by Tucholsky," "Not at the Palace," Bdwy in "Dear World," "Different Times," "Got Tu Go Disco," "Jacques Brel Is. . . ."

MASSI, BERNICE. Born Aug. 23 in Camden, NJ. Bdwy debut 1952 in "South Pacific," followed by "Wish You Were Here," "By the Beautiful Sea," "Can-Can," "The Vamp," "Two for the Seesaw," "Beg, Borrow and Steal," "No Strings," "What Makes Sammy Run?," "Man of La Mancha," "How the Other Half Loves," "I Ought to Be in Pictures," OB in "Kaboom."

MASSMAN, PAIGE. Born Oct. 13, 1946. Graduate Webster Col., Purdue U. Debut 1976 OB in "The Boys from Syracuse," Bdwy 1981 in "Woman of the Year."

MASTRANTONIO, MARY E. Born Nov. 17, 1958 in Chicago, IL. Attended UIl. Bdwy debut 1980 in "West Side Story," followed by "Copperfield."

MASTERS, ANDREA. Born Nov. 16, 1949 in Chicago, IL. Attended Mills Col, Columbia U. Debut 1975 OB in "The Long Valley," followed by "Justice," Bdwy in "The Basic Training of Pavlo Hummel" (1977).

MATHEWS, CARMEN. Born May 8, 1918 in Philadelphia, PA. Graduate RADA. Bdwy debut 1938 in "Henry IV," followed by "Hamlet," "Richard II," "Harriet," "Cherry Orchard," "The Assassin," "Man and Superman," "Ivy Green," "Courtin' Time," "My Three Angels," "Holiday for Lovers," "Night Life," "Lorenzo," "The Yearling," "Delicate Balance," "I'm Solomon," "Dear World," "Ring Round the Bathtub," Ambassador," "Copperfield," "Morning's at 7."

MATHIAS, TIMOTHY. Born Oct. 15, 1957 in Torance, CA. Attended Orange Coast Col. Debut 1981 OB in "Forty-Deuce."

MATTHEWS, ANDERSON. Born Oct. 21, 1950 in Springfield, OH. Graduate Carnegie-Mellon U. Bdwy debut 1975 in "The Robber Bridegroom," followed OB by "Edward II," "The Time of Your Life," "Mother Courage," "King Lear," "Tied by the Leg."

MATTHEWS, BRIAN. Born Jan. 24, 1953 in York, PA. Attended St. Olaf Col., Juilliard. Bdwy debut 1981 in "Copperfield."

MATTSON, WAYNE. Born July 13, 1952 in Rochester, MN. Attended Allan Hancock Col., Pacific Cons. Bdwy debut 1974 in "Lorelei," followed by "Music Is," "They're Playing Our Song."

MAUPIN, SAMUEL. Born Dec. 27, 1947 in Portsmouth, VA. Graduate Va Commonwealth U. Debut 1977 OB in "The Passion of Dracula," followed by "Death Takes a Holiday."

MAXWELL, ROBERTA. Born in Canada. Debut 1968 OB in "Two Gentlemen of Verona," followed by "A Whistle in the Dark," "Slag," "The Plough and the Stars," "Merchant of Venice," "Ashes," "Mary Stuart," Bdwy in "The Prime of Miss Jean Brodie," "Henry V," "House of Atreus," "The Resistible Rise of Arturo Ui," "Othello," "Hay Fever," "There's One in Every Marriage," "Equus," "The Merchant."

MAXWELL, WAYNE. Born Dec. 22, 1939 in Neodesha, KS. Bdwy debut 1976 in "Legend," OB in "Titus Andronicus," "Boy with a Cart," "Kataki," "Long Voyage Home," "The Grass Harp," "Room Service," "Night of the Auk," "Pictures in a Hallway," "A Whitman Portrait," "Too Close for Comfort," "Gay Apprentice," "Dog in a Manger," "The Beheading," "Ah, Men."

MAY, BEVERLY. Born Aug. 11, 1927 in East Wellington, BD, Can. Graduate Yale U. Debut 1974 OB in "Female Transport," followed by "Bonjour, La, Bonjour," Bdwy 1977 in "Equus," followed by "Once in a Lifetime," "Whose Life Is It Anyway?," "Rose."

MAY, DEBORAH S. Born Sept. 28, 1948 in Lafayette, IN. Attended IndU. Am. Consv. Theatre. Bdwy debut 1978 in "Once in a Lifetime," followed by "Romantic Comedy," OB in "Frimbo."

MAYER, JERRY. Born May 12, 1941 in NYC. Graduate NYU. Debut 1968 OB in "Alice in Wonderland," followed by "L'Ete," "Marouf," "Trelawny of the Wells," "King of the Schnorrers," "Mother Courage," "You Know Al," Bdwy in "Much Ado about Nothing" (1972).

McCABE, EILEEN. Born Feb. 4, 1931 in Toledo, OH. Attended Wayne State, Hunter Col. Bdwy debut 1948 in "Park Avenue," followed by "The Chocolate Soldier," "Oklahoma!" (1951), "Musical Chairs," OB in "Anything Goes."

McCARTY, CONAN. Born Sept. 16, 1955 in Lubbock, TX. Attended USCal., AADA/West. Debut 1980 OB in "Star Treatment," followed by "Beyond Therapy."

McCARTY, MICHAEL. Born Sept. 7, 1946 in Evansville, IN. Graduate InU., MiStateU. Debut 1976 OB in "Fiorello!," Bdwy in "Dirty Linens," "King of Hearts," "Amadeus."

McCAULEY, WILLIAM. Born Nov. 20, 1947 in Wayne, PA. Graduate Northwestern U., Goodman Th. Bdwy debut 1974 in "Saturday, Sunday, Monday," OB in "Captive Audiences."

McCLARNON, KEVIN. Born Aug. 25, 1952 in Greenfield, IN. Graduate Butler U, LAMDA. Debut 1977 OB in "The Homecoming," followed by "Heaven's Gate," "A Winter's Tale," "Johnny on a Spot," "The Wedding," "Between Daylight and Boonville," "Macbeth" (LC).

McCORRY, MARION. Born Oct. 10, 1945 in the Bronx, NY. Graduate Hunter Col. Debut 1974 OB in "Ionescapade," followed by "Cappella."

McCOY, BASIA. Born Dec. 15, 1916 in Plains, PA. Graduate Carnegie-Mellon U. Debut 1948 OB in "The Fifth Horseman," followed by "Mary Stuart," "The Crucible," "Knitters in the Sun."

McDERMOTT, KEITH. Born in Houston, TX. Attended LAMDA. Bdwy debut 1976 in "Equus," followed by "A Meeting by the River," "Harold and Maude," OB in "Heat of Re-entry."

McDONALD, BETH. Born May 25, 1954 in Chicago, IL. Graduate Juilliard. Debut 1981 OB in "A Midsummer Night's Dream," followed by "The Recruiting Officer," "Jungle of Cities."

McDONALD, TANNY. Born Feb. 13, 1939 in Princeton, IN. Graduate Vassar Col. Debut OB with Am. Savoyards, followed by "All in Love," "To Broadway with Love," "Carricknabauna," "Beggar's Opera," "Brand," "Goodbye, Dan Bailey." "Total Eclipse," "Gorky," "Don Juan Comes Back from the War." "Vera with Kate," Bdwy in "Fiddler on the Roof," "Come Summer," "The Lincoln Mask," "Clothes for a Summer Hotel."

McDONNELL, MARY. Born in 1952 in Ithaca, NY. Graduate SUNY Fredonia. Debut OB 1978 in "Buried Child," followed by "Letters Home," "Still Life."

McDONOUGH, ANN. Born in Portland, ME. Graduate Towson State. Debut 1975 OB in "Trelawny of the Wells," followed by "Secret Service," "Boy Meets Girl," "Scribes," "Uncommon Women," "City Sugar," "Fables for Friends."

McDOWELL, MALCOLM. Born June 15, 1943 in Leeds, Eng. Debut 1980 OB in "Look Back in Anger."

McGANN, MICHAELJOHN. Born Feb. 2, 1952 in Cleveland, OH. Graduate OhioU. Debut 1975 OB in "The Three Musketeers," followed by "Panama Hattie," BAM Theatre Co.'s "A Winter's Tale," "Johnny on a Spot," "Barbarians," "Midsummer Night's Dream," "The Wild Duck," "Jungle of Cities."

McGOWIN, BRITTAIN. Born Sept. 4, 1954 in Mobile, AL. Attended Chatham Col., RADA, HB Studio. Bdwy debut 1980 in "John Gabriel Borkman."

McGREEVEY, ANNIE. Born in Brooklyn, NY. Graduate AADA. Bdwy debut 1971 in "Company," followed by "The Magic Show," "Annie," "Moony Shapiro Songbook," OB in "Booth Is Back In Town."

McGREGOR-STEWART, KATE. Born Oct. 4, 1944 in Buffalo, NY. Graduate Beaver Col, Yale U. Bdwy debut 1975 in "Travesties," followed by "A History of the American Film," OB in "Titanic," "Vienna Notes," "Beyond Therapy."

McGUIRE, MAEVE. Born in Cleveland, OH. Graduate Sarah Lawrence Col., Cleveland Playhouse. Debut 1968 with LCRep in "Cyrano de Bergerac," followed by "The Miser" "Charades," "Vera with Kate."

McGUNNIGLE, KATHI. Born May 26, 1959 in Whitman, MA. Graduate NYU. Debut 1981 OB in "The Meehans."

McHATTIE, STEPHEN. Born Feb. 3 in Antigonish, NS. Graduate Acadia U, AADA. Bdwy debut 1968 in "The American Dream," OB in "Henry IV," "Richard III," "The Persians," "Pictures in the Hallway," "Now There's Just the Three of Us," "Anna K.," "Twelfth Night," "Mourning Becomes Electra," "Alive and Well in Argentina," "The Iceman Cometh," "The Winter Dancers," "Casualties."

McINERNEY, BERNIE. Born Dec. 4, 1936 in Wilmington, DE. Graduate UDel., Catholic U. Bdwy debut 1972 in "That Championship Season," followed by OB in "Life of Galileo." "Losing Time," "3 Friends," "The American Clock," "Father Dreams."

McINTYRE, BILL. Born Sept. 2, 1935 in Rochester, NY. Debut OB 1970 in "The Fantasticks." followed by "City Junket," Bdwy in "Secret Affairs of Mildred Wild," "Legend," "The Inspector General."

McINTYRE, MARILYN. Born May 23, 1949 in Erie, PA. Graduate PennState, NCSch. of Arts. Debut 1977 OB in "The Perfect Mollusc," followed by "Measure for Measure," "The Promise," "Action," Bdwy 1980 in "Gemini."

Nicholas Martin

Eileen McCabe

Stephen McNaughton

Joanna Merlin

Gregory Miller

McKEEHAN, MAYLA. Born Dec. 8 in Barbourville, KY. Graduate Fla-StateU. Debut 1979 OB in "Big Bad Burlesque," followed by "God Bless You, Mr. Rosewater," "Anyone Can Whistle," "Facade."

McKELLEN, IAN. Born May 25, 1939 in Burnley, Eng. Attended St. Catherine's Col. Bdwy debut 1967 in "The Promise," followed by "Amadeus" (1980).

McLAREN, CONRAD. Born Nov. 13 in Greenfield, IL. Graduate IllWesleyan U. StateUIowa. Debut 1973 OB in "Medea," followed by "Shay," "The Show-Off," "Company," "Time Steps," "Crimes and Dreams," "The Trading Post."

McLERNON, PAMELA. Born March 1 in Lynn, MA. Lowell State Col. graduate. Debut 1975 OB in "Tenderloin," Bdwy in "Sweeney Todd," followed by "Copperfield."

McMURRAY, SAM. Born Apr. 15, 1952 in NYC. Graduate Washington U. Debut OB 1975 in "The Taking of Miss Janie," followed by "Merry Wives of Windsor," "Clarence" "Ballymurphy," "The Connection," "Translations."

McNAMARA, DERMOT. Born Aug. 24, 1925 in Dublin, Ir. Bdwy bow 1959 in "A Touch of the Poet," followed by "Philadelphia Here I Come," "Donny-brook," "Taming of the Shrew," OB in "The Wise Have Not Spoken," "3 by Synge," "Playboy of the Western World," "Shadow and Substance," "Happy as Larry," "Sharon's Grave," "A Whistle in the Dark," "Red Roses for Me," "The Plough and the Stars," "Shadow of a Gunman," "No Exit," "Stephen D," "Hothouse," "Home Is the Hero," "Sunday Morning Bright and Early," "The Birthday Party."

McNAMARA, ROSEMARY. Born Jan. 7, 1943 in Summit, NJ. Attended Newark Col. OB in "The Master Builder," "Carricknabauna," "Rocket to the Moon," "The Most Happy Fella" (CC). "The Matchmaker," "Anyone Can Whistle," "Facade," "Marya," Bdwy in "The Student Gypsy."

McNAUGHTON, STEPHEN. (Formerly Steve Scott) Born Oct. 11, 1949 in Denver, CO. Graduate UDenver, Debut 1971 OB in "The Drunkard," followed by "Summer Brave," "Monsters," "Chase a Rainbow," "Two on the Isles," Bdwy in "The Ritz" (1976), "Shenandoah."

McNEIL, CLAUDIA. Born Aug. 13, 1917 in "Baltimore, MD. Bdwy debut 1952 in "The Crucible," followed by "Simply Heavenly," "Raisin in the Sun," "Tiger, Tiger Burning Bright," "Something Different," "Her First Roman," "Wrong Way Light Bulb," OB in "Contributions," "Raisin."

McROBBIE, PETER. Born Jan. 31, 1943 in Hawick, Scot. Yale graduate. Debut 1976 OB in "The Wobblies," followed by "The Devil's Disciple," Bdwy 1979 in "Whose Life Is It Anyway?"

MERKIN, LEWIS. Born Dec. 18, 1955 in Philadelphia, PA. Attended Cal-StateU. Bdwy debut 1980 in "Children of a Lesser God."

MERLIN, JOANNA. Born July 15 in Chicago, IL. Attended UCLA. Debut 1958 OB in "The Breaking Wall," followed by "Six Characters in Search of an Author," "Rules of the Game," "A Thistle in My Bed," "Canadian Gothic-/American Modern," Bdwy in "Becket," (1961), "A Far Country," "Fiddler on the Roof," "Shelter," "Uncle Vanya," "The Survivor."

MERRILL, DINA. Born Dec. 29, 1925 in NYC. Attended AADA, AMDA, Geo. Washington U. Bdwy debut 1975 in "Angel Street," OB in "Are You Now or Have You Ever Been," followed by "Suddenly Last Summer."

MERRILL, GARY. Born Aug. 2, 1915 in Hartford, CT. Attended Trinity Col. Bdwy debut 1937 in "Brother Rat," followed by "See My lawyer," "This Is the Army," "Winged Victory," "Born Yesterday, "At War with the Army," "Step on a Crack," "The World of Carl Sandburg," "Morning's at 7."

MERYL, CYNTHIA. Born Sept. 25, 1950 in NYC. Graduate InU. Bdwy debut 1976 in "My Fair Lady," OB in "Before Sundown," "The Canticle," "The Pirate," "Dames at Sea," "Gay Divorce," "Sterling Silver," "Anything Goes."

MICHAEL, STEVEN. Born Aug. 31 1957 in Fall River, MA. Attended Pasadena City Col. Attended Ringling Bros. Clown Col. Bdwy debut 1980 in "Barnum."

MICHEL, JOHN. Born Mar. 10, 1935 in Old Town ME. Attended Columbia U. Debut 1953 OB in "Six Who Pass While the Lentils Boil," followed by "Pal Joey," "Caligula," "Lo and Behold," "Curtains."

MILES, ROSS. Born in Poughkeepsie, NY. Bdwy debut 1962 in "Little Me," followed by "Baker Street," "Pickwick," "Darling of the Day," "Mame," "Jumpers," "Goodtime Charley," "Chicago," "Dancin'."

MILES, SYLVIA. Born Sept. 9, 1934 in NYC. Attended Pratt Inst., Actors Studio. Debut 1954 OB in "A Stone for Danny Fisher," followed by "The Iceman Cometh," "The Balcony," "Chekhov Sketchbook," "Matty, Moron and Madonna," "The Kitchen," "Rosenbloom," "Nellie Toole & Co.," "American Night Cry," "It's Me, Sylvia!," Bdwy in "The Riot Act," "Night of the Iguana."

MILGRIM, LYNN. Born Mar. 17, 1944 in Philadelphia, PA. Graduate Swarthmore Col., Harvard U. Debut 1969 OB in "Frank Gagliano's City Scene," followed by "Crimes of Passion," "Macbeth," "Charley's Aunt," "The Real Inspector Hound," "Rib Cage," "Museum," "Bits and Pieces," Bdwy in "Otherwise Engaged," "Bedroom Farce."

MILLER, ANN. Born Apr. 12, 1923 in Chireno, TX. Bdwy debut 1940 in "George White's Scandals," followed by "Mame," "Sugar Babies."

MILLER, ANNETTE. Born Sept. 29, 1956 in Buffalo, NY. Debut 1979 OB in "Fantasy Children," Bdwy in "Five O'Clock Girl."

MILLER, DARLEIGH. Born May 28, 1955 in Seymour, IN. Graduate Ball State U. Bdwy debut 1980 in "The Music Man," followed by "Copperfield."

MILLER, GREGORY. Born Oct. 2, 1954 in Cincinnati, OH. Graduate UMi. Debut 1978 OB in "The Vampire and the Dentist," followed by "The Passion of Alice," Bdwy 1981 in "Inacent Black."

MILLER, MICHAEL. Born Sept. 1, 1931 in Los Angeles, CA. Attended Bard Col. Debut 1961 OB in "Under Milk Wood," followed by "The Lesson," "A Memory of Two Mondays," "Little Murders," "Tom Paine," "Morning, Noon and Night," "Enemy of the People," "Whitsuntide," "Say When," "Case Against Roberta Guardino," "Dandelion Wine," "Museum," Bdwy in "Iva-nov," "Black Comedy," "Trial of Lee Harvey Oswald," "Past Tense."

MILLER, PATRICIA. Born Dec. 1, 1950 in Seattle, WA. Graduate UGa. Debut 1978 OB in "Vanities."

MILLER, VALERIE-JEAN. Born Aug. 22, 1950 in Miami Beach, FL. Bdwy debut 1978 in "Dancin'."

MILLIGAN, JOHN. Born in Vancouver, Can. Attended Bristol Old Vic. Credits include "The Matchmaker," "The First Gentleman," "Lock Up Your Daughters," "Love and Libel," "Man and Boy," "The Devils," "Portrait of a Queen," OB in "One Way Pendulum," "John Brown's Body," "When You Comin' Back, Red Ryder?," "Esther," "Veronica's Room."

MINOT, ANNA. Born in Boston, MA. Attended Vassar Col. Bdwy debut 1942 in "The Strings, My Lord, Are False," followed by "The Russian People," "The Visitor," "The Iceman Cometh," "Enemy of the People," "Love of Four Colonels," "Trip to Bountiful," "Tunnel of Love," "Ivanov," OB in "Sands of the Niger," "Getting Out."

MISTRETTA, SAL. Born Jan. 9, 1945 in Brooklyn, NY. Ithaca Col. graduate Bdwy debut 1976 in "Something's Afoot," followed by "On the 20th Century," "Evita."

MIXON, ALAN. Born Mar. 15, 1933 in Miami, FL. Attended UMiami. Bdwy bow 1962 in "Something about a Soldier," followed by "Sign in Sidney Brus-tein's Window," "The Devils," "Unknown Soldier and His Wife," "Love Suicide at Schofield Barracks," "Equus," OB in "Suddenly Last Summer," "Desire under the Elms," "Trojan Women," "The Alchemist," "Child Buyer," "Mr. and Mrs. Lyman," "Whitman Portrait," "Iphigenia in Aulis," "Small Craft Warnings," "Mourning Becomes Electra," "The Runner Stumbles," "Old Glory," "The Gathering," "Ballad of the Sad Cafe," "One Tiger to a Hill," "The Butler Did It."

MOBERLY, ROBERT. Born Apr. 15, 1939 in Excelsior Springs, MO. Graduate UKan. Debut 1967 OB in "Arms and the Man," followed by "The Millionairess," "A Gun Play," "Shadow of a Gunman," "Heartbreak House," Bdwy in "A Place for Polly," "A Matter of Gravity," "Morning's at 7."

MOLDOW, DEBORAH. Born Dec. 18, 1948 in NYC. Graduate Sarah Lawrence Col. Debut 1958 OB in "The Enchanted," followed by "The Power and the Glory," "The Pursuit of Happiness," "Romance Is."

MOLNAR, ROBERT. Born June 22, 1927 in Cincinnati, OH. Attended Oh-NorthernU, UCin, CinConsv. of Music. Debut 1958 OB in "Hamlet of Stepney Green," followed by "Boys from Syracuse," Bdwy "Camelot" (1980).

MONTELEONE, JOHN. Born Mar. 2, 1956 in Far Rockaway, NY. Attended Dowling Col., NYU. Debut 1981 OB in "The Butler Did It."

MOONEY, DEBRA. Born in Aberdeen, SD. Graduate Auburn, UMinn. Debut 1975 OB in "Battle of Angels," followed by "The Farm," "Summer and Smoke," "Stargazing," "Childe Byron," Bdwy 1978 in "Chapter 2," followed by "Talley's Folly."

MOORE, CHARLOTTE. Born July 7, 1939 in Herrin, IL. Attended Smith Col. Bdwy debut 1972 in "The Great God Brown," followed by "Don Juan," "The Visit," "Chemin de Fer," "Holiday," "Love for Love," "A Member of the Wedding," "Morning's at 7," OB in "Out of Our Father's House," "A Lovely Sunday for Creve Couer," "Summer."

| G. Eugene Moose | Jannet Moranz | Marc Murray | Timothy Near | Ron Nakahara |

MOORE, MELBA. Born Oct. 29, 1945 in NYC. Graduate Montclair State Col. Bdwy debut 1968 in "Hair," followed by "Purlie," for which she received a Theatre World Award, "Timbuktu," "Inacent Black."

MOOSE, G. EUGENE. Born July 23, 1951 in Kilgore, TX. Graduate TxWesleyanCol. Bdwy bow 1975 in "The Lieutenant," followed by "Rex," "Pirates of Penzance," OB in "Nerfertiti," "Annie Get Your Gun" (JB).

MORALES, MARK. Born Nov. 9, 1954 in NYC. Attended Trenton State, SUNY/Purchase. Debut 1978 OB in "Coolest Cat in Town," Bdwy 1980 in "West Side Story," followed by "America."

MORAN, PETER. Born July 3, 1959 in Chicago, IL. Graduate Northwestern U, UCin. Debut 1981 OB in "Sister Aimee."

MORANZ, JANNET. (formerly Horsley) Born Oct. 13, 1954 in Los Angeles, CA. Attended CaStateU. Bdwy debut 1980 in "A Chorus Line."

MORATH, KATHY. Born Mar. 23, 1955 in Colorado Springs, CO. Graduate Brown U. Debut 1980 OB in "The Fantasticks," followed by "Dulcy," "Snapshot," "Alice in Concert," "A Little Night Music."

MORDEN, ROGER. Born Mar. 21, 1939 in Iowa City, IA. Graduate Coe Col., Neighborhood Playhouse. Debut 1964 OB in "Old Glory," followed by "3 by Ferlinghetti," "Big Broadcast," "The Incognita," Bdwy in "Man of La Mancha."

MORENO, RITA. Born Dec. 11, 1931 in Humacao, PR. Bdwy debut 1945 in "Skydrift," followed by "West Side Story," "The Sign in Sidney Brustein's Window," "Last of the Red Hot Lovers," "The National Health," "The Ritz," "She Loves Me," "Wally's Cafe."

MORGAN, MONIQUE. Born May 4, 1955 in Norfolk, VA. Graduate Stephens Col, Wayne State U. Debut 1980 OB in "Transcendental Love."

MORRISON, WILLIAM. Born Mar. 24, 1967 in NYC. Bdwy debut 1980 in "One Night Stand," followed by "Macbeth"(LC).

MORRISEY, BOB. Born Aug. 15, 1946 in Somerville, MA. Attended UWi. Debut 1974 OB in "Ionescapade," followed by "Company," "Anything Goes."

MORSE, ROBIN. Born July 8, 1963 in NYC. Bdwy debut 1981 in"Bring Back Birdie."

MORTON, JOE. Born Oct. 18, 1947 in NYC. Attended Hofstra U. Debut 1968 OB in "A Month of Sundays," followed by "Salvation," "Charlie Was Here and Now He's Gone," "G. R. Point," "Crazy Horse," "A Winter's Tale" "Johnny on a Spot," "Midsummer Night's Dream," "The Recruiting Officer," "Oedipus the King," "The Wild Duck," Bdwy in "Hair," "Two Gentlemen of Verona," "Tricks," "Raisin" for which he received a Theatre World Award.

MOSTEL, JOSHUA. Born Dec. 21, 1946 in NYC. Graduate Brandeis U. Debut 1971 OB in "The Proposition," followed by "More Than You Deserve," "The Misanthrope," "Rocky Road," Bdwy in "Unlikely Heroes," "American Millionaire," "Texas Trilogy."

MUENZ, RICHARD. Born in Hartford, CT., in 1948. Attended Eastern Baptist College. Bdwy debut 1976 in "1600 Pennsylvania Avenue," followed by "The Most Happy Fella," "Camelot."

MUNDY, MEG. Born in London, Eng. Attended Inst. of Musical Art. Bdwy debut 1936 in "Ten Million Ghosts," followed by "Hoorah for What," "The Fabulous Invalid," "Three to Make Ready," "How I Wonder," "The Respectful Prostitute," for which she received a Theatre World Award, "Detective Story," "Love's Labour's Lost," "Love Me a Little," "Philadelphia Story," OB in "Lysistrata," "Rivers Return."

MURCH, ROBERT. Born Apr. 17, 1935 in Jefferson Barracks, MO. Graduate Washington U. Bdwy bow 1966 in "Hostile Witness," followed by "The Harangues," "Conduct Unbecoming," "The Changing Room," OB in "Charles Abbott & Son," "She Stoops to Conquer," "Transcendental Love."

MURPHY, ROSEMARY. Born Jan. 13, 1927 in Munich, Ger. Attended Neighborhood Playhouse, Actors Studio. Bdwy debut 1950 in "Tower Beyond Tragedy," followed by "Look Homeward, Angel," "Period of Adjustment," "Any Wednesday," "Delicate Balance," "Weekend," "Death of Bessie Smith," "Butterflies Are Free," "Ladies at the Alamo," "Cheaters," "John Gabriel Borkman," OB in "Are You Now or Have You Ever Been."

MURPHY, SEAMUS. Born in Philadelphia, PA. Attended Juilliard. Bdwy debut 1967 in "Hair," OB in "Butterfingers Angel."

MURRAY, BRIAN. Born Oct. 9, 1939 in Johannesburg, S.A. Debut 1964 OB in "The Knack," followed by "King Lear," "Ashes," "The Jail Diary of Albie Sachs," "A Winter's Tale," "Barbarians," "The Purging," "Midsummer Night's Dream," "The Recruiting Officer," Bdwy in "All in Good Time," "Rosencrantz and Guildenstern Are Dead," "Sleuth," "Da."

MURRAY, CHRISTOPHER. Born Mar. 19, 1957 in Hollywood, CA. Attended Carleton Col. Debut 1980 OB in "Paris Lights," followed by "Glory! Hallelujah!"

MURRAY, MARC. Born Jan. 25, 1955 in NYC. Attended Ithaca Col., HB Studio. Debut 1978 OB in "Godsong," followed by "Fall of Masada," "The Importance of Being Earnest," "A Marriage Proposal," "Danton's Death."

MUSANTE, TONY. Born June 30, 1936 in Bridgeport, CT. Graduate Oberlin Col. Debut 1960 OB in "Borak," followed by "The Balcony," "Theatre of the Absurd," "Half-Past Wednesday," "The Collection," "Tender Heel," "Kiss Mama," "Mme. Mouse," "Zoo Story," "Match-Play," "Night of the Dunce," "Gun Play," "A Memory of Two Mondays," "27 Wagons Full of Cotton," "Grand Magic," "Cassatt," Bdwy in "P.S. Your Cat is Dead" (1975), "The Lady from Dubuque."

MUSNICK, STEPHANIE. Born Apr. 12, 1950 in Philadelphia, PA. Graduate Villanova U. Bdwy debut 1977 in "Gemini." OB in "As to the Meaning of Words," "Childe Byron."

NADEL, BARBARA. Born Dec. 18, 1947 in New Haven, CT. Graduate Simmons Col. Bdwy debut 1980 in "Barnum."

NAKAHARA, RON. Born July 20, 1947 in Honolulu, HI. Attended UHI, Tenri U. Debut 1981 OB in "Danton's Death," followed by "Flowers and Household Gods."

NASTASI, FRANK. Born Jan. 7, 1923 in Detroit, MI. Graduate Wayne U, NYU. Bdwy debut 1963 in "Lorenzo," followed by "Avanti," OB in "Bonds on Interest," "One Day More," "Nathan the Wise," "The Chief Things," "Cindy," "Escurial," "The Shrinking Bride," "Macbird," "Cakes with the Wine," "Metropolitan Madness," "Rockaway Boulevard," "Scenes from La Vie de Boheme."

NEAR, TIMOTHY. Born Feb. 23, 1945 in Los Angeles, CA. Graduate San Francisco State Col., LAMDA. Debut 1978 OB in "The Immediate Family," followed by "Still Life."

NEIL, ROGER. Born Nov. 19, 1948 in Galesburg, IL. Graduate Northwestern U. Debut 1974 OB in "The Boy Friend" (ELT), followed by "Scrambled Feet."

NELSON, MARK. Born Sept. 26, 1955 inHackensack, NJ. Graduate Princeton U. Debut 1977 OB in "The Dybbuk," followed by "Green Fields," Bdwy 1981 in "Amadeus."

NELSON, P. J. Born Nov. 17, 1952 in NYC. Attended Manhattan Sch. of Music. Bdwy debut 1978 in "Hello, Dolly!," followed by "The Music Man"

NELSON, RUTH. Born Aug. 2, 1905 in Saginaw, MI. Attended AmThLab. Bdwy debut 1931 in "House of Connolly," and other Group Theatre productions, and in "The Grass Harp," "Solitaire," "To Grandmother's House We Go," OB in "Collette," "Scenes from the Everyday Life."

NESBITT, CATHLEEN. Born Nov. 24, 1889 in Cheshire, Eng. Attended Victoria Col. Bdwy debut 1911 in "Well of the Saints," followed by "Justice," "Hush," "Such Is Life," "Magic," "Garden of Paradise," "General Post," "Saving Grace," "Diversion," "Cocktail Party," "Gigi," "Sabrina Fair," "Portrait of a Lady," "Anastasia," "My Fair Lady" (1956 & 1981), "The Sleeping Prince," "Second String," "Romulus," "Uncle Vanya."

NEUBERGER, JAN. Born Jan. 21, 1953 in Amityville, NY. Attended NYU. Bdwy debut 1975 in "Gypsy," OB in "Silk Stockings," "Chase a Rainbow," "Anything Goes."

NEVILLE-ANDREWS, JOHN. Born Aug. 23, 1948 in Woking Surrey, Eng. Attended Westminister Tech. Col. Debut 1973 OB in "El Grande de Coca-Cola," followed by "Bullshot Drummond," Bdwy in "The Elephant Man."

NEWMAN, PHYLLIS. Born Mar. 19, 1935 in Jersey City, NJ. Attended Western Reserve U. Bdwy debut 1953 in "Wish You Were Here," followed by "Bells Are Ringing," "First Impressions," "Subways Are for Sleeping," "The Apple Tree," "On the Town," "Prisoner of Second Avenue," "Madwoman of Central Park West," OB in "I Feel Wonderful," "Make Someone Happy," "I'm Getting My Act Together."

Mary Ann Niles **Don Nute** **Marcia O'Brien** **Conal O'Brien** **Alexandra O'Karma**

NEWMAN, WILLIAM. Born June 15, 1934 in Chicago, IL. Graduate UWa., Columbia. Debut 1972 OB in "Beggar's Opera," followed by "Are You Now," "Conflict of Interest," "Mr. Runaway," "Uncle Vanya," "One Act Play Festival," Bdwy in "Over Here," "Rocky Horror Show," "Strangers."

NEWTON, DOUGLAS. Born July 19, 1954 in Baltimore, MD. Attended Butler U., OhState U. Debut 1981 OB in "Anything Goes."

NEWTON, JOHN. Born Nov. 2, 1925 in Grand Junction, CO. UWash. graduate. Debut 1951 OB in "Othello," followed by "As You Like It," "Candida," "Candaules Commissioner," "Sextet," LCReps, "The Crucible" and "A Streetcar Named Desire," "The Rivals," "The Subject Was Roses," "The Brass Ring," "Hadrian VII," "The Best Little Whorehouse in Texas." Bdwy in "Weekend," "First Monday in October."

NICHOLS, ROBERT. Born July 20, 1924 in Oakland, CA. Attended Coll. of Pacific, RADA. Debut 1978 OB in "Are You Now or Have You Ever Been," followed by "Heartbreak House," Bdwy in "Man and Superman," "The Man Who Came to Dinner."

NIEHENKE, WALTER. Born Sept. 8, 1950 in Philadelphia, PA. Attended Temple U. Debut OB 1977 in "The Confidence Man," Bdwy 1981 in "Pirates of Penzance."

NILES, MARY ANN. Born May 2, 1933 in NYC. Attended Miss Finchley's Ballet Acad. Bdwy debut in "Girl from Nantucket," followed by "Dance Me A Song," "Call Me Mister," "Make Mine Manhattan," "La Plume de Ma Tante," "Carnival," "Flora the Red Menace," "Sweet Charity," "George M!," "No, No, Nanette," "Irene," "Ballroom," OB in "The Boys from Syracuse," CC's "Wonderful Town" and "Carnival."

NIXON, CYNTHIA. Born Apr. 9, 1966 in NYC. Debut 1980 in "The Philadelphia Story" (LC) for which she received a Theatre World Award.

NOONAN, TOM. Born Apr. 12, 1951 in Greenwich, CT. Yale graduate. Debut 1978 OB in "Buried Child," followed by "The Invitational," "Farmyard."

NORTH, ALAN. Born Dec. 23, 1927 in NYC. Attended Columbia U. Bdwy bow 1955 in "Plain and Fancy," followed by "South Pacific," "Summer of the 17th Doll," "Requiem for a Nun," "Never Live over a Pretzel Factory," "Dylan," "Spofford," "Finian's Rainbow," (JB), "Music Man" (JB), "Annie Get Your Gun" (JB), "The American Clock."

NUTE, DON. Born Mar. 13, in Connellsville, PA. Attended Denver U. Debut OB 1965 in "The Trojan Women" followed by "Boys in the Band," "Mad Theatre for Madmen," "The Eleventh Dynasty," "About Time," "The Urban Crisis," "Christmas Rappings," "The Life of a Man," "A Look at the Fifties."

NYE, CARRIE. Attended Stephens Col., Yale U. Bdwy debut 1960 in "Second String," followed by "Mary, Mary," "Half a Sixpence," "A Very Rich Woman," "Cop-Out," "The Man Who Came to Dinner," OB in "Ondine," "Ghosts," "The Importance of Being Earnest," "Trojan Women," "Real Inspector Hound."

O'BRIEN, CONAL. Born July 18 in New Jersey. Graduate Carnegie-Mellon U. Debut 1981 in "Macbeth" (LC).

O'BRIEN, MARCIA. Born Mar. 17, 1934 in Indiana. Graduate IndU. Bdwy debut 1970 in "Man of La Mancha," followed by "Evita," OB in "Now Is the Time for All Good Men," "House Party."

O'BRIEN, SYLVIA. Born May 4, 1924 in Dublin, Ire. Debut OB 1961 in "O Marry Me," followed by "Red Roses for Me," "Every Other Evil," "3 by O'Casey," "Essence of Woman," "Dear Oscar," "Dona Rosita," Bdwy in "Passion of Josef D.," "Right Honourable Gentleman," "Loves of Cass McGuire," "Hadrian VII," "Conduct Unbecoming," "My Fair Lady," "Da."

O'CONNELL, PATRICIA. Born May 17 in NYC. Attended AmThWing. Debut 1958 OB in "The Saintliness of Margery Kemp," followed by "Time Limit," "An Evening's Frost," "Mrs. Snow," "Survival of St. Joan," "Rain," "Rapists," "Who Killed Richard Cory?," Bdwy in "Criss-Crossing," "Summer Brave," "Break a Leg," "The Man Who Came to Dinner."

O'CONNOR, DONALD. Born Aug. 28, 1925 in Chicago, IL. Bdwy debut 1981 in "Bring Back Birdie."

O'CONNOR, KEVIN. Born May 7 in Honolulu, HI. Attended UHi., Neighborhood Playhouse. Debut 1964 OB in "Up to Thursday," followed by "Six from La Mama," "Rimers of Eldritch," "Tom Paine," "Boy on the Straightback Chair," "Dear Janet Rosenberg," "Eyes of Chalk," "Alive and Well in Argentina," "Duet," "Trio," "The Contractor," "Kool Aid," "The Frequency," "Chucky's Hunch," Bdwy in "Gloria and Esperanza," "The Morning after Optimism," "Figures in the Sand," "Devour the Snow," "The Lady from Dubuque."

O'KARMA, ALEXANDRA. Born Sept. 28, 1948 in Cincinnati, OH. Graduate Swarthmore Col. Debut 1976 OB in "A Month in the Country," followed by "Warbeck," "A Flea in Her Ear," "Knitters in the Sun," "The Beethoven."

O'KELLY, AIDEEN Born in Dalkey, Ire. Member of Dublin's Abbey Theatre. Bdwy debut 1980 in "A Life."

OLIVER, LYNN. Born Sept. 18 in San Antonio, TX. Graduate UTx, UHouston. Debut 1970 OB in "Oh! Calcutta!," followed by "In the Boom Boom Room," "Redhead," "Blood," "Two Noble Kinsmen," "Curtains."

O'NEILL, GENE. Born Apr. 7, 1951 in Philadelphia, PA. Graduate Loyola U. Bdwy debut 1976 in "Poison Tree," followed by "Best Little Whorehouse in Texas," OB in "Afternoons in Vegas," "The Slab Boys."

ORBACH, JERRY. Born Oct. 20, 1935 in NYC. Attended Northwestern U. Bdwy debut 1961 in "Carnival," followed by "Guys and Dolls," "Carousel," "Annie Get Your Gun," "The Natural Look," "Promises Promises," "6 Rms Riv Vu," "Chicago," "42nd Street," OB in "Threepenny Opera," "The Fantasticks," "The Cradle Will Rock," "Scuba Duba."

ORIN, RENEE. Born Oct. 25 in Slatington, PA. Attended Carnegie Tech. Debut 1951 OB in "Good News," followed by "The Great Magician," "Riverwind," "Augusta," "Turns," Bdwy in "Plain and Fancy," "Cafe Crown," "Slapstick Tragedy," "Show Me Where the Good Times Are," "Plaza Suite."

ORLANDO, TONY. Born in NYC in 1944. Bdwy debut 1981 in "Barnum."

ORMAN, ROSCOE. Born June 11, 1944 in NYC. Debut 1962 OB in "If We Grow Up," followed by "Electronic Nigger," "The Great McDaddy," "The Sirens," "Every Night When the Sun Goes Down," "Last Street Play," "Julius Caesar," "Coriolanus," "The 16th Round."

O'ROURKE, KEVIN. Born Jan. 15, 1956 in Portland, OR. Graduate Williams Col. Debut 1981 OB in "Declassee."

O'ROURKE, ROBERT T. Born Aug. 20, 1947 in NYC. Graduate Hunter Col., OhStateU. Bdwy debut 1975 in "Kennedy's Children," followed by "Major Barbara," "The Man Who Came to Dinner."

O'SHEA, MILO. Born June 2, 1926 in Dublin, Ire. Bdwy debut 1968 in "Staircase," followed by "Dear World," "Mrs. Warren's Profession" (LC), "Comedians," "A Touch of the Poet," OB in "Waiting for Godot," "Mass Appeal."

OSTRIN, ART. Born Aug. 30, 1935 in NYC. Bdwy in "The Time of Your Life," "Carnival," "Finian's Rainbow," "South Pacific," "Promenade," "Beggar on Horseback," "Irma La Douce," "Slapstick Tragedy," OB in "A Funny Thing Happened on the Way to the Forum."

O'SULLIVAN, MAUREEN. Born May 17, 1911 in Roscommon, Ire. Bdwy debut 1962 in "Never Too Late," followed by "The Subject Was Roses," "Keep It in the Family," "Front Page," "Charley's Aunt," "No Sex Please, We're British," "Morning's at 7."

OWENS, ELIZABETH. Born Feb. 26, 1938 in NYC. Attended New School, Neighborhood Playhouse. Debut 1955 OB in "Dr. Faustus Lights the Lights," followed by "Chit Chat on a Rat," "The Miser," "The Father," "Importance of Being Earnest," "Candida," "Trumpets and Drums," "Oedipus," "Macbeth," "Uncle Vanya," "Misalliance," "Master Builder," "American Gothics," "The Play's the Thing," "The Rivals," "Death Story," "The Rehearsal," "Dance on a Country Grave," "Othello," "Candida," "Little Eyolf," "The Winslow Boy," Bdwy in "The Lovers," "Not Now Darling," "The Play's the Thing."

OWENS, LEE. Born Oct. 30, 1943 in Kansas City, MO. Graduate San Diego State, Juilliard. Debut 1977 OB in "As You Like It," followed by "Country Gentleman," "Uncle Vanya," "Twelfth Night," "Hedda Gabler," "The Seagull," "The Miser," "Winner Take All," "Don Juan in Hell."

PACINO, AL. Born Apr. 25, 1940 in NYC. Attended Actors Studio. Bdwy bow 1969 in "Does a Tiger Wear a Necktie?" for which he received a Theatre World Award followed by "The Basic Training of Pavlo Hummel," "Richard III," OB in "Why Is a Crooked Letter?," "Peace Creeps," "The Indian Wants the Bronx," "Local Stigmatic," "Camino Real" (LC), "Jungle of Cities."

PAGANO, GIULIA. Born July 8, 1948 in NYC. Attended AADA. Debut 1977 OB in "The Passion of Dracula," followed by "Heartbreak House," "The Winslow Boy."

| Dina Paisner | Scott Palmer | Lisa Pelikan | Paul Perri | Elizabeth Perry |

PAISNER, DINA. Born in Brooklyn, NY. Bdwy debut 1963 in "Andorra," OB in "The Cretan Woman," "Pullman Car Hiawatha," "Lysistrata," "If 5 Years Pass," "Troubled Waters," "Sap of Life," "Cave at Machpelah," "Threepenny Opera," "Montserrat," "Gandhi," "Blood Wedding," "The Trial of Dr. Beck."

PALMER, SCOTT. Born Jan. 25, 1953 in San Francisco, CA. Attended Mon-StateU. Bdwy debut 1976 in "Caesar and Cleopatra," followed by "Clothes for a Summer Hotel," OB in "Glory! Hallelujah!"

PAPAS, IRENE. Born Sept. 3, 1929 in Chiliomodion, Greece. Bdwy debut 1967 in "That Summer, That Fall," followed by "Bacchae," OB in "Iphigenia in Aulis," "Medea."

PAPE, JOAN. Born Jan. 23, in Detroit, MI. Graduate Purdue U., Yale. Debut 1972 OB in "Suggs," followed by "Bloomers," "Museum," "Funeral Games," "Getting Out," "Barbarians," "He and She," "The Wild Duck," "Jungle of Cities," Bdwy in "The Secret Affairs of Mildred Wild," "Cat on a Hot Tin Roof," "A History of the American Film."

PARKER, ELLEN. Born Sept. 30, 1949 in Paris, FR. Graduate Bard Col. Debut 1971 OB in "James Joyce Liquid Memorial Theatre," followed by "Uncommon Women and Others," "Dusa, Fish, Stas and Vi," "A Day in the Life of the Czar," Bdwy in "Equus," "Strangers."

PARKER, HOWARD. Born Aug. 3, 1933 in Tampa, FL. Attended Pasadena Playhouse, HB Studio. Debut 1959 OB in "Once Upon a Mattress," Bdwy in "Juno," "Ballroom," "Bring Back Birdie."

PARKER, ROCHELLE. Born Feb. 26, 1940 in Brooklyn, NY. Attended Neighborhood Playhouse. Bdwy debut 1980 in "The Survivor."

PARKER, VIVECA. Born Mar. 7, 1956 in Montgomery, AL. Graduate Catholic U. Debut 1979 OB in "Don Juan Comes Back from the War," followed by "Hitting Town," "Principally Pinter," Bdwy in "John Gabriel Borkman" (1980).

PARRY, WILLIAM. Born Oct. 7, 1947 in Steubenville, OH. Graduate Mt. Union Co. Bdwy debut 1971 in "Jesus Christ Superstar," followed by "Rockabye Hamlet," "The Leaf People," "Camelot" (1980) OB in "Sgt. Pepper's Lonely Hearts Club Band," "The Conjuror," "Noah," "The Misanthrope," "Joseph and the Amazing Technicolor Dreamcoat," "Agamemnon," "The Coolest Cat in Town," "Dispatches," "The Derby."

PARSONS, ESTELLE. Born Nov. 20, 1927 in Lynn, MA. Attended Boston U, Actors Studio. Bdwy debut 1956 in "Happy Hunting," followed by "Whoop-Up!," "Beg, Borrow or Steal," "Mother Courage," "Ready When You Are, C.B.," "Malcolm," "The 7 Descents of Myrtle," "And Miss Reardon Drinks a Little," "The Norman Conquests," "Ladies at the Alamo," "Miss Margarida's Way," "Pirates of Penzance," OB in "Demi-Dozen," "Pieces of 8," "Threepenny Opera," "Automobile Graveyard," "Mrs. Dally Has a Lover," for which she received a Theatre World Award, "Next Time I'll Sing to You," "Come to the Palace of Sin," "In the Summer House," "Monopoly," "The East Wind," "Galileo," "Peer Gynt," "Mahagonny," "People Are Living There," "Barbary Shore," "Oh Glorious Tintinnabulation," "Mert and Paul," "Elizabeth and Essex," "Dialogue for Lovers."

PASSELTINER, BERNIE. Born Nov. 21, 1931 in NYC. Graduate Catholic U. OB in "Square in the Eye," "Sourball," "As Virtuously Given," "Now Is the Time for All Good Men," "Rain," "Kaddish," "Against the Sun," "End of Summer," "Yentl, the Yeshiva Boy," "Heartbreak House," "Every Place Is Newark," "Isn't It Romantic," Bdwy in "The Office," "The Jar," "Yentl."

PATTON, LUCILLE. Born in NYC; attended Neighborhood Playhouse. Bdwy debut 1946 in "A Winter's Tale," followed by "Topaze," "Arms and the Man," "Joy to the World," "All You Need Is One Good Break," "Fifth Season," "Heavenly Twins," "Rhinoceros," "Marathon '33," "The Last Analysis," "Dinner at 8," "La Strada," "Unlikely Heroes," "Love Suicide at Schofield Barracks," OB in "Ulysses in Nighttown," "Failures," "Three Sisters," "Yes, Yes, No, No," "Tango," "Mme. de Sade," "Apple Pie," "Follies," "Yesterday Is Over."

PAUL, DON. Born Oct. 22, 1951 in Chattanooga, TN. Graduate UTn. Debut 1975 OB in "A New Breed," followed by "Streamers," "Bojangles," "The Trial of Dr. Beck."

PAYTON-WRIGHT, PAMELA. Born Nov. 1, 1941 in Pittsburgh, PA. Graduate Birmingham Southern Col., RADA. Bdwy debut 1967 in "The Show-Off," followed by "Exit the King," "The Cherry Orchard," "Jimmy Shine," "Mourning Becomes Electra," "Glass Menagerie," "Romeo and Juliet," OB in "The Effect of Marigolds ...," "The Crucible," "The Seagull."

PEARLMAN, STEPHEN. Born Feb. 26, 1935 in NYC. Graduate Dartmouth Col. Bdwy bow 1964 in "Barefoot in the Park," followed by "La Strada," OB in "Threepenny Opera," "Time of the Key," "Pimpernel," "In White America," "Viet Rock," "Chocolates," "Bloomers," "Richie."

PEARSON, PAULETTA. Born Sept. 28 in NC. Attended NCSch. of Arts, NTxStateU. Bdwy debut 1977 in "Jesus Christ Superstar," followed by "Shakespeare's Cabaret," OB in "Jule Styne Revue," "Sweet Main Street," "Ethel Waters Story," "Helen of Troy," "Frimbo."

PEARSON, SCOTT. Born Dec. 13, 1941 in Milwaukee, WI. Attended Valparaiso U, UWisc. Bdwy debut 1966 in "A Joyful Noise," followed by "Promises, Promises," "A Chorus Line."

PEARTHREE, PIPPA. Born Sept. 23, 1956 in Baltimore, MD. Attended NYU, Bdwy debut 1977 in "Grease," followed by "Whose Life Is It Anyway?," OB in "American Days."

PELIKAN, LISA. Born July 12 in Paris, France. Attended Juilliard. Debut 1975 OB in "Spring's Awakening," followed by "An Elephant in the House," "The American Clock," "The Diviners," Bdwy in "Romeo and Juliet" (1977).

PELZER, BETTY. Born in Berkeley, CA. Graduate StanfordU. Bdwy debut 1979 in "Wing," OB in "Suddenly Last Summer."

PENBERTHY, BEVERLY. Born May 9 in Detroit, MI. Graduate UMi. Bdwy debut 1964 in "Nobody Loves an Albatross," followed by "But Seriously," OB in "Desperately Yours."

PENDLETON, WYMAN. Born Apr. 18, 1916 in Providence, RI. Graduate Brown U. Bdwy "Tiny Alice," "Malcolm," "Quotations from Chairman Mao Tse-Tung," "Happy Days," "Henry V," "Othello," "There's One in Every Marriage," "Cat on a Hot Tin Roof," OB in "Gallows Humor," "American Dream," "Zoo Story," "Corruption in the Palace of Justice," "Giant's Dance," "Child Buyer," "Happy Days," "Butter and Egg Man," "Othello," "Albee Directs Albee," "Dance for Me Simeon," "Mary Stuart."

PENN, SEAN. Born Aug. 17, 1960 in Calif. Bdwy debut 1981 in "Heartland."

PENZNER, SEYMOUR. Born July 29, 1915 in Yonkers, NY. Attended CCNY. OB in "Crystal Heart," "Guitar," "Paterson," "The Possessed," Bdwy in "Oklahoma!," "Finian's Rainbow," "Call Me Madam," "Paint Your Wagon," "Can-Can," "Kean," "Baker Street," "Man of La Mancha."

PEREZ, LAZARO. Born Dec. 17, 1945 in Havana, Cuba. Bdwy debut 1969 in "Does a Tiger Wear a Necktie?," followed by "Animals," OB in "Romeo and Juliet," "12 Angry Men," "Wonderful Years," "Alive," "G. R. Point," "Primary English Class."

PERKINS, PATTI. Born July 9 in New Haven, CT. Attended AMDA. Debut 1972 OB in "The Contrast," followed by "Fashion," "Tuscaloosa's Calling Me ...," "Patch Patch," "Shakespeare's Cabaret," Bdwy in "All Over Town" (1974), "Shakespeare's Cabaret."

PERRI, PAUL. Born Nov. 6, 1953 in New Haven, CT. Attended Elmira Col., UMe., Juilliard. Debut 1979 OB in "Say Goodnight, Gracie," followed by "Henry V," "Agamemnon," "Julius Caesar," "Waiting for Godot," Bdwy in "Bacchae."

PERRY, BARBARA. Born June 22, in Norfolk, VA. Attended LACC, RADA. Bdwy debut 1946 in "Swan Song," followed by "Happy as Larry," " Rumple," "Passionate Ladies."

PERRY, ELIZABETH. Born Oct. 15, 1937 in Pawtuxet, RI. Attended RISU, AmThWing. Bdwy debut 1956 in "Inherit the Wind," followed by "The Women," with APA in "The Misanthrope," "Hamlet," "Exit the King," "Beckett" and "Macbeth," OB in "Royal Gambit," "Here Be Dragons," "Lady from the Sea," "Heartbreak House," "Him," "All the Way Home," "The Frequency," "Fefu and Her Friends," "Out of the Broomcloset," "Ruby Ruby Sam Sam," "Did You See the Elephant?," "Last Stop Blue Jay Lane."

PERRY, KEITH. Born Oct. 29, 1931 in Des Moines, IA. Graduate Rice U. Bdwy debut 1965 in "Pickwick," followed by "I'm Solomon," "Copperfield," OB in "Epicene, the Silent Woman."

PESATURO, GOERGE. Born July 29, 1949 in Winthrop, MA. Graduate Manhattan Col. Bdwy debut 1976 in "A Chorus Line," OB in "The Music Man" (JB).

PETERSEN, ERIKA. Born Mar. 24, 1949 in NYC. Attended NYU. Debut 1963 OB in "One Is a Lonely Number," followed by "I Dream I Dwelt in Bloomingdale's," "F. Jasmine Addams," "The Dubliners," "P.S. Your Cat Is Dead," "The Possessed," "Murder in the Cathedral."

| Ross Petty | Alice Playten | Eddie Pruett | Cleo Quitman | David Purdham |

PETERSON, LENKA. Born Oct. 16, 1925 in Omaha, NE. Attended UIowa. Bdwy debut 1946 in "Bathsheba," followed by "Harvest of Years," "Sundown Beach," "Young and Fair," "The Grass Harp," "The Girls of Summer," "The Time of Your Life," "Look Homeward, Angel," "All the Way Home," "Nuts," OB in "Mrs. Minter," "American Night Cry," "Leaving Home," "The Brass Ring," "Father Dreams."

PETRICOFF, ELAINE. Born in Cincinnati, OH. Graduate Syracuse U. Bdwy debut 1971 in "The Me Nobody Knows," followed by "Grease," OB in "Hark," "Ride the Winds," "Cole Porter," "Pins and Needles," "Hijinks."

PETTY, ROSS. Born Aug. 29, 1946 in Winnipeg, Can. Graduate U Manitoba. Debut 1975 OB in "Happy Time," followed by "Maggie Flynn," "Carnival," "Little Eyolf," "It's Wilde!," "Romance Is," Bdwy in "Wings."

PHILLIPS, CLAYTON. Born Apr. 19, 1950 in Pittsburgh, PA. Graduate Point Park Col. Debut 1979 OB in "Loyalties," followed by "The Broken Heart," "The Hostage."

PHILLIPS, LACY DARRYL. Born Feb. 24, 1963. Attended Lehman Col. Debut 1981 OB in "Raisin."

PIACENTI, VALERIE. Born Dec. 5, in Chicago Heights, IL. Graduate UWi, HB Studio. Debut 1979 OB in "An Open Stage," followed by "Time and the Conways."

PIERCE, HARVEY. Born June 24, 1917 in NYC. Graduate NYU. OB credits include "The Gentle People," "Native Son," "The Country Girl," "Men in White," "To Bury a Cousin," "Time of the Cuckoo" (ELT).

PIERSON, GEOFFREY. Born June 16, 1949 in Chicago, IL. Graduate Fordham U, Yale U. Debut 1978 OB in "Wings," Bdwy 1980 in "Tricks of the Trade."

PIETROPINTO, ANGELA. Born Feb. 5 in NYC. Graduate NYU. OB credits include "Henry IV," "Alice in Wonderland," "Endgame," "Our Late Night," "The Sea Gull," "Jinxs Bridge," "The Mandrake," "Marie and Bruce," "Green Card Blues," Bdwy 1980 in "The Suicide."

PILLARD, DAVID J. Born Sept. 27, 1958 in Hamilton, NY. Graduate Fordham U. Debut 1980 OB in "Twelfth Night."

PINHASIK, HOWARD. Born June 5, 1953 in Chicago, IL. Graduate OhU. Debut 1978 OB in "Allegro," followed by "Marya," "The Meehans."

PLACE, PATRICIA. (formerly Charmian Sorbello) Born Dec. 17, 1930 in Long Beach, CA. Graduate UTx. Bdwy debut 1977 in "Tartuffe."

PLAYTEN, ALICE. Born Aug. 28, 1947 in NYC. Attended NYU. Bdwy debut 1960 in "Gypsy" followed by "Oliver," "Hello, Dolly!," "Henry Sweet Henry," for which she received a Theatre World Award," "George M!," OB in "Promenade," "The Last Sweet Days of Isaac," "National Lampoon's Lemmings," "Valentine's Day," "Pirates of Penzance."

PLUMMER, AMANDA. Born Mar. 23, 1957 in NYC. Attended Middlebury Col., Neighborhood Playhouse. Debut 1979 OB in "Artichoke," followed by "A Month in the Country," "A Taste of Honey" for which she received a Theatre World Award, " Alice in Concert," "A Stitch in Time."

PLUMMER, AMY. Born Apr. 24, 1953 in Forest City, AR. Graduate Elmira Col. Debut 1979 OB in "Love's Labour's Lost."

POLIS, JOEL. Born Oct. 3, 1951 in Philadelphia, PA. Graduate USC, Yale. Debut 1976 OB in "Marco Polo," followed by "Family Business."

POLLARD, GARY. Born Aug. 8, 1951 in Boston, MA. Graduate UFl, Neighborhood Playhouse. Debut 1981 OB in "Redback."

PONAZECKI, JOE. Born Jan. 7, 1934 in Rochester, NY. Attended Rochester U, Columbia U. Bdwy debut 1959 in "Much Ado About Nothing," followed by "Send Me No Flowers," "A Call on Kuprin," "Take Her, She's Mine," "Fiddler on the Roof," "Xmas in Las Vegas," "3 Bags Full," "Love in E-Flat," "90 Day Mistress," "Harvey," "Trial of the Catonsville 9," "The Country Girl," "Freedom of the City," "Summer Brave," "Music Is," "The Little Foxes," OB in "The Dragon," "Museeka," "Witness," "All Is Bright," "The Dog Ran Away," "Dream of a Blacklisted Actor," "Innocent Pleasures," "The Dark at the Top of the Stars," "36," "After the Revolution."

POPPENGER, CAROL. Born Nov. 17, 1937 in Plymouth, MA. Graduate FlStateU, NEConsv. Debut 1979 OB in "Men in White," followed by "The Bald Soprano," "Time and the Conways."

POSER, LINDA. Born Mar. 10 in Los Angeles, CA. Graduate San Francisco State U. Debut 1973 OB in "Call Me Madam," followed by "The Boy Friend," Bdwy in "On the 20th Century," "The Grand Tour," "Onward Victoria," "Copperfield."

POTTER, CAROL. Born May 21, 1948 in NYC. Graduate Radcliffe Col. Debut 1974 OB in "Last Days of British Honduras," followed by "Gemini" (also Bdwy), "Pericles," "The Front Page," "The Devil's Disciple."

PRADO, FRANCISCO. Born Nov. 3, 1941 in San Juan, PR. Graduate UPR. Debut 1977 OB in "G. R. Point," followed by "Julius Caesar," "Coriolanus," "Antony and Cleopatra," "Lewlulu," "Puerto Rican Obituary," "Death Shall Not Enter the Palace."

PREECE, K. K. Born Nov. 14, 1949 in Anna, IL. Graduate Brenau Col. Debut 1976 OB in "Panama Hattie," followed by "Scrambled Feet," Bdwy 1980 in "Canterbury Tales."

PRESNELL, HARVE. Born Sept. 14, 1933 in Modesto, CA. Attended USCa. Bdwy bow 1960 in "The Unsinkable Molly Brown," followed by "Carousel," "Annie Get Your Gun" (JB), "Annie."

PRESS, GWYNN. Born July 28 in NYC. Attended Queens Col. Debut 1975 OB in "The Wild Duck," followed by "Out of Sight," "Romeo and Juliet," "Greenfields," "A New England Legend," "Richard II," "Bird with Silver Feathers," "Playboy of the Western World."

PRESTON, BARRY. Born May 31, 1945 in Brooklyn, NY. Attended UtStateCol. Bdwy debut 1964 in "Something More," followed by "A Joyful Noise," "Bubbling Brown Sugar," "The Five O'Clock Girl."

PRICE, LONNY. Born Mar. 9, 1959 in NYC. Attended Juilliard. Debut 1979 OB in "Class Enemy" for which he received a Theatre World Award, Bdwy 1980 in "The Survivor."

PRIMONT, MARIAN. Born Oct. 2, 1913 in NYC. Graduate NYU. Debut 1957 OB in "Richard III," followed by "The Anatomist," "Come Share My House," "Dona Rosita," "Killings on the Last Line," "Hijinks," Bdwy 1961 in "All the Way Home."

PROVENZA, SAL. Born Sept. 21, 1946 in Brooklyn, NY. Attended Bklyn Col., Juilliard. Debut 1980 OB in "The Fantasticks."

PRUETT, EDDIE. Born July 21, 1951 in Terre Haute, IN. Attended Austin Peay Col. Bdwy debut 1979 in "Sugar Babies."

PRUNCZIK, KAREN. Born July 21, 1957 in Pittsburgh, PA. Attended Pittsburgh Playhouse. Bdwy debut 1980 in "42nd Street."

PUGH, RICHARD WARREN. Born Oct. 20, 1950 in NYC. Graduate Tarkio Col. Bdwy debut 1979 in "Sweeney Todd," followed by "The Music Man," "The Five O'Clock Girl," "Copperfield," OB in "Chase a Rainbow."

PULLIAM, ZELDA. Born Oct. 18 in Chicago, IL. Attended Roosevelt U. Bdwy debut 1969 in "Hello, Dolly!," followed by "Purlie," 'Raisin," "Pippin," "Dancin'," OB in "Croesus and the Witch."

PURDHAM, DAVID. Born June 3, 1951 in San Antonio, TX. Graduate UMd., UWa. Debut 1980 OB in "Journey's End," Bdwy 1981 in "Piaf."

QUITMAN, CLEO. Born Mar. 18 in Edwards, MS. Attended Wayne State U. Debut OB 1964 in "Cabin in the Sky," followed by "American Nite Cry," "Raisin," Bdwy 1971 in "Purlie."

RABB, ELLIS. Born June 20, 1930 in Memphis, TN. Attended Carnegie Tech, Yale. Debut 1956 in "A Midsummer Night's Dream," followed by "The Misanthrope," "Mary Stuart," "The Tavern," "Twelfth Night," "The Importance of Being Earnest," "King Lear," "Man and Superman," "Life in the Theatre," Bdwy in "Look after Lulu," "Jolly's Progress," "Right You Are," "Scapin," "Impromptu at Versailles," "Lower Depths," "School for Scandal," "Pantagleize," "Cock-a-Doodle Dandy," "Hamlet," "The Royal Family," "The Man Who Came to Dinner."

RACHELLE, BERNIE. Born Oct. 7, 1939 in NYC. Graduate Yeshiva U, Hunter Col. OB in "Winterset," "Golden Boy," "Street Scene," "World of Sholom Aleichem," "The Diary of Anne Frank," "Electra," "Nighthawks," "House Party," "Dancing in NY," "Metropolitan Madness," "Incident at Vichy."

RADIGAN, MICHAEL. Born May 2, 1949 in Springfield, IL. Graduate Springfield Col., Goodman Theatre. Bdwy debut 1974 in "Music! Music!" (CC), followed by "Sugar Babies," OB in "Broadway Dandies," "Beowulf."

RADNER, GILDA. Born June 28 in Detroit, MI. Debut 1975 OB in "The National Lampoon Show," Bdwy 1979 in "Gilda Radner—Live from NY," followed by "Lunch Hour."

RAGNO, JOSEPH. Born Mar. 11, 1936 in Brooklyn, NY. Attended Allegheny Col. Debut 1960 OB in "Worm on the Horseradish," followed by "Elizabeth the Queen," "A Country Scandal," "The Shrike," "Cymbeline," "Love Me, Love My Children," "Interrogation of Havana," "The Birds," "Armenians," "Feedlot," "Every Place Is Newark," Bdwy in "Indians," "The Iceman Cometh."

245

Theresa Rakov   Lawrence Raiken   Arleigh Richards   Bill Randolph   Patricia Richardson

RAIKEN, LAWRENCE. Born Feb. 5, 1949 in Long Island, NY. Graduate Wm. & Mary Col., UNC. Debut 1979 OB in "Wake Up, It's Time to Go to Bed," Bdwy 1981 in "Woman of the Year."

RAKOV, THERESA. Born Sept. 6, 1952 in Clarkson, NY. Graduate SUNY/-Fredonia. Bdwy Debut 1978 in "Hello, Dolly!," followed by "The Grand Tour," OB in "Florodora," "Romance Is."

RAMOS, RICHARD RUSSELL. Born Aug. 23, 1941 in Seattle, WA. Graduate UMn. Bdwy debut 1968 in "House of Atreus," followed by "Arturo Ui," OB in "Adaptation" "Screens" "Lotta," "The Tempest," "A Midsummer Night's Dream," "Gorky," "The Seagull," "Entertaining Mr. Sloane."

RAMSAY, REMAK. Born Feb. 2, 1937 in Baltimore, MD. Graduate Princeton U. Debut 1964 OB in "Hang Down Your Head and Die," followed by "The Real Inspector Hound," "Landscape of the Body," "All's Well That Ends Well" (CP), "Rear Column," "The Winslow Boy," Bdwy in "Half a Sixpence," "Sheep on the Runway," "Lovely Ladies, Kind Gentlemen," "On the town," "Jumpers," "Private Lives," "Dirty Linen," "Every Good Boy Deserves Favor," (LC), "Save Grand Central."

RAMSEL, GENA. Born Feb. 19, 1959 in El Reno, OK. Graduate SMU. Bdwy debut 1974 in "Lorelei," followed by "The Best Little Whorehouse in Texas," OB in "Joe Masiell Not at the Palace."

RANDELL, RON. Born Oct. 8, 1920 in Sydney, Aust. Attended St. Mary's Col. Bdwy debut 1949 in "The Browning Version," followed by "A Harlequinade," "Candida," "World of Suzie Wong," "Sherlock Holmes," "Mrs. Warren's Profession" (LC), "Measure for Measure" (CP), "Bent," OB in "Holy Places."

RANDOLPH, BILL. Born Oct. 11, 1953 in Detroit, MI. Attended Allen Hancock Col., SUNY Purchase. Bdwy debut 1978 in "Gemini," OB in "Holy Places."

RANDOLPH, JOHN. Born June 1, 1915 in the Bronx, NY. Attended CCNY, Actors Studio. Bdwy debut 1937 in "Revolt of the Beavers," followed by "The Emperor's New Clothes," "Capt. Jinks," "Nor More Peace," "Coriolanus," "Medicine Show," "Hold on to Your Hats," "Native Son," "Command Decision," "Come Back, Little Sheba," "Golden State," "Peer Gynt," "Paint Your Wagon," "Seagulls over Sorrento," "Grey-Eyed People," "Room Service," "All Summer Long," "House of Flowers," "The Visit," "Mother Courage," "Sound of Music," "Case of Libel," "Conversation at Midnight," "My Sweet Charlie," "The American Clock," OB in "An Evening's Frost," "The Peddler and the Dodo Bird," "Our Town," "Line," "Baba Goya," "Nourish the Beast," "Back in the Race," "The American Clock."

RAPHAEL, GERRIANNE. Born Feb. 23, 1935 in NYC. Attended New Sch., Columbia. Bdwy 1971 in "Solitaire," followed by "A Guest in the House," "Violet," "Goodbye My Fancy," "Seventh Heaven," "Lil Abner," "Saratoga," "Man of LaMancha," "King of Hearts," OB in "Threepenny Opera," "The Boy Friend," "Ernest in Love," "Say When," "Prime of Miss Jean Brodie," "The Butler Did It."

RASCHE, DAVID. Born Aug. 7, 1944 in St. Louis, MO. Graduate Elmhurst Col., U. Chicago. Debut 1976 OB in "John," followed by "Snow White," "Isadora Duncan Sleeps with the Russian Navy," "End of the War," Bdwy in "Shadow Box" (1977), "Loose Ends," "Lunch Hour."

RATHBURN, ROGER. Born Nov. 11, 1940 in Perrysburg, OH. Attended OhStateU, Neighborhood Playhouse. Bdwy debut 1971 in "No, No, Nanette," for which he received a Theatre World Award, followed by "Five O'Clock Girl," OB in "Children of Adam."

REAMS, LEE ROY. Born Aug. 23, 1942 in Covington, KY. Graduate U. Cinn. Cons. Bdwy debut 1966 in "Sweet Charity," followed by "Oklahoma!" (LC), "Applause," "Lorelei," "Show Boat" (JB), "Hello Dolly!" (1978), "42nd Street," OB in "Sterling Silver," "Potholes."

REDFIELD, ADAM. Born Nov. 4, 1959 in NYC. Attended NYU. Debut 1977 OB in "Hamlet," followed by "Androcles and the Lion," "Twelfth Night," "Reflected Glory," "Movin' Up," Bdwy 1980 in "A Life" for which he received a Theatre World Award.

REDFIELD, MARILYN. Born May 2, 1940 in Chicago, IL. Graduate Vassar, Harvard, HB Studio. Debut 1973 OB in "The Rainmaker," followed by "Monologia," "Mod Madonna," "King of the U.S.," "Too Much Johnson," Bdwy in "Chapter 2" (1979).

REED, ALAINA. Born Nov. 10, 1946 in Springfield, OH. Attended Kent State U. Bdwy debut in "Hair" (original and 1977), followed by "Eubie!," OB in "Sgt. Pepper's Lonely Hearts Club Band," "In Trousers."

REED, PAMELA. Born Apr. 2, 1949 in Tacoma, WA. Graduate U Wash. Bdwy debut 1978 in "The November People," followed by "Fools," OB in "The Curse of the Starving Class," "All's Well That Ends Well" (CP), "Seduced," "Getting Out," "The Sorrows of Stephen."

REED, VIVIAN. Born June 6, 1947 in Pittsburgh, PA. Attended Juilliard. Bdwy debut 1971 in "That's Entertainment," followed by "Don't Bother Me, I Can't Cope," "Bubbling Brown Sugar" for which she received a Theatre World Award, "It's So Nice to Be Civilized."

REEHLING, JOYCE. Born Mar. 5, 1949 in Baltimore, MD. Graduate NC Sch. of Arts. Debut 1976 OB in "Hot l Baltimore," followed by "Who Killed Richard Cory?," "Lulu," "5th of July," "The Runner Stumbles," "Life and/or Death," "Back in the Race," Bdwy 1980 in "5th of July."

REEVE, CHRISTOPHER. Born Sept. 25, 1952 in NYC. Graduate Cornell U, Juilliard. Debut 1975 OB in "Berkeley Square," followed by "My Life," Bdwy in "A Matter of Gravity" ('76), "5th of July."

REID, KATE. Born Nov. 4, 1930 in London, Eng. Attended Toronto U. Bdwy debut 1962 in "Who's Afraid of Virginia Woolf?," followed by "Dylan," "Slapstick Tragedy," "The Price," "Freedom of the City," "Cat on a Hot Tin Roof," "Bosoms and Neglect," "Morning's at 7."

REINKING, ANN. Born Nov. 10, 1949 in Seattle, WA. Attended Joffrey Sch., HB Studio. Bdwy debut 1969 in "Cabaret," followed by "Coco," "Pippin," "Over Here" for which she received a Theatre World Award, "Goodtime Charley," "A Chorus Line," "Chicago," "Dancin'."

REMME, JOHN. Born Nov. 21, 1935 in Fargo, ND. Attended UMn. Debut 1972 OB in "One for the Money," followed by "Anything Goes," Bdwy in "The Ritz" (1975) "The Royal Family," "Can-Can."

RENFROE, REBECCA L. Born Nov. 9, 1951 in Alexandria, VA. Graduate UCin. Bdwy debut 1981 in "Bring Back Birdie."

REVILL, CLIVE. Born Apr. 18, 1930 in Wellington, NZ. Attended Rongotai Col. Bdwy debut 1952 in "Mr. Pickwick," followed by "Irma La Douce," "Oliver!," "Sherry!," "The Incomparable Max," "Sherlock Holmes," "Lolita."

REY, ANTONIA. Born Oct. 12, 1927 in Havana, Cuba. Graduate Havana U. Bdwy debut 1964 in "Bajour," followed by "Mike Downstairs," "Engagement Baby," "The Ritz," OB in "Yerma," "Fiesta in Madrid," "Camino Real" (LC), "Back Bog Beast Bait," "Rain," "42 Seconds from Broadway," "Streetcar Named Desire" (LC), "Poets from the Inside," "Blood Wedding," "Missing Persons."

RICHARDS, ARLEIGH. Born Nov. 28, 1949 in Gary, IN. Graduate Swarthmore Col., Neighborhood Playhouse. Debut 1977 OB in "The Crucible," followed by "Fefu and Her Friends," "Romeo and Juliet'

RICHARDS, JESS. Born Jan. 23, 1943 in Seattle, WA. Attended UWash. Bdwy debut 1966 in "Walking Happy," followed by "South Pacific" (LC), "Blood Red Roses," "Two by Two," "On the Town" for which he received a Theatre World Award, "Mack and Mabel," "Musical Chairs," "A Reel American Hero," "Barnum," OB in "One for the Money," "Lovesong," "A Musical Evening with Josh Logan," "The Lullaby of Broadway," "All Night Strut!"

RICHARDSON, IAN. Born Apr. 7, 1934 in Edinburgh, Scot. Attended Royal Scotish Acad. Debut 1964 in "King Lear," followed by "Comedy of Errors," "Marat/Sade" ('65), "My Fair Lady" ('76), "Lolita," OB in "Richard II," "Summerfolk," "Love's Labour's Lost," "He That Plays the King."

RICHARDSON, PATRICIA. Born Feb. 23 in Bethesda, MD. Graduate SMU. Bdwy debut 1974 in "Gypsy," followed by "Loose Ends," OB in "Coroner's Plot," "Vanities," "Hooters," "The Frequency," "Fables for Friends."

RICHERT, WANDA. Born Apr. 18, 1958 in Chicago, IL. Bdwy debut 1980 in "42nd Street" for which she received a Theatre World Award.

RIDDLE, GEORGE. Born May 21, 1937 in Auburn, IN. OB in "Eddie Fay," "The Prodigal," "The Fantasticks," "Huui, Huui," "The Glorious Age," "The Trial of Dr. Beck."

RIEGERT, PETER. Born Apr. 11, 1947 in NYC. Graduate UBuffalo. Debut 1975 OB in "Dance with Me," followed by "Sexual Perversity in Chicago," "Sunday Runners," "Isn't It Romantic," Bdwy 1980 in "Censored Scenes from King Kong."

RILEY, LARRY. Born June 21, 1952 in Memphis, TN. Graduate Memphis State U. Bdwy debut 1978 in "A Broadway Musical," followed by "I Love My Wife," "Night and Day," "Shakespeare's Cabaret," OB in "Street Songs," "Amerika," "Plane Down," "Sidewalkin'," "Frimbo."

| Martin Robinson | Elaine Rinehart | Dylan Ross | Harriet Rogers | David Ruprecht |

RINEHART, ELAINE. Born Aug. 16, 1952 in San Antonio, TX. Graduate NC Sch of Arts. Debut 1975 OB in "Tenderloin," followed by "Native Son," Bdwy in "The Best Little Whorehouse in Texas."

RIORDAN, NAOMI. Born Aug. 25, 1926 in Muskegon, MI. Attended UCLA. Bdwy debut 1949 in "The Velvet Glove," followed by "The Country Girl," "Amazing Adele," "Absurd Person Singular."

RIVERA, CHITA. Born Jan. 23, 1933 in Washington, DC. AmSch of Ballet. Bdwy debut 1950 in "Guys and Dolls," followed by "Call Me Madam," "Can-Can," "Seventh Heaven," "Mr. Wonderful," "West Side Story," "Bye Bye Birdie," "Bajour," "Chicago," "Bring Back Birdie," OB in "Shoestring Revue."

ROBERSON, VIRGIL. Born June 17, 1953 in St. Louis, MO. Graduate UMo, PAStateU. Debut 1979 OB with The Paper Bag Players, followed by "Action," "Caine Mutiny Court Martial," "Principally Pinter/Slightly Satie."

ROBERTS, BILL. Born May 25, 1948 in Sealy, TX. Graduate Sam Huston State U. Debut 1976 OB in "Maggie Flynn," followed by "Twelfth Night," "Murder in the Cathedral."

ROBERTS, ERIC. Born Apr. 18, 1956 in Biloxi, MS. Attended RADA, AADA. Debut 1976 OB in "Rebel Women," followed by "Mass Appeal."

ROBERTS, RALPH. Born Aug. 17 in Salisbury, NC. Attended UNC. Bdwy debut 1948 in "Angel Street," followed by "4 Chekhov Comedies," "S. S. Glencairn," "Madwoman of Chaillot," "Witness for the Prosecution," "The Lark," "Bells Are Ringing," "The Milk Train Doesn't Stop Here Anymore," "Love Suicide at Schofield Barracks," "A Texas Trilogy," OB in "Siamese Connections," "Fishing."

ROBERTS, TONY. Born Oct. 22, 1939 in NYC. Graduate Northwestern U. Bdwy bow 1962 in "Something about a Soldier," followed by "Take Her, She's Mine," "Last Analysis," "Never Too Late," "Barefoot in the Park," "Don't Drink the Water," "How Now, Dow Jones," "Play It Again, Sam," "Promises, Promises," "Sugar," "Absurd Person Singular," "Murder at the Howard Johnson's." "They're Playing Our Song," OB in "The Cradle Will Rock," "Losing Time."

ROBERTSON, LILLIE. Born Sept. 5, 1953 in Houston, TX. Graduate Carnegie-Mellon U. Debut 1979 OB in "The Guardsman," followed by "Casualties."

ROBINSON, MARTIN P. Born Mar. 9, 1954 in Dearborn, MI. Graduate WiState, AADA. Debut 1980 OB in "The Haggadah," followed by "Yellow Wallpaper," "The Lady's Not for Burning."

ROCCO, MARY. Born Sept. 12, 1933 in Brooklyn, NY. Graduate Queens Col., CCNY. Debut 1976 OB in "Fiorello!," followed by "The Constant Wife," "Archy and Mehitabel," "Sweethearts."

ROCKAFELLOW, MARILYN. Born Jan. 22, 1939 in Middletown, NJ. Graduate Rutgers U. Debut 1976 OB in "La Ronde," followed by "The Art of Dining," "One Act Play Festival," Bdwy 1980 in "Clothes for a Summer Hotel."

RODD, MARCIA. Born July 8 in Lyons, KS. Attended Northwestern, Yale. Bdwy debut 1964 in "Love in E-Flat," followed by "Last of the Red Hot Lovers," "Shelter," Bdwy in "O Say Can You See L.A.," "Cambridge Circus," "Mad Show," "Merry Wives of Windsor," "I Can't Keep Running in Place."

ROERICK, WILLIAM. Born Dec. 17, 1912 in NYC. Bdwy bow 1935 in "Romeo and Juliet," followed by "St. Joan," "Hamlet," "Our Town," "The Importance of Being Earnest," "The Land Is Bright," "Autumn Hill," "This Is the Army," "The Magnificent Yankee," "Tonight at 8:30," "The Heiress," "Medea," "Macbeth," "The Burning Glass," "The Right Honourable Gentleman," "Marat/deSade," "Homecoming," "We Bombed in New Haven," "Elizabeth the Queen" (CC), "Waltz of the Toreadors," "Night of the Iguana," "The Merchant," "Happy New Year," OB in "Madam, Will You Walk," "The Cherry Orchard," "Come Slowly, Eden," "A Passage to E. M. Forster," "Trials of Oz," "Close of Play."

ROGERS, GIL. Born Feb. 4, 1934 in Lexington, KY. Attended Harvard. OB in "The Ivory Branch," "Vanity of Nothing," "Warrior's Husband," "Hell Bent fer Heaven," "Gods of Lightning," "Pictures in the Hallway," "Rose," "Memory Bank," "A Recent Killing," "Birth," "Come Back, Little Sheba," "Life of Galileo," "Remembrance," "Mecca," Bdwy in "The Great White Hope," "The Best Little Whorehouse in Texas."

ROGERS, HARRIET. Born Dec. 25, 1910 in St. Regis Falls, NY. Graduate Emerson Col. Debut 1965 OB in "Live Like Pigs," followed by "Richard II," Bdwy in "Richard III" (1979), "Morning's at 7."

ROMAGUERA, JOAQUIN. (a.k.a. Fidel Romann) Born Sept. 5, 1932 in Key West, FL. Graduate Fla. Southern Col. Debut 1961 OB in "All in Love," followed by Bdwy 1979 in "Sweeney Todd."

ROONEY, MICKEY. Born Sept. 23, 1920 in Brooklyn, NY. As a child, appeared in vaudeville with his parents Joe Yule and Nell Brown. Bdwy debut 1979 in "Sugar Babies," for which he received a Special Theatre World Award.

ROSE, GEORGE. Born Feb. 19, 1920 in Bicester, Eng. Bdwy debut with Old Vic 1946 in "Henry IV," followed by "Much Ado about Nothing," "A Man for All Seasons," "Hamlet," "Royal Hunt of the Sun," "Walking Happy," "Loot," "My Fair Lady," (CC '68), "Canterbury Tales," "Coco," "Wise Child," "Sleuth," "My Fat Friend," "My Fair Lady," "She Loves Me," "Peter Pan," BAM's "The Play's the Thing," "The Devil's Disciple," and "Julius Caesar," "The Kingfisher," "Pirates of Penzance."

ROSE, MARGOT. Born July 17, 1951 in Pittsburgh, PA. Attended Yale. NC School of Arts. Debut 1978 OB in "I'm Getting My Act Together and Taking It on the Road."

ROSIN, JAMES. Born Oct. 20, 1946 in Philadelphia, PA. Attended Temple U. Debut 1979 OB in "A Yank in Beverly Hills," followed by "A Force of Nature."

ROSS, DYLAN. Born June 10, 1930 in Racine, WI. Debut 1979 OB in "Frankenstein Affair," followed by "Period of Adjustment."

ROSS, JAMIE. Born May 4, 1939 in Markinch, Scot. Attended RADA. Bdwy debut 1962 in "Little Moon of Alban," followed by "Moon Beseiged," "Ari,"' 'Different Times," "Woman of the Year," OB in "Penny Friend," "Oh, Coward!"

ROSS, LARRY. Born Oct. 18, 1945 in Brooklyn, NY. Attended AADA. Bdwy debut 1963 in "How to Succeed . . .," followed by "Fiddler on the Roof," "Frank Merriwell," "Annie."

ROTH, ANDY. Born Jan. 5, 1952 in NYC. Graduate Brown U., Juilliard. Bdwy debut 1979 in "They're Playing Our Song," OB in "Godspell."

ROTHMAN, JOHN. Born June 3, 1949 in Baltimore, MD. Graduate Wesleyan U, Yale. Debut 1978 OB in "Rats Nest," followed by "The Impossible H. L. Mencken," "The Buddy System."

ROUNDS, DAVID. Born Oct. 9, 1930 in Bronxville, NY. Attended Denison U. Bdwy debut 1965 in "Foxy," followed by "Child's Play" for which he received a Theatre World Award, "The Rothschilds," "The Last of Mrs. Lincoln," "Chicago," "Romeo and Juliet," "Morning's at 7," OB in "You Never Can Tell," "Money," "The Real Inspector Hound," "Epic of Buster Friend," "Enter a Free Man."

ROUTLEDGE, PATRICIA. Born Feb. 17, 1929 in Birkenhead, ENG. Attended ULiverpool, Bristol Old Vic. Bdwy debut 1966 in "How's the World Treating You?," followed by "Darling of the Day," "1600 Pennsylvania Avenue," OB in "The Pirates of Penzance."

RUANE, JANINE. Born Dec. 17, 1963 in Philadelphia, PA. Bdwy debut 1977 in "Annie."

RUBINSTEIN, JOHN. Born Dec 8, 1946 in Los Angeles, CA. Attended UCLA. Bdwy debut 1972 in "Pippin" for which he received a Theatre World Award, followed by "Children of a Lesser God," "Fools."

RUDIN, STUART. Born Dec 16, 1941 in Vancouver, WA. Graduate UWa, EWaStateU. Debut 1974 OB in "Friends," followed by "Great American Stickball League," "Progress"

RUDRUD, KRISTIN. Born May 23, 1955 in Fargo, ND. Graduate Moorhead State U, LAMDA. Debut 1981 OB in "A Midsummer Night's Dream," Bdwy 1981 in "Amadeus."

RUISINGER, THOMAS. Born May 13, 1930 in Omaha, NE. Graduate SMU, Neighborhood Playhouse. Bdwy debut 1959 in "Warm Peninsula," followed by "The Captain and the Kings," "A Shot in the Dark," "Frank Merriwell," "The Importance of Being Earnest," "Snow White," "Manhattan Showboat," "A Stitch in Time," OB in "The Balcony," "Thracian Horses," "Under Milk Wood," "Six Characters in Search of an Author," "Papers," "As to the Meaning of Words."

RUPPRECHT, DAVID. Born Oct 14, 1948 in St. Louis, MO. Graduate Valparaiso U. Bdwy debut 1980 in "Perfectly Frank."

RUSKIN, JEANNE. Born Nov. 6 in Saginaw, MI. Graduate NYU. Bdwy debut 1975 in "Equus," OB in "Says I, Says He,""Cassatt," "Inadmissible Evidence," "Hedda Gabler."

| William Ryall | Fran Salisbury | Nicholas Saunders | Sophie Schwab | James Secrest |

RYALL, WILLIAM. Born Sept 18, 1954 in Binghamton, NY. Graduate AADA. Bdwy debut 1980 in "Canterbury Tales," OB in "Elizabeth and Essex,""Sound of Music"(JB).

RYAN, STEVEN. Born June 19, 1947 in NYC. Graduate Boston U., UMn. Debut 1978 OB in "Winning Isn't Everything," followed by "The Beethoven."

RYDER, ALFRED. Born Jan 5, 1919 in NYC. Bdwy bow 1929 in "Peter Pan," followed by "All the Living," "Jeremiah," "Awake and Sing," "Medicine Show,""Man with Blonde Hair," "Nathan the Wise," "Skydrift," "Yellow Jack," "Ghosts," "Julius Caesar," "Tower Beyond Tragedy," OB in "Uncle Vanya," "Volpone," "Two Character Play."

RYDER, RICHARD. Born Aug 20, 1942 in Rochester, NY. Attended Colgate U, Pratt Inst. Bdwy debut 1972 in "Oh! Calcutta," followed by "Via Galactica," OB in "Rain," "Oh, Pshaw!," "The Dog Beneath the Skin," "Polly," "Lovers," "Green Pond," "Piano Bar," "She Loves Me."

SABIN, DAVID. Born Apr 24, 1937 in Washington, DC. Graduate Catholic U. Debut 1965 OB in "The Fantasticks," followed by "Now Is the Time for All Good Men," "Threepenny Opera," "You Never Can Tell," "Master and Margarita," Bdwy in "The Yearling," "Slapstick Tragedy," "Jimmy Shine," "Gantry," "Ambassador," "Celebration," "Music Is," "The Water Engine," "The Suicide."

SACKS, DAVIA. Born July 10 in Flushing, NY. Attended Dade Jr. Col. Debut 1973 OB in "Swiss Family Robinson," followed by "Zorba," Bdwy in "Fiddler on the Roof" (1976), "Evita."

SAFFRAN, CHRISTINA. Born Oct 21, 1958 in Quincy, IL. Attended Webster Col. Bdwy debut 1978 in "A Chorus Line," followed by "A New York Summer," "Music Man."

SALISBURY, FRAN. Born Feb 9, 1945 in NYC. Graduate Shaw U., Columbia. Bdwy debut 1972 in "Purlie," followed by "Royal Family," "Reggae," OB in "Prodigal Sister," "The Lion and the Jewel," "Sparrow in Flight," Helen," "Broadway Soul," "As to the Meaning of Words."

SALOIS, DORI. Born Nov. 9 1953 in Holyoke, MA. Graduate Lowell U. Debut 1981 OB in "The Butterfingers Angel."

SANAZARO, MARIANNE. Born Nov 9, in St. Louis, MO. Graduate Stephens Col., InU. Debut 1977 OB in "Company," followed by "God Bless You, Mr. Rosewater," Bdwy 1980 in "Annie."

SANCHEZ, JAIME, Born Dec 19, 1938 in Rincon, PR. Attended Actors Studio. Bdwy bow 1957 in "West Side Story," followed by "Oh, Dad, Poor Dad ...," "Midsummer Night's Dream," "Richard III," OB in "The Toilet" "Conerico Was Here to Stay" for which he received a Theatre World Award, "The Ox Cart," "The Tempest," "Merry Wives of Windsor," "Julius Caesar," "Coriolanus."

SANDERS, JAY O. Born Apr 16, 1953 in Austin, TX. Graduate SUNY Purchase. Debut 1976 OB in "Henry V," followed by "Measure for Measure," "Scooping," "Buried Child," "Fables for Friends," "In Trousers," "Girls Girls Girls," "Twelfth Night," Bdwy 1979 in "Loose Ends."

SANTIAGO, SOCORRO. Born July 12, 1957 in NYC. Attended Juilliard. Debut 1977 OB in "Crack," followed by "Poets from the Inside," "Unfinished Women," Bdwy 1980 in "The Bacchae."

SAPUTO, PETER J. Born Feb 2, 1939 in Detroit, MI. Graduate EMiU, Purdue U. Debut 1977 OB in "King Oedipus," followed by "Twelfth Night," "Bon Voyage," "Happy Haven," "Sleepwalkers," "Humulus the Mute," "The Freak," Bdwy in "Once in a Lifetime."

SARGENT, ANNE. Born Nov. 18, 1924 in West Pittston, PA. Graduate Carnegie Tech. Bdwy debut 1945 in "The Late George Apley," followed by "I Know My Love," "The Men We Marry," "The Boy Who Lived Twice," "The Philadelphia Story."

SARNO, JANET. Born Nov 18, 1933 in Bridgeport, CT. Graduate SCTC, Yale U. Bdwy debut 1963 in "Dylan," followed by "Equus," "Knockout," OB in "6 Characters in Search of an Author," "Who's Happy Now," "Closing Green" "Fisher," "Survival of St. Joan," "The Orphan," "Mamma's Little Angels," "Knuckle Sandwich," "Marion Brando Sat Right Here," "Last Summer at Bluefish Cove."

SARRACINO, ERNEST. Born Feb 12 in Valdez, CO. Graduate LACC. Bdwy debut 1946 in "He Who Gets Slapped," followed by "Girl of the Golden West," "At War with the Army," "Filumena!"

SAUCIER, CLAUDE-ALBERT. Born Oct 9, 1953 in Berlin, NH. Graduate Dartmouth Col. Debut 1977 OB in "A Midsummer Night's Dream," followed by "Veronica's Room,"

SAUNDERS, NICHOLAS. Born June 2, 1914 in Kiev, Russia. Bdwy debut 1942 in "Lady in the Dark" followed by "A New Life," "Highland Fling," "Happily Ever After," "The Magnificent Yankee," "Anastasia," "Take Her, She's Mine," "A Call on Kuprin," "Passion of Josef D.," OB in "An Enemy of the People," "End of All Things Natural," "The Unicorn in Captivity," "After the Rise," "All My Sons," "My Great Dead Sister," "The Investigation," "Past Tense," "Scenes and Revelations."

SAXON, JAMES. Born Apr 6, 1954 in Brooklyn, NY. Graduate NYU,AADA. Debut 1980 OB in "Marching Song."

SCARDINO, DON. Born in Feb. 1949 in NYC. Attended CCNY. On Bdwy in "Loves of Cass McGuire," "Johnny No-Trump," "My Daughter, Your Son," "Godspell," "Angel," "King of Hearts," OB in "Shout from the Rooftops," "Rimers of Eldrich," "The Unknown Soldier and His Wife," "Godspell," "Moonchildren," "Kid Champion," "Comedy of Errors," "Secret Service," "Boy Meets Girl," "Scribes," "I'm Getting My Act Together ...,""As You Like It,""Holeville,""Sorrows of Stephen," "A Midsummer Night's Dream," "The Recruiting Officer," "Jungle of Cities."

SCHAUT, ANN LOUISE. Born Nov 21, 1956 in Minneapolis, MN. Attended UMn. Bdwy debut 1981 in "A Chorus Line."

SCHECHTER, DAVID. Born Apr 12, 1956 in NYC. Bard Col. Neighborhood Playhouse graduate. Debut 1976 OB in "Nightclub Cantata," followed by "Dispatches," "The Haggadah," Bdwy in "Runaways" (1978).

SCHLEE, ROBERT. Born June 13, 1938 in Williamsport, PA. Graduate Lycoming Col. Debut 1972 OB in "Dr. Selavy's Magic Theatre," followed by "Hotel for Criminals," "Threepenny Opera," "Penguin Touquet."

SCHNABEL, STEFAN. Born Feb 2, 1912 in Berlin, Ger. Attended UBonn. Old Vic. Bdwy bow 1937 in "Julius Caesar," followed by "Shoemaker's Holiday," "Glamour Preferred," "Land of Fame," "Cherry Orchard," "Around the World in 80 Days," "Now I Lay Me Down to Sleep," "Idiot's Delight," "Love of Four Colonels," "Plain and Fancy," "Small War on Murray Hill," "A Very Rich Woman," "A Patriot for Me," "Teibele and Her Demon," OB in "Tango," "In the Matter of J. Robert Oppenheimer," "Older People," "Enemies," "Little Black Sheep," "Rosmersholm," "Passion of Dracula," "Biography," "The Firebugs."

SCHREIBER, AVERY. Born Apr. 9, 1935 in Chicago, IL. Graduate Goodman ThSch. Debut 1965 OB in "Second City at Square East," followed by "Conerico Was Here to Stay," Bdwy in "Metamorphoses," "Dreyfus in Rehearsal," "Can-Can." (1981).

SCHULL, REBECCA. Born Feb 22 in NYC. Graduate NYU. Bdwy debut 1976 in "Herzl" followed by "Golda," OB in "Mother's Day," "Fefu and Her Friends," "On Mt. Chimborazo," "Mary Stuart."

SCHWAB, SOPHIE. Born Feb 23, 1954 in Miami, FL. Graduate Northwestern U. Debut 1976 OB in "Fiorello!," followed by "King of Schnorrers," "She Loves Me," Bdwy 1980 in "Barnum."

SCOTT, GEORGE C. Born Oct. 18, 1927 in Wise, VA. Debut 1957 OB in "Richard III" for which he received a Theatre World Award, followed by "As You Like It," "Children of Darkness," "Desire under the Elms," Bdwy in "Comes a Day," "Andersonville Trial," "The Wall," "General Seegar," "The Little Foxes," "Plaza Suite," "Uncle Vanya," "Death of a Salesman," "Sly Fox," "Tricks of the Trade."

SCOTT, KEVIN. Born Dec. 10, 1928 in Oakland, CA. Bdwy debut 1952 in "Wish You Were Here," followed by "Carnival in Flanders," "Almost Crazy," OB in "Ralph Roister Doister."

SCOTT, MICHAEL. Born Jan 24, 1954 in Santa Monica, CA. Attended Cal. State U. Debut 1978 (OB and Bdwy) in "The Best Little Whorehouse in Texas," followed by "Happy New Year."

SCOTT, SERET. Born Sept. 1, 1949 in Washington, DC. Attended NYU. Debut 1969 OB in "Slave Ship," followed by "Ceremonies in Dark Old Men," "Black Terror," "Dream," "One Last Look," "My Sister, My Sister," "Weep Not for Me," "Meetings."

SEAMON, EDWARD. Born Apr 15, 1937 in San Diego, CA. Attended San Diego State U. Debut 1971 OB in "The Life and Times of J. Walter Smintheous," followed by "The Contractor." "The Family," "Fishing," "Feedlot," "Cabin 12," "Rear Column," "Devour the Snow," "Buried Child," "Friends," Bdwy in "The Trip Back Down," "Devour the Snow," "The American Clock."

SECREST, JAMES. Born Nov. 17 in Thomasville, GA. Graduate UNC. Debut 1966 in "Girl in the Freudian Slip," OB in "John Brown's Body," "Trial of the Catonsville Nine."

| Marcie Shaw | Martin Shakar | Joan Shepard | Ben Siegler | Leda Siskind |

SEFF, RICHARD. Born Sept 23, 1927 In NYC. Attended NYU. Bdwy debut 1951 in "Darkness at Noon," followed by "Herzl," OB in "Big Fish, Little Fish," "Modigliani," "Childe Byron."

SELBY, JAMES. Born Aug 29, 1948 in San Francisco, CA. Graduate Washburn U. Debut 1978 OB in "The Rivals," followed by "Caligula," "L'Ete," "A Prayer for My Daughter."

SELDES, MARIAN. Born Aug 23, 1928 in NYC. Attended Neighborhood Playhouse. Bdwy debut 1947 in "Medea," followed by "Crime and Punishment," "That Lady," "Tower Beyond Tragedy," "Ondine," "On High Ground." "Come of Age," "Chalk Garden," "The Milk Train Doesn't Stop Here Anymore," "The Wall," "A Gift of Time," "A Delicate Balance," "Before You Go," "Father's Day," "Equus," "The Merchant," "Deathtrap," OB in "Different," "Ginger Man," "Mercy Street," "Candle in the Wind," "Isadora Duncan Sleeps with the Russian Navy."

SELL, JANIE. Born Oct 1, 1941 in Detroit, MI. Attended UDetroit. Debut 1966 OB in "Mixed Doubles," followed by "Dark Horses," "Dames at Sea," "By Bernstein," "God Bless You, Mr. Rosewater," "Sidewalkin'," "Real Life Funnies," Bdwy in "George M!," "Irene," "Over Here" for which she received a Theatre World Award "Pal Joey," "Happy End,." "I Love My Wife."

SERRANO, CHARLIE. Born Dec. 4, 1952 in Rio Piedras, PR. Attended Brooklyn Col. Debut 1978 OB in "Allegro" followed by "Mama, I Want to Sing," Bdwy 1979 in "Got Tu Go Disco."

SERRECCHIA, MICHAEL. Born Mar. 26, 1951 In Brooklyn, NY. Attended Brockport State U. Teachers Col. Bdwy debut 1972 in "The Selling of the President," followed by "Heathen!," "Seesaw," "A Chorus Line," OB in "Lady Audley's Secret."

SETRAKIAN, ED. Born Oct. 1, 1928 in Jenkintown. WV. Graduate Concord Col., NYU. Debut 1966 OB in "Drums in the Night," followed by "Othello," "Coriolanus," "Macbeth," "Hamlet," "Baal," "Old Glory," "Futz," "Hey Rube," "Seduced," "Shout across the River," "American Days," Bdwy in "Days in the Trees," "St. Joan," "The Best Little Whorehouse in Texas."

SEVERS, WILLIAM. Born Jan. 8, 1932 in Britton, OK. Attended Pasadena Playhouse, Columbia Col. Bdwy debut 1960 in "Cut of the Axe," OB in "The Moon Is Blue," "Lulu," "Big Maggie," "Mixed Doubles," "The Rivals," "The Beaver Coat," "Twister."

SEVRA, ROBERT. Born Apr. 15, 1945 in Kansas City, Mo. Graduate Stanford U., UMi. Debut 1972 OB in "Servant of Two Masters," followed by "Lovers," Bdwy 1980 in "Charlie and Algernon."

SEYMOUR, JANE. Born Feb. 15, 1951 in Hillingdon, Middlesex, Eng. Attended Arts Educational Trust. Bdwy debut 1980 in "Amadeus."

SHAKAR, MARTIN. Born Jan. 1, 1940 in Detroit, MI. Attended Wayne State U. Bdwy bow 1969 in "Our Town," OB in "Lorenzaccio," "Macbeth," "The Infantry," "Americana Pastoral," "No Place to Be Somebody," "World of Mrs. Solomon," "And Whose Little Boy Are You," "Investigation of Havana," "Night Watch," "Owners," "Actors," "Richard III," "Transfiguration of Benno Blimpie," "Jack Gelber's New Play," "Biko Inquest," "Second-Story Sunlight," "Secret Thighs of New England Women."

SHANE, HAL. Born Mar. 17, 1948 in Rockaway, NY. Graduate Hofstra U. Bdwy debut 1975 in "Very Good Eddie," followed by "They're Playing Our Song."

SHANGOLD, JOAN. Born Mar. 28 in Albany, NY. Debut 1977 OB in "The Crucible," followed by "Love's Labor's Lost."

SHAPIRO, DEBBIE. Born Sept. 29, 1954 in Los Angeles, CA. Graduate LACC. Bdwy debut 1979 in "They're Playing Our Song." followed by "Perfectly Frank."

SHARKEY, SUSAN. Born Dec. 12 in NYC. Graduate UAZ. Debut 1968 OB in "Guns of Carrar," followed by "Cuba Si," "Playboy of the Western World," "Good Woman of Setzuan," "Enemy of the People," "People Are Living There," "Narrow Road to the Deep North," "Enemies," "The Plough and the Stars," "The Sea," "The Sykovs," "Catsplay," "Ice," Bdwy 1980 in "The American Clock."

SHAW, MARCIE. Born June 19, 1954 in Franklin Square, NY. Attended UIl. Bdwy debut 1980 in "Pirates of Penzance."

SHEA, JOHN V. Born Apr. 14 in North Conway, NH. Graduate Bates Col., Yale. Debut OB 1974 in "Yentl, the Yeshiva Boy," followed by "Gorky," "Battering Ram," "Safe House," "The Master and Margarita," "Sorrows of Stephen," "American Days," Bdwy in "Yentl" (1975) for which he received a Theatre World Award, "Romeo and Juliet."

SHELLEY, CAROLE. Born Aug. 16, 1939 in London, Eng. Bdwy debut 1965 in "The Odd Couple," followed by "Astrakhan Coat," "Loot," "Noel Coward's Sweet Potato," "Hay Fever," "Absurd Person Singular," "The Norman Conquests," "The Elephant Man," OB in "Little Murders," "The Devil's Disciple," "The Play's the Thing."

SHELTON, REID. Born Oct. 7, 1924 in Salem, OR. Graduate U. Mich. Bdwy bow 1952 in "Wish You Were Here," followed by "Wonderful Town," "By The Beautiful Sea," "Saint of Bleecker Street," "My Fair Lady," "Oh! What a Lovely War!," "Carousel" (CC), "Canterbury Tales," "Rothschilds," "1600 Pennsylvania Avenue," "Annie," OB in "Phedre," "Butterfly Dream," "Man with a Load of Mischief," "Beggars Opera," "The Contractor," "Cast Aways."

SHELTON, SLOANE. Born Mar. 17, 1934 in Asheville, NC. Attended Berea Col., RADA. Bdwy debut 1967 in "The Imaginary Invalid," followed by "A Touch of the Poet," "Tonight at 8:30," "I Never Sang for My Father," "Sticks and Bones," "The Runner Stumbles," "Shadow Box," "Passione," OB in "Androcles and the Lion," "The Maids," "Basic Training of Pavlo Hummel," "Play and Other Plays," "Julius Caesar," "Chieftains," "Passione."

SHENAR, PAUL. Born Feb. 12. 1936 in Milwaukee, WI. Graduate UWI. Bdwy debut 1969 in "Tiny Alice," followed by "Three Sisters," OB in "Six Characters in Search of an Author," "Hedda Gabler."

SHEPARD, JOAN. Born Jan. 7 in NYC. Graduate RADA. Bdwy debut 1940 in "Romeo and Juliet," followed by "Sunny River," "The Strings, My Lord, Are False," "This Rock," "Foolish Notion," "A Young Man's Fancy," "My Romance," "Member of the Wedding," OB in "Othello," "Plot against the Chase Manhattan Bank," "Philosophy in the Boudoir," "Knitters in the Sun."

SHERMAN, BRUCE. Born June 20, 1953 in Philadelphia, PA. Graduate UFL., Neighborhood Playhouse. Debut 1976 OB in "The Boys from Syracuse," followed by "The Music Man" (JB), Bdwy in "Snow White." (1979), "Copperfield."

SHIELDS, ROBERT. Born Mar. 26, 1951 in Los Angeles, CA. Bdwy debut 1981 in "Broadway Follies."

SHIMERMAN, ARMIN. Born Nov. 5, 1949 in Lakewood, NJ. Graduate UCLA. Debut 1976 in "Threepenny Opera" (LC), followed by "Silk Stockings" (ELT), "When the War Was Over," "The Possessed," "Principally Pinter," Bdwy in "St. Joan," (1977). "I Remember Mama." (1979)

SHIMIZU, KEENAN. Born Oct. 22, 1956 in NYC. Graduate HS of Performing Arts. Bdwy 1965 in CC's "South Pacific" and "The King and I," OB in "Rashomon," "The Year of the Dragon," "The Catch," "Peking Man," "Flowers and Household Gods."

SHROPSHIRE, NOBLE. Born Mar. 2, 1946 in Cartersville, GA. Graduate LaGrange Col., RADA. Debut 1976 OB in "Hound of the Baskervilles," followed by "The Misanthrope," "The Guardsman," "Oedipus Cycle," "Gilles de Rais," "Leonce and Lena."

SHULL, RICHARD B. Born Feb. 24, 1929 in Elmhurst, NY. Graduate IOStateU. Bdwy debut 1954 in "Black-Eyed Susan," followed by "Wake Up, Darling," "Red Roses for Me," "I Knock at the Door," "Pictures in the Hallway," "Have I Got a Girl for You," "Minnie's Boys," "Goodtime Charley," "Fools," OB in "Purple Dust," "Journey to the Day," "American Hamburger League," "Frimbo."

SIEGLER, BEN. Born Apr. 9, 1958 in Queens, NY. Attended HB Studio Debut 1980 OB in "Innocent Thoughts, Harmless Intentions," followed by "The Diviners," Bdwy 1981 in "5th of July."

SIFF, IRA. Born Feb. 15, 1946 in NYC. Graduate Cooper Union. Debut 1972 OB in "Joan," followed by "The Faggot," "The Haggadah."

SILBER, DAVID. Born Feb. 21, 1953 in New Haven, CT. Graduate Boston U. Debut 1978 OB in "The Changeling," followed by "The Doctor's Dilemma," "The Story of the Gadsbys."

SILVER, SHELDON. Born Nov. 30 in Philadelphia, PA. Graduate Temple U, ILStateU. Debut 1976 OB in "Fiorello!," followed by "Allegro," "Me and Molly."

SIMPSON, THOMAS. Born Nov. 15, 1953 in Chicago, IL. Graduate Grinnell Col. Debut 1977 OB in "Hagar's Children," followed by "Self-Surgery."

SISKIND, LEDA. Born Sept. 16, 1952 in Los Angeles, CA. Graduate UCA. Debut 1978 OB in "Hamlet Revisited," followed by "Why I live at the P.O.," "I Paid My Dues," Bdwy 1980 in "The Suicide."

SKALA, LILIA. Born in Vienna; graduate UDresden. Bdwy debut 1941 in "Letters to Lucerne," followed by "With a Silk Thread," "Call Me Madam," "Diary of Anne Frank," "Threepenny Opera," "Zelda," "40 Carats," "The Survivor," OB in "Medea and Jason," "Gorky."

| Sheila Smith | Cameron Smith | Donna Sontag | Franco Spoto | Pat Stanley |

SLACK, BEN. Born July 23, 1937 in Baltimore, MD. Graduate Catholic U. Debut 1971 OB in "Oedipus at Colonus" followed by "Interrogation of Havana," "Rain," "Thunder Rock," "Trelawny of the Wells," "Heartbreak House," "The Dodge Boys," "Henry V," "Sunset," "House of Blue Leaves," "Every Place Is Newark," Bdwy in "Legend," "On Golden Pond," "Heartland."

SLATER, CHRISTIAN. Born Aug. 18, 1969 in NYC. Bdwy debut 1980 in "The Music Man," followed by "Copperfield," OB in "Between Daylight and Boonville."

SLAVIN, SUSAN. Born Nov. 21 in Chicago, IL. Attended HB Studio. Debut 1968 OB in "The Mad Show," followed by "Dark of the Moon," "Sidnee Poet Heroical," "Wine Untouched," "Motherlove," "Last Summer at Bluefish Cove."

SLOMAN, JOHN. Born June 23, 1954 in Rochester, NY. Graduate SUNY/-Genesco, Debut 1977 OB in "Unsung Cole," Bdwy in "Whoopee!," "The 1940's Radio Show," "A Day in Hollywood/A Night in the Ukraine."

SMITH, CAMERON. Born Aug. 13 in Dayton, OH. Graduate OhU. Debut 1975 OB in "The Three Musketeers," followed by "Twelfth Night," "Fourtune."

SMITH, CATHERINE LEE. Born May 28, 1955 in NYC Juilliard graduate. Bdwy debut 1976 in "Home Sweet Homer," followed by "The Bacchae," OB in "In the Well of the House."

SMITH, DEE DEE. Born June 29, 1958 in NYC.Attended Staten Is. Col. Debut 1970 OB in "The Me Nobody Knows," followed by "Onury," "The Stronger," "The In Crowd," "Poets from the Inside," "Ain't Supposed to Die a Natural Death," "Raisin," Bdwy in "Runaways" (1978.)

SMITH, EBBE ROE. Born June 25, 1949 in San Diego, CA. Graduate San Francisco State U. Debut 1978 OB in "Curse of the Starving Class," followed by "New Jerusalem," "Shout across the River," "Sunday Runners," "After the Revolution."

SMITH, LOUIS. Born Nov. 3, 1930 in Topeka, KS. Attended UWash. Bdwy debut 1952 in "Time Out for Ginger," followed by "The Young and Beautiful." "Wisteria Tress," "Glass Menagerie," "Orpheus Descending," "Stages," OB in "Sunday Dinner," "Present Tense," "The Iceman Cometh," "Harry Outside," "Hillbilly Women," "Touching Bottom," "Tennessee," "After All."

SMITH, LOUISE. Born Feb. 8, 1955 in NYC. Graduate Antioch Col. Debut 1981 OB in "The Haggadah."

SMITH, MOLLIE. Born Mar. 6, 1958 in Portland, OR. Attended Portland State U. Bdwy debut 1979 in "The American Dance Machine," followed by "Brigadoon."

SMITH, REX. Born Sept. 19, 1955 in Jacksonville, FL. Bdwy debut 1978 in "Grease," followed by "The Pirates of Penzance" for which he received a Theatre World Award.

SMITH, SHEILA. Born Apr. 3, 1933 in Conneaut, OH. Attended Kent State U., Cleveland Play House. Bdwy debut 1963 in "Hot Spot," followed by "Mame" for which she received a Theatre World Award, "Follies," "Company," "Sugar," "Five O'Clock Girl," OB in "Taboo Revue," "Anything Goes," "Best Foot Forward," "Sweet Miani," "Fiorello."

SMITROVICH, BILL. Born May 16, 1947 in Bridgeport, CT. Graduate UBridgeport, Smith Col. Bdwy debut 1980 in "The American Clock."

SNELL, DAVID. Born Oct. 4, 1942 in Baltimore, MD. Graduate Hamilton Col., Catholic U. Debut 1970 OB in "Wars of Roses," followed by "Macbeth," "Beggar's Opera," "The Fantasticks," "Bits and Pieces," Bdwy in "Shelter" (1973), "To Grandmother's House We Go."

SNODGRESS, CARRIE. Born Oct. 27, 1946 in Chicago, IL. Attended UNI. Debut 1981 OB in "A Coupla White Chicks Sitting Around Talking."

SNOW, NORMAN. Born Mar. 29, 1950 in Little Rock, AR. Juilliard graduate. Debut 1972 OB in "School for Scandal," followed by "Lower Depths," "Hostage," "Timon of Athens," "Cymbeline," "U.S.A.," "Women Beware Women," "One Crack Out," BAM Theatre Co.'s "A Winter's Tale," "Johnny on a Spot," "The Wedding," Bdwy in "Three Sisters," "Measure for Measure," "Beggar's Opera," "Next Time I'll Sing to You," "Macbeth."

SOD, TED. Born May 12, 1951 in Wilkes-Barre, PA. Graduate King's Col. Debut 1976 OB in "Henry V," followed by "Savages," "City Junket," "A Midsummer Night's Dream," "The Recruiting Officer," "Jungle of Cities," "The Wild Duck."

SONTAG, DONNA. Born Dec. 15, 1952 in Cincinnati, OH. Graduate Cinn-Consv. of Music. Debut 1979 OB in "Big Bad Burlesque," followed by "Sister Aimee."

SOREL, ANITA. Born Oct. 25, in Hollywood, CA. Graduate UUtah, Cal-State/ Long Beach. Debut 1980 OB in "The Time of the Cuckoo" (ELT) followed by "Bourgeois Gentlement."

SOREL, THEODORE, Born Nov. 14, 1936 in San Francisco, CA. Graduate Col. of the Pacific. Bdwy debut 1977 in "Sly Fox," followed by "Horowitz and Mrs. Washington," OB in "Arms and the Man," "Moon Mysteries," "A Call from the East," "Hedda Gabler."

SPENCER, ALEXANDER. Born July 31, 1946 in Cambus, Scot. Graduate Manchester U./ Bdwy Debut 1980 in "Dogg's Hamlet," OB in "American Days."

SPIEGEL, BARBARA. Born Mar. 12 in NYC. Debut 1969 in LCRep's "Camino Real," "Operation Sidewinder," and "Beggar on Horseback," OB in "Feast for Flies," "Museum," "Powder," "The Bleachers," "Nightshift," "Cassatt," "The Rope Dancers."

SPOTO, FRANCO. Born Aug. 12, 1945 in Lincoln, NE. Graduate Oberlin Col. Bdwy debut 1979 in "The Most Happy Fella."

SQUIRE, KATHERINE. Born Mar. 9, 1903 in Defiance, OH. Attended Ohio Wesleyan, Cleveland Playhouse. Bdwy debut 1932 in "Black Tower," followed by "Goodbye Again," "High Tor," "Hipper's Holiday," "What a Life," "Liberty Jones," "The Family," "Shadow of a Gunman," "Traveling Lady," OB in "Roots," "This Here Nice Place," "Boy on a Straight-Back Chair," "Catsplay," "Hillbilly Women," "A Memory of Whiteness," "Hedda Gabler."

STANLEY, FLORENCE. Born July 1, in Chicago. Graduate Northwestern U. OB in "Machinal," "Electra," Bdwy in "Glass Menagerie" ('65) followed by "Fiddler on the Roof," "A Safe Place," "Prisoner of Second Avenue," "Secret Affairs of Mildred Wild," "Fools."

STANLEY, GORDON. Born Dec. 20, 1951 in Boston, MA. Graduate Brown U., Temple U. Debut 1977 OB in "Lyrical and Satirical," Followed by "Allegro," "Elizabeth and Essex," "Two on the Isles," Bdwy in "Onward Victoria" (1980).

STANLEY, PAT. Born Apr. 12, 1931 in Cincinnati, OH. Attended Wm. Woods Jr. Col. Debut 1952 in "Of Thee I Sing," followed by "Carnival in Flanders," "Blue Denim," "The Pajama Game," "Carousel," "Goldilocks," "Fiorello!," "Sunday in New York," "Five O'Clock Girl."

STANNARD, NICK. Born Dec. 2, 1948 in Cohasset, MA. Attended Carnegie-Mellon U. Debut 1975 OB in "Wings," followed by "Beyond Therapy," Bdwy 1979 in "Dracula."

STAPLETON, MAUREEN. Born June 21, 1925 in Troy, NY. Attended HB Studio. Bdwy debut 1946 in "Playboy of the Western World," followed by "Antony and Cleopatra," "Detective Story," "Bird Cage," "The Rose Tattoo" for which she received a Theatre World Award, "The Emperor's Clothes," "The Crucible," " Richard III," "The Seagull," "27 Wagons Full of Cotton," "Orpheus Descending," "The Cold Wind and the Warm," "Toys in the Attic," "Glass Menagerie" (1965 & 1975), "Plaza Suite," "Norman, Is That You?" "Gingerbread Lady," "Country Girl," "Secret Affairs of Mildred Wild," "The Gin Game," "The Little Foxes" (1981).

STARK, MOLLY. Born in NYC. Graduate Hunter Co. Debut 1969 OB in "Sacco-Vanzetti," followed by "Riders to the Sea," "Medea," "One Cent Plain," "Elizabeth and Essex," "Principally Pinter," Bdwy 1973 in "Molly."

STATTEL, ROBERT. Born Nov. 20, 1937 in Floral Park, NY. Graduate Manhattan Col. Debut 1958 OB in "Heloise," followed by "When I Was a Child," "Man and Superman," "The Storm," "Don Carlos," "Taming of the Shrew," "Titus Andronicus," "Henry IV," "Peer Gynt," "Hamlet," LCRep's "Danton's Death," "Country Wife," "Caucasian Chalk Circle," and "King Lear," "Iphigenia in Aulis," "Ergo," " The Persians," "Blue Boys," "The Minister's Black Veil," "Four Friends," "Two Character Play," "The Merchant of Venice," "Cuchulain," "Oedipus Cycle," "Gilles de Rais," "Woyzeck."

STEINBERG, ROY. Born Mar. 24, 1951 in NYC. Graduate Tufts U., Yale. Debut 1974 OB in "A Midsummer Night's Dream," followed by "Firebugs," "The Doctor in spite of Himself," "Romeo and Juliet," "After the Rise," "Our Father," Bdwy in "Wings."

STEINER, SHERRY. Born Sept. 29, 1948 in NYC. Graduate Chatham Col. Debut 1978 OB in "Catsplay," followed by "Safe House," "Frankie and Annie," "The Sorrows of Stephen," "A Winter's Tale," "Barbarians," "The Purging." Bdwy in "Piaf" (1981).

Daniel Stewart

Dorothy Stinnette

Jesse Stokes

Quincella Swyningan

Jay Stuart

STENBORG, HELEN. Born Jan. 24, 1925 in Minneapolis, MN. Attended Hunter Col. OB in "A Doll's House," "A Month in the Country," "Say Nothing," "Rosmersholm," "Rimers of Eldrich," "Trial of the Catonsville 9," "Hot l Baltimore," "Pericles," "Elephant in the House," "A Tribute to Lili Lamont," "Museum," "5th of July," "In the Recovery Lounge," "The Chisholm Trail," Bdwy in "Sheep on the Runway," "Da," "A Life."

STEPHENSON, ALBERT. Born Aug. 23, 1947 in Miami, FL. Attended Boston Consv. Bdwy debut 1973 in "Irene," followed by "Debbie Reynolds Show," "The Act," "A Broadway Musical," "A Day in Hollywood/A Night in the Ukraine."

STERNHAGEN, FRANCES. Born Jan. 13, 1932 in Washington, DC. Vassar graduate, OB in "Admirable Bashful," "Thieves' Carnival," "Country Wife," "Ulysses in Nighttown," "Saintliness of Margery Kemp," "The Room," "A Slight Ache," "Displaced Person," "Playboy of the Western World," "The Prevalence of Mrs. Seal," Bdway in "Great Day in the Morning," "Right Honourable Gentleman," with APA in "Cocktail Party," and "Cock-a-doodle Dandy," "The Sign in Sidney Brustein's Window," "Enemies," (LC), "The Good Doctor," "Equus," "Angel," "On Golden Pond," "The Father."

STEVENS, SUSAN. Born in 1942 in Louisville, KY. Attended Jackson Col., AMDA. Debut 1978 in "The Price of Genius," followed by "A Dream Play."

STEWART, DANIEL. Born June 6, 1957 in Olympia, WA. Attended FLstateU. Debut 1981 OB in "The Miser."

STEWART, DON. Born Nov. 14, 1935 in Staten Island, NY. Attended Wichita U. Bdwy debut 1960 in "Camelot," followed by "The Student Gypsy," OB in "The Fantasticks," "Jo," "Babes in the Woods," "The Music Man" (JB).

STEWART, SCOT. Born March 3, 1941 in Tylertown, MS. Graduate UMiss. Debut 1975 OB in "New Girl in Town," Bdwy 1979 in "Sugar Babies."

STILLER, JERRY. Born June 8, 1931 in NYC. Graduate USyracuse. Debut 1953 OB in "Coriolanus," followed by "The Power and the Glory," "Golden Apple," "Measure for Measure," "Taming of the Shrew," "Carefree Tree," "Diary of a Scoundrel," "Romeo and Juliet," "As You Like It," "Two Gentlemen of Verona," "Passione," Bdwy in "The Ritz," "Unexpected Guests," "Passione."

STINNETTE, DOROTHY. Born May 22, 1933 in Wichita, KS. Graduate Northwestern U. Bdwy debut 1953 in "Solid Gold Cadillac," followed by "New Girl in Town," "Ambassador," "Ziegfeld Follies," "The Man Who Came to Dinner" ('80), OB in "Out of This World," "Leave It to Jane," "The Queen and the Rebels."

STINTON, COLIN. Born Mar. 10, 1947 in Kansas City, MO. Attended Northwestern U. Debut 1978 OB in "The Water Engine" (also Bdwy) for which he received a Theatre World Award, followed by "Twelfth Night," "The Beaver Coat."

ST. DAVID, MARTYN. Born Jan. 14 in Southport, NC. Bdwy debut 1981 in "Heartland."

STOKES, JESSE. Born Jan. 25, 1954 in Norfolk, VA. Attended East Carolina U., HB Studio. Debut 1981 OB in "The Meehans."

STOLARSKY, PAUL. Born Feb. 18, 1933 in Detroit, MI. Graduate Wayne State U, UMich. Debut 1972 OB in "Bluebird," followed by "Let Yourself Go," "Rocket to the Moon," "D.," "My Mother, My Father and Me," "Me and Molly," Bdwy 1980 in "Nuts."

STONE, MAX. Born Oct. 23, 1954 in Greenville, TX. Attended Tx Christian U., SMU. Bdwy debut 1979 in "They're Playing Our Song."

STONEBURNER, SAM. Born Feb. 24, 1934 in Fairfax, VA. Graduate Georgetown U, AADA. Debut 1960 OB in "Ernest in Love," followed by "Foreplay," "Anyone Can Whistle." Bdwy in "Different Times" (1972), "Bent," "Macbeth" (1981).

STOUT, MARY. Born Apr. 8, 1952 in Huntington, WV. Graduate Marshall U. Debut 1980 OB in "Plain and Fancy" (ELT), Bdwy 1981 in "Copperfield."

STOVALL, COUNT. Born Jan. 15, 1946 in Los Angeles, CA. Graduate UCal. Debut 1973 OB in "He's Got a Jones," followed by "In White America," "Rashomon," "Sidnee Poet Heroical," "A Photo," "Julius Caesar," "Coriolanus," "Spell #7," "The Jail Diary of Albie Sachs," "To Make A Poet Black," "Transcendental Blues," Bdwy in "Inacent Black," "The Philadelphia Story."

STRATTON, RONALD BENNETT. Born Jan. 11, 1942 in Philadelphia, PA. Bdwy debut 1959 in "Kiss Me Kate," followed by "Goldilocks," "Happiest Girl n Town," "Subways Are for Sleeping," "Tenderloin," "Kelly," "Her First Roman," "Annie Get YOur Gun," "Mame," "Camelot" (1980).

STREEP, MERYL. Born Sept. 22 in Summit, NJ. Graduate Vassar, Yale. Debut 1975 OB in "Trelawny of the Wells," followed by "27 Wagons Full of Cotton" for which she received a Theatre World Award, "A Memory of Two Mondays," "Secret Service," "Henry V," "Taming of the Shrew," "Measure for Measure," "Taken in Marriage," "Alice in Concert," Bdwy in "Happy End" (1977), "The Cherry Orchard."

STRICKLER, DAN. Born Feb. 4, 1949 in Los Angeles, CA. Graduate CalStateU, Temple U. Debut 1977 OB in "Jules Feiffer's Hold Me!," followed by "Flying Blind," "Coming Attractions."

STROMAN, GUY. Born Sept. 11, 1951 in Terrell, TX. Graduate TX. Christian U. Bdwy debut 1979 in "Peter Pan," OB in "Glory! Hallelujah!"

STRUDWICK, SHEPPERD. Born Sept. 22, 1907 in Hillsboro, NC. Graduate UNC. Bdwy bow 1929 in "Yellow Jacket," followed by "Both Your Houses," "Let Freedom Ring," "End of Summer," "As You Like It," "Christopher Blake," "Affairs of State," "Ladies of the Corridor," "Doctors Dilemma," "The Seagull," "Night Circus," "Desert Incident," "Only in America," "J.B.," "Who's Afraid of Virginia Woolf?," "The Devils," "The Price," "Galileo," "Measure for Measure," "Timon of Athens," "Desert Song," "Eccentricities of a Nightingale," "To Grandmother's House We Go," "Morning's at 7."

STRUTHERS, SALLY. Born July 28, 1948 in Portland, OR. Attended Pasadena Playhouse. Bdwy debut 1981 in "Wally's Cafe."

STRYK, LYDIA. Born Nov. 3, 1958 in DeKalb, IL. Attended London Drama Centre. Debut 1980 OB in "After the Revolution," followed by "Twister."

STUART, JAY. Born in Brooklyn, NY. Bdwy debut 1970 in "Cry for Us All," followed by "Applause," "The Pajama Game," "The Grand Tour," "The Music Man," OB in "A Little Night Music."

STUTHMAN, FRED. Born June 27, 1919 in Long Beach, CA. Attended UCa. Debut 1970 OB in "Hamlet," followed by "Uncle Vanya," "Charles Abbott & Son," "She Stoops to Conquer," "The Master Builder," "Taming of the Shrew," "Misalliance," "Merchant of Venice," "Conditions of Agreement," "The Play's the Thing," "Ghosts," "The Father," "Hot 1 Baltimore," "The Cherry Orchard," "The Devil's Disciple," "Bonjour, La, Bonjour," Bdwy in "Sherlock Holmes" ('75), "Fools."

SULLIVAN, JO. Born Aug. 28 in Mounds, IL. Attended Columbia U. Bdwy debut 1950 in "Let's Make an Opera," followed by "Carousel," "Most Happy Fella," "Wonderful Town," "Show Boat," "Perfectly Frank," OB in "Threepenny Opera."

SUNDSTEN, LANI. Born Feb. 27, 1949 in NYC. Attended Am Col. in Paris. Bdwy debut 1970 in "The Rothschilds," followed by "Tricks," "California Suite," "Scapino," "They're Playing Our Song," OB in "Carousel," "In the Boom Boom Room."

SUROVY, NICOLAS. Born June 30, 1944 in Los Angeles, CA. Attended Northwestern U., Neighborhood Playhouse. Debut 1964 OB in "Helen" for which he received a Theatre World Award, followed by "Sisters of Mercy," "Cloud 9," Bdwy in "Merchant," "Crucifer of Blood," "Major Barbara."

SUTHERLAND, DONALD. Born July 17, 1935 in St. John, New Brunswick, Can. Bdwy debut 1981 in "Lolita."

SWENSON, SWEN. Born Jan. 23, 1932 in Inwood, IA. Bdwy Debut 1950 in "Great to Be Alive" followed by "Bless You All," "As I Lay Dying," "Destry Rides Again," "Wildcat," "Golden Apple," "Little Me" for which he received a Theatre World Award, "Molly," "Ulysses in Nighttown," "Can-Can."

SWYNINGAN, QUINCELLA. Born May 6 in St. Paul, MN. Bdwy debut 1980 in "Your Arms Too Short to Box with God."

SYERS, MARK. Born Oct. 25, 1952 in Trenton, NJ. Graduate Emerson Col. Bdwy debut 1976 in "Pacific Overtures," followed by "Jesus Christ Superstar" (1977), "Evita:" OB in "Under Fire."

TALMAN, ANN. Born Sept. 13, 1957 in Welch, WVa. Graduate PaStateU. Debut 1980 OB in "What's So Beautiful about a Sunset over Prairie Avenue?," Bdwy 1981 in "The Little Foxes."

TANDY, JESSICA. Born June 7, 1909 in London, Eng. Attended Greet Acad. Bdwy debut 1930 in "The Matriarch," followed by "Last Enemy," "Time and the Conways," "White Steed," "Geneva," "Jupiter Laughs," "Anne of England," "Yesterday's Magic," "A Streetcar Named Desire," "Hilda Crane," "The Fourposter," "The Honeys," "A Day by the Sea," "Man in the Dog Suit," "Triple Play," "Five Finger Exercise," "The Physicists," "A Delicate Balance," "Home," "All Over," "Camino Real," "Not I," "Happy Days," "Noel Coward in Two Keys," "The Gin Game," "Rose."

| Maggie Task | Bill Tatum | Mary Testa | Frank Torren | Laurine Towler |

TARLETON, DIANE. Born Oct. 25, in Baltimore, MD. Graduate UMd. Bdwy debut 1965 in "Anya," followed by "A Joyful Noise," "Elmer Gantry," "Yentl," OB in "A Time for the Gentle People," "Spoon River Anthology," "International Stud," "Too Much Johnson," "To Bury a Cousin," "A Dream Play."

TASK, MAGGIE. Born July 4 in Marion, OH. Attended Wright Col. Bdwy debut 1960 in "Greenwillow," followed by "A Family Affair," "Tovarich," CC's "Most Happy Fella" and "Carousel," "Funny Girl," "Kelly," "Anya," "A Time for Singing," "Darling of the Day," "Education of Hyman Kaplan," "Sound of Music," "CoCo," "Sweeney Todd," OB in "Sing Melancholy Baby."

TATE, DENNIS. Born Aug. 31, 1938 in Iowa City, IA. Attended UIowa. Bdwy debut 1970 in "Les Blancs," followed by "The Poison Tree," OB in "Black Monday," "The Blacks," "The Hostage," "Bohikee Creek," "Happy Bar," "Trials of Brother Jero," "Strong Breed," "Goa," "Electronic Nigger," "Black Quartet," "Life and Times of J. Walter Smintheus," "Jazznite," "Cherry Orchard," "Phantasmagoria Historia. . . . ," "Merry Wives of Windsor," "Coriolanus," "The Trial of Dr. Beck."

TATUM, BILL. Born May 6, 1947 in Philadelphia, PA. Graduate Catawba Col. Bdwy debut 1971 in "Man of La Mancha," OB in ELT'S "Missouri Legend" and "Time of the Cuckoo," "Winner Take All?"

TATUM, MARIANNE. Born Feb. 18, 1951 in Houston, TX. Attended Manhattan School of Music. Debut 1971 OB in "Ruddigore," followed by "The Sound of Music" (ELT), Bdwy 1980 in "Barnum" for which she received a Theatre World Award.

TAVARIS, ERIC. Born Apr. 8, 1939 in Fall River, MA. Debut 1959 OB in "An Enemy of the People," followed by "The Prodigal," "In White America," "Butterfly Dream," "Macbeth," "Mummers and Men," "Androcles and the Lion," "The Guardsman," "Leonce and Lena," "Oedipus Cycle," "Gilles de Rais," Bdwy in "The Lincoln Mask" (1972).

TAYLOR, ELIZABETH. Born Feb. 27, 1932 in London, Eng. Bdwy debut 1981 in "The Little Foxes," for which she received a Special Theatre World Award.

TAYLOR, GEORGE. Born Sept. 18, 1930 in London, Eng. Attended AADA. Debut 1972 OB in "Hamlet," followed by "Enemies"(LC), "The Contractor," "Scribes," "Says I, Says He," "Teeth 'n' Smiles," "Viaduct," "Translations," Bdwy in "Emperor Henry IV," "The National Health."

TAYLOR, JEANNINE. Born June 2, 1954 in Hartford, CT. Graduate New Eng. Consv. Debut 1979 OB in "Umbrellas of Cherbourg," followed by "Hijinks."

TAYLOR-MORRIS, MAXINE. Born June 16 in NYC. Graduate NYU. Debut 1977 OB in "Counsellor-at-Law," followed by "Manny," "The Devil's Disciple."

TEITEL, CAROL. Born Aug. 1, 1929 in NYC. Attended AmTh Wing. Bdwy debut 1957 in "The Country Wife," followed by "The Entertainer," "Hamlet," "Marat/deSade," "A Flea in Her Ear," "Crown Matrimonial," "All Over Town," OB in "Way of the World," "Juana La Loca," "An Evening with Ring Lardner," "Misanthrope," "Shaw Festival," "Country Scandal," "The Bench," "Colombe," "Under Milk Wood," "7 Days of Mourning," "Long Day's Journey into Night," "The Old Ones," "Figures in the Sand," "World of Sholom Aleichem," "Big and Little," "Duet," "Trio," "Every Good Boy Deserves Favor"(LC), "Fallen Angels," "A Stitch in Time," "Faces of Love."

TESTA, MARY. Born June 4, 1955 in Philadelphia, PA. Attended URI. Debut 1979 OB in "In Trousers," followed by "Company," Bdwy 1980 in "Barnum."

THACKER, RUSS. Born June 23, 1946 in Washington, DC. Attended Montgomery Col. Bdwy debut 1967 in "Life with Father," followed by "Music! Music!," "Grass Harp," "Heathen," "Home Sweet Homer," "Me Jack You Jill," OB in "Your Own Thing" for which he received a Theatre World Award, "Dear Oscar," "Once I Saw a Boy Laughing," "Tip-Toes," "Oh, Coward!"

THOMAS, RICHARD. Born June 13, 1951 in NYC. Bdwy debut 1958 in "Sunrise at Campobello," followed by "A Member of the Wedding," "Strange Interlude," "The Playroom," "Richard III," "Everything in the Garden," "Fifth of July."

THOMASON, DONNA. Born Feb. 11, 1954 in MO. Graduate Ct. Col. Bdwy debut 1980 in "Annie."

THOME, DAVID. Born July 24, 1951 in Salt Lake City, UT. Bdwy debut 1971 in "No, No, Nanette," followed by "Different Times," "Good News," "Rodgers and Hart," "A Chorus Line."

THOMPSON, EVAN. Born Sept. 3, 1931 in NYC. Graduate UCal. Bdwy bow 1969 in "Jimmy," OB in "Mahagonny," "Treasure Island," "Knitters in the Sun," "Half-Life."

THOMPSON, LAUREN. Born in 1950. Attended PaStateU, Pittsburgh Playhouse. Bdwy debut 1979 in "Dracula," followed by "A Life."

THOMPSON, TRINITY. Born Oct. 4 in Greenwich, CT. Graduate AADA. Debut 1958 OB in "The Time of Your Life," followed by "Toys in the Attic," "Hot 1 Baltimore," "The Crucible," "Misalliance," "LaRonde," "Invitation to a March," "Age of Anxiety," "Under Milk Wood," "Half-Life," "The Beethoven."

THORNE, RAYMOND. Born Nov. 27, 1934 in Lackawanna, NY. Graduate UConn. Debut 1966 OB in "Man with a Load of Mischief," followed by "Rose," "Dames at Sea," "Love Course," "Blue Boys" Bdwy 1977 in "Annie."

THORNTON-SHERWOOD, MADELEINE. Born Nov. 13, 1926 in Montreal, Can. Attended Yale. OB in "Brecht on Brecht," "Medea," "Hey, You, Light Man," "Friends and Relations," "Older People," "Oh Glorious Tintinnabulation," "Getting Out," "Secret Thighs of New England Women," Bdwy in "The Chase," "The Crucible," "Cat on a Hot Tin Roof," "Invitation to a March," "Camelot," "Arturo Ui," "Do I Hear a Waltz?," "Inadmissible Evidence," "All Over!"

THURSTON, TED. Born Jan. 9, 1920 in St. Paul, MN. Attended Drake U. Bdwy debut in 1951 in "Paint Your Wagon," followed by "Girl in Pink Tights," "Kismet," "Buttrio Square," "Seventh Heaven," "Most Happy Fella," "Li'l Abner," "13 Daughters," "Happiest Girl in Town," "Let It Ride," "Sophie," "Luther," "Cafe Crown," "I Had a Ball," "Wonderful Town," "Celebration," "Gantry," "Wild and Wonderful," "Onward Victoria," OB in "Bible Salesman," "Smith," "Fiddler on the Roof," "Celebration," "Turns."

TOBIE, ELLEN. Born Mar. 26 in Chambersburg, PA. Graduate OhWesleyanU, Wayne State U. Debut 1981 OB in "The Chisholm Trail Went Through Here."

TOBIN, NOREEN. Born Feb. 18 in Chicago, IL. Graduate Loyola U. Debut 1980 OB in "The Slab Boys."

TOMEL, CONCETTA. Born Dec. 30, 1945 in Kenosha, WI. Graduate UWisc, Goodman School. Debut 1979 OB in "Little Eyolf," "Cloud 9," Bdwy 1979 in "The Elephant Man."

TOMPKINS, TOBY. Born Sept. 8, 1942 in NYC. Yale graduate. Bdwy debut 1968 in "Man of La Mancha," followed by "The Cherry Orchard," OB in "Hail Scrawdyke," "In White America," "Mirandolina," "A Prayer for My Daughter."

TOOMBS, LEE. Born July 2, 1954 in Memphis, TN. Attended UTn. Bdwy debut 1976 in "Equus," OB in "The Winslow Boy" (1980).

TORMEY, JOHN. Born Aug. 4, 1937 in Willimantic, CT. Graduate Boston U. Bdwy debut 1960 in "Beg, Borrow or Steal," followed by "Bajour," "Marat/deSade," "Mike Downstairs," "Our Town," OB in "Ten by Six."

TORREN, FRANK. Born Jan. 5, 1939 in Tampa, FL. Attended UTampa, AADA. Debut 1964 OB in "Jo," followed by "No Corner in Heaven," "Treasure Island," "Open Season for Butterflies," "Brownstone Urge," "The Meehans."

TORRES, MARK. Born May 7, 1955 in Brownsville, TX. Graduate InU, Temple U. Bdwy debut 1980 in "Amadeus."

TOWERS, CONSTANCE. Born May 20, 1933 in Whitefish, MT. Attended Juilliard, AADA, Bdwy debut 1965 in "Anya," followed by "Show Boat" (LC), "Carousel"(CC), "Sound of Music" (CC '67, JB '70, '71, '80), "Engagement Baby," "The King and I" (CC '68, JB '72, Bdwy '77).

TOWERS, IAN MICHAEL. Born Aug. 21, 1951 in Rockville Centre, NY. Bdwy debut 1979 in "Carmelina," followed by "Onward Victoria," OB in "Florodora."

TOWLER, LAURINE. Born Oct. 19, 1952 in Oberlin, OH. Graduate Stanford U., UCa. Debut 1981 OB in "Godspell."

TRESKO, ELSA. Born Oct. 1 in Vienna. Graduate Vienna Acad. Debut 1970 OB in "The Dirtiest Show in Town," followed by "Art War."

TRIGGER, IAN. Born Sept. 30, 1942 in England. Graduate RADA. Debut 1973 OB in "The Taming of the Shrew," followed by "Scapino," "True History of Squire Jonathan," "The Slab Boys," Bdwy in "Scapino," "Habeas Corpus," "13 Rue de l'Amour."

| Jake Turner | Juanita Tyler | James Umphlett | Benay Venuta | Peter Walker |

TROOBNICK, GENE. Born Aug. 23, 1926 in Boston, MA. Attended Ithaca Col., Columbia U. Bdwy debut 1960 in "Second City," followed by "The Odd Couple," "Before You Go," "The Time of Your Life," OB in "Dynamite Tonight," "A Gun Play," "Tales of the Hasidim," "Wings," "Sganarelle," "Damien."

TRUEMAN, PAULA. Born Apr. 25, 1907 in NYC. Graduate Hunter Col., Neighborhood Playhouse. Bdwy debut 1922 in "Thunderbird," followed by "Grand Street Follies," "Sweet and Low," "Grand Hotel," "You Can't Take It with You," "George Washington Slept Here," "Kiss and Tell," "Violet," "For Love or Money," "Gentlemen Prefer Blondes," "Solid Gold Cadillac," "Mrs. McThing," "Wake Up, Darling," "Family Affair," "Wonderful Town," "Sherry!," "The Chinese," OB in "Sunday Man," "Wilder's Triple Bill," "Postcards," "The Chisholm Trail Went Through Here."

TUCCI, MARIA. Born June 19, 1941 in Florence, It. Attended Actors Studio. Bdwy debut 1963 in "The Milk Train Doesn't Stop Here Anymore," followed by "The Rose Tattoo," "The Little Foxes," "Cuban Thing," "The Great White Hope," "School for Wives," "Lesson from Aloes," OB in "Corruption in the Palace of Justice," "Five Evenings," "Trojan Women," "White Devil," "Horseman Pass By," "Yerma," "Shepherd of Avenue B," "The Gathering."

TUPOU, MANU. Born in 1939 in Fiji Islands. Attended San Francisco State U., ULondon. Bdwy debut 1969 in "Indians," followed by "Othello," "Capt. Brassbound's Conversion," OB in "Madwoman of Chaillot," "Passion of Antigona Perez," "Wedding of Iphigenia," "The Old Glory," "Black Elk Lives."

TURETZKY, JOAN. Born Sept. 26 in Brooklyn, NY. Attended Sullivan Co. Com. Col. Debut 1977 OB in "Counsellor-at-Law," followed by "Merton of the Movies."

TURNER, JAKE. Born May 6, 1953 in Pittsburgh, PA. Graduate Carnegie Tech. Bdwy debut 1980 in "West Side Story," OB in "Tied by the Leg."

TURNER, KATHLEEN. Born June 19, 1954 in Springfield, MO. Graduate Southwest Mo. State. Bdwy debut 1978 in "Gemini."

TWOMEY, ANNE. Born June 7, 1951 in Boston, MA. Graduate Temple U. Debut 1975 OB in "Overruled," followed by "The Passion of Dracula," Bdwy 1980 in "Nuts" for which she received a Theatre World Award, "To Grandmother's House We Go."

TYLER, JUANITA GRACE. Born Mar. 9, 1956 in Brooklyn, NY. Attended Kingsborough CC. Bdwy debut 1980 in "Reggae," followed by "It's So Nice to Be Civilized."

TYRRELL, SUSAN. Born in 1946 in San Francisco, CA. Bdwy debut 1952 in "Time Out for Ginger," OB in "The Knack," "Futz," "A Cry of Players," "The Time of Your Life," "Camino Real," "Father's Day," "A Coupla White Chicks."

UMPHLETT, JAMES. Born Apr. 17, 1945 in Norfolk, Va. Attended HB Studio. Debut 1980 OB in "The Cocktail Party."

VALENTINE, JAMES. Born Feb. 18, 1933 in Rockford, IL. Attended ULondon, Central Sch. of Drama. Bdwy debut 1958 in "Cloud 7," followed by "Epitaph for George Dillon," "Duel of Angels," "Ross," "Caesar and Cleopatra," "The Importance of Being Earnest," Bdwy in "Camelot" (1980).

VALOR, HENRIETTA. Born Apr. 28 in New Cumberland, PA. Graduate Northwestern U. Bdwy debut 1965 in "Half a Sixpence," followed by "Applause," "Jacques Brel Is Alive," "Annie," OB in "Fashion," "Jacques Brel . . .," "A Bistro Car on the CNR."

VAN DEVERE, TRISH. Born Mar. 9, 1945 in Englewood, NJ. Graduate Ohio Wesleyan U. Debut 1967 OB in "Kicking Down the Castle," "Violano Virtuoso," Bdwy in "All God's Chillun Got Wings" (1975), followed by "Sly Fox," "Tricks of the Trade."

VAN DYKE, DICK. Born Dec. 13, 1925 in West Plains, MO. Bdwy debut 1959 in "The Girls against the Boys," followed by "Bye Bye Birdie," "The Music Man" (1980).

VAN NORDEN, PETER. Born Dec. 16, 1950 in NYC. Graduate Colgate U., Neighborhood Playhouse. Debut 1975 OB in "Hamlet," followed by "Henry V," "Measure for Measure," "A Country Scandal," "Hound of the Baskervilles," "Tartuffe," "Antigone," "Bingo," "Taming of the Shrew," "The Balcony," "Shadow of a Gunman," "Jungle of Cities," "Shakespeare's Cabaret," Bdwy in "Romeo and Juliet" (1977), "St. Joan," "Inspector General," "Macbeth."

VANNUYS, ED. Born Dec. 28, 1930 in Lebanon, IN. Attended Ind. U. Debut 1969 OB in "No Place to Be Somebody," followed by "Conflict of Interest," "The Taming of the Shrew," "God Bless You, Mr. Rosewater," "The Chisholm Trail," Bdwy in "Black Terror," "Nuts."

VAN PATTEN, JOYCE. Born Mar. 9 in Kew Gardens, NY. Bdwy bow 1941 in "Popsy," followed by "This Rock," "Tomorrow the World," "The Perfect Marriage," "The Wind is 90," "Desk Set," "A Hole in the Head," "Murder at the Howard Johnson's," "I Ought to Be in Pictures," OB in "Between Two Thieves," "Spoon River Anthology," "The Seagull."

VAN TREUREN, MARTIN. Born Dec. 6, 1952 in Hawthorne, NJ. Graduate Montclair State Col. Debut 1978 OB in "Oklahoma!," followed by "The Miser."

VEAZEY, JEFF. Born Dec. 6 in New Orleans, LA. Bdwy debut 1975 in "Dr. Jazz," followed by "The Grand Tour," "Sugar Babies," OB in "Speakeasy."

VENUTA, BENAY. Born Jan. 27, 1911 in San Francisco, CA. Bdwy debut 1935 in "Anything Goes," followed by "Orchids Preferred," "Kiss the Boys Goodbye," "By Jupiter," "Nellie Bly," "Hazel Flagg," "Copper and Brass," "Dear Me, the Sky Is Falling," "Carousel," "Annie Get Your Gun," "Romantic Comedy," OB in "A Quarter for the Ladies Room."

VESTOFF, VIRGINIA. Born Dec. 9, 1940 in NYC. Bdwy debut 1960 in "From A to Z," followed by "Irma La Douce," "Baker Street," "1776," "Via Galactica," "Nash at 9," "Boccacio," "Spokesong," OB in "The Boy Friend," "Crystal Heart," "Fall Out," "New Cole Porter Revue," "Man with a Load of Mischief," "Love and Let Love," "Short-Changed Review," "The Misanthrope," "Drinks Before Dinner," "I'm Getting My Act Together. . . ."

VIDNOVIC, MARTIN. Born Jan. 4, 1948 in Falls Church, VA. Attended Cincinnati Consv. of Music. Debut 1972 OB in "The Fantasticks," followed by Bdwy in "Home Sweet Homer" (1976), "The King and I" (1977), "Oklahoma!" (1979), "Brigadoon" (1980).

VIPOND, NEIL. Born Dec. 24, 1929 in Toronto, Can. Bdwy debut 1956 in "Tamburlaine the Great," followed by "Macbeth," OB in "Three Friends," "Sunday Runners," "Hamlet" (ELT).

VITA, MICHAEL. Born in NYC. Studied at HB Studio. Bdwy debut 1967 in "Sweet Charity," followed by "Golden Rainbow," "Promises, Promises," "Cyrano," "Chicago," "Ballroom," "Charlie and Algernon," OB in "Sensations," "That's Entertainment," "Rocket to the Moon."

VOGEL, DAVID. Born Oct. 19, 1922 in Canton, OH. Attended UPa. Bdwy debut 1948 in "Ballet Ballads," followed by "Gentlemen Prefer Blondes," "Make a Wish," "Desert Song," OB in "How to Get Rid of It," "The Fantasticks," "Miss Stanwyck Is Still in Hiding," "Marya."

VOSBURGH, DAVID. Born Mar. 14, 1938 in Coventry, RI. Attended Boston U. Bdwy debut 1968 in "Maggie Flynn," followed by "1776," "A Little Night Music," "Evita," OB in "Smith."

WADE, CAROL. Born Dec. 14 in Flint, MI. Graduate Point Park Col., Pittsburgh Playhouse. Debut 1980 OB in "The Beaver Coat," followed by "Twelfth Night."

WADE, STEPHEN. Born Feb. 13, 1953 in Chicago, IL. Bdwy debut 1980 in "Banjo Dancing."

WALDRON, MICHAEL. Born Nov. 19, 1949 in West Orange, NJ. Graduate Columbia U. Debut 1979 OB in "Mary," followed by "Dulcy," "Romance Is."

WALDROP, MARK. Born July 30, 1954 in Washington, DC. Graduate Cincinnati Consv. Debut 1977 OB in "Movie Buff," Bdwy in "The Grand Tour," "Evita."

WALKEN, CHRISTOPHER. Born Mar. 31, 1943 in Astoria, NY. Attended Hofstra U. Bdwy debut 1958 in "J.B.," followed by "High Spirits," "Baker Street," "The Lion in Winter," "Measure for Measure," "The Rose Tattoo" (CC'66) for which he received a Theatre World Award, "Unknown Soldier and His Wife," "Rosencrantz and Guildenstern Are Dead," "Scenes from American Life," "Cymbeline," "Enemies," "The Plough and the Stars," "Merchant of Venice," "The Tempest," "Troilus and Cressida," "Macbeth," "Sweet Bird of Youth," OB in "Best Foot Forward," "Iphigenia in Aulis," "Lemon Sky," "Kid Champion," "The Seagull."

WALKER, PETER. Born July 24, 1927 in Mineola, NY. Bdwy debut 1955 in "Little Glass Clock," followed by "Dear World," "Where's Charley?," "Follies," OB in "Dancing for the Kaiser," "My Old Friends," "Do You Still Believe the Rumor."

WALLACE, TIMOTHY. Born July 24, 1947 in Racine, WI. Graduate UWi., PaStateU. Debut 1976 OB in "Rimers of Eldritch," followed by "Dance on a Country Grave," Bdwy in "King of Hearts," "Five O'Clock Girl."

WALLER, KEN. Born Apr. 12, 1945 in Atlanta, GA. Graduate Piedmont Col. Debut 1976 OB in "Boys from Syracuse," Bdwy in "Sarava," "Onward Victoria."

253

Chris Weatherhead   Denzel Washington   Kate Wilkinson   Ellwoodson Williams   Susan Willis

WALLING, GERALD C. Born June 26, 1928 in Chicago, IL. Graduate Loyola U., Northwestern U. Debut 1980 OB in "The Devil's Disciple."

WALSH, TENNEY. Born Oct. 18, 1963 in New Haven, CT. Attended Yale. Debut 1981 OB in "The Wild Duck."

WALTERS, KELLY. Born May 28, 1950 in Amarillo, TX. Graduate UWash. Debut 1973 OB in "Look, We've Come Through"(ELT), Bdwy in "Candide" (1975), "Canterbury Tales," "Barnum."

WANDEL, PETER. Born Oct. 15, 1955 in Buffalo, NY. Attended SUNY/Purchase. Bdwy debut 1980 in "The Music Man."

WARING, TODD. Born Apr. 28, 1955 in Saratoga Springs, NY. Graduate Skidmore Col. Debut 1980 OB in "Journey's End," followed by "Mary Stuart."

WARREN-COOKE, BARBARA. Born June 6, 1948 in Cincinnati, OH. Graduate St. Francis Col., UMn. Debut 1981 OB in "Anything Goes," followed by "Peanut Man."

WASHINGTON, DENZEL. Born Dec. 28, 1954 in Mt. Vernon, NY. Graduate Fordham U. Debut 1978 OB in "The Emperor Jones," followed by "Othello," "Coriolanus," "Mighty Gents," "Beckett," "Spell #7," "Ceremonies in Dark Old Men," "One Tiger To a Hill."

WASS, TED. Born Oct. 27, 1952 in Lakewood, OH. Attended Goodman School. Debut 1975 OB in "Columbus," Bdwy 1976 in "Grease."

WATERSTON, SAM. Born Nov. 15, 1940 in Cambridge, MA. Yale graduate. Bdwy bow 1963 in "Oh Dad, Poor Dad," followed by "First One Asleep Whistle," "Halfway Up the Tree," "Indians," "Hay Fever," "Much Ado about Nothing," "Lunch Hour," OB in "As You Like It," "Thistle in My Bed," "The Knack," "Fitz," "Biscuit," "La Turista," "Posterity for Sale," "Ergo," "Muzeeka," "Red Cross," "Henry IV," "Spitting Image," "I Met a Man," "Brass Butterfly," " Trial of the Catonsville 9," "Cymbeline," "Hamlet," "A Meeting by the River," "The Tempest," "A Doll's House," "Measure for Measure," "Chez Nous," "Waiting for Godot."

WATSON, DOUGLASS. Born Feb. 24, 1921 in Jackson, GA. Graduate UNC. Bdwy bow 1947 in "The Iceman Cometh," followed by "Antony and Cleopatra," for which he received a Theatre World Award, "Leading Lady," "Richard III," "The Happiest Years," "That Lady," "Wisteria Trees," "Romeo and Juliet," "Desire under the Elms," "Sunday Breakfast," "Cyrano de Bergerac," "Confidential Clerk," "Portrait of a Lady," "The Miser," "The Young and Beautiful," "Little Glass Clock," "Country Wife," "Man for All Seasons," "Chinese Prime Minister," "Marat/deSade," "Prime of Miss Jean Brodie," "Pirates of Penzance," "Over Here," "The Philadelphia Story," OB in NYSF's "Much Ado about Nothing," "King Lear" and "As You Like It," "The Hunger," "Dancing for the Kaiser," "Money," "My Life," "Sightlines," "Glorious Morning," "Hamlet."

WEATHERHEAD, CHRIS. Born Jan. 11, 1948 in Glendale, CA. Attended UCal/Santa Barbara. Debut 1979 OB in"Table Settings," followed by "Death Takes A Holiday."

WEAVER, FRITZ. Born Jan. 19, 1926 in Pittsburgh, PA. Graduate UChicago. Bdwy debut 1955 in "Chalk Garden" for which he received a Theatre World Award, followed by "Protective Custody," "All American," "Lorenzo," "The White House," "Baker Street," "Child's Play," "Absurd Person Singular," OB in "The Way of the World," "White Devil," "Doctor's Dilemma," "Family Reunion," "The Power and the Glory," "The Great God Brown," "Peer Gynt," "Henry IV," "My Fair Lady" (CC), "Lincoln," "The Biko Inquest," "The Price," "Dialogue for Lovers."

WEAVER, SIGOURNEY. Born in NYC in 1949. Attended Yale, Stanford. Debut 1976 OB in "Titanic," followed by "Das Lusitania Songspiel," "Beyond Therapy."

WEBER, FREDRICKA. Born Dec. 22, 1940 in Beardstown, IL. Attended Northwestern U. Bdwy debut 1965 in"Those That Play the Clowns," OB in "Upstairs at the Downstairs," "The Last Sweet Days of Isaac" for which she received a Theatre World Award, "Two."

WEEKS, JAMES RAY. Born Mar. 21, 1942 in Seattle, WA. Graduate UOre., AADA. Debut 1972 in LCR's "Enemies," "Merchant of Venice" and "A Streetcar Named Desire," followed by OB's "49 West 87th," "Feedlot," "The Runner Stumbles," "Glorious Morning," "Just the Immediate Family," "The Deserter," "Life and/or Death," "Devour the Snow," "Innocent Thoughts, Harmless Intentions," "The Diviners," Bdwy in "My Fat Friend," "We Interrupt this Program," "Devour the Snow."

WESTON, JACK. Born in 1924 in Cleveland, OH. Attended Cleveland Play House, AmThWing. Bdwy debut 1950 in "Season in the Sun," followed by "South Pacific," "Bells Are Ringing," "California," "The Ritz," "Cheaters," "The Floating Light Bulb."

WESTON, MARK. Born Feb. 13, 1931 in The Bronx, NY. Attended UWi. Debut 1955 in "Billy Budd," followed by "The Trial of Mary Surratt," "Come Back, Little Sheba," "Time Limit," OB in "36."

WETTIG, PATRICIA. Born Dec 4, in Cincinnati, OH. Graduate Temple U. Debut 1980 OB in "Innocent Thoughts, Harmless Intentions," followed by "The Woolgatherer," "Childe Byron."

WHITE, JANE. Born Oct. 30, 1922 in NYC. Attended Smith Col. Bdwy debut 1942 in "Strange Fruit," followed by "Climate of Eden," "Take a Giant Step," "Jane Eyre," "Once Upon a Mattress," "The Cuban Thing," OB in "Razzle Dazzle," "Insect Comedy," "The Power and the Glory," "Hop, Signor," "Trojan Women," "Iphigenia in Aulis," "Cymbeline," "Burnt Flowerbed," "Rosmersholm," "Jane White Who?," "Ah, Men."

WHITE, TERRI. Born Jan. 24, 1953 in Palo Alto, CA. Attended USIU. Debut 1976 OB in "The Club," followed by Bdwy in "Barnum" (1980).

WHITEHEAD, PAXTON. Born in Kent, Eng. Attended Webber-Douglas Acad. Bdwy debut 1962 in "The Affair," followed by "Beyond the Fringe," "Candida," "Habeas Corpus," "Crucifer of Blood," "Camelot" (1980), OB in "Gallow's Humor," "One Way Pendulum," "A Doll's House," "Rondelay."

WHITTON, MARGARET. (formerly Peggy). Born Nov. 30 in Philadelphia, PA. Debut 1973 OB in "Baba Goya," followed by "Arthur," "The Wager," "Nourish the Beast," "Another Language," "Chinchilla" "Othello," "The Art of Dining," "One Tiger to a Hill."

WIDDOES, KATHLEEN. Born Mar. 21, 1939 in Wilmington, DE. Attended Paris Theatre des Nations. Bdwy debut 1958 in "The Firstborn," followed by "World of Suzie Wong," "Much Ado about Nothing," "The Importance of Being Earnest," OB in "Three Sisters," "The Maids," "You Can't Take It with You," "To Clothe the Naked," "World War 2½," "Beggar's Opera," "As You Like It," "A Midsummer Night's Dream," "One Act Play Festival."

WIEST, DIANE. Born Mar. 28, 1948 in Kansas City, MO. Attended UMd. Debut 1976 OB in "Ashes," followed by "Leave It to Beaver Is Dead," "The Art of Dining," for which she received a Theatre World Award, "Bonjour, La, Bonjour," Bdwy 1980 in "Frankenstein."

WILKINSON, KATE. Born Oct. 25 in San Francisco, CA. Attended San Jose State Col. Bdwy debut 1967 in "Little Murders," followed by "Johnny No-Trump," "Watercolor," "Postcards," "Ring Round the Bathtub," "The Last of Mrs. Lincoln," "Man and Superman," "Frankenstein," "The Man Who Came to Dinner," OB in "La Madre," "Earnest in Love," "Story of Mary Surratt," "Bring Me a Warm Body," "Child Buyer," "Rimers of Eldritch," "A Doll's House," "Hedda Gabler," "Real Inspector Hound," "The Contractor," "When the Old Man Died."

WILLIAMS, ELLWOODSON. Born June 17, 1937 in Jacksonville, NC. Graduate TnAIU. Debut OB 1968 in "Cadillac Dreams," followed by "Land beyond the River," "Voice of the Gene," "Jerico-Jim Crow," "Duet in Black," "Adding Machine" "A Man's a Man," "Cry the Beloved Country," "Mercury Island," "Middle Class Black," "Ceremonies in Dark Old Men," "Murderous Angels," "Get Out," "Triple Play," Bdwy 1971 in "Two Gentlemen of Verona."

WILLIAMS, J. SCOTT. Born Dec. 27, 1957 in Harborcreek, PA. Graduate Bradley U. Debut 1980 in "The Butterfingers Angel."

WILLIAMS, TREAT. Born in 1952 in Rowayton, CT. Bdwy debut 1976 in "Grease," followed by "Over Here," "Once in a Lifetime," "Pirates of Penzance," OB in "Randy Newman's Maybe I'm Doing It Wrong."

WILLIAMSON, NICOL. Born Sept. 14, 1938 in Hamilton, Scot. Bdwy debut 1965 in "Inadmissible Evidence" followed by "Plaza Suite," "Hamlet," "Uncle Vanya," OB in "Nicol Williamson's Late Show," "Inadmissible Evidence."

WILLIS, SUSAN. Born in Tiffin, OH. Attended Carnegie Tech. Cleveland Play House. Debut 1953 OB in "The Little Clay Cart," followed by "Love and Let Love," "The Glorious Age," "The Guardsman," "Dangerous Corners," Bdwy in "Take Me Along" (1959), "Gypsy," "Dylan," "Come Live With Me," "Cabaret."

WILSON, KEVIN. Born May 26, 1950 in Indianapolis, IN. Graduate UMd., HB Studio. Bdwy debut 1977 in "Shenandoah," followed by "Carmelina," "The Most Happy Fella."

WILSON, MARY LOUISE. Born Nov. 12, 1936 in New Haven, CT. Graduate Northwestern U. OB in "Our Town" "Upstairs at the Downstairs," "Threepenny Opera," "A Great Career," "Whispers on the Wind," "Beggar's Opera," "Buried Child," Bdwy in "Hot Spot," "Flora, the Red Menace," "Criss-Crossing," "Promises, Promises," "The Women," "Gypsy," "The Royal Family," "The Importance of Being Earnest," "The Philadelphia Story," "Fools."

WINKWORTH, MARK J. Born July 19, 1948 in Michigan. Graduate Hofstra U. Bdwy debut 1973 in "The Changing Room," followed by "Frankenstein."

William Witter	Janet Wong	John Yost	Debra Zalkind	Brian Zoldessy

WINSTON, LEE. Born Mar. 14, 1941 in Great Bend, KS. Graduate UKs. Debut 1966 OB in "The Drunkard," followed by "Show Boat" (LC), "Little Mahogonny," "Good Soldier Schweik," Bdwy in "1600 Pennsylvania Avenue," "Carmelina," "The Music Man" (1980).

WINTER, ALEXANDER. Born July 17, 1965 in London, Eng. Bdwy debut 1978 in "The King and I," followed by "Peter Pan," OB in "Close of Play."

WISE, WILLIAM. Born May 11 in Chicago, IL. Attended Bradley U., Northern IlU. Debut 1970 OB in "Adaptation/Next," followed by "him," "The Hot Baltimore," "Just the Immediate Family," "36."

WITTER, WILLIAM C. Born Mar. 15, 1950 in Portland, OR. Graduate UWash. Bdwy debut 1980 in "Barnum."

WOHL, DAVID. Born Sept. 22, 1953 in Brooklyn, NY. Debut 1981 OB in "The Buddy System."

WOJEK, ALAINA. Born May 3, 1966 in The Bronx, NY. Bdwy debut 1981 in "Lolita."

WOLPE, LENNY. Born Mar. 25, 1951 in Newburgh, NY. Graduate Geo. Washington U, UMn. Debut 1978 OB in "Company," Bdwy in "Onward Victoria" (1980), followed by "Copperfield."

WONG, JANET. Born Aug. 30, 1951 in Berkeley, CA. Attended UCal. Bdwy debut 1977 in "A Chorus Line," followed by "Bring Back Birdie."

WOOD, KELLY. Born Nov. 10, 1943 in Chicago, IL. Attended San Diego State U. Debut 1963 OB in "Cindy," followed by "As You Like It," Bdwy in "Cactus Flower," "The Sign in Sidney Brustein's Window."

WOODARD, CHARLAINE. Born Dec. 29 in Albany, NY. Graduate Goodman Sch. of Drama, SUNY. Debut 1975 OB in "Don't Bother Me, I Can't Cope," Bdwy in "Hair" (1977), "Ain't Misbehavin'," OB in "Under Fire."

WOODESON, NICHOLAS. Born in England. Graduate USussex, RADA. Debut 1978 OB in "Strawberry Fields," followed by "The Taming of the Shrew," Bdwy in "Man and Superman." (1978), "Piaf."

WOODS, JAMES. Born Apr. 18, 1947 in Vernal, Ut. Graduate MIT. Bdwy debut 1970 in "Borstal Boy," followed by "Conduct Unbecoming," "Trial of the Catonsville 9," "Moonchildren" for which he received a Theatre World Award, "Finishing Touches," OB in "Saved," "Green Julia," "One Act Play Festival."

WOODS, RICHARD. Born May 9, 1921 in Buffalo, NY. Graduate Ithaca Col. Bdwy in "Beg Borrow or Steal," "Capt. Brassbound's Conversion," "Sail Away," "Coco," "Last of Mrs. Lincoln," "Gigi," "Sherlock Holmes," "Murder among Friends," "The Royal Family," "Deathtrap," "Man and Superman," "The Man Who Came to Dinner," "The Father," OB in "The Crucible," "Summer and Smoke," "American Gothic," "Four-in-one," "My Heart's in the Highlands," "Eastward in Eden," "The Long Gallery," "The Year Boston Won the Pennant," "In the Matter of J. Robert Oppenheimer" (LC), with APA in "You Can't Take It With You," "War and Peace," "School for Scandal," "Right You Are," "The Wild Duck," "Pantagleize," "Exit the King," "The Cherry Orchard," "Cock-a-doodle Dandy," and "Hamlet," "Crimes and Dreams."

WOODSON, SALLY. Born Aug. 28, 1951 in St. Louis, MO. Graduate UKs. Debut 1978 OB in "Oklahoma!," followed by "Oh Me Oh My Oh Youmans."

WORTH, IRENE. Born June 23, 1916 in Nebraska. Graduate UCLA. Bdwy debut 1943 in "The Two Mrs. Carrolls," followed by "The Cocktail Party," "Mary Stuart," "Toys in the Attic," "King Lear," "Tiny Alice," "Sweet Bird of Youth," "The Cherry Orchard" (LC), "The Lady from Dubuque," "John Gabriel Borkman," OB in "Happy Days," "Letters of Love and Affection."

WORTH, PENNY. Born Mar. 2, 1950 in London, Eng. Attended Sorbonne, Paris. Bdwy debut 1970 in "Coco," followed by "Irene," "Annie."

WRIGHT, AMY. Born Apr. 15, 1950 in Chicago, IL. Graduate Beloit Col. Debut 1977 OB in "The Stronger," followed by "Nightshift," "Hamlet," "Miss Julie," Bdwy in "5th of July" (1980).

WRIGHT, JENNY. Born in NYC in 1962. Attended Theatre Inst. Debut 1980 OB in "Album."

WRIGHT, MARY CATHERINE. Born Mar. 19, 1948 in San Francisco, CA. Attended CCSF, SFState Col. Bdwy debut 1970 in "Othello," followed by "A History of the American Film," "Tintypes," OB in "East Lynne," "Mimi Lights the Candle," "Marvin's Gardens," "The Tempest," "The Doctor in spite of Himself," "Love's Labour's Lost," "Pushcart Peddlers."

WRIGHT, MAX. Born Aug. 2, 1943 in Detroit, MI. Attended Wayne State U. Bdwy debut 1968 in "The Great White Hope," followed by "The Cherry Orchard," "Basic Training of Pavlo Hummel," "Stages," "Once in a Lifetime" for which he received a Theatre World Award, "The Inspector General," "Richard III," "Lunch Hour."

WRIGHT, TERESA. Born Oct. 27, 1918 in NYC. Bdwy debut 1938 in "Our Town," followed by "Life with Father," "The Dark at the Top of the Stairs," "Mary, Mary," "I Never Sang for My Father," "Death of a Salesman," "Ah, Wilderness," "Morning's at 7," OB in "Who's Happy Now," "A Passage to E. M. Forster."

YACKO, ROBERT. Born Dec. 20, 1953 in Philadelphia, PA. Attended Temple U., Juilliard. Debut 1978 OB in "Oh, What a Lovely War," followed by "The Miser," Bdwy in "Fiddler on the Roof" (1981).

YARNELL, LORENE. Born Mar. 21, 1948 in Los Angeles, CA. Bdwy debut 1981 in "Broadway Follies."

YODER, JERRY. Born in Columbus, OH. Graduate Ohio State U. Bdwy debut 1973 in "Seesaw," followed by "Goodtime Charley," "Chicago," "Best Little Whorehouse in Texas," OB in "Boys from Syracuse."

YOSHIDA, PETER. Born May 28, 1945 in Chicago, IL. Graduate UIll., Princeton U., AADA. Debut 1965 OB in "Coriolanus," followed by "Troilus and Cressida," "Santa Anita '42," "Pursuit of Happiness," "Servant of Two Masters," "The Peking Man," "Monkey Music."

YORK, SUSANNAH. Born Jan. 9, 1941 in London. Attended RADA. Debut 1981 OB in "Hedda Gabler."

YOST, JOHN. Born Jan. 30 in NYC. Graduate CCNY. Bdwy debut 1979 in "Evita."

YOUNG, RONALD. Born June 11, 1941 in Tulsa, OK. Graduate Tulsa U. Bdwy debut in "Hello, Dolly," followed by "Mame," "George M!," "The Boy Friend," "Different Times," OB in "Dames at Sea," "Promenade," "Oh Me Oh My Oh Youmans."

YULIN, HARRIS. Born Nov. 5, 1937 in Calif. Attended USCal. Debut 1963 OB in "Next Time I'll Sing to You," followed by "A Midsummer Night's Dream," "Troubled Waters," "Richard III," "King John," "The Cannibals," "Lesson from Aloes," "Hedda Gabler," Bdwy 1980 in "Watch on the Rhine."

ZAKS, JERRY. Born Sept. 7, 1946 in Germany. Graduate Dartmouth, Smith Col. Bdwy debut 1973 in "Grease," followed by "Once in a Lifetime," "Tintypes," OB in "Death Story," "Dream of a Blacklisted Actor," "Kid Champion," "Golden Boy," "Marco Polo," "One Crack Out," "Tintypes."

ZALKIND, DEBRA. Born Mar. 30, 1953 in NYC. Graduate Juilliard. Appeared with several dance companies before Bdwy debute 1978 in "The Best Little Whorehouse in Texas."

ZALOOM, PAUL. Born Dec. 14, 1951 in Brooklyn, NY. Graduate Goddard Col. Debut 1979 OB in "Fruit of Zaloom," followed by "Zalooming Along," "Zaloominations!"

ZANG, EDWARD. Born Aug. 19, 1934 in NYC. Graduate Boston U. OB in "Good Soldier Schweik," "St. Joan," "Boys in the Band," "The Reliquary of Mr. and Mrs. Potterfield," "Last Analysis," "As You Like It," "More than You Deserve," "Polly," "Threepenny Opera," BAM Co.'s "New York Idea," "The Misanthrope," "Banana Box," "The Penultimate Problem of Sherlock Holmes," Bdwy in "Crucifier of Blood," "Amadeus."

ZAVIGLIA, RICHARD. Born Mar. 25, 1937 in Newark, NJ. Attended HB Studio, AADA. OB in "Skater," "As You Like It," "Life of Galileo," Bdwy in "Chapter Two" (1979), "Passione-'

ZIEN, CHIP. Born in 1947 in Milwaukee, WI. Attended UPa. OB in "You're a Good Man, Charlie Brown," followed by "Kadish," "How to Succeed in Business . . ." (ELT), "Dear Mr G.," "Tuscaloosa's Calling . . .," "Hot 1 Baltimore," "El Grande de Coca Cola," "Split," "Real Life Funnies," "March of the Falsettos," Bdwy in "All Over Town." (1974), "The Suicide."

ZIMMERMAN, MARK. Born Apr. 19, 1952 in Harrisburg, PA. Graduate UPa. Debut 1976 OB in "Fiorello!," followed by "Silk Stockings," "On a Clear Day You Can See Forever," Bdwy in "Brigadoon" (1981).

ZINN, JEFF. Born Dec. 4, 1949 in NYC. Graduate NYU. Debut 1977 OB in "Sexual Perversity in Chicago," Bdwy in "The Suicide" (1980).

ZITKO, PEG. Born Aug. 9, 1950 in St. Louis, MO. Graduate Southern IlU. Debut 1979 OB in "Mary," followed by "But Shirley Fairweather!"

ZOLDESSY, BRIAN. Born Aug. 27, 1953 in The Bronx, NY. Graduate Long Island U. Debut 1978 OB in "The Diary of Anne Frank."

ZORICH, LOUIS. Born Feb. 12, 1924 in Chicago, IL. Attended Roosevelt U. OB in "Six Characters in Search of an Author," "Crimes and Crimes," "Henry V," "Thracian Horses," "All Women Are One," "Good Soldier Schweik," "Shadow of Heroes," "To Clothe the Naked," "Sunset," "A Memory of Two Mondays," "They Knew What They Wanted," "The Gathering," "True West," Bdwy in "Becket," "Moby Dick," "The Odd Couple," "Hadrian VII," "Moonchildren," "Fun City," "Goodtime Charley," "Herzl."

WALLACE ACTON, 76, actor, died of lung cancer Sept. 2, 1980 in Anaheim, Ca. He had appeared in over 25 Broadway productions, including "Twelfth Night," "The Tempest," "Arsenic and Old Lace," "Winesburg, Ohio," "Valley Forge," "Pastoral," "All the Comforts of Home," "Wonderful Journey," "Skipper Next to God," and "Mr. Pickwick." No reported survivors.

C. K. ALEXANDER, 57, actor, producer, director, died of cancer Sept. 2, 1980 in New York City. Born in Cairo, he came to the U. S. in 1946, and subsequently appeared in "Hidden Horizon," "The Happy Time," "Flight into Egypt," "Mr. Pickwick," "Can-Can," "Fanny," "The Matchmaker," "La Plume de Ma Tante," "Rhinoceros," "Carnival," "Tovarich," "Poor Bitos," "Ari," and OB in "The Dragon," "Corruption in the Palace of Justice," "Justice Box," "The Threepenny Opera," "The Cherry Orchard." He is survived by his widow and seven children.

BORIS ARONSON, 81, Russian-born stage designer, died Nov. 16, 1980 in Nyack, NY. He had designed more than 100 productions for Broadway, and won "Tonys" for six of his designs: "The Rose Tattoo," "Pacific Overtures," "Cabaret," "Zorba," "Company" and "Follies." Other credits include "Merchant of Yonkers," "Truckline Cafe," "Detective Story," "I Am a Camera," "Bus Stop," "J. B.," "Incident at Vichy," "Diary of Anne Frank," "Fiddler on the Roof," "The Crucible," "A View from the Bridge," "The Price" and "A Little Night Music." Surviving are his widow and a son.

ADELE ASTAIRE, 82, (nee Austerlitz in Omaha, Ne.) dancer and comedienne, died Jan. 25, 1981 following a stroke in Phoenix, Az. With her brother Fred, she had appeared in 11 musicals, including "Funny Face," "Lady Be Good," "The Band Wagon," "Smiles," "For Goodness Sake," "Apple Blossoms" and "Flying Colors." She retired in 1932 to marry Lord Cavendish and live in Ireland. After his death, she married Kingman Douglass of NYC. After his death in 1971, she moved to Phoenix. She is survived by her brother, and three step-sons.

MIRIAM BATTISTA, 68, actress in theatre and films, died of emphysema Dec. 22, 1980 in NYC. She made her Broadway debut at 3 in "A Kiss for Cinderella," subsequently appearing in "Daddy Long Legs," "A Doll's House," "Short Cut," "The Honor Code," "Hot-Cha!," "Saint Wench," "Our Wife," "An Undesirable Lady," "No More Ladies," "Fools Rush In," "Tapestry in Gray," "Summer Wives," "Prelude to Exile," and "They Knew What They Wanted." She was the lyricist for the musical "Sleepy Hollow." A daughter survives.

BEULAH BONDI, 92, Chicago-born stage, film and tv actress, died of pulmonary complications on Jan. 12, 1981 in Woodland Hills, Ca. After her success on Broadway, she was in great demand as a character actress in films and tv. In 1977 she received an Emmy for her appearance on "The Waltons" series. Her Broadway credits include "One of the Family," "Saturday's Children," "Mariners," "Cock Robin," "Street Scene," "Milestones," "Distant Drums," "The Late Christopher Bean," "Mother Lode," "Hilda Crane," and "On Borrowed Time." She was never married, and leaves no immediate survivors.

RICHARD BOONE, 63, Los Angeles-born actor, died of throat cancer, Jan. 10, 1981 in his home in St. Augustine, Fl. He had displayed his versatility on stage, film and tv, and is best known for his tv series "Have Gun Will Travel." His Broadway credits include "Medea," "The Man" and "The Rivalry." Surviving are his widow, and a son Peter.

KELLY BROWN, 52, Kentucky-born dancer, actor and teacher, died of a heart attack March 13, 1981 while teaching a ballet class in his school in Phoenix, Az. He had been a soloist with American Ballet Theatre, and appeared on Broadway in "Carousel," "Brigadoon," "Shinbone Alley," "Goldilocks," "Chic," "From A to Z," and "Kiss Me Kate." He is survived by his widow, dancer Isabel Mirrow, two daughters, Elizabeth Laing and Leslie Brown, both dancers, and two sons.

WILLIAM CALLAHAN, 54, New York-born former dancer-actor, was found March 18, 1981 mysteriously murdered in a Wisconsin nature preserve. After retiring from theatre, he became a business executive. His Broadway credits include "Something for the Boys," "Mexican Hayride," "Call Me Mister" for which he received a Theatre World Award, "Annie Get Your Gun," "As the Girls Go," "Top Banana," and "Two's Company." His widow, a son and a daughter survive.

GOWER CHAMPION, 61, Illinois-born dancer-choreographer-director, died of a rare cancer of the blood Aug. 25, 1980 in a NYC hospital. His last Broadway hit "42nd Street" opened only a few hours later. He began his career in vaudeville but joined with Marge Belcher to become a popular dance team and nightclub act, as well as husband and wife. They rose to stardom on tv and in films, and had their own tv show. He made his Broadway debut as a director-choreographer with "Bye Bye Birdie" in 1960, for which he received a Tony Award, followed by "Carnival" for which he won a NY Drama Critics Award, and "Hello, Dolly!" that won 10 Tonys in 1964, including his direction and choreography. "42nd Street" brought him another Tony for his choreography, as did "The Happy Time." He also directed and choreographed "I Do, I Do," "Irene," "The Act" and "Sugar." He is survived by his second wife, Karla, and two sons by his first wife.

HAROLD CLURMAN, 78, director, critic, author and teacher, died of cancer Sept. 9, 1980 in his native NYC. After several small parts as an actor, in 1931 he founded the Group Theatre, and directed several of its productions, including "Awake and Sing" and "Golden Boy." After a brief sojourn in Hollywood to direct "Deadline at Dawn", he returned to Broadway. He co-produced "All My Sons" and directed "A Member of the Wedding." In the meantime he had been busy as a writer and critic. In 1974 his memoirs, "All People Are Famous" was published. He was divorced from actresses Stella Adler and Juleen Compton.

BARBARA COGGIN, 41, Tennessee-born actress, died in her sleep, of natural causes, on Jan 19, 1981 in her NYC apartment. For the past two years she had been appearing in "Gemini." Previously she had performed in "Lovely Ladies, Kind Gentlemen," "Poor Murderer," and OB in "The Drunkard," "One for the Money," "Judy: A Garland of Songs," "Rag Doll," "Museum" and "Tune the Grand Up." Her husband, James Butler survives, as do her parents

C. K. Alexander
(1976)

Beulah Bondi
(1953)

Gower Champion
(1980)

MARC CONNELLY, 90, Pennsylvania-born Pulitzer-Prize-winning playwright, died Dec. 21, 1980 in a NYC hospital. His career began as a cub reporter in Pittsburgh, but in 1914 he was sent to Broadway with one of his plays. He got a job with the Morning Telegraph covering the theatre and met playwright George S. Kaufman. Together they collaborated on "Dulcy," followed by "To the Ladies," "Merton of the Movies," "Helen of Troy, N.Y.," "Beggar on Horseback" and "Be Yourself." After his "The Wisdom Tooth" he went to Hollywood and wrote scenarios for several films. In 1930 his play "The Green Pastures" was awarded the Pulitzer Prize. He had also appeared as an actor in a revival of "Our Town" (1945), and in "Tall Story" (1959). At the time of his death, his last play "A Stitch in Time" was in rehearsal. He was married to and divorced from actress Madeline Hurlock.

TAMARA DAYKARHANOVA, 91, Russian-born actress and teacher, died Aug. 2, 1980 in Englewood, NJ. She began her career with the Moscow Art Theatre, and after coming to New York in 1929 she opened a drama school with Akim Tamiroff and Maria Ouspenskaya. she remained head of the school until her retirement in 1971. Her Broadway appearances include "Chauve-Souris," "The House of Bernarda Alba," "The Emperor's Clothes," "Bullfight," "The Three Sisters." No reported survivors.

JEAN DIXON, 85, Connecticut-born stage and film actress, died in NYC Feb. 12, 1981 after a long illness. During her education in Paris, she appeared in bit parts in Sarah Bernhardt's company, and made her Broadway debut in 1926 in "Wooden Kimono," followed by "Behold the Bridegroom," "Anna," "Heavy Traffic," "Final Fling," "Back Here," "June Moon," "Divorce Me, Dear," "Once in a Lifetime," "Dangerous Corner," "Heat Lightning," "Bright Star," "George Washington Slept Here," "The Deep Mrs. Sykes," "The Velvet Glove," "To Be Continued," "Square Root of Wonderful," "The Gang's All Here" her last appearance in 1959. Her husband, Edward S. Ely died in 1980. No immediate survivors.

JAMES S. ELLIOTT, 54, NY-born former actor, director, producer, died of cancer Jan. 12, 1981 in Granada Hills, Ca. He made his Broadway debut as the youngest producer-director (at 17) with "Arlene," followed by "The First Million," "Too Hot for Maneuvers," "Accidentally Yours," "The Rats of Norway," "Prometheus Bound." No reported survivors.

ISOBEL ELSOM, 87, English-born retired stage and screen actress, died of heart failure Jan. 12, 1981 in Woodland Hills, Ca. After moving to NYC, she appeared in "The Outsider," "Ghost Train," "The Mulberry Bush," "People Don't Do Such Things," "The Silver Box," "The Behavior of Mrs. Crane," "American Landscape," "Ladies in Retirement," "Flowers of Virtue," "Hand in Glove," "The Innocents," "The Curious Savage,", "Romeo and Juliet," "The Climate of Eden," "The Burning Glass," "Hide and Seek," "The First Gentleman." Her second husband, Carl Harbord, died in 1958.

MICHAEL ENSERRO, 62, stage, film and tv character actor, died of a heart attack March 4, 1981 in his NYC apartment. After teaching at the Pasadena Playhouse, he came to NYC and made his Broadway debut in 1948 in "Me and Molly," followed by "The Passion of Josef D," "Song of the Grasshopper," "Mike Downstairs," "Camino Real," "Saturday Sunday Monday," OB in "Penny Change," "The Fantasticks," "The Miracle," "The Kitchen," "Rome, Rome," and "The Jar." He had also been seen in many tv commercials, including the crying plumber and the priest in a Ragu spaghetti sauce commercial. He was a member of Actors Equity Counsil. Surviving are a sister and three brothers.

MADGE EVANS, 71, NYC-born stage and film actress, died of cancer Apr. 26, 1981 in her home in Oakland, NJ. After a career as a child actress and model, she made her Broadway debut in 1926 in "Daisy Mayme," followed by "The Marquise," "Our Betters," "Dread," "Philip Goes Forth," "Here Come the Clowns," "The Patriots," She is survived by her husband of 40 years, playwright Sidney Kingsley.

JAN FARRAND, 52, stage and tv actress, died of cancer Nov. 4, 1980 in NYC. She had appeared in "The Relapse," "Love's Labour's Lost," "Misalliance," "Portrait of a Lady," "Tonight in Samarkand," "Othello," "Henry IV Part I," "The Duchess of Malfi," "Right You Are," "Impromptu at Versailles," "The Lower Depths," "The Umbrella," "Song of the Grasshopper," "What the Butler Saw" and "Ladies at the Alamo." She had also appeared on the tv series "Edge of Night." Her husband, Colin MacLachlin, and a brother survive.

FRANCES FULLER, 73, South Carolina-born actress, and former president and director of the American Academy of Dramatic Arts, died Dec. 18, 1980 in her NYC home. After her Broadway debut in 1928 in "The Front Page," she appeared in "Cafe," "Five Star Final," "The Animal Kingdom," "I Loved You Wednesday," "Her Master's Voice," "The Country Wife," "The Coward," "Stage Door," "Excursion," "Home Is the Hero," and "Lady of the Camellias." She is survived by her husband, Worthington Miner, a son, and two daughters.

HELEN GAHAGAN, 79, New Jersey-born former actress and U.S. Representative from California, died of cancer June 28, 1980 in a NYC hospital. A Broadway star at 22 and hailed as one of the world's most beautiful women, went to Europe to sing opera, came back to Broadway, married her leading man, Melvyn Douglas, moved to Calif. and plunged into politics. After 3 terms in the House, she ran for the Senate but was defeated by Richard Nixon, and never ran again. Her Broadway credits include "Shoot," "Manhattan," "Dreams for Sale," "Fashions for Men," "Chains," "Leah Kleschna," "Beyond," "Sapphire Ring," "Enchanted April," "Young Woodley," "Trelawny of the 'Wells," "Diplomacy," "Tonight or Never," "The Dance of Death," "Moor Born," "Mother Lode," "And Stars Remain," "Wind in the Sails," "First Lady" (1952). In addition to her husband, she leaves a son, a daughter, and a stepson.

REGINALD GARDINER, 77, English-born stage and film actor, died of pneumonia July 7, 1980 in his home in Westwood, Ca. He came to the U. S. in 1935 to appear with Beatrice Lillie in her revue "At Home Abroad," followed by "The Show's On," "An Evening with Beatrice Lillie and Reginald Gardiner," "The Little Glass Clock," and "My Fair Lady" in 1964 at City Center. He appeared in over 100 films. Surviving are his widow, and a son.

PAUL GREEN, 87, North-Carolina-born Pulitzer-Prize playwright, and teacher, died of a heart attack at his home in Chapel Hill, N.C., on May 4, 1981. His play "In Abraham's Bosom" received the 1927 Pulitzer; his other Broadway credits include "The House of Connelly," "Roll Sweet Chariot," "Johnny Johnson," "Native Son" adapted with Richard Wright. He also wrote 15 plays to be performed outdoors, including "The Common Glory." He leaves his wife, dramatist Elizabeth Atkinson Lay, a son and three daughters.

Isobel Elsom
(1945)

Michael Enserro
(1970)

Madge Evans
(1936)

**George Jessel
(1945)**

**Sam Levene
(1966)**

**Barbara Loden
(1964)**

HARRY WAGSTAFF GRIBBLE, 90, English-born actor, director, producer, died Jan. 28, 1981 in a NYC hospital. After his Broadway debut in 1916 in "Quinneys," he appeared in "The Merchant of Venice," "Tyrants," "All Men Are Alike," "The Thorntons," and wrote "The Outrageous Mrs. Palmer," "March Hares," "Shoot," "Elizabeth and Essex," "The Royal Virgin," "Meet My Sister," "Perfumed Lady" and "Almost Faithful." Among his directorial credits are "Cherry Pie," "Pleased to Meet You," "After Dark," "Silent Witness," "Cynara," "No More Ladies," "Living Dangerously," "Simpleton of the Unexpected Isles," "If This Be Treason," "Man from Cairo," "The Millionairess," "Taming of the Shrew," "Johnny Belinda," and "Anna Lucasta." He was never married, and left no known relatives.

LOU HOLTZ, 87, San Francisco-born vaudevillian and ethnic comedian, died after heart surgery Sept. 22, 1980 in Century City, Ca. In addition to three editions of George White's "Scandals," he appeared in "The Dancing Girl," "Tell Me More," "Stylish Stouts," "You Said It," "Calling All Stars," "Transatlantic Rhythm," "Laughter over London," "Priorities of 1942," and "Star Time." He is survived by his second wife, and two sons.

PAUL HUBER, 85, character actor, died March 14, 1981 in a NYC hospital. His Broadway credits include "Spanish Love," "Hamlet," "King Lear," "Sure Fire!," "The New Yorkers," "Sailor, Beware!," "I Want a Policeman!," "Johnny on the Spot," "Strip for Action," "Parlor Story," "Decision," "The Immoralist," "Sixth Finger in a Five Finger Glove," "Point of No Return," "One Flew over the Cuckoo's Nest," "Never Live Over a Pretzel Factory." No reported survivors.

PHILIP HUSTON, 72, Virginia-born actor, died July 25, 1980 in NYC. After his 1934 Broadway debut in "Strange Orchestra," he appeared in over 48 plays, including "Macbeth," "Othello," "Catherine Was Great," "The Father," "A Winter's Tale," "With a Silk Thread," "Tower Beyond Tragedy," "The Shrike," "Cyrano," "Richard III," and "Mandingo." He is survived by his actress daughter Dulcie Huston.

LEON JANNEY, 63, Utah-born actor of radio, stage, film and tv, died of cancer Oct. 28, 1980 in Guadalajara, Mex. After making his debut in vaudeville at 2, he became one of the few child actors to enjoy a lifelong career. After many films as a child, and several Our Gang comedies, he returned to vaudeville, then was on radio's "The Parker Family" as Richard for 5 years. He made his Broadway debut in 1934 in "Every Thursday," followed by "Simpleton of the Unexpected Isles," "Parade," "Ah, Wilderness!," "Jazz Age," "Foreigners," "Ghost for Sale," "Days of Our Youth," "The Victors," "School for Scandal," "Flowering Peach," "Measure for Measure," "Country Wife," "Gazebo," "Summer of the 17th Doll," "Call on Kuprin," "Nobody Loves an Albatross," "The Last Analysis," "Kelly," "Three Men on a Horse," and OB in "Threepenny Opera." Surviving are his fourth wife, a son and a step-son.

GEORGE JESSEL, 83, NYC-born comedian and "Toastmaster General," died of a heart attack May 24, 1981 in Los Angeles, Ca. After becoming vaudeville's top attraction, he was starred on Broadway and in films. His greatest stage success was "The Jazz Singer," and other credits are "The Passing Show," "Even in Egypt," "Sweet and Low," "Lost Paradise," "High Kickers," "Show Time," "Red, White and Blue." He was married and divorced four times. Two daughters survive.

ALLYN JOSLYN, 79, Pennsylvania-born radio, stage, film and tv actor, died of cardiac failure Jan. 21, 1981 in Woodland Hills, Ca. His 1922 Broadway debut in "Johannes Kreisler" was followed by "Scaramouche," "Man and the Masses," "The Firebrand," "Head or Tail," "A Lady in Love," "Boy Meets Girl," "All That Glitters," "Arsenic and Old Lace" and "Collector's Item." No reported survivors.

ROBERT LENN, 62, actor-singer-musician, died Jan. 15, 1980 in his NYC apartment. After his 1942 Broadway debut in "Star and Garter," he appeared in "Ballet Ballads," "The Girl from Nantucket," "Hazel Flagg," "High Spirits," "South Pacific," "Whoop-Up," "Along Fifth Avenue," "The Music Man," "Let It Ride," and revivals of "Tovarich," "Brigadoon," "Oklahoma!" and "The King and I." A son survives.

SAM LEVENE, 75, Russian-born character actor on stage and screen, was found dead in his NYC apartment Dec. 28, 1980 apparently from a heart attack. After his 1927 Broadway debut in "Wall Street," he appeared in "Headquarters," "Wonder Boy," "Dinner at 8," "Yellow Jack," "Three Men on a Horse," "Room Service," "Margin for Error," "A Sound of Hunting," "Light Up the Sky," "Guys and Dolls," "The Matchmaker," "Hot Corner," "Fair Game," "Make a Million," "The Good Soup," "Heartbreak House," "Let It Ride," "Seidman and Son," "Cafe Crown," "Nathan Weinstein, Mystic, Connecticut," "Paris Is Out!," "A Dream Out of Time," "Horowitz and Mrs. Washington." A son survives.

BARBARA LODEN, 48, North Carolina-born stage, film and tv actress, died of cancer Sept. 5, 1980 in NYC. After her Broadway debut in 1957 in "Compulsion," she appeared in "Look after Lulu," "The Long Dream," "After the Fall" for which she received a Theatre World Award. OB she was in "Winter Journey," "The Changeling" and "Come Back to the 5 & Dime, Jimmy Dean." She is survived by her husband, director Elia Kazan, and two sons.

MARY MASON, 69, stage and film actress, died of cancer Oct. 14, 1980 in her NYC home. Born Betty Ann Jenks in Pasadena, Ca., she appeared in films before coming to Broadway. Her credits include "Call It a Day," "Brother Rat," "The Sky's the Limit," "Field of Ermine," "Schoolhouse on the Lot," "Aries Is Rising," "Goodbye in the Night," "Charley's Aunt," "Natural Man," and "Cafe Crown." She was the widow of theatrical lawyer John F. Wharton. A daughter by her first husband survives.

JOHN (JACK) McCAULEY, 79, former actor, singer and dancer, died June 18, 1980 in Menlo Park, Ca. His Broadway credits include "Nerves," "White Cargo," "Earl Carroll's Vanities," "No, No, Nanette," "The Gang's All Here," "Hey, Nonny, Nonny!," "The Show Is On," "Johnny on the Spot," "Ziegfeld Follies," "Sing Out Sweet Land," "High Button Shoes," and "Gentlemen Prefer Blondes." He retired from the theatre to manage the Actors Fund and Percy Williams Home for actors in Englewood, NJ. He is survived by his widow, former actress Amy Revere, and a son.

PARKER McCORMICK, age unreported, stage, film and tv actress, died of cancer July 22, 1980 in NYC. After her 1947 Broadway debut as a replacement in the original production of "Harvey," she appeared in "The Tender Trap," "Third Best Sport," "One Eye Closed," "Three Bags Full," and OB in "The Seagull," "Dr. Willy-Nilly," "Marcus in the High Grass," "Play That on Your Old Piano," "Little Boxes," "Divorce of Judy and Jane," "Medea," "Marco Polo Sings a Solo," "Marie and Bruce," and "Time Steps." She was married and divorced four times. Two sons survive.

MARY MICHAEL, 77, Colorado-born stage and tv actress, died Nov. 6, 1980 in Greenwich, Ct. Her credits include "The Barretts of Wimpole Street," "Distant Drums," "Mary of Scotland," "Ceiling Zero," "Wingless Victory," "Accent on Youth," "Madame Capet," "Two on an Island," "Abe Lincoln in Illinois," "Yours, A. Lincoln," "The Damask Cheek," "Portrait in Black," "Mrs. McThing." Survivors include her husband, James L. Farrell, and a son.

PAUL MORRISON, 74, Pennsylvania-born actor and designer, died Dec. 29, 1980 in a NYC hospital. For the past 17 years he had served as a director of the Neighborhood Playhouse. Among his 64 Broadway credits for sets, lighting or costumes are "Thunder Rock," "The Royal Family," "All My Sons," "Golden Boy," "Bus Stop," "What Every Woman Knows," "Affairs of State," "Billy Budd," "On Borrowed Time," "The Tender Trap," "The Nervous Set," "The Price" and "After the Rain." He appeared in "Till the Day I Die," "Paradise Lost," "Case of Clyde Griffiths," "The Skin of Our Teeth." Surviving are a sister and two brothers.

KERMIT MURDOCK, 72, stage, screen and tv actor, died Feb. 11, 1981 in Tenafly, NJ. His theatre credits include "Saint's Parade," "No More Frontier," "Merry-Go-Round," "Just Suppose," "Lamp at Midnight," "The Sun and I," "Bruno and Sidney," "The Strong Are Lonely," "The Man Who Never Died," "The Idiot," "Emmanuel" and "More Stately Mansions." A nephew survives.

ELLIOTT NUGENT, 83, Ohio-born actor-producer-director-playwright, died in his sleep in his NYC home on Aug. 9, 1980. He made his stage debut at 4 with his vaudevillian parents, and his Broadway debut in "Dulcy" in 1921. During the run he married the ingenue, Norma Lee, who died Dec. 12, 1980 at age 81. They are survived by two daughters. He had appeared in "Kempy," "The Wild Westcotts," "The Poor Nut," "By Request," "The Male Animal" which he co-authored with James Thurber, "Without Love," "The Voice of the Turtle," and "Not for Children." Other writing credits include "Dumbbell," "Apartment to Let," "Rising Sun," "Human Nature," "Nightstick," "Fast Service," "The World's My Onion," and "A Place of Our Own." His Hollywood career included over 20 films.

ARTHUR O'CONNELL, 73, NYC-born character actor on stage, film and tv, died of Alt-zheimer's disease May 18, 1981 in Hollywood, Ca. After his Broadway debut in 1943 in "The Army Play-by-Play," he appeared in "How Long Till Summer," "Child of the Morning," "Anna Christie," "Picnic," "Golden Boy," "Lunatics and Lovers," "Comes a Day" and "Remote Asylum." No reported survivors.

BARBARA O'NEIL, 70, stage and film actress, died Sept. 3, 1980 at her home in Cos Cob, Ct. After her debut with the University Players, she appeared on Broadway in "Saint's Parade," "Carry Nation," "Forsaking All Others," "Is Life Worth Living?," "Mother Lode," "Reprise," "Ten Million Ghosts," "Miles of Heaven," "The Willow and I," "Counterattack," "Doctors Disagree," "The Searching Wind," "Affairs of State," "Portrait of a Lady," "The Seagull," "Little Moon of Alban." She is probably best known for her film portrayal of Scarlet's mother in "Gone with the Wind." She is survived by two brothers.

IRWIN PEARL, 35, Brooklyn-born actor, died Nov. 13, 1980 of Hodgkin's disease in a NYC hospital. After his 1970 Broadway debut in "Minnie's Boys," he appeared in "Fiddler on the Roof" (1976 revival), and OB in "Big Hotel," "Ergo," "Invitation to a Beheading," "Babes in Arms" and "The Taming of the Shrew." His widow and two daughters survive.

RACHEL ROBERTS, 53, Welsh stage, screen and tv actress, died of acute barbiturate intoxication on Nov. 26, 1980 in her home in West Los Angeles, Ca. Broadway audiences had seen her in "The Visit," "Chemin de Fer," "Habeas Corpus" and "Once a Catholic." She was divorced from actors Alan Dobie and Rex Harrison. A sister survives.

DOROTHY SANDS, 87, Massachusetts-born stage, radio and tv actress, died Sept. 11, 1980 in Croton-on-Hudson, NY. After her 1924 Broadway debut in "Catskill Dutch," she appeared in "Little Clay Cart," "Exiles," "The Critic," "Grand Street Follies," "The Dybbuk," "The Apothecary," "Romantic Young Lady," "Pinwheel," "The Stairs," "The Seagull," "Half Gods," "Inconstant Moon," "Jeannie," "Papa Is All," "Tomorrow the World," "A Joy Forever," "Misalliance," "Quadrille," "First Gentleman," "Mary Stuart," "Family Reunion," "Whisper to Me," "My Fair Lady," "Come Summer," "Paris Is Out!" "Right You Are," "Bell, Book and Candle," and her one-woman shows "Styles in Acting" and "Our Stage and Stars." In 1959 she received a Tony for her teaching at the American Theatre Wing. A sister and a brother survive.

WILLIAM SAROYAN, 72, prize-winning author of plays, short stories, scenarios and novels, died of cancer May 18, 1981 in his native Fresno, Ca. In 1940 he was awarded the Pulitzer Prize for his play "The Time of Your Life" but refused to accept the monetary reward. Of Armenian descent, much of his work was autobiographical. His other plays include "My Heart's in the Highlands," "Love's Old Sweet Song," "The Beautiful People," "Hello Out There," "Jim Dandy," "Life, Laughter and Tears," "Across the Board on Tomorrow Morning," "Get Away Old Man," "The Cave Dwellers," and "Talking to You." He was twice married to and divorced from Carol Marcus. He leaves a son Aram, and a daughter, actress Lucy Saroyan.

DORE SCHARY, 74, Newark-born playwright, director and producer for stage and film, died in his sleep July 7, 1980 in his NYC home. For Broadway he wrote "Too Many Heroes," "Sunrise at Campobello," "The Highest Tree," "The Devil's Advocate," "One by One," "Brightower," "Herzl," and directed "A Majority of One," "The Unsinkable Molly Brown," "The Highest Tree," "Something about a Soldier," "Love and Kisses" and "The Zulu and the Zayda," most of which he also produced. He was also involved with more than 250 movies. Surviving are his widow, two daughters and a son.

**Parker McCormick
(1980)**

**Barbara O'Neil
(1960)**

**Dorothy Sands
(1974)**

Michael Strong
(1971)

Bobby Van
(1975)

Mae West
(1942)

YUKI SHIMODA, 59, California-born character actor and former dancer, died of cancer May 21, 1981 in UCLA Medical Center. He appeared in over 25 films, and on Broadway in "Teahouse of the August Moon," "Auntie Mame," "South Pacific," "The King and I" and "Pacific Overtures." No reported survivors.

JOE SMITH, 97, NYC-born Joe Sultzer, a comedian for 73 years with his partner Charles Dale, died Feb. 22, 1981 at the Actors Home in Englewood, NJ. Mr. Dale died in 1971. In addition to being vaudeville headliners, they appeared on Broadway in "The Whirl of New York," "Sidewalks of New York," "Mendel Inc.," "The Sky's the Limit," "Summer Wives," "Laugh, Town, Laugh!" and "Bright Lights of 1944." His wife, former singer Mabel Miller, died in 1967. No immediate survivors.

BARTON STONE, 59, Tennessee-born actor on stage, radio, film and tv, died Aug. 25, 1980. He had appeared in "Janie," "The Respectful Prostitute," "Tobacco Road," "The Shrike," "For Keeps," "Show Boat" (LC-1966), and "The Trial of Lee Harvey Oswald."

MICHAEL STRONG, 57, NYC-born actor on stage, screen and tv, died of cancer Sept. 17, 1980 in Hollywood, Ca. After his 1941 Broadway debut in "Spring Again," he appeared in "The Russian People," "I'll Take the High Road," "Thank You Svoboda," "Men to the Sea," "It's a Gift," "The Whole World Over," "Detective Story," "An Enemy of the People," "The Emperor's Clothes," "Anastasia," "A Month in the Country," "The Firstborn," "Rhinoceros," "After the Fall," "Marco Millions," "But for Whom Charlie," "The Changeling," "Incident at Vichy," "Dance of Death," "The Sponsor," and "Taxi Tales." He is survived by his widow, a son and a daughter.

LEE SULLIVAN, 70, NYC-born actor and singer on stage, film, radio and tv, died of cancer May 29, 1981 in Brooklyn. After his 1940 Broadway debut in "Walk with Music," he appeared in "High Kickers," "Let Freedom Sing," "The Time, the Place and the Girl," and "Brigadoon." He was host of radio's "Lee Sullivan's Vest Pocket Varieties," and co-host of tv's "Date in Manhattan." Surviving are his widow and two sons.

TORIN THATCHER, 76, British actor on stage, tv and film, died of cancer March 4, 1981 in his home in Newberry Park, Ca. Born in Bombay, he made his stage debut in London before coming to NY in 1948 in "Edward, My Son," followed by "That Lady," "Billy Budd," "The Firstborn," "The Miracle Worker," "Write Me a Murder," and "Hidden Stranger." He appeared in over 70 films. His widow and a son survive.

DAVID THOMAS, 73, Welsh character actor on stage and film, died Jan. 27, 1981 in a NYC hospital. After his 1930 Broadway debut in "A Night at an Inn," he had roles in "Million Dollar Baby," "Street Scene," "The Cradle Will Rock," "Love Life," "Regina," "Courtin' Time," "Paint Your Wagon," "Can-Can," "My Fair Lady" (for 2148 performances), "All American," "Moby Dick," "Sophie," "Morning Sun," "The Deputy," "On a Clear Day You Can See Forever," "A Time for Singing," "Show Boat," "Soldiers," "Coco," "Lovely Ladies, Kind Gentlemen," "King of Hearts," and "1600 Pennsylvania Avenue." Surviving are his widow, actress Peggy Turnley, his brother, singer Thomas L. Thomas, and a sister.

BOBBY VAN, 47, (nee Robert King in NYC) actor, dancer and comedian on stage, film and tv, died of cancer July 31, 1980 in Los Angeles, Ca. After his 1950 Broadway debut in "Alive and Kicking," he appeared in "On Your Toes," "No, No, Nanette" (1971), 'Red, White and Blue," and "Dr. Jazz." He was seen in many tv shows, and in 9 films. Surviving are his widow, actress Elaine Joyce, and their daughter.

RICHARD WATTS, 82, drama critic, died Jan. 2, 1981 in a NYC hospital of cardiac arrest, following a stroke. He was critic for the New York Herald Tribune and for the New York Post from 1936 to 1976. He took time out from his work as a critic to warn readers about world troubles in Spain, the Far East, Ecuador, Colombia, China, Burma and Malaya. During World War II he was with the Office of War Information. He was born in Parkersburg, WVa. and studied at Columbia U. He was never married, and left no immediate survivors.

MAE WEST, 88, Brooklyn-born playwright and actress on stage, screen and tv, died of natural causes Nov. 22, 1980 in her home in Los Angeles, Ca. She created her own legend by burlesquing sex in vaudeville, on stage, in films, in nightclubs, and on records, writing much of her own material. In a career covering six decades, she became a millionairess. She introduced the shimmy to New York in 1918 in "Sometime," subsequently appearing on Broadway in "The Mimic World of 1921," "Sex," "Pleasure Man," "The Wicked Age," "Diamond Lil," "The Constant Sinner," and "Catherine Was Great," all of which she wrote, and revived several times. She was married briefly to Frank Wallace, a song-and-dance man. A sister survives. Interment was in her family plot in Brooklyn.

EDITH WILSON, 84, (nee Woodall in Kentucky), singer, actress and vaudeville performer, died March 30, 1981 after a cerebral hemorrhage in Chicago, Il. After her 1921 NY debut in "Put and Take," she appeared in "Plantation Review," "Hot Chocolates," "Hot Rhythm," "Shuffle Along of 1933," "Hummin' Sam," "Blackbirds," "Blackberries of 1932," "Memphis Bound," and "Black Broadway" (1980). On radio she was the mother-in-law of Kingfish in the "Amos 'n' Andy" series, and on the tv series she played Kingfish's girl friend. For 18 years she portrayed Aunt Jemima for Quaker Oats Company. She is survived by her husband, Millard Wilson.

HERMAN YABLOKOFF, 77, actor, composer, playwright, director and producer in the American Yiddish theatre, died Apr. 3, 1981 in a NYC hospital. He came to NYC in 1924 after playing children's roles in his native Poland. For the theatre on lower Second Avenue he wrote several productions, including "Der Payatz," "King of Song," "Goldela Dem Bakers," "Mein Veise Blum," "Der Dishwasher," and "My Son and I." He was president of the Hebrew Actors Union, the Yiddish Theatrical Alliance, and the Yiddish National Theatre. Surviving are his widow, actress Bella Mysell, a son and a daughter.

(NOTE: *Miss Fay Sappington was erroneously included in the obituaries of Volume 36 (1979–1980). Apologies are extended.*)

INDEX

265

266

267

271

274

275

278

283